Administrative Practices
In Boys And Girls
Interscholastic Athletics

Administrative Practices In Boys And Girls Interscholastic Athletics

By

JOHN H. HEALEY, Ph.D.
University of North Carolina at Charlotte
Charlotte, North Carolina

and

WILLIAM A. HEALEY, Pe.D.
North Illinois University
DeKalb, Illinois

CHARLES C THOMAS · PUBLISHER
Springfield · Illinois · U.S.A.

Published and Distributed Throughout the World by

CHARLES C THOMAS • PUBLISHER

BANNERSTONE HOUSE

301-327 East Lawrence Avenue, Springfield, Illinois, U.S.A.

© *1976, by* CHARLES C THOMAS • PUBLISHER

ISBN 0-398-03475-3

Library of Congress Catalog Card Number: 75 14081

With THOMAS BOOKS *careful attention is given to all details of
manufacturing and design. It is the Publisher's desire to present
books that are satisfactory as to their physical qualities and artistic
possibilities and appropriate for their particular use.* THOMAS
BOOKS *will be true to those laws of quality that assure a good
name and good will.*

Printed in the United States of America

W-11

Library of Congress Cataloging in Publication Data

Healey, John H
    Administrative practices in boys and girls
interscholastic athletics.

    Bibliography: p.
    Includes index.
    1. School sports. 2. Physical education and
training—Administration. I. Healey, William Albert.
II. Title.
GV346.H4   375'.796   75-14081
ISBN 0-398-03475-3

Dedication

To Dr. Ruth M. Healey . . .
for John—it is mother,
for Bill—it is wife.

PREFACE

INTERSCHOLASTIC ATHLETICS has become an important part of the school life and experience of the average, American high school student regardless of whether the role played is one of a participant or spectator in the program. The increased interest and emphasis on athletic competition for girls add to its importance.

As athletics become more a part of the American way of life, it is only natural that it has found a place in schools throughout the nation. Its contributions to the education of the youth of our country are noteworthy. The benefits derived from such a program are remarkable. This book is based on the premise that interscholastic athletics is an accepted and vital part of the educational program and that its philosophy, its policies, and its operational procedures coincide with those of education as a whole and can be administered in the same manner. It is assumed that by making the program of interscholastic athletics educationally sound that it will gain the support of the community, faculty, and students; that they will view it as an extremely valuable asset in the continuing education of the youth of our country.

Although the carryover value of interscholastic athletics into the everyday life of the average American staggers the imagination and its impact on education is phenomenal, no one can deny that interscholastic athletics is beset with many problems, educationally, socially, and financially. Because it has such a tremendous effect on so many people, the proper conduct of the athletic programs within the school is of the utmost importance. It is of equal importance then to realize that if interscholastic athletics is to assume its rightful place in the American educational system, it must be safeguarded by proper administration, expert management, and dedicated direction. Without this, it cannot succeed, let alone survive.

It is the hope of the authors that this book will serve as a guide to a better understanding of interscholastic athletics and its place in the educational curriculum as well as in the life-style of the American youth. It is also our hope that persons closely associated with athletic programs will discover how to better administer, manage, and conduct them so as to emphasize their contribution, their worth, and their value to a complete education. The book can be used as a resource textbook for those who are learning how or are already engaged in managing, administering, or conducting interscholastic athletic programs. Each chapter gives detailed information relative to a particular area of interscholastic athletics. The value of the book is further enhanced by the inclusion of behavioral objectives and activities which are presented at the end of each chapter. Furthermore, this information can be used effectively in hypothetical situations.

The activities enable the student to gain added practical information which has a direct bearing on the area of interscholastic athletics. The readers of this book should continue to remember that no two situations are the same so that all administrative policies and procedures which are presented must be used in relation to the existing conditions, any or all of which will have a direct bearing on their use and their effectiveness.

ACKNOWLEDGMENTS

T HE WRITERS ARE INDEBTED to many individuals who have contributed to the writing of this book. It would be virtually impossible to list and give personal credit to all of them but their help and efforts are deeply appreciated.

Grateful acknowledgment is given to the many authors, professional organizations and publishing firms of books and magazines who graciously consented to the use of the many quotations, illustrations and other material used throughout the book. These added immeasurably to the authenticity, reliability and verification of the material presented.

A special thanks is given to the Illinois High School Association, the National Federation of State High School Associations and the many other organizations and companies who furnished various forms and diagrams to illustrate particular points of emphasis.

A sincere expression of appreciation is extended to the many schools, athletic directors, coaches, administrators, superintendents, principals and teachers who contributed diagrams, charts, forms and letterheads to illustrate particular points of interest throughout the book.

A special thanks is given to the various high school athletic conferences and officials' organizations who furnished material for various phases of the book.

A sincere expression of appreciation is extended to the many educators, teachers and students who assisted in this undertaking by providing materials from their schools.

Were it not for the professional opportunities and inspiration by several individuals and schools, interest by the authors in professional administration in physical education and athletics might not have been developed. Therefore, appreciation is given to Dr. O. N. Hunter and the University of Utah and Indiana University.

Finally, the authors are indebted to Dr. Ruth Healey who unselfishly gave of her time and effort in typing, editing and proofreading the manuscript.

TABLE OF CONTENTS

Administrative Practices
In Boys And Girls
Interscholastic Athletics

CHAPTER 1

The Relationship of Administration to Interscholastic Athletics

WHAT IS ADMINISTRATION? How is it applied to interscholastic athletics? What is the function of administration in athletics? Does it have a counterpart in other areas? How does athletic administration differ from, and in what ways is it similar to, administration in these other areas? What does the athletic administrator contribute to the program to make it more efficient and workable? What should the responsibilities of the athletic director be? What is his role in respect to the rest of the school program and community problems? What is the administrator's relationship and responsibility to the athletes and academic staff of the school? What is the administrator's role in respect to the athlete? Why is administration necessary? These and other similar questions which confront the administrator, coach, and other school personnel will be answered within the pages of this book.

Administration covers a multitude of events, happenings, and incidents within the educational structure of the school. These must be thoroughly understood if the administrator is to acquire an expertise which will enable him to make the decisions necessary to do his job.

ADMINISTRATION AFFECTED BY SITUATIONS

Administration can never be the same in every situation. Every situation has a past history all of its own and must be dealt with accordingly. While there may be certain established factors which influence the making of decisions, the fact still remains that there are certain habits and ways that characterize the people who will be affected by administrative decisions. Administration must then be affected by past experiences which must be considered. With these facts in mind it can be understood that any kind of administration must deal with the problem as it exists at the present time with all the influences of a particular and unique situation influencing it. All administrative decisions must be made at the exact time and under the exact conditions that the problem exists.

It is understandable that situations differ in the kinds of administrative problems they present. Problems differ in complexity and ease of solution. Some are more easily solved than others. There are certain factors and circumstances that affect the decisions of the person or persons solving each particular problem. No problem can be segregated and solved without taking into consideration these related facts as instruments of solution.

However, even though decision making and problem solving admittedly are influenced by specific factors which are compatable to a special situation, there are certain basic principles that apply to most of these situations.

THE PURPOSE
OF ADMINISTRATION

To say that administration has changed over the years is putting it mildly. Nothing is the same. The theories and beliefs that carried us through the past have undergone radical changes that have affected programs and personnel in all areas of school life. Many of the accepted procedures in the past are now obsolete and are being replaced with new ideas and programs.

The purpose of administration is, therefore, to (1) make plans to help solve future problems rather than wait for them to appear and attempt to solve them at the time they occur, (2) organize, direct, and make use of the talents of those affected quickly and efficiently to accomplish the tasks at hand, (3) direct and inform those involved of the anticipated changes which are to take place in the future, (4) inform and bring small minority groups into the total picture so that their efforts can be coordinated with the total group in a uniform effort to solve problems, (5) coordinate the talents of all the individuals in a total effort and create an *esprit de corps* among the participants.

The ultimate purpose of administration is then to provide a meaningful, purposeful, and gradual change which will bring about the desired results.

DEFINITION
OF ADMINISTRATION

The high school athletic director and coach more than any others in the school system are placed in a position where administrative functions are many and varied. Therefore, it is essential for them to be as familiar as possible with what administration is and with the particular roles the persons who carry out administrative duties have. Since those who are engaged in the administration of high school athletics have

a wide range of administrative duties for many different sports it would seem logical to use the dictionary as a starting point for defining administration. Webster[1] defines administration as, "the management of governmental or institutional affairs."

From this definition one can infer that a person involved in administration is in a position of management. Voltmer and Esslinger[2] state that, "Administration is mainly concerned with guiding human behavior in the service of some goal. Whatever the nature of the organization, it is through human behavior that necessary tasks are accomplished. The crux of administration is managing human behavior."

Most definitions of administration will stress the characteristic of leadership. This seems to be the most important factor in any type of administration and is especially true in the area of high school athletics. This is due, in part, to the wide diversity of roles which constitute athletic administration. The administration of athletics encompasses many sports and the administrator of this program must relate well to all areas of education and athletics in order to have a well-rounded program. All coaches and directors of athletics must have acquired a good definition of athletics on which to base his beliefs of administrative responsibilities. A good administrator must possess good leadership qualities. Good administration will provide leadership opportunities for all individuals functioning within the program, student, and faculty alike. It will provide opportunities for the professional growth of faculty and allow

---

[1] *Webster's New World Dictionary of the American Language* (New York The World Publishing Co., 1968).

[2] Voltmer, Edward and Esslinger, Arthur, *The Organization and Administration of Physical Education* (New York, Appleton Century-Crofts, 1957), p. 1.

them freedom to express and carry out ideas which will be beneficial to the program, the students, and themselves.

Williams[3] makes this statement regarding administration:

> The business of administration is to get things done. It does not exist as an independent specialization concerned with its own purpose and devoted to its own procedures. Its only reason for existence is to make effective the program of the school or institution; in this purpose the administrator attempts to arrange conditions and materials so that teachers can teach better, facilities will be provided and used, and the standards of the program will be realized.

THEORIES OF ADMINISTRATION

Administration is ever changing although unfortunately some of the practices in administration which are in use today are those which have been used in the past. Many of these practices and techniques, however, have been discarded because they no longer could be justified as meeting the needs of present-day society. Others were kept because of tradition, beliefs, and reluctance or resistance to change. There cannot be any real scientific basis for the formulation or development of theories of administration which will meet every situation because every situation is different. This is one of the reasons why administration is so difficult. The administrator is faced with the problem of dealing with the traditions and beliefs of the past many of which are in direct conflict with those of the present. He is also faced with the desire of those persons who wish to push forward into the future and discard both the past and present traditions, beliefs, and ideas as being obsolete and undesirable. This is particularly true in athletics where the

philosophies regarding the place of athletics in the total educational structure of the school can be an issue with many school administrators, faculty, and school boards. Outside pressures can be instrumental in determining administrative behavior and action at all levels. It can influence and set the tone for administrative behavior of those individuals in administration. This is unfortunate because it does not allow the administrator to function to the best of his ability. It hampers progress and leads to corruptness and ineffectiveness of the program itself.

Bucher[4] emphasizes very emphatically the importance of an emergency theory in administration. He comments that:

> It is being recognized increasingly that administration is not a matter of hit or miss, trial and error, or expediency. Instead, a theory of administration is emerging. It is further recognized that from a study of this administrative theory one will gain insights into how to administer and how human beings work most effectively. Administrative theory will also help in the identification of problems that need to be solved if an effective working organization is to exist. Although some educators oppose the idea that a framework of theory can be established, it seems assured that administration is rapidly becoming a science and is thereby characterized by more objectivity, reliability, and a systematic structure of substance.

It is difficult to develop a theory of administration which will stand the test of time and still be functional.

Even though all the available information is known at the time the theory is developed, it will become out-of-date in a short time because of changing conditions. It is not advisable to use facts which are out-of-date. New facts must be learned and the truth sought out on the basis of the

---

[3]Williams, Jesse, *The Principles of Physical Education* (Philadelphia, W.B. Saunders Co., 1964), p. 423.

[4]Bucher, Charles *Foundations of Physical Education*. (St. Louis, C. V. Mosby Co., 1968), p. 50.

facts that presently exist. The results and ramifications of these facts along with their implications and effects on the behavioral patterns of human beings, must result in changes in the thinking of these same humans. As a result, the theories of administration will also change. Halpin[5] sums up what he feels is a good explanation of administrative theory, "An adequate theory would direct the student's attention to processes and relationships rather than to techniques. It would provide him with a framework into which he could place both the future findings of the social sciences and his own experiences in administration."

The administrator must be constantly aware of changing conditions which will, because of their very nature, necessitate a change in behavioral patterns. By working within a framework, he is able to make these changes successfully.

It would be most desirable in administration to formulate a set of principles which could be used to determine: (1) what action should be taken, (2) make decisions which would result in the desired outcomes, and (3) to predict the actions and behavior of all the individuals within the organizational program. While there is still no predetermined principles or guiding rules for action Morphet, Johns, and Reller[6] contrasted the traditional theories of school administration with those which are now emerging. They pointed to the characteristics of emerging theories as follows:

> Leadership is not confined to those holding status positions in the power echelon.

_____
[5]Halpin, Andrew, *Administrative Theory in Education* (Chicago, The Midwest Administration Center, 1958), p. 24.

[6]Morphet. Edgar, Johns, Roe and Reller, Theodore *Educational Administration-Concepts, Practices, and Issues,* (Englewood Cliffs, N.J., by permission of Prentice-Hall, Inc., 1959), p. 64.

> Good human relations are essential to group production and to meet the needs of individual members of the group.
> Responsibility as well as power and authority can be shared. If leadership can be shared, responsibility can be shared.
> Everyone affected by a program or policy should share in decision making with respect to that program or policy.
> The individual finds security in a dynamic climate in which he shares responsibility for decision making.
> Unity of purpose is secured through consensus and group loyalty.
> Maximum production is attained in a threat-free climate.
> The line and staff organization should be used exclusively for the purpose of dividing labor and implementing policies and programs developed by the total group affected.
> The situation and not the position determines the right and privilege to exercise authority.
> The individual in the organization is not expendable. The ultimate purpose of an organization is to meet the needs of individuals in human society.
> Evaluation is a group responsibility.

These characteristics of emerging theories can be easily applied to the field of athletics. It is understandable that, because of the very nature of athletics, it would be very difficult to establish any theories which could be used in all instances. There are, however, certain proficiencies which do apply to the administration of athletics regardless of the situation under which the program is operating. These proficiencies include the ability to purchase equipment, make athletic schedules, prepare budgets, and administer the budget, etc.

These abilities are all necessary for the successful administrator of athletics. They can be learned.

PURPOSE OF THEORY

Why should theory in administration be important to the administrator of athletics? Will this be a help in administering the program? The changing concept of athletics and society in general will create a necessity for the administrator to condition himself to think in terms of change rather than specific techniques which can be used in the administration of the program. Halpin[7] states the following:

> We cannot expect techniques of administration in 1977 to have much resemblance to those current today. Nor can we predict with any degree of confidence, the nature of the techniques which would equip the future administrator to alter the values of those variables subject to his control as other variables beyond his control change in value.

It is necessary then for the administrator to not only know the techniques of administration but to formulate a mental plan of the way in which he will accomplish whatever administrative task needs to be done. This would include a systematic statement of principles or guiding rules for action which would be in keeping with certain existing phenomena which would be compatible to a particular situation. The administrator of athletics must then keep an open mind and be ready to accept changes, after weighing all the evidence, which would affect the athletic program. The purpose of theory is to establish a base or belief from which decisions can be made.

SOURCES OF THEORY FOR ADMINISTRATION

Much of our knowledge of administration has been empirical in nature. It has been learned through trial and error over a long period of time. There are several sources, however, where the knowledge of administration has been forthcoming. Hal-

[7]Halpin, Andrew, *Administrative Theory in Education* (Chicago, The Midwest Administration Center), 1958, p. 22.

pin[8] lists these as primary sources of theory for administration and are as follows: "(1) The comments and reports made by practicing administrators, (2) the survey research of teachers, (3) the deductive reasoning of teachers, and (4) the adaptation of models from other disciplines."

LINES OF INFLUENCE IN EDUCATION

Educational administration and administration of athletics are accomplished through the combined efforts of many individuals. Successful administration is based on the placing of these individuals into responsible positions where he can function the best and be the most productive. Each person's responsibilities should be made clear to him. It is also important that there be good communication between the administrators and other personnel. This will not only help in delegation of authority, but will also give some direction for feedback to the administrator. If this procedure is followed, the basic processes of administration (planning, organizing, directing, coordinating, and evaluating) can be effectively applied to total programs whether they be educational or athletic in nature.

In order to better understand the entire scope of administration, it is necessary to begin with the top level of authority and work down through the entire range of operation. The top administrative agency for education is the federal government.

Immediately below the federal government in administering to education is the state government. State government has for the most part followed a pattern similar to that of the federal government. The amount of money received by the school through state funds is a major factor in determining how much state control over local education will occur. The state's role

[8]*Ibid.*, p. 25.

in educational administration varies from state to state depending upon their particular philosophy regarding state control.

Traditionally, local communities have assumed almost complete authority in administering their local education and athletic programs. Communities usually establish some type of board of education which acts as the main administrative body in that community or district. Such a board of education then acquires the services of a superintendent. This person generally has overall charge of the school program including athletics. In large school districts, he may have several assistants to deal with special programs. Athletics is one of these programs and as such is under the direct control of the superintendent. Directors of these special programs follow in the line of authority. Immediately below these directors are the teachers, business staff, and maintenance staff. Last, but not least, in the line authority are the students.

FUNCTIONS OR PROCESSES OF SCHOOL ADMINISTRATION

The only real justification of administration is to improve and facilitate the instructional program of the school. It does this through organization of all existing facilities within the school in such a way that it makes it possible to program this instruction more effectively. Administration cannot be thought of as an instructional device but rather as a means by which facilities, personnel, and materials can be better organized so that better instruction will result. One of the most important aspects of a successful athletic program is organization. Nowhere in the educational program is good organization so evident and necessary as in athletics because so many people are involved in the program and its results are constantly being placed before the public for evaluation.

According to the American Association of School Administration,[9] the functions of administration are these:

1. To plan ways and means of achieving the purpose of the enterprise.
2. To allocate resources, personnel, and responsibility.
3. To stimulate or motivate such activity on the part of staff members as well as make the maximum contribution to the purposes of the enterprise.
4. To coordinate the activities of various persons and units so that maximum effort is achieved.
5. To evaluate the effects of programs and operations with reference both to the attainment of objectives and to the growth of staff members.

Since the justification or real reason for administration is concerned with getting things done or in the case of education to facilitate the instructional program, it is important to know the way affairs are conducted as well as what is being done. These ways are also known as methods or procedures. They are used by the administrator to perform the duties required of him to obtain the desired outcomes of the program and to attain the stated objectives. These processes can and do apply to administration in the schools and in the athletic programs in every situation. The way in which these processes are carried out or put into practice, however, are never the same in all situations. The similarity changes because of various reasons. The main one is the general makeup of the community in which the school is located. The philosophy of the athletic program is dependent upon the type of support it receives from the community. Questions often asked are, "What is administration? What does it consist of? What are its ingredients? How would you

[9]Educational Policies Commission, *The Structure and Administration of Education in American Democracy* (Washington D. C., National Education Association, 1938), p. 70.

analyze it?" Gulick[10] has broken it down into seven areas or categories,

1. Planning: working out in broad outline the things that must be done and the methods to be used to accomplish the purpose set for the enterprise.
2. Organizing: establishing the formal structure of authority through which work subdivisions are arranged, defined, and coordinated for the defined objective.
3. Staffing: the whole personnel function of bringing in and training the staff and maintaining favorable conditions of work.
4. Directing: the continuous task of making decisions and embodying them in specific and general orders and instructions and serving as the leader of the enterprise.
5. Coordinating: the all-important duty of interrelating the various aspects of the work.
6. Reporting: keeping those persons to whom the executive is responsible informed as to what is going on. This, of course, requires of the administrator that he keep himself and his subordinates informed through records, and inspection.
7. Budgeting: fiscal planning, accounting, and control.

TYPES OF ADMINISTRATORS

Administrators are individuals as are other people. They cannot be placed in a mold so that they will all be the same in their beliefs, their personality. Administrators of athletics are no different in this respect than administrators in other areas. These administrators do, however, all fall into four specific categories or types. Griffiths[11] lists these types as, (1) *laissez-faire*, (2) democratic, (3) hard-boiled autocratic, and (4) father-type.

[10]Gulick, Luther, "Notes on the Theory of Organization," *Papers on the Science of Administration* (New York, Institute of Public Administration, 1937) , p. 13.

[11]Griffiths, Daniel, *Human Relations in School Administration* (New York, Appleton-Century-Crofts, Inc., 1956, p. 148.

The *laissez-faire* administrator allows the department to more or less run itself. Each member does about what he wants to do without any help or direction. The administrator exercises no authority and as a result, the department is weak and its members inefficient with little incentive and low morale.

The hard-boiled autocrat administrator is as the name implies, the type of person who uses the authority which his position gives him to, "throw his weight around." This means that he makes most of the decisions without any imput or help from members of the department. He expects department members to obey his every command without question and believes that he, as the director of the department, has the prerogative to make all decisions and to represent the department in any way he sees fit.

The father-type administrator treats his staff as one of the family. He has their interests at heart and encourages them to bring their problems to him for solution. His treatment of department members is on a friendly, fatherly basis. This promotes excellent *esprit-de-corp* among faculty members and helps to establish high morale.

The democratic administrator makes every effort to enlist the help of every staff member by involving them in all departmental decisions. He makes every member feel that he is an important cog in the machine and that he is a valuable member of the department and one whom they could not get along without. He has regular staff meetings with prepared agendas so that members of the department will be prepared to discuss all issues that come before it. The democratic administrator spends a great deal of his time in involving all personnel in the department in all matters pertaining to it.

IMPORTANCE
OF ADMINISTRATION

Nowhere in the entire school system is good administration as necessary as it is in the athletic program. Nowhere does it assume more importance or affect so many students, parents, and citizens. The administration of interscholastic athletics is important because the individual school cannot control these activities alone. Competitive athletics has grown to tremendous proportions largely because of community and school pride. The administrator of the interscholastic athletic program has a very difficult and intricate job because of the many problems that are inherent in interscholastic athletics.

The administrator must first of all keep the athletic program within the bounds set by professional administrators. The administrator must, at the same time, keep the spectator public happy yet he must not allow them to determine the operation of the program. The administrator must always keep in mind and give cognizance to the fact that the educational and health benefits of the participants are more important than the desires of the spectators. The administrator must keep an open mind and give equal opportunity in every respect to the girls' athletic program. This means that he must understand their needs, their philosophy, and their objectives. The administrator must possess the knowledge and know-how to bring the boys' and girls' programs together in such a way that there will be no partiality shown to either program and that there will be a healthy interrelationship between the two programs. It will require a certain type of administrative leadership to bring about an indispensable condition necessary for the program to perform adequately this unique role.

The word administration means to manage or conduct. Applied to the interscholastic athletics program, administration means giving it direction and conducting and managing all matters pertaining to this program. If applied correctly, then it is necessary to conduct the entire program of education in such a way that lines of responsibility are established in such a way as to make for the most effective organization and conduct of affairs in the department in which the program of athletics is located.

BEHAVIORAL OBJECTIVES

After a person has read this chapter, he should be able to:

1. Explain the purposes of administration and enumerate several which can be applied to an athletic program.
2. Define administration and apply this definition to educational and athletic administration.
3. Enumerate several theories of administration which have emerged the past few years.
4. Explain the purpose of theory as it applies to administration and describe its importance in athletic administration.
5. List several primary sources of theory for administration and explain each.
6. Enumerate the functions of school administration and give examples of how they can be applied to an athletic program.
7. Distinguish between functions and processes in administration.
8. List and analyze the processes of administration.
9. Define and explain administrative leadership and apply it to athletics.
10. Identify several traits which can be used to identify leaders in administration.
11. Explain why democratic administration held by some athletic directors as to be inefficient.

12. Distinguish between democratic, autocratic, and *lassiez-faire* administrators.
13. Compare the forces of personnal motives and reason in solving administrative problems in athletics.
14. Explain and illustrate if democratic action in administration means that all decisions must be arrived at through group discussion and voting.
15. Analyze and justify the statement "Athletics exist for the education of the youth rather than the youth exists for the performance of athletic activities."
16. Outline the most feasible organization for the athletic administration of your local high school.
17. List and explain several reasons why athletic directors fail.
18. Identify the different types of administrators and explain each.
19. Differentiate between athletic administration.
20. Define administration. Differentiate between organization and administration.
21. Explain the purpose of athletic administration.

ACTIVITIES

1. Interview an athletic director to determine his leadership qualities.
2. Observe several athletic directors at work. Does their behavior appear to be more easily understood in terms of the administrator as an initiator of action or as a recipient of action?
3. Talk with several teachers and try and discover the ways in which they attempt to influence the directors with whom they work.
4. Attend a high school athletic staff meeting. Prior to the visit, set up criteria for such a meeting based on these criteria.
5. Visit a high school athletic department and by observation determine the organizational structure.
6. Interview several citizens and find out their opinion as to the place of athletics in the total school curriculum.
7. Interview several athletic directors and try to determine how they judge their success, whom they regard as the people best-fitted to judge their success.
8. Observe an athletic director in a staff meeting. From what he does, interpret his view of the role of authority and the role of the athletic administrator.
9. Interview several athletic directors and attempt to identify how they got their first administrative position.

SUGGESTED READINGS

1. AAHPER: Professional preparation of the administrator of athletics. *Journal of Health, Physical Education, and Athletics,* September, 1970.
2. American Association of School Administrators: *Staff Relations in School Administration.* Washington, D. C., The Association, 1955.
3. Bucher, Charles: *Administration of Health and Physical Education Programs Including Athletics.* St. Louis, Mosby, 1971.
4. ———: Foundations of Physical Education. St. Louis, Mosby, 1968.
5. Burrup, Percy: *Modern High School Administration.* New York, Har-Row, 1962.
6. Campbell, Ronald: *Introduction to Educational Administration.* Boston, Allyn, 1971.
7. Daughtery, Greyson and Woods, John: *Physical Educaton Programs, Organization and Administration.* Philadelphia, Saunders, 1971.
8. Educational Policies Commission: *The Structure and Administration of Education in American Democracy.* Washington D. C., National Education Association, 1938.
9. George, Jack and Lehmann, Harry: *School Athletic Administration.* New York, Har-Row, 1966.
10. Goldman, S.: *The School Principal.* New

York, The Center for Applied Research in Education Inc., 1966.

11. Griffiths, Daniel: *Human Relations in School Administration.* New York, Appleton, 1956.

12. Gulick, Luther: *Notes on the Theory of Organization.* New York, Institute of Public Administration, 1937.

13. Halpin, Andrew: *Administrative Theory in Education.* Chicago, The Midwest Administrative Center, 1958.

14. Havel, Richard and Seymore, Emery: *Administration of Health, Physical Education and Recreation for Schools.* New York, Ronald, 1961.

15. Howard, Glenn and Masonbrink, Edward: *Administration of Physical Education.* New York: Har-Row, 1963.

16. Hughes, William, French, Esther, and Lehsten, Nelson: *Administration of Physical Education for Schools and Colleges.* New York, Ronald, 1962.

17. Knezevich, Steven: *Administration of Public Education.* New York, Har-Row, 1962.

18. Morphet, Edgar, Roe, John and Reller, Theodore: *Education Administration, Concepts, Practices and Issues.* Englewood Cliffs, P-H, 1959.

19. ———: *Educational Organization and Administration.* Englewood Cliffs, P-H, 1967.

20. Peirce, T.M. and Merrill, E.C.: *The Individual and Administrative Behavior,* New York, Har-Row, 1966.

21. Richardson, Deane: Preparation for a career in public school athletic administration. *Journal of Health, Physical Education, and Recreation,* February, 1971.

22. Voltmer, Edward, and Esslinger, Arthur: *The Organization and Administration of Physical Education.* New York, Appleton-Century-Crofts, 1967.

23. Williams, Jesse, Brownell, Clifford, and Vernier, Elmon: *The Administration of Health Education and Physical Education,* Sixth Edition. Philadelphia, Saunders, 1966.

CHAPTER 2

The Place of Interscholastic Athletics In the Educational Curriculum

ATHLETIC ACTIVITIES HAVE been a part of school since the development of the educational system in America. As school systems grew, so did interscholastic athletics. Along with this growth came the problem of administering these programs in a fair and just manner. Although the administration of athletics has improved tremendously over the years, problems still exist that greatly concern today's administrator.

The biggest problem is, of course, as it always has been, the place of interscholastic athletics in the educational curriculum.

A great deal of criticism has been leveled at the interscholastic athletic program over the years. Many individuals have sought to abolish competitive athletics altogether. Others have attempted to include it in the school curriculum as being part of the educational objectives of the program. The latter have been successful, and as a result competitive athletics today does have a place in the curriculum and plays a prominent part in the lives of the young and old alike, both as participants and spectators.

DEFINITION OF INTERSCHOLASTIC ATHLETICS

In order to understand the place of interscholastic athletics in the educational curriculum, it is necessary to define it.

Daughtrey[1] does this by stating, "It is a contest between selected individuals or teams representing two or more schools organized and controlled by school authorities."

It is important to understand the difference between interscholastic athletics and the other phases of sports which are a part of the physical education and intramural program.

The proper understanding will help clarify the place of the interscholastic athletic program and its right perspective within the total educational program of the school.

THE GROWTH OF ATHLETICS IN THE SCHOOLS

The fact that athletics has established itself as a vital part of American education cannot be denied. Its growth from a small beginning as an unwanted part of the program has been encouraging. It has finally become accepted as a vital force in the curriculum of almost every high school in the United States. Its popularity has grown until at the present time its biggest problem is to provide opportunity for all students who wish to participate. However, the growth of athletics within the school

[1]Daughtrey, Greyson and Woods, John, *Physical Education Programs* (Philadelphia, W. B. Saunders, 1971), p. 416.

13

structure has not been without its problems.

There have been three issues in school athletics that have been a problem to school administrators over the years and these problems still exist today to some degree. The first, which is not an issue at the present time, especially on the high school level, is the fact that athletic programs were instigated by the students. Athletics were opposed by the faculty because they felt athletics were not a part of education as it existed at that time. They were forced to compromise. This feeling still exists today to a certain extent.

Another problem is the fact that in the early days of athletic competition in the schools there was a great deal of alumni influence and even interference. Some of these outside influences still exist although it is not a major issue.

The third problem is that of the amateur standing of the athlete. Some of the original problems of school attendance and eligibility are still problems today in the administration of interschool athletics.

Howard and Masonbrink[2] substantiate this thinking in the following statement:

> Competitive sports have been part of popular cultures through the recorded history of mankind. Their part in the lives of people in the United States demonstrates without question that this type of sports activity is an integral part of American culture. The fact of significance to the educator is its place in the educational curriculum.

The program has grown from a few of the so-called major sports to almost every sport known to our American culture. As a result of these increased interests, many schools sponsor several sports teams which include competition of the freshmen,

junior varsity, and varsity level. Athletics on the interscholastic level has "come of age" and its growth in the past few years has become sensational.

Attesting to this fact, a study by Epler[3] brought out the following startling figures:

> In 1937, there were 586 high schools sponsoring six-man football teams. By 1953-54, the six-man game and its eight-man offspring were played in 1,818 schools. The 1964 survey indicates a drop off to 1,297 but this is more than offset by the dramatic increase in eleven-man teams from 9,333 in 1953-54 to 12,922 in 1964. The number of high school baseball teams has grown from 12,261 in 1954 to 13,248 in 1964, a gain of 987. Over the same period the number of schools represented by basketball teams has increased by 659, from 18,453 to 19,112. The most marked gain has been in track and field, from 10,381 to 15,524, an increase of 5,143.

This tremendous and spectacular growth of athletics brought forth serious problems, many of which have been solved over the past few years. There still is a lingering doubt in the minds of many individuals including educators as to the rightful place of athletics in the schools.

In order to place interscholastic athletics in its right perspective in the educational curriculum, the Educational Policies Commission[4] has established the following guidelines for athletics in the schools:

1. We believe in athletics as an important part of the school's physical education program. We believe that the experience of playing athletic games should be a part of the education of all children and youth who attend school in the United States.

---

[2]Howard, Glenn, and Masonbrink, Edward, *Administration of Physical Education* (New York, Harper and Row, 1963) , p. 27

[3]Epler, Stephen, "The Growth of Interscholastic Sports," *The Athletic Journal* (April, 1954), p. 34.

[4]School Athletics—Problems and Policies, *The Educational Policies Commission of the National Education Association of the United States and the American Association of School Administrators* (Washington, D. C., 1954) , p. 3.

2. Participation in sound athletic programs we believe contributes to health and happiness, physical skill and emotional maturity, social competence, and moral values.
3. We believe that cooperation and competition are both important components of American life. Athletic participation can help teach the values of cooperation as well as the spirit of competition.
4. Playing hard and playing to win can help to build character. So also does learning to "take it" in the rough and tumble of vigorous play, experiencing defeat without whimpering and victory without gloating and disciplining one's self to comply with the rules of the game and of good sportsmanship.
5. Athletics may also exemplify the value of the democratic process and of fair play. Through team play the student athlete often learns how to work with others for the achievement of group goals. Athletic competition can be a wholesome equalizer. Individuals on the playing field are judged for what they are and what they can do, not on the basis of the social, ethnic, or economic group to which their families belong.

PURPOSE OF ATHLETICS IN THE SCHOOL PROGRAM

Athletics should occupy a prominent place in the school program of physical education because the games themselves consist of the fundamental activities that are taught in the physical education classes. A vigorous athletic program will provide the individual with the big muscle exercise he needs. It will insure the organic development necessary for good health and physical fitness needed by the growing high school student.

Athletics will also help the high school student to develop a wholesome attitude toward play. It will help to provide the opportunity to develop desirable citizenship and character traits through the relation-

ships obtained in competing. The athlete through participation can help develop an appreciation for good health, sportsmanship, and fair play.

EVALUATION OF ATHLETICS IN EDUCATION

In evaluating the place of athletics in education it must be remembered that athletics exist for the education of the youth rather than the youth existing for the performance of athletic activities. The administration should carry out the athletic program the same as other programs within the school curriculum. Athletic outcomes should contribute to the well being of the participants. It should be an outgrowth of the activities that are taught in the physical education classes and should parallel this program. It should include many youngsters rather than just a few outstanding players.

PRINCIPLES OF ATHLETIC ADMINISTRATION

A principle can be thought of as a "guiding rule for action." If this definition is applied to the administration of athletics, it could mean that there are certain principles or rules which would apply to the administration of the program if educational goals are to be met.

Each school should set up its own principles of athletic administration because local conditions, of course, determine policies to a large extent, and these policies vary in different localities. Policies are dependent upon the size of the department and the administration. Obviously, many of the athletic policies that are formulated for the large department will not be applicable to the small department. The attitude of the administration and the community will have a direct bearing and affect on all policy making. This does not mean, however, that definite principles and procedures should not be established. Sound administration demands uniformity upon which the program can be built. Certain uniform principles can be established. Some of them may be listed as follows.

1. Athletics should be under the jurisdiction of the state athletic association.
2. Athletics should be voluntary for all participants.
3. Participation in the athletic program should not be substituted for physical education.
4. Athletics should be carried out after school hours.
5. Coaches should be bonified faculty members and selected on this basis.
6. The health of the participants should be paramount and hold first priority in all competition.
7. A variety of sports should be offered to take care of the needs of all students.
8. The needs of the student should have preference in the athletic program.

UNDESIRABLE EFFECTS OF ATHLETICS ON THE EDUCATION PROGRAM

When considering the undesirable effects of athletics upon the educational program, it must be remembered that there are underlying causes of these effects. These causes can be the result of unscrupulous individuals who use athletics to exploit their own ego and to accomplish their own desires. This is not the fault of the program but rather those who administer and control it.

The purpose of athletics in the schools should be to further worthwhile educational goals. Financial or professional values should not be used to replace the educational values. For example, football and basketball programs sometimes bring in a great deal of revenue but institutional

policy should not favor these sports by giving the players better equipment or other advantages.

All sports regardless of financial income should be treated alike. Undesirable effects of athletics on the educational program can be eliminated by an alert, aggressive administration without affecting or curtailing the program of athletics. Some of the athletic evils to avoid are brought forth by Lawes Alley[5] as follows:

1. Disruption of the school program.
2. Preoccupation with the outcomes of athletic contests to the extent the effectiveness of the classroom learning situation is impaired.
3. Pressures brought to bear upon teachers to give athletes special privileges with relation to assignments, test grades, and attendance requirements.
4. Undue influence by nonschool persons.
5. Interference with progress toward the reorganization of school districts even though such reorganization would result in greater educational accomplishments at less cost to the elders involved.
6. Exaggerated importance attached to interscholastic athletics.
7. Unwholesome recruiting practices by colleges.
8. The formation of egocentric habits of behavior.
9. A tendency for the nonathlete to become maladjusted in an environment in which the social pressure for athletic achievement is so pronounced.

The Educational Policies Commission[6] lists the following as bad effects of the athletic program on the educational program:

1. Overemphasis on the varsity.
2. Distortions in the educational program
3. Coaches under pressure
4. Financial woes

[5]Alley, Lawes, "Better Start Kicking that Dog Around," *The Physical Educator* (October, 1959), p. 103.

[6]*The Educational Policies Commission of the National Education Association of the United States and the American Association of School Administrators,* p. 4.

5. Recruiting by colleges
6. Involving young players
7. Neglecting the girls
8. Distorting school organization

The perplexing problem of school athletics will persist until present evils are identified and attacked on a broad front. School authorities hold only one sector of this front. Schools can go a long way toward building sound athletic policies. But they cannot do it alone. Communities, too, must help.

Bucher[7] cites the harmful effect that athletics may have upon the student as follows:

1. Ego centered athletes
2. False values
3. Harmful pressures
4. Inequitable use of facilities, leadership and money
5. Distortion of the educational program leading to overspecialization
6. Leadership

An article by Pietrofesa and Rosen points out that athletics have no educational values because of the way in which they are administered. Some of the arguments upon which this belief is founded are that many schools have made a ceremony out of the interscholastic sports program. The sports program has been allowed to become a component of violence. Riots, fighting, and rowdyism are common-place occurrences at many of the athletic contests. Fighting among players is not uncommon. The overemphasis on winning has been allowed to be the dominant force in the athletic program.[8] This destroys one of the main objectives of athletics.

The program should be directed so that it will not interfere with other school programs. It should not be considered as entertainment but rather as an educational endeavor.

Solberg brings out the fact that the high school athletic programs of today are consuming a great deal of time from the students and faculty alike. The costs have skyrocketed. All these facts indicate that the program should be discontinued. He advocates that an intramural program should replace the athletic program because it would accomplish the same outcomes for which the athletic program was designed. Originally, the athletic program was organized to educate the students in attitudes to help motivate and encourage them to stay in school. It has grown in popularity and magnitude and has outgrown its place in the school setting.[9]

DESIRABLE EFFECTS OF ATHLETICS IN THE CURRICULUM

Much has been written about the desirable effects of athletics on individuals of all ages. However, it might be appropriate at this time to stress what some of the outstanding organizations as well as some influential individuals have said about the benefits derived from a program of interscholastic athletics. For example, the American Alliance of Health, Physical Education and Recreation[10] gives the following reasons for including athletics within the educational framework of the school system:

1. Athletics are of historical and social significance in our national culture.
2. Athletics are a means of providing "physical vigor and stamina" necessary

---

[7]Bucher, Charles, *Foundations of Physical Education* (St. Louis, C. V. Mosby Company, 1968), p. 570-572.

[8]Pietrofesa, John and Rosen, Al, "Interscholastic Sports—Misdirected? Misguided? Misnomer?" *Clearing House* (November, 1968), p. 165.

[9]Solberg, James, "Interscholastic Athletics—Tail that Wags the Dog," *Journal of Secondary Education* (May, 1970), p. 238.

[10]Division of Mens Athletics, AAHPER, "Athletics in Education—A Platform Statement," *Journal of Health, Physical Education and Recreation* (September, 1962). p. 25.

for the defense of democracy.

3. Athletics develop habits, attitudes, and ideals requisite to ethical competition and effective cooperation in a free society.
4. Athletics provide a means of healthful and wholesome leisure living.
5. Athletics appeal to youth and can be used to aid in their "harmonious development."

The Educational Policies Commission[11] makes the following comment:

> No motivation for the development of good health and rugged physical condition could be found that would approximate that provided by competitive athletics. The schools have chief responsibility for operating sound athletic activities as part of their total educational programs. Citizens should give support to such activities and programs. But citizens especially need: (a) to understand the effects of existing bad practices on youth, and (b) to withhold their support of malpractice. Although responsibility for such understanding and such self-restraint rests with citizens themselves, educators have responsibility for identifying harmful practices, for formulating constructive programs and for energetically explaining to the public the advantages of the latter.
>
> There is nothing inherently wrong with school athletics. They can be helpful or they can be harmful. Players can learn to cheat and slug, or to play fair and to develop self control. Communities can support constructive programs or become hysterical over public athletic contests. Athletics will be what they are made to be by colleges and communities.

Bucher[12] cites the beneficial impact athletics can have upon the student as follows:

1. Good sportsmanship
2. Cooperation
3. Acceptance of all persons regardless of race, creed, or origin
4. Traits of good citizenship
5. Leadership
6. Followership
7. Additional avenues for social acquaintances
8. Social poise and understanding of self

It is certainly true that athletics is not all good, and those individuals who are the staunch supporters of the program will readily agree. They will also argue that the good effects far outweight the bad. The athletic program is not only justifiable but is extremely advantageous to the youngsters in the school and should be definitely a part of the curriculum. In defense of the program, Cherry and Lawther[13] have this to say:

> Athletics are first of all educational media through which he may train his body so that it responds precisely, quickly, efficiently, and automatically to the impulses from his mind. The contests provide highly competitive and stressful situations. They present realistic and highly emotional experiences, situations in which the individual's physical shortcomings, his ability or inability to adjust to other persons, his emotional reactions, his drive, energy, determination, or lack of it—in short, his personality with all its quirks and ramifications is etched out for examination. Moreover, the heat of the contest will mold this individual, cut some new shape or pattern. He is, under such emotional arousal, more pliable and more subject to change. Herein, of course, lies the absolute necessity for careful guidance.

Donnehl and Razor have emphasized the fact that athletics as an important part of our American culture is difficult to deny,

[11]Educational Policies Commission, *School Athletics, Problems and Policies* (Washington, D. C., National Association of the United States and the American Association of School Administrators, 1954), p. 13.

[12]Bucher, Charles, *Foundations of Physical Education*, p. 567-569.

[13]Cherry, Spurgeon and Lawther, John, "Division of Men's Athletics—Purposes and Projects," *Journal of Health, Physical Education and Athletics* (January, 1963), p. 12.

but it is also important for students to realize that society rewards a winning effort whether it be in athletics, business, or education. Athletics can be of great value to the educational, psychological, and social growth of students, but moderation is the key to that value. Competition on the athletic field tends to lose its educational value when victory is the ultimate goal. Like all educational programs, athletics can be defended only to the extent to which they contribute to established educational goals. Most people will agree that participation in athletics is a wholesome way for students to spend their time out of school.[14]

Personal Health

The health of the individual is becoming increasingly important. Our life styles are changing because luxurious and easy living have become a pattern of life. The individual no longer needs the rugged physique that was needed in years gone by. The working day has been shortened and much of the hard physical labor needed a number of years ago is no longer necessary. Machinery has taken the place of manual labor and the easy life in many instances has been the result. There are increasing signs of minor health disorders which in time can become major. Drugs, alcoholism, and venereal disease have become common place, resulting in a moral decay of our young people. Athletic competition can offset these factors. It can change the attitude of the individual toward the easy life and allow him to enjoy and see the value of the competitive athletics that bring out the survival instinct that has made our country great. Let us be glad that sport is good for health because health is our most valuable

asset and without it life can be very difficult.

Personal Friendships

It probably would be most difficult to point out specific examples but athletics can cause the formation of lasting bonds of friendship. Athletics teaches participants to give freely of themselves and ask nothing in return except the opportunity to participate in the game. Individuals play because it is a natural act of man, one which he enjoys because it gives him relaxation and allows him to express himself and gives him the feeling of well-being. The skills performed in athletics are expressions of the joy of living.

Physical and Mental Fitness

The values of athletics are many and are inherent within the activity, but exploitation through ill-conceived goals and improper administration is common and on the increase. Only through careful philosophical inquiry and practical application can the value be realized.

No one can be an outstanding athlete in any branch of sport without being in perfect physical and mental condition. There is no question that such training fits a person for a place in life. Athletics is a means to an end, that of teaching good sportsmanship, clean play, and the ability to "take it." In order to be a good athlete, a person needs first of all a sound body and a keen, alert mind. The athlete cannot abuse the laws of nature and still have his dream come true. A well-known explorer once said, "If I were to choose a companion for a perilous journey into an unknown region, I would go to a high school and select from their ranks an outstanding athlete. The athlete would be selected on the basis of character, and be one that would suffer in silence for his errors. An individu-

[14]Donnehl, Wayne, and Razor, Jack, "The Value of Athletics," *The Bulletin of the National Association of Secondary School Principals* (September, 1971), p. 65.

al who would stand up in the face of over-whelming odds; and when he could no longer stand, he would finish on his knees."

There have been innumerable books and articles written extolling the virtues of athletics. It is the great youth movement of the world. Its impact on our civilization is immeasurable. Its benefits are unlimited. All over the country at the present time, games are being won and lost and as a result people's lives are being affected one way or another. Meetings are being held, hundreds and thousands of people attend games and banquets and discuss the chances of their team winning from little Po Dunk high school to the Super Bowl and the World Series.

Personal Development

The first real issue of the program of athletics in the high school is the personal development of the participant. This entails the understanding of the skills needed to participate. Every youngster thrills in the knowledge that he can perform physical skills such as kicking the football, and hitting the baseball. Others are satisfied to be adept at playing the piano and the violin. Where does the difference lie? It is satisfying a need. It is serving a purpose when it gives the youngster confidence in his ability to do something better or at least as good as someone else. It is satisfying an ego at a particular time in his life when it is most needed. He knows he has a potential to pass the football and he has gained stature with his fellow man as well as their respect and perhaps in some cases their admiration. He is well thought of and it has made him in many cases a better man. Everyone needs to be well thought of and admired. He needs self-esteem. People will go to great lengths to be noticed, to be pointed out as possessing a specific talent. This talent can be in the form of athletic ability.

Many youngsters would rather be a talented baseball, basketball, or football player than president of the United States.

The greatest force against evil acts is to channel the energy of the youth in the right direction. A good athletic program will do just that.

Emotional Control

We are living in a complex society where close contact with our fellow man brings about differences of opinion. An understanding of one's self in relationship to others is a part of the learning process in athletics. The athlete learns to keep his emotions on an even keel, not to go from the high to the low on the slightest provocation.

Ethical Judgment

No one is born with the knowledge of what is right and wrong. He must learn it. The student learns to know honesty from dishonesty, fair from unfair play on the athletic field. The coaches who have taught players the lessons of life have not received the full support of those critics who believe that the coaches' only interest in the player is to exploit his athletic talents toward a winning season. Anyone who has participated in athletics knows full well the opportunities that exist to help the player decide what is right and what is wrong. Youngsters must have the opportunity to decide and to learn the meaning of justice. There is no better place to experience this than in athletics.

Nowhere else can the lessons of life be taught better than on the athletic field or court. Athletics can teach the youngster how to:

1. Be strong enough to know when he is weak.
2. To be brave enough to force himself to the utmost when he is afraid.

3. To realize that wishes do not take the place of deeds.
4. To be humble in victory.
5. To be proud in defeat.
6. To have a sense of humor.
7. To set his goal high.
8. To master himself before he attempts to master others.
9. To reach into the future but not to forget the past.
10. To not be lead along the path of ease and comfort.
11. To control his temper.
12. To realize the importance of being on time.
13. To smile when he was the most discouraged person in the world.
14. To work out problems by himself.
15. To form friendships that money could not buy.
16. To learn to know himself.
17. To learn to know God.

Paul Briggs,[15] superintendent of schools in Cleveland, Ohio, expresses his views on the value of athletics for urban youth by making the following statement:

> From my experience over the years as a high school administrator, as a member for about eight or ten years of an executive committee of a high school athletics governing board, a member of a state board, and many other associations —I have found that physical education and athletics do something for young people that cannot be equaled anywhere else in the school. I have seen young men and young women, but more particularly young men, heading straight for trouble—academic trouble, personal trouble, trouble with the law, and more. Then when they came into a real experience in physical education or athletics, they seem to begin to find themselves. I have seen young men change and I have seen so many success stories

come out of the athletic plan that I cannot help but stand here this morning as perhaps the strongest advocate of any of the city superintendents of America in behalf of a revitalized and effective program of physical education, health, recreation, and athletics.

Motivation

Athletics many times is the motivating force that keeps a student in school. His love for participation and competition keeps him in school and out of trouble. Brigg's[16] comments that in a study in Cleveland, Ohio, that principals of five inner city schools were asked to review the records and find out what had happened in the last few years to the boys involved in athletics. One principal related the following success story about what took place in one school located in an area where it was unsafe to walk three blocks at night, an area where violence and trouble were in great abundance, extremely commonplace and almost a way of life.

> The principal of that inner city high school said that in the last three years, 161 boys have gone out for football and of that 161, not one dropped out of school—not one. Twelve of the boys got scholarships and went on to college. There were 45 basketball participants with no dropouts, and 18 of them went on to college on scholarships; 89 in track with not one dropout and nine of them got special scholarships; 32 in tennis with one dropout; 64 in baseball, with three drafted by professional teams and one dropout. The statistics of this school during a three-year period show that there were 391 athletes with two dropouts, within a setting where 60 percent of the general student body drop out.

People who are not close to the issues do not fully realize the real benefits of the athletic program within the high school.

---

[15]Briggs, Paul, "The Opportunity to be Relevant," *Journal of Health, Physical Education and Recreation* (May, 1970), p. 41.

[16]Briggs, Paul, "The Opportunity to be Relevant," *Journal of Health Physical Education and Recreation* (May 1970), p. 43.

They cannot comprehend the purposes of such a program because they do not understand it. They see only the superficial aspect of the program, the expenses, the problems connected with crowd control, the divergence away from the issues of learning and education. These critics fail to realize and comprehend that there are real, important, and worthwhile relationships within the athletic programs that may not be seen. These critics do not understand the objectives and benefits of such a program.

EFFECT OF ATHLETICS ON YOUTH AND SOCIETY

The effect of athletics on our present-day society is astounding. People must realize that they are participating in a program for youth that is unmatched in this country. Why is this important? How can it be a vital force in the preservation of our youth at a time when drugs are threatening the very existence of our country and draining the very life blood of our great nation. If we analyze its importance, we can see a force of good that is unmatched in this country for the cultivation of virtues that are desperately needed for the preservation of the youth of this country and a vital force that depicts the good and wholesome life that somewhere along the line has been lost or discarded as being unneeded, unwanted, and unnecessary.

We can argue at length that athletes are for the few, talented individuals. We can argue the benefits of the championship games and the merits of the bowl games. We can become so engrossed in the problems of eligibility and conference rules that we lose sight of the real values of the athletic program and what it does for the participant as well as the nonparticipant and the community. What are these benefits? They are not complex in nature. They

are the things we have tried to teach and provide our youth with throughout the ages. They coincide with the concepts upon which our country was founded: the personal development of the youth; the development of the social, physical, and psychological aspects of young people to help them better fit into society as responsible, worthwhile citizens; ones that will make their mark on the world while making it a better place to live for future generations. Athletics will provide them with a base upon which to build these ideals, ambitions, and dreams. It will provide them with a frame of reference, something they can hold on to, something good, wholesome, and clean.

The division of men's athletics[17] of the American Alliance for Health, Physical Education, and Recreation emphasized the place of interscholastic athletics in the education program by listing the following principles:

1. Interscholastic and intercollegiate athletic programs should be regarded as integral parts of the total education program and should be so conducted that they are worthy of such regard.
2. Interscholastic and intercollegiate athletic programs should supplement rather than serve as substitutes for basic physical education programs, and intramural athletic programs.
3. Interscholastic and intercollegiate athletic programs should be subject to the same administrative control as the total education program.
4. Interscholastic and intercollegiate athletic programs should be conducted by men with adequate training in physical education.
5. Interscholastic and intercollegiate athletic programs should be so conducted that the physical welfare and

---

[17]Division of Men's Athletics, Athletics in Education, a Platform Statement, *Journal of Health, Physical Education and Recreation* (September, 1962), p. 27.

safety of the participants are protected and fostered.

6. Interscholastic and intercollegiate athletic programs should be conducted in accordance with the letter and the spirit of the rules and regulations of appropriate conference, state, and national athletic associations.

THE FUTURE OF ATHLETICS IN THE SCHOOL

The future of interscholastic athletics as an educational force in the school is dependent upon the establishment and development of strong, defensible principles and procedures which govern the administration of the program. Every program in the school is justified only by its contribution to the education of the student. If athletics does not fulfill its mission in this respect, it should not be a part of the program because activities should be selected only on the basis of their contributions to the education of the whole child.

If interscholastic athletics is to fulfill its destination as a contributing force in the education of the youth, then it must be established under uniform principles which will guide it toward this goal. It should be an integral part of the curriculum of the school and, therefore, should be administered in the same manner. This means that even though the athletic director administers the athletic program, he or she is still responsible to the administration and the administration must justify the athletic program in terms of what it contributes to the education of the students. If the purpose of education is to better fit the individual to take his place in society, it would be reasonable to assume that the best preparation for developing broad interests, wholesome recreation, and socialized living after school days is to experience these during school days. School athletics offer these opportunities. There must be some phase of the educational program which is designed to develop those capacities which will help the student to adjust to the stress of present-day living. Athletics has long been a motivating force for good among the youth of America. As Briggs[18] so aptly put it in discussing what athletics means to the youth in the ghetto:

> I stand here as a superintendent of schools thoroughly convinced that we must be active in physical education, health, recreation, and athletics. We've got to double the programs of America. We've got to use our programs to break the isolation of the ghetto. We've got to use our programs to keep the children in school, to teach them discipline, to teach them how to live with each other— a team approach. We've got to use the wholesomeness of the athletic field to do these things.
>
> I come from a school system that has just completed building four new high schools, all with big plants and facilities for athletics and physical education. Another high school is under construction; two on the drawing boards will open within two years; seven large Olympic-size swimming pools are under construction this year; two additional high school gymnasiums are under construction this year. We're putting our money where our mouth is, because we believe in health, physical education, and recreation. It costs so much money to conduct junior high athletic programs that we cannot support them. So what do we do? We turn the junior high school youngster onto the street at the moment in his life when he has the greatest desire to be a member of some kind of team.

The ability to mold the forces of good and fight the forces of evil through the programs of athletics both for the participant and the spectator are tremendous.

The Educational Policies Commission[19]

---

[18]Briggs, Paul, "The Opportunity to be Relevant," p. 45.

[19]*School Athletics—Problems and Policies*, *Educational Policies Commission* and *The American Association of School Administrators* (Washington, D.C., 1954), p. 81.

has summarized the place and value of interscholastic athletes very aptly in the following manner:

1. Each school or school system should identify clearly the goals it seeks for its athletic program. School personnel should invite the cooperation of students and other citizens in identifying these goals.
2. Athletics should fit harmoniously into the rest of the school program with respect to purposes, schedules, budgets, and demands on the time and attention of the students and staff.
3. Programs of athletic education will succeed in preparation to the extent to which they are infused with variety and appeal, matched to the varying needs and interests of different children scheduled to permit maximum participation and supported with adequate funds, facilities, and leadership.
4. The core of the program at all levels should be the athletic instruction and play for all pupils in regular classes in physical education.
5. Athletic games, in all cases, should be played with emphasis on fun, physical development, skill and strategy, social experience, and good sportsmanship.
6. High pressure competition, with over emphasis on the importance of winning, should not be sanctioned in any part of the school programs.
7. Girls should share equally with boys in facilities, equipment, and funds allocated to athletic activities.
8. Boys interscholastic athletics should be governed by the same authorities that control other parts of the school program, at both local and state levels.
9. Local school authorities should give consistent support in letter and in spirit, to the rules and standards developed by the several state high school athletic associations and by similar bodies.
10. State departments of education should become increasingly active in efforts to focus attention of educators and laymen on the needs for desirable educational objectives and effective controlling policies for interscholastic athletics.
11. Boards of education should establish policies for financial support of interscholastic athletics that will free the interscholastic program from dependence on gate receipts.
12. A school's athletic activities should be in harmony with the rest of the total school program with respect to aims and outcomes.

Further evidence of the value of athletics stated by the Division of Men's Athletics of the American Association of Health, Physical Education, and Recreation[20] is stated as follows:

Athletics when utilized properly serve as potential educational media through which the optimum growth — physical, mental, emotional, social, and moral—of the participants may be fostered. During the many arduous practice sessions and in the variety of situations that arise during the heat of the contests, the players must repeatedly react to their own capabilities and limitations and to the behavior of others. These repeated reactions and the psychological conditioning that accompanies them, inevitably result in changes—mental, as well as physical—in the players. Because each contest is usually surrounded by an emotionally charged atmosphere and the players are vitally interested in the outcome of the game, the players are more pliable and, hence, more subject to change than in most educational endeavors. To ensure that these changes are educationally desirable, all phases of athletics should be expertly organized and conducted.

It is the desire of many youngsters to excel in athletics. To them athletics is a tremendous, motivating force and many will sacrifice things to develop a high degree of fitness. They will endure long hours of vigorous exercise and practice to acquire the necessary skills to make them champions. This rigorous training has a direct effect on their attitude toward life and to-

---

[20]A.A.H.P.E.R., "Athletics in Education — A Platform Statement." *Journal of Health Physical Education and Recreation* (Sept, 1962) p. 24.

ward society in general.

The Division of Men's Athletics[21] justified its belief that participation in athletics should be included in the educational experiences of students with the following statements:

> Because athletics are of historical and social significance in our national culture . . .
>
> Because athletics provide a primary means through which may be developed and maintained the physical vigor and stamina required to defend successfully our concept of freedom, and to realize fully our potential as Americans . . .
>
> Because athletics provide a primary means through which may be developed the habits, attitudes, and ideals requisite to ethical competition and effective cooperation in a free society . . .
>
> Because athletics provide a primary means through which may be utilized in a healthful and wholesome fashion the leisure of our citizens and youth . . .
>
> Because athletics have a powerful appeal for young people during their formative years and can be utilized to further the harmonious development of youth . . .

The students have, through athletics, made a real contribution to American education. The students were responsible in the beginning, for the development of athletics in school life. It was through their continued effort and interest that athletics thrived and grew and eventually became a part of the total educational curriculum and gained its rightful place as a contributor to the education of the whole child. School men, slowly at first, began to understand the value of competitive athletics. They realized that it is a part of man's nature to compete, and that this will profoundly affect his attitudes, his abilities, his values and appreciations. Because of

this, athletics should be of tremendous value in the education of youth.

It is interesting to note that as far back as 1951 Scott[22] made the following statement in respect to the heritage and place of athletics in the schools:

> Despite the unfortunate system that has been permitted to develop in the conduct of the program of competitive sports, there is some hope that the problems of athletics can be solved. The heritage of interscholastic and intercollegiate athletics has been such that the program has been considered something separate and apart from the general educational curriculum. Despite this heritage, however, there is increasing evidence that the true value of competitive athletics as a method of education is gaining wide recognition among educators. It is significant that in those schools and colleges that have come to understand the educational, rather than a business venture, the true worth of competitive athletics is revealed.

Athletics has a terrific responsibility. The football field, the basketball court, the baseball field, and the tennis court are the laboratories of life. The athletic fields are the places where life's lessons are taught and where they are learned best. These are the places where people learn to play fairly, to play cleanly, to fight hard. The participants learn to take it as well as to dish it out. The leaders of our youth should realize before it is too late the potentialities existent in the athletic programs within our schools which can be used to fight the evils which are threatening our society.

BEHAVIORAL OBJECTIVES

After a person has read this chapter, he should be able to:

1. Predict some of the trends which may occur in the future in the professional

---

[21]A.A.H.P.E.R., Division of Men's Athletics, *Athletics in Education,* A Platform Statement, *Journal of Health Physical and Recreation* (Sept., 1962) , p. 25.

[22]Scott, Harry, *Competitive Sports in Schools and Colleges* (New York, Harper and Brothers, 1951) , p. 125.

preparation of interscholastic athletic directors.

2. Explain the early beginnings of interscholastic athletics and analyze its role in present-day society.

3. Enumerate some of the criticisms of interscholastic athletics.

4. Visualize the functions of a good interscholastic program and the promotion of school discipline.

5. Apply the contributions which athletics makes to the lives of young people. Analyze the benefits which are made by athletics.

6. Appraise the relationship between vigorous exercise and disease.

7. Recognize the importance leadership of interscholastic athletics has in our present-day society.

8. Predict the role that interscholastic athletics will play in the next ten years. Justify these predictions.

9. Cite several examples whereby athletics can develop character and good citizenship through participation.

10. Explain the role the Educational Policies Commission has played in the development of interscholastic athletics.

11. Analyze the growth of the interscholastic athletic program in the past few years.

12. Explain the role of athletics in relation to the use of leisure time.

13. Enumerate some of the benefits of the interscholastic athletic program.

14. Analyze the statement, "educational leadership in athletics" with concrete examples.

15. Enumerate several factors which directly influence the program of athletics and show how they may affect the program.

16. Enumerate and explain the most important factors in a good interscholastic athletic program.

17. Enumerate several factors which influence the development of a good interscholastic athletic program and explain the implications of each.

18. Differentiate between the aims and goals of the elementary and high school athletic program.

19. Detect and identify any evidence which supports the belief that interscholastic athletics are on the upsurge.

20. Explain the importance of leadership in interscholastic athletics.

21. Select several desirable standards for evaluating interscholastic athletics in schools.

22. Differentiate between aims, objectives, and outcomes in the development of the interscholastic athletic program.

23. Identify some of the administrative guidelines that should guide the conduct of interscholastic athletics in the schools.

24. Identify some of the relations between moral behavior and athletic competition.

25. Identify some of the contributions that athletic sports make to the lives of young people. Explain the benefits that are derived from athletics.

26. Analyze some of the characteristics of a good athletic program.

27. Explain what is the chief source of agitation for championship contests.

28. Explain how athletics promote good school discipline.

29. Identify the reasons for the persistence of interscholastic athletics in spite of many adverse forces that have attempted to abolish it.

30. Define athletics. Differentiate between the trivial or vital aspects of athletics in American life.

ACTIVITIES

1. Debate the issue: What is the role of interscholastic athletics in modern education?

2. Debate the issue: Why do boards of education fail to support interscholastic athletics?

3. Interview a number of athletic directors to determine what it is about their work that either makes them feel uncomfortable or what leads to a state of uneasiness about their work.

4. Debate the issue: Limitations should be placed on athletics if they are to be a part of education.

5. Compile a list of the possible contributions to the traditions of interscholastic athletics make to American life.

6. Attend a meeting of the board of education in your local community in which the athletic program is being discussed. List your criteria for the effectiveness of such a meeting and evaluate this meeting in terms of them.

7. Debate the issue: Does athletics contribute to human needs?

8. Develop or prepare some standards for evaluating the interscholastic program.

9. Debate the issue: Athletic competition should be coeducational.

10. Debate the issue: Are there major and minor sports?

11. Debate the issue: Competition for both girls and boys should be allowed on the same varsity teams.

12. Debate the issue: Can state high school championship tournaments be justified?

13. Secure the dropout records of the local high school and determine whether there seems to be a correlation between dropouts and a lack of an athletic program.

SUGGESTED READINGS

1. A.A.H.P.E.R.: Athletics in education — A platform statement. *Journal of Health, Physical Education, and Recreation,* September, 1962.

2. Alley, Louis: Better start kicking that dog around. *The Physical Educator,* October, 1959.

3. Bucher, Charles: *Administration of Health and Physical Education Programs.* St. Louis, Mosby, 1971.

4. Bucher, Charles: *Foundations of Physical Education,* St. Louis, Mosby, 1968.

5. Briggs, Paul.: The opportunity to be relevant. *Journal of Health, Physical Education, and Recreation,* May, 1970.

6. Cherry, Spurgeon, and Lawther, John: Division of Men's Athletics—Purposes and Projects. *Journal of Health, Physical Education, and Athletics,* January, 1963.

7. Dannehl, Wayne, and Razor, Jack: The Value of Athletics. *National Association of Secondary School Principals* September, 1971.

8. Daughtrey, Greyson, and Woods, John: *Physical Education Programs,* Philadelphia, Saunders, 1971.

9. Division of Men's Athletics: Athletics in education, a platform statement. *Journal of Health, Physical Education, and Recreation,* September, 1962.

10. Editorial: It matters . . . How you play the game. *Physical Education News Letter,* May 15, 1964.

11. Epler, Stephen: *The Growth of Interscholastic Sports,* Englewood Cliffs, P-H, 1962.

12. Frank, Dick: Spectator sports: Opportunity or nightmare? *The Bulletin of the National Association of Secondary School Principals,* May, 1971.

13. Greenwood, Edward: Emotional well being through lifetime sports: *Journal of Health, Physical Education, and Recreation.* December, 1967.

14. Kaech, Arnold: The point of sport, its whole importance, its true meaning. *Scholastic Coach,* March, 1971.

15. Keller, Irvin: School athletics—Its philosophy and objectives. *American School Board Journal,* August, 1966.

16. Kennedy, Joseph: Interscholastic sports— A balanced viewpoint. *The Clearing House,* April, 1969.

17. Lehmann, Harry and George, Jack: *School Athletic Administration.* New York, Har-Row, 1966.

18. Lockhart, Aileene and Slusher, Howard: *Anthology of Contempory Readings.* Dubuque, W. C. Brown, 1966.

19. Masonbrink, Edward and Howard, Glenn: *Administration of Physical Education.* New York, Har-Row, 1963.

20. Mehn, Duane: Athletics and values. *Coach and Athlete,* November, 1971.

21. Olds, Glenn: In defense of sports. *Journal of Health, Physical Education, and Recreation,* January, 1961.

22. Pietrofesa, John and Rosen, Al: Interscholastic sports — Misdirected? Misguided? Misnomer? *Clearing House,* November, 1968.

23. Resick, Matthew, Seidel, Beverly, and Mason, James: *Modern Administration Practices in Physical Education and Athletics.* Reading, A-W, 1970.

24. Slusher, Howard: *Man, Sport and Existence.* Philadelphia, Lea & Febiger, 1967.

25. Solberg, James: Interscholastic athletics, tail that wags the dog? *Journal of Secondary Education,* May, 1970.

26. South American Federation of YMCAs: Character Values in Sports and Games. *Journal of Health, Physical Education, and Recreation,* November, 1960.

27. *The Educational Policies Commission.* School Athletics, Problems and Policies: Washington, D.C., 1954.

28. Wilton, W.M.: An early consensus on sportsmanship. *The Physical Educator,* October, 1963.

CHAPTER 3

Philosophy of Athletics

Interscholastic athletics attracts millions of people and has grown tremendously popular over the years. It is one of the most thoroughly enjoyed activities in America. It is a recreational pastime for many people, and an opportunity for the participants to learn the lessons of life in a controlled environment under the supervision of experts. Despite its popularity, there is a great deal of confusion and misunderstanding over the philosophies, goals, and objectives of interscholastic athletics. This is partly true because the people in charge of the program have not outlined its real purpose and the philosophy under which it is administered.

To fully understand the philosophy and objectives of the present-day athletic program, one must understand the history of athletics and how athletics was first introduced by the students. For many years athletics was not a part of school programs as it is now. Administrators turned their heads because they did not want to see the abuses that crept into the program due to outside influences. They did not want to "face up" to the decisions that needed to be made to bring the program under their direction. This continued, as history will show, until finally athletics was brought under the control of the school administration where it flourished and grew to be an integral part of the educational program. Its educational values are now accepted as being equal in every respect to other programs within the school. Athletics has established a firm foundation and is now a contributing force in the education of our youth.

To definitely state a philosophy of athletics which will apply to every high school situation is impossible. This is true because a philosophy is the result of the thinking and beliefs of one or a number of individuals. If these individuals are in direct control of athletics at the top level of administration it will most certainly have a direct bearing on the athletic program at the lower high school level. The philosophy dictated by the board of education, the superintendent, and the principal will in turn reflect the thinking and attitude of the athletic director, as well as the athletic coaches of the high school athletic teams. This, in turn, will permeate the thinking of the athletes, the faculty, as well as the students themselves. Even though this is true, it is necessary that an athletic philosophy for every school be formulated and that this philosophy be in writing and made known to the community, faculty, and students.

FORMULATING A PHILOSOPHY OF ATHLETICS

Formulating a philosophy of athletics should be an important and initial step in establishing a program of athletics in the high school. Who should develop this philosophy? Why should the philosophy be developed? What should the philosophy include?

Ideally, the selection of an athletic

philosophy should be the responsibility of a committee made up of persons who might be affected by the program or will be involved in implementing the program. This committee might include the superintendent, the principal, the athletic director, one or two coaches, a faculty member not connected with athletics, a school board member, a parent association representative, and a student body representative who preferably is on some athletic squad.

This committee should serve as a sounding board to air ideas on what should be included in the philosophy. When all the ideas have been presented and positive discussion exhausted, a smaller committee which is appointed by the original committee should take the ideas and draw up the philosophy for the program. Upon its completion and its approval by the original committee, the philosophy should be made a part of the total educational philosophy and then published so that all persons affected will be familiar with it.

Why all this bother? Why a philosophy? As Frankel says, "Philosophy is a systematic effort to clarify and coordinate our beliefs and to integrate them with our actions."[1] In this world of increasing awareness and questioning, everything must be justified. Athletics is no different. If anything, it requires more justification than many other areas because it is in the eye of the public so much. For that reason, the belief that athletics is an integral and equal part of the educational process must be evaluated as to whether that belief is real and is being carried out in the educational process. Formulating and studying the philosophy of athletics provides this type of evaluation and furnishes a justification of the program in the public view.

The first consideration in formulating the philosophy is, "What should that philosophy be?" The real question, however, is, "What should athletics be?" Athletics should consist of five basic and important points. These are participation, improvement, achievement, interaction, and enjoyment.

A youngster's participation in athletics should be as valuable to his total educational experience as math or English if it is considered valuable enough to be included in the program. For this reason all students should be encouraged to participate equally and with the same opportunities.

Improvement is the underlying aim of education. Thus, it must be a main point in a philosophy of athletics. Through participation and instruction there must be the opportunity for improvement.

Closely coordinated with improvement is achievement. Goals must be set which the student can reach and in which he can feel satisfaction. As the philosopher Xenophon states, ". . . what a disgrace it is for a man to grow old without ever seeing the beauty of which his body is capable."[2]

The fourth point which should be included in an athletic philosophy is interaction. Athletics is interaction with the coach, with the fans, with the teammates, and with the opposition. Whether conflict or teamwork, the athlete is confronted with a social situation where he must learn to conduct himself in an appropriate manner.

The last aspect of a philosophic dialogue on athletics should include enjoyment. After all, athletics are just glorified games in the public view. The athlete, even though the physical torment and desire to excel is there, still enjoys playing the game.

---

[1]Frankel, Charles, "A Review for the Teacher . . . Philosophy", *National Education Association Journal* (December, 1962), p. 51.

[2]Xenophon, cross quoted from: Bucher, Charles, *Foundations of Physical Education* (St. Louis, The C. V. Mosby Co., 1964), p. 129.

If not, participation would not be held in as high a regard as it seems to be. Weiss[3] comments, "Athletics are many things. They afford the opportunity for many people to excel in and through the use of the body." In doing so, they allow for social interaction and enjoyment that contributes to the total development of the individual and his education.

ATHLETIC PHILOSOPHIES

Keller[4] has commented on several philosophies which have come about as a result of rules, controls, or standards that have guided the interscholastic programs.

The first is one on which the entire program of athletics is based, and is that . . .

Interscholastic athletics is a part of the total educational program and as such contributes to the development of desirable learning habits and outcomes in knowledge, skill, and emotional patterns. Because of this, the athletic program can be justified as a contributing part of the educational curriculum.

Another philosophy stems from the fact that as administrators realized the educational values of athletics, they become interested in providing these opportunities to all the students instead of a selected few. They did this by establishing programs in physical education and making it compulsory. Thus all students benefited. With the development of trained teachers of physical education, came better programs. Gradually the philosophies of physical education and athletics blended together and the objectives became similar—that of the education of the 'whole' child.

Another philosophy of athletics, which has caused major concern among schoolmen and one which has caused a great deal of anxiety on their part, is the emphasis on making money from athletic contests through gate receipts. This type of philosophy can lead only to trouble because in order to obtain gate receipts a winning team is necessary. People will not come to see a loser. In order to produce a winner, abuses creep in and soon the educational values have disappeared and the program is no longer justifiable as being part of the school curriculum.

Still another philosophy which is popular in the United States is the one which typifies the olympic idea of play for fun. There is a similarity between this idea and the idea behind the interscholastic athletic program in as much as none of the participants received any monetary rewards. All athletes who participate but receive no monetary reward are amateurs. These include high school athletes representing different organizations. School athletes are amateurs but all amateur athletes are not school athletes. While they are similar in this respect, they do not have the same philosophy or objectives.

Interscholastic athletics has grown and flourished over the years because school administrators have made them a part of the educational curriculum. They have insisted that if athletics is to be part of the educational program then it must contribute to the education of the youth; otherwise it cannot be justified. To better accomplish this purpose, more work needs to be done to better inform boards of education so that they will have a better insight and understanding of the purpose, objectives, and philosophy of interscholastic athletics. If this can be done, athletics will continue to flourish in the high schools throughout America.

SAMPLE ATHLETIC CODE OF ETHICS

Philosophy

We believe that interscholastic athletics are an integral part of the school's total curriculum.

[3]Weiss, Paul, *Sport: A Philosophic Inquiry* (Carbondale, Illinois, Southern Ilinois University Press, 1969) p. 36.

[4]Keller, Irvin, "School Athletics—Philosophy and Objectives" *American School Board Journal* (August, 1966) , p. 22.

We believe that participation in athletics should be a part of the total educational experience for all youths who attend high school.

We believe that participation in a sound athletic program contributes to the development of health and happiness, physical skills, emotional maturity, social competence, and moral values.

We believe that a sound athletic program teaches the participants the value of cooperation as well as the spirit of competition so important to our society. The student athlete learns to work with others for the achievement of group goals.

We believe that the spirit of play and the will to win are valuable to the development of a healthy mind.

We believe that the ability to "take it" in vigorous play, experiencing defeat without whimpering, and victory without gloating, and disciplining one's self to comply with the rules of the game and of good sportsmanship, are necessary to the development of sound character.

We believe that athletics are a wholesome equalizer because individuals are judged for what they are and for what they can do, not on the basis of the social, ethnic, or economic group to which their families belong.

The coaches at high school have agreed that a definite framework of conduct for athletes is essential in attaining quality in athletics. This framework is written as an Athletic Code of Ethics.

As a member of an athletic team, there are certain things we feel each boy or girl should do to make our teams the best. If you have a sincere desire to be the BEST you will have no trouble living up to these few simple regulations.

Eligibility

Grades must be maintained through proper utilization of regular and athletic study hall periods. Proper attitude and example maintained in the classroom at all times. One should have a knowledge and compliance of the High School Athletic Association rules.

Behavior

As athletes at high school your behavior, athletically and socially, should be beyond reproach. Since you are representing the coaches, teams, students, and the good name of the high school, you are expected to be respectful, courteous and well-behaved on and off the competitive areas.

Training Rules

As an athlete you are expected to maintain proper rest, food, and general health habits. During a normal week day, you are expected to be in your home no later than 10:30 P.M. which is curfew time. On a night before a contest you should be in bed no later than 10:30 P.M.

Smoking and Drinking

One of the most rigid training rules which MUST be obeyed is the "NO SMOKING-NO DRINKING" rule. This training rule is quite clear and carries with it the implication that "NO boy or girl may drink or smoke and still participate in the high school athletic program."

Violation, to any degree of this rule, whether in or out of season will NOT BE TOLERATED at the high school. Violations could result in suspension or expulsion from a team. The head coach, principal, and athletic director will decide in severe cases.

These rules are in effect during the summer vacation months, holiday periods, etc. as well as during the school term.

Conduct

Since you are representing your school, community, and athletics, you are expected to conduct yourself properly at all times, on and off the playing field, and in the community. Remember, *good sportsmanship* is to be followed at all times!

Dedication

Each athlete must be willing to sacrifice and dedicate himself to sports. The athlete should be aware that nothing worthwhile is accomplished without hard work, application, and a sincere desire to succeed. The athlete must also realize that he must work "out of season" as well as during the time he participates. He must also be willing to sacrifice his own personal "whims" or desires for the good of the group or team.

Language

Use language which is socially acceptable. Profanity or vulgar talk will not be tolerated on or off the field at any time. *Speak ENGLISH!* The use of such words only displays lack of control, ignorance, not high moral standards which all athletes must attain.

Respect

The athlete is to show respect for coaches, teachers, officials, spectators, school facilities, and equipment.

Absence and Tardiness

If the athlete is in school, he or she is expected to practice unless excused by the coach. Do not send word by way of another student or player that you cannot make practice. *See your COACH personally!*

a. Two unexcused absences will bring disciplinary action

b. The third unexcused absence will mean dismissal from the team

c. Two tardinesses will equal one unexcused absence

(These rulings, a, b and c, may be altered by the coach.)

Appearance

As a member of our teams we want to be proud of your appearance. Boys are expected to dress neatly and keep the hair short and well-groomed. Hair cuts shall be obtained periodically so as to keep the hair short enough on the sides and back of the neck and one inch above the eyebrows. Dress on the day of a contest is up to the desires of the coach in charge.

OBJECTIVES
OF THE ATHLETIC PROGRAM

Keller[5] has indicated that after the school board in cooperation with the school officials and with input from the community has formulated a philosophy for interscholastic athletics, then the objectives should be carefully worked out. He has suggested that a school athletic program should include the development of the following goals for its youth.

1. An understanding of why the school offers a program of athletics.
2. A knowledge of the values that athletics have for the individual and for society.
3. An understanding of the rules essential to playing the games and to being intelligent spectators.
4. The ability to think both as an in-

---

[5]Keller, Irvin, *American School Board Journal*, p. 23.

dividual and as a member of a group.

5. Faith in the democratic processes.
6. Realization of the values of group ideals.
7. Improved motor skills.
8. Better health and physical fitness.
9. An appreciation of wholesome recreation and entertainment.
10. The desire to succeed and to excel.
11. High moral and ethical standards.
12. Self-discipline and emotional maturity.
13. Social competence.
14. A realization of the values of conforming to rules.
15. Respect for the rights of others and for authority.
16. High ideals of fairness in all human relationships.

With interscholastic athletics as they exist at present, it is apparent that athletic objectives should be written for the participant, the school, the student body, and the community. By objectives are meant the goals or the ends to be realized, and in athletics especially it is important that the goals be thoroughly understood by all parties. Those involved must know in advance what is anticipated during the coming year. This does not mean that the sole objective of athletics is winning a definite number of games or winning the conference in all sports. Neither is it to be assumed to mean that the year is to be considered a success or failure on the number of wins that the teams experienced. It could mean that the objectives consisted of setting up a series of contests with neighboring schools which had as their objective friendly rivalry, the formulating of new friendships, the perfection of playing skills, the development of good sportsmanship, and the improvement of community relationships. It is difficult to imagine that such a program would not be considered successful even though not one contest resulted in a win.

Areas of Interest in Formulating Philosophies

There has been a great deal of confusion and misunderstanding regarding the philosophy of athletics. The people delegated to formulate the philosophies of athletics have not made it clear to the public the beliefs, outcomes, objectives and goals upon which the philosophies are based. Philosophies will vary considerably in the different schools. The goals and beliefs of people represent many divergent points of view. There are certain areas in the administration of interscholastic athletics which have a tendency to affect the establishment of philosophies more than do others, and administrators must determine or at least make a firm commitment on their feelings regarding these areas in the athletic program. In making these decisions, they determine the philosophy or direction the department is to take.

EXPLAINING THE PHILOSOPHY OF THE ATHLETIC PROGRAM

The philosophy of athletics will be somewhat different in every school. Therefore, a plan for explaining the philosophy of each particular school should be the responsibility of the school board, the administration, and the individual coaches. A meeting, open to the general public, should be held during which time a member of the board of education should give a statement of the school's philosophy of athletics and education. The athletic director should state the goals and objectives of the school's athletic program at this meeting. This could be followed by having the head coach of each sport state his personal philosophy and individual goals for his particular sport. An opportunity for a question-and-answer period with the school personnel should be held.

This type of meeting will promote

public interest and understanding of inter-scholastic athletics at the high school level. It will give the coach the opportunity to meet with parents personally, something that is not done enough at the high school level.

A SAMPLE PHILOSOPHY OF ATHLETICS FOR THE SCHOOL

The program of interscholastic athletics should teach sound citizenship through the practice of good sportsmanship. It should develop desirable social traits, cooperation, and dependability. It should provide opportunities for students to compete in a variety of sports at their own levels of ability and provide opportunities for the development of desirable student leadership and teamwork.

The most important values should be the provision of a wholesome outlet for superior athletes, respect for authority, learning the spirit of the rules through hard work and sacrifice, attainment of physical fitness through good health habits, the joy and experience of keen competition, and the desire to excel.

These activities should be properly supervised to provide a variety of athletic experiences so that the participant may derive the maximum educational and physical values from his experiences.

It is expected that each participant will develop and improve his performance through dedication to the sport in which he is participating and that he will practice and develop a positive mental attitude toward his teammates and coaches.

The teachers, coaches, student body, and community expect the athletes who participate in the program to maintain the following standards:

1. All acts of insubordination and/or non-compliance are handled by the coach of the team involved at the time the act

occurs. The coach should determine what measures are appropriate.

2. It is neither the duty nor the desire of interscholastic athletics to deprive a student-athlete of his or her right to express individuality. Certain sports do, however, have prescribed codes which are designed to take into consideration the health and safety of the athlete. It is expected that those athletes who wish to compete in these activities will consider all regulations and conform to them. In cases where the sport has no prescribed code on the matter of hair styles, treatments, or athletic apparel the decision of what is reasonable and appropriate to insure the safety and physical welfare of the student athlete shall be made by the coach. If in the judgment of the coach an athletes' hair style, treatment, or athletic apparel either disrupts the learning situation and/or places the safety and physical welfare of the student athlete in jeopardy, the coach should request that the student take appropriate remedial action.

It the student athlete fails to comply within a reasonable length of time, the athlete should be suspended from further interscholastic competition until the problem is corrected.

3. The American Medical Association and the American Alliance of Health, Physical Education, and Recreation have issued a statement on the health hazards connected with the use of tobacco products, particularly cigarette smoking. Concerned educators share the position of these associations and make every effort to discourage student athletes from the habitual use of tobacco products.

It is therefore recommended, except in cases with extenuating circumstances, that any student-athlete reported as having been seen using tobacco products, be counseled by their coach, and if after a more complete study of the circumstances substantiates the allegation, the coach *may* suspend the athlete from further interscholastic participation for that sport season.

4. The use of alcoholic beverages by an athlete is also discouraged, and upon receipt of information from a reliable source regarding the use of alcoholic beverages the coach should immediately counsel the athlete involved. If no extenuating circumstances exist and the coach feels enough substantiating evidence is available, the athlete involved may be suspended from participation for that sport season.

5. The use and/or abuse of drugs by a student athlete, unless prescribed by a physician, should result in the suspension of that athlete from further interscholastic participation for a period of at least one sport season. The period of suspension may be extended if the use and/or abuse of the drugs has in someway impaired the student's ability to function within the normal activity and expectations of the athletic program.

When a coach is made aware that an athlete is using and/or abusing drugs, he should counsel the athlete involved. If in the opinion of the coach enough substantiative evidence is available to warrant suspension, the athlete should be suspended and directed to the appropriate school authorities for further counseling and guidance.

In situations involving any of the five areas of clarification either the student athlete or the coach of the team involved may request in writing a hearing by the Athletic Review Board. (The Athletic Review Board should consist of three faculty members selected at large, the high school principal and the athletic director.

The request should be sent to the athletic director as resident *pro tem* of the Athletic Review Board. Upon receipt of this letter the athletic directors should set up a meeting of the athlete and his or her parents, and the Athletic Review Board. The board should review the testimony of all persons involved and either confirm or disapprove the responsive action of the coach.

The Athletic Advisory Board should request the Athletic Review Board to meet whenever it is necessary to insure the student athlete of due process of his or her right to appeal what he considers to be an unsubstantiated judgement by his coach. It should also be the wish of the Advisory Board that the coach use the Review Board when in the coach's opinion extenuating circumstance exists that merit the Review Board's consideration for reinstating an athlete.

This also includes cheerleaders. When a cheerleader is dropped, inform the athletic director why this has happened.

This statement of philosophy and objectives should also be written out in letter form and sent to parents of prospective interscholastic athletes. For the parents to better understand the general philosophy and objectives of interscholastic athletics, a brief history of athletics should be presented. In this history of athletics it should be pointed out that athletics evolved from student interest rather than school initiative. It should also be pointed out that rivalry of students is a natural phenomena just as it is in the business world and life. The eligibility of contestants as well as the rules and regulations of the sport should be explained. Lastly, the role of athletics in education and its priority as an educational experience rather than some other less desirable attributes, should be explained.

The Relationship of Interscholastic Athletics to the Physical Education Program

Interscholastic athletics should be a part of the physical education program. It depends heavily on the physical education programs and consequently there should be a good relationship between interscholastic athletics and the total physical education program.

LEADERSHIP IN THE INTERSCHOLASTIC ATHLETIC PROGRAM

Leadership is an important aspect of the athletic program. The youth of today hear different answers to the same questions from many sources yet they are expected to make decisions on these questions. The interscholastic athletic program can provide the constructive and positive leadership that will help the youth to make the right decisions. The athletic coach has, without question, a profound effect on the athletes who play for him. He has a wonderful opportunity to help mold their characters and influence their decisions on moral and citizenship issues because of the close association he has with them under emotionally charged situations.

Reeves[6] has suggested that:

. . . many of the boys lack the guidance and leadership at home so they look to the coach for this. For this reason the coach must have the qualities that the boys will look up to. Characteristics frequently found in good coaches are (1) a vigorous and inspiring personality, (2) a

good personal appearance, (3) good taste in personal grooming (4) a love for sports, (5) an ability to plan and organize, (6) emotional stability, and (7) a strong character that will set himself up as an example to the boys both on and off the field.

The coach is constantly in the public eye and his or her personal conduct is always open to scrutiny. The coach is a good subject of conversation at all levels, personal and professional, so he must conduct himself at all times with this in mind. The entire interscholastic program is an "open window" for the people of the community to look into and compare the way it is conducted with other aspects of the entire school program.

In order to provide the public with the correct image of the athletic program as being a part of the education program, the coach should identify himself with the administration and faculty. In order to provide the overall leadership that is so necessary for the youth of today, the coach must be a complete individual in all school affairs. He must display leadership in all educational endeavors and not only in athletics. He must participate in all school activities to the extent that the athletes will acknowledge other areas in education as being important because of the coaches' identification with them. This is the type of leadership that the youth needs from the coach. It will not only enhance his image with the athlete but with the faculty, the administration, and the community. If the coach can do this, he will become the most valuable person on the faculty.

The Role of the School Board in Athletics

Each and every local school board has a definite responsibility to help shape, formulate, and finally implement a justifiable philosophy concerning the total ath-

[6]Reeves, Fred, "Educational Leadership of the Athletic Coach," *Coach and Athlete* (January, 1968), p. 18.

letic program. Once the philosophy is formulated, more specific objectives have to be defined and the athletic program planned.

The cardinal athletic principles as set forth by the Educational Policies Commission[7] should:

1. Include a program that closely follows the general instruction program and articulates with other departments of the school,
2. Accommodate a number of students to justify the amount of money spent and merit the warrant of more,
3. Let these funds not interfere with the efficiency of any other school project,
4. Confine school athletic activities to events sponsored only by proper school authorities,
5. Set reasonable season limits and offer a variety of sports,
6. Avoid elements of professionalism and commercialism,
7. Avoid all-star games,
8. Include educative exercises to reach all nonparticipating students to keep them informed and interested,
9. Encourage intramural activities to students below the high school level,
10. Demand respect of rules and policies under which the school conducts its programs.

In the end, the philosophy of any athletic program should have the well-being of the student as its main objective. The parents should be kept well-informed as they are the supporters and financers of the athletic program, and they are the building blocks if the athletic program is going to reach its full potential.

Too often the formulation of the philosophy and objectives of the school's athletic program is done by the academic faculty. The superintendent, principal, and especially the board of education should really understand the philosophy and the most worthwhile objectives of athletics. This understanding can help them make wise and meaningful decisions regarding finances, facilities, and the correct choice of personnel needed to meet the previously mentioned objectives to the fullest extent.

The Role of the Principal in Athletics

While the principal has very little input in formulating a philosophy of athletics for the school system, he is directly affected because it is his responsibility to implement the policies and carry out the philosophy as set forth by the school board and the superintendent. The principal's role is that of a chief communicator. He presents the school's philosophy, its purposes, its programs, its problems, and its progress to the general public. He is the go-between for the school and the community. He must be diplomatic, understanding, intelligent, and cooperative in dealing with the general public. He must be a communications expert and be able to present a true picture to the general public.

The Role of the Superintendent in Athletics

Certainly the superintendent of schools sets the tone for athletics in any school system. He is the figure head, and as such he governs, he approves, and he vetoes all requests. His philosophy, beliefs, and desires concerning the athletic program have a great deal to do with the type of program which will be put into affect. The success or failure of the program is in direct proportion to the enthusiasm which he displays regarding it. A superintendent who is enthusiastic, who is an avid fan, and supporter of the athletic program enhances its success considerably. He should attend the games as often as he can because his

[7]Educational Policies Commission, *School Athletics: Problems and Policies* (Washington, D.C., National Education Association of the United States, 1954), p. 98.

very presence at the games indicates his approval of the program.

The Role of the Student in Formulating a Philosophy

The student has become an increasingly important individual in the formulation of philosophies and objectives for the interscholastic athletic programs. They have become involved in the organizing, developing, and administering of these programs. The administrators can no longer sit back and make all the decisions without having the desires of the student in mind. To begin with, in the early days of athletics, the student was in complete control. Gradually they lost control. The past few years have brought about a desire on the part of the student to become more involved in the formulation of policies. The pressure is now on the administration, and they must offer programs in which the students will want to participate and establish a philosophy which will coincide with the beliefs of the student. Students are becoming more involved as time goes on and their ideas should be considered.

The Relationship of Outside Organizations to the Athletic Program

Outside organizations in the form of booster clubs, quarterback clubs, fathers' clubs and even the parent-teacher organization can be a tremendous help to any athletic program if they are properly conducted. They can also be a detriment to the program if their efforts are misguided and their members feel that their primary function is to direct and run the high school athletic program. A good relationship between these outside organizations and the individuals in charge of the high school athletic program can bring about highly beneficial results. Probably the best examples of outside organizations that work closely with school athletic officials is the booster club or the quarterback club. The membership in these clubs is generally made up of parents and people in the community who are interested in the athletic program. The main objective of these clubs is to help the athletic program in any possible way. This usually consists of money-making projects. These projects take the form of booster-club tag days, seat cushion sales, etc. The money obtained by these clubs is usually used in purchasing some of the fringe benefits for the program which ordinarily would not be purchased, such as movie cameras, etc. They usually do not raise money to support the athletic budget.

These clubs are also vitally concerned with bettering the relationships between coaches and parents. These clubs generally hold weekly meetings during the season and monthly meetings in the off-season. Usually a movie of the preceding game is shown and a question-and-answer period is conducted between the parents and the coach. This gives both parties an awareness of how things are being run.

Other outside organizations are involved in the athletic program. These groups are made up of people in the community and their function is different than the booster club as they act as the line of communication between the coach and the people in the community. Coaches are asked to speak at these organizations, and as a result better communication is obtained between the athletic department and the general public.

The most important contribution made by outside organizations is the improvement of communications between the coaches and parents, and the coaches and the people within the community who are interested in the school and especially the athletic program.

SEPARATE DIRECTORS OF ATHLETICS AND PHYSICAL EDUCATION

There are many conditions which affect the athlete as well as the physical education department in the school. The physical size of the school has much to do with both the programs and the staffing. The number of activities offered in the physical education program and the number of sports offered in athletics is in direct proportion to the number of students and the amount of money available to finance them. There are several methods used to administer the athletic programs in the high school.

One method of administering the athletic and physical education programs is to have the two positions filled by one person. However, this person must be able to devote full time to the duties of both positions. In this way, the total program would be directed or organized using the same philosophy. Participants in the program would benefit more from the total involvement in physical education and sports. A second method is to have an athletic director who is a physical education teacher but is not head of the department. Another physical education teacher is head of the department and the two work together. In this situation, either or both might coach one or more sports as well as being director. With separate roles, more than one philosophy develops and the students benefit from varied ideas. Perhaps having only the one area of responsibility allows the person to devote his complete energy to it. A third method would be to have an athletic director who is not connected with the physical education department at all. This person must work with the physical education staff, but he does not necessarily make the two programs coincide. The first and third methods of assigning an athletic director, would work out well in either a large or small school. The second method would need to be applied in a large school with both a large physical education staff and a large coaching staff. There are almost as many different ways to provide an athletic director and physical education department head as there are schools and districts. Some districts believe in separation of duties; others believe in a conglomeration of duties. Each method of staffing has its merits when the needs and assets of the individual district are considered.

THE PLACE OF THE ATHLETIC COUNCIL IN THE ATHLETIC PROGRAM

The athletic council as a part of the interscholastic program is pretty generally accepted as a necessary part of the total program. The membership of this organization varies considerably. It usually is composed of coaches, administrators, faculty, and students. Its function is to establish policies or rules concerning the conduct, eligibility, appearance, training rules, and the like that are to be followed by anyone who is actively a part of the school's athletic program. This then would include athletes, trainers, and managers. A second and vital part of the function of this group would be to interpret the rules that they have established as they apply to specific situations that may arise during the school year.

In the past many of the problems involved in a high school athletic program were brought about by the fact that either the athlete did as the rules required or he was not allowed to remain in the athletic program. There was no thought as to the degree of failing to meet the rules or extenuating circumstances involved in any individual case. There was no thought about the fairness of the rule or family circumstances that might affect the given situation. Edwards comments in his book, *Sociology of Sport,* that the life of the athlete is as regulated as that of the student in the classroom, and the coach is the sole authority.[8]

However, since the early sixties, our society has changed dramatically so that past values and practices are not accepted (especially by the youth of the nation) just because it happens to be the way it has always been done. Today, youth is willing to accept authority, if it can be justified, that is, if it can be shown that the procedures that athletes should follow are necessary in terms of their performance, safety, or health. Another trend today seems to be to give students more of a voice in major decisions which will affect them in some way. This has been true for some time in other areas of education and is evident now in the athletic program where student input is being experienced through the athletic council.

Athletic councils are concerned about questions concerning training rules, (Why have any? Are they being enforced? Do they really deal with the health and safety of the athlete?) questions on eligibility rules, (What is the relation between grades and participation? Why have any rules? How does this compare with the school's philosophy of education?) and many other questions concerning the athlete's conduct and appearance.

Because athletes are the ones being most directly affected by the decisions of the athletic council and because of the pressure of the times, more athletes were placed on the council. The athletes then became part of a group making and enforcing the rules. The athletic council became an enforcer of the rules in that it had the responsibility of determining the guilt or innocence of anyone in question of having possibly broken a rule.

The philosophy and aim of the council should be to provide a way for the faculty and students to participate in the conducting and control of the interscholastic program in the school. The council should also have the opportunity to serve in an advisory capacity to the principal and athletic director in the preparation of the budget.

The council is responsible for setting up provisions for the unification of training rules and their implementation. The membership on the council should consist of the following people: All head coaches, the principal and assistant principal, student representatives, faculty members, and director of athletics.

SAMPLE ATHLETIC COUNCIL TRAINING RULES

The purpose of the athletic council is to further athletics in Bridgewater High School and to make them representative of the total school program. It is the belief, therefore, of the council that it has the right to expect the athletes representing Bridgewater High School to live by and abide by the following rules which represent the beliefs of the majority of students.

I. No member of Bridgewater High School athletic team will partake of alcoholic beverages, smoke, or use illegal drugs at any time during his or her high school career.

II. Each athletic squad will elect a member of that squad to represent them on the athletic council.

III. Each coach of a varsity athletic team will represent that team on the athletic council.

IV. The athletic director will represent

[8]Edwards, Harry, *Sociology of Sport* (Homewood, Illinois, The Dorsey Press, 1973) , p. 120.

the department of athletics on the athletic council. He will be a nonvoting member but will conduct all meetings.

V. If a coach has reason to believe that a member of his squad has or is violating a training rule, he should initiate action immediately to learn if this is true. This is done by first confronting the athlete with the charge. The coach will then inform the director who in turn will inform the principal. After this has been done the following actions should be instigated.

A. The coach will decide if further action should be taken. If he feels the athlete is innocent, the charges are dropped and the athlete and principal are so informed.

B. If the coach is convinced that the athlete is guilty, the coach will pursue the accepted disciplinary procedure which is stated in the code. He will inform the athletic director and the school principal of his action.

C. If the coach is undecided as to the guilt or innocence of the athlete, he will ask for a meeting with the athlete and the athletic director. If the problem cannot be resolved to the satisfaction of all concerned parties the athletic director will inform the principal and he in turn will call a meeting of the athletic council at which time the final decision will be made. Neither the coach or the elected squad representative of the sport involved will vote on this issue.

1. The voting must be done by secret ballot. It must be a yes or no vote. The votes will be opened and counted by the athletic director. If the vote indicates that the athlete is innocent, the charges will be dropped and the athlete will become eligible immediately. If the athlete is found to be guilty, he will be disciplined according to the code.

D. Any person will be allowed to attend the council meeting providing he has made arrangements to do so through the high school principal; otherwise, the only persons allowed to attend this meeting will be those persons directly involved along with the parents or guardians of the athlete.

E. The athletic council will be involved only with the rules on smoking, drinking, and use of illegal drugs. Individual squad rules will be dealt with directly by the head coach of the particular squad.

F. Offenses

1. The first offense will automatically suspend the athlete from the first 50 percent of the games.

2. If the offense is committed during the season, he would be suspended from 50 percent of the remaining games.

3. If the offense is committed during the season after 50 percent of the games have been played, he would be suspended from 50 percent of the remaining games.

4. If the offense is committed during the off-season, he would be suspended from the first scheduled sport in which he previously had participated.

5. The coach can request the athletic director to allow the athlete to continue to practice with the team. However, he may be deprived of this privilege at any

time upon the decision of the coach.

6. The second offense will result in the athlete being suspended from all athletic contests and all practices for a period of one year.

7. The third offense will result in the athlete being permanently suspended from all athletic participation.

PROBLEMS IN INTERSCHOLASTIC COACHING

There are many problems that must be faced by the coach today but the most important ones center around the question of civil rights. Does the coach, for example, have the right under law to enforce personal grooming and standards of dress rules on the athlete? Does he have the right to enforce any rule on the athlete that is contrary to those which do not apply specifically to all other students (such as curfew hours, eating habits, etc.) ?

Veller found in his survey that an overwhelming number of coaches (82%) disagreed with the statement: A member of an athletic squad should be able to dress (hair, beard, sideburns, clothes) any way he wishes.[9]

A recent court case in California decided in support of the coaches' right to enforce regulations on grooming and dress.[10] Another problem facing the coach of today is the black athlete or minority groups. The black athlete has made his presence felt and the coach must make every effort to see to it that he is given fair

[9]Veller, Don "Survey '71 Highlighting the Problems and needs of the Coaching Profession," *The Athletic Journal* (October, 1971) , p. 58.

[10]The Journal of Health Physical Education and Recreation, "The Coach and the Courts," *The Journal of Health Physical Education and Recreation* (June, 1970) , p. 10.

and uniform treatment. The coach must select the players purely on the basis of their ability and make certain he shows no partiality because of race, creed, or color.

It is the responsibility of the coach to formulate a philosophy which will coincide with that of the school and the community. He cannot build a philosophy which in any way will show partiality.

The Academic Teacher as a Coach

The expanding interest in athletics in the high schools has brought about a shortage of persons who are *qualified* to coach the various sports which are offered. It has become administratively difficult to employ certified physical educators for every coaching assignment in the school system. The need for professionally qualified and certified coaches to coach the athletic teams in the schools has become acute. The problem, of course, lies in the fact that there are many more coaches that are needed to coach the athletic teams than there are people needed to teach physical education in many of the schools throughout the country. This situation often results in the assignment of unqualified people to coach the athletic teams. The reflection on the physical education department in a situation such as this is understandable. However, the real damage is done to the student athletes who suffer the ill effects of the lack of qualified instruction.

This dilemma has resulted in many colleges offering the coaching minor with the hope that this will provide a solution to the problem. Several states have established requirements for a coaching certification program for coaches who are not certified in physical education.

There are differences of opinion among physical educators and school men relative to the certification of academic teachers who want to coach athletics. There is some speculation as to whether academic teachers should coach at all.

The Coach as a Faculty Member

Many coaches are criticized because of their seemingly general attitude or apathy regarding their obligations as a faculty member. Often times this is an unfair criticism. However, there are many coaches who feel that they do not have to attend meetings, be on committees, and do extra duties as other teachers do. They feel no obligation to support many of the issues that are vital to the staff as a whole and, for that matter, to themselves also. They expect the other staff members to carry the load because they themselves are too busy coaching. This attitude is resented by many faculty members and rightly so.

If the coach is a member of the faculty, and in most instances he is, and if he is teaching on the high school level, he is morally obligated to carry his full share of faculty duties if he expects to be a member of that faculty.

However, in defense of this attitude among a few coaches, it can be said that this is the exception and not the rule. Most coaches make an effort to attend faculty meetings because they feel that it is to their interest to do so. It is true, however, due to the pressures placed upon a coach to win, that scheduled practices in most cases interfere with faculty meetings. A coach can remedy this situation by rescheduling practice on days of staff meetings.

Sometimes there are ill feelings toward the coach among some of the teaching staff because the coach and his players receive more publicity than any other group in the school. Also, the coach generally makes a better salary than any other teacher. Unfortunately, these very same people who are jealous of the coaches' salary do not take into consideration the many, many hours involved in this coaching activity. A good way for the staff to share part of the limelight is to give them some responsibility such as chaperoning trips, speaking at pep rallies, and invitations to banquets. At the same time, teachers can increase their salary through different athletic events by ways of crowd control, ticket takers, score keepers, timers, and judges.

Philosophy for Coaching Compensation

Today, everything we do is measured in dollars and cents. Justification for extra pay for coaches should be readily accepted by all people involved when the extra number of working hours and outside pressures are accounted for. Time spent in preparation, actual practice time, and time spent in game participation represent many added hours, for which coaches should be rewarded beyond the regular teaching salary. This does not mean, however, that money is the ultimate reward that coaches strive for. Coaches would not be coaches if this were true. Coaches have a great inner feeling for the athletes that they coach; they enjoy working with and guiding the talents of young athletes. They experience a great personal pride in defeating the competition that they play. If this were not true, then the great coaches in the coaching field would be doing some other type of work. Yet with today's great emphasis on winning, how else can a coach be shown that his time and effort have not been for naught if not by extra pay. The contributions by the people in the coaching field in regard to educational and social values for young players must also be considered by those who do not favor the extra-pay-for-extra-work idea.

Most boards of education feel that all members of the coaching staff should receive extra compensation for their coaching duties. Along with this, most administrators expect that each coach should teach a like number of classes as do the other faculty members. They have followed the philosophy of setting up a schedule of coaching pay differentials. The schedule makes clear the differential differences for head and assistant coaches' pay.

THE IMPORTANCE OF GOOD SCHEDULING

Scheduling of athletic events parallels very closely the philosophy of athletics as set forth by the school authorities. This applies particularly to the number of games played, the dates on which they are played, and the time at which they are played. The first consideration in scheduling, of course, is the guidelines which are set forth by the state association. These must be strictly adherred to. The second consideration in developing the schedule, if the school belongs to a conference, is the conference games. Usually conference games are scheduled about two or three years in advance in an effort to get the best officials. Scheduling these games so far in advance gives the athletic director an opportunity to find good nonconference opponents. In the case of basketball it provides an opportunity to look for a suitable tournament in which to participate.

Some schools have a large number of season ticket-holders and like to play as many home games as possible. When scheduling nonconference basketball games, most schools like to have a two-year contract where each team plays on the home floor once. Some items that need to be considered when scheduling the nonconference opponents include: Are they competitive? Do they have a good athletic facility? How many miles would there be in traveling? Do they have a good reputation for sportsmanship and will the game

attract spectators?

If at all possible, the ideal schedule would be one in which the educational objectives of the athletes come first. The schedule should be one in which the least amount of time from school is lost.

THE CONDUCT OF ATHLETES AND ATHLETIC TEAMS

The responsibilities of the athletic director, the coach, and the player have undergone a great change over the years. The coach of twenty-five years ago, to use an old expression, would, "literally turn over in his grave," if he were to observe present-day practices and procedures. The rules and regulations under which he operated for so long no longer exist. The athlete of today is more sophisticated, more aware of his rights to do his thing and his right not to conform to established rules which are set up by the coach. It is unfortunate that many of our present-day athletes feel that their rights are their rights no matter what else has to be taken into consideration. In their opinion, being an athlete is a right and not a privilege. Fortunately it has been stated in many courts throughout the land that this idea is wrong. The courts have upheld the premise that participation in athletics is special and can be held apart from other areas of education. It has been a very prevalent belief of many people over the years that athletes should live by a certain set of rules and observe certain rules of conduct. Many athletes do not wish to do this. They do not want to cooperate, and sacrifice for the common good. It would almost seem like they want the best of two situations. This is unfortunate because there are as Dr. Cramer[11] points out, in an article entitled "Athletics and Higher Edu-

---

[11]Cramer, John, "Athletics and Higher Education" *Scholastic Coach* (November, 1972), p. 74.

cation," benefits that should be derived from athletics other than physical or mental. Under moral he lists "courage, decision making, self control, discipline, responsibility, and dependability." Under social is listed "cooperative effort, loyalty, self-sacrifice, public spirit, and good citizenship." The interpretation of these items is that not only should they be learned but they must be practiced within the realm of athletic competition.

The coach is not always right and the rules that he or she may wish the athletes to observe may not always seem to be fair. However, if an athlete's conduct and responsibilities are to meet the beliefs, such as those presented by Cramer, then the athlete must realize that at some period of time he will not have things exactly his way, but must realize that he must abide by the rules for the good of everyone concerned. It should always be remembered, however, that this is a two-way street; if the coach expects work and dedication, the athlete has an equal right to expect the same from the coach. Once the coach-player relationship is established the desired conduct should be forthcoming.

A quote from Harvard physiologist, Walter B. Cannon, sums up the needed attitude.[12]

> The high standards of honor and fairness in sport; its unfailing revelation for excellence without distinction of class, wealth, race, or color; the ease with which it becomes an expression of the natural feelings of patriotism; the respect which victory and (honorably) borne defect inspire in competitors and spectators alike; the extension of acquaintance and understanding which follows friendly and magnanimous rivalry among strong men who come together . . . each of these admirable features of athletic contests . . . might be enlarged upon.

---

[12]Cramer, John, "Athletics and Higher Education" *Scholastic Coach* (November, 1972), p. 74.

The conduct of athlete, coach, and team can be summed up briefly. Common sense, morality, social awareness, and healthy physical attitudes are the common goals. When these goals are kept in sight, the program cannot fail.

BEHAVIORAL OBJECTIVES

After a person has read this chapter, he should be able to:

1. Explain why the leadership of athletics is of such great importance.
2. Identify some of the arguments for and against the use of tax funds for the support of interscholastic athletics.
3. Explain several ways in which students may participate in the administration of the athletic program.
4. Formulate a workable plan for explaining the philosophy of interscholastic athletics to parents.
5. Explain and analyze the responsibility of the superintendent, the principal and the board of education for the athletic program.
6. Explain the importance of the principal and how he can cooperate in the program of athletics in the high school.
7. Explain the role of the parent in the interscholastic program.
8. Compare the role of the high school principal and athletic director and superintendent in promoting the athletic program.
9. Think of an instance where a student may have disagreed with the athletic director of a school. Describe the situation briefly, tell what the director did, tell what should have been done and try to indicate the nature of the inner factors which lie behind the two different kinds of behavior.
10. Describe the principal's role in the supervision of athletics. Explain why this role is sometimes very difficult.

11. Describe the procedure which could be followed in formulating a philosophy of athletics.
12. List several areas of athletics which should be considered in formulating a philosophy of athletics.
13. Using your own words construct a philosophy of administration in athletics.
14. Explain why the philosophy of education is the basis for the belief that athletics are a part of physical education.
15. Develop a philosophy of athletics.
16. Describe the superintendent's role in the supervision of the athletic program.
17. Explain the part the parent-teacher association should play in the athletic program.
18. Identify the most difficult problems in interscholastic athletic coaching today. Explain how these problems may change in the future.
19. Compile several important items that enter into the making of a good athletic schedule.
20. Name and describe several philosophies which guide the athletic program.
21. Identify and describe several attributes as goals for a good athletic program.
22. Formulate and justify a philosophy for athletes in a small urban school.

ACTIVITIES

1. Interview a principal of a high school concerning his major duties and activities pertaining to the athletic program.
2. Draw up a constitution for a boys' athletic association or a lettermen's club.
3. Spend a day visiting the athletic department of the high school. How does the philosophy of athletics in this school compare with your own?
4. Form a panel and discuss the issue: Athletic gate receipts should be or should not be considered school funds.

5. Debate the issue: The control of athletics should be in the hands of the director of athletics or the school board.
6. Chart the qualifications needed for students under consideration for a cheerleader position, a lettermen's club member, a student-athletic council member.
7. Interview a principal, board member, superintendent, athletic director, and coach concerning their philosophy of interscholastic athletics and its place in the school curriculum.
8. Write to several high schools in different sections of the country requesting their policies pertaining to interscholastic athletic programs.
9. Using outside readings determine an outstanding coach's philosophy of athletics and physical education.
10. Express in writing your personal philosophy concerning athletics.
11. Debate the issue: Is it possible to adopt a single philosophy for physical education and athletics on a high school level?
12. Investigate the different professional athletic associations and state their philosophy of athletics.
13. Make a survey of an athletic department of a school system and determine the philosophy of the athletic program.
14. Develop a set of standards which would apply to an athletic program in high school.
15. Debate the issue: Training rules for athletes should be no different than those imposed on any other student attending school.
16. Write about an incident that occurred in your local school which you can remember. Give your analysis of the problem presented in the incident and

the procedure you would employ in its solution.

17. Visit the local high school and using your own objectives of athletics determine how you would change the program.

18. Write a 500-word article on your philosophy of athletics based on present-day beliefs of youngsters.

SUGGESTED READINGS

1. Abinanti, Abby: The communications media and women in sports. *Journal of Health, Physical Education and Recreation,* January, 1971.

2. Bonnette, Allan: Should there be separate curricula for coaches? *Physical Educator,* October, 1969.

3. Bucher, Charles: *Administration of Health and Physical Education Programs.* Saint Louis, Mosby, 1971.

4. Cramer, John: Interscholastic athletics and higher education. *Scholastic Coach,* November, 1972.

5. Davis, T.: Should high school coaches be teachers of physical education or some other academic subject? *Journal of Health, Physical Education, and Recreation,* January, 1962.

6. DeBacy, Diane, Spaeth, Rue, and Busch, Roxanne: What do men really think about athletic competition for women? *Journal of Health, Physical Education, and Rerceation,* November, 1970.

7. Editorial: The coaches and the courts. *The Journal of Health, Physical Education, and Recreation,* June, 1970.

8. Educational Policies Commission: *School Athletics: Problems and Policies.* Washington, D.C., The National Education Association of the United States, 1954.

9. Edwards, Harry: *Sociology of Sports.* Homewood, Dorsey Pr, 1973.

10. Field, Charles: Faculty and coach relationship. *Coach and Athlete,* October, 1971.

11. Frankel, Charles: A review for the teacher . . . . philosophy. *National Educators Journal,* December, 1962.

12. Grieve, Andrew: *Directing High School Athletics.* Englewood Cliffs, P-H, 1963.

13. Grzebien, Albert: Communication and the coach. *The Athletic Journal,* January, 1969.

14. Hixson, Chalmer: *The Administration of Interscholastic Athletics.* New York, Lowell Pratt, 1967.

15. Keller, Irvin: School athletics—Its philosophy and objectives. American, School Board Journal August, 1966.

16. Lawther, John: The role of the coach in American education. *Journal of Health, Physical Education, and Recreation,* May, 1965.

17. McKenney, Wayne: Certification of coaches—The Missouri approach. *Journal of Health, Physical Education, and Recreation,* October, 1970.

18. Mehn, Duane: Athletics and values. *Coach and Athlete,* November, 1971.

19. Prato, Douglas: The personal approach in coaching. *The Journal of Health, Physical Education, and Recreation,* January, 1971.

20. Reeves, Fred: Educational leadership of the athletic coach. *Coach and Athlete,* January, 1968.

21. Santoro, Joel, and Thurston, James: Coaches' salaries: Two approaches, *Journal of Health, Physical Education, and Recreation,* April, 1968.

22. Sheets, N.L.: Current status of certification of coaches in Maryland. *Journal of Health, Physical Education, and Recreation,* June, 1971.

23. Smith, Willie: One man's philosophy of coaching. *Journal of Health, Physical Education, and Recreation,* October, 1971.

24. Teper, Lynn: Letters to the editor. *Journal of Health, Physical Education, and Recreation,* May, 1970.

25. Tutko, Thomas and Richards, Jack: *Psychology of Coaching.* Boston, Allyn, 1971.

26. Vanderzoswaag, Harold: *Toward a Philosophy of Sport.* Reading, A-W, 1972.

27. Veller, Don: Survey '71 highlighting the problems and needs of the coaching pro-

fession. *The Athletic Journal,* October, 1971.

28. Veller, Don: Vital relationships for the coach. *The Athletic Journal,* November, 1968.

29. Weiss, Paul: *Sport: A Philosopher Inquiry,* Carbondale, Southern U Pr, 1969.

30. Welch, Everett: The athletic council. *The Athletic Journal,* February, 1956.

31. Wilson, Larry and Bailey, James: Why interscholastic athletics? *The Coaching Clinic,* Englewood Cliffs, P H, 1969.

CHAPTER 4

The Relationship of the Boys' and Girls' Athletic Program

PERHAPS THE BIGGEST CHANGE that has taken place in interscholastic athletics in the past decade is the change in philosophy regarding women and competitive athletics. Whether this attitude has developed because of the changing role of women in present-day society, or because women have come to realize the inherent benefits of wholesome, athletic competition to the physical and mental well-being of the participant, is not easily understood. Although this changing attitude regarding competitive athletics for girls is new and a complete reversal from former attitudes and beliefs, it has reached a point where major decisions must be made relative to the future of girls' and women's athletics in our society and especially in the schools.

Williams[1] makes the following comment which partially explains this change in attitude:

Modern liberalism has brought to women greater freedom in the choice of a vocation and in numerous other matters. Thus, she shares with her brother opportunities to engage in politics, industry, the professions, homemaking, recreation, and in fact, practically all functions of citizenship toward which education is focused. Under such conditions it is difficult to support the view

that the interschool athletic competition for girls should be abolished and at the same time subscribe to the policy that there are educational values to be derived from interschool athletics for boys not attainable to the same degree in other forms of public school education. Consistent judgment would appear to recommend similar policies for both girls and boys.

Cheska[2] gives the following reasons for girls' and women's increased interest in sports:

Several reasons have contributed to increased sports participation by girls in our country: (1) change of attitude toward the human body as an instrument of expression not represssion; (2) emancipation of women politically, socially, economically and sexually; (3) increase of usable time for sports participation because of decrease of home maintenance and child rearing tasks for both mother and child; (4) equal educational opportunities for both sexes; (5) urbanization which provides concentration of sports facilities, instruction, equipment and participants; (6) rapid, efficient transportation to sports facilities; (7) mass communication media placing status on sport excellence by reporting and on participation through advertising propaganda; (8) earlier introduction of coeducational sports activities in

---

[1]Williams, Jesse, Brownell, Clifford, and Vernier, Elmon, *The Administration of Health, Education, and Physical Education* (Philadelphia, W.B. Saunders Co., 1958), p. 216.

[2]Cheska, Alyce, "Current Developments in Competitive Sports for Girls and Women," *Journal of Health, Physical Education, and Recreation* (March 1970), p. 89.

school and recreational situations; (9) interest of men as well as women in providing leadership for girls' sport programs; (10) clothing manufacture emphasis on sports clothes for girls and women; (11) manufacture and distribution of more and varied sports equipment; and (12) more instruction providing sports competition, as political units, youth agencies, churches, schools, and colleges, specific sports organizations and commercial business.

For as long as can be remembered, sports and athletics has always been a "man's world" and women just "looked on." They looked upon sport as something only the men could do, and there was no place for the woman. Sport was a test of manhood in many respects and certainly was not an activity for the women. However, the desirable effects of sports for girls was not always disputed by everyone for there were those people who were ardent supporters of sports for girls. Among the individuals one voice was heard again and again in her arguments for girls' participation in sports as a step forward and a means by which girls could assume a new role in our culture and economy. The voice was that of Thelma Bishop.[3] In 1960 she made the following observation:

> The future of sports for girls and women is promising, difficult, full of changes that must be evaluated. The course chosen must be more than right; it must be best. New roles for women in our culture stimulate us to build new concepts of womanhood. As psychological and cultural barriers to participate in sports by girls and women are broken down, the division for girls' and women's sports is challenged to stimulate participation and upgrade the kinds of experience available to girls and women through sports.

In 1959, Williams, Brownell, and

Vernier[4] stated that:

> Widespread differences of opinion exist relative to athletic competition for girls. At one extreme are those who favor an interscholastic program for girls which approximates the type of organization found in the average boys' senior high school. At the other extreme is a group which contends that competition for girls should be restricted to participation in social games with the 'desire to win' element largely removed.

There are others who contend that competitive athletics will actually harm the woman physically. This has long since been proven false, and it is now an accepted fact that physical excercise and athletic competition is not harmful to either sex. Substantiating this thinking is William's[5] comment that, "If girls are to be restricted from engaging in interschool competition while boys are encouraged to do so, the reasons for such restriction must be found in the different sexes, rather than in significant differences in biological needs and interests."

Gradually more and more girls and women have become interested in sports until the time has finally arrived when the interscholastic program for girls must be given full recognition and full support. If all the things that have been said about the values of interscholastic athletics are true for the boys, then these same values are existent and obtainable for the girls. There are some people that still are solidly against athletic competition for girls because they feel that it is not womanly to sweat and that vigorous exercise will build large muscles and that it will make the woman less feminine. However, Malumphy[6] dis-

---

[3]Bishop, Thelma, "Girls and Womens Sports," *Journal of Health, Physical Education and Recreation* (April 1960), p. 94.

[4]Williams Jesse, Brownell, Clifford, and Vernier, Elmon, *The Administration of Health, Education, and Physical Education,* p. 215.

[5]*Ibid.*

[6]Malumphy, Theresa, "Personality of Women Athletes in Intercollegiate Competition," *Research Quarterly,* (October 1968), p. 617.

putes this suggestion in the following observation:

> The effect of participation on the female
> image depends on the participant her-
> self. Femininity was seen to be enhanced
> by participation in tennis, golf, fencing,
> archery, competitive swimming, synchro-
> nized swimming, and gymnastics. Girls
> who played basketball, field hockey, soft-
> ball, volleyball, badminton, and bowling
> were less sure that participation en-
> hanced the feminine image.

Fortifying this belief the National
Association of State High School Associations[7] has made the following statement:

> Recently the American Medical Associa-
> tion released the results of a study point-
> ing out that the health benefits of whole-
> some exercise are as great for women as
> they are for men. It announced that
> women who maintain a high level of
> health and fitness can meet family and
> career responsibilities more effectively
> and can pursue vocational interests more
> enjoyably.

PHYSIOLOGICAL DIFFERENCES BETWEEN BOYS AND GIRLS

Women have traditionally been placed
in the role of the homemaker. The man
had assumed the role of protector and provider. He was the person who sallied forth
into the world and brought home the
necessities of life. The woman was left in
the home to take care of the children and
"run" the home. The man was the ag-
gressor and the protector. Because the
mode of life has changed, the role of man
has changed. Society has placed women in
the same role as men in many areas of life.
The opportunity to enjoy and participate
in athletics is one of these areas. However,
there is still considerable controversy that
because of physiological differences men

and women should not compete against
each other. Lacey[8] substantiates this belief
by commenting on the following statement
made by three panelists from the University of Minnesota:

> Some of the sexual differences relevant
> for athletic competition are obvious;
> others are only marginal. Some of those
> most commonly recognized are:
>
> 1. Males are taller than females.
> 2. Women have narrower shoulders
>   than men.
> 3. Women have a lower center of
>   gravity.
> 4. Women's arms and legs are pro-
>   portionately shorter than men's.
> 5. The women's pelvis is wider and
>   shallower.
> 6. Women have more adipose tissue
>   and less lean body mass.
> 7. The male's ability to supply oxy-
>   gen to working muscles is larger.
> 8. Women are less able to adapt to
>   heart stress.
> 9. Women have less hemoglobin than
>   men.

The most reliable data on the relative
physical potential of men and women in
sport deals with aerobic (oxygen) capacity and strength. Men have about 20 to
25 percent more oxygen capacity than
women. This is important because the
more oxygen an athlete can supply to
working muscles, the greater the capacity
for efficient energy to make those muscles
work. This capacity is not important for
all kinds of sport activities; in those
events where high oxygen is not necessary, strength and power are important.
Women, again find themselves at a disadvantage.

Hult[9] has the following comment about
the sexual differences between males and
females in athletic competition:

> The muscular strength component in

---

[7]National Federation of State High School Association. *Official Handbook* (Chicago, Illinois,
1972-1973), p. 28.

[8]Lacey, Carol, "Three University Panelists Conclude Females Appear Weaker in Strength, Endurance," *St. Paul Pioneer Press* (Sept. 29, 1973).

[9]Hult, Joan, "Separate but Equal Athletics for
Women," *Journal of Health, Physical Education
and Recreation* (June 1973), p. 57.

athletic events prevents even well-trained female athletes from reaching the attainment levels of male athletes. The muscle mass of women does not exceed or even begin to be equal (on the average) to that of males. However, in physical performance that does not test strength, but demands factors of strategy, reaction time, coordination, flexibility, and perhaps even endurance, female athletes are developing qualities similar to those of male athletes. The lack of muscle mass, however, which is one of the factors not affected by culture and which makes females different, is very apparent in sports.

One important biological aspect of women's participation in sports is brought out by Gendel,[10] "It is important to remember that compared to men, women are biologically stronger in their resistance to illness and death. Because of fewer illnesses and disabilities, women could show more consistent and prolonged participation in sports and further develop their aptitude for endurance."

Erdelyi[11] comments on participation of the female in sports during the menstrual period, which is a concern of many people, "It is generally concluded that participation in all sports activities before, during or after menstruation causes no deleterious effect on the normal menstrual cycle."

Engle brings out some interesting facts which she substantiates through H. Royer Collins,[12] chief of sports medicine and an orthopedic surgeon at the Cleveland Clinic which has a definite bearing on the effects of the health and childbearing future of the girl who ventures onto the athletic field. Collins contends that:

All the latest medical evidence indicates there's no reason why females shouldn't participate in sports, but there are still a lot of old wives' tales about this. For instance, some people say girls may damage their reproductive organs by competing in jumping events. There's no proof to substantiate this at all. In fact, many gynecologists believe such activity improves muscular support in the pelvic area.

Other biological facts which substantiate the belief that competition in sports is no more harmful to girls than to boys, and some of the comparison is further brought forth by Collins[13] in the following statements:

Male reproductive organs are actually more vulnerable to injury than females because they're external. The uterus and ovaries are much better protected by nature since they're internal organs. Females who play contact sports, however, probably should shield their breasts.

Female bones aren't more fragile, just smaller. An active girl will have the same strong bones as her male counterpart.

Most girls do have less muscle mass, possibly because they rarely exercise to develop their muscles. But even when put on a weight-training program, most girls don't seem to develop the bulging muscles males do. This is because of male and female hormones, and the more muscular girls you see produce more male hormones than others.

The female's lung capacity is smaller because of her smaller size.

ADMINISTRATIVE AGENCIES FOR GIRLS' ATHLETICS

Because of the increasing interest in girls' and women's athletics, several governing agencies came into being and as a result became instrumental and influential

---

[10]Gendel, Evalyn, S. MD., "Physicians, Females, Physical Exertion, and Sports," Proceedings, Fourth National Institute of Girl's Sports (Washington, D.C., AAHPER, 1968), p. 9

[11]Erdelyi, G., "Gynecological Survey of Female Athletes," *The Journal of Sports Medicine and Physical Fitness* (September 1962), p. 179.

[12]Collins, Roger H., "The Greening of Girls Sports," *Nations Schools* (September 1973), p. 30.

[13]*Ibid.*

in the progress of girls' and women's interscholastic programs. Women have always felt the effects of opposing forces which have attempted to govern their athletic programs. For many years the Division of Girls' and Women's Athletics was the dominant force. This organization was an arm of the American Association of Health, Physical Education, and Recreation and, as such, was dominated by it in respect to the place of interscholastic athletics for girls in the school curriculum. The change in philosophy in recent years in regard to interscholastic athletics for girls has resulted in a quest for power between the several agencies which, heretofore, have been instrumental in their own way in the governing of the girls' interscholastic athletic program. This has resulted in dramatic changes in the administration of the girls' programs. Whether or not the change in philosophy toward competition for girls had any influence on the resultant outcome is noteworthy.

The Influence of the Division of Girls' and Women's Sports on Girls' Athletics

The Division for Girls' and Women's Sports was an outgrowth of many previous organizations. The first attempt at establishing standards of conduct for girls and women's sports came out of the conference on physical training at Springfield, Massachusettes, on June 14, 1899. The establishment of the Women's Basketball Rules Committee occurred in 1907, and in 1916 the first women's athletic committee was appointed by the American Physical Education Association, now the American Alliance for Health, Physical Education, and Recreation. This was a milestone for those women who were working hard for recognition. The National Amateur Athletic Federation was established in February, 1923, and under the able leadership of Mrs.

Herbert Hoover, the Women's Division of the National Amateur Athletic Federation was formed. It was a beginning, and this organization worked diligently through the twenties and the thirties for recognition and ways to obtain proper supervision and promotion of girls' and women's sports and games. Its efforts were recognized as the Women's Division of the National Amateur Athletic Association was joined by the Women's Athletic Section of the American Physical Education Association.

Finally, in 1940 a merger of the Women's Division of the National Amateur Athletic Federation and the National Section on Women's Athletics was accomplished.

In 1958 the efforts of this group were recognized and the American Association for Health, Physical Education, and Recreation brought them into their organization as the Division of Girls' and Women's Sports. The girls' and Women's sports programs have always recognized the fact that athletics is and should be a part of the physical education program. This belief has been carried out for many years and still is the philosophy under which many of the programs still operate. This organization has developed and controlled the many and varied sports activities in the girls' athletic program. It supports the view that athletic competition for girls is desirable because it helps to achieve educational and recreational objectives. It supports the idea that athletics should be available for all girls and not the few who happen to be highly skilled.

Hult[14] makes the following comment on the purpose of the DGWS:

> The DGWS subscribes to the belief that teams for girls and women should be provided for all girls and women who

---

[14]Hult, Joan, *Journal of Health, Physical Education and Recreation*, p. 57.

desire competitive athletic experiences. Funds, facilities, and staff should be available for the conduct of these programs. While positive experience for the exceptional girl or woman competitor may occur through participation in boys' and men's competitive groups, these instances are rare and should be judged acceptable only as an interim procedure for us until women's programs can be initiated.

The DGWS was recognized by many of the state associations as the governing body of the girls' interscholastic athletic program. However, because of interproblems, conflicts grew. There were differences of opinion among the women as to what direction the program should move. Should it be a highly, competitive program and be one equal to the boys' in every respect, or should it hold to the old ideas of play for fun? Because of the rapid, almost overnight demand for the competitive and equal programs idea for the girls, the Division of Girls' and Women's Athletics was not able to cope with the growth problem that it faced. Because the division seemed to be caught in this struggle of conflicting ideas and because the need for rule changes for the various sports was not being met, the National Amateur Athletic Federation wrote the current guides governing women's sports. Probably, if the women had used the men's program as a guide and profited from the men's experiences, this move would not have taken place. Because of the differences of opinion and an unwillingness of certain individuals to use the men's rules as a guideline, the conflicts arose and resulted in the National Federation assuming the leadership role; the results will be interesting to observe. It may take many years before men and women coaches will be able to solve their differences, but the end result will benefit all athletes, both boys and girls.

It should be pointed out that the membership of both the National Federation and the state associations are made up of high schools who are already sponsoring and administering high school activities. All decisions are related to these member schools.

The DGWS[15] has taken the following stand on girls' and women's athletics:

> The DGWS recognizes that separate sports programs for girls while on the increase, can rarely be equated with boys' teams in terms of funding, staffing, and use of facilities. This is partly true due to the long held societal prejudice that participation by girls in organized athletics is unladylike and, in fact, harmful to the physical and social development of the female. The DGWS believes that sports programs in high schools and colleges should be an outgrowth of the physical education program, and should provide a variety of opportunities for participation and appropriate competition for all students. Funds, facilities, equipment, and staff should be made available for girls' and women's programs on the basis of parity with boys' and men's programs. The DGWS further believe it is essential that women physical educators, coaches, and athletic directors be involved in the planning, developing, and administration of girls and women's sports programs and be included on boards and councils which develop policies for girls athletics.
>
> The DGWS believes that those responsible for the administration of sports programs for girls and women should be concerned with training adequate numbers of women officials and with developing minimum certification standards for coaches of girls and women's teams. The DGWS feels that there must be a united effort if female students are to be given the opportunity for high level performance, achievement, and competition within the framework of girls' and women's varsity sports.

The DGWS does not support the claim that girls are physiologically or socially harmed by participation in sports, and the current approach of society toward the role of girls and women repudiates such outdated ideas and practices.

Purpose

The purpose of the Division for Girls' and Women's Sports is to foster the development of sports programs for the enrichment of the life of the participant.

Functions

The Division of Girls' and Women's Athletics[16] aims for the promotion of a desirable women's sports programs through:

1. Formulating and publicizing guiding principles and standards for the administrator, leader, official, and player.

2. Publishing and interpreting rules governing sports for girls and women.

3. Providing the means for training and rating officials.

4. Disseminating information on the conduct of girls' and women's sports.

5. Stimulating, evaluating, and disseminating research in the field of girls' and women's sports.

6. Cooperating with allied groups, interested in girls and women's sports in order to formulate policies and rules that effect the conduct of women's sports.

7. Providing opportunities for the development of leadership among girls and wo-

men for the conduct of their sports programs.

The Influence of the National Association of Girls' and Women's Sports on Girls' Athletics

In order to more efficiently administer and conduct the girls' and women's sports program, a new organization called the National Association of Girls' and Women's Sports (NAGWS) was formed. It is felt that this new structure will be more flexible, more democratic, and be able to reach all its members more adequately. This is an attempt on the part of those individuals interested in the girls' and women's athletics to upgrade this program in view of the present emphasis on the girls' and women's athletics. It will include the following organized groups: the Association for Intercollegiate Athletics for Women, a secondary school person representing interscholastic interests; the National Coaches Associations, the state Division of Girls' and Women's Sports Chairperson; the student membership of AAHPER; Affiliated Boards of Officials; and organizations with club sports, intramural, or sport interest focus.

The N.A.G.W.S. is interested in building sport programs for all levels of education. It will attempt to help individual school districts to effectively make the necessary changes within their own schools to comply with the Title IX of the Education Amendments Act of 1972.

The N.A.G.W.S. is an organization within the alliance structure of the American Alliance for Health, Physical Education, and Recreation. It actually came into being in 1973 and it was formed out of recognition for the need to develop, encourage, foster, and support sports programs for girls and women.

---

[15]Division for Girls' and Women's Sports, "Sports Programs for Girls and Women," *Journal of Health, Physical Education, and Recreation* (April 1974) , p. 12.

[16]The Division for Girls' and Women's Sports, American Association of Health, Physical Education and Recreation, *Philosophy and Standards for Girls' and Women's Sports* (Washington, D.C., 1972) , p. 2.

Purpose

The N.A.G.W.S.[17] has stated that this organization will attempt to promote desirable sports programs for girls and women and that these programs will be specifically enhanced through fulfillment of the following purposes:

1. Formulate guiding principles, standards, and policies for administrators, leaders, and players.
2. Provide for evaluating and rating officials.
3. Provide for improvement in coaching of girls' and women's sports.
4. Provide means for disseminating, encouraging, and stimulating information on athletic training for girls and women.
5. Disseminating information on the conduct of girls' and women's sports.
6. Stimulating, evaluating, and disseminating research in the field of girls' and women's sports.
7. Formulate, publish, and interpret rules governing sports for girls and women.
8. Encourage and support state A.G.W.S. structures.
9. Share in and cooperate with the interests of other A.A.H.P.E.R. structures and substructures in promoting girls' and women's sports.
10. Cooperate with allied groups interested in girls' and women's sports in order to formulate policies and rules that affect the conduct of girls' and women's sports.
11. Increase public understanding of the need for sound programs for girls' and women's sports.
12. Hold national conferences and meetings supporting conferences, workshops, clinics, and institutes on girls' and women's sports.
13. Conduct activities consistent with the purposes of the American Alliance for Health, Physical Education, and Recreation.

The Influence of State High School Associations on Girls' Athletics

There is a divergence of beliefs within the different states regarding the supervision and control of all interschool activities in which its member schools may engage. From the time interscholastic activities were introduced in the school programs they were primarily athletic in nature. However, since that time, many of the state associations have assumed the responsibility of supervising and conducting other activities, such as music, dramatics, speech, etc. in an attempt to make all these activities an integral part of the total educational program. Most states have, therefore, attempted to make adaptations so as to include a program of athletics for girls. This program will assume a larger part of the total picture with the continued growth of the girls' athletic program.

The National Association of State High School Associations[18] makes this comment regarding the administration of girls' athletics:

It is logical to assume that the organization responsible for conducting successful programs for boys should logically assume responsibility for administering wholesome programs for girls. State High School Associations are the logical agencies for sponsoring interscholastic athletics for girls. Their membership consists of high schools which have experience in developing educational pro-

---

[17]American Alliance of Health, Physical Education, and Recreation, *National Association for Girls and Women in Sport,* Bylaws (Washington, D. C., 1974).

[18]National Federation of State School Associations, *Official Handbook,* p. 28.

grams in competitive athletics. Existing organizations can make adaptations to include a program of athletics for girls which will satisfy educational objectives. Within each state, the needs may be slightly different as they are in the boys' program.

Many secondary schools have decided to place the girls' interscholastic athletic programs in the hands of the various state associations and the National Federation of State High School Associations. This is a logical move because these associations are both in the business of administering interscholastic athletics and other extra-mural programs and are well equipped with personnel and in every other way to conduct the girls' program. The addition of the girls' expanded program can be done without too much difficulty. The state associations have always had the legal right to govern the girls' interscholastic program, and it is logical to assume that they will continue to do so. The administrative machinery is already in operation for conducting the boys' program so it would be only requiring slight changes in personnel to assume the leadership of the girls' program also.

The Influence of the National Federation of State High School Associations on Girls' Athletics

The National Federation of State High School Associations has provided leadership and encouragement for a strong program of athletic competition for girls. As far back as 1964, this organization made a study as to the feasibility of increasing the program in girls' athletics. It passed a resolution urging state high school associations to explore the idea of including girls' programs in interscholastic athletics. The need for responsible leadership of these programs was recognized and this leadership could come only from school

personnel if it was to be kept within the educational structure of the school community. The girls' program of athletics could profit from a thorough study of the outcomes of the boys' program throughout its history. In this way it might be able to divorce itself from some of the outside influences and pressure groups which over the years have caused problems for the boys' program. The National Federation of State High School Associations[19] makes the following comment regarding the administration of girls' athletics:

> The National Federation believes that the interscholastic sports program for girls must be designed to stimulate and encourage participation by the girls so that they may enjoy values resulting from interscholastic competition. In this regard, definite standards must be adapted to provide that these values do accrue. The girls' program must be an integral part of the curriculum. Therefore, the high schools and their organization should administer local and state-wide programs.

The Influence of Title IX on Girls' Athletics

Title IX of the Education Amendments Act which was enacted by both houses of Congress and signed by the president in June, 1972, prohibits sex discrimination in education programs or activities. "No person in the U.S.," it states, "shall on the basis of sex be excluded from participation in, be denied benefits of, or be subjected to discrimination under any education program receiving federal financial assistance." The impact of this law can be tremendous and change the program of interscholastic athletic programs drastically. It will make sexual discrimination in schools illegal. The old image of the boys' team taking preference over the girls' team will disap-

---

[19]National Federation of State High School Associations, *Official Handbook,* p. 29.

pear and their efforts will bring about an integrated athletic program which will be in line with other school departments. Sex discrimination will end as equal opportunities for the girls are provided in all areas of interscholastic athletics.

There will be repercussions and problems which will arise as the integration of these programs moves forward. The solution seems to hinge on the question: Is it more desirable for girls to vie for positions on the team? Equality of opportunity can be put into writing but can it be put in effect if only one team is fielded which will, without question be completely dominated by males? Ability in athletics cannot be determined by putting words on paper which makes it necessary for girls to compete against boys on an interscholastic team. The outcome can be predetermined and it could well be that the boys will completely dominate, with the exception of a few isolated cases, where numbers are the important factor and there are not enough boys to fill all the positions on the different athletic teams. It could also mean that there could be more boys on the girls teams in the traditional girls' sports such as field hockey. If the equality of opportunity is to be reached there needs to be more work done in the area of girls' sports and not attempt to find the answer by having them compete against boys.

Collins[20] justifies this belief in the following comment:

At the high school level boys are bigger than girls and usually faster and stronger, we in medicine are against the mismatching of youngsters because a 180-pound boy who hits a 120-pound boy or girl is likely to hurt him. Kids should be evenly matched according, to weight, size, strength and speed. I'm not against girls competing in contact sports if they so desire, but if they compete against

other girls, they'll be better matched and their chances for serious injury will be greatly diminished. Noncontact sports are another story, though. I see no reason why qualified girls shouldn't compete against boys in sports like tennis and golf.

Title IX will provide girls with the same opportunity to enjoy the athletic competition which has brought so much satisfaction and benefits to boys. However, most every one will agree that physically girls cannot compete successfully against the boys in all athletic activities. As Collins[21] so aptly puts it in the following statement, "Naturally, you can't expect a 110-pound girl to run as hard or lift as much as a 180-pound man. This same girl, however, can certainly compete in the same sports as boys and develop her lung capacity, cardiorespiratory efficiency, and musculature."

Title IX has focused a great deal of attention on sex discrimination in athletics and has been responsible for exploding the myth that competitive athletics was not only physically harmful to girls but morally bad as well. Many organizations have not only recognized the benefits of athletic competition for girls but have gone on record as supporting this type of program. The National Education Association[22] has recently advocated this practice and at the 1974 NEA Annual meeting in Chicago, delegates to the representative assembly passed the following resolution:

The National Education Association believes that, at all educational levels, female and male students must have equal opportunity to participate in athletic programs.
The association urges that athletic funds for facilities, equipment, and remuneration of staff must be equally allocated between female and male programs.

---

[20]Collins, Roger H., "The Greening of Girls' Sports," p. 30.

[21]Collins, Roger H., "The Greening of Girls' Sports," p. 30.

[22]"National Education Association, "*Today's Education* (November-December, 1974) , p 55.

The Changing Concept of Athletic Competition for Girls and Women

The administration of interscholastic athletics can undergo tremendous change as a result of Title IX. The regulations will affect the selection of sports, the levels of competition, provisions for equipment or supplies, scheduling of games and practice times, travel and *per diem* allowance, award of athletic scholarships, opportunity to receive coaching and instruction, assignment of coaches, provision of locker room, practice and facilities, provision of medical facilities and services, publicity, etc. There needs to be equality of opportunity for girls to compete in interschool athletics but not at the expense of either their program or the boys' program. Each program must provide a framework of competition which will be beneficial to both boys and girls. One should complement the other but neither should jeporadize the objectives of either program. Each should provide large numbers of boys and girls the opportunity to participate in competitive athletics.

Desire on the part of women for a program of competitive athletics is natural because it reflects the general attitude of the people toward equalization of opportunities for everyone regardless of age, sex, color, or religion. While there are many pros and cons concerning interscholastic competition for women, it must be remembered that it is not only coming but it is already here. The problems it brings with it will no doubt, further complicate the interscholastic athletic scene. It will mean the sharing of facilities, personnel, and finances. There will be direct conflicts with the existing boys' programs because it will mean sharing on an equal basis those things the boys have had all by themselves for these many years. It will mean the development of a philosophy which will spell out the competitive guidelines which will be followed in regard to boys and girls competing on the same teams. It will mean a breakdown in the attitude of school boards, administrators, and the community in regard to the present pressure on boys' athletics for winning, at least for a while. Presently this aspect of the boys' program does not coincide with that of the girls. But placing them together will necessarily mean a change of philosophy one way or the other. These are problems that need to be solved and will be solved. Much depends on the attitude of the men toward the women's competitive athletic program. This is brought out very forcefully by DeBacy[23] in the following statement:

> As future athletic directors and administrative officers, men physical education majors will be instrumental in formulating policies, making decisions and providing the logical support which can cause desirable competitive athletics for girls and women to flourish or perish. The usual departmental coexistence of men and women involved in both physical education and athletics make it imperative that the staff provide a supportive atmosphere for all phases of the program. The success of this whole new venture in competition hinges on a receptive attitude on the part of the men involved.

It will take years to determine to what extent girls' athletics should be a part of the athletic picture. There are arguments for and against. Lambert[24] has presented some of these as follows:

[23]Debacy, Diane L., Spaeth, Ree, and Busch, Roxanne, "What Do Men Really Think about Athletic Competition for Women?" *Journal of Health, Physical Education and Recreation* (November, 1970), p. 29.

[24]Lambert, Charlotte, "Pros and Cons of Intercollegiate Athletic Competition for Women: A Middle of the Road Position Paper, *"Journal of Health, Physical Education, and Recreation"* (May, 1969), p 77.

FOR:

1. It is coming whether we want it or not.
2. If the schools do not take it over, some agency with possibly less ability and lower standards will.
3. If women do not coach these athletes and sponsor these events, men will. Girls should be coached and officiated by women who understand girls' limitations.
4. There are very highly skilled women coaches who want to teach these highly skilled girls.
5. We can control it by carefully devising and adhering to policies.
6. There is nothing wrong with competition *per se*. It is the best way to build a high degree of skill.
7. The highly skilled girls should have a chance to participate in high level competition. She does not now have that opportunity.
8. There is no reason why physcial education in the schools should develop everyone to only a moderate degree of skill. We should develop each to the highest degree of skill possible for her.
9. Interscholastic competition will not make girls any more aggressive and masculine than they would have been without the competition.
10. The development of an athlete of either sex is the development of top physical conditioning as well as skill.

AGAINST:

1. Our culture likes feminine looking and acting girls. Interscholastic competition often toughens them and makes them social misfits.
2. The place and purpose of sports in the education of a woman is not served by interscholastic competition.
3. Psychologically, women and girls should not have to put up with the pressures of interscholastic competition.
4. Interscholastic competition is a jungle of trouble for which women are not prepared.
5. Physical educators cannot control interscholastic competition. It will be controlled by administrators and pressure from the general public.

6. Interscholastic and/or collegiates lead to cut-throat competition among the girls for a place on a team.
7. Interscholastic competition leads to situations where a teacher's job depends upon her win-loss column.
8. With pressure to produce a winning team, teachers will find that something must suffer—classes, lesson planning, intramurals.
9. Interscholastic and/or collegiate competition with audiences is entertainment business not education.
10. Interscholastic and/or collegiates is expensive, in time, money, facilities and equipment for the benefit of only a few girls. It also increases the administration responsibility and load.

It must be remembered that if girls' athletic programs do become as organized as the boys' programs, and nothing indicates that it cannot if the girls' basketball program in the state of Iowa is any example; then the women are going to be expected to coach them. This means that they will be working long hours after school, and that they are to be judged (as the coaches of the boys' athletic teams have been and still are judged) on winning. The girls' athletic coaches will be competing for the girls' interest in other areas, such as music, dramatics, etc. This will all mean a terrific adjustment to the situation in which the women find themselves. In the past girls played for the fun of it and no one was particularly concerned with which team won the game. The playday type of athletic competition will be gone and taking its place will be a highly competitive athletic program with winning as the primary objective. The popularity of girls' athletics may increase to the point where professionalism will develop and girls' professional teams may compete for the spectator with the boys.

Regardless of all the arguments for and against interscholastic athletic competition for girls, a change is in the offing. The change will definitely affect the athletic programs in all schools and the biggest change will be in the existing financial structure. Equal programs for both boys and girls will mean equal expenditure of funds. To bring this about would require either an increase in money which is presently being appropriated for the existing program for the boys or a curtailment of the present expenditure. However, to deny girls the use of equal tax funds, facilities, and their rights to engage in athletic competition is discriminatory, and it appears that this is very definitely in the process of undergoing a drastic change. The same arguments that have been used for years to justify the extensive programs in interscholastic athletics for boys are now being used for establishing a similar program for the girls.

It must be remembered that in most cases the boys' sports program developed from a one- or two-sport project and gradually over the years other sports were added until many schools now have as many as ten sports. In contrast, the girls' program has suddenly mushroomed overnight from nothing to a comparable program which the boys now have. This has and will place a strain on facilities and will place a strain on money and personnel, because the boys have had the full use of these for years. The boys' programs are going to have to adapt; their monopoly will be broken. There will need to be a closer relationship between the boys' and girls' departments. Each will need to better understand the other's problems. There will need to be better coordination of personnel, more sharing of facilities, better planning of programs, better organization of equipment, and supplies and most of all, better cooperation between everyone concerned.

Even though the boys' program of interscholastic athletics seems threatened by the rapid surge forward of the girls' program, it is only realistic to make plans for the solution to these problems. The lack of communication between the two departments must be bridged. The men must attempt to help the women get their program off the ground and to help steer them clear of the pitfalls that the men have encountered.

The major concern among the women is that their program does not follow the same pattern as did the men's and as a result may lose its original good intentions due to the public pressure on winning. The women and also the men, in so far as is possible, are greatly concerned with the overall physical, mental, social, and emotional development of the participant. The women are at this point determined to preserve this objective. They want to start out slowly so that this development and educational value will always be present in their program. However, it is going to be difficult to stem the tide of feeling which exists for equal programs immediately.

Men receive very little compensation other than self-satisfaction for their efforts to produce a winning team. If they do not win, public pressure will be brought to bear to have them replaced.

There are many problems which the women must meet and solve before their program can be successful. The men's program is firmly entrenched and in most communities will receive first priority. This means that the sharing of personnel, facilities, and money will need to be made. It is understandable that in order for the women's program to survive, it is vital that male coaches and men outside of the athletic program support it. DeBacy[25] brings out this point very forcefully in the following statement:

A natural desire and motivation for com-

[25]DeBacy, Diane L., Spaeth, Ree and Busch, Roxanne, "What Do Men Really Think about Athletic Competition for Women?" p. 28.

petition in a woman will be totally stifled by male disapproval, direct or indirect. Hopefully, men will exert a positive influence on the future of women's competition by encouraging female participation, by helping to upgrade standards of play, and providing adequate facilities and financing for high level competitive experiences. As future directors and administrative officers, men physical education majors will be instrumental in formulating policies, making decisions and providing the logistical support which can cause desirable competitive athletics for girls and women to flourish or perish . . . . The usual departmental coexistence of men and women involved in both physical education and athletics make it imperative that the staff provide a supportive atmosphere for all phases of the program. The success of this whole new venture in competition hinges on a receptive attitude on the part of the men involved.

It is natural for women to want to engage in physical movement in the form of competitive athletics. They do not want in any way to be the cause of the curtailment of the men's program but rather to have a good one of their own which will meet the needs of girls.

The women have one point in their favor. They have watched the men's program develop over the years and are in a position to profit from mistakes. The men should do all they can to share their experiences and understanding to help the women develop a good program. The men should join hands with the women in an all-out cooperative effort to help them develop a high-level athletic program of interscholastic athletics that will afford girls the opportunity to enjoy and benefit from the outcomes of such a program. The men should help them develop a program which reflects the women's philosophy of what interscholastic athletics are for and should be.

Because of the existing circumstances in present-day society in reference to the civil rights movement and the role of the female, it appears that many of the policies of the past regarding interschool athletics are likely to change. This change will not only affect the athletic system, but other policies within the entire social structure of our society.

Although the growing program of girls' interscholastic athletics will present financial, personnel, and faculty problems and a decided change in the total picture of interscholastic athletics, it will in no way affect the administration of the program whether it is in girls' athletics, boys' athletics, or a combination of both. Therefore, this book is written with this thought in mind. The administrative practices discussed can apply, with minor revisions, in any or all three cases. These minor revisions can take care of socially accepted practices which must be recognized and dealt with in present-day society. Other than the kinds of problems brought about because of differences in sex, the interscholastic athletic program itself can be administered in the same manner and by either or a combination of sexes. The administration practices which are used to administer the program will generally apply for both sexes except where direct competition against each other in specfic contact sports will, of necessity, require a revision in some of these practices.

Blauforb[26] has made the following comment, regarding the increased emphasis on girls' athletics, some of its benefits, and the fact that it will improve, not hinder the boys' program. She states that:

> In the Houston School District, girls are involved in six competitive sports locally; four, on a statewide basis. In response to a survey, parents gave over-

[26]Blauforb, Marjorie, "Equal Opportunity for Girls in Athletics," *Today's Education* (November-December, 1974) , p. 55.

whelming approval to girls' participation in a competitive athletic program. Participation by students is enthusiastic, and although no large sums of money are available, the school board is constantly increasing funds available for girls' sports. Boys' sports have not suffered, according to some observers.

Several school districts in northeast Ohio have a long-standing pattern of varsity sports for girls. They participate in eight or even 10 sports with apparent community approval. As these programs have developed with local support, there has been no outcry that the girls' program was eclipsing the boys' sports activities.

Iowa has had a girls'athletic league for more than 50 years. Wayne Cooley, the executive director of this league, says that girls have a better chance for good competition with Iowa's pattern of two leagues, one for girls and one for boys. For the most part, the same gate fees are charged for girls' and boys' events, although when admission prices have been increased, those for girls' events have been increased before those for boys' events. Television coverage and television fees for girls' events are more than double those for boys'.

Girls' and boys' teams are often scheduled to play at the same place on the same day so that they may travel together. The team that is having a winning season gets the choice place on the program, so the boys may lead off in some years and the girls, in other years.

Cooley believes that while less money is being made on boys' sports now, properly administered girls' sports can in fact be a new form of revenue. Total annual revenues for the program sponsored by the Iowa Girls High School Athletic Union doubled between 1969 and 1974.

Administrators faced by requests to upgrade the high school girls' sports program have most often offered lack of funds as an excuse for not doing so. Since funding for athletic programs for boys in public schools varies, no panacea exists to solve the financial problems related to a good girls' program.

One big city director claims that upgrading programs for girls has helped with the funding for the boys' programs in his district. Others from smaller districts say that they have had to rework their budgets, bring out old uniforms and make all kinds of economies in order to support an adequate girls' sports program. But they do it. And they are proud of their girl athletes at the high school level.

It seems obvious that the time has come for enlarged programs for girls' sports and that informed parents support them.

Murray[27] sums up the place of women in athletics very adequately in the following comments:

I don't really feel that the woman in athletics is a problem, but rather a solution to a problem—the woman in athletics is the result of a crying need for the highly skilled sportswoman to express herself. Until recently, a small percentage of American women were permitted to excel in sport. Women are proving to be fine athletes, and I am pleased that I have an opportunity to coach some outstanding women athletes. Women in sport is a 'now thing.' Women are constantly searching for opportunities for pursuit of excellence as they compete in sport.

To those who still wonder if women should be in athletics please be receptive to our plea. Women are involved in sport and they do wish to excel. They are competitive.

I do believe that women athletes are more self-directed and dedicated to excellence than the women of the past. This in itself is an indication of their desire and need for a fine sports program.

BEHAVIORAL OBJECTIVES

After a person has read this chapter, he should be able to:

1. Explain the changing role of women in today's society and apply this to interscholastic athletics.

[27]Murray, Mimi, "The Woman in Athletics," *Journal of Health, Physical Education, and Recreation* (January 1974), p. 65.

2. Identify several reasons which have contributed to the increased sports participation by girls in recent years.
3. Identify and analyze three reasons for the increase of girls' participation in sports and apply these reasons to a specific situation.
4. Distinguish between the past and present philosophy of competitive athletics for girls.
5. Predict the future of competitive athletics for girls and justify this prediction with concrete fact.
6. Propose several sports in which girls are able to compete successfully against boys and explain why.
7. Distinguish between the Division of Girls' and Women's Sports and the National Association of Girls' and Women's Sports.
8. Analyze the statement: It is logical to assume that the organization responsible for conducting successful programs for boys should logically assume responsibility for administering wholesome programs for girls.
9. Distinguish between the influence of the National Federation of State Associations and the State Associations in girls' interscholastic athletic programs.
10. Predict the future administration pattern of the program of girls' interscholastic athletics.
11. Compare the relationship of the Division of Girls' Athletics and the Division of Men's Athletics within the administrative structure of the American Alliance of Health, Physical Education, and Recreation.
12. Explain the influence Title IX will have on the girls' interscholastic athletic program in the future.
13. Predict the outcome of girls' and boys' competing on the same interscholastic athletic teams.
14. Recognize some of the problems which may arise concerning the interscholastic competition for girls in the future.
15. Identify and explain some of the direct conflicts the girls' interscholastic athletic program might have with the existing boys' program.
16. Recall several pro's and con's regarding girls' interscholastic athletic competition and explain each.
17. Distinguish and explain one of the main concerns which the women have regarding the girls' interscholastic athletic program compared to the boys' program.
18. Identify and explain several biological differences between boys and girls which will definitely affect comparable athletic competition.
19. Enumerate several of the controversial issues between the philosophy of the women and men regarding interscholastic athletic competition. Analyze each.
20. Explain the change in attitude and the apparent reversal in attitude with the women in regard to athletic competition.
21. Explain why in the past athletics was a man's world.
22. Analyze the statement that: The effect of athletic participation on the female image depends on the participant herself.
23. Compare the physical attributes of man against woman in athletic competition in various selected sports.
24. Compare the education values in interscholastic athletics in the boys' and girls' programs.

ACTIVITIES

1. Interview the girls' physical education teacher in the local high school concerning girls competing in an interscholastic athletic program.

2. Express in writing your personal philosophy concerning girls' athletics.
3. Develop a set of standards for a girls and boys athletic program in a small high school.
4. Form two groups and debate the issue: Girls and boys should (or should not) play on the same basketball team in high school.
5. Arrange to have a high school coach or athletic director talk to the class regarding problems concerning the implications brought about by Title IX.
6. Visit a large high school and relate back to the class what you found in regard to the girls' athletic program.
7. Write to several high schools in different sections of the country requesting information on the girls' interscholastic program in their school.
8. Survey several high school coaches and obtain their opinion on the effect Title IX will have on their program.
9. Talk with several parents who have boys or girls engaged in athletics and obtain their reactions to their participating again each other on a competitive basis.
10. Talk with several boys who are high school athletes and obtain their reaction regarding their competing against girls.

SUGGESTED READINGS

1. Andrews, Leta: The role of girls' sports in public education. *Proceedings of National Federation's Fourth Annual National Conference of High School Directors of Athletics*, December, 1973.
2. Bell, Mary: Are we exploiting high school girl athletes? *Journal of Health, Physical Education, and Recreation,* Feb. 1970.
3. Bishop, Thelma: Girls' and women's sports. *Journal of Health, Physical Education, and Recreation,* April, 1960.
4. Cheska, Alyce: Current developments in competitive sports for girls and women. *Journal of Health, Physical Education, and Recreation,* March, 1970.
5. Crudo, Angelo and Reed, Kathy: No! You can't have the gym. *Journal of Health, Physical Education, and Recreation,* September, 1973.
6. DeBacy, Diane, Spaeth Ree and Busch Roxanne: What do men really think about athletic competition for women? *Journal of Health, Physical Education, and Recreation,* November, 1970.
7. Erdelyi, G.: Gynecological survey of female athletes. *The Journal of Sports, Medicine, and Physical Fitness,* September, 1962.
8. Gendel, Evelyn S.: Physicians, females, physical exertion and sports. *Proceedings Fourth National Institution of Girls' Sports,* Washington, D.C., A.A.H.P.E.R., 1968.
9. Gilbert, Bill, and Williamson, Nancy: Sport is unfair to women. *Sports Illustrated,* May 28, June 4, June 11, 1973.
10. Helmker, Judith: *High School Girls' Athletic Associations.* Cranbury, A.S. Barnes, 1970.
11. Hult, Joan: Separate but equal athletics for women. *Journal of Health, Physical Education and Recreation,* June, 1973.
12. Hutton, Linda: Needed: Women athletic trainers. *Journal of Health, Physical Education, and Recreation,* January, 1972.
13. Lacey, Carol: *Three University Panelists Conclude Females Appear Weaker in Strength Endurance.* St. Paul, St. Paul Pioneer Pr, September 29, 1973.
14. Lambert, Charlotte: Pros and cons of intercollegiate athletic competition for women: A middle of the road position paper. *Journal of Health, Physical Education, and Recreation,* May, 1969.
15. Langdon, Brenda: Use of facilities and financing girls' interscholastics—Where there is a will there is a way, *Proceedings of National Federation's Fourth Annual National Conference of High*

School Directors of Athletics, December, 1973.

16. Malumphy, Theresa: Personality of women athletes in intercollegiate competition. *Research Quarterly,* Oct. Vol. 39, 1968.

17. Murray, Mini: The woman in athletics, *Journal of Health, Physical Education, and Recreation,* January, 1974.

18. National Federation of State High School Associations: *Official Handbook.* Chicago, 1972-1973.

19. The role of girls' sports in public education. *Proceedings of the National Federation of Athletic Directors Conference,* 1974.

20. Roy, Patricia: Training women coaches and officials. *Proceedings of National federation's Fourth Annual National Conference of High School Directors of Ath-letics,* December, 1973.

21. Should girls play on boys' teams? *Good Housekeeping,* October, 1969.

22. Snyder, Art: Boys and girls together in sports? *Science Digest,* April, 1971.

23. Stutzman, Sandra Jean and McCullough, Charles: Two points of view—Did D.G.W.S. fail? *Journal of Health, Physical Education, and Recreation,* January, 1974.

24. Ulrich, Celeste: She can play as good as any boy. *Phi Delta Kappan,* October, 1973.

25. Williams, Jesse, Brownell, Clifford, and Vernier, Elmon: *The Administration of Health, and Physical Education.* Philadelphia, Saunders, 1958.

26. Wilson, Hally: Women athletic trainers. *Journal of Health, Physical Education, and Recreation,* May, 1973.

CHAPTER 5

The Levels of Control in Interscholastic Athletics

EARLY BEGINNINGS

THE TIGHT CONTROL over interscholastic athletics has been responsible in part for its success. This control was brought about by dedicated and far-sighted men who were keenly aware of the benefits which a sound athletic program, under the direct control of educational agencies, would bring to the youth of America. We have much to thank them for, as well as those men who are presently carrying on this work and presenting those ideas that were first pioneered. These men believed from the beginning that athletics should be a part of the school curriculum and a segment of the whole system of education, not an entity unto itself. Therefore, it should be administered by means similar to other areas of the school curriculum. There were, and still are, however, problems in athletics which do not apply to education and are in fact foreign to other areas or departments within the school structure. This is due in part to the tremendous interest of persons outside the school. Often they are influential citizens within the community who sometimes use their influence and position to dictate the policies under which the school athletic program operates. Fortunately, these cases are isolated due in part to the rigid administrative controls of national, state, and local organizations.

These national, state, and local organizations have assumed control over the interscholastic athletic programs to such an extent that most all of the interscholastic athletic programs in the high schools throughout the country are played under uniform rules and regulations which make the competition fair and equal in most respects. This was not always the case, however, for in the early days, it was not uncommon for teachers, principals, and even janitors to play on the high school team. Whitten,[1] the first executive secretary of the Illinois High School Association, gives this description of an incident that occurred:

> It seems to have been a generally accepted rule that team members should actually be students in the schools they represented on the athletic field. But gross violations of even this elementary principle of good sportsmanship were said to be common enough. If occasion seemed to warrant it, the butcher or the blacksmith's apprentice or the village's budding pugilist was drafted to add strength to the team. A city superintendent of one of the larger cities of Illinois told me himself that in the early days when he was coach in a Northern Illinois city, his football team seemed to be getting rather the worst of it in a game with a neighboring school. Whereupon, he rushed to the dressing room, donned

[1]Whitten, Charles, *Interscholastics* (Chicago, The Illinois High School Association, 1950), p. 3.

a uniform, and substituted himself in the line. His team, he reported, did much better thereafter.

It seems that there were no age limits, no scholastic requirements, and even membership in the school was subject to very vague interpretations. Whitten[2] tells of another case in point:

> In one case which came under my observation, two football players, whose chief qualification for the game must be expressed in terms of tonnage, took only spelling in their school and were required to be present only ten minutes per day. I have no evidence that they were required even to 'carry' the spelling.

A statement by Wagenhorst[3] brings out a very interesting practice that existed in the early days of interscholastic competition and resulted in regulations being made by the state associations to counteract such practices.

> Previous to the spring of 1895, representatives of various Wisconsin high schools had engaged in interschool contests, especially in baseball games. As competition between the schools became known, the temptation increased to use players who were not really enrolled at the time of a game. Perhaps a graduate was taken along with the nine, or some boy who had attended school, but had left to go to work. From using such players, it was an easy step to secure the services of a good player of about high school age living in the same town. Apparently, some principals either winked at such practices or remained in blissful ignorance. Other principals became disgusted and wished to abolish athletics in the high schools as a form of corruption which needed a drastic remedy.

The athletic program in most schools developed from the desire of the students to form teams and compete against other schools. This worked fine to begin with until the overwhelming urge to win at any cost took over. This situation brought forth many of the evils inherent in the program, some of which still exist today. As a result, athletics in the early days was in direct conflict with the stated purpose of the schools. As the desire for winning increased, the athletic program drifted further and further away from the control of the school officials. Outside influence crept in and gradually took over. In many instances, some school officials were happy to relinquish this responsibility, but there were others who saw the evils that could result. These administrators attempted to keep the athletic program within the realm of school control and still prevent it from interfering with the educational aspects of the school program. They selected faculty members to oversee and regulate the programs. As the programs grew, the question of who was going to accept the financial responsibility of paying for the program presented itself. This, in turn, brought up the question of gate receipts. Winning teams resulted in more people wanting to see the games. More people meant more money. So the emphasis was placed on winning teams. This in turn led to unethical practices by faculty and players alike. As a result of the malady, it soon became apparent that the athletic programs would need to be brought under the direct supervision of the school administration if the teams were to represent the school.

Much of the damage had already been done, however, and to this day, some of the evils which existed in the early days of the interscholastic athletic program still exist even though the athletic program is an official school function in almost every instance. It has changed due to the efforts of school authorities. Athletics has become an intricate part of the total school pro-

[2]*Ibid.*, p. 4.

[3]Wagenhorst Lewis, *The Administration and Cost of High School Interscholastic Athletics* (New York, Bureau of Publications, Teachers College, 1926), p 3.

gram. Its goals, objectives, and outcomes are identical in almost every respect to those of general education. Interscholastic athletics has performed its function and will continue to expand its possibilities and eventually take its rightful place in the educational program under the supervision and guidance of educational leaders.

There were numerous attempts in the early years to establish some uniformity in policies which could be used to govern competition in athletics. These organizations were powerful enough to override any local decisions which might have been made by enterprising persons whose desires were of a personal nature, detrimental to the program, or contrary to educational aims and objectives. They acted as stabilizing influences on interscholastic athletics.

These organizations were not instantly successful, and it took the combined energy and intelligence of many individuals to enable them to function and perform the many tasks they do today.

STATE CONTROL OF ATHLETICS

As a result of these types of situations, conferences and leagues were formed in the larger cities. Consequently, uniform procedures were developed which resulted in more equal and fair competition. It was generally understood that if interscholastic athletics were to survive, drastic action had to be taken. Those people who were in favor of such a program realized that it had to have the full support of the school administration if it was to succeed. Local control had failed because of various reasons, the biggest one being, of course, the desire of some to disregard the rules in their efforts to win. Control at a higher level was necessary and efforts were begun to bring this about.

It is interesting to note that Wagen-

horst[4] wrote as far back as 1926 that:

The attempt to control and regulate high school interscholastic athletic contests through state-wide organization was forced upon school administrators through pressure of circumstances. The administration of interscholastic athletics, when left solely to local authorities or sectional groups, has been generally unsatisfactory—a source of constant friction and misunderstanding. Coincident with the growth and extension of these school activities state-wide control and regulation have developed.

As competition grew and more and more schools began fielding teams, it seemed apparent that the control of school athletics should be in the hands of a single board and this should be preferably statewide. The state of Wisconsin was one of the first states to take this historic step when a group of far-sighted school administrators established the first set of rules and procedures to govern all interscholastic contests within the state.

Purposes and Functions of the State Association

The purposes and functions of the state associations vary from state to state, but there are some general functions for all. Daughtrey and Woods[5] list these functions as follows:

1. Determining eligibility and contestants
2. Establish regulations for conducting contests
3. Interpreting rules for playing
4. Developing insurance plans
5. Handling registration and classifications of officials
6. Conducting tournaments and meets
7. Establishing athletic standards

[4]Wagenhorst, Lewis, *The Administration and Cost of High School Interscholastic Athletics*, p. 3.

[5]Daughtrey, Greyson, and Woods, John, *Physical Education Programs* (Philadelphia, W. B. Saunders, 1971) , p 433.

8. Providing judicial service
9. Providing service
10. Sponsoring workshops and clinics.

Although there are wide differences in the stated purposes and functions of state associations as an examination of handbooks will verify, it is apparent that each association has as its main purpose and function that of furthering interscholastic athletics within the schools, whether they be large, small, private, or public. They are interested primarily in a sound athletic program which is a part of the total school program. They are interested in equal athletic competition, safe playing conditions, protection, and safety of the players.

ILLINOIS HIGH SCHOOL ASSOCIATION

11 S. LA SALLE ST., CHICAGO 60603

APPLICATION FOR SANCTION

OF

GIRLS INTERSCHOLASTIC SPORTS AND RELATED ACTIVITIES

(Make in duplicate and submit both copies.)

Conditions of Sanction:

The school applying for sanction agrees:

1. To conduct the meet strictly in accordance with the rules of Division B of the Illinois High School Association.
2. To use as major officials who receive remuneration only those who are registered with the Illinois High School Association and who are in good standing, and to report on officials promptly after the meet.
3. To supply the data asked for below.

Data to be supplied by applicant

Kind of meet for which sanction is requested:...................................... (Sports days, play days, workshops, tennis, etc.)

List of Schools to participate: (If not determined at this time, send list as soon as known.)......................................

A fee of..................will be charged each participant to cover the expense of......................................

The activity will begin at................o'clock and will end at............... o'clock on...................... (Date)

The program will include:......................................

Description — Approx. Cost

School Awards:...................................... $ ....

Individual Awards:......................................

Name of manager in direct charge:......................................

Illinois High School Association
11 South LaSalle Street, Chicago, Illinois 60603

Date:......................................, 19........

I accept the foregoing conditions of sanction and on behalf of...................................... (Institution conducting the meet)

I hereby apply for sanction of the IHSA for the .... (Name of meet)

to be held in......................(City)..........at...................(Gymnasium or Field)..........on......................, 19........

......................................, Principal

......................................High School

......................, Ill...............(Zip Code)

Sanction GRANTED / WITHHELD Date acted on:......................................, 19........................

By......................................, Exec. Sec.
ILLINOIS HIGH SCHOOL ASSOCIATION

Figure 1. Reprinted with permission from the Illinois High School Association.

Each association has a handbook in which is stated its aims, objectives, purposes, functions, and goals. Many of the state associations have more than the athletic programs under their jurisdiction. Some exercise control over music, dramatics, and academic programs. However, Daughtrey and Woods[6] explain that the objectives of all of these associations are general in nature and include the following, "(1) to regulate and control interschool competition, (2) to contribute to the educational growth of high school students, (3) to improve the quality of amateur competition, (4) to protect the interests of member schools, and (5) to promote a more wholesome attitude toward all interschool competition."

Types of State Associations

There are three basic types of state associations.[7] The first and most numerous type is the voluntary state association. This type of association usually limits competition to member schools with certain specifications that schools must meet to qualify for membership. The second type are state associations affiliated with state departments of education. The third type is the university-directed association in which the control is vested in some large state university. An example of this type is in the state of Texas. Daughtrey[8] indicates that:

> Some of the states that have voluntary associations are Washington, Kansas, Indiana, Florida, and Pennsylvania. Associations affiliated with state departments of education place legal control of the interschool program with the state. This plan has been in effect in the state of Michigan since 1924. In 1925, the

[6]Daughtrey, Greyson, and Woods, John, *Physical Education Programs,* p. 433.

[7]Forsythe, Charles, and Keller, Irvin, *Administration of High School Athletics,* 5th ed., (Englewood Cliffs New Jersey, by permission of Prentice-Hall, Inc., 1972), p. 49.

[8]Daughtrey, Greyson, and Woods, *Physical Education Programs,* p. 433.

New York Board of Regents made athletics in New York a definite part of the physical education program. The state association in South Carolina, Virginia, and Texas are affiliated with the state universities in these states and are examples of highly organized associations with administrative control exercised by the the state university.

The organizational setup of state associations is similar in some respects, and basically all are organized to serve similar purposes as best they can. One reason for a difference is the fact that they encompass different activities and deal with different areas within the school program. Another difference is the fact that the organization may serve schools of different sizes, classes, or geographic districts. This poses a problem of proper representation within the organization. However, regardless of these differences, each state has a handbook which contains the rules and procedures under which the association operates.

Voluntary Associations

Most of the state associations fall under the category of voluntary associations. Voluntary indicates that the schools are not required to belong to the association but must meet certain requirements to become a member. These requirements vary with each state but fundamentally include such items as organization setup, finance, and faculty status of athletic coaches. All schools are required to abide by the rules established by boards of control. These boards of control are elected and represent geographic regions or areas within the state.

State Association and Departments of Education

There are some states where the athletic program is under the direct jurisdiction of the state department of instruction.

Usually, a separate association for athletics exists and all business pertaining to athletics is carried out through this association. Yet, it is more or less a branch of the state department of instruction and under the direct supervision of the state superintendent of schools. Usually, the athletic association has its own officers who are elected from geographical areas and based on school enrollments. For all practical purposes, the athletic association is a separate entity which engulfs both physical education and athletics, yet its decisions and rules must be approved by the state department of instruction. The athletic association also receives the support and encouragement of the state department of instruction in the enforcement of its rules and regulations. Complete cooperation is necessary for the proper functioning of this type of athletic control. On the surface this plan appears to place more emphasis on the educational aspects of the athletic program. Whether or not this is true is controversial especially if the athletic associations, under the voluntary program, have the right leadership.

Associations Under University Control

The university type of association control is not popular and places the high school athletic program under the direct supervision of the state university. There are only a few states where this type of organization exists. The amount of control varies in each state.

Forsythe and Keller[9] point out that:

> Typical states that have a voluntary type of organization include Washington, Colorado, Kansas, Illinois, Wisconsin, Indiana, Connecticut, Florida, Pennsylvania, and Alabama.
>
> States that have the athletic associa-

---

[9]Forsythe, Charles, and Keller, Irvin, *Administration of High School Athletics*, p. 49.

tions connected with the state department of education include Michigan and New York.

States that have university directed state associations are Texas, South Carolina, and Virginia.

NATIONAL CONTROL OF ATHLETICS

The National Federation of State High School Associations

As the interscholastic program grew and became a part of the educational program, a need developed for the organization and regulation of the program on a national level. It was not a desire of those persons interested in the national organization to take over the state associations but rather to try and obtain uniformity of interscholastic competition throughout the United States. It was with this in mind that the original idea developed from a small beginning and grew into the present organization. The National Federation has attained tremendous stature over the years and has been a guiding force for better interscholastic athletics throughout the schools of the United States. Its influence is felt nationally and much of the credit for keeping interscholastics within the school structure belongs to the efforts of those dedicated people affiliated with the National Federation of State High School Associations.

In respect to the beginning of the National Federation and the need for such an organization, Scott[10] makes the following comment:

Following the same pattern established by the colleges, high school athletic associations were established at the turn of the century in many of the states. Since matters tended to be elastic in athletic affairs, each state association de-

[10]Scott, Harry, *Competitive Sports in Schools and Colleges* (New York, Harper and Brothers, 1951), p. 35.

National Federation of State High School Associations

INTERSTATE ALL-STAR GAME SANCTION APPLICATION

NOTE: Make application to your home state high school association executive officer. He will complete the procedure and forward to the National Federation. Each school will receive signed copy if sanctioned.

National Federation of State High School Associations   P.O...........

400 Leslie St., Elgin, Illinois 60120   Date................... 19......

On behalf of ....
                     (School or group conducting the Meet)

I hereby apply for National Federation sanction for the...........
                                                (Name and Kind of Contest)

...........to be held at...........

on..........., 19.......

The meet will be managed by...........
                          (Name of school conducting Meet)

We desire to invite recent high school graduates from the following states only...........

The number of players that will probably compete in this contest is:...........

The reasons for desiring to sponsor this contest are: ....

Contest conditions include the following:
1. Each competitor must have graduated from a high school which is a member in good standing in its State High School Association (or an affiliate as provided by the State Association), and his participation in the contest must not violate any rule of that Association or of the National Federation. His right to participate is void if his participation is found to be contrary to the State or National rules.
2. Each competitor must have been, at the time of his graduation, eligible under rules of his own State Association.
3. The game will be administered under playing rules, officiating procedures and safety requirements approved by the National Federation as meeting the specifications of the various athletic accident benefit associations and each player must have reasonable athletic accident insurance.
4. Awards and expense payments will be limited to such as will not destroy the college eligibility of any player.
5. No entry will be accepted for any competitor from any state or section of a state not included in the list of states for which sanction is granted.

Signed:...........   Official Position:...........

RECOMMENDATION OF HOME STATE EXECUTIVE

P.O...........   Date..........., 19......

I recommend that this contest be (SANCTIONED) (NOT SANCTIONED). I have sent endorsement blanks to each state named in the application.

Signature of State Executive...........

State...........

OFFICIAL ACTION OF NATIONAL FEDERATION

Elgin, Illinois,..........., 19......

This contest is hereby sanctioned for the states of ....

You should not invite boys from states or sections not included in this list.

By...........   OF THE NATIONAL FEDERATION
     (Authorized Signature)   THE EXECUTIVE COMMITTEE

(These blanks may be obtained from any state association office.)

500 10/71

Figure 2. Reprinted with permission from the National Federation of State High School Associations.

veloped along the lines that seemed to be indicated by local conditions. Accordingly, widely divergent practices were developing in high school athletics. A need was clearly indicated for some overall organization which could standardize eligibility rules and practices in the conduct of interscholastic athletics. Accordingly in May, 1920, the then secretary of the Illinois High School Athletic Association, L. W. Smith, invited representatives of neighboring states to a meeting in Chicago to discuss the problem. As an outgrowth of this meeting the Midwest Federation of State High School Athletic Associations was formed. The immediate success of this organization indicated a need on the national level. In 1922, therefore, the name was changed to the National Federation of State High School Athletic Associations. The functions of this organization are: to get

STATE SECRETARY'S ENDORSEMENT
FOR INTERSTATE MEET OR INTERSECTIONAL GAME

NOTE: When the home state secretary receives an APPLICATION FOR SANCTION, he should sign and send it to the National Office. At the same time he should execute and sent one of these ENDORSEMENT sheets to each involved state secretary, who will sign and forward it to the National Federation Office.

Home State of Proposed Contest:........................ Date this Endorsement is sent:........................

To Executive Officer of........................
(Neighboring State)

On behalf of........................
(School or group conducting the Meet)

Mr........................
(Position)

has applied for National Federation sanction of........................
(Name and Kind of Meet or Game)

.... to be held at........................
(Give Facility and Address)

.... on........................, 19....

He desires to invite schools from the following states:........................

....

Total No. of schools to be invited:........................

Reasons:........................

The Contest Manager has agreed to adhere to all the conditions of sanction as listed on the National Federation Application blank and on the Interstate Contract form and our home state (heartily approves) (endorses) (tolerates) the meet (or intersectional game).

The National Federation will approve the sending of invitations to your schools only if you endorse it. Please check endorsement below and return entire sheet to the National Federation office promptly.

Yours truly,

Executive Officer of Home State

National Federation of State High School Associations   Date:........................
400 Leslie Street, Elgin, Illinois 60120

I ☐ ENDORSE   ☐ DO NOT ENDORSE the above meet (or intersectional game) for
(Mark Correct Item):

  ☐ 1. Any of our schools
  ☐ 2. Schools within .... miles
  ☐ 3. ....

We ☐ REQUIRE   ☐ DO NOT REQUIRE that our schools send eligibility lists for contest direct to our state office for approval before they are forwarded to the meet manager.

Comment:........................

Signed:........................   State:........................
30M 8/71

Figure 3. Reprinted with permission from the National Federation of State High School Associations.

National Federation of State High School Associations

DISTANT INTERSTATE GAME SANCTION APPLICATION

NOTE: Make application in triplicate and send all copies to your home state officer. He will forward all three to the National Federation. Each school will receive signed copy if sanctioned.

National Federation of State High School Associations   P.O.........................
400 Leslie St., Elgin, Illinois 60120

                             Date........................19....

On behalf of ....at........................
(High School)   (Address)

I hereby apply for National Federation sanction for an interstate........................game for which
(Name of Sport)

one of the team will travel in excess of 600 miles (round trip). The proposed game (or games) would be:

1st game with........................at........................on........................19....

2nd game with........................at........................on........................19....

The game is sponsored by........................
(Name of School or Promoting Organization)

The reasons for desiring to compete in this distant contest are:........................

....

Contest conditions include the following:

1. Each school guarantees its membership and good standing in its own state high school association and also guarantees that participation in this contest will not violate any rule of that association or of the National Federation. The game contract is void if such membership is terminated or if participation is found to be contrary to the state or national rules.
2. Each contestant will be eligible under rules of his home state association.
3. The game will be administered under playing rules and safety requirements approved by the National Federation as meeting the specifications of the various athletic accident benefit associations.
4. If either party fails to fulfill its contract obligations, that party shall make amends in accordance with terms fixed by the National Federation executive committee after consultation with the executive officer of the states involved.
5. Only officials approved by the home state office shall be used. They will be proposed by the home school at least 5 days before the contest and approved by the visitors not later than the day before the contest.

Signed:........................   Official Position:........................

RECOMMENDATION OF HOME STATE EXECUTIVE

        P.O........................Date........................, 19....
  : I recommend that this meet be (SANCTIONED) (NOT SANCTIONED). I have sent statement to the neighboring state association officer.

                    Signature of State Executive........................

                    State........................

OFFICIAL ACTION OF NATIONAL FEDERATION

              Elgin, Illinois,........................, 19....

Sanction for the above game to be played in accordance with the conditions as outlined is hereby granted.

By........................   THE EXECUTIVE COMMITTEE
  (Authorized Signature)   OF THE NATIONAL FEDERATION

(These blanks may be obtained from any state association office.)
'IM 8/71

Figure 4. Reprinted with permission from the National Federation of State High School Associations.

agreement on rules of eligibility; to prescribe conditions of interstate competition; to exchange and pool experience in the interest of improving athletic competition; to adapt the sports and sports equipment to the participants; and to maintain research and consultant services for the benefit of all who are interested in interscholastic competition.

The National Federation of State High School Associations as it is now called consists of fifty individual high school athletic and/or activity associations and the association of the District of Columbia. Its growth has been phenomenal and it now represents 22,000 high schools and approximately 9,500,000 secondary students. Since Mr. L. W. Smith was elected secretary-treasurer, three men have served in this capacity, C. W. Whitten, H. V. Porter, and the present executive secretary, Clifford B. Fagan.

Purpose

The purpose of the National Federation is stated in its constitution:[11]

> The object of this Federation shall be to protect and supervise the interstate interests of the high schools belonging to the state associations, to assist in these activities of the state associations which can be best operated on a nationwide scale, to sponsor meetings, publications, and activities which will permit each state association to profit by the experience of all other member associations, and to coordinate the work so that waste effort and unnecessary duplication will be avoided.

George and Lehmann[12] suggests that:

[11]National Association of State High School Associations *Official Handbook* (1972-73), p. 8.

[12]George, Jack, and Lehmann, Harry, *School Athletic Administration* (New York, Harper and Row, 1966), p. 241.

National Federation of State High School Associations

CONTRACT FOR INTERSTATE GAMES OR MEETS

Place_____, Date_____, 19____

This CONTRACT is made and subscribed to by the Principals and Athletic Managers of the _____High School

and of the_____High School, for_____contests in_____to be played as follows:

	City	Date	Day	Hour	(Name of Sport)	Hour

First Team Contest_____Preliminary Game_____

First Team Contest_____Preliminary Game_____

Financial Terms:_____

1. Each school guarantees its membership and good standing in its own state high school association and also guarantees that participants in this contest will not violate any rule of that association or of the National Federation. The game contract is void if such membership is terminated or if participation is found to be contrary to the state or national rules.
2. Each contestant will be eligible under rules of his home state association.
3. The game will be administered under playing rules and safety requirements approved by the National Federation.
4. If either party fails to fulfill its contract obligations, that party shall make amends in accordance with terms fixed by the National Federation executive committee after consultation with the executive officers of the states involved.
5. Only officials approved by the home state office shall be used. They will be proposed by the home school at least 14 days before the contest and approved by the visitors not later than 7 days before the contest.

_____   _____   _____   _____
(Principal)   (Manager)   (School)   (State)

_____   _____   _____   _____
(Principal)   (Manager)   (School)   (State)

NOTE: List suggested Registered officials on the back. The visitors should scratch those not acceptable and number the others in the order of preference.

5M 8/72

Figure 5. Reprinted with permission from the National Federation of State High School Associations.

The original purpose of the organization was to secure proper adherence to the eligibility rules of the various state associations in interscholastic contests and meets.

The purposes have been accomplished in many respects and the desired results have been accomplished. Desired regulations for interstate contests and tournaments have been adopted, and a high degree of control over athletics has been accomplished.

The program of the National Federation is based on the belief that the athletic activities of the high school must be protected and this can be done through strong national and state associations. The justification that athletics is an integral part of the educational curriculum and the increasing popularity of athletics necessitates strong methods of protection to insure this philosophy. Therefore, it is necessary for administrators to formulate organizations such as the National Federation to accomplish this purpose.

The National Federation, because of its tremendous growth, has been able to exercise a strong influence on the formulation of policies and plans for the athletic program in high schools. It is probably the largest organized athletic organization in the world. Its contributions have been outstanding.

The legislative body of the National Federation is the National Council which consists of one member of each member state association. Each member of the council must be an officer in his respective state association or a member of the State Board of Control. The executive body is the executive committee which consists of eight members, one from the eight election

National Federation of State High School Associations

APPLICATION FOR SANCTION OF INTERNATIONAL COMPETITION

NOTE: Applications are to be initiated by the executive officer of the host state not later than 60 DAYS PRIOR TO THE DATE OF THE FIRST COMPETITION. Make application to the executive secretary of the National Federation.

National Federation of State High School Associations   P.O._____
400 Leslie St., Elgin, Illinois 60120

Date_____

On behalf of _____
(School or group conducting international competition)

I hereby apply for National Federation sanction for competition involving _____
(Sport)

team from _____, consisting of _____ to be held
(Visiting Country)   (Meet, tour, or tournament)

at _____ on _____
(Facility and address)   (Date)

The competition will be managed by _____. The team
(Name of organization conducting)

from _____ will be in the United States from _____ to _____. The
(Country)   (Date)   (Date)

schools involved in this international competition are as follows: (List all hosting schools.)

(School)   (Date)   (School)   (Date)

_____
_____
_____
_____

The visiting team from _____ will be managed by _____, whose
(Country)   (Name of director)

title and address are as follows: _____

CONDITIONS OF COMPETITION as follows have been agreed to by the visiting team manager and all schools involved in the competition:
1. Each school guarantees its membership is in good standing in its own state high school association, and also guarantees that participation in this contest will not violate any standard of or the National Federation.
2. Each participant representing a United States high school will be eligible under the rules of his home state association.
3. Foreign competitors shall qualify as amateurs and if students, comply with the eligibility standards prevalent in the host state concerning age, year in school, etc.
4. Competition in the United States shall be administered under those playing rules and safety requirements approved by the National Federation.
5. The program of competition will not conflict with either the academic or interscholastic regulations adopted by the state high school associations or with the scholastic or athletic program of the schools.
6. A complete financial report involving all phases of the competition will be filed with the National Federation and the involved state associations within 30 days following final competition.
7. The competition has been sanctioned by the appropriate international amateur sports governing body.

Host State Executive Officer _____ State _____

OFFICIAL ACTION OF THE NATIONAL FEDERATION

Elgin, Illinois _____ 19____

Sanction for the above competition to be played in accordance with the conditions as outlined is hereby granted.

By_____ THE EXECUTIVE COMMITTEE OF
(Authorized Signature)   THE NATIONAL FEDERATION

(These blanks may be obtained from any state association office.)

1M 10/71

Figure 6. Reprinted with permission from the National Federation of State High School Associations.

HOST SCHOOL'S APPLICATION
FOR SANCTION OF NON-ATHLETIC INTERSTATE EVENT

NOTE: Make application to the executive officer of the state in which the meet is to be held at least 30 DAYS PRIOR TO THE DATE the meet is to be held.

National Federation of State High School Associations   P.O._____
400 Leslie St., Elgin, Illinois 60120

Date_____, 19____

On behalf of _____
(School or Organization Sponsoring the Event)

I hereby apply for interstate sanction of the following non-athletic event:

_____, to be held at _____
(Name and Kind of Event)   (Location)

on _____, 19____. The meet will be managed by _____
(Name of School Conducting the Event)   (Manager)

We desire to invite schools from the following states only:_____

_____ (List schools to be invited on back.) The number of schools which will probably compete is _____

Awards to be given are: _____ Approximate cost per award_____

Entry fees to be charged are: _____

The contest manager has agreed to the following conditions:
1. Each school guarantees its membership in good standing in its own state high school association and also guarantees that participation in this contest will not violate any standard of that association.
2. Each participant shall be eligible under the standards of his own home state association.
3. Awards shall be limited to those permitted by the state association with the most restrictive award rule.
4. No entry shall be accepted for any competitor from any state or section not included in the list of states from which sanction is received.
5. File in the state office a complete financial and participation report.

Date_____ Signed:_____
(Principal or Superintendent)

School_____ Address_____

APPROVAL OF HOME STATE EXECUTIVE OFFICER

P.O._____Date_____, 19____

This application for sanction is hereby approved and we recommend that it be sanctioned. Endorsement blanks have been sent to each state association sponsoring non-athletic activities from which schools have been invited. We request authorization for schools from the listed states to participate.

Signature of State Executive_____

State_____

OFFICIAL ACTION

Elgin, Illinois_____, 19____

This meet is hereby sanctioned for the states of _____

_____

DO NOT INVITE schools from _____ nor any other state not included in the above sanctioned list.

By _____ NATIONAL FEDERATION

(These blanks may be obtained from any state association sponsoring non-athletic activities.)

10M 8/71

Figure 7. Reprinted with permission from the National Federation of State High School Associations.

---

sections as outlined in the constitution. Their election is by the National Council at their annual meetings.

The National Federation Conference of High School Directors of Athletics

This organization is composed of high school athletic directors throughout the United States. The conference came about at the request of the representatives of the fifty state, high school athletic or activity associations which constitute its membership. The conference is held each year at various cities throughout the United States and is an in-service program for administrators of interscholastic athletics. It pro-vides for direct contact with high school athletic directors through state-wide workshops and national conferences. It provides these people with added knowledge and expertise which enables them to execute proper administration of interscholastic athletic programs at the local, state, and national levels. The conference provides the directors with the information that enables them to best carry out the responsibilities of their position. The conference provides a needed service and is liberally subsidized by the National Federation. Its impact on interscholastic athletics is very real and it is another first in the administration of interscholastic athletics as it relates to the total educational curriculum.

CONFERENCE CONTROL
OF ATHLETICS

The conference is an important aspect of interscholastic athletic control. Very few schools involved in an athletic program do not belong to a conference.

Control Aspects of the Conference

There are several ways in which the conference can exert an influence in the control of interscholastic athletics. Some of these ways are as follows:

1. It enables one school to become acquainted with schools through athletics.
2. It assures suitable competition.
3. It provides an opportunity to acquire competition with schools of approximate equal size.
4. It provides an opportunity to acquire competition where travel is not great.
5. It provides an opportunity to be involved in competition where league championships are at stake.
6. It provides an opportunity to become involved in competition where individuals from the school are recognized for their achievements in the conference.
7. It enables a group of schools to work closely with state and national associations.
8. It insures uniform rules and regulations for athletic competition.
9. It enables schools to establish better crowd control at all games.
10. It insures a complete schedule.

Principles of Conference Control

Every conference must provide a code of principles and a set of operational procedures for member schools to follow. This will assure equality and equal opportunity for all the schools involved.

There are many control principles and operational procedures to be dealt with in the administration of interscholastic athletics. The following controls and procedures are evident in most conferences:

1. MEETINGS: Administrators and members gather on prescribed dates for the purpose of transacting the athletic business of the conference.
2. OFFICIALS: Uniform rules as to how officials conduct contests in all sports are established. Their eligibility to officiate the sport is determined as well as how much they are paid. Uniform rating procedures are established.
3. AWARDS: Procedure and control of awards will vary from conference to conference. Specifications are made as to the kind of award (trophy, medal, ribbon, etc.) to be given for specific events or contests and levels of competition. For instance, in a swimming conference championship, the varsity might receive medals for the individual finalists while sophomores might receive ribbons for the individual finalists. Some conferences have strict rules forbidding the giving or receiving of awards by member schools. For example, no school should be allowed to purchase or accept from any outside organization or any individual a trophy for an athletic conference championship won by any team, except the conference award on the varsity level.
4. CONDUCT OF CONTESTS: General conduct of all athletic contests are established. Items such as bands, mechanical noisemakers and signs, movies and electronic devices, opening time of gates, smoking, spotters, towels, and teams in the locker room and bench must receive uniform consideration. Practices will vary from conference to confer-

ence. A good example of this is the supervision of students at athletic contests. A faculty member (preferably a representative of the administrative staff) should be appointed by each participating school superintendent or principal to take the responsibility for student conduct at games played away from home. This procedure will help unify and strengthen practices of good sportsmanship and ethical conduct among all students in the conference schools. It would be helpful if the school faculty representative of the visiting school would report to the host superintendent or principal and make his identity and whereabouts known.

5. SCHEDULES: The contest schedules for all conference schools should be made up by the athletic directors and approved by the principals of the conference schools. Other items such as schedule limitations, change of dates for contests, postponed contests, and preliminary games should also be taken care of in the same way so as to avoid any confusion and misunderstanding.

6. LIMITATION OF SEASON AND PRACTICE: Conferences will vary as to the number of practices allowed before the season begins as well as the length of the season in each sport. All conference schools must abide by the state requirement in this respect; however, they may impose more stringent restrictions if they wish to do so.

7. ASSIGNMENT CHAIRMAN: There should be specific qualifications for this man, such as being a faculty member of one of the member schools, not an active coach, athletic director, or official, etc. His duties would usually be the assignment of officials for the conference athletic events.

8. TICKETS AND ADMISSIONS: The confer-

ence will usually charge an admission for students and adults for conference contests.

9. REGULATIONS FOR THE DIFFERENT SPORTS: Rules and regulations for each interscholastic sport in the conference have their own individual interpretations and will not be discussed. It should be mentioned that there may be differences in rules between the different sports and differences in rules between the same sports in different conferences.

LOCAL CONTROL OF ATHLETICS

The high school athletic program should be organized and carried on under the rules, regulations, and recommendations of the State High School Association, the National Federation of State High School Associations, the American Alliance for Health, Physical Education, and Recreation, the National Association of Secondary School Principals, and the rules and regulations of the conference to which the school belongs as well as the local school board.

The essential difference between a good athletic program and a poor one is its purpose. Schools exist for educational purposes and the athletic program should be organized and administered on the basis of educational values. Athletics contribute to educational objectives and aid in establishing standards of behavior that represent the best in good citizenship. In addition to stressing the will to win, athletics, to be considered worthwhile, should also result in the acquiring of such virtues as truthfulness, fair play, honesty, modesty, give-and-take, courtesy, self-discipline, courage, generosity, self-restraint, and loyalty. These virtues cannot be achieved by the athlete if he sees the coaches cutting corners.

A program of athletics at the inter-

TABLE I
ATHLETIC DEPARTMENT

WEEKLY SCHEDULE
WEEK OF _____   *COACHES*
SPORT_____ SQUAD_____   _____
                                            _____
                                            _____
                                            _____

Check this list for any errors. Please return this list *with the scores* to the Athletic Office no later than the following Monday.

DATE OF ACTIVITY _____
HIGH SCHOOL SCORES _____
OPPONENT _____
OPPONENT'S SCORE _____
LOCATION
OF ACTIVITY _____
LEAVING TIME _____
TIME OF ACTIVITY _____
OFFICIALS   1._____
RATING
  1. Sup.   2._____
  2. A. Ave.
  3. Ave.   3._____
  4. B. Ave.
  5. Poor   4._____
BUS TIME _____
COMMENTS:

scholastic level should be offered which makes it possible to give recognition to boys and girls of all sizes and ages. Sports which have a great carry-over value for later, lesiure-time activity, should be included in the program.

Responsibility for Controls

The local control of interscholastic athletics is the responsibility of many individuals. The local control is vested in the school district which includes the board of education and the school administration itself. The size of the school district is the determining factor in the number of people involved.

Importance of Local Control

The importance of the local school administrative control is apparent because

without this local control, there could be no interscholastic athletics. The measure of success of the program of interscholastic athletics is the responsibility of the local organization or administration. Therefore, the main responsibility falls on the superintendent and/or the principal. With all the other responsibilities of the administration, athletics is under the administration's control more than most people think. The major decisions and policies concerning athletics are theirs. The administrators have the difficult job of keeping a balance of emphasis on the different parts of the entire educational system. Athletics must not receive too much attention in relation to the rest of the various parts of the entire educational system. It should not, however, be put aside or receive no attention at all.

Interscholastic athletics are a part of the educational system and should be considered as such.

Daughtrey[13] has this to say about athletic control:

> One of the problems confronting teachers and administrators is the control of the interschool program. The program is designed primarily for the participants, the student body is of secondary importance, and the public should be the last to be concerned with the interschool athletic program. It is when this control is assumed by the community that trouble arises. Several principles that should be brought to the attention of the community are:
>
> 1. Communities should realize that control of, and responsibility for school athletics rests entirely with school authorities.
> 2. School athletics should furnish a recreational opportunity for the general public only insofar as a community is willing to see that programs are conducted solely for the benefit of student competitors and student spectators.
> 3. Communities should judge the success of the season on the number of participants and spectators, new skills required and good citizenship and good sportsmanship taught, rather than on number of games won and lost.
> 4. Communities constantly should keep in mind the fact that, primarily, an athletic contest is a part of a school program because of its educational implications. When it ceases to have educational value it should cease to be a school function.
>
> Community support is desirable for the success of any school program in interschool athletics. Keeping the public informed is one sure way of gaining this support.

Principles of Local Control

There are some principles of control that the local administration should be aware of and vitally concerned about. First, the administration must realize that interscholastic athletics should be an integral part of the school system and should operate in harmony with the objectives and aims of secondary education. Athletics should neither be considered a necessary evil or be placed in the spotlight and overshadow everything else.

The superintendent along with the board of education has the responsibility of establishing the athletic policy of the school and relating this policy to the community or district. The athletic policies of a school must be well known and understood by the public if good school-community relations are to be kept and problems are to be avoided. The superintendent can best do this by informing the public in various ways as to the worth and value of the athletic program. He can cite other successful programs and indicate new trends as evidence of the worth of local program and policies.

There are some considerations in relation to the control of athletics which must be considered in formulating athletic policy. Such things as amount and quality of facilities and equipment are important when considering the number ond limitations of sports at the school. The quality and number of available coaches is another consideration. According to Esslinger,[14] "The major problem confronting interscholastic athletics in the United States is the fact that approximately one fourth of all head coaches of junior and senior high school teams have had no professional preparation for such a responsibility."

The criteria for selecting head coaches that are qualified for the job should include a major in physical education along

---

[13]Daughtrey, Greyson, *Methods of Physical Education and Health in Secondary Schools* (Philadelphia, W. B. Saunders and Co., 1967), p. 478.

[14]Esslinger, Arthur, "Certification for High School Coaches," *Journal of Health, Physical Education and Recreation* (October, 1968), p. 42.

with some actual playing experience on the varsity level in the sport that he is expected to coach. However, it seems that many of today's head coaches do not meet these requirements. This is one of the major problems that an administrator faces today when formulating the school's athletic policy regarding the selection of coaches.

Another consideration in regard to control is the relationship of facilities and personnel to intramural sports and interscholastic sports. The emphasis given to each area is quite a challenge to the administrator. Methods of financing athletics is another consideration in formulating policy. Other considerations would include an athletic injury insurance plan, the length of schedules in all sports, and how much authority to give the coaches in such matters as game contracts, eligibility, schedules, and selection of personnel.

Although the administration is responsible for the control of athletics to a great degree, the responsibilities can be split up through the various administrative levels in the school.

THE SUPERINTENDENT AND CONTROL OF ATHLETICS

The superintendent must be able to justify interscholastic athletics in terms of meeting education goals and objectives.

Philosophy

The superintendent must assume the responsibility and leadership in determining the philosophy of athletics within the school system. The board of education must be well aware of the superintendent's attitude toward athletics before he is hired because he is the person who will guide the program, influence the faculty, and place athletics within the total program structure. He must see the athletic program

as being an integral part of the framework of the educational system if it is to be successful. He must have an intimate knowledge of the values of athletics and request that written policies regarding the place of athletics within the educational structure be formulated.

Written Policies

The superintendent has the responsibility of establishing written policies as to the duties of all school personnel involved in the program of athletics. These people would include head coaches, assistant coaches, athletic directors, business managers, etc. The duties of all these people should be spelled out in detail. Included in these written policies should be a clearly defined statement regarding the place of physical education in relation to athletics.

Evaluation Procedures

The superintendent should also assume the responsibility of determining evaluation procedures regarding all personnel connected with the athletic program. This should be done in cooperation with the principal and athletic director. This might involve some very difficult decisions because the nature of athletic problems involves winning and losing which in itself many times can be catastrophic.

Public Relations

The superintendent is in a position to deal directly with the general public, and it is his responsibility to assume the leadership role in this respect. He is the frontman and the one who "calls the shots." He must be tactful in his dealings, yet he must "take a stand" on issues of major importance whenever it is necessary to do so.

Facilities

The superintendent can spare himself untold grief by establishing written policies regarding various aspects of the program. This procedure could apply very well in the use of facilities both by the general public and members of the school staff.

Financing

The financing of the athletic program is one of the major concerns of every school administrative staff. The cost of every phase of the school program has skyrocketed the past few years, and the athletic program certainly is no exception. Superintendents are cost conscious and rightly so. The superintendent should be well versed in school financing and be able to justify the expenditures necessary to carry on a well-rounded athletic program. To do this, he should formulate a detailed plan under which he will operate. He should have this plan in writing and it should be stated in writing if the funds to support the program are to come from general revenue, gate receipts, or both. He should have an understanding with the board of education as to how the athletic program is to be financed and then act accordingly.

Athletic Injuries

Another area of great concern in the athletic program is injuries. The superintendent must have absolute control over this vital area and he should do this by establishing written policies which are approved by the board of education with the help of the school lawyer.

Responsibility to the Board

The superintendent also exercises control over the athletic program by his direct association with the board of education. He must report directly to them and be directly accountable to them. He must secure their approval for the establishment of all policies and procedures.

Leadership

It is the responsibility of the superintendent to provide leadership in formulating the policies and procedures under which the department of athletics must operate. Complete cooperation between coaches, athletic director, principal, and teachers is vital if the program is successful. The superintendent must provide this leadership.

THE PRINCIPAL AND CONTROL OF ATHLETICS

The principal must assume his full share of the responsibility of administering the athletic program. By virtue of his position as principal, he can exercise certain controls over the athletic program.

Philosophy

The principal will indicate his philosophy of athletics by his actions. The principal must, however, regard athletics as a part of the total school curriculum and in reality as being just another subject that is being offered in the total program. He has the responsibility of projecting athletics in a favorable light to the student body. He must show the students that he, himself, thinks that athletics is worthwhile and justifiable in every respect. He should attend as many contests as possible. He should also commend any person who shows good citizenship and sportsmanship in relation to athletics.

This person must know the athletic policies of the school and be able to project them to the public. He must keep his school informed on happenings pertaining to matters discussed at meetings he attends whether it be at the conference or state level. And finally, this is the person that does the busy paper work required such as securing officials and preparing contrasts.

The local control of athletics is not the same at all schools. One big determining factor is differences in school size. Organization of control at the local level has to be different because of school size. There are three basic school sizes today. They are the small or "one-man" school, the medium-size school, and the large school.

The "one-man" department in the small school will have an organizational control that is far from being complex. In this situation, one man may coach every sport that is offered (possibly football, basketball, and baseball) and will assume the responsibility.

Duties of the Principal

The principal is in closer contact with the athletic situation than either the board of education or the superintendent. Therefore, he must assume the leadership role in the administration of the program. His role will be different from that of the superintendent and athletic director as he will be more or less the "watch dog," whose duties will be the enforcement of the state association regulations.

The principal is in direct daily contact with the athletic program and must consider it as a part of the school curriculum. Because of this, the principal will be called upon to be responsible for the many details connected with the proper administration of an athletic program. Consequently, he will be held accountable to the superintendent for the conduct of the athletic program within his school just as he is accountable for every other program that is part of the school curriculum.

Player Eligibility

The principal has access to the academic as well as the personal records of all the students. It would seem logical, therefore, to expect the principal to be responsible for the determination of the eligibility of all athletes. He can delegate this authority to anyone of his chosing, and this is often done by his secretary or office help. In the last analysis, however, the principal is held responsible for the eligibility of all athletes. He must first determine the eligibility and then enforce the policies and regulations established by local, state, and national agencies.

Responsibility of Staff

Even though the principal is held accountable for administering the athletic program within the limits of his responsibility, he must delegate many of the tasks to other staff members. Many of the details will, if necessary, be assigned to those individuals who are most capable of working in the area of athletics.

Conduct of Athletes

The principal is responsible for the conduct of the athletes as well as the other students while they are in school. He should, therefore, be aware of what takes place during practice, as well as during the game. He should visit the practice sessions as he does other classes and meet with the coaches periodically so that they may exchange viewpoints regarding any phase of the athletic program. If the athletic program is an actual part of the entire school program, it should be supervised in the same manner and function under the same regulations.

Conduct of Students

The principal is responsible for the conduct of all students during the game. He should make every effort to educate the students as to the principles of good sportsmanship. This can be done with the cooperation of other faculty members, coaches, and students through the use of posters, assemblies, and talks by various team members.

Athletic Program Responsibilities

The principal, in cooperation with the athletic director, is responsible for many of the factors that are a part of the athletic program. This could include the payment of game officials, scheduling of games, work schedules for custodians, maintenance and groundsmen, hiring of ticket takers and sellers, assigning the use of facilities for practice and games, hiring of scorers and timers, arranging for the hiring of a physician to be present at all games, etc.

Enforcement of School Philosophy

The principal should be ever mindful of the school philosophy regarding the athletic program. He should continually point out to students, coaches, and parents alike what athletics are for and how they fit into the general pattern of education in his particular school. He should stand behind his coaches at all times in the enforcement of the rules of the game.

Staff Selections

Most principals will have a voice in the selection of all staff members including the athletic coaches. Due to the very nature of the athletic program and because the principal will of necessity be working very closely with all athletic personnel, it is natural that he should be vitally interested in the selection of all coaches. It is important if they are to work together harmoneously that the principal's and the coach's philosophy of athletics is somewhat similar, and that their personalities are compatible. The wise superintendent will solicit the help of the principal when hiring the athletic coach.

THE ATHLETIC DIRECTOR AND CONTROL OF ATHLETICS

The direct control of the athletic program on a local basis is, of course, in the hands of the athletic director. Most of the administrative details of carrying out the program are the responsibility of the athletic director. He or she in turn is directly responsible to the immediate superior, the principal.

Scheduling of Games

The director of athletics may delegate this responsibility to the coaches, but he is responsible for the final disposition of the contract and gives final approval for the games. He signs the contract and determines if the date on which the contest is to be played does not conflict with other school functions.

Transportation

The transporting of the athletic teams to contests is of major importance because of the pressure of the times and the chance of legal implications in case of accidents while in transit. This responsibility usually belongs to the director of athletics and is under his direct supervision and control.

Hiring of Officials

The hiring of officials should be under the direct control of the athletic director and not the coach. This policy will relieve the pressure which might be present if the coach had this responsibility. Usually the names of acceptable officials are given to the director by the coaches who, as a group, have approved them at an earlier date.

Supervisory Control

The supervision of coaches as well as other department personnel is the responsibility of the athletic director. He or she should carefully scrutinize the actions of these persons and report findings to the principal.

Eligibility

The eligibility of the players, as has been mentioned previously, is under the direct control of the principal. However, the athletic director must assume the responsibility of seeing to it that the principal obtains the names of all players so that their records can be scrutinized.

Contracts

The principal usually signs the contracts for all athletic contests, although often this is done by the athletic director or both. Usually the athletic director will fill out the contract stating the terms and send it along to the principal for his signature.

Medical Examinations

The medical examination is an important aspect of any interscholastic athletic program. This is the responsibility of the athletic director. He or she, in turn, works very closely with the coach of each sport. No student should be allowed to participate unless he has fulfilled the necessary physical requirements and has a physician's permission. Many schools will not allow the player to draw any athletic equipment unless he has a physician's permit to engage in the particular sport.

Equipment and Supplies

The athletic director usually has initial control over all equipment and supplies. However, the coach of each sport generally determines the type of equipment that is purchased and to whom the equipment should be issued.

Bucher[15] has this to say about the ad-

ministration:

> The school administrator is the one responsible for the educational program in his school; and as such, he should be the expert in and the leader for educational athletics. He has within his power the potential to utilize athletics as an educational medium or have them serve as a means of entertainment for the multitudes, to stress knowledge and understanding, or gate receipts, and to recognize the unique value of athletics as an educational experience for our boys and girls, or see them as a way of gaining newspaper headlines. School administrators are the persons responsible for the total in-class and out-of-class educational programs that go in their schools. Such a responsibility cannot be relegated to the coach, the alumni, or the enthusiastic community-minded citizen.

THE ATHLETIC COUNCIL AND CONTROL OF ATHLETICS

The athletic council, as a local control group in interscholastic athletics, has an important place in the total athletic picture. Its functions, while mostly of an advisory nature, are those which deal primarily with controversial problems which are a constant concern to the administrators of the athletic program. The athletic council is primarily a policy-making body, and its duties vary with each particular school. Usually, the council acts as a "watch dog" on all athletic matters.

Composition of the Athletic Council

The composition of the athletic council will be different in some respects depending upon the situation in which it operates.

Welch[16] suggests, for example, that:

> The Council in their school is made up of the superintendent, principal, football coach, basketball coach, baseball coach, all assistant coaches, track coach, equipment manager, the financial advis-

---

[15]Bucher, Charles, "Needed: A New Athletic Program," *The Physical Educator* (October, 1966), p. 100.

[16]Welch, Everett, "The Athletic Council," *The Athletic Journal* (February, 1956), p. 26.

ors, and the athletic director. The girls' physical education director is an ex-officio member, meeting only when business pertains to her program. All other faculty members are invited to meet with the council any time they have problems pertaining to an athlete or athletics, or any other member of the faculty who might be interested in athletics, but cannot engage in coaching for one reason or another. Many times it has been found that those people not actively engaged in coaching, offer excellent suggestions which the coaches fail to see because they are so close to the program.

In many situations the composition of the council might be made up of the administration, the coaches, and all faculty members interested in athletics.

Size of Athletic Councils

The control of athletics differs in all schools and some more than others. The size of the school is often the determining factor in the type of control experienced. Naturally in the small school the staff will be composed of few members. In fact, often one person will do all of the coaching and assume the duty of athletic director. The athletic control council in this situation may include the athletic director, the superintendent, a faculty and student representative, and possibly a school board member. The problems encountered are usually not nearly as complex and do not require a lot of formality. Problems can be solved more quickly because there are fewer people involved in the decision making.

The medium-size school will have a larger athletic control council due to its size and the greater number of students involved in the program. The board in this situation may be made up of the superintendent and/or principal, some faculty members, selected student representatives, the athletic director, the coaches, and possi-

bly a school board member. Meetings will take place more frequently because there will be problems arising and more formality will be required.

The large school athletic control council will have more members. Responsibility is more evenly divided and the council will be composed of the superintendent and principal, the athletic director, the coaches and their assistants, some faculty members, the head of the physical education department, selected student representatives, and possibly some school board members. Procedures here are quite formal because of the number of people involved and the divided responsibility.

Purpose of the Athletic Council

The purpose of the athletic council is to serve as an advisory board in counseling the administration in determining policies, principles, and standards for the operation of the school athletic program and to determine rules, regulations, and operating procedures which will best contribute to the desired outcomes of the athletic program.

Membership of the Athletic Council

Membership of the athletic council should consist of all head coaches, the athletic director, two faculty members appointed by the principal, the dean of boys, the assistant principal, the principal, and two students. The principal should be the permanent chairman and the coordinator should be the vice-chairman.

Meetings of the Athletic Council

Regular meetings of the council should be held shortly after the fall, winter, and spring seasons in November, March, and May respectively. Special meetings should be called by the principal or coordinator if there is a need. Minutes should be kept by an appointed member of the council and distributed to the members.

Functions of the Athletic Council

The problems confronting the athletic department in any school are generally of a very complex nature. The following functions can be considered as the problems confronting the athletic council:

1. To serve as an advisory committee to assist in solving departmental problems,
2. To determine criteria for athletic awards and to approve or disapprove award recommendations by the coaches,
3. To discuss and propose matters of league interest and make recommendations for league or conference attention,
4. To work closely with the board of education,
5. To rule on all schedules,
6. To rule on all budgets for each sport,
7. To determine what to charge for admission to athletic contests,
8. To determine the cost of season passes,
9. To determine who shall receive complementary tickets,
10. To determine matters of policy,
11. To determine the expenditure of money,
12. To determine eligibility procedures,
13. To instigate a fair and just method of selecting cheerleaders,
14. To present a unified front to the public on all athletic decisions.

The athletic council handles so many problems concerning the athletic program that it is impossible to list many of the less important duties.

The attempts at controlling interscholastic athletics over the years has been a gradual process starting from a situation where the program was under the control

TABLE II

LACOMA HIGH SCHOOL

Lacoma, Iowa

District 91

NAME _____   CLASS _____

TRAINING RULES — ADOPTED FEBRUARY, 19_____

This uniform code of training rules has been adopted by our Athletic Council at Lacoma High School for all athletes. All of our coaches are obligated to help enforce these rules for all squads. Those players who are members of our athletic teams:

1. Shall not use or attempt to use tobacco.
2. Shall not use or attempt to use alcoholic beverages.
3. Shall not misuse or attempt to misuse any drugs.

Athletes who violate the above training rules will be excluded from the season in which the violation occurs plus three consecutive seasons. This suspension may be appealed by the athlete at the conclusion of the sport season following the sport season during which the violation occurred. For a second violation a player will be excluded from all athletics for one calendar year (365 days) with no appeal provision.

There will be four sport seasons: Fall, Winter, Spring & Summer in assessing penalties for training violations.

Any athlete who, in the coaches' opinion, demonstrates poor behavior not conducive to the spirit of sportsmanship and good citizenship shall be subject to the disciplinary action, including possible exclusion or suspension from athletics.

SIGNED _____   SIGNED _____
PARENT   STUDENT ATHLETE

DATE _____

of nonschool personnel to the present time where the program is under the direct control of the school administration. The program at the present time is a reflection of the type of men who guided the program, not only in its formative years, but also at the present time. These men have made interscholastic athletics an integral part of the educational curriculum in the schools of America. The future of this program holds much in store for the young people who are fortunate enough to take advantage of it.

BEHAVIORAL OBJECTIVES

1. Distinguish between some of the problems which exist in interscholastic athletics as opposed to those in other areas within the school curriculum.
2. Recall and explain the early beginnings in the control of interscholastic athletics as opposed to those controls which exist today.
3. Identify some of the problems confronting interscholastic athletics in the early years of its existence.
4. Evaluate and compare the function or goal of interscholastic athletics with other school programs and education in general.
5. Summarize the early beginnings of leagues and identify some of their purposes and reasons as to why these leagues were formed.
6. Identify the types of state associations and explain the distinguishing characteristics of each.
7. Recall the early history of the National Federation of State High School Athletic Associations and identify some of its purposes.
8. Recall some of the rules required for membership in the National Federation of State High School Associations and conclude why they are important.
9. Explain the organizational structure of the National Federation of State High School Associations.
10. Select three recommendations for the regulation of athletic contests which the National Federation has made and apply them to actual school situations.
12. Predict the role the National Federation will have in the future of the interscholastic athletic program.
13. Recall several ways in which an athletic conference can exert an influence in the control of interscholastic athletics. Select the most important one and explain why.
14. Explain several control principles which are common to every athletic conference.
15. Explain the importance of local administrative control of interscholastic athletics.
16. Identify several principles of local control in interscholastic athletics that the administration should be aware of.
17. Analyze the responsibility of the superintendent in determining the philosophy of athletics in the school. Apply this philosophy to a particular school system.
18. Identify and explain the responsibilities of the principal in administering the athletic program in the school.
19. Identify and explain the responsibilities of the athletic director in administering the athletic program in the school.
20. Explain the responsibilities and the purpose of the athletic council in the athletic program.
21. Visualize or predict what the future control of athletics in the school will be in light of the civil rights movement.
22. Recall several services which the athletic board performs in the high school

athletic program.

23. Distinguish between the duties and the personnel of the athletic council in the small, medium, and large high school.
24. Compile a list of responsibilities or duties that would be appropriate for the athletic council in the high school.
25. Analyze several functions of the athletic council and apply them to a local school.
26. Identify the names and explain the functions of the most important national, state, and sectional organizations promoting interscholastic athletics in educational institutions.
27. Explain the functions of influential organizations promoting interscholastic athletics.
28. Explain how the local athletic director can use the national and state athletic associations.
29. Explain the functions of the National Federation of State High School Associations, and the local associations.
30. List several athletic administrative problems and name the organizations which could be called upon to solve them.
31. Identify the role of the state association and the National Federation in interscholastic athletics.
32. Identify the responsibilities of the local board of education in the conduct of interscholastic athletics.
33. Explain the role of the athletic council in interscholastic athletics.
34. Describe the purposes of the National Federation of State High School Associations.
35. Enumerate the advantages of belonging to a state high school athletic association and the National Federation of State High School Associations.
36. Describe the services provided to coaches by professional organizations.
37. Explain the advantages of the athletic conference.
38. Identify several professional coaches' organizations and explain their purposes.

ACTIVITIES

1. Write a 500-word article on the life of H. V. Porter.
2. Write a letter to the superintendent of schools in the school district where you graduated from high school and ask him to provide you with:
   a. a copy of the organization chart showing the organization of the athletic program,
   b. discuss the organizational charts in class and determine their strengths and weaknesses.
3. Visit a local secondary school and examine the athletic program in regard to the following:
   a. duties of the athletic council,
   b. duties of the athletic director,
   c. duties of the principal,
   d. area of athletic control.
4. Talk with an athletic director from a small, medium, and large high school and ask his opinion as to the types of athletic control in their school system.
5. Obtain the conference handbook from several conferences and make comparisons on the type of controls exercised by them.
6. Talk with a high school athletic director about the advantages of belonging to an athletic conference as opposed to not belonging.
7. Obtain a National Federation handbook and discuss its contents in class.
8. Formulate a set of rules for an athletic council in a large high school.
9. Talk with a student member of a high school athletic council relative to his position on the council.

10. Talk with a superintendent of schools relative to his philosophy of athletics and its place in the school curriculum.
11. Outline a plan for the organization control of an athletic program in a large high school.
12. Study the organizational structure of the athletic department of the schools in your hometown. Describe the role of the athletic director and the coaches in relation to the administration.
13. Write to the state superintendent of schools and find out if there is a state athletic director and just what his duties are.
14. Visit a neighboring school system and by observation and interview determine the organizational structure of the athletic department in relation to the physical education department.
15. Observe an athletic director in a staff meeting or a meeting of the advisory council. From what he does, interpret his view of the role of authority, and the role of the director.
16. Diagram the organizational setup of the small, medium, and large high school athletic department.
17. Write a letter to the principal or superintendent of schools and ask him for an organizational chart of the athletic department. Discuss these charts in class.
18. Debate the issue: What is the role of the athletic council in the conduct of interscholastic athletics?
19. Debate the advantages and disadvantages of membership in an athletic conference.

SUGGESTED READINGS

1. Albo, Eugene: Athletic associations call the tune for school boards, but the music isn't all sour. *American School Board Journal*, February, 1972.
2. Avidesion, Charles and McCook, Joseph: Develop a functional athletic council. *Scholastic Coach*, September, 1956.
3. Bucher, Charles: *Administration of Health and Physical Education Programs Including Athletics*. St. Louis, Mosby, 1971.
4. Bucher, Charles: Needed: A new athletic program. *Physical Educator*, October, 1966.
5. Daughtrey, Greyson and Woods, John: *Physical Education Programs*. Philadelphia, Saunders, 1971.
6. Esslinger, Arthur: Certification for high school coaches. *Journal of Health, Physical Education, and Recreation*, October, 1968.
7. *First Yearbook of Wisconsin Interscholastic Association*. 1924.
8. Forsythe, Charles and Keller, Irvin: *Administration of High School Athletics*. Englewood Cliffs, P-H, 1972.
9. Forsythe, Charles: *The Athletic Directors Handbook*. Englewood Cliffs, P-H, 1956.
10. George, Jack, and Lehman, Harry: *School Athletic Administration*. New York, Har-Row, 1966.
11. Hackensmith, C. W.: *History of Physical Education*. New York, Har-Row, 1966.
12. *Illinois High School Association Handbook*, Chicago, 1971-72.
13. *National Federation of State High School Associations Official Handbook*. 1972-73.
14. Resick, Matthew, Siedel, Beverly and Mason, James: *Modern Administrative Practices in Physical Education and Athletics*. Reading, A-W, 1970.
15. Rice, Emmett, Hutchison, John and Lee, Mabel: *A Brief History of Physical Education*. New York, Ronald, 1958.
16. Voltmer, Edward and Esslinger, Arthur: *The Organization of Physical Education*. New York, Appleton, 1967.

CHAPTER 6
Administrative Policies in Athletics

WEBSTER[1] DEFINES A policy as, "any governing principle, plan or course of action." Applied to a department of athletics in the high school this could mean that a policy is similar in effect to a principle which is described as a "guiding rule for action." Administration is described by Webster as, "managing, conducting or directing." Using the terms together this could be interpreted to mean that administration in any form is governed by decisions. Most decisions in administration are in turn based on policies which have, to some degree, been formulated beforehand.

One of the weaknesses of democratic administration is the fact that there is a lack of consistency in making decisions on problems that are relatively the same. There must be policies formulated that can be applied to the solution of problems which are similar in nature although the problem may exist at different times under different circumstances. The policies, on the other hand, should not be so rigid and stereotyped that they lose their effectiveness because they cannot possibly apply to all situations. Therefore, it is necessary to formulate policies which can be altered, at least, so that they can be applied to the administration of most organizations.

What then are the reasons for formulating policies?

REASONS FOR FORMULATING POLICIES

1. To avoid duplication of goals and outcomes by establishing policies which reflect the philosophy of the department.
2. To provide uniformity of purpose and utilization of staff effort for a common cause.
3. To bring about a philosophy upon which to build a strong administrative organization.
4. To enable the department personnel to arrive at decisions or solutions to problems by using a set of rules formulated specifically for a particular situation.
5. To allow problem solving on a local basis by formulating policies which apply to local situations.
6. To avoid any personal bias if any one person is affected differently so that he may feel discriminated against, or affected adversely.
7. To guide the less experienced personnel in any decision making they need to make in the execution of their duties.
8. To make sure that departmental policies are in accord with those established for all other departments.

Forsythe[2] has justified the establishment

---

[1]*Webster's New World Dictionary* (New York, The World Publishing Company, 1968), p. 1131.

[2]Forsythe, Charles, and Keller, Irvin, *Administration of High School Athletics*, 5th ed. (Englewood Cliffs, New Jersey, by permission of Prentice-Hall, 1972), p. 142.

of policy making by stating that:

> If an established and well-defined athletic policy is in existence in a school it can be pointed to constantly as the objective of the school program. It should include both the interschool and intramural programs, as well as the attitude of the administration toward such common controversial problems as girls and junior high school interscholastic athletics, awards, schedules and finances. General policies known ahead of time may alleviate many difficult situations.

FORMULATION OF POLICIES

Democratic administration and policy making demands representation and input from those individuals who are affected by it and governed by its application. This means then that meetings with discussions by these individuals are necessary. Representatives from various organizations may present their viewpoint regarding the problems which exist in particular situations. Other individuals in similar situations may present their viewpoint. Suggestions as to a policy which could be applied to each situation is suggested. As a result, a compromise may result but a policy will be formed which can be applied to both situations based upon definite rules of conduct. These rules of conduct are based on the beliefs of the people they represent. These beliefs should be the underlying bases for the formulation of all policies which govern the athletic department. These policies will provide direction for the operation of the athletic program.

Scott[3] has the following comment regarding the formulation of policies:

> The need for policies in athletics will be suggested from many sources. One such source will be the institution itself. The policies and procedures which the insti-

tution has established for the conduct of its affairs will, of course, dictate the policies which may be developed for the Conduct of Athletics. The philosophy and purpose of the institution as a whole will be reflected in its policies with reference to such matters as curriculum, scholastic requirements, degree of emphasis on student activities, the balance between athletics and other activities on the campus, facilities and equipment available for athletics, the salary range of professional personnel, and the number and quality of faculty members.

Guidelines for the Formulation of Policies

Because the policies will determine the direction and outcomes of the department, great care should be taken to formulate them. Because it will be cooperative effort of many individuals, certain guidelines should be established. Some of these are as follows:

1. The establishment of policies should be the task of many individuals in order to take advantage of as much input as possible from as many people as possible who are concerned with the program.

2. Policies should be flexible. It should be remembered that all situations are not the same; therefore, policies which are broad in scope should be given preference.

3. Policies should be placed in the possession of every staff member. Each new staff member should receive a complete explanation by the director of each policy.

4. Policies should be revised and changed whenever it is needed to meet any arising problems. They should not remain static.

5. Every staff member should be given the opportunity to contribute according to his or her individual talents.

6. Problems should be anticipated and pro-

---

[3]Scott, Harry, *Competitive Sports in Schools and Colleges* (New York, Harper and Brothers, 1951), p. 230.

visions for adjustments in programs and personnel should be ready for immediate implementation.

7. Policies are not the answer to every problem. Too few are perhaps better than too many. Too many can complicate and restrict administration of the program. Too few will not provide the proper guidelines for efficient administration. The goal is to have the correct number and the right ones.

Determination of Policies

No two schools will have the same problems and no two situations are identical. Problems will vary as a result of many conflicting interests, beliefs, and financial involvements. However, there are some common problems that all schools share in athletics for which general policies can be established with the stipulation that they can be altered to fit the local situation. Consequently, policies may not always be the same, although they can be general in nature.

Forsythe[4] lists these common problems as follows:

1. The relationship and division of available facilities and personnel between intramural and interscholastic athletics.
2. The number of sports activities in which the school can offer (a) proper teaching and coaching; (b) adequate equipment; (c) satisfactory playing facilities.
3. Educationally justifiable athletic schedules; length of them and frequency of games.
4. Methods of financing the athletic program.
5. Determining whether girls' interscholastic athletics should be part of the program.
6. The place of junior high school athletics in the general athletic program.

7. The student and faculty relation in the organization for the control of athletics.
8. Understanding of the relation of the local school to its league and state athletic association.
9. The policy of the school in the care of, and payment for athletic injuries.
10. Delegation of authority to coaches or faculty managers in matters pertaining to contracts, eligibility, equipment, schedules, officials, and the like.

POLICY-MAKING ORGANIZATIONS OR GROUPS IN INTERSCHOLASTIC ATHLETICS

There are four organizations designed to set up policies which govern the administration of interschool athletics. These organizations are (1) the National Federation of State High School Associations, (2) the state associations, (3) the conferences, and (4) the local authorities. The policies of all these organizations differ yet all are concerned with having better interscholastic athletic programs.

The National Federation and Its Philosophy and Basic Beliefs

The National Federation is made up of state associations. These associations united to secure the benefits derived from cooperative thinking and the cooperative effort of all individuals interested in high school athletics. These benefits are the result of the pooling of ideas and the cooperative action which in turn, eliminates duplication of work. Member state associations' programs must be administered in accordance with the following basic beliefs:

Interscholastic athletics shall be an integral part of the total secondary school educational program that has as its purpose to provide educational experiences not otherwise provided in the curriculum, which will develop learning outcomes in the areas of knowledge, skills and emotional patterns and will

---

[4]Forsythe, Charles, and Keller, Irvin, *Administration of High School Athletics*, p. 143.

contribute to the development of better citizens. Emphasis shall be upon teaching 'through' athletics in addition to teaching the 'skills' of athletics.

Interschool athletics shall be primarily for the benefit of the high school students who participate directly and vicariously in them. The interscholastic athletic program shall exist mainly for the value which it has for students and not for the benefit of the sponsoring institutions. The activities and contests involved shall be psychologically sound by being tailored to the physical, mental, and emotional maturity levels of the youth participating in them.

Any district and/or state athletic meet competition to determine a so-called champion shall provide opportunities for schools to demonstrate and to evaluate the best taught in their programs with the best taught in other schools and in other areas of the state.

Participation in interscholastic activities is a privilege to be granted to those students who meet the minimum standards of eligibility adopted cooperatively by the schools through their state associations and those additional standards established by each school for its own students.

The state high school association and the National Federation shall be concerned with the development of those standards, policies, and regulations essential to assist their member schools in the implementation of their philosophy of interscholastic athletics. Interschool activities shall be kept in proper perspective and must supplement the academic program of the schools.

Nonschool activities sponsored primarily for the benefit of the participants in accordance with a philosophy compatible with the school philosophy of interscholastics may have value for youth. When they do not interfere with the academic and interscholastic programs and do not result in exploitation of youth, they shall be considered as a worthwhile supplement to interschool activities.[5]

It is necessary to develop a full understanding of the need for observance of local, league, sectional, state, and national standards in athletics.

The State Association and Guiding Policies

The state associations came into being before the National Association. The National Association being an outgrowth of state associations attempted to unify procedures and regulations for interscholastic activities. Each state association has a handbook which explains thoroughly the policies and rules under which they operate. While not all state association policies are the same, there are many that pertain to the same areas of interest. The schools are not obligated or forced to join the state associations. However, most of them become members because they realize the benefits derived from belonging to such an organization.

The purpose of the state association is to establish sensible and educationally sound controls over the athletic program. To do this each association establishes guiding policies which are used as guidelines. An example would be those of the Illinois High School Association[6] which are listed as follows:

1. The Board of Directors shall (a) encourage economy in the school time of the pupil and teacher personnel for interscholastic activity purposes, (b) encourage economy in expenses of interscholastic activities, (c) discourage long trips for large groups of students, (d) encourage the proper evaluation of time devoted to activity supervision by teachers in terms of the total daily teaching load and (e) encourage the proper evaluation of pupil participation in activities in terms of the total scholastic pupil load.

---

[5]National Federation of State High School Associations, *Official Handbook* (Elgin, 1972-73).

[6]Illinois High School Association, *Official Handbook* (Chicago, Illinois, 1973-74), p. 11.

2. In order to carry out the provisions of the Constitution, the Board of Directors requires that sanctions must be secured from the IHSA Office for all meets, tournaments, festivals or other assemblies of student representatives from four or more member high schools.
3. It shall be the policy of the Board not to sanction any activity conducted or sponsored by any national or interstate organization or by any organization or group wholly or in part outside of the state of Illinois except that it may at its discretion sanction:
   a Such activities as are directly conducted or sponsored by some department of the United States Government.
   b Such intra- or interstate activities as involve the participants in a negligible amount of travel and which do not require any cash deposit or fee from the school or the individual participant, either as direct or indirect membership or entry fees, or in payment for any incidental service or privilege.
   c Purely community or local activities involving areas that would not require extensive travel and expense or undue absence from school on the part of the participants even though the community may involve portions of more than one state.
4. It is the clear obligation of principals, coaches, faculty representatives, boards of education and all official representatives of member schools in all interscholastic relationships to practice the highest principles of sportsmanship and ethics of competition. The Board of Directors shall exercise its authority to penalize any member school whose representatives may violate this obligation.

The Conference and Guiding Policies

The conference is established to build sound relationships and to promote better understanding and goodwill between schools in athletics. The value in membership in the conference is the aid it renders to the arranging of schedules, declaring of league championships, maintenance and preservation of records, and the approval of officials. It provides opportunity for local competition without excessive team travel and aids in interschool relationships through exchange assemblies, etc. Membership in the conference implies abiding by all established rules and regulations.

As far back as 1936 Williams[7] made the following observation:

> Conferences have been important factors making for steady improvement of conditions in the administration of school athletics in that they have tended toward establishing uniformity of procedure, aim and point of view in the correlation of athletics to the primary purpose of the school. Equality if competitive opportunity is essential. These conferences have been formed in order that athletic departments may work together in checking vicious practices and in directing athletics in such a way that school boards will regard them as educational resources to be encouraged.

Conferences of schools are formed in athletics as well as in other school activities for the purpose of promoting equalized competition of the sort that will result in benefits for all the students. The benefits derived from an athletic conference are many and are in direct proportion to the policies which are formulated to govern and administer the activities which are to be engaged in between the conference schools.

Each conference will have different policies dependent upon the attitudes and desires of those people who are designated to formulate, establish, and administer them. These attitudes and desires are in turn dependent upon local conditions

[7]Williams, Jesse and Hughes, William, *Athletics in Education* (Philadelphia, W. B. Saunders Co., 1936), p. 148.

existing in the immediate area in which the conference is formed and in which it will function. These conditions among others will include the financial structure of the community, facilities, philosophy of the people, and administration in respect to the place of athletics in the school curriculum and the locality.

I. Suggested Policies for Conference Meetings

A. The conference athletic directors should meet each month to transact athletic business of the conference.

B. The chairmanship of the athletic directors should rotate annually in the same order as the chairmanship of the conference superintendents.

C. The secretary of the athletic directors should be from the same school as next year's chairman of the conference superintendents.

D. Meetings of the head coaches to determine the all-conference teams should be held as follows:
   1. Football—Monday following the last conference game.
   2. Basketball—Monday following the last conference game.
   3. Baseball—Monday following the last conference game.

E. An annual coaches golf meet may be held the last Friday in May at 4:00 P.M.

F. All-Conference Dinner
   1. An all-conference dinner should be held annually in the first week of October. The place to be determined in the all-conference calendar should be approved the last meeting of the conference superintendents held in May of each year.
   2. The philosophy of the all-conference dinner should support the ideal of bringing together different groups who would then have future meetings within the conference and set up competitions or festivals during the school year. This can be implemented by using the long list of eligible persons.

II. Suggested Conference Policies for Administrators

A. They should see that the athletic program is closely articulated with and operated on the same basis as other departments of the school.

B. They should see that there is sufficient faculty or police supervision at all games to properly handle the crowds.

C. They should see that rules governing coaching practices as stated in these by-laws and as provided in the rules and regulations of the high school association are obeyed.

III. Suggested Conference Policies for Athletic Directors

A. The athletic directors of the conference should meet when there is a need to transact the athletic business of the conference.

B. The chairmanship of this group should be rotated among the directors annually according to an established pattern. An athletic director should not be a chairman in his first year.

C. A secretary should be elected by

the athletic directors.

D. The chairman should preside at all meetings of this group. The secretary should compile the minutes of the meetings, have them duplicated, and should send to each school sufficient copies for athletic directors and the members of the board of control of the conference.

E. The conference assignment chairman or statistician should receive the results of all conference contests and compile the official standings for conference records. The results of conference contests should be forwarded promptly to the assignment chairman or statistician in the form required by him. The athletic director of each school should send all conference contest results from his school to the conference assignment chairman or statistician every Monday.

F. The athletic directors should receive all proposals from the various coaches' groups for consideration.

G. The recommendations of the athletic directors pertaining only to their conference should be submitted to the board of control of their conference for action.

H. Recommendation of the athletic directors pertaining to conference regulations should be submitted to athletic directors for action.

I. Only the athletic directors or their delegated representatives and the chief administrators of the member schools may attend their conference athletic directors' meetings, except upon official invitation by the majority of the athletic directors of the member schools.

IV. Suggested Conference Policies for Coaches

A. A coach should study the by-laws of the association.

B. The coach should be responsible for good sportsmanship in the school and the community. He should, therefore, be a good example to the players of his teams. At no time in their hearing should he use profane language.

C. The coach should not visibly or audibly protest the decisions of officials during the game or in any place where a crowd might see or hear him.

D. The coach should avoid a display of temper.

E. The coach should not smoke at any time on the field or playing area or before players.

F. The coach should not go on the field or playing area during a game except with the permission of an official.

G. The coach should not allow any player who is known to be physically unfit to participate in any practice or contest.

H. The coach should assume responsibility for controlling any improper language or conduct of his players on the field and in the locker rooms.

I. The coach should be responsible for the care of the locker room on all trips.

J. The visiting coach should assume responsibility for players' conduct before, during, and after the contest.

K. Each coach should instruct players in the proper method of paying respect when the colors are presented at the opening of a contest.

L. Head coaches or their representatives should meet regularly according to the accepted schedule, unless a majority of coaches request that no meeting be held. Expenses should be allowed only for the meetings having conference approval.

M. Schedule of meetings of conference head coaches.

1. Baseball—The Monday before or after the last regularly scheduled conference game.
2. Basketball—The Monday preceding the last regularly scheduled conference game.
3. Cross Country—The Monday preceding the conference meet or the Monday after the State Cross Country meet.
4. Football—The Monday following the last conference game.
5. Golf—During the week preceding the conference meet.
6. Gymnastics—The Monday after the state gymnastics meet.
7. Soccer—The Monday following the last conference contest.
8. Swimming—Between October 15 and the starting date for swimming practice, but not before the new rule books are available.
9. Tennis—During the week of the conference meet.
10. Track—During the week of the conference meet.
11. Wrestling—The Monday following the state wrestling meet.
12. Meetings other than those listed above may be called at the request of the conference athletic directors.

N. The chairmanships of the coaches' groups should rotate annually among the head coaches of the conference schools, according to the established rotation.

O. The chairman should preside at all meetings and should send all recommendations to each athletic director of his own conference.

P. Order of business for conference meetings

1. Roll call
2. Minutes of the previous meeting
3. Reports of standing committees
4. Reports of special committees
5. Special reports
6. Unfinished business
7. New business
8. Adjournment

V. Suggested Conference Policies for Both Coaches and Athletic Directors

A. They should do everything possible to educate the crowd to understand the rules, penalties, and strategies of the game, thus encouraging sports appreciation among the spectators.

B. They should avoid pregame statements to the press which might be misleading to opponents or the public.

C. They should encourage competition in events which are sponsored and approved by proper school authorities.

D. They should resist at all times the encroachment of highly commercialized and professional entrepreneurs into the high school athletic program.

E. They should assign a school representative to meet officials before a game, to arrange for their privacy before and after the game, and during halftime, and to provide for the caring for their needs.

F. Athletic directors should be responsible for the organization and administration of all contests.

VI. Suggested Conference Policies for Awarding Trophies

A. All trophies should be purchased by the president-secretary of the conference and have the following characteristics:
1. Two standard trophies should be used for all sports, changing only the figure to represent the sports involved.
2. The trophy should be approximately seventeen inches in height, costing a certain amount for the varsity, and a similar trophy thirteen inches in height, costing a certain amount for frosh-soph teams.
3. Total cost of trophies in any

one year should be determined at the beginning of that year.

B. Medals should be awarded for the first three places in conference track and ribbons for fourth and fifth places. Frosh-soph cross-country carries no award trophies, medals, or ribbons.

VII. Suggested Conference Policies for Student Admission to Games

A. Players on frosh-soph teams should pay regular student admission charges to games which they attend away from home, unless they are dressed as a team member and are eligible to participate in the game.

B. All conference events should have a set student fare and a set admission for adults. These prices should apply to all conference activities for which a charge is made.
The board of control of each conference should provide funds for the purchase of suitable awards for the individual winners in all contests conducted by the conference, and for championship teams. Medals, ribbons, etc. should be purchased by a representative of the conference with money provided by the board of control of that conference from the general fund. These awards should be purchased for all sports in which the conference meets are held and should be ready for distribution at the time of each conference event.

VIII. Suggested Conference Sportsmanship Code Policies

A. WHEREAS, the high school association has, as a basic objective, the aim to stress the cultural values, the appreciation, and the skills involved in all interscholastic activities, and to promote cooperation and friendship, and

B. WHEREAS, it is the clear obligation of principals, coaches, faculty representatives, and all official representatives of state high schools in all interscholastic relationships to practice the highest principles of sportsmanship and ethics of competition, and

C. WHEREAS, the high school association does not permit mechanical noise makers at the state basketball tournament.

D. THEREFORE, be it resolved that the home schools of the conference shall adopt the following policy:

1. If the host school band performs at a conference football or basketball game, the school song of both the host school and the visiting school should be played prior to the beginning of the national anthem.

2. All banners and signs should carry no derogatory remarks against the opposing school.

3. All host schools should encourage their fans to extend to both participant teams common foul-line courtesy.

4. The use of mechanical noise makers, such as horns, sirens, cow bells, or band instruments should not be allowed.

5. Visiting schools should not bring banners to be displayed or posted at the host school.

6. In all football contests, if the goal posts are to be decorated, one goal post should be decorated with the colors of the host school and the other goal post should be decorated with the colors of the visiting school.

7. Students and fans of all home schools of the conference should be encouraged to participate only in those acts which will tend to promote cooperation and friendship among the students and schools in the conference.

IX. Suggested Policies for Conference News Officials

A. There should be a certain person appointed or designated as the official person to distribute the information about the happenings of the conference to the news media.

X. Suggested Conference Policies for the Appointment of Officials

A. A conference assignment official with the cooperation of the athletic directors should engage officials for the conference activities in the following sports:

1. Varsity and frosh-soph football

2. Varsity and frosh-soph basketball

3. Varsity and frosh-shop baseball

4. Varsity and frosh-soph wrestling

5. Varsity and frosh-soph swimming

6. It should be the responsibility of each local school to secure new officials following cancellations.

7. A specified fee plus expenses should be established.

XI. *Suggested Conference Eligibility Policies*

A. Conference eligibility rules should apply to contests between member schools.

B. Eligibility should be certified under state high school association rules.

C. No player should be given permission to play or practice with outside teams if he or she is at the same time a member of a high school team.

D. Changing teams

1. For the purposes of interpretation three levels of competition may be recognized and used here as examples.
   a. Varsity and junior varsity
   b. Sophomore
   c. Freshman

2. A player should be allowed to make only one change in the level for conference competition during any one season, except in wrestling where two moves may be permitted. Any movement downward should occur prior to the last two conference dual contests.
   a. For the purposes of interpreting this rule, a player is not a member of the squad until he plays in conference competition with that squad.

b. No player should be allowed to take part in a junior varsity contest following participation in any of the first three quarters of a varsity contest until the next varsity contest has been held in that sport or until five days have elapsed, whichever may occur first.

c. Whenever a level of competition between the two schools competing does not exist, a player may make a move downward or upward without constituting a move.

E. Suggested participation policies for sports teams are as follows:

1. No player should be allowed to be a member of teams in two different sports or on two different levels of competition in the same sport at the same time.

2. No player should be allowed to play on any two different levels in the same sport within any twenty-hour period.

3. No player should be eligible for freshman competition after he or she is sixteen or has attended two semesters; no player should be eligible for sophomore competition after he is seventeen, or has attended four semesters, except that when a freshman reaches his or her sixteenth birthday or when a sophomore reaches his or her seventeenth birthday after the date set for the start of practice in the fall, winter, or spring

sport, he or she may complete the season of the sport in which he or she is participating. The permissive date set by the conference for the start of practice should be the date accepted for the start of the season.

4. No award winners from the previous season should be allowed to take part in intramurals in that sport prior to the start of the next season.

XII. Suggested Conference Scheduling Policies

A. Each conference should regulate the scheduling in any sport in which the majority of the member schools of that conference compete.

B. All schedules should be drawn by the athletic directors of the member schools of each conference subject to approval by the board of control of that conference.

C. In conference competition, the preliminary contest should be paired as the home team does in its regular conference schedule.

D. The official schedules of each school should be construed as contracts and carry the same binding obligations as the state high school contracts.

E. Schools should change the date of a contest only by mutual consent and upon approval by the majority vote of the athletic directors of the conference involved when unusual circumstances indicate it advisable. All schools of the conference should be notified of such changes.

F. A contest should be postponed by mutual agreement because of severe weather conditions or other emergencies. Postponed contests should be rescheduled according to regulations established for a specific sport or, if none, established at the earliest date possible and practicable.

XIII. Suggested Conference Limitation of Seasons and Practicing Policies

A. No player should be allowed to participate in more than one practice session per day on school days.

B. Whenever a school's athletic facilities are opened to the general student body for free recreational use outside of that sport season and if a coach of that sport is supervising the activity, then award winners in that sport should be barred; but if anyone not coaching that sport is supervising, then anyone should be allowed to participate.

The Local School and Guiding Policies

Local conditions, beliefs, and philosophy will determine policies within each local school and as a result those under which the athletic program is to function. It is important, therefore, to understand the organizational structure of a school system under which a school is administered and operates so that one may see how the goals set forth by the administration can be accomplished in all departments and how the athletic program must operate within this organizational framework and under the direction of an administrator.

Organization is a process of systematically establishing proper relationships within an administrative structure. This is necessary in every school system if it is to function effectively and efficiently. Schools are divided administratively into three major functions (1) instruction, (2) educational services, and (3) business management. We are interested in administration as it pertains to instruction and its effects on the athletic program.

The organizational chart shown is a typical example of the administrative structure of a school system which encompasses three high schools. On studying this chart it should be remembered that, as has been mentioned previously, all athletic policies made by local administration must coincide with and be subservient to both national and state regulations.

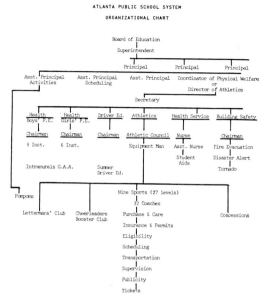

Figure 8.

I. The Board of Education's Responsibility for Local Policy Making in Athletics

The board of education members are the elected representatives of the people and are responsible to them. They are elected for their stand on and belief in certain issues. Their philosophy regarding athletics should be made known to the general public as it will definitely effect the policies which they will make for the operation of the athletic program.

The board of education has control over and is responsible for the interscholastic program. They should administer the program in the same manner as any other program within the school. By so doing they are in essence demonstrating that athletics is a part of the educational curriculum and should be treated and administered as such.

The board of education is direct-

ly responsible to the people. It is the educational agency for the educational system. Because of this, its duties in athletic matters should be considered to be the same as for general education.

A. Legal responsibilities

The board should assume all of the legal responsibility for conducting the school.

B. Representation

The board should represent the will of the people and act in accordance with the interest of the people in mind.

C. Education opportunity

The board should promote the use of educational development and cultural growth of all the people in the community.

D. Management

The board should require the school to operate in an economical manner and to see that financial affairs are conducted and meet the highest standards of integrity and business practice.

E. Levels of function

The board should provide the superintendent, principal, etc. with a framework of operation for administering the schools.

F. Communication

The board should keep the people well-informed at all times on all facts concerning the schools.

G. Education

The board should defend and support education at all times.

II. The Superintendent's Responsibility for Local Policy Making in Athletics

The superintendent is a representative of the board and as such he is responsible for the athletic program and to some extent the policies which govern it. It is his responsibility to keep the board of education members informed about the program and to carry out their wishes regarding it. He should be completely aware of the conduct of the athletic program as to its philosophy, its purpose, its aims, and its outcomes. He should attempt in every way possible to implement a program of interschool athletics that is in complete harmony with other extracurricular programs within the school system. It is his responsibility to provide leadership and wisdom to those whose task it is to establish policies which will be used by all programs throughout the school system as well as those which govern the athletic program.

As a legal representative of the board of education, the superintendent's duty is to set the level of importance given to athletics. It is his responsibility to keep the athletic program on a sound educational basis. He should present athletic policies to the board of education for their approval. He should assume the responsibility of informing the public as to the athletic policies under which the program is operating.

The superintendent's duties will vary according to the size of the school system, ranging from the larger schools, where all duties are delegated, to the smaller schools, where he may be both the administrative and executive officer. In either case it is his duty to have set up a definite school policy and have a complete understanding of that policy by all concerned.

It should be the responsibility of the superintendent to develop ways and means of executing efficiently the policies adopted by the board of education. He should recommend to the board appointments of coaches and other persons who are given responsibility for handling athletics.

He should consider for approval all policies and procedures recommended by the staff through the athletic director and principal.

III. The Principal's Responsibilities for Local Policy Making in Athletics

The principal is the watchdog of interschool athletics. He is directly responsible for the program. He is in direct contact with the athletic director and the coaches. He signs the eligibility sheets, approves the budget and generally makes all decisions affecting the program that cannot be decided by the athletic director or the coach. The principal is the go-between with coaches and faculty, with parents and coaches, with superintendent and athletic director, and sometimes between athletic director and coaches. The principal often times handles many of the details associated with the program. He also keeps the superintendent informed about the program and strives to keep harmony between students, faculty, athletes, and coaches, whenever and wherever it is needed. The principal quite naturally assumes the largest share of responsibility in conducting the athletic program.

The principal usually is the official representative of the school and is directly responsible for the general attitude of the student body and the conduct of the athletic affairs by the business manager, athletic director, and the coach.

He is the administrative head of interscholastic athletics just as he is of all other activities in the school. As principal he should help implement athletic policies as stipulated by the board of education and the superintendent. The principal is recognized by the state association as head of the school in all matters pertaining to interscholastic athletics, and as such is responsible to them for the conduct of the school's athletic activities. The principal is in charge of the enforcement of the regulations and policies of the state associations. It is his responsibility to act as a go-between for coaches, parents, and community.

IV. The Athletic Director's Responsibility for Local Policy Making in Athletics

The athletic director is charged with the responsibility of providing the leadership necessary to carry out the program. His leadership will be instrumental in developing and maintaining the type of program that is in keeping with the philosophy, aims, and objectives of the total school curriculum. It is his responsibility to work closely with the principal and to follow the guidelines established by the administration and board relative to the type of athletic program desired by the people in the community. He should enlist the help of all the coaches, the principal, and superintendent to establish the policies upon which to operate the athletic program. After the formulation of the policies, the director must see that they are carried out. He is responsible to the superintendent, the principal, and the business officer for the school district.

The athletic director, because of his or her training and qualifications, has become increasingly important in directing the athletic program. He or she is expected to recommend policies to the principal who in turn submits them to the superintendent. He or she is directly responsible to the principal.

The athletic director assumes complete responsibility of directing the athletic program. His duties encompass many areas for which he is held accountable. He is in an excellent position to meet the public and because of this he should act as a buffer between the coach and the public. His enthusiasm should be contagious as he should be a super salesman for the program.

V. *The Faculty Manager's Responsibility for Local Policy Making in Athletics*

The size of the school determines to a large extent the type or kind of athletic administration which is used. The small school will usually combine the duties of the athletic director and physical education director. The large school will separate the duties. Often the athletic director is an academic teacher. However, there are some schools that prefer to have a person who is removed from the duties of athletic director or coach to assume the duties of managing the athletic program. This person is called the athletic manager and while he is not directly involved in policy making he is in a position, because of his duties as faculty manager, to initiate a great deal into any decision making which might take place within the athletic department. It is, therefore, his role to be cognizant of this fact and attempt in every way to enter into discussion which will result in decision making and departmental policy making.

VI. *The Athletic Coach's Responsibility for Local Policy Making in Athletics*

The athletic coach is affected more than anyone else by policy. He should, therefore, be vitally concerned because his success as a coach depends upon the existence of poli-

cies which coincide with his philosophy of coaching. The coach will also be directly affected, because his actions and decisions, which are often governed by policy, are made known to the general public and administration far more readily than other teachers or personnel in the school system.

The coach should then take an active part in policy making and should insist that his voice be heard in any policy making in the athletic program.

Wilson[8] has commented on the importance of policy because of the complexity of modern-day coaching and large coaching staffs. This in itself necessitates the formation of policies which can be used as guidelines to avoid discord among coaching staffs, unless policies are established and are made known to each coach, problems and misunderstandings will come up. In order to avoid this type of situation, Wilson has suggested that definite and concrete policies be formulated and followed by the staff in regard to the following categories:

1. Coaching relationships
2. Relationships with Parents
3. Relationships with Administrators
4. Relationships with the Squad
5. Relationships with College Staffs
6. Relationships with the Community
7. Relationships with the Faculty.

High school athletic coaching can be very satisfying if the coach enters into it with the proper prospective. Basically, the coach enters this profession because he loves to coach, to

---

[8]Wilson, Emerson, "Policy Avoids Problems in Prep Coaching Staffs," *Coach and Athlete* (June, 1965), p. 14.

work with young people, and believes in athletics. Obtaining fame and fortune, for the most part, is negligible.

School athletics should be amateur competition. Athletes and coaches alike must get both joy and pleasant satisfaction from the program rather than any materialistic reward.

The interscholastic athletic program that exists today is of greater value than ever before though it needs more selling than ever. The best salesman is the athlete who is already happily and energetically involved in the program and who sees some purpose in what he is doing. The coach must always remember that he is dealing with young people during a period in life in which they are most unstable and unpredictable but also very pliable and impressionable. Patience is essential during this period of the person's life.

The effectiveness of an athletic coach will be measured primarily by his contribution to physical, social, and character education. The educational outcome of the athletic program depends to a great extent on the preparation, character, and ideals of the coaches in charge. The coach is in a strategic position to influence not only his teams but the entire student body as well.

The coach may not be striving to win a popularity contest but he must be respected and be a leader. His discipline must be firm, consistent, and tempered with fairness. His rules must be considerate and reasonable and must not be empty threats. Once made, they must be enforced.

Good standards of behavior are necessary for the successful coach. His own language, decorum, dress, and habits influence his athletes, and he should insist on high standards of conduct among them. It is not expected that coaches live exactly as they expect their athletes to, but a good example is valuable and important.

It is essential that the coach study and keep up to date with his sport. Skills, techniques, systems, theories, rules, virtually everything changes in athletics (some sports more rapidly and completely than others). It is the coach's duty to know the rules of the conference and the state association. The spirit of the rules is as important as the words. It is also important that the coach know, understand, and practice the ethics of his profession.

Interscholastic athletics should be closely coordinated with the general instructional program and properly articulated with other departments of the school. As a part of the curriculum, school athletics should be conducted only by school authorities so that definite educational aims may be achieved. Basically, athletics is an extention of the physical education program; therefore, it is necessary that the academic teacher-coach have a reasonable grasp and appreciation of the total physical education program. Otherwise, he will have difficulty orienting himself and his athletic squads.

Coaches must recognize that their primary jobs are their regular classes, study halls, etc. The teaching of these classes cannot justifiably be slighted, neglected, short-cut, or sacrificed in favor of athletic coaching assignments.

All coaches need an appreciation of the values involved in equipment and facilities. A keen sense of responsibility in the coach is necessary if the athletes are to have the same.

A real team spirit is of utmost importance in the coaching staff. Mutual help and cooperation are needed if the program is to be a success. No asset is of greater importance to the staff than loyalty. This loyalty to the other coaches, faculty, and community will solve many problems.

VII. The Coaching Staff's Responsibility for Local Policy Making

A. All members of the coaching staff should consider the teaching of character, self-discipline, respect, honesty, responsibility, and sacrifice just as important as winning.
B. They should strive to win at all times, but not at the cost of injury to an athlete or by breaking any rules.
C. Each athlete who participates should be inspired by the coach with a tremendous desire to win.
D. Each member of the staff whether he be the head coach or assistant should be dedicated to his job. The long hours and tense situations are considered a part of the job.
E. Every member of the coaching staff should be concerned with an over-all, successful athletic program, not with just the sport he is coaching.

Departmental Policies

Suggested Scheduling Policies

1. The director of athletics should personally approve all contracts for athletic contests in which a school participates.
2. Regulations established by the state and the conference should be observed before contracts are issued. Conference scheduling is usually automatic.
3. Nonconference contests should be scheduled for convenience and local interest. The director should continually strive to schedule contests which are educationally sound and will serve the best interests of the school and its students.

Suggested Supervision Policies

1. *All* coaches should be responsible for supervising *all* athletes when they are in the school activity areas.
2. *The coaches should be fully responsible* for each and every athlete on the squad whether it be in the locker room, play area, training room, or elsewhere *from the time he or she enters the building until he or she leaves.* The coach should arrange his practice and activities so that supervision can be carried out on every occasion.
3. The coach should make it clear to the players when and where they are to enter the building or activity area for practice or games. The coach should be sure that he is present to supervise *when they arrive.* The athletes should clearly understand that they are not to enter the building or areas until the coach is present. Coaches should make every effort to be at the school prior to the arrival of his opponents.
4. Following a practice or contest the coach should not leave the building until all players are out of the build-

TABLE III
SPRING ATHLETIC SCHEDULE
WEEK OF _____

BASEBALL

DAY	DATE	LEVEL	OPPONENT	TIME	PLACE	FACILITY TO BE USED & COMMENTS

TRACK

DAY	DATE	LEVEL	OPPONENT	TIME	PLACE	FACILITY TO BE USED & COMMENTS

TENNIS

DAY	DATE	LEVEL	OPPONENT	TIME	PLACE	FACILITY TO BE USED & COMMENTS

ing. These athletes should understand that they are not to reenter the building after the coach is gone.

5. When busses are used to transport squads a coach should ride the bus and be responsible for the riders' conduct. He or she should inspect the bus *before* and *after* the squad is on the bus and fix responsibility for any possible damage.

6. When a trip is made to another school the coach should inspect the locker room that is used by the team both *before* and *after* his squad uses it. He or she should report any irregularities.

7. On a trip to a contest or at a home contest the coach should inform all players of proper dress and decorum that should be adhered to.

8. After practice and games the coach should be sure that all equipment is

GLENBARD WEST HIGH SCHOOL

ATHLETIC EVENTS

SPORT _____ YEAR _____

DAY MO.	VARSITY	JR. VARSITY	SOPHOMORE	FRESHMAN
Mon.				
Tue.				
Wed.				
Thu.				
Fri.				
Sat.				
Mon.				
Tue.				
Wed.				
Thu.				
Fri.				
Sat.				
Mon.				
Tue.				
Wed.				
Thu.				
Fri.				
Sat.				
Mon.				
Tue.				
Wed.				
Thu.				
Fri.				
Sat.				
Mon.				
Tue.				
Wed.				
Thu.				
Fri.				
Sat.				
Mon.				
Tue.				
Wed.				
Thu.				
Fri.				
Sat.				

Figure 9.

accounted for and storage rooms are locked.

9. The athletic team locker room, training room, and conference room should be kept closed and considered off limits to all students during the school day with some exceptions as noted below:

A. No player should enter the locker room before school in the morning unless he or she has bulky equipment to be put away and then he or she may be admitted only *under the direct supervision of a coach.* The coach assuming this responsibility should stay with the player and relock the door upon leaving. No books, coats, or other personal items should be left in the locker room. The only things to be stored in the locker room should be athletic equipment.

B. During the day no students should enter this area unless they are under direct and continued supervision of a coach. No player should use the area during the school day without a *prearranged* request. When the purpose is completed the player should leave immediately. These visits may be necessary for such purposes as whirlpool treatments, weight checks for wrestling, etc. Exception to this may be for *bona fide* student (leaders) instructors that the players' physical education department head may assign there.

C. When a player is found violating these rules he or she should be reported to the coach for discipline. Any player who is discovered in the area and who is not on an athletic squad should be referred immediately to the dean's office.

Suggested Equipment Room Policies

1. The equipment manager should have final authority in the equipment room.

2. Head coaches should inform the equipment manager of their needs and any plans which concern him, *well in advance.* He or she cannot be present to serve the athletes at all times.

3. *All* equipment taken from the equip-

ment room should be checked out through the equipment manager. Only equipment authorized for a sport by the director of athletics should be checked out. If any authorized equipment is taken out by a coach when the equipment manager is not present, the coach should make written notice of it at all times.

4. Managers should be assigned by the coaches to help in the equipment room as needed. The room should not be a loafing place and managers should stay out except when working there.

5. If the equipment room is unlocked by a coach in the absence of the equipment manager *the coach should remain there and actively supervise until he* locks the door.

6. Where need is indicated the head coach of a sport should be issued a key to the equipment room. The key should remain in his or her possession except when the head coach of another squad may need it at night or on a day when the equipment manager is not in attendance. No manager or athlete should have possession of the key *at any time.*

7. Coaches should make arrangements well ahead of time for checking out equipment to squads.

8. Game uniforms should be checked out for each contest. They should also be checked in again the same way *as soon as possible* after the contest. If the uniforms need to be kept overnight after a contest, *the coach should be responsible for seeing that the equipment is properly cared for.*

9. Players who have lost equipment should be required to pay for it. Notices should be posted and dis-

ciplinary action taken if not paid within a reasonable length of time.

Suggested Athletic Equipment Policies

Each member of the athletic staff should be conscientiously concerned about the care of all athletic equipment. Regardless of whether he is coaching a particular sport or not if he sees any team members mistreating equipment he should bring it to the attention of the coach in charge as well as to the athletic director. Good athletic equipment is expensive but with proper care it will last a long time. Along this same line anytime a member of the staff sees a player outside of school wearing athletic equipment that player should be told that he is wearing stolen equipment and it should be returned at once.

Each coach should be responsible for the equipment the team is using. For example, all freshman football coaches should be responsible for the equipment issued to freshman football players, junior varsity coaches for junior varsity players, etc. At the end of the season the coaches of each respective team should see to it that the equipment is returned. He should stress at all times that it is the responsibility of all players to take care of all equipment that is issued to them. The players who are careless concerning their equipment should be reprimanded and in some cases penalized in order to impress upon them the importance of taking care of equipment which was purchased by the school for their use.

Student managers are a valuable aid to the coach in the care of athletic equipment and supplies. The coach should make certain that the student he selects as manager is loyal, trustworthy, hardworking, and a good student and *wants* to be a student manager. *Good managers* are a tremendous asset to any athletic program; therefore, proper selection of these players is important.

Suggested Equipment Purchasing Policies

All purchasing of athletic equipment should be made through the office of the director. No expenditures should be authorized by any individuals or coaches.

The director of athletics should obtain price quotations, where it is feasible, on all items of equipment to be purchased. Care should be taken that equipment that is to be purchased should be specified by catalog numbers so that the suppliers are quoting on comparable items.

The director of athletics should work with and follow suggestions and recommendations made by coaches relative to specifications of equipment.

Suggested Financial Statement Policy

A financial statement should be prepared by the director of athletics. At his discretion, he may elect to prepare such a statement at the conclusion of each season. He or she should enlist the help of the coaches whenever possible.

This statement should be distributed to the athletic council, board of education, superintendent of schools, the assistant superintendent of schools, and those members of the faculty who wish such a statement.

Suggested Budget Policies

The budget for interscholastic athletics should be prepared by March 15 of each school year. Each coach should prepare his requests for the annual budget and submit them to the director of athletics.

This budget should not include any items of expense assumed by the board of education, such as utilities, field and building maintenance, additional facilities, construction, etc.

Once the budget has been adopted the director of athletics should guide the program within the limits dictated by the budget.

Suggested Training Room Policies

1. *All* coaches should be responsible for seeing that the training room and its supplies and equipment are properly used.
2. All players should keep out of this area unless they need attention.
3. Athletes should use only designated supplies.
4. Reserve supplies should be kept in a locked cabinet. This cabinet is to be unlocked *only* by a coach. He should get his needs taken care of and see that the cabinet is immediately relocked.

Suggested Team Roster Policies

Team rosters should be given to the athletic director ten days before the first contest, complete with correct numbers.

Suggested Team Results Policies

Coaches should be responsible for seeing that the game results of their teams are turned in to the director by 8:30 A.M. the first day after a contest.

Suggested Athletic Team Transportation Policies

All athletic team members should travel by public carrier which is designated and contracted for by the school if at all possible.

Suggested Athletic Publicity Policies

Each coach should be responsible for the team's publicity. This should be done in close cooperation with the athletic director.

TABLE IV
RIDGE HIGH SCHOOL STUDENT ATHLETIC TRAINING CODE

This is an athletic code I shall practice while attending Ridge High School:

to plan to sleep eight to ten hours each evening

to dress wisely, neatly, and in conformity with the school code of dress

to be well groomed. All students, regardless of length of hair are encouraged to try out for any interscholastic athletic team at Ridge High School. Subsequently if in the judgment of the head coach long hair is deemed detrimental to an athlete's safety, welfare, or performance, the student shall be requested to either cut his hair or hold it back. Upon refusal by a student to this reasonable request by a coach, the student shall be dropped from the team.

At every opportunity the coach shall explain the implication of long hair as it relates to the sport involved and its effect upon a student's health, safety, welfare, and performance.

to spend school nights and pregame contests at home

to avoid the use of harmful drugs, tobacco and alcohol at all times

to eat well-balanced meals

to try to eat a regular meal at least two hours prior to the game and practice periods

to postpone postgame meal for an hour in order to permit proper digestion

to keep myself in good physical condition throughout the year

to drink water during hot weather and confine activity to prevent heat exhaustion

to keep the body clean by taking a shower following all practice and games

to give my best effort in order to develop the best, competitive physical and mental fitness

to know and observe the rules and regulations of the high school

to practice in word and deed that which is best in the American character — competition, loyalty, morality, self-reliance, self-sacrifice, and the responsibilities of self-discipline.

TABLE V
RIDGE HIGH SCHOOL
STUDENT ATHLETIC CODE OF ETHICS

As an athlete who represents Ridge High School, I pledge to conduct my personal life so that it demonstrates and supports loyalty and belief in the following code of ethics:

to assume the responsibilities, privileges, and obligations of being an athlete.

to practice health, training routines, and regulations by maintaining physical fitness, proper eating, and sleeping habits and the abstention of alcohol, tobacco, and drugs.

to agree that academic studies is the priority, not athletics.

to understand that success in athletics results only when there is dedication to hard work and desire on a year-round basis.

to promote team harmony and spirit by avoiding special interest groups and cliques.

to sacrifice personal glory for the cause of team unity and endeavor.

to seek those relationships with my peers which bring credit to me and my school.

to realize that all members of the team have a unique role and contribution to make.

to remember that a good athlete will strive to tap his own capacity to achieve, regardless of criticism and even in a losing cause.

to remain with the team from the first day and until the season is completed.

to be cognizant that an athlete should never place a limit on what can be done.

to give more to the team than you receive.

to be a leader by the worthwhile things you do, and say.

TABLE VI
GENOA COMMUNITY HIGH SCHOOL
SAMPLE ATHLETIC TRAINING CODE

Dear Parents:

We are writing this letter to explain the athletic training code for all players participating in athletics at _____ High School. We believe in the valuable results of mental and physical development for all players who participate in athletics. To achieve this goal, we must emphasize *TRAINING*. We believe that it is not a good policy to have players in athletics who will not train.

All athletes participating on school teams will be required to abide by the training rules and regulations listed below. Violations of the training code will be administered as outlined:

1. SMOKING, DRINKING OF ALCOHOLIC BEVERAGES

   PENALTY—1ST OFFENSE: Minimum penalty is suspension for one calendar athletic contest week or two athletic contests. The penalty will be served immediately following the violation. If the violation is not during the sport season, the penalty will be served the first contest week of the player's sport season.

   A letter will be mailed to the parents informing them of the violation and the penalty. A conference with the head coach and athletic director will be arranged if requested by the parents.

   PENALTY—2ND OFFENSE: Minimum penalty is suspension from the Genoa High School athletic program for one calendar year.

2. There shall be NO STEALING, which includes items taken from other schools. There shall be no wearing of athletic equipment from other schools.

   PENALTY—1ST OFFENSE: Suspension for one athletic contest. (If this should happen during the off-season the suspension will begin during his sport season.)

   PENALTY—2ND OFFENSE: Suspension from all sports for one calendar year.

3. INSUBORDINATIONS

   Such infractions as conduct, attitude, unexcused absence from practice, etc. will be taken care of by the head coach.

4. ADMINISTRATIVE INFRACTIONS

   Any infraction which results in suspension from the school, by the school administration, automatically removes the boy from the athletic program until he is properly reinstated.

   It is understood by the athletic director and the head coaches of the various sports, that head coaches may establish additional stricter rules for the sport they are coaching. If such rules are established the coach will notify his team members of such rules.

5. If a student is not in school attendance by 12:00 P.M., he cannot practice or participate in an athletic contest on that school day.

TABLE VII
ATHLETE TRAINING RULE PLEDGE

Name_____

We are aware of the Bridgeport Athletic Council's training rule which became effective in the school year of 19____.

No ATHLETE may smoke tobacco or drink alcoholic beverages throughout the entire year once he has become a member of a squad. If he is detected doing so *at any time,* he shall be suspended from membership in all athletic squads from the time of detection to the beginning of the next year's sport season in which he was detected.

All athletes shall be expected to keep reasonable hours as outlined by the head coach.

The rule becomes effective for every athlete the first time he tries out for an athletic squad. It is enforced from that time on regardless of whether school is in session or whether he is a squad member at the time.

SIGNED_____
Student Athlete

SIGNED_____
Parent or Guardian

TABLE VIII
DUNBAR HIGH SCHOOL
ATHLETIC CONTEST RESULT RECORD

Name of Opponent _____ Date _____
Sport _____ Squad _____ Contest played: Home — Away
Score: Dunbar High School _____   Opponent: _____

Officials:						
(1)	_____	(Excellent)	(Good)	(Fair)	(Poor)
(2)	_____	(Excellent)	(Good)	(Fair)	(Poor)
(3)	_____	(Excellent)	(Good)	(Fair)	(Poor)
(4)	_____	(Excellent)	(Good)	(Fair)	(Poor)

Game Comments: _____

_____

_____

_____
Coach's Signature

Suggested Athletic Injury Policies

1. All injuries no matter how slight they may be, should be considered seriously and not ignored until they have been taken care of.

2. The coach has a strong moral and *legal obligation* to make sure that injuries receive prompt and satisfactory treatment. This should not be left up to a student manager or bystander.

Suggested Policy on Dropping an Athlete from the Team

Coaches should keep regular and accurate attendance of squad members. When a player is dropped from a squad for any reason, notification of this fact should be made using the proper form and given to the director of athletics *immediately*. The athletic department office should then notify the people involved. The coach should also direct the equipment man to pick up the dropped player's equipment.

Suggested Scouting Policies

1. The head coach should assign scouting duties.
2. These assignments should be distributed as equally as possible with each staff member assuming his share of the responsibility.
3. Scouting assignments for each week should be given to the director of athletics at the beginning of the week.
4. Mileage should be paid if coaches' cars are used for scouting. The head coach should make reservations for use of the school cars whenever possible. Minor expenses for scouting should be paid. Car expenses should be paid for only one car to any one destination. Expenses should be paid only for scouting authorized by the conference.

Suggested Coaches Accepting Gifts Policies

Coaches should not accept or receive gifts or favors from students, parents, or

UNDER $50 ONLY

UNDER $50 ONLY
If over $50, use
4-part form

TABLE IX
JACKSON TOWNSHIP HIGH SCHOOL
REQUEST FOR TRAVEL REIMBURSEMENT

NAME _____

CAMPUS   N   S   DEPARTMENT _____
      (Circle)

DATE OF TRAVEL _____

PURPOSE OF TRAVEL _____
_____

DESTINATION _____

EXPENSES: (Attach receipts for room, transportation, and other items when possible.)

                                                                AMOUNT

        Room   _____

        Transporation (Reimbursement shall not exceed
        the round trip air-coach fare from Chicago).
        (Shorter trips by car shall be reimbursed at 10
        cents a mile.)   _____

        Other   (Please list)   _____
                                                       _____
                                                          _____

                     TOTAL REQUEST FOR REIMBURSEMENT $_____

SIGNED: _____   DATE _____

DEPARTMENT CHAIRMAN: _____   DATE_____
       (Signature indicates amount has been budgeted)

— —

                                  FOR OFFICE USE

                                      VENDOR NUMBER _____

                                      INVOICE NUMBER _____

                                      ACCOUNT CHARGED _____

                                      AMOUNT _____

                                      AUTHORIZATION _____

other individuals. Appreciation can be shown by the spirit of cooperation in the relationship that is enjoyed through working together. Tangible evidence in the form of a gift is unnecessary. Students and/or parents should not collect money or set aside funds for gifts to be given to the coaches. Such collections may create problems for the student and/or parents and also for the coach receiving the gift. Oral or written statements of appreciation are adequate and are always in good taste.

Disbanding of Squads Policies Suggestions

1. At the conclusion of each sport season, the coach should make plans for the checking in of all equipment. Arrangements should be made with the equipment man, with the athlete's being informed fully as to when and how this is to be done.

2. Many schools require each coach to fill out a season summary report for each sport. These report forms should be carefully filled out and given to the athletic director immediately after the season is completed.

   It would be logical to assume that *all* members of a school coaching staff will not have the same goals or objectives in relation to training rules. Many coaches object to being policemen and believe that too many rules and regulations are sometimes detrimental and defeat the purpose of a good program of athletics. In most *successful athletic programs* the players themselves will see to it that all team members abide by the rules and regulations.

Athletic Staff Policies on Athletes' Behavior Suggestions

One of the greatest faults that some coaches have is not recognizing responsibilities. For example, behavior around the team he is coaching such as poor discipline, team members "horsing around" in practice, not listening when the coach is talking, improper behavior in school, on the bus, or away on trips. Once a player becomes a member of a team the coach should be concerned about that player's behavior at *all* times and not just when the coach is supervising the player at practice or during a game.

The player should never be permitted to use bad language. By the same token, the coach should never use bad language in front of the players. It cannot be expected that the athletes will refrain from using bad language if they hear the coach using it.

The coaching staff should strive at all times to help each athletic participant to be a top notch person. This means in the classroom as well as in athletics. Players do not respect the coaches who do not keep discipline; in fact, they lose respect for them. If a coach is sincere, he makes his players abide by any rules and insists on *each* player being a top-notch individual. That coach will long be remembered after the personality seeker is forgotten.

Sometimes, under existing conditions, it is difficult for some coaches to enforce rules and regulations because they are afraid the players will not like them but it is better to lose *affection* than *respect*. Usually the player that loses affection for a coach because of a reprimand is not the type of player he wants on the team anyway.

Coaching Clinics Attendance Policies Suggestions

At various times during the year coaching clinics are held throughout the state. It is assumed that all members of the staff in order to increase their knowledge of the

TABLE X
FOOTBALL POLICIES FOR PLAYERS

The following is a list of policies which each athlete will be expected to adhere to:
Training Rules

All players must obey the law and be gentlemen in and out of school. The above mentioned covers most everything that will occur in regard to training rules. Drinking will be prohibited at all times under any circumstances.

On the night before a game players should be home by 9:59 P.M. This should preclude attending other games the night before.

The penalty for violation or abuse of rules will be commensurate with the severity of the violation.
Classroom

Every athlete should do his best in school to achieve high academic standing.
Practice

Every player must attend practice sessions religiously and arrive promptly. If he is unable to attend practice because of an unforseen circumstance, he should notify the coach as soon as possible. He must attend practice sessions to be eligible for the first game.

If an athlete misses practice twice in a row without a valid excuse he will be dropped from the squad. If an athlete is chronically absent he will be dismissed.

Players are expected to be on the field twenty minutes after the last bell rings. Penalty for unexcused tardiness will be one lap for every minute he is late. Laps will be run after practice.

When he enters the practice or game field his helmet should be on.
Equipment

Every player will be required to pay for equipment that is lost. He must not leave his gear on the floor unless he wants to run laps. Part of being an athlete is being responsible. His name should be on the helmet in the back. He should see the manager if the name comes off and be sure to get a new one.
Locker Room

It is imperative that all players keep their area clean. Use the waste baskets for tape, paper etc. Keep the equipment off the floor. Do not wear muddy cleats into the locker room. Keep lockers locked.

Towels will be left by the shower. Take one and only one towel; make it easy on yourself and the team. Use the drying area to dry off to help keep the locker room as arid as possible. Put your towel in the towel basket when you are finished with it.

No horseplay in the shower or locker room. Get showered, dressed, and leave.

Read the bulletin board daily.
Managers and Managers Room

Stay out of medicine kits, equipment kits, and managers' room. If you need something, ask for it. Managers are to serve you and not be your servants.
Insurance, Physicals Etc.

No one is to practice without a physical or insurance or waiver of insurance form signed by parents or guardian. Every player is required to have a mouthpiece and wear it. A fifteen-yard penalty will be imposed if he does not wear it in the game and four laps in practice if he does not wear it.
Injuries

Report any injury to the coaching staff immediately so a report can be made out.
Traveling to Games

Squad members are expected to go and return with the players bus unless some exception should come up.

Bus will leave at a specific time; so every player must be at school in plenty of time to pack his gear. He should call the school if he has car trouble, etc.

Conduct on the bus — Each player is expected to conduct himself properly or he will not be riding the players bus. If that does not work out, he will come in on Saturday and do a little road work.

Every player is expected to dress in proper attire. If he is not sure what that is, we will draw up a dress code that will include a shirt and tie. He is representing the school and community at home and away.

Winning a Letter

Winning a letter is contingent on playing in games, attending practice regularly, and finishing the season in good standing. If a player is injured he can help us in some capacity if it is at all possible.

Dismissal from the Squad

If a player is dismissed from the squad he must turn all his equipment in immediately. He checked it out so he must check it back in.

General Information

It is not necessary to be taped unless the player has had a previous injury.

Ankle wraps are available.

Get plenty of rest and take salt tablets in warm weather.

Profanity, dirty play, and illegal tactics will not be tolerated on the field. A fifteen-yard penalty and out of game will be the result of being profane and dirty.

Do not yell and criticize the officials.

Do not be a hot dog by trying to bait the opponent.

When told to do something, do it on the double.

No talking when a coach is addressing a player.

We feel that since the players are representing the high school they should present a neat appearance.

No beards and mustaches during the season will be tolerated.

If a player is a chronic complainer or has an alibi for everything, then football is not his game. The coach will decide who plays. To win it is necessary to play as a unit. The strength is in the pack and not the wolf.

Players should eat at regular hours and drink plenty of liquids in warm weather.

Players should eat at least 3½ hours before the game. Avoid greasy food and include plenty of carbohydrates in your diet.

---

sport or sports they are coaching, would deem it, not only desirable but important to attend such clinics. It should be the recommendation of the director of athletics that they do so. If at all possible the school should provide financial assistance to coaches to attend these clinics.

Personal Property Policy Suggestions

Most schools carry a deductable insurance policy; therefore, any items lost or stolen up to the cost of the deductable ($50.00) will not be covered. If personal items are used on school premises, they should be well secured.

Policies Regarding the Relationship Between Staff Members Suggestions

It should be the policy of the school athletic department that any time a sports activity is taking place, all staff members whether they are coaching in that activity or not should feel and should be made to feel they are a part of that activity. So many times, and it is not always the coach's fault, a staff member who is not busy with a sport during an off season contributes nothing to any other phase of the athletic program except to his own sport. So many times, unless they are paid as we would pay other faculty members who are not on the staff, coaches who are not busy, are not interested in helping his fellow coaches.

If a member of the coaching profession is only in it for the money he will receive, it is very likely he will die poor. However, the coach should be paid just as other faculty members are paid. There are times, however, when a little help from other members of the coaching staff, not busy with coaching a sport at that particular time would be greatly appreciated by the other coaches. If, however, the only time the coach contributes something to the program is when he is going to be compensated for it, the program will face a dismal failure.

Suggested Policies Regarding Athletic Officials

All officials who are contracted to officiate games should be registered with the state association. All officials that are contracted for varsity games should be on the state approved list.

Contest officials should be hired by the director who should seek the mutual confidence and agreement of all persons involved. The head coaches of football and basketball should comply with the state's request for the rating of officials at the end of the season. If a coach feels that a certain official should not be contracted for future games, he should notify the director of athletics in writing. Criticism of officials by coaches should be done in an ethical fashion and never in public.

Suggested Practice Session Policies

The head coach should be responsible for outlining specific duties for his staff and to provide the leadership and direction that is necessary for successful training programs.

The coach or his assistant should be physically present during the entire period of practice that requires the presence of all or one of his team members. At no time should a coach leave the practice area and place responsibility for the team on a student. Responsibility of practice sessions should extend to the use of equipment, facilities, and materials. Well-organized and understood practice sessions should help eliminate any deviations from sound educational philosophies. Whenever practice or contests calls for the use of board of education property after custodian hours, the head coach should be responsible for the security of the facilities and the building.

Suggested Publicity and Promotion Policies

There are various and sundry means by which any activity can be promoted. The basic mediums which a school may use are posters, schedule cards, newspapers, and radio. In a sense, each coach is a press agent and should bear in mind during requested interviews that their statements will be published and read by people who are for or against the school's program. These statements should be weighed carefully before they are given to the press.

Press releases should be submitted to the director of athletics. Telephone or personal interviews are not considered as press releases. Coaches should be encouraged to prepare press releases for the school paper. The publications department usually welcomes prepared pre- and postgame releases. Complete understanding between individual coaches and the publications department should result in news releases of the type best desired by both parties.

Suggested Physical Education Class Attendance Policies for Athletes

All students should be required to attend all physical education classes in which they are enrolled even though they are members of an athletic team. This has been the subject of much controversy among coaches.

Suggested Meals and Lodging Policies

The athletic director should determine the justification of providing meals and lodging as well as the amount to be spent if this is needed in case of a trip. The coach should handle all financial transactions and turn in an accurate accounting of all monies spent along with receipts.

Suggested Dismissal Time for Athletic Contests Policies

Any coach in charge of an athletic team that is dismissed from school early because of an impending contest should submit a list of players to be excused to the attendance office before 8 A.M. the day of the contest. The time to be dismissed should be determined before the season starts in cooperation with the athletic director and the principal.

Suggested Medical and Insurance Plans Policies

Usually the public schools will not assume any responsibility or liability relative to doctor or hospital expense. Athletics are a voluntary program in which the student may participate if he so desires but he does so at his own risk of injury. This policy should be explained to all students participating in the program by each coach. They should emphasize that neither their name or that of the school should be used where medical expense is involved. Medical bills received by the school or the board of education should be returned to the coach for an explanation.

A physical examination and parent's consent should be required of every player before he or she is allowed to participate in

practice sessions or games. Each coach should check each player personally to ascertain that these requirements have been fulfilled for their self-protection. An attempt should be made each year for group examinations to be given at some date during the week prior to the opening of football practice. This examination should be held for all students at a nominal cost in cooperation with the doctors of the community who favor such a plan.

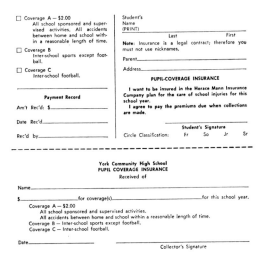

Figure 10.

Students who are engaged in the athletic program should be urged and encouraged to enroll in commercial insurance plans. It must be remembered, however, that because coaches encourage students to enroll in a program of insurance or benefit plan, those acts in no way implicate the coach, school, or board of education for liability in case of an injury.

Several Athletic Accident Benefit Plans are offered to member schools to assist intramural, physical education, and athletic programs to meet at least part of the costs of injuries incurred by registered students, provided the activities involved are conducted according to insurance plan regulations. Neither a state association nor the insurance plan always guarantees the payment of costs of all injuries. It is expected that claims for scheduled benefits usually will be paid in full. It must be understood, however, that it is impossible to distribute more money for injury claims than is paid in by schools in membership and registration fees.

give him full protection.

When school buses are used, the following general rules should be observed:
1. A coach should travel with the bus.
2. There should be no eating or smoking on the bus.
3. Team members should remain in their seats and conduct themselves in a manner that will promote good safety factors.

TABLE XI
PALO HIGH SCHOOL
PALO, NEBRASKA
Insurance Request Form
TO THE PRINCIPAL
PERMISSION TO PARTICIPATE IN ATHLETICS

We hereby request that _____
(Name of participant)
be permitted to participate in _____,
(Name of sport)
one of the athletic activities offered by the high school. It is understood that the school cannot accept full responsibility for a student's welfare, and therefore, one of the following insurance coverages must be subscribed to before he/she is permitted to participate in the athletic program at the high school.

    A. Regular school accident insurance _____
    B. 24-hour school accident insurance _____
    C. Other accident insurance (Policy No. _____).
        (Company _____)
In case of emergency we may be reached at 1._____
                                       2._____

_____   _____
     Student Signature   Parent or Guardian Signature

_____
     Student Address
All overnight trips must have 24-hour school
accident insurance or comparable coverage.

Suggested Transportation Policies

Travel to all athletic events should be made by school bus if at all possible. If for some reason a coach wishes to use his automobile for transporting a student or students, this should be cleared with the director of athletics. The coach should be sure that either the school or he himself has adequate insurance coverage which will

4. Windows should remain closed unless permission is otherwise granted.
5. Nothing should be stuck out of or thrown from a window.
6. The bus should be recognized as a part of the school system and no conduct should be allowed in it that reflects upon the individual, the team, or the school.

7. The team should cooperate and help the driver in every way possible.

It is recommended that coaches permit only qualified personnel transportation privileges. Players who travel to the game in the team bus should be expected to return the same way.

Suggested Liability Policies

The school laws differ in many states regarding the duty of the school to:
1. Exercise precautionary diligence in operating gymnasiums, athletic fields, and play areas.
2. Be constantly on the alert for unsafe conditions and practices in and around the school.
3. Maintain a policy of correcting defects and changing unsafe practices as soon as they are noticed.
4. Make a detailed investigation and appropriately written report of every accident which occurs.

Suggested Maintenance of Facilities and Grounds Policies

Many school systems are limited in personnel that can be used for the upkeep of grounds and facilities. Considerable amounts of time and expense are saved if coaches give thoughtful consideration to their use of facilities. A little attention before and after some practice sessions by players and managers will help solve many problems. The cooperation of all people vitally concerned with the program can overcome many obstacles. Requests for special maintenance services should be made to the athletic office in writing.

Suggested Policies Regarding Cheerleaders

The cheerleaders and other booster functions are efforts of the school at large to promote spirit and morale. They are self-directed bodies which have no responsibility to or from the athletic department. They should be counseled by a school appointed advisor and should be directly responsible to the school principal.

Suggested Athletic Banquets Policies

If there is an annual banquet, it should be promoted by the athletic department. The school should sponsor one such banquet annually and it should be held in honor of all sports award winners for that school year.

It is the best policy not to encourage special banquets for championship teams but rather to have all athletes at one time in the spring of each year.

Suggested Policies Regarding Varsity Club

Almost every high school has a varsity club. Its contribution to the athletic program is in direct proportion to the efforts contributed by the students and the leadership provided by the administration. It can be a guiding force in the athletic program or it can be just another club. If it is to be successful, it must have a strong constitution and show no favoritism to either boys or girls.

The Constitution of the Varsity "O" Club

Article I—Section 1

The name of the organization shall be the Varsity "O" Club.

Article II—Section 1

The objectives of the club shall be:
1. To promote good fellowship among varsity athletes.
2. To take an active part in high school activities, especially those pertaining to athletics.

3. To be of service in any way for the good of the school.
4. To foster a wholesome attitude toward all rival schools.
5. To aid in the development of school spirit.
6. To promote good sportsmanship in all athletic contests.
7. To protect and elevate the standard of and toward the varsity "O".
8. To promote a social program.
9. To support the athletic policies for all athletic teams.
10. To promote scholarship among athletes.

Article III—Section 1 (Membership)

Membership in the club shall be limited to all athletes who have earned a varsity major letter.

Article III—Section 2

All members shall be major letter winners, except present charter members who are continuing in a sport or sports in which they won letters, or by mutual agreement of the two coaches involved for athletes to switch sports.

Article III—Section 3

Upon winning a varsity letter the winner named will be brought before the club for a vote. He must be approved by two-thirds majority of the members present, providing it is a *quorum*.

Article III—Section 4

All Varsity "O" Club members shall become honorary members upon graduation.

Article III—Section 5

The coaches and athletic director shall be honorary members.

Article III—Section 6

Boys and girls shall be eligible to become members of the Varsity "O" Club.

Article III—Section 7

Three unexcused absences a semester shall automatically drop a member.

Article III—Section 8

Any member who fails to uphold the rules and regulations of the Varsity "O" Club shall be recommended for removal by the membership committee. A two-thirds majority vote will dismiss such a member. He shall automatically be excluded from all Varsity "O" Club activities and become ineligible for remembership for one semester.

Article III—Section 9

No dues will be required of the members.

Article IV—Section 1 (Wearing Sweater or Jacket)

It shall be traditional that every Friday shall be declared letter day and every member is to wear his "O"; however, letter sweaters may be worn to school on any other day.

Article IV—Section 2

Only the person earning the award will be allowed to wear it.

Article IV—Section 3

Only high school awards are to be worn on the school premises.

Article IV—Section 4

Members must be active in at least one sport during the school year, unless disabled.

Article V—Section 1

Officers shall be: president, vice-president, secretary, treasurer, sergeant at arms, and advisors.

Article V—Section 2 (Duties)

The president shall preside at all meetings. He must prepare an agenda and perform all the duties required of him by this constitution. He shall appoint all standing and special committees. He shall appoint a representative from each sport to constitute the board.

The vice-president shall be the varsity club parliamentarian and assist the president in parliamentary decisions. He shall perform the duties of the president in his absence. He shall be responsible for all committees appointed by the president.

The secretary shall take minutes of all meetings and shall aid the president when necessary in the preparation of the order of business.

The treasurer shall keep records of "O" club expenditures with the assistance of an advisor. He shall assist in counting the money taken in at the concessions and other "O" club projects.

The sergeant at arms shall assist in keeping order at the meetings.

The officers and the board shall administer the affairs of the "O" club.

The advisors shall assist in guiding the program of the "O" club.

Article V—Section 3

The club shall have the following committees appointed by the president:

A. Membership
B. Publicity
C. Projects
D. Initiation
E. Social
F. Constitution

Article V—Section 4

No member shall be eligible to hold office until he has been a member of the club for at least one semester.

Article V—Section 5

Officers shall serve for a term of one year and be eligible for reelection to the same office for a second term only.

Article VI—Section 1

Regular meetings shall be held during the school year, the time and place to be designated by the president. Special meetings shall be called by request of the president.

Article VI—Section 2

A quorum shall consist of one half (50%) of the total membership of the club.

Article VI—Section 3

The order of business at regular meetings shall be:
1. Roll call
2. Reading of minutes of the previous meeting.
3. Reports of boards and standing committees.
4. Reports of special committees.
5. Special orders
6. Unfinished business
7. New business

Article VII—Section 1

The constitution, by-laws and rules of order that have been adopted may be amended at any regular business meeting by three-fourths majority of the quorum.

Amendment I

The Varsity "O" Club court shall exist for the purpose of hearing cases of members who have been recommended to them by the membership committee for dismissal from the club. The court shall consist of president, vice-president, secretary, treasurer, sergeant at arms, two advisors, and the chairmen of the six standing committees. (The court then is a total of 13 people). The president shall act as chief justice and only vote in case of a tie.

Amendment II

Any member of the club who is dropped from a sport or quits a sport other than the sport in which he or she won a varsity letter which brought him or her a membership must have his case tried by the Varsity "O" Club court. If the reasons are found to be justifiable, the membership shall be continued. If the court finds the reasons are not sound and justified, he or she shall be suspended from all club activities and the case shall be turned over to the membership committee with recommendations for dismissal from the club.

Suggested Policies for Most Valuable Player Selection

The task of selecting the most valuable player at the end of the season in any sport is a complex problem, and one that can have many repercussions if not done correctly and consistently for all sports. It is advantageous, therefore, to establish policies which will be uniform for every sport in so far as is possible. Many schools allow the players themselves to select the most valuable player. However, unless some guidelines are established for the players to follow in their selection, it degenerates into a popularity contest and does not prove a thing. There should be no differentiation between the requirements for boys and girls. The requirements should be the same. One such plan is offered here.

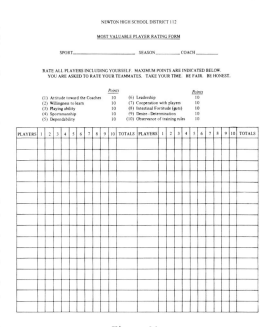

Figure 11.

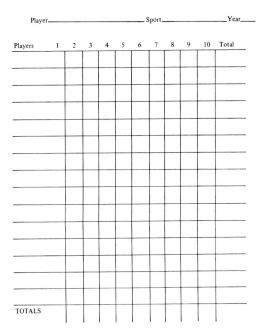

Figure 12.

Suggested Tournament Play Policies

Inasmuch as most state associations issues its tournament information and materials to the various coaches, it should be their responsibility to follow through on completing the arrangements for participating. The coach should be sure that he meets entry deadlines, etc. The athletic office should cooperate in every way to expedite clerical and mechanical procedures.

Suggested Policies Regarding the Marching Band

The band director should be responsible for all phases of work done by members of the marching band.

Suggested Staff Policies Concerning Athletic Injuries

It is of primary importance for each staff member to remember, even though, he may have had courses in preparation for coaching, such as the care and treatment of athletic injuries, health education, first aid, kinesiology, and anatomy that he is not a medical doctor. There are many instances and circumstances when small minor injuries can be treated by the athletic staff. Injuries such as minor sprains, scratches, burns, etc. can be handled by the coach in charge. If first-aid supplies are available they should be used.

Any injury which occurs that the coach in charge feels he cannot treat should be brought to the attention of the doctor. The athletic participants' health and welfare should be the prime responsibility and concern of the athletic staff.

Suggested Staff Loyalty Policy

Attempts are made constantly to eliminate or deemphasize athletics. This would be unjustified under any circumstances. However, as a result, athletics are being carefully scrutinized by many people as to their place in the school curriculum and in society in general. It should be brought to the attention of all athletic participants that the athletic program must be a good one in every way. This does not necessarily mean a winning season always, although winning solves many problems. It does mean that stress should be placed on the more important aspects such as behavior of athletes, academic endeavors, behavior of coaches, wasteful spending of money, etc. Every school is interested in having the best, all-around sports program in the state. The efforts, philosophy, and actions of the athletic staff will play a large role in accomplishing that goal. Every school wants to have one of the finest athletic staffs in the state, and this can be accomplished also if staff members are constantly thinking along the same lines. The staff must display loyalty to the board of education, principal, director of athletics, and fellow coaches. This is the prime requisite for a good staff member. The ability to get along with other staff members *at all times* regardless of the situation is an important requisite to a good coach, not the ability to win ball games. *All* staff members should be eliminated who cannot be loyal to their superiors and find it difficult or impossible to get along with their colleagues. There are too many other pressures to have to put up with unsatisfied staff members who in reality would be dissatisfied in any situation because of their personality.

All staff members should at all times make a tremendous effort in every way to have a successful athletic program as well as having a well-organized harmonious athletic staff.

BEHAVIORAL OBJECTIVES

After a person has read this chapter, he should be able to:

1. Define administrative policies in inter-

scholastic athletics.

2. Identify the reasons for establishing policies in the administration of interscholastic athletics.

3. Explain how policies are formed.

4. Identify and explain several guidelines which can be used in the establishment of policies.

5. Identify the policy-making organizations in interscholastic athletics and differentiate between their duties.

6. Recall several specific duties of each governing organization and apply them to a local situation.

7. Distinguish between philosophy and objectives in interscholastic athletics and give a concrete example of each.

8. Distinguish between the policies which affect the athletic director to those of the athletic coach.

9. Recall several policies which affect all coaches.

10. Analyze several policies which affect only head coaches.

11. Explain the purpose of a sportsmanship code and its adoption by a conference.

12. Summarize the reasons for a conference admissions policy.

13. Formulate a sportsmanship code based on present-day beliefs in conduct and civil rights.

14. Predict several changes in sportsmanship codes which might occur in the near future as a result of the civil rights movement.

15. Select one policy in scheduling which might be universal and question its reliability in terms of its justification.

16. Recall the basic policies which apply to administrators and add any others which might be important.

17. Select one policy in scheduling as being most important and defend this choice.

18. Explain the limitations on practice and competition.

19. Recall several policies regarding the conduct of athletic contests and apply them to a local situation.

20. Propose any policies which might be beneficial in the conduct of contests and which would result in a change for the better.

21. Explain what is meant by the scope of interscholastic athletics on the local level.

22. Differentiate between the board of education, the superintendent, the principals, the athletic director, the faculty manager, and the head coaches' responsibility in policy making in interscholastic athletics.

23. Select several coaching staff policies and discuss each.

24. Explain the policies regarding injuries.

25. Explain the use of the training room.

26. Recognize the concern of the athletic director for organizational, management, and evaluative practices by the staff in the conduct of the program.

27. Explain how the policies of school administration affect the athletic policies.

28. Propose some arguments for and against a plan of allowing the conduct of interscholastic athletics to be under the supervision of the student council as are some of the other extracurricular activities.

29. Indicate who is responsible for the conduct of interscholastic athletics and explain why.

30. Explain the purpose of a guide for interscholastic athletics for the high school. Explain its contests and reasons for its establishment.

31. Select the most desirable administrative policies that should be used as guides in the promotion of the interscholastic athletic programs.

32. Explain how the policies of the school

administration affect the interscholastic athletic program.

33. Determine a fair and equitable plan for the distribution of complementary tickets for the basketball season.
34. Prepare a list of policies which should be used in making the athletic schedule.

ACTIVITIES

1. Form two groups and debate the issue: (1) Should the coach or players formulate training rules, (2) should the coach or players administer them, (3) should the coach or players judge them?
2. Debate the issue: Should conferences make uniform policies governing interscholastic athletics or should each school make their own as they see fit?
3. Arrange for the athletic director of the local high school to speak to the class regarding conference policies and the problems encountered in administering them.
4. Write for copies of the several state association handbooks and compare the policies in several areas.
5. Seek the opinion of several athletic directors regarding their philosophy of athletics and make a comparison.
6. Study several high school administrative organizations and report the findings to the class.
7. Write to several large and small high schools for their organizational plan and compare them.
8. Make all arrangements and plans for a conference dinner including the agenda of activities and discussions which might take place during the meeting.
9. Arrange to have a head coach talk to the class regarding problems concerning conference policies and their enforcement.
10. Arrange to help at a high school athletic event and obtain first-hand knowl-

edge on how policies can be helpful in administering the event.

11. Visit a college or high school training room and relate back to the class on what you found.
12. Arrange for a high school head coach to talk to the class and explain his coaching staff organizational policies.
13. Arrange for a school board member to talk with the class and explain his role in policy making.
14. Arrange for the principal to explain his role in policy making.
15. Visit a high school and talk with the athletic director regarding the handling and purchasing of equipment.
16. List a set of policies to be used as a guide for the director and student council in establishing a satisfactory system of athletic awards.
17. Compile a list of administrative policies for the conduct of an interscholastic program of athletics.
18. Outline the contents of a coaches manual.
19. Prepare a list of policies to be used for workers at athletic contests, such as police, cheerleaders, ticket takers, etc.
20. Prepare a list of policies that should guide the director of athletics in the conduct of athletic teams on trips.
21. Develop a coach's manual for an athletic department in a school of five hundred.
22. Debate the issue: Athletic policies should be made with the welfare of all the students in mind or to make money to finance the athletic program.
23. Write to several high schools in different sections of the country requesting information on their school and conference scouting regulations.

SUGGESTED READINGS

1. American Association for Health, Physical Education and Recreation: *Admin-*

istration of High School Athletics. Washington, D.C., The Association of Health, Physical Education, and Recreation, 1962.

2. Daughtrey, Greyson and Woods, John: *Physical Education Programs*. Philadelphia, Saunders, 1971.

3. Division of Men's Athletics: Athletics in education, a platform statement. *Journal of Health, Physical Education, and Recreation*, September, 1962.

4. Educational Policies Commission: *School Athletics, Problems and Policies*. Washington, D. C., National Education Association and American Association of School Administrators, 1954.

5. Forsythe, Charles and Keller, Irvin: *Administration of High School Athletics*. Englewood Cliffs, P-H, 1972.

6. George, Jack F. and Lehman, Harry A.: *School Athletic Administration*. New York, Har-Row, 1966.

7. Grieve, Andrew, *Directing High School Athletics*. Englewood Cliffs, P-H, 1963.

8. Havel, Richard, and Seymour, Emery: *Administration of Health, Physical Education and Recreation for Schools*. New York, Ronald, 1961.

9. Hixson, Chalmer: *The Administration of Interscholastic Athletics*. New York, Lowell Pratt, 1967.

10. Illinois High School Association: *Official Handbook*. Chicago, 1971-72.

11. Kelliher, M.S.: Successful athletic administration. *Journal of Health, Physical Education, and Recreation*, November, 1957.

12. National Federation of State High School Associations: *Official Handbook*, Chicago, 1972-73.

13. Resick, Matthew, Siedel, Beverly, and Mason, James: *Modern Administrative Practices in Physical Education and Athletics*, Reading, A-W, 1970.

14. Sells, James: Need a staff policy book? *The Physical Educator*, May, 1961.

15. Thomas, Eugene: The role of athletics in education. *Administration of High School Athletics—Report of a National Conference*, American Association for Health, Physical Education and Recreation. Washington, D.C., December, 1962.

16. Williams, Jesse and Hughes, William: *Athletics in Education*. Philadelphia, Saunders, 1936.

17. Wilson, Emerson: Policy avoids problems in prep coaching staffs. *Coach and Athlete*, June, 1965.

CHAPTER 7

Legal Liability in Athletics

SPORTS ARE INCREASING in popularity throughout the world, and they are fast becoming an American way of life. As a result of the emphasis being placed on sports, their value both mentally and physically, the problem of injury to the participants has presented itself. Bird[1] estimated in 1970 that:

> There will be in excess of 552,000 sports injuries in the United States elementary and secondary schools. Football will account for about 67 percent or 368,000 of the injuries with basketball a distant second at 13 percent or 68,000. Accidents included here are those requiring a doctor's attention or causing at least one-half day's absence from school.

As a result of these accidents or injuries to the athletes, those people supervising these activities are placed in a very vulnerable position. Many times these accidents are the result of negligence. People are more likely to bring suit today than they would a few years ago even though the accident is not the fault of the coach.

It has been suggested that one of the most lucrative areas for lawyers today is legal liability, especially cases which involve physical educators.

Rice[2] generally concurs with the idea that this is true in the following comment:

---

[1]Bird, Patrick, "The Coach and the Courts," *The Athletic Journal* (October, 1970) , p. 62.

[2]Rice, Sidney, "A Suit for the Teacher," *Journal of Health, Physical Education and Recreation* (November, 1961) , p. 24.

In the United States anybody can be sued for almost anything at any time. American judicial history has recorded cases in which teachers have been forced to defend themselves and, in some instances, pay heavy judgments from their meager, hard-earned salaries.

VULNERABILITY OF COACHES FOR LIABILITY

Coaches are more vulnerable than ever before in the eyes of the law for civil tort liability (injury or wrong caused to one party by another party). Professional publications and the daily newspapers contain a growing number of stories on civil actions which have been filed against coaches for student injuries resulting from negligence. It is imperative that the coach be aware of the manner in which the law generally views his or her professional role.

Howard[3] summarizes this viewpoint very adequately in the following statement:

> Litigation of all kinds appears to be on the increase and school litigation is no exception. Teachers are not expected to know all the many laws, regulations, and court decisions pertaining to the operation of the public schools. However, the very nature and responsibilities of the teaching profession, involving as it does care and supervision of children, make it desirable for teachers to be aware of what may or may not be areas of liability.

Interpretations of law have tended to

---

[3]Howard, Alvin, "Teacher Liability and the Law," *The Clearing House* (March, 1968) , p. 411.

favor the injured party more and more the past few years. Suits to recover damages have become more and more common. A very high percentage have been won by the complainant.

The awards have steadily risen. Schools, as well as persons, have lost much of the protection afforded them a few years ago. It, therefore, is important that schools and coaches afford themselves maximum protection. They should be constantly vigilant and should exercise every precaution to avoid any action that will result in an injury to a player and result in a law suit.

The coach is very vulnerable in case of injury to the player. He or she should do everything within his or her power to insure safety for the athletes. In order to avoid being charged with negligence, Grimsley[4] has suggested that the coach follow Augustus Steinhelber's Chairman of the School Law Unit of the United States Office of Education, list of reminders of appropriate actions for the coach to take in order to meet the legal definition of acting as a reasonably prudent and careful teacher.

It is unfortunate that many coaches are not aware, or at least many of them put it out of their minds until something happens, that they are responsible for injuries suffered by players under their supervision. The courts in recent years have ruled in favor of the player in many instances. The permit from the parent or guardian to participate no longer affords the coach protection or absolves him from blame if the player is injured. If negligence can be proven, and it can with increasing frequency, the coach can be held liable. The courts have ruled that the parent or guardian cannot sign away the rights of a minor

---

[4]Grimsley, Jimmie, "Legal Liability of Injured Pupil," *Physical Education* (October, 1969), p. 104.

when there is a possibility of injury to the player.

Suits Against Coaches

Most suits involving coaches are those which constitute an action of unintentional injury. The charge in most suits is, of course, negligence, which is the failure to act as a reasonably prudent and careful person would act under similar circumstances. As a result, the player sustains an injury or even death.

PROOF OF NEGLIGENCE

The proof of negligence results when a coach does not act as a reasonable and careful person would in the same situation. Therefore, the coach must thoroughly understand what he is doing, how it is to be done, and why it is to be done in the way he is teaching the particular skill. If he can show, in case of a suit against him, that the way in which he was teaching the skill is the generally accepted way to teach it, he cannot be proven negligent. He must also show that the skill was not dangerous and was within the capabilities of the player performing it. The coach must not allow participation of the kind that is not definitely a part of the skill required to play a particular game. The activity should be the kind that the player would learn the fundamentals of the game. For instance, in teaching the game of football, tackling would be one fundamental that would be taught. It is important that it be taught in such a manner that injury to the player will be avoided. Teaching techniques should be used that are accepted and used by those considered to be expert teachers. If unacceptable methods are used, and the player is injured, the coach could be held liable. An example of this could be to allow a player to be tackled from the blind side or lining the players up ten yards apart and have them charge at each other at full speed. The coach should also be sure to demonstrate (either himself or by a class member or on film) the correct technique in performing the skill. These are all precautions against injury and possible suit. The coach is not liable, regardless of the injury to the player, if he is not negligent. An example of the following case[5] shows the value of these precautions. A suit was filed because the player, who weighed only 140 pounds, was tackled simultaneously, and very hard, by two players who hit him from opposite sides. The injury occurred after six weeks of practice. He was an inexperienced player. He claimed that he had not been given proper instruction and that he was wearing poor and improper equipment. He claimed the injury resulted due to negligence by the coach because of these facts.

The court ruled the boy had had football playing experience in junior high school.

> The coach was an expert teacher of football fundamentals as testified to by experts. The fact that he was tackled hard did not necessarily cause the injury. Furthermore, just how hard is being tackled hard? The athlete was aware that the equipment was poor but accepted it even though he knew this. The player also was aware of the fact that football was a contact sport and he might be injured. He was not forced or required to participate but did it of his own free will. Consequently, he had no cause for complaint and had to assume the risk of injury.

In cases of minor injuries, the coach can be placed in a very vulnerable position. When an injury occurs, the coach must administer first aid because a doctor is not always available on the practice field or court. He should be careful not to overstep his abilities and training for if he does, negligence can be proven and he is placed in a position where he can be liable and involved in a court action. On the other hand, if he fails to perform first aid, he can also be liable. In either case, his only recourse is that he acts as a prudent person would act under similar circumstances and conditions. The coach should protect himself by following these steps and use good judgment: (1) act as a prudent person, (2) have a physician present at all contests, and (3) follow the first-aid handbook.

The following case studies illustrate how the coach can be held liable in case of injury to the player:

> In a New Jersey case[6] (Duda vs. Gaines) a coach was sued for not seeking immediate attention for a shoulder injury sustained by a boy in football practice. The case was tried under the stipulation that the defendant's duty was limited to the summoning of medical aid in a situation where an emergency existed. The boy threw his shoulder out of place; the coach put it back, and sent the boy to a school physician. Several days later, the boy again threw his shoulder out, and again the coach put it back. This time the coach told the boy he couldn't play the rest of the year, but it wasn't necessary to see a physician a second time. In making the latter statement, the coach was skating on thin ice, but the court didn't hold him liable, ruling that the second situation wasn't an emergency and didn't indicate that the boy was in urgent need of attention.

In a California case[7] (Bellman vs. San Francisco High School District) it was clearly pointed out that some sort of physical examination must be given to pupils entering athletic activities. If a coach does

---

[5]Vandrell vs. School District No. 260, Malhuer County, 376P. 2nd 402.

[6]Shroyer, George, "Coaches Legal Liability for Athletes Injuries," *Scholastic Coach* (December, 1964), p. 18.
[7]*Ibid.*

not require pupils to have an examination yet compels them to participate in certain kinds of exercise without determining in advance their aptitude for the sport, he would be considered negligent. This is especially true when he knows of a condition, such as a knee injury. The examination should be done prior to practice or a contest. No coach wants to take the chance of being a party in a liability suit for a possible injury or physical defect which the player may have had previously. A physical examination, therefore, is the coach's only safe protection against this type of liability suit, as well as the athletes' only health protection.

> In another case (Welch vs. Dunsmuir Joint High School District) a boy suffered an injury to his back in a football game. The boy was unable to get up and walk off the field, but several other boys carried him from the field by his arms and legs. The boy became a quadriplegic. The court ruled that the boy was removed from the field in a negligent manner which aggravated and worsened the original injury. The court, therefore, awarded the boy $206,804 for damages. Permanent injury and payment for damages may have been prevented if proper first-aid measures had been taken. It seems that most people would agree that, first, the boy should have been placed on a stretcher in a proper manner and carried from the field, instead of having been carried from the field by outstretched arms and legs; and secondly, a physician should have been in attendance and readily should have been available to take charge of all injuries.[8]

If the complainant expects to win the case, he must prove that the coach was negligent in his duty. To do this, the complainant must (1) show that he has a right to expect certain conditions to exist which will be in the interest of the athlete's welfare, (2) the coach failed to recognize and

observe this right, and (3) the person was a victim of the coach's actions or his failure to act as a reasonable and prudent person would under similar circumstances.

Negligence cannot be thought of as something the person has neglected to do and as a result an injury occurred. Liebee[9] puts it this way, "The so-called reasonable, prudent person against whom the jury measures the defendant is, of course, a creature of the mind. He is an ideal; the good citizen doesn't daydream while approaching a dangerous spot in the road."

Voltmer and Esslinger[10] make the following comment regarding negligence:

> There can be no liability for injury unless negligence can be shown. Negligence is considered the failure to act as a reasonably prudent person would act under the circumstances. Negligence will not arise unless there is a duty towards a person which is disregarded. The teacher is in *loco parentis* (in the place of the parent) and thus must act in relation to the pupil as a reasonably prudent and careful parent would under the circumstances. Courts interpret a reasonably prudent person to be one who would anticipate danger or accident. Negligence is gauged by the ability to anticipate danger. If such foresight is reasonable, failure to seek to prevent the danger is negligence.
>
> The teacher is not always liable when an accident occurs even though he has been negligent. The negligence must be directly responsible for the injury suffered before a suit can be successfully brought. If the injured person failed to act as a reasonably prudent individual should have acted under the circumstances and if this negligence contributed to the accident, any negligence on the part of the teacher is cancelled.

[8]*Ibid.*

[9]Liebee, Howard C., "Tort Liability for Injuries to Pupils" (Ann Arbor, Michigan, *Campus Publishers*, 1965), p. 10.

[10]Voltmer, Edward and Esslinger, Arthur, *The Organization and Administration of Physical Education* (New York, Appleton-Center Crofts, 1967), p. 480.

Athletes generally cannot collect for injuries incurred either in practice or in a contest because their consent to such possible reasonable chance of injury amounts to an assumption of risk which will defeat the suit.

Gold and Gold[11] make the following comment regarding the reasonable man and administering first aid:

> Although the law may set a duty upon physical educators to administer first-aid in an emergency to a seriously injured pupil, this is not a license to act imprudently. In undertaking to give first-aid, a teacher assumes the responsibility to administer it in a careful and acceptable manner and not in a slovenly or haphazard fashion.
>
> A teacher who has administered first-aid to a pupil suffering an injury in class may find himself involved in a lawsuit, based upon allegations that he negligently and carelessly administered first-aid, resulting in injuries or aggravation of the original injury. To determine whether the first-aid administered by a physical educator was negligent, the courts apply what is known as 'the reasonable man' test. This proposition has been succinctly stated in a case by the Supreme Court of California. 'The standard of care required by an officer or employee of a public school is that which a person of ordinary prudence, charged with his duties, would exercise under the same circumstances.

In the case of the athletic coach it would mean that the manner in which the coach cared for the player at the time of the injury would be judged by the court in comparison to what a reasonably prudent and careful coach would do under the same type of conditions, situation, and circumstances. Testimonials from doctors and outstanding coaches who would come under the category of experts would be used as evidence as to whether the coach acted as a

prudent and reasonable person. If the testimony of these people indicated that the first-aid given was proper, then the coach would not be held liable. If the first aid was not the type that would not have been given by other coaches under the same conditions and was not the right kind as judged by the doctors, the coach could be liable. All coaches should be constantly alert to players' injuries and should exert extreme caution in allowing a player to participate while injured and after an injury.

Playing a pupil who is ill is a negligent act by a coach. The coach who knowingly or unknowingly sends an injured player into a game is held negligent. If the coach does not know of the injury, he is negligent for his ignorance.

Every coach should have an understanding of his responsibilities under the law in regard to legal liability for his or her acts.

LIABILITY OF THE SCHOOL DISTRICT

Usually the school district is not held liable for negligence caused by its teachers or employees provided there are no laws to the contrary. The reason for this being, the school district is an agent of the state. Its duties are performed as a state or governmental agent for the benefit of the public. Some state laws, however, indicate that the state is responsible for providing competent leadership and a safe environment. However, according to Shroyer,[12] "The courts have started to change their attitudes on this issue; California, New York, Washington, Illinois, Minnesota, and Wisconsin have already held districts liable or have warned the districts that they will be held liable for their torts."

[11]Gold, Sandra, and Gold, Gerald, "First Aid and Legal Liability," *Journal of Health, Physical Education and Recreation* (January, 1963), p 43.

[12]Shroyer, George F., "How's Your Liability Insurance?" *School Management* (September, 1963), pp. 91-96.

This could result in a change of attitude in regard to, "Who is suing whom?" It could result in the district being sued rather than the coach if for no other reason but financial. The district would have the money and in most cases the coach would not.

Feld[13] stresses the fact that:

The school district may be guilty of negligence if one of its teachers performs an act which in the opinion of the court an ordinarily careful prudent teacher under the same circumstances would not perform. The teacher can also be negligent if he or she fails to act where an ordinarily careful and prudent teacher would have taken action.

LIABILITY STATUS OF STATES

Liability laws like other laws differ from state to state. The coach should be aware of his state's laws and know how they will affect him in case of injury to a player which results in a law suit. There is increasing evidence that the school district will not be responsible for negligence on the part of its employees. This is not fair in many respects, but never-the-less it is true, and the smart coach will protect himself in cases where the state is immune from liability and as a result the blame may be shifted upon him.

Grieve[14] makes the following comment which reflects the attitude of the various states:

In any discussion of the legal aspects of athletic activities, it must be realized that there are variations in the statutes of the various states regarding the immunity of school districts. It is not the purpose of this article to discuss the various legal viewpoints which exist throughout the fifty states, but it would be wise to mention the present trend toward the elimination of immunity for school districts in the area of negligence. Over the past few years, the tendency has been to hold the school district responsible for providing a safe environment for school functions. Each year legislative action in various states has indicated that school districts should be held liable for negligent acts, and athletics, due to the nature of the activities, has become a prime target for such legal action.

Bird[15] has categorized the states regarding their liability status:

Group I. In fifteen states, the laws have been repealed which gave the states immunity. The school districts in these states are most likely to be sued while the individual is least likely to be sued. These states are Arizona, California, Connecticut, Hawaii, Illinois, Iowa, Massachusetts, Minnesota, Nevada, New Jersey, New York, Oregon, Utah, Washington, and Wisconsin.

Group II. There are some states, according to the courts that are immune from liability if they do not purchase insurance and the states that do purchase insurance are liable only up to the amount of the insurance. Those states are Arkansas, Idaho, Indiana, Montana, New Mexico, North Carolina, North Dakota, Vermont, and Wyoming.

Group III. The individual is most likely to be sued directly rather than the school district in the remaining states. In other words, these states are afforded the most protection against being sued for negligence.

Liebee[16] has stated the following in regard to the doctrine that the state can do no wrong,

The courts and legislatures in some states have (a) abolished the immunity of school districts; (b) enacted legislation that permits districts to purchase liabil-

---

[13]Feld, Lipman, "Who's Responsible for What?" *School Management* (March, 1972), p. 29.

[14]Grieve, Andrew, "Legal Considerations on Equipment and Facilities," *The Athletic Journal* (February, 1967), p 38.

[15]Bird, Patrick, "The Coach and the Courts."

[16]Liebee, Howard C., *Tort Liability for Injury to Pupils* (Ann Arbor, Campus Publishers, 1965), p. 1.

ity insurance protecting districts; (c) enacted legislation that permits districts to purchase liability insurance protecting employees of the districts during their employment; (d) enacted 'save harmless' statutes; and (e) legislated methods of recovery other than common 'tort law.'

Voltmer and Esslinger[17] make the following observation regarding the states' liability:

> The prevailing principle of law in the United States is that a school board is not liable for injuries suffered by students or others during their attendance in school unless there is a statute imposing such liability. New York and California have such statutes. Thus, in these two states, school boards can be sued when injuries result from the negligence of school personnel. School boards are exempt from such lawsuits in the remainder of the states. In these states, public institutions are considered as performing a governmental function. In the exercise of a governmental function, a municipality is generally held to be exempt from liability suits for the negligence of its servants. This freedom from suit stems from the legal doctrine that the king (and now the state) can do no wrong. It is obvious that if school boards could be readily sued for damages because of negligence of school personnel that the entire educational program could be halted or disrupted if heavy damages were awarded a plaintiff.
>
> Private schools and colleges do not share the immunity which public educational institutions have. They are liable for the acts of their employees committed within the scope of their employment, and if a negligent act results in an injury to the person or property of another, the school can be held.

Rice[18] makes the following comment regarding the states' liability:

> Since legal liability is a matter which

must eventually be decided by the courts, it is both impractical and impossible to formulate 'rules' by which to guide one's actions. There are, however, a few well-established principles of common law which are significant.

It has been rather well-established by the courts that a school district, or a school board, in the absence of a specific statute, is not subject to liability for injuries sustained by pupils during their attendance at school. Historically, this principle has its roots in the theory that education is a function and that the municipality (school district) acts as an agent of the state. As agent, there is delegated to it, or imposed upon it, powers and duties to be performed exclusively for the people. A municipality is generally held exempt from liability in failure to exercise these powers or for exercising them in a negligent manner. Such immunity is based upon the philosophy that the state is sovereign, and being sovereign, cannot be sued without its consent. It is further held that a designated agency of the sovereign, the municipality likewise immune.

PROTECTION AGAINST SUIT

The legal aspects in case of injuries in athletics is becoming a very definite factor in coaching and to those individuals connected with interscholastic athletics. "I'll sue him!" How often have you heard this expression in the past few years? It is becoming increasingly popular to sue. Consequently, the coach needs to protect himself. He can do this by (1) realizing and admitting that there are many things that he does daily which would perhaps place him in a position where he could be sued; (2) educating himself as to what these possibilities are and try to avoid them; (3) knowing his legal rights; and (4) protecting himself against being sued by carrying liability insurance.

Most coaches are too involved in winning and too interested in the young players they are coaching to even think that they

[17]Voltmer, Edward, and Esslinger, Arthur, *The Organization and Administration of Physical Education* (New York, Appleton-Century Crofts, Inc., 1967), p. 484.

[18]Rice, Sidney, "A Suit for the Teacher"

could be involved in a law suit for negligence. They cannot imagine themselves being negligent. How could anyone think that of them when they are putting everything into their job and making an all-out effort to win? How could anyone think that they could ever do anything that would jeopardize the health and well-being of their players? Why, that would be heresy of the worst kind. But it can happen, it has happened, and it will happen again. Therefore, the coach must prepare for this eventuality. He does this by understanding all there is to know about legal liability and how it applies to him.

High School Athletic Insurance As a Means of Protection

There are certain situations where the school may wish to provide, either at school expense or student expense, coverage for athletic activities. The available coverage will vary depending on what the school or student wants as protection. There are a few states that have their own insurance plan for athletics. There are various private insurance companies that offer a limited number of policies. Usually it is normal for a company in the student insurance business to offer to the school a plan of coverage which would include a school-time policy, a twenty-four-hour policy, and a high school interscholastic football policy, each with identical benefits with the possible exception of a lesser medical maximum in the football policy. The school-time policy provides coverage to the student while traveling to and from school, while attending school, and while participating in school activities, except those activities specifically excluded.

Within the high school athletic insurance area, actually a very limited number of policies do cover this particular type of risk since the basic student policies available to school systems cover most athletic activities as well as academic and social activities of the school.

The one area commonly excluded from the student policies is high school interscholastic football. There is, therefore, a great number of policies offered to cover this situation. Other sporting activities are, on occasion, excluded and these would include soccer, wrestling, ice hockey, etc. However, this type of broader exclusion of interscholastic sports under a student policy would be classified as the unusual situation as opposed to the normal.

The basic forms of student insurance coverage offered to school systems cover most sports, such as baseball, basketball, etc. The one sport that is normally not covered is football although it is often extended to other contact sports. To complement the student policies, a football policy is offered, normally with benefits identical or very similar to the student plans. Separate sports policies are available.

Although the idea of providing coverage for injuries in the interscholastic athletic program is excellent, there are some drawbacks. Scott[19] has suggested that:

(1) the benefits generally do not cover the cost of caring for the injury;

(2) the premiums are frequently paid by the parents, who are not always able to afford the expense or who are not in sympathy with the program;

(3) the benefits do not cover all activities or hazards encountered in the broad program of physical education;

(4) the program does not provide for all students;

(5) insurance plans sometimes are limited to member schools of the state high school athletic association and, in other cases to members of the athletic teams only.

---

[19]Scott, Harry, "Competitive Sports in Schools and Colleges" (New York, Harper and Brothers, 1951), p. 331.

SCHEDULE

Policy Number: S92ECS

Policy Date:

Expiration Date:

Term Premium:

Name of School:

Mutual of Omaha

Dodge at 33rd Street
Omaha, Nebraska 68131

MUTUAL OF OMAHA INSURANCE COMPANY

(Herein called the Company)

THIS IS A LIMITED POLICY READ IT CAREFULLY

Hereby insures persons (herein individually called the Insured) for whom the required premium has been paid in advance to the Company or its authorized representative and agrees to pay the benefits described in this policy, subject to its provisions, for injuries received while the Insured is:

(1) participating in scheduled parctices or games of interscholastic football while under the supervision of an authorized representative of the school;
(2) traveling directly to and from such scheduled practices or games in an authorized vehicle furnished by the school.

PART A. DEFINITIONS

"Injuries" means accidental bodily injuries received by the Insured while this policy is in force as to the Insured, which result, independently of sickness and all other causes, in (a) loss of life, limb or sight and/or (b) expense incurred for hospital and professional services specified in this policy.

"Hospital" means a place licensed as a hospital (if licensing is required by law), which is operated for the care and treatment of resident inpatients and which has a graduate nurse always on duty, and a laboratory and an operating room (both on the premises) where major surgical operations are performed by persons legally qualified to do so. In no event, however, will the term "hospital" mean a hospital or an institution or part of such hospital or institution which is licensed as or used principally as a clinic, convalescent home, rest home, nursing home or home for the aged, or treatment center for drug addicts or alcoholics.

"School" means the school named in the Schedule; however, if more than one school is covered by this policy, the term "school" shall mean the individual school where the Insured is enrolled.

"Authorized Vehicle Furnished by the School" means a school bus, a bus chartered by the school, or a private automobile arranged for in advance by the school for the transportation of a group of pupils, which is supervised and attended by the person designated by school authorities.

PART B. BENEFITS FOR HOSPITAL AND PROFESSIONAL SERVICE

When injuries result in treatment by a legally qualified physician beginning within thirty days after the date of the accident, the Company will pay the expense incurred up to the usual, reasonable charges normally made within the geographic area where treatment is performed for necessary Services and Supplies listed below, but not to exceed the specified limits for each accident nor $5,000.00, in the aggregate, for each accident.

Services and Supplies

1. Treatment by a physician (other than X-ray – see Part B 3 for X-ray):
   (a) For treatment of a fracture or dislocation or for performing suturing or a cutting operation. (Subluxation or internal derangement shall not be deemed a dislocation.)
   (b) For treatment of other injuries (when no fracture, dislocation, suturing or cutting operation is involved) – up to $6.00 for the first treatment and $5.00 for each subsequent treatment, including physical therapy, but not to exceed ten treatments.

Form S92ECS – Series 3538S

NONRENEWABLE FOOTBALL INJURY POLICY

   (b) For treatment of other injuries (when no fracture, dislocation, suturing or cutting operation is involved) – up to $5.00 for each treatment, including physical therapy, but not to exceed ten treatments.
2. Dental treatment – up to $50.00 for treatment and/or replacement of each sound, natural tooth.
3. X-ray (other than dental) – up to one of the appropriate amounts (the most expensive) in the following schedule:
   (a) Skull $20.00
   (b) Sternum, jaw, spine, pelvis or ribs 15.00
   (c) Shoulder, elbow, arm, scapula, clavicle, leg, hip, knee, ankle or wrist 10.00
   (d) Hand, foot, nose, fluoroscope or any other X-ray not listed 7.50
4. Hospital services:
   (a) Hospital room and board – up to the usual daily charge.
   (b) Hospital furnished medical services or supplies (X-ray only as specified in item B 3).

   Payment for hospital expense incurred while the Insured is a resident bed patient shall be made only for such expense which is not compensable under any other insurance policy or service contract.
5. Professional ambulance service – up to $25.00.
6. Orthopedic appliances – up to $25.00.
7. The services of a private duty nurse (R.N. or L.P.N.) or a physiotherapist during hospital confinement as a resident bed patient.

Benefits are payable under this Part B only for service or treatment performed and supplies furnished within the fifty-two-week period immediately following the date of the accident.

PART C. SPECIFIC LOSS ACCIDENT BENEFITS

When injuries result in any of the following specific losses within one hundred eighty days from the date of the accident, the Company will pay for loss of:

Life	$2,000.00	One Hand or One Arm	$2,500.00
Both Hands or Both Arms	7,500.00	One Foot or One Leg	2,500.00
Both Feet or Both Legs	7,500.00	Either Eye	1,000.00
Both Eyes	7,500.00		

Loss in every case referred to above of hand or hands, or foot or feet, shall mean severance at or above the wrist joint or ankle joint, respectively; and loss of arm or arms, or leg or legs, shall mean severance at or above the elbow joint or knee joint, respectively; the loss of eye or eyes shall mean the total and irrecoverable loss of the entire sight thereof. Only one of the amounts (the largest applicable thereto) named in this Part C will be paid for injuries resulting from one accident, and shall be in addition to any other benefits for such accident.

PART D. EXCEPTIONS AND LIMITATIONS

Benefits are not payable for: (a) the cost of eyeglasses, contact lenses or examinations for either, (b) the cost of drugstore prescriptions, (c) injuries caused by an act of declared or undeclared war, (d) treatment or repair of hernia, (e) the services of any person employed or retained by the school and (f) injuries for which any benefits are payable under workmen's compensation or employer's liability laws.

PART E. POLICY PROVISIONS

1. **Entire Contract; Changes**: This policy, including the endorsements and the attached papers, if any, constitutes the entire contract of insurance. No change in this policy shall be valid unless approved by an executive officer of the Company and evidenced by an endorsement on the policy or by amendment to the policy signed by an authorized representative of the school and the Company. No agent has authority to change this policy or to waive any of its provisions.

2. **Time Limit on Certain Defenses**: The application of the school is not a part of this policy and no statement of the school shall be used to void the policy or to deny a claim for loss incurred.

3. **Notice of Claim**: Written notice of claim must be given to the Company within twenty days after the occurrence or commencement of any loss covered by the policy, or as soon thereafter as reasonably possible. Notice given by or on behalf of the Insured or the beneficiary to the Company at Omaha, Nebraska, or to any authorized agent of the Company, with information sufficient to identify the Insured, shall be deemed notice to the Company.

4. **Claim Forms**: The Company, upon receipt of a notice of claim, will furnish to the claimant such forms as are usually furnished by it for filing proofs of loss. If such forms are not furnished within fifteen days after the giving of such notice, the claimant shall be deemed to have complied with the requirements of this policy as to proof of loss upon submitting, within the time fixed in the policy for filing proofs of loss, written proof covering the occurrence, the character and the extent of the loss for which claim is made.

5. **Proofs of Loss**: Written proof of loss must be furnished to the Company at its said office within ninety days after the date of the loss for which claim is made. Failure to furnish such proof within the time required shall not invalidate nor reduce any claim if it was not reasonably possible to give proof within such time, provided such proof is furnished as soon as reasonably possible and in no event, except in the absence of legal capacity, later than one year from the time proof is otherwise required.

6. **Time of Payment of Claims**: All indemnities payable under this policy will be paid immediately upon receipt of due written proof of loss.

7. **Payment of Claims**: Indemnity for loss of life and any other accrued indemnities unpaid at the Insured's death will be payable to the estate of the Insured; however, if the Insured is a minor, such indemnity will be payable to the natural parents or guardian of the Insured.

All other indemnities will be payable to the Insured; however, if the Insured is a minor, the Company will pay such indemnity to his parents, guardian or other person who is actually supporting him. Any payment made by the Company in good faith pursuant to this provision shall fully discharge the Company to the extent of such payment.

8. **Physical Examinations and Autopsy**: The Company at its own expense shall have the right and opportunity to examine the person of anyone covered under this policy when and as often as it may reasonably require during the pendency of a claim hereunder and to make an autopsy in case of death where it is not forbidden by law.

9. **Legal Actions**: No action at law or in equity shall be brought to recover on this policy prior to the expiration of sixty days after written proof of loss has been furnished in accordance with the requirements of this policy. No such action shall be brought after the expiration of three years after the time written proof of loss is required to be furnished.

10. **Change of Beneficiary; Assignment**: The right to change of beneficiary is reserved to the Insured and the consent of the beneficiary or beneficiaries shall not be requisite to surrender or assignment of this policy or to any change of beneficiary or beneficiaries, or to any other changes in this policy.

11. **Conformity with State Statutes**: If any time limitation of this policy with respect to the bringing of an action at law or in equity is less than that permitted by the law of the state in which the Insured resides at the time this policy is issued, such limitation is hereby extended to agree with the minimum period permitted by such law.

PART F. ADDITIONAL PROVISIONS

1. **Persons Eligible**: Persons eligible for insurance under this policy shall include all persons who are actively participating in the football program of the school.

2. **New Insureds**: New athletes will be insured for injuries received after names and the required premium have been submitted to the Company or its authorized representative.

3. **Term of Coverage**: The term of this policy begins on the Policy Date at 12:01 a.m., Standard Time of the place of the school, and ends at 12:01 a.m., the same Standard Time, on the Expiration Date.

4. **Consideration**: This policy is issued in consideration of the payment in advance of the Term Premium for the term ending on the Expiration Date.

5. **Notice of Annual Meeting**: The Annual Meeting of the Company will be held at 10 a.m. on the second Saturday after the first day of February at the Home Office of the Company.

IN WITNESS WHEREOF, MUTUAL OF OMAHA INSURANCE COMPANY has caused this policy to be signed by its President and Secretary.

T. J. Skutt — Secretary

J. D. Minton — President

Countersigned by:

____
Licensed Resident Agent

Figure 13. Reprinted with permission from Mutual Insurance of Omaha.

The advantages of an insurance plan, however, far outweigh the disadvantages and it is almost paramount that some kind of plan be used. Scott[20] lists some of these advantages:

(1) it assists families in meeting the financial crisis brought on by an injury;
(2) it provides for immediate diagnostic and medical attention thus preventing complications;
(3) it produces a safety consciousness among the students and faculty, thus tending to reduce the incidence of accidents and the severity of injuries;
(4) it aids the educational institution in discharging what it may regard as a moral responsibility with respect to accidents incurred in school-sponsored activities;

[20]*Ibid.*, p. 332.

SCHEDULE

Mutual of Omaha.
FARNAM AT 33rd STREET
OMAHA, NEBRASKA 68131

Policy Number: 510S
Policy Date:
Expiration Date:
Sport:
Term Premium:
Maximum Benefit:
Deductible Amount:
Policyholder:

MUTUAL OF OMAHA INSURANCE COMPANY
(Herein called the Company)

Hereby insures the persons of the Policyholder (herein individually called the Insured) and agrees to pay the benefits described in this policy, subject to its provisions, for injuries received while the Insured is:

1. Participating in scheduled practices or games of a sport named in the Schedule of this policy while under the supervision of an authorized representative of the Policyholder.
2. Traveling directly to or from such scheduled practices or games as a member of a group attended and supervised by an authorized representative of the Policyholder.

PART A.   DEFINITIONS

"Persons of the Policyholder" means persons for whom the required premium has been paid in advance to the Company or its authorized representative.

"Injuries" means accidental bodily injuries received by the Insured while this policy is in force as to the Insured and which result, independently of sickness and all other causes, in: (a) loss of life, limb or sight or (b) expense incurred for hospital and professional services specified in this policy.

"Hospital" means a place, other than a convalescent, nursing or rest home, having accommodations for resident bed patients, a laboratory, a registered nurse always on duty, and operating room where surgical operations are performed by a legally qualified physician or physicians.

PART B.   BENEFITS FOR HOSPITAL AND PROFESSIONAL SERVICE

When injuries result in treatment by a legally qualified physician or surgeon beginning within thirty days after the accident date, the Company will pay the expense incurred in excess of the Deductible Amount, if any, but not to exceed the usual and customary charges for necessary: (a) treatment by a legally qualified physician or surgeon, (b) treatment of injuries to sound, natural teeth, (c) professional ambulance service, (d) X-rays, (e) orthopedic appliances, (f) hospital care or service and (g) services of a registered graduate nurse (R.N.) during a period of hospital confinement as a resident bed patient, but such payment shall not exceed the Maximum Benefit for each accident and is subject to the following conditions and limitations:

(1) Benefits for dental care, including X-ray, shall not exceed $100.00 for each accident;
(2) Benefits for professional ambulance service shall not exceed $25.00 for each accident;
(3) Benefits for orthopedic appliances shall not exceed $20.00 for each accident;
(4) Benefits under this Part are provided only for care, service or treatment performed and appliances furnished within the first two week period immediately following the accident date.

PART C.   SPECIFIC LOSS ACCIDENT BENEFITS

When injuries result in any of the following losses within one hundred eighty days from the date of the accident, the Company will pay for loss of:

Life $1,000.00	One hand or one arm $500.00
Both hands or both arms 1,000.00	One foot or one leg 500.00
Both feet or both legs 1,000.00	Either eye 500.00
Both eyes 1,000.00	

Loss in every case referred to above of hand or hands, or foot or feet, shall mean severance at or above the wrist joint or ankle joint, respectively; and loss of arm or arms, or leg or legs, shall mean severance at or above the elbow joint or knee joint, respectively; the loss of eye or eyes shall mean the total and irrecoverable loss of the entire sight thereof. Only one of the amounts (the largest applicable thereto) named in this Part C will be paid for injuries resulting from one accident, and is in addition to any other benefits for such accident.

PART D.   EXCEPTIONS AND LIMITATIONS

This policy does not cover: (a) the cost of eyeglasses (including contact lenses) or examinations therefor, (b) drugstore prescriptions, (c) injuries caused by war or any act of war (declared or undeclared), (d) hernia, (e) medical treatment by any person employed or retained by the Policyholder, (f) diathermy, light or short-wave treatment, ultrasonic therapy, hydromassage, or any other form of physical therapy, (g) injuries for which any benefits are payable under workmen's compensation or employer's liability laws.

Form 510S - Series 2446S   BLANKET ATHLETIC INJURY POLICY

Figure 14. Reprinted with permission from Mutual Insurance of Omaha.

(5) it provides for the annual health examination of many students; and
(6) it encourages participation in all phases of the sports program.

Ashton[21] has this to say about insurance:

Several high school athletic associations have developed group accident insurance plans. In plans such as these, parents are given the opportunity to carry such insurance under reasonable premiums. Probably the best known of these plans is that of Wisconsin, with its option of group or individual plan. In some of these insurance plans, all phases

---

[21]Ashton, Dudley, *Administration of Physical Education for Women* (New York, The Ronald Press, 1968), p. 118.

Mutual of Omaha.
The Company that pays
Mutual of Omaha Insurance Company
Home Office: Omaha, Nebraska

When treatment is completed or whichever period is less, mail this completed form (both sides) with bills to:

POLICY NO.

WILLIAM C. HAYES, General Agent
457 ROCKFORD TRUST BLDG.
P.O. BOX 419
ROCKFORD, ILL. 61105

STUDENT ACCIDENT REPORT
TO BE COMPLETED ON ALL APPLICATIONS FOR BENEFITS
(ALL QUESTIONS MUST BE ANSWERED)

Name of student _____ Age _____ Grade _____ Homeroom _____
Address _____
Name of parent or guardian _____ Address _____
Name of school _____ Address _____
Name of school system or district _____
Date of injury _____, 19___ Hour _____ a.m. _____ p.m.
Date accident reported to school officials _____, 19___ Hour _____ a.m. _____ p.m.
Nature of injury _____
Student injured was at a school sponsored activity as a: Participant ☐ Spectator ☐
If student was engaged in a sports event, was it: Intramural athletics ☐ Interschool athletics ☐
Please furnish name of school authority supervising activity of injured student at time of accident:
Name _____ Title _____
On date of accident, state time student was scheduled to report to school _____ Hour _____ a.m. _____ p.m.
On date of accident, state time student was scheduled to be dismissed from school Hour _____ a.m. _____ p.m.
What specific activity was involved? _____
Was the activity sponsored and supervised by the Insured's school? Yes ☐ No ☐
Type of school applicant attends: Elementary ☐ Junior high ☐ High ☐ Other _____

DESCRIBE FULLY HOW AND WHERE THE ACCIDENT TOOK PLACE
Where did the accident happen? _____
How did the accident happen? _____
Is applicant covered by workmen's compensation or employer's liability? Yes ☐ No ☐
Date of this report _____ Signature of school official _____

COACH MUST COMPLETE FOR INTERSCHOLASTIC ATHLETIC INJURIES IF COVERED BY POLICY
Name of sport _____ Senior high team ☐ Junior high team ☐
I hereby certify that the applicant is insured for the sport in which he was injured and that the injury occurred as follows:

Dated _____, 19___
Signature of coach

REVERSE SIDE MUST BE COMPLETED ON ALL APPLICATIONS FOR BENEFITS

Figure 15. Reprinted with permission from Mutual Insurance of Omaha.

of competition sports plus the regular physical education program are covered. In other plans, varsity athletics only, or specifics such as football only, constitute the coverage. Administrators and coaches must be alert to the implications in the various types of insurance coverage and should offer information to the general public regarding the possibilities for such coverage as far as local rulings make this action possible. If the insurance program is subscribed to through local auspices, applications, premium collection, and accident claims must be processed and machinery set in motion to care for the details.

Glossary of Terms on School Liability

In order to better understand the legal terms involved, it is necessary to be familiar with the most common words and phrases

UNITED INSURANCE COMPANY OF AMERICA
SCHOOL ACCIDENT REPORT

When completed, send this form and attached bills to:
american youth
P.O. Box 122
River Forest, Illinois 60305

IMPORTANT—This form should be completed in full within 30 days after the accident and mailed promptly with all itemized bills to the office indicated at the right. If additional expense is incurred, the bills may be forwarded at a later date as they are received.

PLEASE COMPLETE THIS FORM FULLY TO AVOID ANY DELAY IN PROCESSING THIS CLAIM

PART I — Verification by School Official

Name of School | Policy Number
Address of School (Street) | (City and State) | (Zip)
Name of School System or District (if different)
Name of Insured Last | First | Initial | Grade | Age
Insured's name appears on Page No. | Line No. | of School Insurance Listing Sheet

ACCIDENT
Date of Accident 19 | Time of Accident ☐ A.M. ☐ P.M.
Time School Started on Day of Accident | Time Dismissed
Description of Accident: How and Where did it occur?
Description of Activity (If Athletics, Name Sport and state if Interscholastic, Intramural or Other)

INJURY
Describe Injury

DiJ accident happen while under the attended supervision of a teacher or other school official? ☐ Yes ☐ No
If yes, list name and title of supervisor

This is to certify that the above information is correct to the best of my knowledge, that the above Claimant is insured by the policy, and that the insurance was in effect on the date on which the accident occurred.

Signed ____________ Title ____________ Date ____________

PART II — To be completed by Parent or Guardian (then forward to Doctor for completion)

Name of Parent or Guardian (provider — head of household)
Address (Street)
(City and State) | (Zip)
Employed by (Name of Company) | (Occupation)
Address (Street) | (City) | (State)
Date of Birth of INSURED STUDENT | (Mo. | Day | Yr.)

AUTHORIZATION DATED ____________, 19____. I hereby authorize any hospital, physician, or other person who has attended or examined me or my dependent, to disclose when requested to do so by the UNITED INSURANCE COMPANY OF AMERICA, or by its representative, any and all information with respect to any illness or injury, medical history, consultation, prescription or treatment, and copies of all hospital or medical records. A photostatic copy of this authorization shall be considered as effective and valid as the original.

Approved by: ____________ Physician   Signed ____________ Parent or Guardian

SG 7-1 Rev 71

Figure 16. Reprinted with permission from the American Youth, River Forest, Illinois.

pertaining to liability.

Assumption of risk is a term designating a person's voluntary involvement in a hazardous situation, with full knowledge of the dangers attendant upon his action.

Attractive nuisance is any unguarded, dangerous contrivance, apparatus, building, or condition of land which a child may be expected to use or with which he is likely to play.

Comparative negligence is a more recent and amiable concept relating to contributory negligence. In the application of this principle, the courts have the prerogative of assigning a percentage of fault to both the defendant and the plaintiff and apportioning the damages accordingly.

Contributory negligence is a charge brought against a plaintiff who has failed to exercise ordinary care to prevent an injury that he subsequently sustains through the actionable negligence of another.

Damages is a term designating the compensation, recompence, or satisfaction, awarded by a court to a person injured through another's wrongful act.

Forseeability is a term applied when a reasonably prudent person could have foreseen the harmful consequences of his act, the actor, in disregarding the foreseeable consequences, is liable for negligent conduct. This is the general rule. Applying it to the teacher-pupil relationship, we may say that if a reasonably prudent teacher could have foreseen that a pupil might be injured by some act of his own or another's, the teacher is liable if he disregards these foreseeable consequences.

In loco parentis is a phrase describing one who acts in place of a parent and assumes a guardian's responsibility for a child.

Last clear chance is a term designating a final opportunity to prevent injury to another, who through his own negligence has placed himself in a dangerous situation.

Liability is a legal responsibility, an obligation that is enforceable by court action.

Malfeasance is a term usually applied to the misconduct of an official to indicate the performance of an illegal act.

Masfeasance is the improper performance of a lawful act.

Negligence is the failure to act as a reasonably prudent person would act under the specific circumstances involved.

Nonfeasance is the failure to perform a legal duty.

Plaintiff is the person who initiates legal action against another; the person who is suing for damages.

Propriatory function, as applied to a school, is an activity conducted for financial profit, such as a football game that is open to the public. In contrast, a governmental function, like public education, is intended for the benefit of all and is not conducted for monetary gain, even though a fee may sometimes be charged to cover expenses.

Proximate cause is that which directly produces a specific result without intervention from any independent cause in the natural sequence of events.

Quasi-public corporations are municipal bodies granted certain limited powers by the state.

Res ipae loquitur is a term designating a self-evident situation, one that speaks for itself. It is applied when the defendant's negligence is presumed upon proof that the instrumentality causing the injury was in the defendant's exclusive control and that the accident is one which ordinarily would not happen in the absence of negligence.

Respondent superior is a phrase denoting the tenant that an employer is legally responsible for the acts of his agent.

Self-place statutes are laws requiring the proper construction and maintenance of buildings.

Save harmless statute is a law requiring the school district to recompence a teacher who is held liable for injuries resulting from negligence.

Stare decisis is a term meaning to stand by settled matters, to follow the precedent established in previous cases.

Tort is held to be a civil wrong, other than one arising out of a breach of contract, for which wrong the court will provide a remedy in the form of an action for damages. Legal test of a tortious act include the following:

1. The existence of a legal duty of one person to another,
2. a breach of that contract,
3. a causal link between the breach and

the distress of the injured party.

As a matter of law, the courts will ask the following three questions whenever a person alleges that a tort has been committed against him.

1. Did the defendant owe the plaintiff a duty?
2. Was there a breach of duty owed?
3. Was the breach the proximate cause of the plaintiff's injury?

Vis Major is a term applied to an inevitable accident; an occurrence caused by a superior or irresistible force, such as lightning or a hurricane, that could not have been prevented by reasonable foresight, experience, care, or an act of God.

Some of the acts which can be considered as negligent according to Garrison[22] are as follows:

ACTION WHICH CAN BE DEEMED NEGLIGENT ACTION

1. It is not properly done; appropriate care is not employed by the actor.
2. The circumstances under which it is done creates risks, although it is done with care and precaution.
3. The actor is indulging in acts which involve an unreasonable risk of direct and immediate harm to others.
4. The actor sets in motion a force, the continuous operation of which may be unreasonably hazardous to others.
5. He created a situation which is unreasonably dangerous to others because of the likelihood of the action of the third person or of inanimate forces.
6. He entrusts dangerous devices or instruments to persons who are incompetent to use or care for such instruments properly.
7. He neglects a duty of control over third persons who, by reason of some incapacity or abnormality, he knows to be likely to inflict intended harm upon others.

[22]Garrison, Cecil, "Have You Acted Negligently Today?" *Athletic Journal* (December, 1958), p. 10.

8. He fails to employ due care to give adequate warning.
9. He fails to exercise the proper care in looking out for persons when he has reason to believe they may be in the danger area.
10. He fails to employ appropriate skill to perform acts undertaken.
11. He fails to employ appropriate skill to his preparation to avoid harm to others before entering upon certain conduct where such preparation is reasonably necessary.
12. He fails to inspect and repair instruments or mechanical devices used by others.
13. His conduct prevents a third person from assisting persons involved through no fault of his own.
14. His written or spoken word created negligent misrepresentation.

FACTORS NECESSARY FOR PROOF OF NEGLIGENCE

Resick, Seidel and Mason[23] reveal that anyone can sue anyone else for negligence. This would be a common practice if it was easier to prove negligence. The law states that a person is innocent until proven guilty. Fortunately, this holds true in the case of proving negligence. Most of the time it is very difficult to offer enough concrete evidence to prove negligence. Several factors must be present.

First, the defendant must have a duty toward the plaintiff. In essence, this means that a person is not obligated to help a stranger under any conditions even though the person's life may be in danger. It can be readily seen that this would not apply to the athletic coach because the players are under his supervision and direction. He is hired to do this job; therefore, he has an obligation and a duty to help the player as a prudent person would do.

Second, a tort or wrong has been committed against the plaintiff. This wrong could include his health, property, or character.

Third, the defendant must have failed to perform his duty by doing nothing at a time when the plaintiff needed help. The defendant may have walked away from the scene to avoid helping the plaintiff or stood by and did nothing. In either case, he is negligent.

Fourth, the defendant in his efforts to avoid trouble by not helping the plaintiff when help was needed may have created a situation or event which would cause another situation to take place. This event or situation would then result in a tort or wrong to a person. A chain of events could take place all or any of which would cause a tort or wrong and be the result of the first act of not helping the person.

BASIS OF LIABILITY SUITS

Coaches and athletic directors should be constantly alert for possible injury to any athlete under their supervision. There are some sports, however, that are more conducive to injury because of the very nature of the activity. The contact sports, of course, are good examples although other sports, such as swimming can provide circumstances where injury can easily occur. Tourney[24] has listed several of these categories of basis for suit with examples of each which apply specifically to swimming.

CATEGORIES OF BASIS FOR SUIT

1. Failure to provide safe facilities.
2. Failure to provide safe equipment.
3. Failure to provide safety equipment.
4. Failure to supervise.
5. Failure to post signs or warnings.

[23]Resick, Matthew, Seidel, Beverly, and Mason, James, *Modern Administrative Practices in Physical Education and Athletics* (Reading, Massachusetts, Addison-Wesley Publishing Co., 1970), p. 55.

[24]Tourney, John, and Clayton, Robert, *Aquatic Instruction* (Minneapolis, Burgess Publishing Co., 1970), p. 213.

6. Failure to comply with laws.
7. Failure to provide security.
8. Failure to perform duties.
9. Improper action.
10. Lack of action.
11. Failure to administer properly.

ELEMENTS IN A SUIT

There are several elements which must be in evidence for the successful maintenance of a suit which is based on negligence. Liebee[25] lists these as follows: " (1) Duty to conform to a standard of behavior which will not subject others to an unreasonable risk of injury; (2) Breach of that duty, failure to exercise due care; (3) A sufficiently close causal connection between the conduct or behavior and the resulting injury; and (4) Damage or injury resulting to the rights or interest of another."

Since coaches can no longer enjoy immunity in many states because they are employed by the school district, they must depend upon themselves and perform their duties in such a way that they will not be taken to court in suits for damages. However, even though they may exercise great precaution and make every effort possible to avoid acts which could eventually be construed as negligence on their part, there are times when this may be impossible. Therefore, in spite of the fact that he acts as a reasonable and prudent person, the coach may be sued. There are times when certain conditions exist which result in some negligence. Even though this may be true, he still may avoid liability through certain legal defenses.

Rice[26] states that:

Perhaps the best protection, since liability is a personal matter, can be attained through an insurance policy. Such coverage can be provided by most insurance companies on an individual basis or through group liability plans at a very nominal cost. It should be thoroughly understood, however, that such protection does not in any way decrease the responsibility of the teacher for the welfare of his students.

LEGAL DEFENSES WHICH MAY BE USED AGAINST NEGLIGENCE BY THE COACH

If the coach is sued for negligence, the law provides him with certain legal means by which he can be protected. These defenses are as follows:

Act of God: The circumstances and conditions surrounding the accident were beyond the control of the coach.

Assumption of Risk: The athlete is participating in the sport voluntarily and is not forced to do so. By doing so, he assumes a certain responsibility for an accident which might happen to him.

Contributory Negligence: The athlete could have avoided the injury if he himself had acted as a prudent person of his own age and in similar circumstances would have acted. The action could be either direct or indirect.

The Lack of Proximate Cause: The athlete is injured and the coach moves him. Later the athlete reinjures his back at home. The coach cannot be held responsible.

Players' Legal Rights

The possibility that a person may be injured at any time is accepted. However, every person has the right to expect that he will be protected from an injury caused by others. It is, therefore, important that the individuals entrusted with the coaching of interscholastic athletics be responsible people and will act as prudent persons at all times and in all situations. The law requires this to be done or the person will be held liable. It is necessary that the per-

---

[25]Liebee, Howard, *Tort Liability for Injury to Pupils*, p. 8.

[26]Rice, Sidney, "A Suit for the Teacher."

sons hiring athletic personnel select only those persons who are qualified and trained to assume the responsibility that goes along with the coaching of interscholastic athletics. The coaches should be trained to accept this responsibility.

It is important to remember, however, that many accidents are unavoidable, and many accidents happen through no fault of the coach but rather because of the very nature of the activity being engaged in. The school or coach cannot and should not be expected to insure the students' safety at all times. However, if the coach can forsee a possible harmful outcome while the athlete is under his supervision and does not act as a prudent person would act to prevent the accident from happening, he could be negligent in his duty. The proof of this negligence could be determined by the fact that he should have anticipated the consequences of certain actions, which would result in injury to the athlete.

Any example of this type of negligence could be in the use of faulty equipment which resulted in injury to the user. The coach should inspect the equipment at regular intervals and not permit the athlete to use the equipment if it is found to be defective. The coach must always be on the alert for situations which would result in injury to the players. This is part of his job and he had better do it well. He should instruct the players in the right way to perform all activities.

Waivers and Consent Slips

Many coaches are under the assumption that a statement from the parent giving his or her permission for his son or daughter to engage in athletics obsolves the coach of all responsibility in case of injury to the player. Nothing could be further from the truth. If the player is injured and the coach is negligent, he can be sued and dam-

ages can be collected. The consent slip only offers protection from the standpoint of showing that the player has the parents' permission to engage in an activity.

The waiver is an agreement whereby one party waives a particular right. When the parent signs such a paper, he waives the parents' right to sue in case of injury. The parent cannot waive the rights of the player to sue if he is under eighteen years of age.

Many schools require all players to obtain waivers and consent slips from their parents which, when signed by the parents, supposedly release the school from any injury claim if injury occurs.

These waivers will not hold up in court. Their value lies in the fact that the parent in most cases is unaware that he has any grounds for sueing as he believes that he has signed this right away by signing the waiver.

Most schools require the athletes to fill out a parents' permission form and have it signed by a parent or legal guardian. It should be the responsibility of the coach of each sport to be sure that each player participating has turned in a parents' permission form. Once these forms are collected by the coach, they are filed by the athletic director.

Bula[27] suggests that:

> Many coaches are operating in the belief that if they obtain the written consent of the parents or guardians to allow their sons or charges to compete in the sport which they are coaching that they are relieved of all responsibility toward the player. Nothing is further from the truth because the parent or guardian cannot legally sign away the rights of a minor when there is a possibility of the child being injured.

---

[27]Bula, Michael, "The Personal Liability of the Coach and Physical Education Teacher," *Athletic Journal* (June, 1965), p. 46.

TABLE XII
LAKE HIGH SCHOOL
Genoa, Illinois
ATHLETIC DEPARTMENT

Parent's Permission

I want my son, _____, to have the privilege of
participating in _____ during the 19____ to 19____ school year.
I will strive to help my son abide by the Lake Athletic Conduct Code. I understand that my
son is to participate in the school-time insurance program offered through the school, or I
must present to the school verification of insurance coverage.

Be it understood that the school is not legally responsible for the result of any injury received
by a student while participating in any athletic event.

_____
(Parent's Signature)

FOR ELIGIBILITY PURPOSES

Name _____

Name _____

      last   first given name

Birth Record: _____

      month   day   year   county   state

Physical Examination: _____

            month   day   year

Participation Record: 1   2   3   4   5   6   7   8   Semester Number
                          (Please circle one)

Number of Season: 1   2   3   4
                    (Please Circle)

Do you live in School District #108? _____

Did you pass all subjects last semester? _____

YOU MUST HAVE SCHOOL INSURANCE TO PARTICIPATE

Please check one (football — two must be checked)

_____Regular Insurance

_____Round-the-Clock Insurance

_____Football Insurance

TABLE XIII
LENA HIGH SCHOOL DISTRICT 122
ATHLETIC PARTICIPATION REQUEST FORM

Student's Name _____

I request permission to participate in the interscholastic sport of _____

_____

_____
Student's Signature

Age _____   Grade _____   Date of Birth _____

Birthplace _____

            City   County   State/Country

Height _____   Weight _____

My son has my permission to participate in the interscholastic sport of _____

_____

Parent's Signature

* * * * * * * * * * * * * * * * * * * *

MEDICAL ELIGIBILITY FORM

Student's Name _____

I have examined the applicant and find he is physically fit to participate in the interscholastic sports named on the top of this form (excluding those that have been crossed out). Should he wish to change sports during the year, he may _____, he may not _____ do so without examination.

Comments:

_____   _____

Date of Examination   Physician's Signature

TABLE XIV

PALO HIGH SCHOOL

Palo, Nebraska

ATHLETIC PARTICIPATION PERMIT

Athlete's Name _____

PARENTS' OR GUARDIANS' WAIVER FORM

To whom it may concern:

This is to certify that I give my permission for my son/daughter _____

(name)

to engage in athletics at Palo High School.

I will assume all responsibility for any injury that he or she may receive while participating during practice, during games or while traveling to and from practice or games.

I will also cooperate in every way possible to allow my son/daughter to attend practice sessions and games regularly and to encourage and motivate he or she to perform to the maximum of his or her capacity so that he or she may receive the maximum benefit from athletic participation.

Signature _____

Parent or Guardian

Date _____, 19_____

TABLE XV

JERSEY HIGH SCHOOL DISTRICT NO. 45

PARENT CONSENT (Athletics)

I hereby give consent for ....

(Full Name)

to have the privilege of participating in the Genoa High School Interscholastic Athletic Program during the school year of 19...., 19...., except as noted below.

To the best of my knowledge he has no physical condition that would cause him to be endangered by such participation.

It is understood that the School District assumes no financial responsibility for accident.

My son will be responsible for all equipment issued to him.

....

Signature   (Parent or Guardian)

Exceptions:

ATHLETIC INSURANCE WAIVER

We accept responsibility for ....
for any accident incurred or for any injury while participating
in competitive sports at Glenbard High School. This is the
waiver to allow our son to participate without taking out insurance through the school.

....
Parent's Signature

STUDENT
FORM NO. 079

Figure 17.

Liability Prone Areas in Athletics

Athletics, because of its very nature, results in injuries to the participants. As a
result situations are created whereby the
person supervising them can be the defendant in suits for negligent acts. Because of
this, it is advisable for the athletic director
and the athletic coach to be aware of these
possibilities and the areas where they most
frequently occur. It is impossible to pinpoint every area where an injury may occur or give an example of every situation
which could result in a negligent act.
There are, however, several areas which
could be thought of as danger areas or
areas which are most likely to create situations which could result in injury and a
resultant lawsuit against the coach for
negligence.

Selection and Use of Coaching Techniques

Every coach should be careful to use
only accepted procedures and proven techniques in his teaching. For example, in
teaching a player how to tackle in football,
he needs to know the exact technique that
is used by the experts as an acceptable
teaching method so that if an injury occurs, he can defend his position as being
one in which he was using an acceptable

TABLE XVI
FORM TO BE USED FOR PROTECTION AGAINST LIABILITY
WAIVER FORM

Date _____

We, _____ are the parents or guardian
of _____, and in consideration of the special
benefits of the athletic program being afforded at _____
High School, we hereby permit _____ to participate in
_____
and we hereby release the aforesaid high school and all coaches from any liability whatever to the undersigned which results from any injury which may be sustained by the said
_____, on account of his participation in
_____
or in transportation connected therein.

We further agree that if there is reason for any action which might be by the aforemen-
tioned player as a result of any injury received during his participation in the above mentioned activities or in the transportation to and from the contests, that we will be personally
responsible to the high school, the Board of Education, and any coaches, and will hold them
harmless against any judgment recovered in any such action against them or either of them.

Signed this _____ day of _____, 19_____

_____
Signature of Parent or Guardian

_____
Address

TABLE XVII
*TRAINING RULES AND CONSENT FOR PARTICIPATION
IN BORK HIGH SCHOOL ATHLETICS*

I hereby give consent for _____ to
have the privilege of participating in the Bork High School Interscholastic Athletic Program
during the school year 19_____ to 19_____. To the best of my knowledge, he has no physical
condition that could cause him to be endangered by such participation. It is understood that
the school district assumes no financial responsibility for accidents. My boy will be responsible
for all equipment issued to him. He also agrees to the following training rules approved by
the Board of Education.

Boys who are members of Bork Athletic Squads shall not use, or attempt to use, or aid
and abet anyone else to use tobacco, alcoholic beverages, or any form of narcotics other than
prescribed by a physician. Athletes who violate the above training rules will be excluded from
athletics for a minimum of six months from the date of violation, or for two sports seasons
following the one in which the violation occurred, whichever penalty may seem most appropriate to a specific case. For a second violation a boy may be excluded from athletics for approximately one year, or more specifically until the following year at the beginning of the
particular fall, winter, spring, or summer sports season in which the second violation occurred.

The summer vacation period is regarded as a conditioning period for all athletes. As
applied to the training rules, the summer period will be regarded as the equivalent of the
fall, winter, or spring sports seasons in assessing penalties for training violations.

Any athlete, who in the coach's opinion, demonstrates poor behavior not conducive to the
spirit of sportsmanship and good citizenship, shall be subject to disciplinary action, including
possible exclusion or suspension from athletics.

(Signed) _____   (Signed) _____
                    Parent   Athlete

TABLE XVIII
*CENTRAL HIGH SCHOOL
ATHLETIC PARTICIPATION PERMIT AND AGREEMENT*

Name _____ Grade_____ Phone_____
Address _____ Family Doctor _____
Date of Birth _____ Place of Birth _____
                                                                    City and Sate

Item 1: I hereby request permission to participate in the following sports:

_____

I certify that I have read the bulletin on rules and conduct required of athletes. I
promise that I will observe the rules and will conduct myself as a gentleman and
sportsman at all times.

_____
                    Athlete's Signature

Item 2: I approve of my son's request to participate in the sports named above. I have read
the rules and regulations also and approve of them. It will be my intention to cooperate in this program. I have also read and approve the statements covering my
responsibilities in the area of insurance coverage.

_____
                    Parent's Signature

TABLE XIX

LAKE HIGH SCHOOL

Genoa, Illinois 60172

Authorization to Engage in Extra-Curricular

Activities Without Securing Accident Insurance

The undersigned, being the parent or guardian of _____,
a student at Lake High School, does hereby request that said student be permitted to engage
in _____ extracurricular activity for the
school year of 19_____ to 19_____ without taking out the accident insurance which is normally required of students participating in such activity and does hereby certify as follows:

    1. That the undersigned understands that such accident insurance
        can be secured covering such student upon payment of premium.

    2. That said student is covered by the provisions of other insurance
        which provides benefits in case of accident and that such cover-
        age will be continued on said student during said school year.

DATED: _____, 19_____.

                                                         Parent (or Guardian)

TABLE XX

CENTRAL HIGH SCHOOL

SAMPLE BOYS ATHLETIC PROCEDURES

I. *General Information — The athlete should:*

    1. Have an annual physical examination verifying fitness for athletic competition.

    2. Have written permission of parents to compete.

    3. Attend practice regularly and on time.

    4. Schedule appointments for doctor and dentist, tutors, and others away from practice
        hours except in emergency.

    5. Be present in school all day on day of games.

    6. A boy may participate in only one sport at a time and may transfer from one sport
        to another during the season only with the consent of the coaches involved and the
        athletic director.

    7. When the team travels by bus, athletes must go with the team and are not permit-
        ted to use private cars for return trips except to leave with parents and with coaches
        permission.

    8. When enroute to and from a scheduled contest, athletes not attired in team uni-
        forms shall dress neatly. Grub attire is not permitted.

II. *Injuries and Insurance*

If a boy should be injured, a parent will be notified at once. Immediate care will be
provided and the boy will be taken to the team doctor or one will be brought to him
unless parents have requested otherwise. Notify athletic director. Medical treatment must
be given within thirty days.

Insurance for athletes is voluntary for each participant. The school system does not require insurance coverage for athletes. It should be the responsibility of each family to
determine if it wishes to purchase such insurance which the school makes available or
provide coverage through their home policy (check to see if football is excluded) or to
assume the liability without insurance.

The cost of the insurance for football will be $9.00. Other forms of athletics are included
in the regular school insurance. It is available at a cost of $5.00. In each case, the insur-
ance is $25.00 deductible. Students (male or female) of member high schools of the Illi-
nois High School Association are covered by a catastrophe accident insurance policy while
engaged in interscholastic activities while under the jurisdiction of IHSA and school

supervision. Up to $100,000.00 is payable (after satisfaction of $5,000.00 deductible). Coverage is afforded while engaged in participation, including practice, in interscholastic sports and activities under the jurisdiction of IHSA as well as supervised travel in school or school-furnished vehicles.

III. *Athletic Code*

In order to teach the ideals of good sportsmanship and respect for rules and authority; in order to establish leadership, team pride, teamwork, and team discipline; in order to eliminate disruptive influences in the locker room, on the training field, on the playing field, and on trips both on and off the school grounds; and in order to provide conditions which promote health and safety for the individual team unit and opponents, the following principles are established:

A. Grooming — It is recommended that all athletes follow these principles on grooming.

1. No beards, goatees, or moustaches.
2. Hair should be cut so the eyes, ears, and neck are unobstructed at all times. Sideburns should not extend beyond the bottom of the ear and should be neatly trimmed.

B. Citizenship

1. An athlete representing Wheaton Central High School must exemplify the highest standards of moral integrity and good citizenship both in and out of school. Any behavior that violates this principle is unacceptable.

C. Training Rules

1. The consuming of alcoholic beverages of any kind during the entire year (12 months) is prohibited.
2. The use of tobacco or marijuana in any form during the entire year (12 months) is prohibited.
3. The illegal use of drugs in any form during the entire year (12 months) is prohibited.
4. Reasonable hours may be determined by the coach and Athletic Director.

All violators will be dismissed from the sport activity plus *six weeks into the next sport season.* A second offense will mean one year dismissal.

---

procedure well within the capabilities of the player.

Use of Poor Equipment

The coach can be held liable if a player is injured because of poor equipment even though he is not aware that the equipment is not in acceptable condition. He should, therefore, make a systemized check on all equipment especially in the contact sports, such as football. All equipment found to be dangerous in any way should be reported in writing to the proper authorities and the use of such equipment should be discontinued immediately.

Supervision

This area alone has been the source of many liability lawsuits against coaches. Parents expect their children to be properly supervised at all times especially in areas and activities where injury potential is great as is true in athletics. Any violation of conduct in this area will bring on possible suits. The first rule of thumb, as it applies to supervision, is that no coach should ever leave the playing area whether it be indoors or outdoors under any condition. If he is alone, he should make arrangements ahead of time to care for any injury that may occur that will necessitate removing the player from the area. He should be observant at all times and be constantly aware of his responsibilities as a supervisor.

Playing and Practicing Conditions

Every coach should be continually aware of and constantly alert to the dangers which exist on the practice field and playing court which could cause injury to the participants. These dangers can take varied forms and can include everything from "chuck holes" on the practice field to protrusions on the basketball court. The coach should assume the responsibility to correct and remove any and all obstacles that could cause injury to the players. He should report these conditions in writing to his immediate superiors and keep a copy of this report in his own file for his own protection in case of a liability suit.

Playing Areas

Usually the coach has little to say regarding where the team practices or even plays the game. He accepts what is there and makes the best of what he has. There are instances, however, even though the playing area is "fraught with danger," whereby he might improve or alleviate a dangerous situation which might result in an injury to a player. It is his responsibility to remove these dangers if at all possible because he can, even in situations such as those described above, be held liable in case of injury. An example would be having two games played simultaneously on a small area with the playing areas overlapping.

Classification of Players

Unequal competition has long been a problem in athletics and probably has been the cause of numerous injuries, many of which have gone unnoticed and unchallenged. However, a coach is liable if it can be proven that he matched two players of extreme unequal ability against each other and one is injured as a result. He can also be held liable if he requires or forces a player to perform beyond his capabilities. Liability for negligence may also result if the coach fails to realize the danger of injury when he permits players of apparent unequal ability to participate in the activity.

Leaving Equipment Unattended

All equipment should be put away after use whenever possible. This removes the temptation for a person, who happens to be passing by, to use the equipment and sustain a serious injury. If the equipment is unavailable for use, no one can be injured. The coach should not leave the equipment or facility unattended between practice sessions as this is an open invitation for someone to use it.

Use of Protective and Preventive Equipment

All coaches should insist that players use the protective equipment provided for their use. Failure to use this equipment often takes place during practice sessions but seldom during a game. Not having the equipment is bad enough, but having it and not using it is nondefensible.

Poor Organizational Procedures

The coach should select activities and organize practice procedures in such a way that there is little danger of injury to the players during the confusion of carrying out their assignments. This can happen when players run into each other when moving in opposite directions because of lack of space or poor organization in assigning duties.

Improper Treatment of Personal Information

All personal information regarding players which is accessible and available to the coach should be treated with utmost confidence.

Revealing any of this information without the express consent of the players themselves can constitute grounds for suit.

Transportation

Accidents involving transportation of athletes differ considerably from those in other areas of school activity. There is also a wide difference in the laws of each state regarding school transportation. However, states seem to have adopted a more liberal attitude in the past few years. The danger of the coach being sued for injuries resulting in transportation accidents has tempted Grieve to suggest that, students should travel only in bonded common carriers and if they do travel in private cars, the coach should abide by the liability laws of the state. Students should never be allowed to transport athletes in their own cars or drive anyone else's car to transport athletes.[28]

THE REASONABLE AND PRUDENT PERSON

Augustus Steinhilber,[29] Chairman of the School Law Unit of the United States Office of Education, has originated a list of

[28]Grieve, Andrew, "Legal Aspects of Transportation for Athletic Events," *Athletic Journal* (March, 1967) p. 64

[29]Steinhilber, Augustus, "A Reasonably Prudent and Careful Physical Educator," *Annual Safety Education Review* (1966), p 34.

reminders of appropriate actions for the coach in order to meet the legal definition of acting as a reasonably prudent and careful person.

1. Know the health of your player if he has to engage in highly strenuous activities.
2. Require a medical examination for player participation following a serious illness.
3. Inspect all equipment at regular intervals.
4. Do not expose players to possible injury by using defective equipment.
5. Conduct all practice and games in a safe area.
6. Foresee possible injury if practice or game is improperly conducted.
7. Analyze your coaching methods for the safety of your players.
8. Assign only qualified personnel to participate and supervise an activity.
9. Keep the activity within the ability level of the players.
10. Perform the proper act in the event of injury.
11. Do not diagnose or treat injuries.
12. Instruct the players before allowing them to perform the activity.
13. Keep an accurate record of all accidents and action taken.
14. Use school buses or public utility motor vehicles to transport members of athletic teams to and from contests.
15. Cooperate with the administration in making arrangements for adequate care of injured players in emergency situations.
16. Let the athletic trainer serve only in the area that he is qualified.
17. Fulfill your duty to supervise in situations in which the risk of harm is exceptionally high and in those situations in which it is reasonable to foresee that injury might occur if that supervision is not provided.

The number of participants in interscholastic athletics has increased tremendously over the past few years. This, of course, results in the opportunity to have many more injuries. It means that each coach will have more players under his supervision at a time when lawsuits have become very popular. The coach must then be more aware of his responsibility and liability for any injuries to players that might result from negligence on the part of the coach. Every coach has a responsibility to each of his players. He must protect himself because he must be aware of the liability laws. He must conduct his program in such a way that there will not be any occasion for legal action against him because of negligence on his part. To protect himself he should observe the following rules as set up by Steinhilber.[30]

CLASS SAFETY CODE FOR THE TEACHER
1. Have a proper teaching certificate.
2. Operate and teach at all times in the scope of your enjoyment.
3. Provide safeguards to minimize dangers.
4. Inspect equipment and facilities.
5. Notify proper authorities of dangerous equipment in use.
6. Provide sufficient instruction in the use of all equipment.
7. Be sure all activities are approved by the administration.
8. Do not force a pupil to perform an act which he feels he is unable to do.
9. Act properly and use discretion in giving first aid to an injured pupil.
10. Exercise due care in practicing your profession.

First Aid

It is the responsibility of every coach to be thoroughly familiar with standard first aid procedures for common injuries. The following practices should be readily adhered to:

1. In case of serious injury, do not move the victim.
2. Elevate the feet if this can be done without causing further injury.
3. Keep the victim warm.
4. Send a reliable person to get help. This help can consist of:
   a. Call parents to ascertain what they want done.
   b. If they cannot be reached or if they permit, call the fire department and request an ambulance.
   c. If the school nurse is not present, send for her.
   d. If the victim can be safely moved, he should be moved to the training room. Continue to follow proper precautions.
   e. If medical attention is necessary, seek the parents' help or advice.
   f. In cases of questionable need of medical attention, the athlete should be driven home and the parents informed of what has happened. If at all possible, a parent should pick up the athlete.
   g. Do not leave the player alone; do not expect others to care for him. It is the coach's responsibility.
   h. Under no circumstances should the coach give medical advice.

Gold and Gold[31] make the following comment in respect to rendering first aid to a student:

First aid should only be rendered by the instructor in an emergency in which there is a serious injury. In the absence of such emergency the physical educator should not attempt to act but should see that the pupil is brought to the attention of the school nurse or physician and that his parents are notified. When first aid is administered in an emergency situation, this is as far as the physical educator should go—he must not continue treatment of the injury. This is a rule which should be strictly followed by physical education instructors so as not to render themselves liable for any negligence involved in treating an injury. The physical educator should confine himself to first aid treatment—preserving

[30]*Ibid.,* p 43.

[31]Gold, Sandra, and Gold Gerald, "First Aid and Legal Liability."

life and limb, alleviating the pain of the victim, and making him as comfortable as possible. He should not perform the functions of diagnosis, prescription, or treatment, for this is the practice of medicine and must be left to a duly licensed and qualified physician.

An attempt by a teacher to administer treatment, in the absence of an emergency, will make him personally liable for negligence if the treatment proves harmful to the pupil. Although the physical educator may be wholly qualified to render first aid, any medical treatment or prescription to an injured pupil would leave the instructor open to a negligence suit if his actions prove detrimental.

Accident Report Form

All schools have some sort of accident report form. Each time there is an accident the coach should complete this form and file it with the athletic director and principal. This should be done on the same day of the accident.

TABLE XXI
UTOPIA TOWNSHIP HIGH SCHOOL DISTRICT 87
ACCIDENT REPORT

To be made out in TRIPLICATE
(2 copies to Business Office
1 copy School file)

School _____ Date _____

Child's Name _____

Address _____

Grade _____ Teacher _____

Time of Accident _____ If parents were called, what time? _____

Place _____

Description of Accident _____

_____

_____

_____

_____

_____

Disposition of Case _____

_____

_____

_____

Name of Doctor Called _____

School Follow Up _____

_____

_____

_____

Signature of Principal _____

JEFFERSON HIGH SCHOOL
—School Injuries— Date _____

Time In	Name	Injury	Treatment	Ins. Rept.	Follow-Up	Time Out

Figure 18.

The proper procedure should be followed when filing school insurance claims:
1. Coach fills out the accident report.
2. Coach turns in the report to the athletic director.
3. The athletic director signs it and turns it in to the business office.
4. The business office types up the claim form and mails it to the home.
5. The parents mail the claim form and any bills to the insurance company.
6. At no time should the coach accept bills for a student's injury.

The Medical Examination

The medical examination is one of the most important aspects of the athletic program. It is necessary and also important that many schools have an adequate medical examination for their athletes. In many of the smaller schools, there is no medical examination. This can lead to possible law suits if the athlete is injured because the school is obligated to provide the medical examination. Even with the proper medical examination, there is always the possibility of injury.

No athlete should be allowed to participate in any way until evidence of the physical examination form has been presented to the coach or to the school. Most states require a physical examination of each student who participates in interscholastic sports. This physical examination must have been made during the current year, normally after July 1.

The preseason medical examination is only the beginning of the athlete's proper medical care. This initial screening is to determine if the athlete is able to participate in athletics and is only the beginning of health supervision which should be continued throughout the entire season. The purpose of the preseason examination is to determine the athlete's fitness to participate in rigorous sports.

The primary duty of the team physician is to organize and carry out the preseason physical examinations, and to follow the team health progress throughout the season. The trainer should coordinate the entire athletic medical program. He should

---

TABLE XXII

PROVISO EAST TOWNSHIP HIGH SCHOOL

Athletic Department

Date _____

This is to certify that _____ is a member
of the _____ squad in _____. He is to receive medical attention by
                            Sport
the school doctor.
Nature of Injury _____

_____

_____

_____

Signature of Coach _____
This form must be returned to the coach upon return to school accompanied by a report from the Doctor to the coach.

TABLE XXIII

PALO HIGH SCHOOL ATHLETIC ASSOCIATION

Parent's Agreement as to Medical Treatment

Date _____, 19_____

I, the undersigned, do hereby consent and agree that _____
_____, a student in Palo High School, and
participating in _____ may be attended and
                              (sport)
treated for any and all injuries and/or disabilities received by him incident to his, or her, participation in any manner in said sport during the season thereof for the year 19_____ - _____,
by the physician or physicians who may be engaged for such purpose by the Palo High School Athletic Association with the understanding that if I am not satisfied with such medical attention and services, I may at my expense procure the same from a physician or physicians of my own selection.

I understand that the medical services that may be provided by the Palo High School Athletic Association are wholly voluntary and that such Association is not obliged to provide any such services whatsoever.

_____
Parent or Guardian

ATTEST:

_____
     High School Principal

follow the physician's directives in first aid, injury prevention, injury treatment, and rehabilitation.

Today it is part of an athlete's preparation for participation in sports that he have a preseason medical examination. This must be stressed to the parents and the school authorities. It should also be a part of the school's coordinated medical supervisory plan to have the services of a physician available for all athletic contests. The physician should be provided with desirable conditions for handling injuries. The ideal situation is to have an office or a curtained area in which he can examine the athletes. There should be a phone in the training room and on the field.

Important parts of a medical plan include talks with the coaching staffs.

TABLE XXIV

REPORT OF PHYSICAL EXAMINATION

(All records are confidential. This form shall be kept in the files of the examining physician.)

JOPLIN PUBLIC SCHOOLS   JOPLIN, ILLINOIS

Name _____ Weight _____ Height _____

I. *CASE HISTORY AND HEALTH RECORD* (To be filled out by examinee)

Have you had the following:

1. Surgical operation since previous examination _____. If so state nature: _____

2. Severe accident? _____ If so, state nature: _____

3. Have you been vaccinated for smallpox? _____ Date of last successful vaccination _____ Diphtheria Immunization: _____ Date _____ Negative Shick Test: Date _____ Polio Immunization: Date _____ Tetanus Immunization: Date _____

4. Underline diseases you have had: smallpox, chickenpox, whooping cough, mumps, measles, German measles, scarlet fever, diphtheria, influenza, pneumonia, tuberculosis
Other Diseases _____

5. Are you subject to: frequent headaches, dizziness, fainting spells, colds, persistent cough, rheumatic conditions, marked nervousness? (Underline)

6. Are you under the care of an oculist? _____

7. Do you have any known physical defects? _____

Signature of Employee

II. *CASE REPORT ON PHYSICAL EXAMINATION*

(Chest X-rays will be provided through the auspices of the Tuberculosis Institute of Chicago and Cook County.)

1. Nose_____ Throat_____ Ears _____ Thyroid_____

2. Teeth: Hygiene _____ Repair_____

3. Heart: Rhythm_____ Blood Pressure: Systolic_____ Diastolic _____ Pulse Rate before exercise _____ After _____

4. Nervous System _____

5. Digestive System _____

6. Skin _____ 7. Posture _____

8. Feet _____ 9. Orthopedic Defect _____

10. General health and appearance _____

11. Hemoglobin _____ Kahn _____

12. Urinalysis _____

REMARKS _____

_____M.D.

Signature

(Every item of the above report is to be examined as specified.)

TABLE XXV

PHYSICIAN'S STATEMENT REGARDING PHYSICAL EXAMINATION

Joplin Public Schools
District No. 29
390 North Wright Street
Joplin, Illinois

This is to certify that on _____, I made a medical examina-

(date)

tion of _____, including examination

of blood (hemoglobin and Kahn test) and urinalysis.

The last medical history and the results of this examination and laboratory tests have been recorded on the form supplied to me by the Board of Education, and the record is on file in my office.

Comments: _____

_____

_____

From the history and examination, I consider the examinee to be free from any communicable disease or any physical or mental condition which might interfere with the efficiency of the examinee or which might endanger the health of pupils or adults in the schools.

Signed_____M.D.

Address_____

City_____

Tel. No._____

1. The law of the state of Illinois requires that these examinations to be done by a physician licensed in Illinois to practice medicine and surgery in all its branches.

2. No medical service, no immunizations or vaccinations, and no examination beyond the scope of the examination shown on the *Report of Physical Examination* should be billed to the school district. These are the financial obligations of the examinee.

3. According to the law of the state of Illinois, the cost of the physical examination for new employees shall rest with the employee. Subsequent examinations as are required by the Board of Education are at the expense of the school district and the bill should be mailed to the school at the above address.

4. This form when complete should be mailed to the Joplin Public Schools, 390 North Wright Street, Joplin, Illinois.

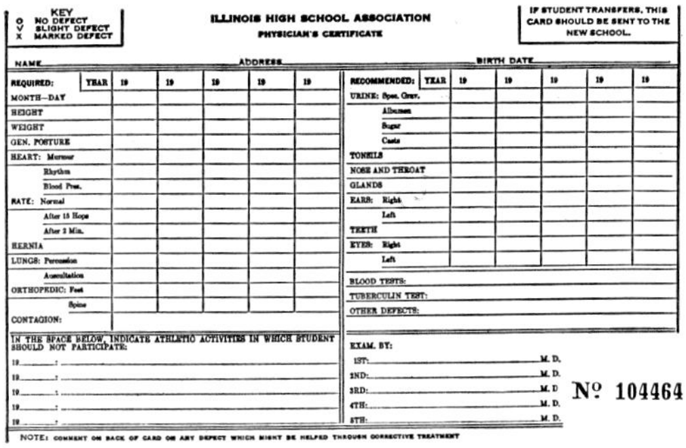

KEY
O NO DEFECT
V SLIGHT DEFECT
X MARKED DEFECT

ILLINOIS HIGH SCHOOL ASSOCIATION
PHYSICIAN'S CERTIFICATE

IF STUDENT TRANSFERS, THIS CARD SHOULD BE SENT TO THE NEW SCHOOL.

NAME ADDRESS BIRTH DATE

REQUIRED:	YEAR	19	19	19	19	19
MONTH—DAY						
HEIGHT						
WEIGHT						
GEN. POSTURE						
HEART: Murmur						
Rhythm						
Blood Pres.						
RATE: Normal						
After 15 Hops						
After 2 Min.						
HERNIA						
LUNGS: Percussion						
Auscultation						
ORTHOPEDIC: Feet						
Spine						
CONTAGION:						

RECOMMENDED:	YEAR	19	19	19	19	19
URINE: Spec. Grav.						
Albumen						
Sugar						
Casts						
TONSILS						
NOSE AND THROAT						
GLANDS						
EARS: Right						
Left						
TEETH						
EYES: Right						
Left						

BLOOD TESTS:
TUBERCULIN TEST:
OTHER DEFECTS:

IN THE SPACE BELOW, INDICATE ATHLETIC ACTIVITIES IN WHICH STUDENT SHOULD NOT PARTICIPATE:
19____:
19____:
19____:
19____:
19____:

EXAM. BY:
1ST: M. D.
2ND: M. D.
3RD: M. D
4TH: M. D.
5TH: M. D.

Nº 104464

NOTE: COMMENT ON BACK OF CARD ON ANY DEFECT WHICH MIGHT BE HELPED THROUGH CORRECTIVE TREATMENT

Figure 19. Reprinted with permission of Illinois State High School Association.

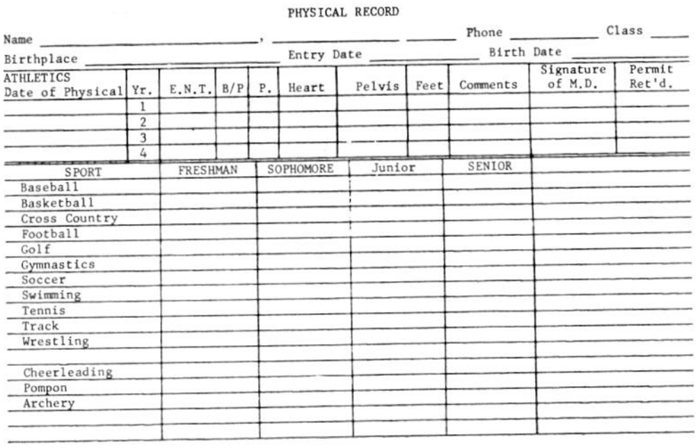

PHYSICAL RECORD

Name ________, ________ Phone ________ Class ____
Birthplace ________ Entry Date ________ Birth Date ________

ATHLETICS Date of Physical	Yr.	E.N.T.	B/P	P.	Heart	Pelvis	Feet	Comments	Signature of M.D.	Permit Ret'd.
	1									
	2									
	3									
	4									

SPORT	FRESHMAN	SOPHOMORE	Junior	SENIOR
Baseball				
Basketball				
Cross Country				
Football				
Golf				
Gymnastics				
Soccer				
Swimming				
Tennis				
Track				
Wrestling				
Cheerleading				
Pompon				
Archery				

Figure 20.

Medical Records

The order that these forms are in represent the order in which they will be used in keeping track of the athletes' injuries.

Voltmer and Esslinger[32] have this to say about the medical examination:

> The medical examination is the first and most important measure to be considered in the proper health supervision of athletics. In many of the smaller high schools, no examination whatsoever is given. A five-minute examination in which the pupil does not even strip cannot be considered satisfactory. If the examination is to be thorough enough to eliminate all possibility of injury, special attention should be devoted to the age, weight, nutrition, bones, feet, eyes, nose, throat, abdomen, glands, heart, lungs, and general health of every individual. This should include a urinalysis and blood pressure test. It is needless to say that the records of these examinations should be kept and referred to when necessary.

Injury Report Forms

The following is an example of a typical injury report form that may be used to inform the school nurse *immediately* after a boy has suffered an injury that requires treatment other than the squad training room.

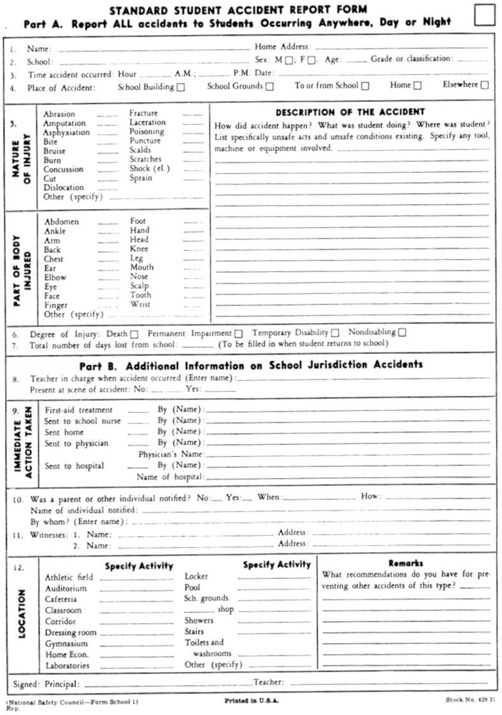

STANDARD STUDENT ACCIDENT REPORT FORM
Part A. Report ALL accidents to Students Occurring Anywhere, Day or Night

1. Name: ________ Home Address: ________
2. School: ________ Sex: M ☐; F ☐. Age: ____ Grade or classification: ____
3. Time accident occurred: Hour ____ A.M.; ____ P.M. Date: ________
4. Place of Accident: School Building ☐ School Grounds ☐ To or from School ☐ Home ☐ Elsewhere ☐

5. NATURE OF INJURY: Abrasion, Amputation, Asphyxiation, Bite, Bruise, Burn, Concussion, Cut, Dislocation, Other (specify), Fracture, Laceration, Poisoning, Puncture, Scalds, Scratches, Shock (el.), Sprain

PART OF BODY INJURED: Abdomen, Ankle, Arm, Back, Chest, Ear, Elbow, Eye, Face, Finger, Other (specify), Foot, Hand, Head, Knee, Leg, Mouth, Nose, Scalp, Tooth, Wrist

DESCRIPTION OF THE ACCIDENT
How did accident happen? What was student doing? Where was student? List specifically unsafe acts and unsafe conditions existing. Specify any tool, machine or equipment involved.

6. Degree of Injury: Death ☐ Permanent Impairment ☐ Temporary Disability ☐ Nondisabling ☐
7. Total number of days lost from school: ____ (To be filled in when student returns to school)

Part B. Additional Information on School Jurisdiction Accidents

8. Teacher in charge when accident occurred (Enter name): ________
Present at scene of accident: No: ____ Yes: ____

9. IMMEDIATE ACTION TAKEN
First-aid treatment ____ By (Name): ________
Sent to school nurse ____ By (Name): ________
Sent home ____ By (Name): ________
Sent to physician ____ By (Name): ________
Physician's Name: ________
Sent to hospital ____ By (Name): ________
Name of hospital: ________

10. Was a parent or other individual notified? No: __ Yes: __ When: ____ How: ____
Name of individual notified: ________
By whom? (Enter name): ________
11. Witnesses: 1. Name: ________ Address: ________
2. Name: ________ Address: ________

12. LOCATION
Specify Activity: Athletic field, Auditorium, Cafeteria, Classroom, Corridor, Dressing room, Gymnasium, Home Econ., Laboratories
Specify Activity: Locker, Pool, Sch. grounds, ____ shop, Showers, Stairs, Toilets and washrooms, Other (specify)
Remarks: What recommendations do you have for preventing other accidents of this type? ____

Signed: Principal: ________ Teacher: ________

(National Safety Council—Form School 1) Rep. Printed in U.S.A. Stock No. 429 21

Figure 21. Reprinted with permission from the National Safety Council.

Emergency Procedure in Case of Injury

Since it is extremely difficult to have a physician and/or ambulance at the scene of every game, the following procedures are to be followed.

[32]Voltmer, Edward, and Esslinger, Arthur, p. 279.

Serious type of injury (head, neck, back, internal) :

1. Send someone to call a physician or ambulance. A list of names and numbers should be provided each coach prior to the start of the season.
2. Keep calm and do not be hurried into moving the injured person.
3. Be sure nothing is done that will cause further injury to the athlete.
4. Keep onlookers away from the injured.
5. Make the injured athlete as comfortable as possible and cheer him in any way possible.
6. Avoid letting the patient see his own injury.
7. Administer only reasonable, prudent first aid (whatever emergency aid the situation dictates).
8. Contact a parent immediately for instructions, if possible, before the athlete is taken to emergency.
9. If a parent cannot be reached, the head coach or designated assistant is to accompany the athlete (or follow the ambulance in his own car) to the hospital. The coach is to remain with the athlete until a parent or responsible guardian appears at the hospital.
10. Anything that happens to an athlete that potentially endangers life or limb of the individual is to be considered an emergency.
11. All questionable injuries should be referred to a physician.
12. No athlete is to be given any internal medication by coaches unless authorized to do so by a physician—in writing.

**INDIVIDUAL
EMERGENCY INFORMATION**

ATHLETE'S NAME_____

PERSON TO CONTACT
IN CASE OF EMERGENCY_____   PHONE NO._____

FAMILY PHYSICIAN_____   PHONE NO._____

REMARKS_____

_____

_____

Figure 22.

Minor injuries (burns, cuts, sprains, etc.) :

1. Each squad should always have a first-aid kit available. These should at all times be properly equipped with the proper first-aid supplies. All necessary supplies are available from the athletic director or equipment manager.
2. If necessary, inform athletes of ice treatment procedure.
3. All questionable injuries should be referred to a physician.

General:

1. Any injured player is to be taken care

TABLE XXVI
GENOA EAST HIGH SCHOOL

Information for use in case of emergency

Name _____   Phone _____

Address _____

Name of your Doctor _____   Phone _____

Hospital preferred _____

In event of illness or accident notify:

Name _____   Phone _____

Address _____   Relationship _____

If no answer from above, contact:

Name _____   Phone _____

Address _____   Relationship _____

PROCEDURES FOR REPORTING ALL ATHLETIC INJURIES

In case of athletic injuries, the coach and/or trainer shall be notified immediately. An accident report is then completed on the injury by the person to whom it was reported and kept on file in the Health Service Office. This procedure will be followed whether student insurance coverage applies or not.

Family Physician:_____Phone:_____

Place of Employment:

      Mother:_____Phone:_____

      Father:_____Phone:_____

I (do) (do not) grant permission to the school to transport the named student to a medical center or hospital in case of emergency when the parent(s) or physician listed cannot be reached.
Other instructions:_____

_____

I understand that all athletic injuries will be reported to the Coach and/or trainer.

_____   _____
Date   Signature of Parent or Guardian   *(over)*

Figure 23.

6. Do not use injured players.

There are several ways by which a coach may protect himself from being sued for negligence.

1. He must be careful at all times that he is doing the proper thing under the circumstances.
2. He should not leave himself open to a lawsuit by leaving practice at any time.
3. He should not administer medical treatment that he is not qualified to give.
4. He should know the health status of his players at all times.
5. He must know what to do in case of an

TABLE XXVII
FULTON HIGH SCHOOL DISTRICT 122
INJURY REPORT FORM

SCHOOL _____

DATE _____

THIS CERTIFIES THAT _____

IS A MEMBER OF THE _____

SQUAD, IS TO RECEIVE MEDICAL ATTENTION BY THE SCHOOL NURSE.

DESCRIPTION OF INJURY _____

_____

_____

of immediately. The head coach and his assistants should be responsible to see that this is done without delay.

2. All accidents requiring medical attention are to be reported to the athletic director the following morning at the latest.

3. Head coaches are responsible to fill out proper accident forms in the nurse's office *the following school day at the latest.*

4. Involved coaches should make a follow-up call to parents on all injured players.

5. Acknowledge all treatment and recommendations of physician.

emergency.

6. He should take appropriate safety precautions at all times.

7. He should provide students with adequate safeguards in the form of oral and written instructions.

8. He should not ask students to perform activities beyond their level of competence.

9. He should always fill out an accident report in detail on any injuries occurring to athletes.

10. He should have all students complete participation or travel permits.

11. He should never allow student drivers to drive cars on athletic trips.

TABLE XXVIII
TOWNSHIP HIGH SCHOOL DISTRICT 214
STUDENT ACCIDENT REPORT
SCHOOL COPY — *DO NOT MAIL*

Name _____ Sex _____ Age _____ Grade_____

Address _____ Town _____

Name of Parent or Guardian _____

Date of Accident _____ Time of Accident _____AM/PM

Description of Accident: How and where did it occur? _____

Nature of injury, and what part of body injured _____

Description of activity: What was student doing at time of injury? _____

If athletics, NAME SPORT _____

Was it practice for or participation in interscholastic event? _____

Did the accident happen in P.E. class? _____

AT SCHOOL   AT OR AWAY FROM SCHOOL

In building _____   School sponsored activity _____

On grounds _____   Activity of social nature _____

                                  During lunch hour _____

TRAVELING

To/from school _____

To/from activity _____   _____

School bus _____   Signature of coach or teacher in charge

Private auto _____   Date _____

TABLE XXIX
LENA HIGH SCHOOL DISTRICT 122
Injury Information Request Form

In case of injury during hours when the medical office is closed we will need to know how to contact a student's parents or a responsible adult.

PARENT OR GUARDIAN — Home Phone _____

PARENT OR GUARDIAN — Phone where they might be reached if they are not at home

_____

INFORMATION ON NEIGHBOR who might be of help if parent or guardian cannot be reached:

Name _____ Phone _____

Address _____

FAMILY PHYSICIAN

Name _____ Phone _____

Address _____

— — — — — — — — — — — — — — — — — — — —

If I cannot be reached in an emergency, I give my permission to have _____

_____ seek medical attention for my child at the Unnversity of Chicago Clinics or elsewhere, if necessary.

Signature of Parent or Guardian

TABLE XXX
STATEMENT OF WITNESS TO INJURY

Witness _____ Address _____

Age _____ Rank _____ Class _____

Name of one injured _____ Injured's Official Class _____

Date of Accident _____ Time _____ Day of Week _____

    A. Description of Accident

        1. Describe the position from which you witnessed the accident:

_____

_____

_____

        2. Describe the position where the accident occurred:

_____

_____

_____

        3. Describe what you saw:

_____

_____

_____

        4. Additional remarks, if any:

_____

_____

_____

        5. Signature of Witness _____

TABLE XXXI
PARK VIEW HIGH SCHOOL
Park View, Nebraska
REQUEST FOR PERMISSION TO PARTICIPATE IN INTERSCHOLASTICS

We hereby request that _____, age _____

be permitted to participate in interscholastic _____ in the

Park View High School. As an inducement to the granting of this permission, we undertake;

    1. To carry SCHOOL ACCIDENT INSURANCE _____

       OR

       Accident Insurance for the above-named student in the amount

       of $_____

    2. To agree to bear full financial responsibility with respect to any injuries which he may sustain in connection with such scholastic

    3. To hold Park View High School and its Board of Education harmless for any claim, loss, cost, or expense growing out of any injury which he may sustain in such participation

                          *Father _____

                          *Mother _____

                          Student _____

Name _____ Year in school *Frosh Soph Junior Senior*

                                                  (circle one)

Address _____ Telephone No. _____

        (street)   (city)

Date of birth _____ County and State of Birth _____
Date of last Doctor's Certificate _____
How many years have you gone out for this sport? _____
Were you on another varsity or frosh - soph team during this school year? _____
Which sport _____ Do you have an activity ticket? _____

SUBJECTS	INSTRUCTORS
1._____	_____
2._____	_____
3._____	_____
4._____	_____
5._____	_____
6._____Physical Education (Period)_____	_____

Coach's initials _____

*When necessary a guardian may sign in place of the parent.

BEHAVIORAL OBJECTIVES

After a person has read this chapter, he should be able to:

1. Define negligence and explain how it applies to athletic coaching.
2. Select an area of coaching and identify by an example of how a coach could be negligent in his teaching methods.
3. Explain and identify the procedures the coach must follow in using first aid.
4. Identify and explain several cases where the coach was sued for negligence.
5. Explain the position of the courts in regard to the liability of the school district.
6. Identify several states whose laws protect them from liability in case of injury to a player.
7. Explain the doctrine that, "the state can do no wrong."
8. Identify and explain several ways in which the coach can protect himself against suit.
9. Define tort liability and apply it to coaching.
10. Analyze what is meant by proof of negligence and recall several ways in which this must be done if the person being sued is to be found negligent.
11. Recall and analyze several elements of a suit which is based on negligence.
12. Recall and explain several actions which can be deemed negligent action.
13. Select several of these actions and apply them directly to athletic coaching.
14. Identify and explain several factors necessary for proof of negligence.
15. Choose several areas in athletics where injuries are likely to happen and explain how these injuries can be avoided.
16. Identify and analyze the legal defenses which may be used against negligence by the coach.
17. Explain what is meant by players' legal rights and give examples.
18. Differentiate between waivers and consent slips and explain the purpose of each.
19. Recall several ways in which a coach may act reasonably and with prudence and apply them to actual situations.
20. Identify several safety codes which a coach should do to avoid negligence.
21. Develop a waiver form to be used as protection for the coach in case of injury to the athlete.
22. Distinguish between the statement of witness to injury and a protection

against liability form.

23. Explain and demonstrate by example the importance of the medical examination for athletics.
24. Summarize the ways in which a coach may protect himself from being sued.
25. Explain how a director might possibly avoid being negligent in performance of his professional duties.
26. As an athletic director in a high school, prepare a brief digest of all the legal factors needed by coaches under your jurisdiction.
27. Explain the legal, financial, and moral responsibilities of coaches for the prevention and care of injuries in athletics.
28. Explain some of the disadvantages of commercial insurance plans for athletes.
29. Evaluate the responsibility of the school to carry insurance on the students participating in athletics.
30. Summarize the responsibilities of the principal, athletic director, and coach in instigating an athletic insurance program for athletes.
31. Identify and explain several ways in which the athletic director can safeguard the health of the athlete.
32. Explain the importance of a knowledge of first aid by the coach who is handling young athletes.
33. Evaluate the importance of and explain the functions of a team physician.
34. Describe three or more hazardous areas in athletics with regard to legal liability.
35. Describe in detail an ideal insurance plan for an interscholastic athletic program.
36. Explain in your own opinion the best way to conduct the physical examinations for athletes.
37. Describe the advantages of a good ath-

letic insurance policy.

38. Explain why it is important for the athletic director to have a good knowledge of athletic insurance.
39. Explain several ways in which the community can help in safeguarding the health of the athlete.

ACTIVITIES

1. Visit a school and make a check list of all the areas of potential negligent action.
2. Talk with an athletic director at the local school. Find out what precautions he takes against negligence.
3. Talk with a local lawyer and obtain his advice on several facts pertaining to negligence. Report this to the class.
4. Formulate a letter to a principal or board of education pointing out an existing area of possible potential negligent action.
5. Arrange for a high school principal to speak to the class on what the responsibilities of the school district is regarding liability.
6. Arrange to have a head coach talk to the class regarding arrangements for taking care of injured athletes.
7. Visit a high school training room and find out what is being done in the way of providing first aid to athletes.
8. Debate the issue: The coach and not the school should be liable for the injury to a player if negligence can be proven on the part of the coach.
9. Debate the issue: The coach should withhold information regarding an injury to a star player.
10. Construct a table of possible insurance coverage for athletic activities.
11. Prepare a policy regarding insurance for interscholastic athletics.
12. Develop an acceptable insurance plan covering injuries incurred in athletics.

13. Interview a trainer from a nearby high school.
14. Bring in an insurance agent to talk to the class about athletic injury indemnity insurance.
15. Construct a checklist of safety procedures for the local high school.
16. Interview a school physician for the local high school.

SUGGESTED READINGS

1. Appenzeller, Herb: *From Gym to the Jury.* Virginia, The Michie, 1970.
2. Ashton, Dudley: *Administration of Physical Education for Women.* New York, Ronald, 1968.
3. Baker, Boyd: Physical education and the law. *Physical Educator,* May, 1972.
4. Bucher, Charles: *Administration of Health and Physical Education Programs.* St. Louis, Mosby, 1971.
5. Bula, Michael: The personal liability of the coach and physical education teacher. *Athletic Journal,* June, 1965.
6. Carlson, Gordon: I'll be suing you coach. *School Executive,* April, 1957.
7. Chambliss, Jim and Mangin, Connie: Legal liability and the physical educator. *Journal of Health, Physical Education, and Recreation,* April, 1973.
8. Feld, Lipman, Who's responsible for what? *School Management,* March, 1972.
9. Garrison, C.: Have you acted negligently today? *Athletic Journal,* December, 1958.
10. Gauerke, Warren: *School Law.* New York, The Center for Applied Research in Education, 1965.
11. Giles, Warren: Liability of Coaches and Athletic Instructors, *Athletic Journal,* February, 1962.
12. Gold, Sandra and Gold, Gerald: First aid and legal liability. *Journal of Health, Physical Education, and Recreation,* January, 1963.
13. Grieve, Andrew: Legal aspects of spectator injuries. *The Athletic Journal,* April, 1967.
14. Grieve, Andrew: Legal aspects of Transportation for athletic events. *The Athletic Journal,* March, 1967.
15. Grimsley, Jimmie: Legal liability of injured pupil. *The Physical Educator,* October, 1969.
16. Howard, Alvin: Teacher liability and the law. The Clearing House, March, 1968.
17. Leibee, Howard: *Tort Liability for Injury to Pupils,* Ann Arbor, Campus, 1965.
18. National Education Association, Research Division: *The Teacher's Day in Court,* Review 1968.
19. Resick, Matthew, Seidel, Beverly, and Mason, James, *Modern Administrative Practices in Physical Education and Athletics. Reading,* A-W, 1970.
20. Rice, Sidney: A suit for the teacher. *Journal of Health, Physical Education, and Recreation,* November, 1961.
21. Shroyer, George: Coach's legal liability for athletic injuries. *Scholastic Coach,* December, 1964.
22. Shroyer, George: How's your liability insurance? *School Management,* September, 1963.
23. Steinhilber, Augustus: A reasonably prudent and careful physical educator. *Annual Safety Education Review,* American Association of H.P.E.R. Washington D.C., 1966.
24. Tourney, John and Clayton, Robert: *Aquatic Instruction.* Minneapolis, Burgess, 1970.
25. Voltmer, Edward and Esslinger, Arthur: *The Organization and Administration of Physical Education.* New York, Appleton, 1967.

CHAPTER 8

The Staff

THE STAFF OF ANY organization, whether it be in industry or education, contributes more to the organization's success than any other factor. If this is true, then, great care should be taken in the selection and retention of these most important persons. This is perhaps more true in education than in any other profession because it deals with our most important commodity, the youth of our country. These young people should be placed in good hands, and given instruction, guidance, and counseling by competent faculty who have not only the interest of the student at heart, but the country as well. Voltmer and Esslinger[1] emphasize this point in the following statement, "No school can be greater than its staff, nor can a program advance beyond the vision of those who administer it." The interscholastic athletic staff members certainly are no exception to this rule. The staff, not the buildings, determines the worth of a school. Fine equipment and excellent buildings in which the student may spend his time are admirable, but without adequate instruction and guidance, he will find it difficult to learn. A good athletic staff that realizes the importance of athletics in the life of the high school student will keep in mind the tremendous educational possibilities of athletics in the life

of the student when they are properly conducted and act accordingly.

THE SELECTION OF STAFF MEMBERS

Each position demands specific qualifications. Age, professional preparation, experience, personality, skills, appearance, and personal habits are a few of these qualifications that are usually considered.

The selection of the personnel is the base upon which a competent staff is built. It is probably the most important single responsibility of the school administrator. In order to secure the best qualified people in any department and for any particular position requires a great deal of energy, and know-how from the administrator. Certain guidelines and procedures must be established and followed so that the administrator knows just what qualifications the candidate must have to fill the position. Haphazard selection based on prejudices, favoritism, and political influences should never be the basis for selection. It will eventually destroy a school system and a department. It will never result in a situation which will assure good working conditions and be conducive to getting the job done.

Staff Selection Procedure

The larger the school system the greater turnover there will be in coaching personnel. Even though the school may be small

---

[1]Voltmer, Edward, and Esslinger, Arthur, *The Organization and Administration of Physical Education* (New York, Appleton Century Crofts, 1967), p. 156.

with few coaching placements each year, it is necessary to establish recognized and acceptable selection procedures. It is important that these selection procedures follow the guidelines set up for fair employment as established by the federal government.

The following procedures may be used in the process of selecting coaching personnel:

PREPARATION OF JOB DESCRIPTIONS: This description should state the required qualifications, including the person's age, certification requirements, education, and experience.

ADVERTISING THE POSITION THAT IS OPEN. The position should be described with as much detail as possible. The duties that are to be performed by the applicant should be stated so that there will be no misunderstanding. The length of time the employment is for, the number and kinds of coaching duties, and the salary should be stated.

The location and size of the school should be described as well as the type and size of the community. Living conditions should be described within the community. Facilities, equipment, and working conditions in the school should also be given. Many schools will state the philosophy and objectives of the school as well as the financial condition of the school district. It is important to give the candidates as complete a picture as is possible.

Needed requirements and qualifications of the applicant should be specifically stated. These should include a request for degree requirements, professional preparation in specific areas, and coaching experience.

Each position requires specific qualifications; therefore, each job description will be different in some respects, some more than others.

CONSTRUCTION OF THE APPLICATION FORM: The application form should obtain information relative to name, sex, age, birth place, height, weight, address, telephone number, and other personal data.

The form should obtain all information regarding the applicant's abilities, educational preparation, experience, outstanding achievements, and names of persons who may be contacted as references and recommendations.

There should be a space on the application form to allow the applicant an opportunity to list additional information of a personal nature.

SELECTION OF CANDIDATES: Usually several promising candidates are selected for personal interviews after a careful screening process. This is done by the board of education in the small school and by the superintendent, principal, or director of athletics or all three if the school is large. Often, however, there are outstanding candidates who do not apply and must be sought out and requested to apply for a particular position. The staff can be selected by using four sources of information: (1) recommendations of others, (2) placement bureaus, (3) teachers agencies, and (4) advertisements.

FINAL SELECTION OF APPLICANT: The final decision as to the successful candidate should be made after due process. This information should be kept confidential until the proper time is chosen for its release.

NOTIFICATION OF SUCCESSFUL AS WELL AS UNSUCCESSFUL CANDIDATES: The successful candidate should be notified as soon as possible. This should be done before the news media is informed. This will give the successful candidate an opportunity to notify his employers and resign his position before they hear of his appointment via the news media. This is only common courtesy.

The unsuccessful candidates should also

TABLE XXXII
BRIDGEWATER COMMUNITY UNIT SCHOOL DISTRICT NO. 25
Bridgewater, Illinois

JOB DESCRIPTION

Position Open:	Director of Athletics and Head Basketball Coach
Qualifications:	1. Master's Degree
	2. Experience in administration and coaching
	3. Evidence of ability to provide democratic leadership to a diverse faculty
	4. Ability to work cooperatively with administrators for the good of the school
	5. Ability to coach basketball
Salary and Rank:	Starting salary of _____ with salary increases according to schedule.
Starting Date:	September 1, 19____
Responsibilities:	1. Coordinate and develop:
	a. The overall interscholastic athletic program
	b. Provide leadership for the coaches of both boys and girls in all sports
	c. Develop a program of inservice training for all coaching personnel
	d. Act as head basketball coach
	e. Be responsible for all purchasing in the Athletic Department
Location and Setting:	Bridgewater is a city of 30,000 population, located in Illinois midway between Potomac and Creston. It is a public supported school with an enrollment of 1700 students. The school is five years old and is located three miles from the city in a rural setting on an eighty acre tract of land. The athletic facilities are excellent and the equipment is adequate. The administration and community are all staunch supporters of the athletic program. The school staff consists of one hundred with an athletic staff of ten. The population of the community is predominately German. The community has ten city parks with a swimming pool, picnic grounds, a city owned golf course, and five recreational facilities.
	The aim of the Bridgewater High School athletic program is to aid the home and the school in helping boys to become better citizens.
Procedure:	Send letter of application and up-to-date credentials to Mr. John Smith, Superintendent of Schools, Bridgwater, Illinois.

TABLE XXXIII
PALOS HIGH SCHOOL DISTRICT 290
PALOS, OREGON
JOB DESCRIPTION
DISTRICT ATHLETIC DIRECTOR

I. Qualifications
   A. Education;   MA degree in Educational Administration and full certification for secondary teaching preferred
   B. Experience;   Experience as a teacher, coach, and athletic director or assistant athletic director

II. Terms of Contract   Ten-month contract with a .28 differential on the district base salary for teacher entering the district

III. Job Goal   To provide each enrolled student of secondary and middle school age an opportunity to participate in an extracurricular athletic activity that will foster physical skills, a sense of worth and competence, a knowledge and understanding of the pleasures of sport, and the principles of fair play

IV. Relationship to Chain of Command:

     Direct responsibility to the Superintendent of Schools and the Board of Education through Administrative Channels

V. Specific Job Responsibilities:

A. He shall provide leadership in selection, employment, and assignment of all coaches at high school and middle school levels in conjunction with the personnel office, district principals, and head coaches concerned. Attention must be given to filling teaching openings as well as coaching vacancies.

B. He shall organize and administer all athletic programs for both boys and girls in the district. This includes the head coach — middle school coach coordination of objectives and skills leading to high school participation.

C. He shall be responsible for budgeting for all athletics and the recommendation of types and amount of equipment and supplies and allocation to departments and schools.

D. He shall be responsible for proper public relations related to the athletic program and shall represent the Palos School District at Harlem Fan's Club meetings.

E. He shall be responsible for establishing good athletic relations among schools with whom Palos schools compete. He shall be responsible for needs of visiting teams as appropriate: meals, dressing rooms, towels, etc.

F. He shall play a key role in developing and promoting principles of good sportsmanship.

G. He shall contract with all athletic officials and initiate requisitions for their payment.

H. He shall schedule and contract for all interschool contests in athletics with careful attention to district school calendars.

I. He shall arrange for all interschool transportation for athletics and also for practice sessions involving transportation. He shall arrange for the needs of coaches and athletes when distance and time necessitate such.

J. He shall represent the Palos High School at all home and away contests, where possible, and represent the school at conference and state meetings.

K. He shall coordinate and arbitrate inner school and inner district conflicts relating to the use of gyms, fields, rooms, and practice areas.

L. He shall be responsible for development of the high school intramural program and act as consultant to middle schools in this capacity.

M. He shall be responsible for the pool areas in both schools and shall schedule life guards and pool supervisors for outside use of these facilities.

N. He shall supervise the care and up-keep of all district athletic equipment.

O. He shall codify district athletic training rules and regulations and promote equitable administration thereof.

P. He shall coordinate rules governing issuing of letters and awards and preside at award programs.

Q. He shall organize and administer summer athletic programs should such develop in the future.

R. He shall be directly responsible for district adherence to IHSAA rules and regulations and shall make sure that athletes are eligible and that proper eligibility lists are issued on schedule.

S. He shall actively promote continuing participation of athletes from middle schools and work toward development of skill sequences in the middle schools leading to high school participation.

T. He shall be responsible for having a doctor present at home athletic contests where required by IHSAA.

U. He shall schedule physical examinations for athletes.

V. He shall be responsible for administering the insurance program covering school athletes and be responsible for processing all reports, clinics, etc.

W. He shall develop and place in operation appropriate rules and regulations governing conduct of athletic activities.

X. He shall keep records of the results of all junior and senior high school athletic contests, and maintain a record file of all award winners, stating the date and type of award, including athletic scholarships.

The above specific areas of responsibility should not be considered all inclusive. The athletic director should be alert for important aspects of the position not specifically detailed in this compilation of duties. Much is expected in individual initiative in this position.

TABLE XXXIV
TOWNSHIP HIGH SCHOOL DISTRICT 420
PALO, OHIO

Job Description for
Division Head of Physical Education, Driver Education
Athletics and Health

Introduction

The division head plays an integral and important role in the formation and administration of school policies in District 420. He will supervise all the teachers in the division in which he is head. He will work with teachers and administrators in establishing desirable working relationships among all staff members. The division head will be alert to the development of the educational program within the framework of the philosophy of the school district. The division head will be responsible for the subject areas which fall under a particular area. He will be responsible for his areas as well as for creating and maintaining a wholesome working relationship within the division. He will be responsible for leadership and coordination of professional growth activities of teacher within his division.

Duties

1. *Selection of New Teachers*
   a. Review applications and credentials of prospective teachers.
   b. Interview potential candidates.
   c. After the interviews, make recommendations to the building principal for the candidate to be hired.

2. *Assistance to Teachers*
   a. Keep in touch with the members of his division during the summer.
   b. Along with building principal write welcome letters to new teachers.
   c. Inform new teachers of their teaching assignments.
   d. Offer to assist new teachers in securing textbooks, course outlines, etc.
   e. Assist building principal in planning workshop activities within the division.
   f. Encourage teachers to bring their questions to him by being constantly available — give an answer or assist them in finding the answer.
   g. Receive oral or written reports from administration on student discipline and classroom control problems encountered by teachers.

3. *Evaluation of Teachers*
   a. Complete all the requirements on teacher evaluation as designated in the evaluation instrument.
   b. Submit written evaluations to building principal as called for in the evaluation calendar.
   c. Confer with teachers after each visit and discuss their evaluation with them.
   d. Confer with the principal on a regular basis regarding teachers within his division.
   e. Complete and submit evaluations on all coaches including recommendations for changes in coaching assignments.

4. *Informing Teachers*
   a. Keep teachers informed of professional developments in the field.
   b. Read materials and route them to members of his division.
   c. Stimulate members to develop for publication new approaches, material usage, and successful teaching experiences.
   d. Encourage division members to participate on professional meetings and when requested, to serve on committees, panels, etc.
   e. Encourage all division members to mark and route good articles related to area of specialization so that all may be informed.

5. *Coordination among Areas of Division*
   a. Work with resource teachers in coordinating use of facilities, equipment and supplies.
   b. Supervise and maintain proper record keeping — Example: grading procedures within division.
   c. Plan with resource teachers educational programs that will enhance the curriculum.

6. *Scheduled Meetings by Administration*
   a. Attend all meetings called for division head by the administration.
   b. Inform administration during meeting of questions arising from within division requiring clarification.
   c. Inform members of division of information discussed during meetings and see that any action items are carried out.

7. *Divisional Meetings*
   a. Schedule and conduct monthly and special department or division meetings.
   b. Prepare and distribute agenda after consulting with resource teacher to each member of the department or division in time for it to be studied before the meeting.
   c. Prepare and distribute minutes of meetings to building administrators, absent department or division members, and resource teachers in subject area within his division not covered by a particular meeting.

8. *Interpretation of Administrative Policies*
   a. Interpret administrative policies, bulletins, and brochures to members of his division.

9. *Evaluation of Instructional Equipment*
   a. Advise the administration as to the merits of certain instructional equipment —
      1. Desirability
      2. Price in relation to quality
      3. Versatility
      4. Quantity

10. *Supervision of Division Budgets*
    a. Prepare the budget in cooperation with the building principal, the resource teacher, and members of his division.
    b. Initiate all requisitions for the division — approve and submit them to the business clerk.
    c. Communicate with the business clerk throughout the school year as to the status of division budgets.
11. *Preparation of Annual Inventories*
    a. Direct the preparation of annual inventories of physical education and athletic equipment and supplies.
    b. Complete the inventories and submit to the building principal at the end of of the school year.
12. *Curricular Duties*
    a. After consulting with the division members and resource teachers, present this information to the curriculum committee on new courses and revision of present courses. This involves the consideration of:
        1. Textbooks
        2. Classroom reference books
        3. Materials other than textbooks
        4. Equipment
        5. Preliminary outlines
    b. Provide outlines for each course in the department or division as requested by the administration.
        1. Conduct continuous evaluation of course outlines.
        2. Revise outlines in light of the evaluations.
13. *Division Schedule*
    a. Assist in the preparation of class and teacher assignment schedule for his division.
    b. Submit this schedule to the administration upon request.
14. *Substitute Teachers*
    a. Assist substitute teachers
        1. Furnish the lesson plans of the absent teacher
        2. Supply a textbook
        3. Provide a class list if possible
        4. Counsel when needed
        5. Report to the principal on the desirability of continued employment of a substitute teacher.
        6. When a substitute is not needed the division head either takes the class or makes other suitable arrangements.
15. *Public and Community Relations*
    a. Work closely with the following people or agencies:
        1. Continuing Education
        2. Local Park District
        3. Local Junior College
        4. Local Booster Clubs, (banquets, projects, etc.)
16. *Athletic Programs — Boys and Girls*
    a. Liabilities
    b. Counseling of Students
        1. Counseling — provide an open-door policy for counseling of the student athlete or student.
        2. Administrative Processing of Athletes into and out of the athletic program.
    c. Supervision of Coaches

1. Supervise coaching assignments in all sports for boys and girls
2. Supervise athletic sports for boys and girls
3. Assignment of duties and responsibilities, and aid in acquiring suitable coaches
4. Responsible for the conduct of coaches at all athletic contests and practices.
5. Assist coaches in details particular to their sport.
6. Liaison between coaches and administration.

d. Act as the principal's representative to the I. H. S. A.
   1. Prepare and certify eligibility lists every three weeks
   2. Obtain sanctions
   3. Correspond with the State Office on Athletic Policies
   4. Read and interpret the By-Laws of the I. H. S. A.
   5. Act as a resource person to the principal on issues brought up at the conference state or national level
   6. Represent the school at all conference meetings.

e. Budget Responsibility
   1. Prepare budgets for all sports for bid list
   2. Prepare all disbursement of funds for payment of all bills
   3. Keep an account of all money spent in all sports
   4. Keep an account of all receipts for contests where admission is charged
   5. Submit financial reports as required

f. Insurance Responsibility
   1. Prepare accurate lists for insured and waiver athletes
   2. Keep lists up to date and accurate
   3. Be responsible for accident claims (forms)
   4. Inform all parents on all accidents to their children
   5. Follow up on accident reports whenever this is necessary

g. Care of Equipment
   1. Be responsible for the safe use of equipment
   2. Be responsible for record keeping, inventories, etc.
   3. Be responsible for marking, repair, laundry and replacement of equipment involving preseason and postseason play
   4. Meet salesmen and purchase equipment for all sports

h. Facilities
   1. Be responsible for the preparation (supervision) of facilities for all athletic events
   2. Be responsible for the coordination of use of various facilities
   3. Be responsible for the building security when school is not in session

i. Public and Community Relations
   1. Work closely with the following people or agencies:
      Continuing Education
      Local Park Districts
      Local Junior College
      Local Boosters Clubs (banquets, projects, etc.)

j. Scheduling of Athletic Events
   1. Schedule contests for all sports
      Send out game contracts for all contests

k. Conduct of Athletic Events
   1. Secure officials through the assignment chairmen
   2. Secure police for all events where admission is charged (football and basketball)

3. Secure doctors and ambulance for football games
4. Be present for every athletic event conducted at home
5. Arrange for bus transportation for all away events and for some home events

l. Professional Meetings
   1. Attend meetings at all levels to keep abreast of the latest changes, innovations, rules, etc.
   2. Attend meetings involving girls' athletics, cheerleaders, and other meetings which involve the athletic department

m. Girls' Athletics
   1. Conduct an athletic program for girls contingent upon student interest, facilities available, and ability to staff the programs.
   2. Obtain schedules from Girls' Athletics Coordinator and after approved at building level, submit to Mid-Suburban League Athletic Directors for approval
   3. Coordinate with Girls' Athletic Coordinator facilities, budget, awards and transportation
   4. Check with Girls' Athletic Coordinator eligibility of all girl participants
   5. Check with Girls' Athletic Coordinator insurance status records of all girl participants
   6. Supervise requests for sanctions and officials' contracts
   7. Attend along with Girls' Athletic Coordinator all meetings representing the school

n. Inventory Equipment
o. During tournament play be responsible for
   1. Securing teams
   2. Hiring officials
   3. Conducting pretourney meetings
   4. Arranging for local workers — police
   5. Releasing publicity to building reporter or newspapers
   6. Accounting for money taken at the gate

---

be informed at the same time as the successful candidate. They should not be informed via the news media.

The person chosen for the position should be placed on the list of faculty so that he will receive all school materials prior to the beginning of the school term.

Criteria for the Selection of Staff

When attempts are made to determine which factors in the selection of staff members are of greater importance such as personality, interest, formal education, experience, etc. it is possible to at least establish criteria for the selection of staff members, in a less-than-random fashion.

Source material in this area propose a number of criteria which may be useful in the task of selection. For example, Voltmer[2] recommends that, ". . . the chief considerations in selecting a coach are: personality traits, training, experience, and health." Bates[3] proposes a number of criteria for selection. In order of importance, they are as follows:

1. personal interview,

---

[2]Voltmer, Edward and Esslinger, Arthur, *The Organization and Administration of Physical Education,* p. 157.

[3]Bates, Aubrey, "Selection of Men Teachers of Physical Education," *Research Quarterly* (May, 1954), p. 129.

A CHECKLIST FOR SELECTING A COACH					
5 POINTS – HIGHEST RATING					
4 POINTS – FOURTH HIGHEST RATING					
3 POINTS – THIRD HIGHEST RATING					
2 POINTS – SECOND HIGHEST RATING					
1 POINT – LOWEST RATING					

CRITERIA	COACH 1	COACH 2	COACH 3	COACH 4	COACH 5
Personality					
Education qualifications					
Experience					
Appearance					
Teaching Skill					
Organizational Skill					
Leadership					
Knowledge					
Public Relations					
Religion					
Community Relations					
Family Status					
Scholastic Record					
Athletic Record					
Educational Interests					
Rapport with Faculty					
Attitudes to Education					
Attitudes to Administration					
Other					
Total Points					

Figure 24.

2. observation in a teaching situation,
3. reference letters,
4. college transcript,
5. record of participation in sports,
6. statement of philosophy regarding teaching,
7. professional and civic activities,
8. written exams, and
9. performance of skill tests.

Still another viewpoint regarding the professional personnel conducting athletics was issued by the AAHPER[4] in 1962. This statement provides further evidence as to the importance of a good staff.

Athletics at every level should be con-

ducted by professionally prepared personnel of unquestionable integrity who are dedicated to the task of developing their charges to the highest degree possible—mentally, physically, and morally. In addition to a knowledge of athletics, such personnel should have a knowledge of (1) the place and purpose of athletics in education, (2) the growth and development of children and growth, (3) the effects of exercise on the human organism, and (4) first aid. Certain basic competencies in physical education, specifically applicable to the welfare and success of participants in competitive sports, should be a minimum prerequisite for teaching or coaching athletics at any level.

There have been various studies made in an attempt to classify the numerous characteristics which have been more beneficial or the qualifications most needed by those persons engaged in teaching physical education and coaching athletics. For example, the National Conference on Undergraduate Preparation in Health, Physical Education, and Recreation[5] adopted the following list of personal qualifications:

1. Faith in the worth of teaching and leadership
2. Personal concern for the welfare of all people
3. Respect for personality
4. Understanding children, youth and adults and appreciating their worth
5. Social understanding and behavior
6. Community-mindedness
7. Interest in and aptitude for teaching and leading
8. Above-average mental abilities
9. Above-average health
10. Voice of good power and quality
11. Effective use of language
12. A sense of humor
13. Energy and enthusiasm sufficient to the requirements of effective leadership.

---

[4]AAHPER. Athletics in Education—A Platform Statement, *Journal of Health, Physical Education and Recreation* (September, 1962) , p. 59.

[5]National Conference on Undergraduate Professional Preparation in Health, Physical Education and Recreation, *The Athletic Institute* (Chicago, 209 South State Street, 1948) , p. 7.

Probably the best teaching is done in coaching. A. S. Barr[6] lists the following qualities of successful teachers: "resourcefulness, intelligence, emotional stability, consideration, buoyancy, objectivity, drive, dominance, attractiveness, refinement, co-operativeness, and reliability." He also lists three other categories of qualities, namely "knowledges, attitudes, and skill."

THE ATHLETIC DIRECTOR
Personal Qualifications

Although training and experience is a highly important factor, directors of athletics should not be selected entirely on this basis. Training itself will not assure success. An athletic director must possess certain desirable personal qualities which are conducive to the human relationships involved in improving the coach-player situation in athletics. There are many factors involved in determining the success of an athletic director; however, personal qualities should perhaps be regarded as the most important. It would probably be impossible to cite a single personality trait which would include the director's complete personality and one which would be considered as the most important in all cases or situations. It would be safe to say that the effectiveness of the athletic director's personal qualities would depend upon the situation. Therefore, it is important that the successful athletic director should possess as many strong personal traits as possible if he or she is going to be successful. What are these personal traits? It is difficult to list all of the ones that would contribute to the success of an athletic director. Certain qualities such as sympathetic understanding, ability to instill confidence, and professional enthusiasm are a few that would, without question, con-

<hr>

[6]Barr, A S., "Characteristics of Successful Teachers," *Phi Delta Kappan* (March, 1958), p 282.

tribute to the success of the director.

The person selected to direct a program of athletics should possess high standards of character and personality. The very nature of the duties require them to be good leaders. A good leader should possess sound judgment, logical thinking, common sense, and the ability to discriminate between right and wrong. The athletic director should look the part. He or she should possess vigorous health and keep fit in order to withstand the rigorous schedule required for successful leadership.

The director should also possess a pleasing personality. He is the front man, the person who acts as a go between, the trouble shooter; therefore, he must be the type of person who is well liked. He should possess such traits as enthusiasm, friendliness, cheerfulness, industry, self control, integrity, dependability, and cooperation.

The successful athletic director, be he man or woman, must understand human nature and realize that people are all different and will react differently to different circumstances and conditions. He should be tolerant and realize that the capabilities of people are not all the same, that some are more capable than others and as a result will do a better job. He must be understanding and be interested in people's problems. He must cultivate the trust and gain the respect of people by being understanding and displaying a willingness to help them. He should exhibit such qualities as patience, loyalty, friendliness, tolerance, reliability, tactfulness, sincerity, and a good temperament.

The athletic director should also be interested in what he is doing. He must be completely *sold* on his job and promote athletics at every opportunity. He should welcome and take every opportunity to work toward having a harmonious department.

Bucher[7] gives the following personal qualifications of the administrator:

1. Integrity
2. Ability to instill good human relations
3. Ability to make decisions
4. Health and fitness for the job
5. Willingness to accept responsibility
6. Understanding of work
7. Command of administrative technique
8. Intellectual capacity.

One of the important aspects of the training of the athletic director is the fact that the person selected may be the director for both the boys and girls program. This, of course is extremely important because he must have the right philosophy which will correspond to that of the school and community. He will need to be diplomatic in all of his decisions and be able to work harmoniously with both the men and women staff members.

Educational Qualifications of the Athletic Director

There has been a need in recent years, because of public interest in interscholastic athletics, for individuals who have special educational preparation in the administration of athletics. Many colleges offer courses and preparation for the administration of physical education but not in the administration of athletics. Because of this situation a joint committee of AAHPER[8] developed a program of professional preparation at the graduate level for those individuals who planned to go into the administration of athletics. The committee recommended the following competencies which would include an awareness and understanding of:

1. The role of athletics in education and our society and the rules, regulations, policies, and procedures of the various governing bodies
2. Sound business practices as related to athletic administration
3. Administrative problems as related to equipment and supplies
4. Problems related to facilities
5. School law and liability
6. The factors involved in the conduct of athletic events
7. Good public relations techniques
8. Staff relationships
9. The health aspects of athletics
10. The psychological and sociological aspects of sports
11. The need of the interpretation of research

Richardson[9] stresses the importance of formal training in athletic administration in the following statement:

As sports programs continue to grow, an athletic director must have breadth and depth of knowledge to give proper leadership. The creation of a professional organization such as the National Council of Secondary School Athletic Directors, a council of AAHPER's Division of Men's Athletics, comes under the general heading of in-service education. This organization will grow in size and strength and will exert a powerful influence on secondary school athletics. The Minnesota State High School Athletic Directors Association, another professional group organized approximately three years ago, has also made great strides in solving common problems.

The major topic for consideration here, however, is for the professional preparation of the athletic director. One approach is to identify the competencies needed by the athletic director. He is a man of many hats. In the past, and in many cases in the present, he has also been a teacher, a coach, a principal, an

[7]Bucher, Charles, *Administration of Health and Physical Education Programs* (New York, The C. V. Mosby Co., 1971) , p. 94-96.

[8]Joint Committee on Physical Education, "Professional Preparation of the Administrator of Athletics," *Journal of Health, Physical Education, and Athletics* (September, 1970) , p. 20.

[9]Richardson, Deane, "Preparation for a Career in Public School Athletic Administration," *Journal of Health, Physical Education, and Recreation* (February, 1971) , p. 17.

equipment manager and/or a caretaker. Yes, some athletic directors still line the fields and pull out the bleachers. As the position becomes more sophisticated and complicated, it will move toward a full-time position with the holder being responsible for important decisions.

The director of interscholastic athletics should understand the position women have now taken in present-day society. He must realize that women have a natural desire to excel. Physiologically they will benefit from athletic competition. If the director is a man, he must prepare himself by taking courses from women instructors so that he may understand the philosophy, aims, and objectives of interscholastic athletics from the women's point of view.

The director of athletics is in a position to make decisions that will affect the lives of many people. Many of these decisions will also affect the pocketbook of the taxpayers. He should, therefore, have ability in several areas.

Richardson[10] states that:

> The Professional Preparation Panel of the AAHPER has endorsed a document entitled 'Professional Preparation of the Administrator of Athletics,' a comprehensive recommendation by a committee which studied this problem for several years. The statement was published in the September, 1970, issue of the *Journal of Health, Physical Education, and Recreation.*
>
> The statement recommends that the candidate for admission to a graduate program in athletic administration should have been a player, a coach, or an administrator in athletics. The last two seem valid; however, having been a player only might not qualify one for admission to a graduate program in athletic administration. A person directing coaches should have had coaching experience himself, so that he knows firsthand the problems, temptations, trials, tribulations, ecstacies and despairs of the coach.

[10]Richardson, Deane, "Preparation for a Career in Public School Athletic Administration," p. 18.

THE COACH

Personal Qualifications of the Coach

There are certain personal qualifications that are generally accepted for those persons working in athletics. First of all, a coach should look the part; he or she should show their commitment and dedication to the way of life they represent. Chain smokers, overweight people, and poorly dressed people do not portray the kind of image needed to motivate the young athlete to live the clean life. If the coach asks the athlete to train and sacrifice the so-called pleasures of life, he himself should also be willing to do the same. Personality and personal appearances are things that can be improved.

While it is true that personality traits are different in all persons, never-the-less it is a pretty well-accepted fact that the possession of desirable personality traits are very important and necessary for those individuals engaged in coaching athletes. Because of the very nature of athletics, with its pressure of competition uppermost in the minds of coaches and players alike, it stands to reason that this will bring about close personal relationships. Coaches are in a position to exert a great deal of influence on the lives of the young people they come in contact with. Any actions which these people commit will usually have a tremendous impact on the minds of the young athletes.

It is, therefore, extremely important that those individuals entrusted with the responsibility of coaching interscholastic athletic teams be of high ethical and moral character with exceptionally high standards of personal conduct.

They should, along with strong personal qualifications, possess the following attributes: (1) they must be true educators, (2) they must possess enough motor skill to demonstrate the correct form in performing the skill, (3) they must possess fine leadership qualities, and (4) they must identify with and relate well to the players.

It should be remembered that the coach is the key to the many benefits derived from participation in the athletic program. The influence of athletic coaches on the lives of those young athletes in whom they come in contact is immeasurable. Many of the athletes will pattern their own lives on what the coach has taught them. The athletic coach in many cases has been their ideal and they believe in what he has told them and the things he stands for.

It must be remembered that the situations in which these young athletes are placed are not the same as the situation which exists in the academic classrooms. These athletic situations are highly charged with emotion and the decisions relative to right and wrong are directly related to winning and losing. Therefore, both the coach and player are faced with making decisions while in a highly emotional state of mind. Unless the coach and athletic director are stable, level-headed individuals, these decisions can result in patterns of conduct which will greatly influence the behavior of the players for years to come. In many cases it could establish a pattern of life for the participant which would lead to cheating and mistrust instead of helping the player to respond constructively and act in the socially accepted fashion.

The people conducting the athletic programs in the high schools of America are in many ways in an enviable position. Because they exert a tremendous influence on the young people, they have a tremendous responsibility. Let them use it well and carefully. If they assume this responsibility they must measure up. It is, therefore, important that personal qualifications be kept in mind in selecting the athletic director and coach of interscholastic athletics.

Unless these kinds of people are conducting the interscholastic athletic program and it is administered as an integral part of the educational curriculum, it is very difficult to justify its existence.

Although there are wide differences of opinion among school men as to the desired personal qualifications of an interscholastic athletic coach, the following are suggested or desirable:

1. Enthusiasm
2. An ability to get along with high school students, yet keep their respect and demand perfection within their ability limits.
3. Good health
4. A willingness to learn and to accept constructive criticism
5. A willingness to help form and implement department policies in:
   A. Training habits
   B. Athletic code
   C. Discipline
   D. Budget
   E. School time lost
   F. Emphasis on one sport over another in relationship to what is good for the athlete
6. A willingness to be an active and dedicated builder of a well-balanced athletic program with major emphasis being placed on whatever is best for the athletes
7. A well-groomed appearance with clean personal habits
8. A friend to all and a parent to none
9. A willingness to agree and emphasize that athletes should budget their time in the following order:
   A. Education
   B. Home membership (includes church)
   C. Athletics
   D. Social functions
10. A philosophy that coaching is done for reasons other than monetary return

Educational Qualifications of the Coach

It is difficult to determine what makes a successful coach. There are so many intangibles. Probably the sole measure of the worth of an individual as a coach or administrator of athletics is whether or not he gets the job done. Even though this may be true, there are certain characteristics that are accepted as being the true measure of the person most likely to succeed in certain professions. Teaching is one of these professions. Formal education of a certain type is generally accepted as beneficial and necessary in the preparation of teaching personnel. The athletic coach is no exception. He too must be qualified, using methods that have been proven successful.

The head coach has many roles, some more important than others. None is more important than his ability to organize and establish a pattern for the entire program in which he is in charge.

For example, one of the concerns of the head coach is to obtain a well-qualified and dedicated staff; one which will function smoothly, efficiently, and as a unit. It is the head coach's role to not only provide the leadership but also to come up with new ideas and innovations which will place his program in front. The head coach should also make wise use of facilities and provide for a good competitive and attractive schedule. He or she should at all times be conscious of providing the best for the team so they can perform at maximum capacity.

Singer[11] stresses the following attributes or determiners of success in coaching:

Experience
    Previous coaching
    Athletic participation
Personal qualities
    Common sense

Intelligence
Dedication
Leadership
Decision making
Character
Human relations
    Sensitivity to others
    Respect for others
    Ability to communicate
    Ability to be an inspiration to others
    Ability to organize
    Ability to motivate others
Education
    College preparation
    Courses in physiology, psychology, sociology, kinesiology, coaching, administration, etc.
    Knowledge gained from books, articles, and research

Bucher[12] makes the following observation about the qualifications of coaches, "About one fourth of all coaches in the junior and senior high schools in this country have no professional preparation. The only qualification many coaches have is the fact that they have played the game or sport in high school, college or the professional ranks."

Bucher[13] makes the following comment regarding current practices in coaching:

Although coaching is generally recognized as being most important to young people, there does not seem to be any consistent pattern for preparing persons for such a position. In fact, in some communities All-American mention, a file of newspaper clippings, a long winning streak, and a shelf full of trophies seem to be the important criteria for selection.

Bucher[14] gives the following essential qualities of a coach:

Expert Knowledge of the Game
    A coach should be an expert in the

---

[11]Singer, Robert, *Coaching, Athletics, and Psycology* (New York, McGraw Hill, 1972), p. 4.

[12]Bucher, Charles, *Administration of Health and Physical Education Programs*, (St. Louis, The C. V. Mosby Co., 1971), p. 239.

[13]Bucher, Charles, "Professional Preparation of the Athletic Coach," *Journal of Health, Physical Education, and Recreation* (Sept., 1959), p.27.

[14]*Ibid.*, p. 28.

game he supervises. This means he has knowledge of techniques, strategy, rules, offenses, defenses, skills, and other information basic to the sport.

Understanding the Participant

The coach needs to understand how a youth functions at his particular level of development. This implies an appreciation of such facts as: skeletal growth, muscular development, organic development, physical and emotional limitations, and social needs. It also means a personal concern for the total physical, mental, and moral welfare of youth.

Skill in the Art of Teaching

The coach should be a master of teaching players not only the basic fundamentals of the game but also such factors as the importance of thinking clearly, making right decisions, understanding healthful and balanced living, and being a good sport. He knows the laws of learning, how to present material most effectively to the age group with which he is working, and how to apply sound psychological principles to his field of work.

Desirable Personality and Character

The coach should possess such traits as patience, understanding, kindness, courage, cheerfulness, affection, sense of humor, energy, and enthusiasm. He should be able to withstand pressure from forces not interested in educational athletics. His character should be beyond reproach and his example one which mothers and fathers would like to have their sons emulate.

There are numerous factors and developments which affect the qualifications of athletic coaches. The most important one seems to stem from the fact that there is a great demand for people who are qualified to coach. This situation has developed because of the tremendous expansion of the athletic programs in all areas of education and all grade levels. This is particularly true, however, in the high school where many schools support several sports in various levels of competition. This increase of interest among the students for more ath-

letic sports and a greater number of teams in each sport creates a need for more qualified coaches. The girls' program alone has accelerated the demand for coaching talent tremendously.

Another development which is brought about by the greater need for qualified coaches is the concern of the parents for the safety and health of their children. All parents want their children to be properly supervised by well-trained, knowledgeable coaches while they are engaged in athletic sports that involve the risk of injury. The parents are also concerned about whether the supervisor is highly qualified in first aid and care of injuries should an injury occur. Few parents and few administrators want students to be under the supervision of any coach unless he is highly qualified in these areas.

Coaches must be prepared who are more adaptable, more courageous, more enduring, and more knowledgeable than was previously necessary.

In the past few years there has been a push in many colleges and universities to train young men to coach athletics. This has been brought about because (1) there has been a demand for coaches who can teach academic courses and coach athletics and (2) there is a demand for this special type of training.

For example, the Department of Physical Activities at the University of California, Santa Barbara,[15] has recently installed a program for training athletic coaches at the secondary school level. The idea was the result of a study conducted by the California Interscholastic Federation in which it was found that many interscholastic coaches were unprepared. The program at Santa Barbara was designed to

---

[15]Breyfogle, Newell, "A New Dimension in Training Athletic Coaches," *Coach and Athlete* (August, 1969), p. 20.

provide training for those individuals who wished to teach an academic subject and coach. This new idea for training athletic coaches could be the solution for preparing the secondary school coach so that it is no longer necessary to have a major in physical education in order to coach athletics.

They suggest a minor in coaching which would include courses, such as:

1. Foundations of athletics
2. Psychology of coaching
3. Medical aspects of athletics
4. Practicum in athletic coaching
5. Theory of team and individual sports
6. Advanced analyses of team sports
7. First aid
8. Appreciation of sports
9. Officiating
10. Life saving
11. Water safety
12. Methods of conditioning in athletics
13. Student teaching in coaching

There are many opinions of what makes an ideal coach. An ideal coach in one situation would not be in another. It depends to a large extent as to what is wanted in the various situations in which the coach is working. Evaluating the worth of a coach by one group of people would not bring the same results as an evaluation by another group in a different situation. However, Newman[16] believes that there are some characteristics that are common to all coaches and has suggested the following:

1. The coach should be a true educator.
2. The coach should possess the motor ability level high enough to enable him to demonstrate or serve as a model.
3. The coach should be aware of the physical and mental needs of the participants.

4. The coach should have the ability to communicate.
5. The coach should be a leader.
6. The coach should be devoted to the profession.
7. The coach must have as a primary objective the utilization of sports as an educational force.

Certification of Coaches

If athletics is a part of the educational curriculum and if there is concern over the qualifications of teachers in the academic area, then there should be equal concern over the qualifications of athletic coaches. Recently there is evidence of some interest in many states to upgrade the qualifications of athletic coaches. In March, 1969, Oehrlein and Segrest[17] conducted a survey to find the states that required coaches to be certified above and beyond that of a regular teacher, what the requirements were and the states that have plans for future requirements. The survey revealed that forty-five states made no special requirements but that seventeen states were exploring the possibilities. There were six states that specified special training for coaches, and these states were Colorado, Indiana, Louisiana, Minnesota, Nebraska, and North Dakota. The requirements varied in nature from a major or minor in physical education to requiring special courses in various areas such as first aid, anatomy, etc. Twenty-eight states had no special requirements for coaches and were not intending to develop any.

Still another survey of special certification requirements for athletic coaches of high school interscholastic teams was made by members of the coaching certification committee of Illinois Association for Pro-

[16]Newman, Dick, "The Philosophical Concept of an Ideal Coach," *Coach and Athlete* (January, 1969), p. 22.

[17]Oehrlein, Tommy and Segrest, Herman, "A Survey of Certification Requirements for High School Athletic Coaches," *Coach and Athlete* (April, 1970) , p. 32.

fessional Preparation in Health, Physical Education, and Recreation.[18]

The study showed that fifty states required that coaching personnel be licensed or certified for teaching usually at the secondary level. Forty-one states have no certification requirements for coaching. Several of the forty-one states, however, indicated that they assume or stress that the coach should have professional preparation in health and physical education. Several of the state departments of public instruction strongly indorse collegiate playing experience as valuable preparation for coaching. Nine states require some sort of coaching certification requirement.

There have been other states that, because of their individual concern within their own state boundaries, have conducted studies which have resulted in their making recommendations for certification of interscholastic coaches for their own states. In checking the recommendations which have been made by these states, invariably the educational requirements include basic courses in the science area, such as kinesiology, physiology, and athletic training along with the theory of coaching and administration. Usually the physical education major will include these areas. For example, the state of Missouri[19] has recently recommended the following minimum standards for certification of coaches who are not certified in physical education:

Courses and Experiences

	Hours
Kinesiology	3
Prevention and care of athletic injuries	2
Scientific bases of conditioning or exercise physiology	3
Coaching theory and a minimum of intercollegiate athletics	2
Administration of interscholastic athletics or physical education	3
Sports officiating	2
Total	15

The Illinois Association for Professional Preparation in Health, Physical Education, and Recreation[20] has gone on record as recommending the establishment of certification standards for teachers of other subjects who desire to coach. These standards would apply only for coaching. This group advocated the following certification standards:

1. Minimum certification standards for coaches.
   All head coaches of autonomous teams must meet state certification standards. It is recommended that all assistant coaches be encouraged to make progress toward certification.
2. Certification for coaching
   a. Major or minor in physical education or
   b. Coaching major or minor.
   c. Fifteen semester hours in:
      1. Medical aspects of athletic coaching
      2. Principles and problems of coaching
      3. Theory and techniques of coaching
      4. Kinesiological foundations of coaching.
      5. Physiological foundation of coaching.

The concern for adequate certification of interscholastic coaches is not confined only to the state level. While it is true that each state exercises almost complete jurisdiction and autonomy over the educational offerings within the immediate boundaries

[18]Coaching Committee of Illinois Association of HPER. "A Survey of Special Certification Requirements for Athletic Coaches of High School Interscholastic Teams," *Journal of Health, Physical Education, and Recreation* (September, 1970), p. 14.

[19]McKinney, Wayne and Taylor, Robert, "Certification of Coaches: The Missouri Approach," *The Journal of Health, Physical Education and Recreation* (Oct., 1970), p. 50.

[20]Illinois Association for Professional Preparation, "A Rationale for Certification of High School Coaches in Illinois" *Journal of Health, Physical Education and Recreation* (Jan., 1971), p. 55.

of the state, with the exception of local control, many national organizations can and do make recommendations and suggestions regarding their profession. These organizations are usually not political in nature. Their membership is composed of people from every state and they are interested only in the betterment of their profession. Their decisions are invariable, based entirely on the needs of the participant and how the recommendations they make fulfill the requirements of the educational program.

The AAHPER division of men's athletics is such an organization and has long been aware of the lack of preparation of high school coaches. As a result, a task force was set up to study and make recommendations pertaining to the certification of coaches. The results of this study made by Esslinger[21] indicated the following:

1. The best way to liquidate unqualified coaches is for each state to establish certification standards for teachers of academic subjects who wish to coach.
2. These standards should be designed for coaching not teaching physical education.
3. The standards should include the basic understandings without which no one should coach.
4. The basic courses should include the following:
   a. Medical aspects of athletic coaching
   b. Principles and problems of coaching
   c. Theory and techniques of coaching
   d. Kinesiological foundations of coaching
   e. Physiological foundations of coaching

Duties of Athletic Director

The high school athletic director should have the responsibility of organizing

---

[21]Esslinger, Arthur, "Certification of High School Coaches," *Journal of Health, Physical Education and Recreation* (October, 1968) , p. 42.

and implementing an interscholastic sports program which will bring the greatest educational benefit to the students. In the performance of these duties he or she usually is directly responsible to the high school principal.

The athletic director should recommend members of the certified staff to the principal for the various coaching positions. He or she should evaluate coaching performances and provide leadership and guidance to the coaching staff by conducting appropriate coaches' meetings. These meetings should allow the staff members the opportunity to become involved in the planning of the total program and provide the opportunity to establish and maintain communication between the different coaches and the various sports. Good rapport and constant communication among coaches is of the utmost importance if such a program is to succeed.

It should be the responsibility of the athletic director to assign teams in both practice and regular season contests to available facilities, draw up schedules with assistance from varsity coaches, assign officials to all home contests and arrange transportation when necessary. He also should coordinate the conduct of home contests with the appropriate assistant building principal.

The athletic director should also be responsible for developing a system to determine the eligibility of interscholastic participants and for coordinating contest sanctions for all high school athletic activities.

The high school athletic director should make himself available to all personnel (principals, coordinators of athletics) responsible for sports activities for consultation in matters pertaining to athletics.

Many of the duties, such as those which exist in the varsity athletic program, will first be done by the coach and then approved by the athletic director. The expanded girls' programs have doubled his duties.

The duties of the director of athletics will be determined to a large extent by the size of the school and by the philosophy of the school. In the large school many of the duties can be delegated and shared by coaches and members of the coaching staff. In some instances many of the responsibilities can be given to a competent secretary. The duties suggested here will include all those which could be the responsibility of any director whether he would be in a large or small school.

The director should act as a liaison person between the principal and the athletic program. It should be the duty of the director to expedite the policies which will enable the total athletic program to operate smoothly and lead to the achievement of this area and the total school program.

The athletic director should represent the school at all meetings that arise in the area of athletics which are approved by the principal. Other duties of the athletic director include the following.

Payment of Officials

The details of the payment should be worked out in advance and put into the official's contract so that both the administrator and the official have them in writing. Probably the best method of paying the official is by check so that the department will receive a receipt acknowledging payment. The check should be mailed immediately after the playing of the contest and acknowledgement should be given by either the athletic director or head coach after the game as to when the official can expect it.

Mailing of Eligibility Records

Current eligibility sheets must be exchanged between schools and mailed approximately one week in advance of the contest. This list can be compiled and sent by either athletic director or principal. The week period will allow the athletic director of the school ample time to check up on any peculiarities and the coach enough time to study the sheets and plot a game strategy.

Partcipation Records

A competent person should be placed in charge of participation time. If this is not possible, this duty should fall on some other competent person, such as a manager. Rough drafts can be kept and later recopied into coach's and athletic director's records. Mimeographing results for both spectator and player immediately following the contest is desirable.

Injuries

At games, especially in contact sports, professional help should be available when possible for both home and visiting squads. A plan should be worked out in case of major emergencies as far as transportation and care is concerned. The home school should provide a first-aid table to be used by both squads for minor injuries, cuts, and bruises. During practice sessions, minor cuts, and injuries can be taken care of on the spot. Here again, a plan should be worked out in case of major injury. If possible, a trainer could be a welcome addition to a staff. Injuries to the head should always be checked out by a physician before the player takes the field. At the high school level, it may help to have a school physician who would work in conjunction with the staff in determining corrective methods in recovering from an injury. In any case, the coach must be well versed in first-aid procedures.

Visiting Team Courtesies

The athletic director should make visitors as comfortable as possible and oversee visitors' privileges, such as locker room space, locks, and towels by assigning people to these tasks. The visitors should know where to go before they get to the school. Once the team gets to the school, a manager could be appointed to show the visitors where to go. Before the contest, coaches, captains, and team should be introduced.

Public Relations

This is a very big part of the athletic director's responsibility. This is a year-round job and the athletic director must always be on the ball to take care of this. He must be a salesman of his program, not only the interscholastic athletic program but the entire program of physical education. He must do a job with the students, parents, community, and all others he comes in contact with. He must let the people know exactly what is happening so they can become interested.

Preparation of Facilities

Although the athletic director is in charge of this, the individual coaches usually do most of the work themselves. However, the athletic director should check the facilities before each contest.

Scheduling

At the high school level, the scheduling is left almost entirely up to the athletic director. The schedules should be balanced and home and away contests should be within easy traveling distance. Natural

rivals should be retained and the coaches should be consulted when the schedules are being made.

Game Contracts

This is the sole duty of the athletic director. He should make sure that the contracts are sent out in plenty of time to have secured the officials before the contest.

Orientation of New Staff Members

It is very important that all new staff members are instructed as to the exact procedures pertaining to department policies. The director should assume the initiative in this important function.

Serving on Nonathletic Committees

The involvement of other faculty members in the athletic program can be brought about by the director becoming involved with other faculty committees.

Interpret the Athletic Program to the Faculty and Community

The director is in an excellent position to reach the faculty and community by speaking at clubs, P.T.A., and faculty meetings.

Interpret Conference and State Rules to the Athletic Staff

Most of the information regarding conference and state rules goes to the athletic director. He in turn should pass this information on to all the coaches.

Preparation of Eligibility Lists

The director usually will obtain the names of the athletes participating in a particular sport from the coach and, after checking it carefully, send the list on to the principal.

Work Out a Student Manager System

A uniform student manager system should be worked out by the department. The director should oversee this area and correct any injustices which might occur from time to time.

Purchase and Care of Equipment

A great deal of money can be saved by using good techniques in the purchasing of new equipment. Only well-known brands should be used and the "instant bargains" should be avoided as they often are deficient in quality. A good athletic director will use his experiences and contacts to learn which equipment is a good buy. By carefully watching and taking care of the equipment, the athletic director will also be able to make it last much longer.

Preparation of Budgets

This can be a very touchy problem between the athletic director and the coaches of the various sports. Naturally, they will be trying to get as much money as possible and it is important that the athletic director develops a good relationship with these people so that a reasonable budget can be reached. It is up to the athletic director to gain the confidence of the board and be able to show them that the money is not being wasted.

Ticket Sales and Finances

In this area, most of the actual work will be done by teachers or other help. However, the athletic director must supervise the activities and make sure everything balances and runs smoothly.

Securing Officials

Good officiating is the key to any well-run athletic contest and the athletic direc-tor should have some sort of record as to the ratings of the various officials available. After choosing the officials, he should make the final arrangements as far as travel, ac-commodations, times, and salary are con-cerned. It is very important to make sure everything with the officials runs smoothly so that the athletic director and the school can have a good reputation with the offi-cials.

Arranging Team Travel

In high school, most of the travel does not include an overnight stay; however, if it should be necessary, the athletic director can arrange for a motel or hotel. Most of the travel will be done by car or bus so the athletic director must secure reliable ve-hicles and drivers and take care of the money for gasoline.

Arrangements for Scouting

Here, the athletic director must work closely with the coaches in arranging for scouting, and he must be in contact with the opposing schools so that reasonable rules and accommodations for the scouts can be made. When a cut in the physical education budget is declared, it usually comes in this area, so the athletic director must make sure that the money and man-power is being used to the maximum.

Supervision of Coaching Staff

The athletic director is always going to have problems with his staff, but he must try to develop a good relationship among all of the staff. The athletic director must settle differences among the coaches and help solve problems within each sport. He must be a supervisor and a friend, and cer-tainly must have the confidence of the coaches below him.

Administration of
Home Athletic Events

Although almost all of the various jobs will be taken care of by different school personnel, the athletic director should make a check on all things before the contest begins. He or she should also be present at the contest to take care of any unforeseen problems that arise.

A detailed list of the duties of the athletic director could include the following:

1. Guide the formulation of a philosophy for the department.
2. Help to formulate and determine policies for the department.
3. Determine the teaching load of coaches.
4. Arrange for medical or physical examinations for all participants in athletics.
5. Arrange for insurance coverage.
6. Help in the organization and implementation of the booster or quarterback club.
7. Oversee gymnasium and athletic field maintenance.
8. Schedule departmental meetings.
9. Make staff recommendations and references.
10. Coordinate crowd control procedures for athletic contests.
11. Represent the staff members on all personal matters.
12. Maintain office procedures.
13. Assign secretarial staff duties.
14. Assume leadership in public relations.
15. Serve on athletic committees.
16. Prepare lists of approved officials.
17. Interpret phases of athletic program to the administration.
18. Assist coaches where necessary.
19. Attend conferences and clinics.
20. Edit all material for publications.
21. Promote joint school and community activities.
22. Do research.
23. Delegate responsibilities for all home interscholastic events to faculty help or students as needed.
24. Schedule transportation for games.
25. Work with the respective head coaches in regards to duties and assume responsibilities of student managers and trainers.
26. Assume responsibilities for all game contracts.
27. Assist the principal in the selection of the athletic staff.
28. Carry out all policies set forth by the state association.
29. Work with the coaches to set up a code of conduct for athletes. This may be done under the direction of the principal and/or superintendent with the approval of the school board or athletic board.
30. Work with each coach to assure a smooth, functioning athletic program.
31. Make sure officials have shower and dressing room facilities.
32. Request security and custodial help if necessary.
33. Develop athletic disciplinary policies with the help of all coaches.
34. Delegate duties to noncoaches within the department.
35. Assign responsibility to coaches.
36. Cooperate with the physical education department in assigning teaching duties to coaches.
37. Encourage and advise staff members in matters of professional growth.
38. Plan new facilities.
39. Establish rules for use of facilities.
40. Take care of all official correspondence pertaining to athletics in the school.
41. At the beginning of a sport season, obtain from coaches completed:
    a. physical examination cards,

b. parents' consent cards,
c. paid athletic insurance receipts,
d. eligibility clearance for contestants, and
e. master eligibility sheet of complete squad.

These are to be accurately tabulated and filed by the athletic coach and kept up to date during the season. This material must be in the hands of the athletic director before any student may compete in a contest.

42. Review financial statements of each game.
43. Keep records of all games and financial transactions.
44. Review returned bid list and list acceptable bids.
45. Write orders for checks.
46. Arrange for cleaning and repairing of equipment during and at the end of season. The head coach should have a voice as to the kind and price range of equipment to be purchased.
47. Carry out business of Athletic Board of Control.
48. Act as representative (along with the principal) of the school at all conference athletic meetings.
49. For safety sake periodically check athletic equipment and facilities with the coaches.
50. Secure competent officials. Make out all check requests for payment of officials. Issue contracts for all officials.
51. Formulate a list of athletic events that will require additional administrative supervision. Collaborate with the building principal to assign such people.
52. Observe practices and confer with coaches on athletic problems.
53. Bring to the attention of all coaches new books, clinics, current research on new equipment, trends, and practices.
54. Plan agendas and conduct regular meetings with head coaches.
55. Participate in the evaluation of all coaches.
56. Participate in the recruitment of coaches.
57. In cooperation with the head coaches, recommend the assignments of assistant coaches.
58. Communicate with board of directors for the use of their golf courses and tennis courts.

The director is the "hub" around which the entire program revolves. His job is to oversee the program in its entirety and make sure that it is coordinated in such a way that it will fulfill the needs of the students and contribute to the educational values of the school system.

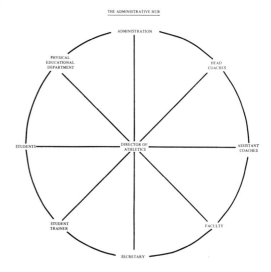

Figure 25.

Duties of Head Coaches

The main function of a head coach should be to properly prepare students to compete in interscholastic athletic activities and help develop a student's best character.

Coaches should be responsible for the

actions of students or observers under their jurisdiction during practice and competitive events both home and away.

They should assure that all participants are adequately equipped, and they are responsible and accountable for developing a training program that will provide wholesome competition in interscholastic sports with an attitude that winning is important, but not everything.

Their qualifications should include considerable training in the sport with which they work, plus the ability to make sound judgments. High school teaching experience should be mandatory. In the case of football, all coaches should be asked to begin practice before school begins in the fall.

They should be responsible and accountable for the supervision of students transported by commercial or private vehicles.

The person assigned as head coach should be directly responsible and accountable to and under the supervision of the athletic director. This person, with his assistants, should be responsible for the supervision of all levels of the activity. The assistant coaches are assigned at the discretion of the head coach working with the athletic director.

The head coaches should be responsible and accountable for the total season's schedule and in recommending and assisting the athletic director in developing the season's schedule.

They should be responsible for recommending the ordering of new equipment and supplies to the athletic director and for the cleaning, checking of inventory, storing, securing, and repairing of all equipment.

They should put into force the athletic policy of the school under the direct supervision of the athletic director.

The head coach should be responsible for the entire program on all levels of his sport.

The head coach should work with the athletic director to establish scheduling and nonconference contests. The coach should advise, suggest, and request, but the final decision should rest with the athletic director.

The head coach should be responsible for the positioning of men on his staff.

He should work with the director to arrive at the best arrangement. In the event that the head coach prefers that a given individual not work on his staff, he should be able to show reason for this.

The following is a list of areas of concern:

1. Determine the budget of the team: After determining the total budget of his team, the coach should give a statement of it to the athletic director.

2. Counsel the players: The coach should act as a counselor at times and help the players with any personal problems that they might have.

3. Attend coaching clinics: It is a duty of a coach to attend coaching clinics so that he may increase his knowledge about that particular sport. New ideas and techniques of the sport are presented in these clinics.

4. Have good knowledge about injuries: A good coach should have the knowledge to determine what type of injury a player has and how to apply first aid to this injury. Most schools do not have a trainer, and therefore, the coach must take care of all injuries that do occur.

5. Design game strategies: The coach should use films, visual aids along with practice sessions to determine strategies for upcoming games.

6. Plan, organize, and direct practice sessions: A coach who is not well organ-

ized is never successful.

7. Make and study scouting reports: Essential practice to a successful season.

8. Design game strategies: Each coach should pattern his game strategy around the quality of players he has and the weaknesses and strengths of the opposition.

9. View films: This is one method of improving as a coach and as a team.

10. Plan game strategy: Each game usually demands a different type of strategy which the coach is responsible for formulating.

11. Schedule games: Usually, in a small school the coach will schedule his own games, but in a larger school this is the athletic director's responsibility.

12. Cooperate with and educate sports writers: Good public relations are essential to any coach and program.

13. Select, purchase, and maintain sports equipment: Only in a small school will this exist.

14. Attend coaching clinics: Essential to all coaches who want to better themselves through the use of newer and better methods.

15. Evaluate players.

16. Deliver speeches at athletic banquets as well as civic gatherings.

17. Obtain and evaluate game officials: Again, this would only be the responsibility of the small school coach.

18. Plan and supervise team trips: The athletic director and coach should work hand-in-hand in this respect.

19. Obtain ticket takers, scorers, police, and concessionaries for games: Again, only in a small school situation.

20. Assume responsibility for the behavior of players at games: Control and the discipline of his ball players are essential to successful team output.

21. Prepare notices.

22. Prepare budget for his sport.

23. Interview salesmen.

24. Conduct coaches' meetings.

25. Develop coaching assignments.

26. Work in harmony with other coaches.

27. Organize and supervise practices.

28. Work out trip itinerary.

29. Classify squad members.

30. Help new coaches.

31. Prepare for practice games.

32. Construct playbooks for coaches.

33. Help plan new facilities.

34. Check on all equipment for safety.

35. Check on instructional materials.

36. Inventory all equipment at end of season.

37. Make plans for issuing equipment.

38. Establish an award system.

39. Arrange press meetings.

40. Be responsible for all equipment issued to his sport.

41. Turn in eligibility lists at the designated time.

42. Know and abide by the school rules.

43. Know and abide by the conference and state rules.

44. Turn in accident reports when they are needed.

45. Turn in post-game summary.

46. Call in all scores for contests to radio and news media.

47. Cooperate with other conference coaches.

48. Maintain athletic squadroom discipline.

49. Abide by opening and closing dates in his respective sports season.

50. Turn in parent's permission forms as designated.

51. Make sure that each athlete is covered by school insurance and has a verification of insurance form before being allowed to participate in games or practice sessions.

52. Make sure that each athlete turns in a physical examination form before be-

ing allowed to participate.

53. Conduct himself so that he will be above criticism at all times.

54. Attend all conference meetings.

55. Bill all athletes for lost or damaged equipment.

56. Turn in a written evaluation of each of his assistant coaches to the athletic director and principal at the end of the season.

57. Attend as many staff meetings as possible.

58. Attend the all-sports banquet.

59. Supervise the locker room and practice areas before and after practice.

60. Arrange a scouting schedule for assistant coaches.

61. Present a season summary including contest results, award winners, records for the sports, conference standings, and other pertinent data to the athletic director.

62. Arrange to meet visiting teams as they arrive.

63. Prepare the area used for practice and games with the help of the custodial staff.

64. Rate officials and turn in the results to the director.

65. Assume the responsibility for the action of the members of the team he coaches, both on the bus and on the field.

66. Leave the building only after the last player from the group has left.

67. Check the locker room, storage areas, and practice areas before leaving the building. This includes lights, windows, doors, etc.

68. Make sure that each athlete is thoroughly conditioned for participation.

69. Explain and enforce strict training rules for his squad.

70. Be responsible for the team's dress and behavior in games, practice sessions, trips, locker rooms, or on any occasion

where the personnel he is coaching is taking part as a team representing his school.

71. Issue equipment to his squad. It is taken for granted that an efficient system of issuing equipment will be thoroughly organized *before* the season begins. The head coach, assistant coaches, equipment manager, and student managers all should be part of this organization.

72. Instruct his squad as to proper care of their equipment on the field, in the locker room, and on trips.

73. See that equipment is cleaned and properly stored at all times.

74. Cooperate with athletic director in providing publicity materials to the newspapers, radio stations, and other schools.

75. Assume a strong leadership in directing his assistants. There must be no doubt as to who is responsible for the successful running of his team.

76. Take a personal interest in players and their problems, do counseling whenever and wherever necessary.

77. Promote morale and team spirit. Stress the benefits derived from wholesome athletic competition.

78. Make trips of athletic teams a reward for the boys who have worked and actually earned the distinction of belonging on the recognized reserves or varsity teams. He must make the trip a privilege and an honor for deserving athletes.

Veller has commented on the importance of good rapport between the head coach and the assistant.

The assistants play a vital part in any success the head coach may have. The head coach's success is in direct proportion to the help he receives from his assistants. This is why he should have some input in the selection of his assistants. The assistant should receive recognition in every way possible by the head coach. This should be done publicly and in front of the squad. It will indicate that the head coach has confidence and trust in the assistant, and it will enhance his position with the players. The head coach should never under any circumstances reprimand an assistant coach publicly.[22]

Duties of Assistant Coaches

The main function of assistant coaches is to help the player to become a better athlete and to assist the varsity coach in the many details of coaching. He should work closely with the varsity coach and should at all times stand ready to carry out any assignments given to him by the varsity coach. Assistant coaches should also assume their full share of responsibility for the actions of the players under his supervision at practice and during games.

Assistant coaches should also observe at all times that players are properly equipped and be responsible for helping to develop a training program in cooperation with the head coach. He should help to develop a good *esprit-de-corps* among the players as well as the staff.

Assistant coaches should be responsible and accountable to assume their share of responsibility and accountability for the supervision of players being transported to and from contests or practice sessions. They should be responsible for supervision of all players under their jurisdiction and any others assigned to them by the head coach.

An important function of assistant coaches is helping and assisting the head coach in developing the season schedule.

The assistant coaches should be responsible for recommending to the head coach

the ordering of new equipment and supplies and for the cleaning, inventorying, storing, securing, and repairing of all equipment as assigned by the head coach.

The assistant coach should be loyal to his head coach, his school, and to the program.

The assistant coach should be thoroughly familiar with the responsibilities of the athletic director and the head coach. Their responsibilities have a direct bearing on the actions of the assistant coach.

The following is a list of areas of responsibility. Many of these duties will be similar to those of the head coaches:

1. Know and abide by the school rules.
2. Know and abide by the state rules.
3. Know and abide by the conference rules.
4. Turn in eligibility lists as designated.
5. Turn in parents' permission forms as designated.
6. See that each player is covered by insurance.
7. See that each player has a physical examination.
8. Turn in accident reports immediately.
9. Turn in game summaries.
10. Prepare season summaries.
11. Attend staff meetings.
12. Attend the all-sports banquet.
13. Be responsible for locker room conduct.
14. Meet visiting teams.
15. Prepare areas used for practice and games.
16. Rate officials.
17. Be responsible for acts of the team on trips.
18. Leave the building last after practice and games.
19. Check locker room after practice and games.

Cousy and Power have made the following observation regarding the role of

[22]Veller, Don, "Head Coach and Assistant Rapport," *Athletic Journal* (April, 1968), p. 66.

the assistant coach. The head coach's philosophy should coincide with that of his assistant's. Assistants should be eager to carry out their duties. If he does a good job the head coach should make him feel that he is an intricate part of the entire organization. The assistant should be made to feel that his contribution is appreciated and necessary. He should be given a voice in the planning and the responsibility of carrying out assignments. The assistant cannot be effective if he has knowledge that he is not respected or his advice is not taken. The assistant, on the other hand, should not try to "run the show." He must listen and carry out the plans the head coach has made.[23]

Duties in Girls' and Women's Athletics

Regardless of the administrative philosophy, it is essential that a woman be the administrative head in charge of the girls' program. This position is usually given the title of coordinator. The function of this position is to prepare and advise the women coaches in respect to student participation in all contests governed by the rules of the conference, state, and national competition. Usually the girls' coordinator will be directly responsible to the athletic director. She is responsible for the arrangements and supervision of all activities and needs of all the participants. The girls' coordinator should be responsible for the total season's schedule and for recommending and assisting the athletic director in formulating it.

The girls' coordinator should be responsible for recommending the ordering of new equipment and supplies and for the maintenance, inventory, storage, securing,

[23]Cousy, Bob and Power, Frank, *Baseball Concepts and Techniques* (Boston, Allyn and Bacon, 1970), p. 8.

and repairing of all existing equipment.

She should be responsible to the athletic director and the person in charge of building use for the scheduling of all events and practices and the supervision, maintenance, and security of all the facilities at all times. She should also assume the responsibility of providing for game officials and faculty help at contests.

Women Coaches

The role of the women coaches should be to direct and provide athletic experiences for students engaged in interscholastic competition and to help develop the student's best character.

Women coaches should be responsible for the actions of students or observers under their jurisdiction during practice and contests. Each coach should be responsible for the maintenance of her respective uniforms and equipment during her season and in making any recommendations for the purchase of new equipment or supplies.

Women coaches should be required to furnish all necessary data for eligibility lists to the athletic coordinator, supply a transportation schedule with time desired, supervise locker rooms, report game results, attend staff meetings and in-service programs, and maintain safety practices concerning participant's involvement.

Cheerleader Director

The function of the position of cheerleader director should be to properly prepare students to participate in cheerleading performance. Cheerleading experience is helpful. Understanding of cheerleading is mandatory. The director should be responsible for teaching routines, developing performance of style, and helping to develop the student's best character. She should be directly responsible for the arrangement and supervision of all activities, practices and performances, pep assemblies, contests, trips, and clinics.

The cheerleader director should be directly responsible and accountable to the appropriate building principal and the athletic coordinator. She should assume the responsibility for providing the necessary format in conducting the rules and regulations in establishing the try-outs for the different cheerleading squads each year. The cheerleader director should be responsible to the athletic coordinator and the assistant principal in charge of the building for the scheduling of all events and practices and the supervision, maintenance, and security of the facilities at all times.

The cheerleader director should be responsible for the actions of students or observers under her direction during practice and competitive events both home and away. She should be responsible and accountable for the supervision of students transported by school or private vehicle which also includes the careful supervision of cheerleaders when involved in activities that require accommodations for staying overnight.

The cheerleader director should assume the responsibility of selecting the cheerleaders. There are various ways in which the cheerleaders can be chosen. Care should be taken that it does not result in a popularity contest. To avoid this, a committee of faculty and students can be formed for the express purpose of selecting the cheerleaders strictly on a prearranged merit basis.

Tryouts for the varsity, junior varsity, and sophomore cheerleaders can be held each spring. Frosh cheerleaders can be selected through tryouts in the fall. In addition to leading cheers at athletic events, the cheerleaders can make posters advertising athletic games, decorate the field and gym for home events, and cooperate with the lettermen's club and pep club in the development of school spirit. Scholastic requirements for cheerleading should be the same as for membership on an athletic team. Cheerleaders should be dropped when it is in the best interest of the school, squad, or the individual. The cheerleaders should be selected on the basis of total points awarded for poise, appearance, agility, originality, form, personality, and leadership.

At the tryouts, the candidates should lead cheers which they have learned and also go through the appropriate maneuvers to the school song. The candidates should be called out at random and asked to perform individually. They should be judged on a five-point scale, five being high.

The criteria for judging the candidates could be appearance, personality, enthusiasm or pep, knowledge of cheers, attitude, and agility.

Once elected to the cheerleading squads, the students should conform to rules and regulations similar to those to which an athlete should conform. Absences from three games which are unexcused are grounds for automatic suspension from the team. A cheerleader should receive an excused absence from a game if he or she presents a doctor's certificate stating that he or she was ill or injured and unable to cheer for that contest. Absences from two practices in a week should make the cheerleader ineligible for the next game. Smoking while in uniform should result in the cheerleader being automatically dropped from the squad. A cheerleader's grade average should be C or better to remain eligible to cheer. Receiving a D in one subject should make a cheerleader ineligible in spite of the fact that he or she might have enough A's to counterbalance the D. The cheerleader should not be allowed to cheer until that D becomes a C or better. The grade should be raised in two six-week periods or the cheerleader should be dropped from the squad.

Suggested Requirements for Cheerleader Selection and Procedure

Cheerleading tryouts shall be held each spring for the high school girls and those eighth grade girls interested in it. Five girls should be selected for each squad. Freshmen and sophomores should try out for the frosh-soph squads; juniors and seniors should try out for varsity. Anyone may try out for the wrestling squad.

Cheerleaders should be selected from a panel of judges (equal number of adults and high school students). No one having an immediate relative trying out should be a judge. The cheerleading advisor should be in charge of getting the adult judges. The student council should select the student judges.

A contestant may try out for any number of squads that do not conflict in sport seasons. Wrestling and basketball tryouts should be first; football tryouts one week later.

One alternate should be selected for frosh-soph and varsity basketball, football, and wrestling.

Specifications: They should try out by number, not name 1—5 scale (5 is high)

1. Three jumps
2. One group cheer (groups picked by random numbers)
3. One individual cheer (This should be picked from a box of numbers right before the contestant goes out.)
4. One splits, one cartwheel (roundoff, etc.)

5. Appearance (mainly smile, hair, neatness, enthusiasm)

Pom Director

The responsibility of the position of pom director should be to prepare students to represent their school in an effort to provide spirit, enthusiasm, and interest in various athletic activities.

The sponsor should be responsible for teaching routines, developing performance of style, and to become involved in developing the student's best character.

The pom director should be responsible for the conduct and actions of students under her direction during practice and competitive events both home and away. Supervision of all practices, rehearsals, and game performances is essential and necessary.

The pom director should assume the responsibility for determining the method of selection and in establishing the try-outs and practice schedule for pom squads each year.

The pom director should be responsible to the athletic coordinator and the principal in charge of building for the scheduling of all activities and practices and the supervision, maintenance, and security of the facilities at all times.

Duties of the Ticket Manager

The ticket manager's function should be to serve the student body and the community with the best possible procedures for the disposition of tickets to high school events.

He should be responsible for the actions of the students and workers under his jurisdiction at the home events.

He should arrange for the printing and sale of tickets and the deposit of money for all high school events where admission is charged with the exception of student sponsored activities.

The ticket manager should be responsible for the banking of all monies from the sale of tickets and expected to keep an accurate account of this money.

The ticket manager should work closely with the athletic director and the assistant principal in charge of the budget in regard to all aspects of ticket sales.

There are no special qualifications required for this assignment. However, the person selected should have some seniority on the staff so that he is familiar with facilities and procedures and be able to make sound judgments.

The ticket manager should be directly responsible and accountable to and under the supervision of the athletic director.

The ticket manager should arrange for employment of all ticket takers and ticket sellers who will also serve as crowd control assistants and who will be directly responsible to the ticket manager.

Attitudes Toward Extra Pay for Coaching

The attitude of most school boards toward extra pay for coaches is favorable. They feel that coaches should be paid for all the extra time they spend coaching athletic teams. The question is, how much should be paid for each sport, and what should the difference be for each coach. For example, there are those who would believe that the basketball coach has a longer season compared with football; basketball seasons run approximately five months whereas football lasts only two to three months. Track (both indoor and outdoor) runs five months whereas baseball runs only 2.5 months. Other comparisons can be cited which would tend to indicate an unfairness regarding time spent, number of athletes to handle, inequity in number of assistants, and others. The situation is such that it could be argued endlessly.

Many argue for a salary schedule for coaching like that used by administrators in payment of the academic staff; a maximum and minimum sum of money should be offered to coaches. For example, a coach could start at a minimum amount of money and reach the maximum after a certain number of years. In other words, the increments for coaching should be paid in accordance with experience just as in teaching. Pay scales should be established with education and experience being the main ingredient. If experience is important in academic teaching, many individuals contend that it means as much if not more in coaching.

The advocates of extra pay for coaching contend that it is not good reasoning to assume, for example, that if a man as an educator is worth five dollars per hour during the school day, and either no pay, token pay, or twenty-five cents to a dollar per hour working two to three hours with the same students after the regular school day, that this is as it should be.

Coaching is not a part-time job for a part-time person. It has problems and demands preparation. Just as the regular classroom teacher must spend extra hours preparing his or her subject matter or keeping up with the latest trends in the field, a coach must do likewise. There is little room for mediocrity in the coaching profession where the standard of measurement is primarily the won and lost record. There are those who feel that coaches are entitled to extra pay for their coaching responsibilities primarily because of the preparation and education necessary to do a competent job. The hours are long, and certainly athletics are a very important part of the school curriculum just as are the academic subjects. To substantiate this statement Santoro[24] makes the following observation:

[24]Santoro, Jack "A Salary Schedule for Coaches," *Journal of Health, Physical Education, and Recreation* (April, 1968) , p. 31.

The philosophy of physical education teachers is that coaching is teaching. Physical educators believe that sports are an integral part of the students' total education and that interscholastic activities provide an area where athletic development can be realized under competent guidance. Those students with exceptional athletic potential have the opportunity to achieve excellence by working closely with a well-trained specialist in an educationally controlled situation.

Unfortunately, many communities do not share the 'teaching' philosophy of coaching, and coaching salaries have not been increasing in proportion to teaching salaries. In some areas, coaches still receive no payment at all. As communities become aware of the educational values sports offer America's youth and as they recognize the importance of qualified personnel in their school system, this pattern is bound to change.

Methods of Payment for Extra Coaching Duties

Teachers everywhere are taking a more aggressive attitude toward the conditions under which they work. Money has become a more significant factor. They are no longer willing to spend extra hours doing after-school work without pay. Coaching is placed in a different category, however, because much or most of a coach's extra work is after school or evenings or Saturdays. What is adequate compensation for this extra time and effort? Should there be a relationship between the pay and the effect the coach has on the lives of the players? If the principle of extra pay for extra duty is acceptable, how can a pattern of extra pay for coaching be worked out? A realistic approach to the problem would be to arrange the pay schedule so that the amount of extra pay the coach receives for coaching would gradually increase as his base pay as a teacher increases. For example, if he receives 1,000 dollars for coaching and his base pay is 10,000 dollars, this would mean that he would be receiving 10 percent of his salary for coaching. If his base pay would be raised to 10,200 dollars the next year he would receive 1,020 dollars for coaching. This would continue until the maximum salary is reached. If he were teaching in a system that has a salary schedule, his coaching pay would increase with each year that he stays in the system and in coaching.

There are always those persons, however, that will question the percentage allowance given for coaching. At best it is a guess on the part of those people burdened with the task of deciding what the percentage should be for each sport.

Index and Formula Method

Thurston[25] developed a formula which takes into consideration length of school day, time spent on coaching per year, and the experience and education of the coach. This plan also takes into consideration that the coaching salary should be tied in with the base salary. In using a plan of this kind it is necessary to determine an index which is based on the factors mentioned above.

This system of determining the index is unique in many ways because most indexes are determined by the number of years on the staff. The index used by Thurston brings into being the time factor in a different and more realistic manner. It stresses the actual time spent on each particular activity and uses this as the determining factor in judging the amount of money that should be given for that particular sport.

Another method of determining extra pay for extra services is given below. This shows a comparison of the differential pay

[25]Thurston, James, "A Formula for Extra Duty," *Journal of Health, Physical Education, and Recreation* (April, 1968), p. 32.

This index was determined by using the following formula and the activity used was basketball.

$$\frac{\text{Amount of time spent in activity (basketball) per day}}{\text{amount of time in normal school day}} \times \frac{\text{amount of time spent in the activity (basketball) during year}}{\text{length of normal school year (month, weeks, days)}} = \text{Index}$$

$$\frac{\text{2-hour practice playing time per day}}{\text{8-hour normal day}} \times \frac{\text{5-month long season}}{\text{10-month school year}} = \text{Index}$$

or

$$2/8 \times 5/10 = .125$$

The base salary is multiplied by the index to arrive at the amount of money given for coaching basketball. If the base salary was $10,000 and this was multiplied by the index of .125 the basketball coaching differential would be $1250. There could be added indexes also. For example .02 for pressure, .002 for responsibility, .03 for a winning season, and .003 for liability.

This would bring the index to .180. This would allow $1,800 for coaching basketball.

for different activities. All the activities are grouped, classified, or categorized. Each area is assessed on a rating scale with A being the lowest and J being the highest according to the following information.

The index used for determining the amount of money given for an activity is based solely on the teacher's experience. This index is then applied to the base salary to obtain the teacher's index salary.

This type of extra pay formula requires an evaluation and a definition of all the extracurricular activities. The evaluation is based on the following criteria.

a. The number of participants. Also considered is whether they are male or female, all age groups, or would they be primarily seniors, juniors, sophomores, etc.

b. The pressures involved and the pressure of leadership demanded by the number of assistants and responsibility. General pressure in the activity itself, crowd control, community pressure, etc.

c. Injury risk. Practically all sports have an injury risk; but some are definitely more injury prone than others.

d. Working conditions in lieu of supervision factors.

e. Equipment involved; the care of it, the accountability, servicing, value, type, and amount.

f. Length of seasons and number of contests. Interest here is not in comparing twenty-two contests to twenty as five is to three etc. but what about the length of the season, how much work is involved with weekends, vacations, evenings, after school, before school, etc.

g. Travel and bus supervision responsibility.

h. Extra meetings that are involved; seeding meetings, conference meetings, scouting, films, etc.

Schedule of Possible Differential Payments

To determine a differential, multiply the appropriate differential index by a 7000 dollar starting salary. An individual's vertical placement is determined by his experience (number of years) in the differential position.

TABLE XXXV
SALARY DIFFERENTIAL INDEX

	A	B	C	D	E	F	G	H	I	J
1	.020	.030	.040	.050	.060	.070	.080	.090	.100	.110
2	.022	.033	.044	.055	.066	.077	.088	.099	.110	.121
3	.024	.036	.048	.060	.072	.084	.096	.108	.120	.132
4	.026	.039	.052	.065	.078	.091	.104	.117	.130	.143

Differential Positions by Schedule Classification

(Dollar Value)

Classification A

1st Year—$140

2nd Year—$154

3rd Year—$168

4th Year—$182

High School Sophomore Class Advisor

Director of All Grade Honor Band

Activity Photographer

Classification B

1st Year—$210

2nd Year—$231

3rd Year—$252

4th Year—$273

High School Speculum (Business)

High School Junior Class Advisor

Stage Scenery—Junior High School

High School Girls' Swim Program

Dramatics—Junior High School

Newspaper—Junior High School

High School Audio-Visual Coordinator

High School Girls' Club Advisor

Classification C

1st Year—$280

2nd Year—$308

3rd Year—$336

4th Year—$364

Activities Director—Bardwell

8th Grade Assistant Football Coach

8th Grade Assistant Basketball Coach

Junior High School Student Council

High School Assistant Cheerleader Coach

High School Girls' Intramurals

High School Speech Activities

Junior High Intramurals

Junior High School Audio-Visual
    Building Coordinator

7th Grade Flag Football Coach

7th Grade Basketball Coach

High School Assistant Pom Pom Coach

High School G.A.A.

High School Pep Club

Director of Junior High Orchestra

Classification D

1st Year—$350

2nd Year—$385

3rd Year—$420

4th Year—$455

High School Student Council

9th Grade Assistant Football Coach

9th Grade Assistant Basketball Coach

Junior High School Assistant Track Coach

8th Grade Football Head Coach

8th Grade Basketball Head Coach

High School Pom Pom Head Coach

Public Address

High School Auroran

High School Speculum (Editorial)

Elementary Intramural Supervisor

Junior High Vocal Music

High School Assistant Cross-Country

High School Cheerleader Head Coach

High School Debate Head Coach

Classification E

1st Year—$420	3rd Year—$504
2nd Year—$462	4th Year—$546

Director of Junior High Bands
Assistant Sophomore Football Coach
Assistant Sophomore Basketball Coach
9th Grade Football Head Coach
High School Assistant Track Coach
Junior High School Track Coach
High School Intramural Supervisor
High School Assistant Band Director

Junior High School Wrestling Coach
Golf Coach
Tennis Coach
Sophomore Baseball Coach
Cross-Country Coach
Assistant Wrestling Coach
Sophomore Track Coach
High School Senior Class Advisor

Classification F

1st Year—$490	3rd Year—$588
2nd Year—$539	4th Year—$637

High School Stage Design
High School Assistant Football Coach
High School Assistant Basketball Coach
Sophomore Head Football Coach

Sophomore Head Basketball Coach
After-School Elementary Athletic
   Supervisors

Classification G

1st Year—$560	3rd Year—$672
2nd Year—$616	4th Year—$728

Director of High School Dramatics

Junior High Athletic Director

Classification H

1st Year—$630	3rd Year—$756
2nd Year—$693	4th Year—$819

Director of High School Vocal Work
Director of High School Orchestra
High School Head Baseball Coach
Ticket Manager

High School Head Track Coach
High School Head Wrestling Coach
High School Head Swimming Coach

Classification I

1st Year—$700	3rd Year—$840
2nd Year—$770	4th Year—$910

Director of High School Band

Classification J

1st Year—$770	3rd Year—$924
2nd Year—$847	4th Year—$1001

High School Head Basketball Coach

High School Head Football Coach

Increases beyond the maximums might be granted in those instances where the board of education, upon recommendation of the superintendent, deems it to be in the best interests of the district.

Lump Sum Payment

One of the most frequent methods used to pay teachers for extra duties is the lump sum payment. This is being used in many school systems. This method does not allow for any correlation between the payment and base salary schedule. It is unrealistic because it forces certain individuals to determine the worth of each activity. Who is to say which activity is the most important? How much is each activity worth in dollars and cents? Who is to determine and on what basis, that coaching the football team is worth 100 or 1000 dollars? Who is to determine whether football coaching is worth more than track coaching or tennis coaching? Be that as it may, this system is used in many schools. The following coaching salary schedule indicates the amount given for the various sports for a period of five years. Most schools using this type of lump sum payment do not go beyond the five-year period.

TABLE XXXVI
SAMPLE COACHING SALARY FOR DIFFERENT SPORTS

GROUPS	FIRST CONTRACT	SECOND CONTRACT	THIRD CONTRACT	FOURTH CONTRACT	FIFTH CONTRACT
A					
Head Football	$ 700	$ 800	$ 925	$1,050	$1,150
Head Basketball	700	800	925	1,050	1,150
Head Track	700	800	925	1,050	1,150
B					
Head Wrestling	675	775	900	1,025	1,125
Head Gymnastics	675	775	900	1,025	1,125
Head Baseball	675	775	900	1,025	1,125
C					
Assistant Football	450	525	600	700	775
Assistant Basketball	450	525	600	700	775
Assistant In/Out Track	450	525	600	700	775
D					
Head Cross Country	425	500	575	675	750
Assistant Gymnastics	425	500	575	675	750
Assistant Wrestling	425	500	575	675	750
Assistant Baseball	425	500	575	675	750
E					
Head Tennis	400	450	525	575	625
Assistant Out Track	400	450	525	575	625
Head Golf	400	450	525	575	625
F					
Assistant Cross Country	300	350	400	450	500
Assistant Tennis	300	350	400	450	500

TABLE XXXVII
COACHES SALARY SCHEDULE ($7,200 Base)

	Step I 1st & 2nd year	Step II 3rd & 4th year	Step III 5th & 6th year	Step IV 7th year
FOOTBALL				
$15 for each of 2				
days prior to practice				
Head Varsity Coach	11% – 792	12% – 864	13% – 936	14% – 1008
Grade 7 - 8	7% – 504	8% – 576	8½% – 612	9% – 648
Assistant Varsity	7% – 504	8% – 576	8½% – 612	9% – 648
Head Sophomore	6% – 432	7% – 504	7½% – 540	8% – 576
Assistant Sophomore	7% – 504	8% – 576	8½% – 612	9% – 648
Head Junior High	6% – 432	7% – 504	7½% – 540	8% – 576
Ass't 9th Grade	5% – 360	6% – 432	6½% – 468	7% – 504
CROSS COUNTRY				
Head Varsity Coach	5½% – 396	6½% – 468	7% – 504	8% – 576
Assistant	4½% – 324	5% – 360	5½% – 396	6% – 432
BASKETBALL				
Head Varsity Coach	11% – 792	12% – 864	13% – 936	14% – 1008
Assistant Varsity	7% – 504	8% – 576	8½% – 612	9% – 648
Head Sophomore	7% – 504	8% – 576	8½% – 612	9% – 648
Assistant Sophomore	6% – 432	7% – 504	7½% – 540	8% – 576
Head 9th Grade	6% – 432	7% – 504	7½% – 540	8% – 576
Ass't 9th Grade	5½% – 396	6½% – 468	7% – 504	7½% – 540
Head 7th & 8th Grade	5% – 360	6% – 432	6½% – 468	7% – 504
Ass't 7th & 8th Grade	4½% – 324	5½% – 396	6% – 432	6½% – 468
WRESTLING				
Head Varsity Coach	10% – 720	11% – 792	12% – 864	13% – 936
Assistant	6% – 432	7% – 504	7½% – 540	8% – 576
Head Junior High	6% – 432	7% – 504	7½% – 540	8% – 576
Ass't Junior High	5% – 360	6% – 432	6½% – 468	7% – 504
TRACK				
Head Varsity Coach	9% – 648	10% – 720	11% – 792	12% – 864
Assistants	5% – 360	6% – 432	7% – 504	8% – 576
Head Junior High	5% – 360	6% – 432	7% – 504	8% – 576
Assistants	4% – 288	5% – 360	6% – 432	7% – 504
BASEBALL				
Head Varsity Coach	8% – 576	9% – 648	10% – 720	11% – 792
Assistant Varsity	4½% – 324	5½% – 396	6½% – 468	7½% – 540
Head Sophomore	4½% – 324	5½% – 396	6½% – 468	7½% – 540
Head Junior High	4½% – 324	5½% – 396	6½% – 468	7½% – 540
Assistants	4% – 288	5% – 360	6% – 432	7% – 504
GOLF				
Head Varsity Coach	5% – 360	6% – 432	7% – 504	8% – 576
TENNIS				
Head Varsity Coach	5% – 360	6% – 432	7% – 504	8% – 576

TABLE XXXVIII
JACKSON HIGH SCHOOL DISTRICT 130
— GIRLS INTERSCHOLASTIC ATHLETIC SALARY SCHEDULE —

	Contract 1	*Contract 2*	*Contract 3*	*Contract 4*	*Contract 5*
Tennis	300.00	350.00	400.00	450.00	500.00
Gymnastics	300.00	350.00	400.00	450.00	500.00
Badminton	300.00	350.00	400.00	450.00	500.00
Archery	234.00	273.00	311.00	350.00	389.00
Track	234.00	273.00	311.00	350.00	389.00
Bowling	167.00	195.00	222.00	250.00	278.00
Fencing	167.00	195.00	222.00	250.00	278.00

G.A.A. SPORTS DAYS — INTRAMURAL SALARY SCHEDULE

9 weeks		9 weeks		9 weeks		9 weeks	
Field Hockey	150.00	Volleyball	150.00	Basketball	150.00	Softball	150.00
Intramural	75.00	Intramural	75.00	Intramural	75.00	Intramural	75.00

Coordinator: 350.00

Summary

Practically all schools now have some type of extra pay for extra services. There are a few that still consider extra services should be included in coaching as part of the job. This practice, however, is no longer prevalent in most school systems. For example, a study appearing in the NEA Research Bulletin comments that the practice of giving extra pay for extra duties is widespread; it is safe to conclude that in a majority of school systems there are informal provisions for extra pay not included in the salary schedule. Almost 53 percent of the fifty-nine systems studied included supplementary schedules for both athletic and nonathletic activities, but less than 4 percent provided supplements only for nonathletic activities.[26]

The concept of extra compensation for such duties has become more prevalent in recent years and has been widely accepted as general practice in many school systems. In a day and age when everything that is done is measured in dollars and cents it is a little ridiculous to assume that a professional person, whether he be a teacher, coach, lawyer, or doctor, should be expected to donate his time and effort and receive nothing in return. The real differences of opinion in this respect are not in whether extra pay for extra work should be given but in the amount paid, the method of payment, and the differential pay that should be awarded for coaching the various sports. The accepted procedure for giving extra pay in the past was to pay a specific amount for each sport, with the assistant coach receiving a smaller amount. More recently schools have given considerations for coaching experience the same as teaching experience. In this way the longer a coach coaches, the more money he receives.

Coaching is teaching, and only through

[26]Thurston, James, 'Extra Pay for Extra Duties," *N. E. A. Research Bulletin* (May 1963), p. 51.

sound administrative policies, qualified staff, proper coaching load, and just and adequate compensation can it serve its purpose to education.

Grieve and Myers[27] make the following observation about extra compensation for coaching:

> There are a number of reasons why substantial evidence must be presented so that teachers will receive extra compensation for coaching. Numerous articles have appeared dealing with methods which may be used to arrive at the amount of extra remuneration for specific coaching duties, but very few provided solid information on why such extra compensation is necessary.
>
> In reference to time required it would be that time which extends beyond the normal teaching day. Those teachers who are not assigned such extra duties would be finished for the day. Many teachers who are not involved in coaching indicate that they do a great deal of work at home. There are two important factors which may be used to counteract the argument. First, they are at home. Second, a coach has a considerable amount of work to do at home also.
>
> An individual who receives compensation for coaching, or for that matter any other extra curricular activity, is being paid for expert teaching. One who is involved in coaching should have extensive training in this important educational area and a great deal of his time as an undergraduate student was undoubtedly spent in acquiring the necessary knowledge.

BEHAVIORAL OBJECTIVES

After a person has read this chapter, he should be able to:

1. Distinguish between the terms selection and retention as applied to teachers and outline a workable plan of selection.

---

[27]Grieve, Andrew and Myers, David, "Why Should There Be Extra Compensation for Coaching? *The Athletic Journal* (March, 1969), p. 78.

2. Identify and explain several criteria for selection of an athletic coach.
3. Distinguish between the personal and educational qualifications of the athletic coach and identify several examples of each.
4. Explain why it is important that coaches possess strong personal qualifications.
5. Identify and explain in order of importance several personal qualifications of the athletic coach.
6. Select in order of importance the educational requirements necessary for the individual to qualify himself as an athletic coach.
7. Explain the difference between the personal qualifications of the athletic coach and the academic classroom teacher.
8. Propose a plan for the certification of interscholastic athletic coaches which can be defended.
9. Distinguish between the director of athletics' special qualifications and those of the athletic coach.
10. Choose three competencies of the athletic director and demonstrate by example how each is applied to the interscholastic athletic program.
11. Distinguish between the base and index as it is applied to teachers' salaries.
12. Differentiate between percentage of the base pay and the use of the index for determining extra pay for extra duties.
13. Select several factors or criteria which are used to determine the index to be used for extra pay for extracurricular activities.
14. Compare the years of experience with the time factor in determining the index.
15. Select three of the most important duties of the athletic director and apply them to an actual situation.

16. Distinguish between the general duties of the athletic director and the athletic coach.

17. Explain the relationship between the athletic director, head coach, and assistant coach.

18. Identify and analyze the factors that determine the duties of the athletic director.

19. Identify and explain several of the overlapping duties of the athletic director and athletic coach and apply each of them to an actual situation.

20. Select and explain the main duty of the head coach.

21. Differentiate between moral and legal responsibilities of athletic coaches.

22. State in order of priority the five most helpful administrative duties for the director of athletics.

23. Develop a workable and fair method for establishing a supplementary pay scale for coaches.

24. Set up a program for the preparation of high school athletic coaches which will be satisfactory.

25. Prepare a list of qualifications for the athletic director and the coach.

26. List all the factors that all staff members should be aware of in maintaining good relations within the department.

27. Formulate a course of study for the preparation of the athletic director and the coach.

28. Identify the most important parts of an athletic director's preparation program. Comment upon the need for increasing or changing the requirements for the athletic director and coaching preparation program.

29. Identify several traits of high school coaches and athletic directors in order of importance.

30. Explain the role of the athletic director in establishing values for the athletic program.

31. Define coaching as a profession.

32. List some of the most promising professional opportunities to the successful high school athletic director and coach.

33. Select a proper procedure for the selection of a football coach.

34. Explain the importance of leadership in athletics. Compare the different types of leaders.

35. Select the most desirable qualifications for the director of athletics in order of importance.

36. Explain the problems encountered with the physical education teacher as coach and academic teacher as a coach.

37. Identify the competencies of the athletic director and the coach.

38. Identify and explain several reasons for extra pay for coaching.

39. Define extra pay for extra services.

40. Compile the essential qualifications of an athletic director, an athletic coach.

41. Enumerate and explain the areas of responsibility of the athletic director and the coach in conducting their program.

42. Analyze the effects of the different types of athletic directors on the personnel within the department as well as the departmental policies.

43. Analyze the responsibilities of the athletic director for staff improvement, and program improvement.

44. List some of the reasons for low staff morale. How can this be improved?

45. Suggest an ideal procedure for the relationship of the superintendent, principal, and board of education in the selection of the athletic director.

46. Present the pro's and con's of extra pay for extra duties.

47. Cite any mandatory legislation with reference to athletic coaching that has been enacted in your state.

48. Appraise the role of motivation in the behavior of an athletic director.
49. Identify the problems involved in the selection of athletic coaches in contrast to classroom teachers.
50. Describe and contrast the employment of classroom teachers to that of coaches in terms of the following: methods of evaluation and contractual agreement.

ACTIVITIES

1. Develop a differential pay schedule for coaches using a scientific method for determining it.
2. Visit a local secondary school and determine the duties of the athletic director, head coach, and assistant coach.
3. Write several superintendents of schools of varying sizes and request copies of their differential pay systems.
4. Interview five interscholastic coaches to determine what their opinions are relative to extra pay for coaching.
5. Attend an interscholastic athletic contest. Observe some of the duties of the assistant coach in comparison with the head coach.
6. Interview five teachers of music, dramatics, and band to determine their attitude toward extra pay for extra services.
7. Survey your local secondary school and submit a report to the class on the educational qualifications of the athletic staff.
8. Talk with a coach and find out how many hours a day he spends on coaching and determine his hourly wage for this activity.
9. Write to several school superintendents and ask them to send you their application for position forms.
10. Talk with several seniors who are planning on coaching after graduation as to their expectations as to what amount of money they will receive for coaching.
11. Select a number of school districts in your area and seek to identify the competencies and personal and prestige traits which are associated with or which figure in their appointment to the athletic directorship.
12. Interview several athletic directors and try and determine how they judge their success.
13. Attend an athletic staff meeting of a high school in your hometown and determine what type of director is in charge.
14. Talk with several coaches in your local school system and try to discover the ways in which they attempt to influence the director of athletics with whom they work. See if you can determine why the coaches choose to use one tactic rather than another. What insights does this information provide you into understanding administrative behavior?
15. Write to several schools requesting salary increments for the coaches of various sports.
16. Examine several university programs leading to certification as an athletic director and a coach. What opportunities do these programs provide for connecting theory with practice and for obtaining familiarity with the world of practice?
17. Interview a number of athletic directors to determine the ways in which they try to influence members of their staffs. Focus your discussion with these directors on concrete examples, and seek to identify what conditions prompted the directors to use one particular influence mode in preference to another.
18. Go with an athletic director and ob-

serve his behavior in all the activities in which he is engaged in fulfilling his professional responsibilities for the day. Try to analyze his behavior in terms of the assumptions, values, and beliefs that seem to underlie his behavior.

19. Interview a number of athletic directors in your area and attempt to identify how they happened to get their first directorship. From their perspective, what factors seemed to be important in their being appointed? What factors seemed unimportant?

20. Check with several school districts and find out the criteria which are used to select the athletic director and the coaches.

21. In several local school districts make an effort to describe the procedures for assessing the athletic director's competencies.

22. Talk with a number of athletic directors and attempt to find out what they regard as the sources of joy and pleasure in their work.

23. Write to several high schools in different sections of the country and obtain information regarding their differential pay schedule.

24. Visit a high school. Identify the director of athletics, duties of the athletic council, the duties of the director of athletics, and the duties of the student manager.

25. Outline a practical plan for the athletic director to follow to improve himself professionally.

26. Debate the pros and cons of the policy of extra pay for extra service.

27. Survey a football practice session in a secondary school and determine the coaching techniques.

28. Write to several schools, requesting outlines of the duties of the director of athletics and the coaches.

29. Observe several athletic directors at work. Does their behavior appear to be more usefully understood in terms of the administrator as an imitator of action or as a recipient of action? Support your conclusion.

30. Develop a differential pay schedule for extra duties.

SUGGESTED READINGS

1. A.A.H.P.E.R.: Athletics in education—A platform statement. *Journal of Health Physical Education and Recreation,* September, 1954.

2. Alba, Abelardo: To hire or not to hire an inexperienced coach. *Athletic Journal,* May, 1972.

3. Anonymous: It it worth it? *Journal of Health, Physical Education, and Recreation,* June, 1969.

4. Ashenfelter, John: One coach's philosophy of coaching. *Journal of Health, Physical Education, and Recreation,* February, 1965.

5. Auxter, David and Nicolau, Anthero: The role of the assistant coach. *Athletic Journal,* March, 1965.

6. Barr, A.S.: Characteristics of successful teachers. *Phi Delta Kappan,* March, 1958.

7. Basic Issues: Should high school coaches be teachers of physical education or teachers of some academic subject? *Journal of Health, Physical Education, and Recreation,* January, 1962.

8. Bates, Aubrey: Selection of men teachers of physical education. *Research Quarterly,* May, 1954.

9. Breyfogle, Newell: A new dimension in training athletic coaches. *Coach and Athlete,* August, 1969.

10. Bryant, Paul: *Building a Championship Football Team.* Englewood Cliffs, P-H, 1960.

11. Bucher, Charles: *Administration of Health, Physical Education, and Recreation.* New York, Mosby, 1971.

12. Bucher, Charles: Professional preparation of the athletic coach. *Journal of Health, Physical Education, and Recreation,* September, 1959.

13. Bunn, John: *The Basketball Coach.* Englewood Cliffs, P-H, 1961.

14. Coaching Committee of Illinois Association of Health, Physical Education, and Recreation: A survey of special certification requirements for athletic coaches of high school interscholastic teams. *Journal of Health, Physical Education, and Recreation,* September, 1970.

15. Cousy, Bob and Power, Frank: *Basketball Concepts and Techniques,* Boston, Allyn, 1970.

16. Daughtrey, Greyson: *Effective Teaching in Physical Education.* Philadelphia, Saunders, 1973.

17. De Groot, Dudley: Have we ignored coaching as a profession? *Journal of Health, Physical Education, and Recreation,* April, 1966.

18. Drew, Gwendolyn: Certification of coaches. *Journal of Health, Physical Education, and Recreation,* April, 1966.

19. Erickson, Donald: The school administrator. *Review of Educational Research,* October, 1967.

20. Esslinger, Arthur: Certification for high school coaches. *Journal of Health, Physical Education, and Recreation,* October, 1968.

21. ———: Extra pay for extra duties. *NEA Research Bulletin,* May, 1963.

22. Grieve, Andrew and Myers, David: Why should there be extra compensation for coaching? *The Athletic Journal,* March, 1969.

23. Hixson, Chalmer: *The Administration of Interscholastic Athletics.* New York, Lowell Pratt, 1967.

24. Howard, Glen and Masonbrink, Edward: *Administration of Physical Education.* New York, A. S. Barnes, 1964.

25. Hughes, William and French, Esther: *The Administration of Physical Education.* New York, A. S. Barnes, 1962.

26. Illinois association for professional preparation. A Rationale for certification of

High School Coaches in Illinois, *Journal of Health, Physical Education, and Recreation,* January, 1971.

27. Joint Committee on Physical Education: Professional preparation of the administration of athletics. *Journal of Health, Physical Education, and Recreation,* September, 1970.

28. Maetozo, Matthew: Required specialized preparation for coaching. *Journal of Health, Physical Education, and Recreation,* April, 1971.

29. Malone, Wayne: A checklist for evaluating coaches. *Coach and Athlete,* October, 1966.

30. McKinney, Wayne and Taylor, Robert: Certification of coaches: The Missouri approach. *Journal of Health, Physical Education, and Recreation,* October, 1970.

31. National Conference on Undergraduate Professional Preparation in Health, Physical Education and Recreation. Chicago, The Athletic Institute, 1948.

32. N E A Research Division: Extra pay for extra duties. *N E A Research Bulletin,* May, 1963.

33. Newman, Dick: The philosophical concept of an ideal coach. *Coach and Athlete,* January, 1969.

34. Oehrlein, Tommy and Segrest, Herman: A survey of certification requirements for high school athletic coaches, *Coach and Athlete,* April, 1970.

35. Richardson, Diane: Preparation for a career in public school athletic administration. *Journal of Health, Physical Education, and Recreation,* February, 1971.

36. Rynda, Gil: The role of the head coach. *The Coaching Clinic,* September, 1969.

37. Santoro, Joel: A salary schedule for coaches. *Journal of Health, Physical Education, and Recreation,* April, 1968.

38. Schaible, Harold: The importance of the director of athletics. *Ohio High School Athlete,* November, 1964.

39. Seets, Norman: Current status of certification of coaches in Maryland. *Journal of Health, Physical Education, and Recrea-*

tion, June, 1971.

40. Sells, James: Essential competencies for the athletic director. *Journal of Health, Physical Education, and Recreation,* May-June, 1961.

41. Singer, Robert: *Coaching, Athletics and Psychology.* New York, McGraw, 1972.

42. Thurston, James: A formula for extra duty. *Journal of Health, Physical Education, and Recreation,* April, 1968.

43. Tope, Donald: *A Forward Look—The Preparation of School Administrators.* Bureau of Educational Research, University of Oregon, 1970.

44. Tutko, Thomas and Ogilvie, Bruce: The role of the coach in motivation of athletics, *Motivators in Play, Games and Sports.* Springfield, Thomas, 1967.

45. Veller, Don: Head coach and assistant rapport. *The Athletic Journal.* April, 1968.

46. Veller, Don: Vital relationships for the coach. *The Athletic Journal,* November, 1968.

47. Voltmer, Edward and Esslinger, Arthur: *The Organization and Administration of Physical Education.* New York, Appleton, 1967.

CHAPTER 9

Contest Management

A VERY IMPORTANT PHASE of athletic administration is contest management. This task can be more difficult in some situations than in others because of personnel, equipment, facilities, and time. The administration of interscholastic contests is a complicated and detailed undertaking and involves careful planning from start to finish if it is to be successful. Organization is the key word in contest management because of the many requirements that are necessary to properly administer an interscholastic contest of any kind.

The cooperation of all personnel is needed and careful attention to details and the strict adherance to proper procedures are paramount in contest management.

Importance of Contest Management

Good administration of an athletic contest is a reflection of the total administration of the school system. Therefore, it is of great importance. Good administration contributes more to the success of a contest than any other one thing.

Wise and thoughtful planning of every detail can do a great deal to make the contest a success. The contest should be in keeping with the educational values and goals considered important for the entire school. When properly conducted, an athletic contest can be a potent force in the education of both participants and spectators. If there has been a good job of planning, the contest will be a success; but if

there has been poor or inadequate planning, it can result in hard feelings and dissatisfaction among players, coaches, spectators, and officials.

George and Lehmann[1] stress the importance of game management in the following statement:

> Efficient management is necessary in order to make the best use of practice time and to insure the businesslike conduct of the interscholastic schedule. Athletic management involves having site and equipment in a state of readiness and all personnel concerned fulfilling their particular functions at the right place at the right time. The administration of interscholastic contests is a highly complex procedure and involves everything from an original contact concerning a possible future game to the payment for personal services following the conclusion of a contest.

Public attention is often focused on the athletic program. People come to see an athletic contest and have a tendency to judge how the school is administered by how the athletic contest is administered. If it is administered in a slip-shod and haphazard manner, then this is indicative of how the other departments within the school are administered. In many instances the reputation of a school may be measured by the manner in which its athletic contests are conducted. Certainly, here is a

[1]George, Jack, and Lehmann, Harry, *School Athletic Administration* (New York, Harper and Row, 1966), p. 292.

golden opportunity to show the public how well the school is being administered and conducted. This should not be difficult if policies and procedures are well established before hand. If this is true, then it will be just a routine matter to follow these procedures and make the athletic contest a business-like and well-organized sports event. The general public, as well as the players, have a right to expect a well-administered contest.

Resick, Siedel and Mason[2] suggest that:

> The efficient management of interscholastic contests is a necessity. The importance of careful planning of home interscholastic athletic events cannot be overestimated. At such events the school is the host not only to local students and adults but to visitors from other communities. The school authorities are obligated to those who support the team and purchase tickets to present an efficiently planned sports contest.

Responsibilities of the Athletic Director

The athletic director is usually the one upon whose shoulders the administration of the contest rests. It is one of his most important responsibilities. He has two distinct tasks to perform. He must organize or set up the contest, and he must administer it or see that it functions properly. He must cooperate with other departments wherever necessary in order to create harmony. It is the director's responsibility to delegate authority and responsibility wherever it is needed. He should also place responsible people in key positions. He must of necessity assume the major share of the work and responsibility. It takes the efforts of all the people involved to assure a well-run contest. Each person should have

specific tasks to perform and should be under the direct supervision of the director and work closely with him. The number of workers needed to administer the contest should be determined by the director and will depend upon the type of contest itself. The duties of each worker should be determined by the director and will be dependent to some extent on the abilities of the personnel and the desires of the director. The smoothness with which the contest is run off will be in direct proportion to the efficiency of the workers. The success of the contest administratively depends to a great extent upon the work of the helpers and the policies established as guidelines.

Administrative Considerations

There are many administrative considerations pertinent to management of an interscholastic varsity athletic contest. Some of the important ones will be discussed in this chapter.

Scheduling of Contests

One of the main duties of the athletic director and coach is the scheduling of games. Scheduling of games can make the difference between a winning or losing season. The placing of teams in the schedule at the right time will allow the team and the coach an opportunity to prepare for each particular team in the proper manner. The importance of this cannot be overestimated. The better teams on the schedule should not all be played in succession but should be spaced throughout the schedule. This is very difficult with the conference teams because these games are scheduled on a rotating basis several years in advance. There is, however, an opportunity to schedule the nonconference games within the conference schedule.

There are several regulatory agencies

[2]Resick, Matthew; Siedel, Beverly; and Mason, James; *Modern Administrative Practices in Physical Education and Athletics* (Reading, Mass. Addison-Wesley, 1970), p. 139.

that must be taken into consideration when developing the schedule as they will definitely have a very important bearing on any decisions which are made regarding the schedule. These agencies are the state associations, the National Federation of State High School Associations, the conference to which the school belongs, and the local school board. All have definite rules and regulations which must be adhered to in formulating any type of athletic schedule. All the regulations set up by these organizations in regard to scheduling of games are for the mutual benefit of all concerned parties.

The schedule should be prepared with the advice of the coach, the athletic council (if there is one), and the principal. The schedule should not only reflect the educational philosophy of the school, but contests should be scheduled only with other schools that have similar philosophies. Every attempt should be made to schedule contests with teams from other schools of approximately the same educational requirements, size of student body, and financial circumstances. Every effort should be made to compete with schools in the same class. In order to obtain the best educational results, teams should be evenly matched, with each having an equal chance to win.

The athletic director should, with these things in mind, consider the schedule from a long-range point of view and should evaluate the following factors in developing the schedule:

1. The philosophy of the school regarding the athletic program
2. Organizational regulations
3. Distance in travel
4. Facilities
5. Number of practice sessions allowed
6. Date of first practice
7. Date of first game
8. Date of last game
9. Number of games allowed
10. Number of games allowed in a specific period of time
11. Night games
12. Policy of releasing students from classes
13. Games on holidays and vacation periods
14. Amount of money available
15. Overnight trips
16. Availability of opponents of equal ability
17. Rivalry between schools
18. Interstate competition
19. Postseason games
20. All-star games
21. Intersectional competition
22. Number of sports an athlete may be permitted to participate in
23. Guarantees
24. Conflicts with other school programs
25. Days on which games may be played

Accommodations for Housing

When a high school team stays overnight, a responsible individual should be appointed by the host school as director of reservations. His job is to contact all motels and hotels in the area to ascertain the types of accommodations available. The following information must be obtained regarding the motel or hotel and sent to the athletic director or principal of the competing school or schools.

1. Name of motel or hotel
2. Location
3. Number of units available
4. Name of manager
5. Telephone number
6. Rates

The school authorities should deal directly with the hotel or motel.

Gulfport Municipal Separate School District

Gulfport, Mississippi

Date

MEMO: HOUSING FACILITIES AND RESERVATIONS

TO: Participants of _____ Invitational
       Wrestling Tournament

       This letter states necessary information regarding housing
and reservations of your athletes, coaches, etc. during the
tournament.

       Please note that all school officials should deal directly
with the management of the establishment. The host school will
not be responsible for, nor will it make, reservations for any
guest school.

Name of *Hotel or Motel	Location	No. Units	Manager	No.	Special
Hilton*	Lincolnway	150	W. Meyer	6-4176	15.00
Ramada	Farnsworth	150	B. Hopkins	6-5132	18.00
Holiday Inn	Lake Street	100	G. Rine	6-1822	17.50
Western	Rt. 50	50	J. Bell	6-9604	19.50
Ramble Inn	Rt. 25	50	F. Smith	6-7303	21.00

Sincerely yours,

Meet Director

aa

Figure 26.

Selection of Help

Careful consideration and thought must be given to the selection of help. In selecting individuals for various positions, their efficiency and cooperativeness are the important items that must be taken into consideration. The following personnel can be selected from the faculty and/or coaches from nearby schools who are willing to make their services available:

1. Team scorer and assistant
2. Chief clerk and assistant
3. Announcer
4. Artists
5. Director of student workers
6. Director of reservations
7. Director of admissions
8. Custodian of awards
9. Custodian of numbers
10. Lounge supervisor
11. Trainer and/or nurse
12. Director of meals
13. Ticket takers
14. Ticket sellers
15. Crowd supervisors

Competent students, chosen from the athletic club, can fill the following positions:

1. Runners
2. Scoreboard
3. Mat
4. Dressing room
5. Welcoming
6. Program

Instructions for All Student Workers

1. The success of the contest depends to a great extent upon you.
2. You are representing your coaches and your school.
3. You have been chosen by your coaches for your dependability; do not let them down.
4. You are *hosts* to the visiting athletes and coaches. Make them feel at home.
5. Report in at least thirty minutes before the contest.
6. Keep a neat, clean appearance at all times.
7. Be polite and courteous to everyone.
8. If you see something unusual or something that needs improving, do not hesitate to tell the proper individual.

LOCKER ROOM ATTENDANTS

1. Meet the visiting team when they get off the bus and show them to their lockers.
2. Be polite; they are guests in your school.
3. If two attendants are assigned to each room, then only one need remain in the room at one time.
4. If you see anyone who apparently is not sure where he is to go, ask him if you can be of help.

RUNNERS

1. You are the only means of communication between the event and the official

scorer and clerk.

2. Pick up the cards and numbers for the next event, take them to the proper place and pick up the results of the previous event; return them to the main table.
3. Wear proper attire at all times.
4. Be alert. Do not hold up an event.

SCORERS

1. Get the contestant's number from the runner and insert if in the scoreboard.
2. Be sure to know the correct number of each contestant. Have a program with you at all times.
3. Keep alert; all eyes are upon you.
4. Do not be influenced by anyone except the scorer at the table.
5. Keep your mind on your job; it is an important one.

MESSENGERS

1. Sit in the designated area and be a

gentleman.

2. Be ready to go on errands as necessary.
3. Be ready to help any tournament official who may need you.

USHERS

1. Assist public to find their seats.
2. Help maintain order and conduct.
3. Pass out programs.
4. Give necessary information when asked.
5. Be courteous.
6. Dress so that you can be identified as an usher.

Contracts for Contests with Opposing Schools

Contracts constitute a business-like way of administering all athletic events. The signing of a contract with another school is the first step in a series of events which finally culminates in the contest, perhaps a month, a year, or several years from the

---

ILLINOIS HIGH SCHOOL ASSOCIATION

N⁰ 19386

CONTRACT FOR ATHLETIC CONTESTS

This contract is drawn under supervision of the Illinois High School Association and must be used in arranging games between member schools.

_____, Ill., _____ 19____

This CONTRACT is made and subscribed to by the Principals and Coaches or Athletic Directors of the_____

High School and of the_____ High School, for_____ contests in_____ to be
played as follows:
(Name of Sport)

| | City | Date | Day | Hour | | Hour |

First Team Game_____ Preliminary Game_____

First Team Game_____ Preliminary Game_____

The rules of the Illinois High School Association are a part of this contract. The suspension or termination of its membership in the IHSA by either of the contracting parties shall render this contract null and void.

Financial terms:_____

_____

_____

| PRINCIPAL | COACH OR ATHLETIC DIRECTOR | SCHOOL |

| PRINCIPAL | COACH OR ATHLETIC DIRECTOR | SCHOOL |

Note 1. List suggested Registered officials on the back of this sheet. The visiting school Principal should scratch those not acceptable and number the others in the order of preference.
Note 2. When one Principal is new to the system he should be notified near the beginning of the school year of existing contracts.

Figure 27. Reprinted with permission from the Illinois High School Association.

National Federation of State High School Associations

CONTRACT FOR INTERSTATE GAMES OR MEETS

Place.., Date.., 19........

This CONTRACT is made and subscribed to by the Principals and Athletic Managers of the ....High School

and of the..High School, for................contests in................................to be played as follows:

(Name of Sport)

	City	Date	Day	Hour		Hour
First Team Contest..					Preliminary Game................	
First Team Contest..					Preliminary Game................	

Financial Terms:..

1. Each school guarantees its membership and good standing in its own state high school association and also guarantees that participants in this contest will not violate any rule of that association or of the National Federation. The game contract is void if such membership is terminated or if participation is found to be contrary to the state or national rules.
2. Each contestant will be eligible under rules of his home state association.
3. The game will be administered under playing rules and safety requirements approved by the National Federation.
4. If either party fails to fulfill its contract obligations, that party shall make amends in accordance with terms fixed by the National Federation executive committee after consultation with the executive officers of the states involved.
5. Only officials approved by the home state office shall be used. They will be proposed by the home school at least 14 days before the contest and approved by the visitors not later than 7 days before the contest.

------------------------------ ------------------------------ ------------------------------ ------------------------------
    (Principal)   (Manager)   (School)   (State)

------------------------------ ------------------------------ ------------------------------ ------------------------------
    (Principal)   (Manager)   (School)   (State)

NOTE: List suggested Registered officials on the back. The visitors should scratch those not acceptable and number the others in the order of preference.

5M 8/72

Figure 28. Reprinted with permission from the National Federation of State High School Associations.

date the contract was signed. The expanse of time from the signing of the contract to the actual playing of the contest is such that without a contract specifying certain conditions, these conditions could be either forgotten or misinterpreted. The contracts should be filed in a place where they are accessible at short notice.

Usually the state associations will furnish standard state contracts while the National Federation will furnish contracts for all interstate contests.

State Sanction of Tournaments and Meets

In order to keep a tight control on the scheduling of athletic contests, most states require all tournaments and meets involving more than two or more schools to obtain permission to conduct them. Under ordinary conditions this permission which must be obtained from the state association is granted with little or no hesitancy. However, this practice does keep a check on any irregularities, such as bringing teams from long distances resulting in the students missing classes for a long period of time.

Agreements for Contests

It is wise to have contract terms in writing. This lessens the chance for misunderstandings of terms between the two schools engaged in athletic contests. The contract document should be signed by authorized representatives of the competing schools.

Arrangements for Parking and Police Protection

Because of the laxity in the enforcement of rules, it would seem that the presence of uniformed police is the best way

TABLE XXXIX
CONTEST AGREEMENT FORM

I. OFFICIALS
   A. Referee _____
   B. Umpire _____
   C. Field Judge _____
   D. Head Linesmen _____
   E. Timer _____

II. BANDS
   A. Each band will be given equal time _____ minutes between halves. Details will be worked out by the band directors from the various schools.
   B. There will be no admission charge for band members.
   C. The band will pay its own trip expenses.

III. SEATING ARRANGEMENTS
   A. Students of visiting team will sit on the east bleachers center. Adults of the visiting team will sit on either side of the students. Signs will indicate where people are to sit.

IV. TRANSPORTATION
   A. Visiting teams will pay their own expenses.

V. FINANCES
   A. All expenses are to be paid by the visiting team with the same arrangements for a return game the following year at the visiting team's home field.

VI. TICKETS
   A. Ticket prices shall be:
      Students _____ (with identification)
      Adults _____
   B. Visiting team will be given _____ complimentary tickets.
   C. _____ student _____ adult tickets will be sent to _____.
      Unsold tickets and money will be sent to _____.
   D. There will be no charge for band members.

VII. SAFETY AND HEALTH PRECAUTIONS
   A. Home team will arrange to have a doctor, ambulance, and stretcher on the field.
   B. Home team will furnish police protection.

VIII. GAME ADMINISTRATION
   A. Home team will furnish and operate: announcer, scoreboard operator, ticket sellers and takers, concessions.
   B. Phones will be provided from the bench to the press box.
   C. Visiting press men must stay in press box.
   D. Photographers must have permission to be on sidelines.
   E. Radio coverage for visiting team will be provided facilities.
   F. One spotter from each school is to be provided for the field announcer, newspaper men, and radio announcer.

XI. TOWELS
   A. Towels will be furnished by the home team.

X. DRESSING ROOM
   A. The dressing room will open at _____.

B. Visiting team will use dressing room _____.

C. Home team will use dressing room _____.

D. Attendants will be furnished by the home team.

XI. BALL

A. The official ball will be a _____ and will be furnished by the home team.

XII. UNIFORMS

A. The home team will wear _____ jerseys, _____ pants and _____ helmets

B. The visiting team will wear contrasting colors.

XIII. MISCELLANEOUS

A

B.

C.

D.

(signed)

_____

Principal

---

to handle both the parking and police protection problem. This takes the responsibility away from the school officials and places it on the police.

Cheerleaders

Cheerleaders play an important part in interscholastic athletic contests. They add color and enthusiasm to the event. This is especially true in the team games such as football and basketball. It is important, however, that the best cheerleaders are used and that they be selected on a competitive basis.

The uniforms worn by the cheerleaders should be supplied by the school, but the cheerleaders should assume the responsibility for cleaning and up-keep of the uniform. They might have the option of purchasing the uniform at the conclusion of the season.

The cheerleaders may wear their uniforms to school the day of the contest. This is to stimulate interest and to make the students aware of the upcoming game.

Bands

Bands lend a great deal to any athletic contest and provision should be made for their accommodations when possible. Special seating arrangements should be made for them so that there will be as little inconvenience as possible after they arrive at the scene of the contest. Reserved seats for the band should usually be in the end zone so that when the band leaves the stands, it will not interfere with the viewing of the game by the spectators. There must be a spirit of cooperation between the coach of the athletic event and the band director. The opportunity for the band to perform before a large audience, such as at a football or basketball game is usually appreciated. Therefore, an understanding regarding the amount of time used by the band should be thoroughly agreed upon so that the band does not consume too much time. Also, the coach and the band director should get together and work out times that the band can use the field to practice marching.

ROGERS HIGH SCHOOL
NEWPORT, RHODE ISLAND

CHARLES H. TOBIN
PRINCIPAL

ATHLETIC DEPARTMENT

JOHN J. TOPPA
Athletic Director

Date _____

Mr. _____
Band Director, _____
_____, _____

Dear Sir:

We are looking forward with pleasure to having the _____
High School band visit us on _____. There is certain
information that you should have so that your visit here will be
more enjoyable. Please pass this information on to all concerned.

Please instruct your bus driver to park on the parking lot
west of the playing field, enter the west gate marked "Gate C,"
and sit in the west stands reserved for band members. Ushers will
be present to show you to your seats.

All band members in uniform will be admitted free of charge at
the west pass gate.

You will be allowed ten minutes to perform. Your band will
assemble for the half time performance under the west goal post
approximately four minutes before the half ends.

We want to make your visit in _____ as pleasant as
possible and should you wish further information, please do not
hesitate to contact me.

Sincerely,

Athletic Director

Figure 29.

Operator of Duplicating Equipment

Coaches and the media should be provided with the results of the athletic event as soon as possible after the contest has been completed. A special room with duplicating equipment should be provided for this service.

Concessions

The concessions are usually taken care of by one of the school organizations such as the varsity club. Permits should be obtained from the city Board of Health. Certain rules pertaining to the area in which food and drink may be taken should be made and enforced.

Sportsmanship

The sportsmanship of the home fans is the responsibility of the host school. The administration should attempt to teach the students how to act at the contests and make them feel that the school they are opposing in the athletic contest is their guest and should be treated accordingly.

Restroom Facilities

Restrooms are a must. These facilities should be available to the general public and should be plainly marked and easily accessible. They should be kept clean at all times.

Availability of Entrances and Exits

All exists should be plainly marked and should conform to all fire regulations.

Proper Supervision of Facilities

All facilities should be properly supervised. Some of the supervision may be done by faculty. It is absolutely necessary that visiting team locker rooms be attended so that vandalism and stealing can be eliminated as much as possible.

Game Management Duties in Specific Sports

All contests require management. However, the duties involved in managing these contests will not be the same although many duties may be similar in nature. These duties are performed by many individuals but the main responsibility lies with the director.

In order to better understand the duties involved in the administration of a contest, the following information is provided for administrating a football game. The administration of a football contest involves many individuals and not all of these individuals will be on the athletic staff. Many of the duties required in the administration of the football game itself must be coordinated with other individuals, such as the band director, chairman of the homecoming committee, and any other activity which could be a part of the game in one

TABLE XL

NORTH JACKSON HIGH SCHOOL DISTRICT 130

Concessions Report Form

Date _____   Event _____

Sales	Units	Unit Price	Total
Soda	_____	_____._____	_____._____
Hot Dogs	_____	_____._____	_____._____
Candy	_____	_____._____	_____._____
Popcorn	_____	_____._____	_____._____
_____	_____	_____._____	_____._____
_____	_____	_____._____	_____._____
Total Sales	_____		_____._____ _____._____

Cost of Sales			
Soda	_____	_____._____	_____._____
Hot Dogs	_____	_____._____	_____._____
Candy	_____	_____._____	_____._____
Popcorn	_____	_____._____	_____._____
_____	_____	_____._____	_____._____
Cost of Items	_____		_____._____ _____._____

Profit on Sales   _____._____

Expenses

_____	_____	_____._____	_____._____	_____._____
_____	_____	_____._____	_____._____	_____._____
_____	_____	_____._____	_____._____	_____._____

Total Expenses   _____._____   _____._____

Net Profit   _____._____

TABLE XLI

SPORTSMANSHIP RATING FORM

Date _____ 197__

_____ vs. _____

(Team Rated)

Visitors rate home teams; home groups rate visitors.

LOCATION OF THE CONTEST _____

Rating Scale: 100-90   (Good Sportsmanship)
                             89-80   (Fair Sportsmanship)
                             79-70   (Poor Sportsmanship)
                             Rate each division separately

I.   .... GENERAL BEHAVIOR OF SPECTATORS.
II.   .... SPORTSMANSHIP DISPLAYED BY MEMBERS OF THE TEAM.
III. .... PROFESSIONAL SPIRIT DISPLAYED BY COACH.
Scored by: ....Spectator   ....Coach   ....Player   ....Official

Spectators:
    Did they conduct themselves in a commendable manner?
    Did they control their tempers and avoid starting quarrels and fights?

Did they accept the rulings of the officials in a sportsmanlike manner?

Team Sportsmanship:
   Did they play a clean game and avoid display of temper and use of foul language?
   Did they show friendliness toward opponents and readily accept rulings of the officials?

Coach:
   Was he calm and sportsmanlike with professional poise under pressure?
   Did he make the most of limited facilities or other handicaps?

---

way or another. All these activities must fit in the game pattern so that everything functions smoothly the day of the game.

Organization and good administration is the key to success. Good administration is easily recognizable and the better it is, the better the results will be.

Records of Eligibility

No contest should be played with another school unless eligibility lists are exchanged. This practice protects both schools. The principal should be responsible for this duty or he can delegate this task to someone. However, regardless of who performs this task, the principal must assume all responsibility. Some conferences have a special eligibility form which is used and this is entirely satisfactory providing all the necessary information is included and the eligibility requirements are equal or more rigid than the state requirements.

New Records Made by Participants

The administrator of any contest should assume the responsibility of providing the necessary arrangements to make official any records that may result from playing the contest. Every participant has a right to expect that any record he breaks is official and can be entered in the record books as being authentic and official. For example, provisions should be made to have qualified statisticians on hand to record yards gained, passes caught, and

tackles made in a football game.

The administrator of the track meet should make certain that the lanes are measured correctly and that a wind meter is in position plus any other requirements that are necessary to make any record-breaking performances official. Not every facility will be one in which records can be obtained because some facilities will not be the official size, length, etc. However, every administrator of an athletic contest should strive to make it possible in any way he can to arrange for and guarantee recognition of any new records that are made.

Athletic Officials

Athletic officials are the subject of conversation before, during, and after the season. The selection of officials is an important aspect of game administration and should be given serious consideration by every coach and athletic director.

Most conferences or leagues have a rating sheet which is sent to each school after the season. The officials are rated by the coaches for that season. Upon the coaches' recommendations of ratings, the officials may be rehired to officiate for the following year. One method of accomplishing this task is to have the officials for conference competition in football and basketball assigned by a conference chairman of the particular sport. The varsity head coaches should also use a rating system when forming the list of officials. The director or chairman should assign officials

National Federation of State High School Associations
400 Leslie St., Elgin, Illinois 60120

**INTERSCHOLASTIC TRACK & FIELD RECORD
APPLICATION**

NOTE: Fill blanks and secure signatures on 5 (8 for relay) copies. Send all 5 (8 for relay) to your state high school athletic officer. He will sign them and if a state or national record is involved, he will forward them to the National Federation for signature of the National Committee. In all cases, one copy will be returned to the school for framing or filing. It is permissible to submit original and photostats.

To The Committee on Interscholastic Records:
    Application is hereby made for a Conference, State or National CHAMPIONSHIP RECORD in the (Event) ....
                                                        The performance was in the (name of meet) ....

Sanctioned by .... State High School Association and (if interstate) by National Federation. Held
at (place) .... on (date) ....
Full name of competitor for whom record is claimed (Give all full names if for a team): ....
                                                                Age in: Yrs. . , . Mo. .
                                                                Age in: Yrs. .... Mo. .
                                                                Age in: Yrs. .... Mo. .
                                                                Age in: Yrs. .... Mo. .
This competitor is an eligible member of the .... High School
of (place) .... , said high school being a qualified member of the ....
.... State High School Association under whose rules the school competed. The claimed
record was (time, height or distance) .... Was the record established
in competition limited exclusively to high school contestants? .... How many high schools were represented in
the meet? ....
Signed: ....
        (Claimant (or captain if for a team))   (Principal of the high school)

* * * * *
ENDORSEMENT BY SECRETARY OF STATE HIGH SCHOOL ATHLETIC ASSOCIATION
The foregoing track and field meet was sanctioned by the home State High School Association and conducted in compliance with the National Alliance Rules.
Secretary .... High School Association

STATEMENT OF REFEREE. I am acquainted with the Officials who have attached their signatures on the reverse side. I believe they are competent and that they acted conscientiously and in good faith. The conditions were official in every way. An anemometer or anemometers, as prescribed by rule, was used and there was no tailwind (for sprint, hurdles, running long jump or triple jump) exceeding 4.473 miles per hour at any time during the performance. I cordially recommend the claim to the National Interscholastic Records Committee for .... record.
                                                    (Conference, State or National)
(Note: The referee should state any exceptions he desires to make to the foregoing statement. He should also describe the condition of the field or track, the force and direction of the wind and any other matters which might in any way influence the outcome.)
Anemometer reading (actual M.P.H.) ....
Weather ....
Track and field condition ....
Signed .... Referee's Address ....

* * * * *
CERTIFICATE
BY COMMITTEE ON INTERSCHOLASTIC RECORDS
The foregoing application was considered by the .... Committee on Interscholastic Records
                                        (Conference, State or National)
on (date) .... , 19 .. and the performance was accepted as a .... record
                                                    (Conference, State or National)
.... Conference Chairman (For Conference Record)
.... State Executive
.... National Executive (For State or National Record)
2M 1/71

Figure 30. Reprinted with permission from the National Federation of State High School Associations.

from this list. The officials should be contacted at least two seasons in advance by the athletic director. About a week or ten days before the contest, the home school should remind the official of the date, time, and place of the contest, and the duty he is to perform. All contracts should be explicit regarding the fee and the number of games to be officiated on a given date. The number of officials to be used and their fees should be set according to the conference regulations. For nonconference competition, officials should be contracted by the athletic director upon recommendation of the head coach. All officials should be paid by the athletic director or head coach immediately following the contest.

All officials should be registered with the state association for the current season. A regular filing system for officials' contracts should be maintained and contracts should be available for scrutiny at all times.

Evaluation of Officials

All officials should be evaluated. Competent evaluators are necessary as well as a valid method of evaluation. The same person should do the evaluating each time.

Many conferences have standard forms which are used by the evaluators. Most coaches want uniform officiating and the only way this can be accomplished is to insist on having all officials make their calls on the same basis each time the calls are made.

Publicity and Promoting the Athletic Program

It is especially important that the athletic department maintain a good public relations program. The best publicity is a good program in each sport. The students themselves recognize good or poor instruction and will generally let parents and friends know about it.

In order to further the athletic program, the administration should use the following media:

1. Efficient and loyal staff members who defend school policies and programs
2. The daily newspaper
3. The school newspaper
4. The local radio and television stations
5. Assembly programs
6. Demonstrations
7. Public speeches
8. Interviews by staff personnel
9. Posters, pictures, and team schedules placed throughout the town or immediate area and in local business establishments
10. School rallies

TABLE XLII
FAIRFIELD HIGH SCHOOL DISTRICT NO. 66
Press and Radio Information Form

Football: _____ vs _____
              Home Team   Visiting Team

Date _____ Time of Contest _____

Season Record:
    Home Team: Won _____   Lost _____
    Visiting Team   Won _____   Lost _____
Head Coach:
    Home Team _____
    Visiting Team _____
Assistant Coaches:
    Home Team _____   _____
    Visiting Team _____   _____
Athletic Director:
    Home Team _____
    Visiting Team _____
Trainer _____
Principal _____
Coaching Record _____
    Years coaching _____ Won _____ Lost_____
Band Director _____
Cheer Leaders: _____   _____

_____

11. A parent booster club

12. A postseason booklet with lettermen, record holders, and statistics

13. Coaches visiting area grade schools recruiting for their program

14. Many athletic awards—school letters, medals, etc.

15. Publicizing outstanding athletes

16. Team or school slogans

17. Banquets—end of season

18. An award assembly

19. A parents' night at a home contest

20. A preseason introduction of players to town and school for all sports of that particular season

21. Cheerleaders wearing their uniforms to school the day of an athletic contest

22. Athletes wearing coat and tie to school the day of a contest

23. Pep club members placing motivational signs on athletes' lockers the day of the contest

24. Student body wearing school colors to school the day of an athletic contest

25. School joining the National Athletic Scholarship Society

Programs

It is an obligation of the school to furnish programs for the spectators of the game. The determining factor in furnishing a program is that a person cannot tell one player from another without the aid of a program which specifies a given number for each participant. The type of equipment worn by the players, especially the headgear and face mask, makes it difficult to recognize each participant by face. Also, the distance which separates the spectator from the players and the number of players going in and out of the game all contribute to the difficulty of identification.

The announcer, no matter how good he is, will have a difficult time trying to keep the spectators informed as to who is playing and who has just left the game; consequently a program is needed. The program need not be very elaborate, although some schools do make up special programs for special games (homecoming, parents' night). It basically should be simple but informative.

Advertising can be the key as to how large the program may be. Not a lot of advertising is suggested for the simple reason that the purpose of the program is for spectators to enjoy and understand the game better. Advertising should be used only to cut down the price of the program. No one should be pressured into subscribing to an ad just so no hard feelings will be produced.

Some determining factors in deciding upon what type of program should be used are (1) importance of the game, (2) the size of the student body, and (3) the size of the community. The best policy is to make the program simple, informative, and at as low a cost as it is possible without making it look cheap.

Gathering Material for the Program

The athletic director must work cooperatively with the coach and the person in charge of printing the program in gathering material for the program. He can be a liaison person between these two people. He has access to the records of individual players and most of the information which will be used in the program.

Program Sales Arrangements

The sale of programs can be handled very well by one of the school organizations. The organization can work on a commission basis which will serve as an incentive for them to make some money for their organization. Many times the varsity club will use this as a money-making adventure. Other organizations such as the 4-H or the key club will help out.

Release of Game Results

The director of athletics should be responsible for arranging the means by which the game results are released. A definite plan should be devised with the same person carrying out this duty each time. A definite plan of action will assure correct game results and immediate release of these results.

Public Address System

The public address system and a good announcer can add immeasurably to the enjoyment of any athletic contest. Care should be taken to select an announcer who understands the game and is willing to announce every game or contest so that he gets to know the players. A good announcer will arrive at the game far enough in advance of the starting time to study the opponent's roster, their record and get a good idea of the strength of the opposition in certain positions.

Telephone System

Telephones have become a very important coaching aid and this should be provided to the visiting coach.

Scouting the Game

Scouts from opposing teams should be given the same privilege as the press and photographers covering the game. A place should be reserved for scouts in the press box for the game. Most schools recognize this mutual courtesy.

Game Ushers

In many schools members of the letterman's club handle the job of ushering.

Lettermen command the respect of the students and the adults in the community and the system works very well. In a large school, if there is a problem with the crowd and if money is available, the school officials may wish to pay faculty members to handle the ushering duty.

Game Attendance by a Physician

Since injuries have become a problem in sports, it has become necessary for the school to provide a physician at all athletic contests. The physician should be available at the end of the contest in case of injuries that are not reported during the contest. Many schools have physicians at the varsity games but none at the minor or reserve games. School officials must realize that serious injuries can occur in these games as well as the varsity games.

Student managers and coaches should know the telephone numbers of both the hospital and school physician. Each school should have a definite procedure or policy about handling injuries in athletics. If an injury does occur and the player is taken to the hospital, the coach should accompany the player and stay there until the player's parents arrive. Parents feel better when they know that their child has someone there to take care of him and comfort him. After the injury occurs, the coach should report it to the school and the athletic director.

Chain Gang, Down Box, and Officials

Many schools pay competent faculty members to work the down box and the chain. These people should be individuals who understand football and know the rules of the game. Before the game, the officials should confer with the three members of this unit to instruct them in their duties. It is a coach's duty before the season

to make sure he has these important people lined up to work the games.

Maintenance of the Field

The person in charge of maintenance should assume the responsibility of preparing the field prior to the start of the game and to assist the coaches in every way possible so that the game will progress smoothly and on time. The grass should be cut and the field lined the day before the contest. The custodians should be responsible for placing yard markers as well as end zone markers. Custodians should be available to assist managers in unlocking doors, gates, etc.

Other Student Manager Duties the Day of the Game

1. Take care of the visiting team and officials
2. Have the game uniforms ready for use
3. Have gum or oranges ready for halftime use
4. Have the score book ready and appoint an efficient scorekeeper
5. Check the timers for clocks and horn
6. Give the ball to head official fifteen minutes before the game
7. Check chalk or blackboards in both coaches' dressing rooms
8. Put first-aid kits in the proper places
9. Collect the game uniforms
10. Present the checks to the officials
11. Record plays, downs, yardage, etc.

Pregame Warm Up

Provision should be made for both teams to warm up before the game. Plenty of time should be allowed for this important and necessary aspect of the game. Timing is very important. All special events should be cleared from the field thirty minutes before game time.

TABLE XLIII
GENEVA HIGH SCHOOL DISTRICT 95

WORK ORDER   Date _____
DESCRIPTION OF MAINTENANCE NEEDED:

_____
_____
_____
_____

SCHOOL _____

               (person requesting order)

               (approved by)

DIRECTIONS FOR WORKMEN:

_____
_____
_____

WORK DONE BY   _____
DATE COMPLETED   _____
TIME ON JOB   _____
COMMENTS: _____
              _____

Scoreboard

Qualified operators, knowledgeable in the sport, should be placed in charge of the scoreboard.

Protection of the Field and Spectators

Continuing effort should be made to keep spectators away from the playing area. This should be done from the standpoint of safety as well as allowing players necessary freedom of movement along the sidelines. Restrictions must be placed on spectators so that problems will not arise in case of a close game. If the field is not fenced, either police or qualified authorities should be used to keep spectators away from the field.

Organization of the Players on the Bench

All players should be required to sit on the benches provided for them. There should be enough benches to accommodate both teams on their respective sides of the field. Seating arrangements of the players, trainers, managers, and assistants is entirely up to the head coach. He will usually arrange his team to facilitate substitutions.

If the coaching staff is large enough, it might be a good idea to organize these individuals in regard to specialized responsibilities in a game situation. Since substitutions are often a problem, possibly one coach should be placed in charge of organizing personnel. One way to facilitate this might be to work out prearranged seating charts indicating where each player is seated according to his position. As players report into the game, notations are made on the chart indicating which player is now in the game.

Halftime Arrangements

Halftime arrangements should be made so that each team has a separate place to

AKRON HIGH SCHOOL DISTRICT 112
ANNOUNCER'S PLAYER IDENTIFICATION CHART

SCHOOL

L E No.	L T No.	L G No.	C No.	R G No.	R T No.	R E No.

Q B No.

L H No.	F B No.	R H No.

COACH _____

ASSISTANT COACHES _____

CAPTAIN _____

Figure 31.

report for instruction and rest. These areas should be large enough that the squad can be split into groups allowing coaches to talk to each group without interruption.

Statistician

This person should have some knowledge of football, the personnel on the team, and the basic formations both offensive and defensive. He should be a person who would be very close to the team, most preferably an assistant coach on the staff. He should be seated on the bench near the head coach. The statistician's assignments would be to record the play-by-play progress of the game and indicate which team has possession of the ball, the play used, and the defensive pattern used against it. Finally, he should indicate yardage gained or lost and make any necessary comments.

TABLE XLIV
JERSEY HIGH SCHOOL DISTRICT NO. 45
GAME STATISTICS REPORT

_____ vs. _____ at _____

Date _____

(month)   (day)   (year)

Scoring:
    1st quarter
    2nd quarter
    3rd quarter
    4th quarter

	Home Team	Opponents
Final Score	_____	_____
First Downs	_____	_____
Passing	_____	_____
Passes Completed	_____	_____
Number of Fumbles	_____	_____
Fumbles Recovered	_____	_____

Injuries _____

Officials: Referee _____ Umpire _____ Linesman _____

General Remarks About the Game: _____

_____

(Signed) _____

Athletic Director

Safety Precautions

All precautions necessary for a safely administered football game are the responsibility of the coach and the athletic director. Under no circumstances should a player who has not passed or taken a medical examination be allowed to participate in a football game.

The playing field should be checked prior to the game to make sure that it is free of rocks, stones, or any other hazard which could result in a physical injury to a player. The field itself should not be allowed to harden because of dryness. It should be watered daily during the season.

Advance Sale of Tickets

The director, in cooperation with the principal, will determine if the advance sale of tickets is necessary. Advance sale may not be necessary for regular season games. However, if the team is in conference contention, it may be wise to have an advance sale of tickets.

Distribution of Complimentary Tickets

The practice of issuing complimentary tickets can lead to trouble if not supervised very carefully. Such tickets should not be handed out indiscriminately and in order to avoid hard feelings, a policy governing the distribution of complimentary tickets should be formulated ahead of time by the administration. Such decisions should not be the sole perogative of the athletic coach or director.

Handling of Money from Gate Receipts

The money obtained from gate receipts should be banked as soon as possible. The person assigned to this duty should be accompanied by a uniformed policeman at all times after leaving the premises and on the way to the bank or school office vault.

Arrangements for Payment of Help

The help should be paid by check. Accurate records should be kept of all money used to pay help, regardless of whether they are students or adults. Receipts should be required whenever possible. The money spent is public funds and an accounting can be required at any time.

Sending of Pertinent Information to Visiting Team

A letter should be sent to the visiting school at least one week in advance of the game giving detailed information regarding the color of the jerseys the home team will wear, the type and color of the ball to be used, the starting time of the game, the location of the field and dressing facilities, ticket information, and any other pertinent information which is relevant to this particular game.

Letter or Postal Card Reminder to Officials

The conscientious athletic director will save himself the untold grief and embarrassment of having an official not show up for a game if he will send the official a letter or card reminding him of the game he is to officiate. The card or letter should inform the official of the date, place, time of the contest, and other pertinent information. He should ask for a verification from the official.

Forwarding of Eligiblity List to Opponents

Forwarding eligibility lists to the opponent school is the responsibility of the principal. However, because of its importance, the athletic director or coach should check periodically to make sure this is being done. This is a state regulation in most states.

Players' Physical Examination

Every player should have a physical examination before he is issued any equipment. How this is done varies with individual schools. Some schools designate a specific time and physician to give this examination. Others require the player to be examined by his family physician. Either practice is entirely satisfactory, but it must be done for the protection of the player and the school officials.

Scorers and Timers

The scoring and timing is extremely important in a football game. Many conferences now require the timer and scorer to pass written examinations before they are allowed to score or time a game. The best persons available should be encouraged to perform these important tasks. Their services should be obtained far in advance of the start of the season. Competent substitutes should be secured to take their places if they cannot perform their duties at any particular time.

Opening of Facilities

Provision must be made for the opening of all facilities that are to be used for the game. Usually arrangements are made for the custodian to perform this task although it could very well be the athletic director or the coach. The facilities should be opened at least thirty minutes before game time. A time schedule should be worked out for ticket sellers, takers, student workers, trainer, physician, etc. to arrive at the game site.

Cleanliness of Facilities

An inspection of all facilities should be carried out far enough before game time so that if they are not clean, this situation can be remedied. Unclean facilities can cause embarrassment to school authorities and so, in the best interests of everyone, a thorough check should be made to make sure facilities are clean in all areas.

Preparation of Game Equipment

Preparing the field equipment for a football game is an important detail in game management. The person placed in charge of this duty should be given proper instructions before the season starts as to how this should be done. He must have a thorough knowledge of the rules; for example, to properly place the yard markers. He must know where to place benches and other necessary equipment which will be needed for the game. He cannot learn this ten minutes before game time. He must know it long before the game starts. He should be given these instructions from either the coach or athletic director.

There are always those last-minute details that come up before the game and which have not been taken care of previously. The director should be aware of this happening and provide for it.

Special Seats for Athletic Director as the Trouble Shooter

The director should always be seated in the same seat so that he can be found easily should he be needed for any reason whatsoever. This seat should be situated in an area which can be easily accessible and one from which he can leave hurriedly and not be too conspicuous when he does leave. It should be situated so that he can leave and return without disturbing too many people.

Seats for Special Guests and Dignitaries

It is important to provide special guests and dignitaries the courtesy of complimentary tickets. Usually several seats are set aside for this purpose. It avoids embarrassment and costs very little.

Reserve Seats for Scouts

Most schools now scout their opponents unless the conference in which the school is a member forbids this practice. If it is allowable, then seats which must be situated in a good location should be provided. Letters should be sent to competing schools informing them of the procedure used to obtain tickets for scouting purposes.

Reserved Parking for Guests and Officials

Nothing is more aggravating than to be a guest at an athletic event and not be able to find a parking place within a reasonable walking distance from the field. Special parking spaces should be provided for all invited guests such as dignitaries, board members, competing school principals, etc. It creates good public relations with a minimum of effort.

Officials should be able to park their cars close to the field if at all possible.

Police Protection for Officials

Often it is necessary to arrange for a police escort on and off the field. Officials have on occasion been attacked by fans and such incidents should be avoided at all costs. There should be some pregame planning. No school should subject an official to this kind of treatment and every effort should be made to prevent it.

Provision for Paging Doctors and Spectators Expecting Calls

There are some people, particularly doctors, who may be called from the game by an emergency. There may be others. This can be taken care of very easily (avoiding the practice of calling the individual by name) by having them stop at the ticket office as they enter the gate and giving them a number. If they are wanted for any reason, the number is called instead of paging the person by name.

Lost and Found Room

There are always articles lost and found at any public gathering and it is a good public relations gesture to provide a means by which people can turn the found items in to a specific area. This room should be clearly marked and easily accessible to the public.

Coat Check Room

The weather will be a determining factor as to whether a coat check room will be needed. Many people may bring heavy coats, rain apparel, and blankets to a football game. Often this equipment is not needed and there is no place to leave it except in the car. A coat check room will be appreciated on these occasions.

Postgame Activities

Often activities are scheduled after the game in order to help avoid any unpleasantries which sometimes occur because of the overaggressiveness of some of the spectators. These activities can take the form of band maneuvers, a rugby game, Pop Warner football, etc. which will divert the attention of the fans and thereby help them forget any unpleasantness which may carry over from the game.

Cleanup After the Game

Provisions should be made by the director to have the premises cleaned as soon after the game as possible. Arrangements should be made with the custodial staff to perform this task. This can be done on a game-to-game basis or for the entire season.

Securing of All Facilities After the Game

The director should make arrangements to secure all of the facilities after the game

BAY SHORE PUBLIC SCHOOLS
RAYMOND R. HOWARD, *Superintendent of Schools*

516-665-1700

DEPARTMENT OF PHYSICAL EDUCATION
102 EAST MAIN STREET, BAY SHORE, NEW YORK 11706

WILLIAM W. MAHON
Director of Health, Physical Education
and Recreation   Date

Dear Coach:

    I received your letter asking for information on local
restaurants and I am listing several that are satisfactory and
can accommodate your team:

    1. Wrigley's Restaurant
       122 Mosby Street
       Telephone 312-6011

    2. The Best   Specialize in home cooking.
       119 Olive Street   Price Range $3.50-$5.00
       Telephone 312-9999   No reservations

    3. The Owl   Family style
       121 Freeman Street
       Telephone 312-9100

    4. Earls' Place
       190 Monroe Street
       Telephone 312-6500

    5. The Ritz   Special in chicken
       0001 Bankers' Row   Reservations
       Telephone 312-1000

    6. The Millionaire Club Specialize in steaks
       1200 Dollar Avenue   Reservations
       Telephone 312-6600   Price Range $6.00-15.00

    These are all nice restaurants and serve good meals. It is
recommended that the restaurant be contacted at least a week in
advance.

                       Best of Luck

                       Director of the Meet

hh

Figure 32.

with the head custodian, the head coach or do it himself. This may mean overtime pay for the custodian but it must be done because of vandalism and liability.

Pregame Meal

Very few high schools will furnish their players with a pregame meal except, perhaps, on special occasions. Should this be true, however, the coach or director should make the necessary arrangements ahead of time to save time and eliminate any upsetting confusion before the game.

Parent's Permission-to-Play-Cards

Many schools require the written permission of the parent or guardian before the player is allowed to participate in any athletic activity. This is especially true with football.

This practice is handled in different ways one of which is to have the player take the card home himself, have his parents sign the card, and return it to the ath-

letic director or the coach. Another method is to have the card mailed to the parent with the parent signing or not signing the permit and returning the card by mail.

Football Check List

A check list of duties should be made and posted where everyone can see it. Students will then be aware of what they will or should be doing as part of a team administering the game. The duties will vary depending upon the size of the school, the administrative set-up, the maintenance set-up and the financial structure of the school. This check list information should be made available to all persons involved in plenty of time for them to acquaint themselves with all the details and facts needed to do an excellent job. Alternate plans should be made in case of bad weather on the day of the contest.

CHECK LIST

CHECK LIST

I. Game week
  A. Workers
    1. ( ) All arrangements for workers should be made as well as the time they are to begin and the place they are to be. These workers would include among others. ( ) police, ( ) ticket takers, ( ) ticket sellers, ( ) scorers, ( ) timers, ( ) concession helpers, ( ) parking.
    2. ( ) Call and schedule police.
    3. ( ) Send letters to officials giving instructions.
    4. ( ) Arrange for public address system as well as announcer.
    5. ( ) Assign manager and give him his duties. Assign student host for visiting team.

TABLE XLV
JENSON CONSOLIDATED HIGH SCHOOL   *PARENT PERMISSION SLIP*

Dear Parents:

As you know, many students taking part in the various athletic programs at Jenson Consolidated High School, practice outside of regular supervised practice sessions. It is important that you understand that neither a coach, the administration, or the school board can assume any responsibility for unsupervised practices.

Boys at Jenson Consolidated High School have the opportunity to participate in the following sports on an interscholastic basis: football, cross country, basketball, gymnastics, wrestling, track, baseball, golf, and tennis.

— —

PARENT APPROVAL AND RESPONSIBILITY FOR ATHLETIC PARTICIPATION IN JHS

NAME _____ YEAR 19_____ - 19_____
       Last   First

BIRTH DATE _____ Frosh_____ Soph._____ Jr._____ Sr._____
      Month/   Day/   Year

BIRTH PLACE _____
          County   /   State

FAMILY DOCTOR _____ PHONE NUMBER _____

PARENTS' NAME _____ PHONE NUMBER _____

PARENTS' ADDRESS _____

What school did student attend last year? _____

It is with my full knowledge and consent that my son, _____

participates in interscholastic athletics, playdays, and sportsdays under the guidance of a certificated teacher. I accept the fact that the coach, administration, or school board cannot be responsible for any injury incurred in practice my son may do outside of the school sponsored program.

School insurance is required of all athletes. The cost of this insurance is $36.00. It should be understood, in case of an injury, that medical expenses may not be covered completely. Rather, benefits will be provided as limited and described in the policy.

As a parent, I agree to help my son live up to the athletic code established by the athletic council.

Date _____ Signature of Parent _____
                                  SIGNATURE OF

DATE OF PHYSICAL _____ PARTICIPANT _____

---

6. ( ) Send letter to scorer and timer.

7. ( ) Call and remind attending physician to be present at game.

8. ( ) Arrange for custodians for locker rooms.

B. Publicity

  1. ( ) Newspaper releases

  2. ( ) Have posters placed in proper places.

  3. ( ) Give program material to school printing department.

4. ( ) Send letters with necessary information and tickets to press and radio.

5. ( ) Check on halftime entertainment.

6. ( ) Check on flag-raising ceremony.

7. ( ) Check on seating arrangements for most valuable persons.

C. Equipment

  1. ( ) Send out all laundry and equipment.

2. ( ) Return all laundry.

3. ( ) Prepare and ready all game uniforms.

4. ( ) Prepare and ready all other game equipment: ( ) balls, ( ) scoreboard, ( ) scorebooks, etc.

5. ( ) Prepare and ready officials equipment: ( ) yard markers, ( ) watches, ( ) down markers, ( ) timer's gun.

6. ( ) First-aid equipment and stretcher.

D. Organization

1. ( ) Send a letter of information to visiting team.

2. ( ) Finalize all accommodations for visiting team.

3. ( ) Prepare all materials for ticket taking.

4. ( ) Prepare all requests and materials for concession stand.

5. ( ) Make arrangements for pregame meal for players.

6. ( ) Make arrangements for pregame sale of tickets.

E. Facilities

1. ( ) Check on all facilities including: ( ) bleachers, ( ) rest rooms, ( ) team benches, ( ) playing field, ( ) scoreboards, ( ) ticket facilities, ( ) concession facilities, ( ) press facilities, ( ) fences, ( ) goalposts, ( ) dressing facilities, ( ) officials' dressing room.

2. ( ) Arrange for lining of the field.

3. ( ) Check with organization responsibile for field and goalpost decoration.

4. ( ) Check on repairing all facilities.

5. ( ) Arrange for seats for dignitaries.

II. Game Day

A. Workers

1. ( ) Meet with all workers prior to the game.

2. ( ) Make final phone call to physician.

3. ( ) Have special meeting with police and supervisors.

4. ( ) Meet with ticket takers and provide them with all necessary materials including change.

5. ( ) Meet with concession workers.

6. ( ) Make final check with principal.

7. ( ) Check with student hosts for both teams.

B. Publicity

1. ( ) Check on public address system.

2. ( ) Check on halftime entertainment.

3. ( ) Make final arrangement for materials for announcer.

4. ( ) Make final check with person in charge of refreshments for press.

5. ( ) Check on student help in press box.

6. ( ) Check on person in charge of record keeping.

7. ( ) Check on programs.

8. ( ) Check on ushers.

C. Equipment

1. ( ) Check on trainer supplies.

2. ( ) Issue game equipment and uniforms.

3. ( ) Arrange for issuing towels, orange juice, etc. to visiting team.

4. ( ) Arrange for officials equipment: ( ) whistles, ( )

time gun, ( ) down mark-
ers, ( ) yard markers, ( )
scorebook.

D. Administration

1. ( ) Make out checks for the following: ( ) officials, ( )
guaranties, ( ) ticket sellers
and takers, ( ) police, ( )
all workers.

2. ( ) Check receipts after game.

3. ( ) Deposit gate receipts in

bank.

4. ( ) Write letters of thanks to all
workers.

E. Facilities

1. ( ) Make final check on scoreboard.

2. ( ) Make final check on public
address system.

3. ( ) Issue keys to appropriate
people.

4. ( ) Check all facilities.

TABLE XLVI
INSTRUCTION FOR FACULTY HELP AT FOOTBALL GAMES

I. Please report no later than assigned time to Mr. Bill Smith at southgate. Mr. Smith's job is to:

A. Confirm or sometimes change your assignment and answer whatever questions you may have.

B. Give you a badge for identification.

C. Issue materials necessary for your job.

II. *Admissions*

A. Gates

1. South gate.

2. West gate. (Gate to be closed and locked at beginning of fourth quarter of varsity game.)

B. Admissions

1. South gate.

a. Ticket purchases. Fifty cents for children under high school age; one dollar for *all* others.

b. District 88 passes.

c. League passes.

d. *Visting student* tickets. Have on them the name of the school, principal's signature, date of game. Confiscate and do not admit if incorrect. Collect.

e. Addison Trail activity passes. Punch out designated number. Not trans-ferable.

f. Press passes. *Professional press only.* One reporter and one photographer from a paper. Keep record. Be sure to look at press passes.

g. Player passes. Similar to visting student passes. Collect.

h. Local and visiting cheerleaders in costume.

i. Season tickets for booster club members. Good only for adult whose name appears on pass. Punch proper space.

2. West gate

a. Players in uniform.

b. Managers and coaches with sideline passes.

c. Player passes.

d. High school football squads. Lists provided. These boys are to be check-ed through in an orderly fashion or not to be admitted.

C. Pass-out checks.

Pass-out checks supplied for the gates may be issued to anyone leaving the field to get to the main building and back. Should students persist in frequent trips in and out of the field, exercise your best judgment in determining their necessity. If not necessary, do not issue passes. These pass-outs are not considered transferable, however, you may not always be able to detect these possible abuses.

III. Sidelines
  A. Allow *no one* on sidelines except those with sideline passes. Those entitled to passes are:
    1. Coaches
    2. Managers
    3. Physicians
    4. Statisticians deemed necessary by the coach.
    5. Only *one* student photographer from a *school* and only one professional press photographer from a paper shall be allowed on the sidelines. (Reporters are to be in stands.)
  B. Sideline passes are to be worn so they are visible.
  C. Only people authorized to be outside of coaches box are two statisticians.
  D. Only band members and director are to be allowed in stands at north end.

IV. Conduct of Fans
  A. Conduct that is detrimental to welfare of other fans, athletes, coaches, officials, etc. is not to be tolerated.
  B. Our association does not permit the use of mechanical noisemakers, including musical instruments. Confiscate them if you detect them at the gates or inside.
  C. Students or others detected in acts very dangerous (Shooting of firecrackers, throwing implements, etc.) are to be ordered off the grounds after identification is recorded.
  D. A policeman is on duty if needed for help in serious situations.
  E. No mobile signs or placards are allowed within the field enclosure. Fixed banners will be allowed if they are put in such a position that they do not bother anyone and if they are not suggestive or offensive. No banner which makes any statement about opponents will be allowed. Banners may only make statements about exhibitor's school.

TABLE XLVII
NEWELL HIGH SCHOOL DISTRICT 112
FOOTBALL ASSIGNMENT BLANK

Date _____ Day _____ Opponent _____ Date _____

Ticket Takers _____ _____ _____ _____

Ticket
Sellers _____ _____ Guest Register _____

Officials
Usher _____ Opponents Usher _____ Score Board _____

Head Car
Parker _____ Bench Manager _____ Public Ad. System _____

Gate
Guards _____ _____ _____

Line
Officials _____ _____ _____

Registered _____ _____ _____
Officials

Field   Player
Markers _____ _____ Benches _____

Other
Jobs _____

Game
Squad _____ _____ _____
      _____ _____ _____
      _____ _____ _____
      _____ _____ _____
      _____ _____ _____
      _____ _____ _____
      _____ _____ _____
      _____ _____ _____
      _____ _____ _____

NEWELL HIGH SCHOOL DISTRICT 112
ROSTER WORKSHEET

NAME	NUMBER WHITE	NUMBER DARK	CLASS	POSITION	HEIGHT	WEIGHT	LETTERMAN

Figure 33.

BEHAVIORAL OBJECTIVES

After a person has read this chapter, he should be able to:

1. List several of the crucial problems in game management.
2. Explain what is meant by administrative practices in contest management.
3. Analyze the key responsibilities of the athletic director in athletic contest management.
4. Recall and explain several reasons why there should be good athletic contest management.
5. Identify several athletic administrative considerations and explain their importance in contest management.
6. Identify several ways in which the faculty can serve in contest management.
7. Distinguish between a contract for an athletic official and a game contract between schools.

TABLE XLVIII
NEWELL HIGH SCHOOL DISTRICT 112
FOOTBALL RECORD BLANK

_____ vs. _____		Field _____	Date _____
		Conference _____	

HOME TEAM		VISITING TEAM	STATISTICS	WE	THEY
_____	LE	_____	First downs	_____	_____
_____	LT	_____	Pass attempts	_____	_____
_____	LG	_____	Completed	_____	_____
_____	C	_____	Intercepted	_____	_____
_____	RG	_____	Fumbles	_____	_____
_____	RT	_____	Recovered	_____	_____
_____	RE	_____	Penalties	_____	_____
_____	QB	_____	Yards gained	_____	_____
_____	LHB	_____	rushing		
_____		_____	Yards lost		
_____	RHB	_____	rushing	_____	_____
_____		_____	Yards gained	_____	_____
_____	FB	_____	passing		
_____		_____	Field goals	_____	_____
_____		_____		_____	_____
_____		_____	Safeties	_____	_____
_____		_____		_____	_____
_____		_____		_____	_____

		STATISTICS	1	2	3	4
_____	_____	SCORE				
_____	_____	WE	__	__	__	__
SUBSTITUTES — BACK FIELD		THEY	__	__	__	__
_____	_____					
_____	_____					
_____	_____					

8. Explain the purpose of the sportsmanship rating form.

9. Explain why the supervision of facilities has become a most important item in contest management.

10. Explain the importance of using the correct procedure in applying for an athletic record that has been established.

11. Develop a check list for a conference track meet.

12. Explain why it is important that the coach be consulted in contracting athletic teams.

13. Summarize the publicity for a football game.

14. Identify and explain several duties of the football manager.

15. Explain the bench organization of the players for a football game.

16. Explain the importance of police protection during a football game.

17. Analyze the purpose of the telephone system used by coaches during a football game.

18. Prepare a contract for an official.

19. List the most difficult problems encountered by the athletic director in the preparation of the yearly calendar.

20. Propose a check list of details which the director of athletics should attend to before the closing of the school term.

21. Explain how students can help in the conduct of the athletic program.

22. Outline the procedures to be followed by an athletic director in bettering the

NEWELL HIGH SCHOOL DISTRICT 112
TEAM INFORMATION (FOOTBALL)

SCHOOL _____ DATE _____

COACH _____ ASSISTANTS _____

CONTESTANTS	NUMBER	POSITION	HEIGHT	WEIGHT	LETTERMAN	YEAR IN SCHOOL

Figure 34.

athletic program.

23. Explain several important considerations for formulating interschool athletic contracts.

24. Develop a plan for the operation of concessions at the athletic contests.

25. Compile and analyze some of the advantages of belonging to an athletic conference.

26. Prepare a check list for the athletic director and coach for all sports.

27. Prepare a list of the duties for the student managers of all sports.

ACTIVITIES

1. Survey the interscholastic program in a school, including several games and list the crucial problems that arise.

2. Survey the interscholastic program in a local school.

3. Visit a local school and observe an athletic contest with specific regard for administrative and organizational techniques.

4. Plan and outline a complete track meet.

5. Set up a complete plan for the reception of a visiting team.

6. Write a letter to an athletic official requesting his services for a particular contest.

7. Work out a plan for taking and selling tickets for the football game at the local high school.

8. Write letters to teachers asking for their help in selling and taking tickets.

9. Set up policies and arrangements for issuing passes, selling food, and crowd control for the basketball games at the local school.

10. Write a letter to the local police chief soliciting his help for the home football games in crowd and traffic control.

11. Talk with the local athletic director regarding his arrangements for taking care of player or spectator injuries.

12. Write to several schools and find out what their policies are in regard to payment of various types of workers at athletic contests.

13. Talk with the local athletic director and find out what the financial arrangements are for concessions.

14. Plan and set up an eight-team basketball tournament.

15. Make an administrative check list for a gymnastic meet.

16. Make a survey of the administration of a local school system and report your findings to the class.

17. Make out a pregame and postgame check list for several sports, both for coach and manager.

18. Design a football program.

19. Indicate several methods of producing game programs.

20. Develop a checklist for the administration of a football game.

SUGGESTED READINGS

1. A.A.H.P.E.R.: *Administration of High School Athletics.* Washington, D. C., American Association for Health, Physical Education, and Recreation, 1962.
2. A.A.H.P.E.R.: *Coaches Handbook—A Practical Guide for High School Coaches.* Washington, D. C., 1960.
3. Daughtrey, Greyson, and Woods, John: *Physical Education Programs.* Philadelphia, Saunders, 1971.
4. Educational Policies Commission: *School Athletics.* Washington, D. C., National Educational Association and American Association of School Administrators, 1954.
5. Forsythe, Charles: *The Athletic Director's Handbook.* Englewood Cliffs, P-H, 1956.
6. George, Jack F. and Lehmann, Harry R.: *School Athletic Administration.* New York, Har-Row, 1966.
7. Gilbert, Clark: Hosting a high school basketball tournament. *School Activities,* February, 1964.
8. Grieve, Andrew: *Directing High School Athletics,* Englewood Cliffs, P-H, 1963.
9. Healey, William: *Coaching and Managing High School Basketball.* Danville, Interstate, 1961.
10. Healey, William: *The Administration of High School Athletic Events,* Danville, Interstate, 1961.
11. Hixson, Chalmer: *The Administration of Interscholastic Athletics.* New York, Lowell Pratt, 1967.
12. Hughes, William, French, Esther, and Lehsten, Nelson: *Administration of Physical Education for Schools and Colleges.* New York: Ronald, 1962.
13. Kelliher, M. S.: Successful athletic administration. *Journal of Health, Physical Education, and Recreation,* November, 1957.
14. Razor, Jack: Game management. *Athletic Journal,* April, 1971.
15. Razor, Jack: Hosts for athletic contests. *Clearing House,* Jan., 1971.
16. Resick, Matthew, Siedel, Beverly, and Mason, James: *Modern Administrative Practices in Physical Education and Athletics,* Reading, A-W, 1970.
17. Scott, Harry: *Competitive Sports in Schools and Colleges,* New York, Har-Row, 1951.
18. Voltmer, Edward and Esslinger, Arthur: *Organization and Administration of Physical Education.* New York, Appleton, 1967.
19. Williams, Jesse: *Athletics in Education.* New York, Saunders, 1930.
20. Williams, Jesse: *The Administration of Health Education and Physical Education.* Philadelphia, Saunders, 1958.

CHAPTER 10

Eligibility

Value of Athletic Eligibility

THERE ARE MANY different opinions, viewpoints, and skepticisms regarding athletic eligibility. Most educators will agree that athletics contribute to the total education of the individual. Its values are many and its inclusion in the educational curriculum is endorsed by the vast majority of educators as desirable.

It is extremely important, however, that careful scrutiny be given to the athletic programs in the schools to make sure that they fulfill their mission and accomplish the purpose for which they were intended. Certain guidelines which govern and control both the program and the participants are necessary. One of these guideline controls is eligibility. Because of its importance and its impact on both the administration and philosophy of the program, extreme care should be taken to insure that the eligibility regulations established by federal, state, and local associations are rigidly enforced.

Grieve[1] comments that:

Generally, two basic types of eligibility systems will be found in the high schools. The first is based upon the adherence to set standards. A specific level of achievement is demanded of students and if they don't achieve the level then they are declared ineligible from participation in activities. This type of system can create difficulties. There are differences in the abilities of the students, yet the system makes no such recognition. A second method bases eligibility requirements on standardized tests, I.Q.'s and individual opinions. A student can test well but not do well in the classroom. The peculiarity of eligibility systems is that in most schools the only activity which is directed by an eligibility system is the athletic program.

Reasons for Eligibility Requirements

There must be rules and regulations in the conduct of any well-organized program of activities. These rules must meet with the approval of the majority of people concerned. This is the American way of life and has resulted in eligibility rules being introduced to provide like standards in athletics. Regulations have been established which are similar in nature for all schools. These regulations result in and bring about a feeling of fairness in all contests between schools as all the contestants are meeting the same standards in order to compete.

The eligibility of high school athletes is and has been a difficult problem for everyone. It is almost impossible to set up uniform rules governing athletic eligibility in high schools which will be the same for every athlete in every school system.

Eligibility requirements are established for two reasons: (1) to provide fair and equal competition and (2) to make athletics a part of the general overall educational program. It is imperative that the

---

[1]Grieve, Andrew, "Why Eligibility Regulations?" *The Athletic Journal* (October, 1968), p. 64.

school authorities comply with the eligibility rules and make them a part of the educational program if athletics is to succeed in establishing itself as a part of this program.

There are, however, some serious problems that can be brought about by the formulation and enforcement of eligibility rules by school authorities. Undesirable as is may seem to many individuals, it can solve many problems which can ultimately develop if the proper steps are taken to establish a uniform, workable system which not only is fair for everyone but also meets the national, state, conference and local regulations.

While the National Federation does not specify or spell out any specific eligibility rules which shall be enforced by all state associations and all high schools, it does indicate in the National Federation handbook several rules which might apply to all states such as age, years of competition, transfer, etc. It is the prerogative of each state to formulate and enforce its own set of rules. The formulation of these rules are the result of the combined efforts of administrators and coaches alike. The enforcement of these rules is excellent and there has been numerous occasions where court cases have been held; often the decision has been handed down in favor of the state's right to enforce these eligibility rules. The eligibility rules and regulations will differ from state to state. Fundamentally, however, the purposes are the same. Whether one believes that the student should be allowed to participate in athletics regardless of his academic achievement or whether he must adhere to certain academic standards is incidental. The student athlete is representing the school, and because of this, he should be a representative that exemplifies the attributes of the student body as a whole. This means that

the student athlete should be a worthy representative, one that can be respected for his conduct both on and off the field.

Therefore, the fairness of depriving a student participation in athletics because he failed in English, math, or history can be argued. His participation in athletics could provide the motivation that is necessary to not only keep him in school but to make a passing grade in English, math, and history.

It must be remembered, however, that the athlete is representing his school and his conduct should be such that it will bring honor to the school as well as to himself.

The value of athletics as a motivating force is brought out very vividly in the following comment by Briggs,[2] and his version of the affects of eligibility on the urban athlete:

> Let's look at the requirement for eligibility in athletics in the urban setting. If athletics does for boys what I know it does, let's not eliminate a boy simply because he is having academic problems. You're not going to save him that way—not our city boys and probably few other boys. I'm convinced that the inner city boy who is saved by athletics is one who has an experience that shakes him to his bones—the kind of experience he has never had before that molds him into part of a team, a dynamic team. He stands tall and straight and is admired by the kids of the ghetto because here is one who can make it. And that soon begins to spill over into the academic area. But if he hasn't made the academic first, we do not allow him to get into the mainstream of athletics. I submit to you this is wrong; this is absolutely wrong and it had better change.

Even though the rules of eligibility are usually set up by state or conference bodies,

[2]Briggs, Paul, "The Opportunity to be Relevant," *The Journal of Health, Physical Education, and Recreation* (May, 1970), p. 44.

the basic rules begin with the coach and player relationship. This type of athletic code encompasses more than eligibility because it generates honor and trust and exacts a certain responsibility from each member of the team. It makes playing on the team a privilege. It says, in so many words, that the athlete must be in complete control of himself both on and off the field. On the field he is obligated to abide by the rules and decisions of the officials and display good sportsmanship. He must maintain satisfactory grades and good attendance in the classroom and display good citizenship and respect for fellow students and faculty. He must act like a gentleman in the community and on trips. He must be a good representative of the school, community, and coaches. He must keep himself in good physical condition. The athlete will learn to realize that athletics is more than playing a game. It is an opportunity to teach fair play, sportsmanship, and citizenship and provides the participant with the opportunity of learning a new way of life.

Benefits Derived from Eligibility Requirements

1. More uniformity can be established between competing schools.
2. Definite regulations are made known to all persons concerned.
3. Standards and rules can be more easily enforced by state and local associations.
4. Pressures can be taken off the local administration because of established rules which must be adherred to.
5. Better relationship can be made between schools because each is functioning under the same eligibility requirements.
6. Even though each school can establish its own maximum eligibility requirements, it is possible for each school to

require the minimum standards without undue pressure to lower them from outside sources.
7. All students are treated the same, and no exceptions are made regardless of who the person may be.
8. Relations between competing schools are enhanced because each school knows the other school must abide by the same rules under which they are functioning.
9. The general public can also be made aware of the fact that all schools must adhere to the same state, athletic eligibility regulations.

WILMINGTON HIGH SCHOOL RED DEVILS

"STATE CHAMPS"   "STATE CHAMPS"   3RD PLACE
BASKETBALL   FOOTBALL   State Tournaments
1971-1972   1971-1972   1970-1971

FLIGHT "A" CONFERENCE FLIGHT "A" CONFERENCE 2ND PLACE
Champions in Football   Champions in Basketball State Tournaments
1971-1972   1970-1971   1972-1973
                       1972-1973

Date

Dear Parent:

Your son/daughter has expressed interest in competing on one of our athletic teams. We are pleased that your child has decided to avail himself/herself of the instruction and coaching of our fine staff. There is little doubt that your child can learn valuable lessons through competitive athletics that cannot be gained through the educational classroom.

To obtain maximum benefits from an athletic sports program, a child must strive for his or her peak physical condition. It is then extremely important that the student obtain sufficient rest at night and a well-balanced diet. Squad members are not permitted to smoke or drink, and violation may cause suspension from the squad.

Our athletic team candidates must present a physical examination card signed by a physician and attached sheet of eligibility requirements also properly signed.

All squad members are to be covered by the pupil insurance plan. All claims are made by the parent to the insurance company.

Your student will be issued equipment for participation in an athletic sport. At the end of the season the equipment must be returned and lost equipment paid for.

Attendance at all practice sessions is mandatory and only absences for emergencies will be excused.

We are confident that your son/daughter will enjoy this opportunity to participate in our athletic program.

Sincerely,

Athletic Director

Figure 35.

Types of Eligibility

There are two types of eligibility. (1) Those dealing with schools and (2) those dealing with the individual athlete. Although all rules pertaining to schools are not the same in every state, many of them are similar in nature. The National Federation of State High School Associations has been very instrumental in bringing about uniformity in many of these rules, some of which can be listed as follows:

1. Member schools should compete only against other member schools.
2. All schools should use contracts for contests furnished them by the state associations.
3. All schools should place a limit on the value of awards that are given to athletes.
4. All schools should abide by the state ruling and require a specified number of days of practice prior to the first athletic contest.
5. Member schools should exchange eligibility lists before a specified time and prior to each contest.
6. Each school should limit the number of games played in each sport.
7. Coaches of all sports should be certified teachers and members of the faculty.
8. Schools should not participate in post-season games.
9. The length of the season should be limited to the dates set up by each state association.
10. Schools should not hold spring football practice.

The eligibility requirements for the individual athlete vary somewhat in the different states. However, there are many similarities that are common to most state high school associations. Some of these are listed below. The athlete must:

1. Be enrolled in the school at the time he is representing that school as a participant on an athletic team.
2. Pass a physical examination by a qualified physician according to the standards set forth by the state association.
3. Abide by the transfer rule as set up by the state association.
4. Have the written permission of the parents or guardian to participate in the athletic program.
5. Qualify himself as an amateur by the rules laid down by the state association.
6. Refrain from participating on any team other than the school team during the course of the regular season.
7. Compete only a specified number of semesters according to the rule set up by the state association.
8. Be scholastically eligible according to school and state regulations.
9. Meet the minimum and maximum age requirement.
10. Be enrolled in a certain number of subjects each semester.
11. Be passing in a certain number of subjects the previous semester.

There are those individuals who are firm in their belief that as long as a student is allowed to remain in school, that student should be allowed to participate in sports. Others believe that an athlete should be required to abide by certain rules and regulations because he is representing the school. Whatever the belief may be, it must be remembered that the athlete does assume certain responsibilities while a member of a school athletic team, and that he does represent his fellow students while a member of that team. He should represent them as a student and a citizen as well as an athlete.

Organizations Determining Eligibility Requirements

There are basically four organizations that determine the eligibility of a student to participate in athletics on the high school level. These organizations are (1) the National Federation of State High School Associations; (2) the individual state associations; (3) the conferences to which teams belong; and (4) the local organization.

The by-laws of the National Federation contain two basic rules which govern the eligibility of players and allow them to represent a school in any interstate contest. (1) His school must be a member of the state athletic association of his home state and he must comply with all eligibility rules of such association. (2) He must be an amateur in accordance with the amateur rule is formulated by his home state athletic association.

The National Federation also sets up minimum eligibility standards which it recommends but does not require state associations to use. For example, the student is considered to be ineligible if (1) he has reached his twentieth birthday, (2) he has attended a four-year high school eight semesters, or a senior high school six semesters, or has graduated, (3) he has failed to do passing work in at least fifteen periods per week, (4) he has lost his amateur standing, (5) he has, after becoming a member of a high school squad, taken part in an independent contest where admission is charged, (6) he transfers from one school to another without a corresponding change in his parents' residence, (7) he has transferred from one school to another for athletic purposes because of undue influence by anyone connected with the school, (8) he enrolled later than the beginning of the eleventh school day of the semester, (9) he accepts from any source a sweater, jersey, or any other award exceeding one dollar in value other than those usually given, such as medals, trophies, fobs, letters, and other athletic insignia, (10) he has not been promoted to the ninth grade, (1) he has not presented during the year a physician's certificate that he is physically fit for athletic competition, and (12) he, after having been certified as being eligible in football and basketball, attends any school, camp, or clinic organized in such a way that its entire purpose or a part of its purpose is to provide coaching or organized training in such sport.

The National Federation of State High School Associations has helped the state high school athletic associations bring about various rules of eligibility. It is not the intention of the National Federation to dictate these rules of eligibility because the local school can and often does enact a more stringent rule if it is not in conflict with state rules. The rule can be more stringent but not less. For example a school could enact an eighteen-year-old playing rule but could not allow a twenty-year-old boy to participate.

The State Associations

The state associations are primarily concerned with sports direction and the establishment of controls in the athletic programs within the schools. Unless these controls are established and enforced it is conceivable that the program in some instances would get out of control. Many schools could without these controls engage in and condone many undesirable excesses in their athletic competition. This would result in the undermining of the entire program and result in the breakdown of the philosophy and objectives of the athletic program as an integral part of the educational curriculum. Without rules and guidelines to follow, school authorities would encounter many difficulties from those individuals who wish to exploit the athletes and the school athletic programs. These individuals wish to center the attention on the few rather than on the welfare of the many who would be benefited by a well-rounded school activity.

There are still some schools that are not affiliated with their state association. There are advantages and disadvantages in being a member of the state association.

The advantages are listed by Resick, Seidel and Mason[3] as follows:

1. Establishment and enforcement of regulations for the conduct of contests
2. Maintenance of athletic accident or insurance plans
3. Registration and classification of athletic officials
4. Publication of magazines and bulletins
5. Establishment of athletic standards
6. Acting as a final authority to whom questions may be addressed, controversies presented, and appeals made

State regulations, therefore, relieve outside pressure on school authorities to lower standards, so it is possible for an athlete to participate and to eliminate criticism from other schools that their standards of eligibility are higher. It also saves the administration a great amount of time as the rules are more or less "cut and dried" and therefore, rulings do not need to be made on each specific case as the problem arises.

Most of the state regulations regarding eligibility are general and are concerned with such factors as age, school work, type of school, number of seasons played, registration, absenteeism, outside contests, awards, attendance at coaching clinics, physical examinations, school districts, postseason and all-star games, and starting dates for practice.

All the states have rules which deal specifically with the eligibility of the athletes and most of these rules are similar in nature. Close scrutiny of the athletic program is provided by state associations, and all schools are directly responsible to the state associations. Some examples of the eligibility rules of a state association are given here as an illustration to give the reader an idea of the attempts being made

to provide for fair and uniform competition between schools.

1. PRESENT SCHOLASTIC STANDING: He shall be doing passing work in at least fifteen hours of high school work per week. (Passing at least 3 major subjects.)
2. PREVIOUS SEMESTER'S RECORD: He shall have credit for fifteen hours of high school work for the previous semester. (Pass 3 major subjects.)
3. REVIEW: A subject taken for review for which he has already received credit cannot be used toward eligibility.
4. SUMMER SCHOOL: Courses taken in summer school cannot be used for eligibility.
5. ATTENDANCE: If he shall have been in attendance ten days or more during any semester, he shall be counted as having been in attendance in school said semester.
6. NUMBER OF SEASONS OF PARTICIPATION: He shall be eligible for eight semesters. He shall not be eligible for more than four seasons of participation in any sport.
7. TRANSFERRED STUDENTS: In case he is transferred from another high school district, he shall not be eligible for one year unless his parents are residents in the same district to which he is transferred. If his parents are residents of the district to which he is transferred, he shall become eligible immediately if the transfer occurs at the beginning of the semester, or after one month's attendance within a semester.
8. PLAYING UNDER AN ASSUMED NAME: In the event he contests under any name other than his own during his high school course, he shall be ineligible for competition for the period of one school year.

[3]Resick, Matthew, Seidel, Beverly, Mason, James, *Modern Administration Practices in Physical Education and Athletics* (Reading, Mass., Addison-Wesley Publishing Co., 1970), p. 126.

9. PARTICIPATION ON INDEPENDENT TEAMS: If, while a member of a school squad in any sport, he plays a match game on any team other than a team representing his own school without the previous written consent of the principal, he shall be ineligible from the date of such match game through a period equivalent to one whole semester. All of this time shall be made up of time in which the student is in actual attendance in the high school.

10. INELIGIBLE PLAYERS: He shall not be allowed to appear at any interscholastic athletic contest in the athletic uniform of his school if he is not eligible.

11. PHYSICAL EXAMINATIONS: No student shall be eligible to compete in any interscholastic sport unless, within the current school year and preceding either a game or practice, he shall have filed with his high school principal a certificate of physical fitness issued by a competent physician.

12. PENALTY OF MISBEHAVIOR DURING CONTEST: Any student in any school may be barred from participating in interscholastic athletic contest for gross violation of the ethics of competition or the principles of good sportsmanship.

13. AGE: A contestant will become ineligible for further competition in freshman sports when he reaches his sixteenth birthday. In sophomore sports he becomes ineligible when he reaches his eighteenth birthday. In junior varsity and varsity he must be under twenty.

14. ATHLETIC AWARDS: He must never have accepted any medal, cup, trophy, or other athletic award of any kind having a value of more than two dollars, except a letter awarded by his school, either as direct or indirect compensation for athletic knowledge or skill or in consequence of being on an athletic team. This rule does not prohibit the acceptance of medals, cups, or trophies in athletic meets or tournaments in which three or more schools participate.

15. BREAKING TRAINING RULES: A player dropped from an athletic squad due to breaking training rules set up by the administration and athletic department of the high school shall be dismissed from all school athletics for an indefinite period.

There may be special consideration in some states regarding parents who do not live in the school district. Some conferences require the parents to live in the district unless it is the student's last year in school and then special consideration is given. There have been cases when a student transferred schools and the parents were already living in the school district which the student transferred to. Then the students' parents, in order for the student to compete in athletics, moved into a different house, either across the street or somewhere else in the district. This complies with preceding requirements, regarding athletic eligibility, which stated that the parents must move. This may seem to be a violation of the spirit of the rules but is legal.

Eligibility Records

It is the responsibility of the director of athletics and the principal in each school to make sure that accurate records are kept on each participant so that a school is not embarrassed by finding out after a game or games have been played that a player was not eligible. This type of situation not only necessitates forfeiture of the game but creates a bad impression and sometimes resentment and bad feelings between the schools involved and the people in the community. These eligibility forms should be kept up to date and should be filed in the principal's office so that they are accessible when needed. The eligibility lists of other schools should also be filed.

The state associations furnish many of the forms that are necessary in regard to eligibility. This is done for several reasons, the most important one being that of uniformity.

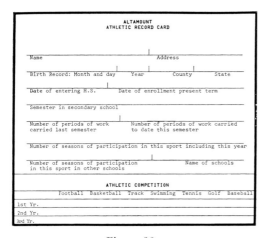

Figure 36.

Importance of Permanent Eligibility Records

This is an age of mobility. Thousands of families are moving from city to city in different parts of the country and from one part of the city to another. Many of the children involved will be athletes, but before they can be a playing member of an athletic team, they must establish their eligibility in conformance to state and local regulations. This requires constant vigilance and continued effort on the part of school authorities burdened with the task of obtaining, maintaining, and keeping permanent eligibility lists for all athletes. Some of the necessary information such as

name, address, and previous school attended can be supplied by the student himself. All other information must be obtained from the school or schools the student previously attended. This information would include the number of semesters in school, number of seasons of participation in all sports, age, credits earned each semester, etc. Every school should have a complete record of the above information on file not only for their own use but also because it should be available to send to other schools upon request. A plan should be worked out and put into effect by the school authorities whereby a continuous and complete season by season record of every athlete in every sport is kept up to date. This plan should be uniform and clear enough so that different people can use and understand it.

Often school authorities can be involved in decisions on the eligibility of athletes that will result in a case being brought into court. The past few years have brought about changes in attitude in regard to rules regulating the eligibility of athletes. Students and parents no longer accept decisions made by administrators and coaches without challenging them. Johnson[4] brings out this idea very forcefully by suggesting that:

> Students now are challenging the courts on eligibility. It is a commonly accepted theory now that the courts opinion strongly suggests that eligibility regulations must be reasonable and that the court will exercise its own judgment as to the reasonableness of the rule rather than simply deferring to the opinion of the officials who wrote the rule. The courts are becoming more lenient and more and more people are questioning the rules.

---

[4]Johnson, Page, "The Courts and Eligibility Rules: Is a New Attitude Emerging? *"Journal of Health, Physical Education, and Recreation* (February, 1973), p 34.

TABLE XLIX
JENSON HIGH SCHOOL DISTRICT NO. 94
ELIGIBILITY CARD

Name _____   _____

Birth Record _____   _____   _____   _____   _____
                  (Month)   (Day)   (Year)   (County)   (State)

Date of Physical Examination _____   _____   _____
                                      (Month)   (Day)   (Year)

Participation Record — 1 — 2 — 3 — 4 — 5 — 6 — 7 — 8 — Semester Number
                                    (Please Circle)

Number of Season — 1 — 2 — 3 — 4
                         (Please Circle)

Do you live in School District #94? _____

Did you pass all subjects last semester? _____

-------------------------- **ATHLETIC**   Phys. OK _____
            Sport   **ELIGIBILITY DATA**   Ins. OK _____

1. Name _____ Phone No. _____
2. Parent's Name _____
3. Address _____
4. Date of Birth_____
            Month   Day   Year
5. Place of Birth_____
            City   County   State
6. Names of other high schools you attended:
   _____ How long_____
7. How many semesters have you participated in high school athletics including this one? _____
8. How many semesters have you been in high school, **including** this one?
   _____
9. How many subjects did you pass last semester? _____
10. How many subjects are you now **carrying**? _____
11. When did you enter Glenbard? _____
12. How many seasons (including **this** one) have you played:
    a. Football _____ b. Cross Country _____ c. Basketball _____
    d. Wrest'ing _____ e. Gymnastics _____ f. Tennis _____
    g. Baseball _____ h. Track _____ i. Golf _____
Form No. 010

Figure 37.

Eligibility Lists

It is standard practice for all schools to exchange eligibility lists before each contest. This is usually a state requirement and the list includes all players who are eligible to participate in the upcoming contest between the two schools. This list is sent several days prior to the contest. These forms are usually provided by the state association so that the forms are uniform. The school principal or superintendent is required to sign this form indicating that all the players are eligible; it is his responsibility.

-------------------------   -------------------------
    Student's Name   Subject

-------------------   ---------------- 19____-19____
   Teacher's Name   Semester

ELIGIBILITY CARD

Evaluate and initial the correct column indicating progress from the 1st day of the current semester through the last day of the:

	Passing	Danger of Failing	Failing
2nd week	_____	_____	_____
4th week	_____	_____	_____
6th week	_____	_____	_____
8th week	_____	_____	_____
10th week	_____	_____	_____
12th week	_____	_____	_____
14th week	_____	_____	_____
16th week	_____	_____	_____
18th week	_____	_____	_____
End of semester	_____	_____	_____

Form No. 031

Figure 38.

Importance of Eligibility Lists

It is of extreme importance that the information needed for the preparation of the eligibility lists be gathered some time before the season begins and that it be done by a responsible person under the direct supervision of the principal. The gathering of this information should not under any circumstances ever be done by the athletic director or the coach. This can be a very laborious, tedious, and exacting task. There can be clerical errors made unless the person making out the list is capable and experienced. Errors can, however, be minimized greatly by gathering the data needed early in the season and sending this information in the form of the eligibility list to the opposing schools in time for them to be checked. Unless accurate year-to-year records are kept, mistakes can be made in regard to age, number of seasons of competition, semesters of enrollment, scholastic standing, number of hours being carried, enrollment in school prior to the game, etc. It is very rare that the records of any student are tampered with or changed so that he would be eligible. Usually it is a clerical error or a misunderstanding of a rule that constitutes the mistake. If a discrepancy is detected by authorities in either school, it should be reported immediately and every effort should be made to rectify it before the game is played.

Giving Eligibility Information to Players

Every effort should be made to disseminate the information regarding eligibility to the prospective athlete. Many times he is ignorant of the fact that he is violating a rule which may prevent him from ever competing on a high school team. This has happened to many players who inadvertently accepted money, a gift, or played on a professional team without realizing the dire consequences of such an act. It is, therefore, the responsibility of the school via the director of athletics and the coach to inform the player what he can and can-

NORTH JACKSON HIGH SCHOOL DISTRICT 130

ELIGIBILITY WORKSHEET

SPORT

YEAR _____

NAME	BIRTHDATE	COUNTY	SEM.	SEASON

Figure 39.

not do in order to protect his eligibility. This can be done in various ways. Probably the most popular one being the use of posters which are provided by most state associations. Some states also provide the schools with handbooks, bulletins, and other information which can be given to the students or posted on the school bulletin boards for viewing by the students. These rules can also be placed on athletic bulletin boards and in all locker rooms. Every precaution should be taken and every effort be made to inform and acquaint the student with the rules which will affect his eligibility. Many schools have the player sign a statement that he has read the rules and understands them. However, this is not always fool proof as many students will sign the statement even though

TABLE L
INFORMATION SHEET
ACTIVITIES ELIGIBILITY

Name _____ Telephone Number _____

Parent's Name _____

Address _____

                 Number   Street   Village

Date of Birth _____

                Month   Day   Year

Place of Birth _____

              City   County   State

I have attended high school for _____ semesters (including this semester).

I have been on the _____ squad in high school for _____
years (including this year).

Present Program — Omit study, gym, music, and counselor.

Period	Subject	Teacher
Homeroom		
1		
2		
3		
4		
5		
6		
7		

he has not read the rules. It will, however, many times prevent the student from intentionally violating a rule.

Transfer Forms

Most states provide standard forms which will contain the necessary information regarding the transfer student. The school authorities fill in the necessary information which in turn can be obtained from the permanent record which they should have on file for every athlete.

The Conference Associations

Each conference will have many different rules which the member schools feel fit their particular situation and fulfill their needs and philosophy. These rules are minor in nature, however, and always follow the general rule pattern set up by the state association. For instance, one requirement could be that no player's name may appear on the eligibility sheets of two different sports at the same time. Another rule might be that if a player competes in a varsity contest, he may not compete in a frosh-soph contest until another varsity contest is played, providing he did not compete in the second varsity contest.

Some conferences are, however, very specific in stating their additions to the rules already set up by state associations. For instance, one conference may prescribe the following additions which are typical in the rules which concern coaches in their efforts to equalize competition.

ILLINOIS HIGH SCHOOL ASSOCIATION
ATHLETIC DIVISION
ELIGIBILITY CERTIFICATE

N⁰ 92515

Data for a contest in_____between the_____High School,

_____, Illinois, and the _____High School, _____,

Illinois, to be held at _____ on _____, 19___

Game will be played at _____ and called at _____
A.M.
P.M.

(Park, Play Ground or Gymnasium)

OFFICIALS

OFFICIALS LISTED BELOW will be used in this game as agreed between the two schools. If not previously agreed upon they will be considered accepted unless protested by visiting school immediately upon receipt of this notice. (By-law A-II-11.)

(Not To Be Filled By Visiting School)

NAME	ADDRESS	POSITION

ELIGIBILITY LIST

I hereby certify that each person whose name appears below is a bona fide student in regular attendance at the_____

_____ High School, _____, Illinois; that he completed fifteen or more hours of recognized high school work in the last preceding semester he was in any high school; that he has successfully carried fifteen or more hours during the present semester from the beginning up to the date of this certificate; that the following tabulated data are correct; that he has complied in all respects with the requirements of the Illinois High School Association, and is eligible to participate in interscholastic contests under said rules.

Name of
Coach_____ Dated_____ Signed_____ Principal of_____ H.S. ___

PLAYING NO.		NAMES OF CONTESTANTS	BIRTH RECORD		Date of Enrollment for Present Term	(Based on) (Grades 9-12) IS NOW IN		Date of Latest Doctor's Certificate	Check if Parents Do Not Live in District
White	Dark		Mo., Day, Yr.	County and State		Sem. (No.)	Season (No.)		

LIST CONTINUED ON REVERSE SIDE

PLAYING NO.		NAMES OF CONTESTANTS	BIRTH RECORD		Date of Enrollment for Present Term	(Based on) (Grades 9-12) IS NOW IN		Date of Latest Doctor's Certificate	Check if Parents Do Not Live in District
White	Dark		Mo., Day, Yr.	County and State		Sem. (No.)	Season (No.)		

DATA ON ATHLETES WHOSE PARENTS DO NOT LIVE IN THIS DISTRICT

NAMES OF CONTESTANTS	ADDRESS OF PARENTS	ELIGIBLE BECAUSE (USE NUMBERS)
		1. Lives in non-high district normally tributary to this school but outside of any elementary district conducting a 2-yr. or 3-yr. H.S.; or if within such district has completed the 2-yr. or 3-yr. course.
		2. Has been ruled eligible by the IHSA Board of Directors (or IHSA Office) because:
		a) He is a transferred student who has been in attendance one full year or more and whose tuition has been paid as required under By-law A-I-13.
		b) Waiver has been granted under notes following By-law A-I-12.
		c) Parents have moved out of the district within the current school year.
		d) Other reason (explain).

Figure 40, A & B. Reprinted with permission from the Illinois High School Association.

ILLINOIS HIGH SCHOOL ASSOCIATION

Attention Athletes!

You Are Not Eligible:

1. If you are nineteen (19) years of age or over. (See By-law A-I-9 for exceptions)
2. If you do not have credit for fifteen (15) hours of work earned during the last semester, or if you are not currently passing fifteen (15) hours of work per week for high school credit. (See By-law A-I-3 for exceptions)
3. If you have attended more than eight (8) semesters after entering the ninth grade. Ten (10) days attendance constitutes a semester. (See By-laws A-I-4 and 10)
4. If you have participated in a given sport for all or parts of four (4) seasons. (See By-law A-I-11 for exceptions)
5. If you have competed under an assumed name. (See By-law A-I-17)
6. If you were not enrolled and in attendance at school by the beginning of the eleventh school day of the current semester. (See By-law A-I-1 for exceptions)
7. If you have been absent more than ten (10) consecutive school days during the current semester. (See By-law A-I-8 for exceptions)
8. If, during the school year and while a member of a school athletic squad, you have competed on a non-school team in any interscholastic sport. You are a member of a school squad until your school participates in its last contest in that sport. (See By-law A-I-18)
9. If you have played on any college or university team, on any "all-star" football or basketball team, or during the school year on any "all-star" baseball team. (See By-laws A-I-6 and 19)
10. If, after entering a member school, you have played on a team with a paid player. (See By-law A-I-15)
11. If, after entering a member school, you have accepted for athletic achievement any medal, cup, trophy or other athletic award exceeding $5.00 in value, cash or material rewards. (See By-laws A-I-15 and 16 for exceptions)
12. If you attended a Coaching School, Camp or Clinic in any interscholastic sport between August 1 and the end of the school year. You may have attended a Coaching School, Camp or Clinic during the summer provided no faculty representative from your school was an instructor. (See By-law A-I-21 for exceptions)
13. If you do not have a licensed physician's certificate of physical fitness issued within one year preceding your current participation. (See By-law A-I-22)
14. If your parents do not live in the school district in which you are attending high school. (See By-laws A-I-12 and 13 for exceptions)
15. If you were a member of a high school football or basketball squad and have played in a post-season football or basketball game except intramural. (See By-law A-I-24)

CAUTION: You should not attend any organizational meetings, participate in practice sessions or interscholastic contests except during the regular seasons as provided in By-law A-II-16.

NOTE: By-laws are published in the Official IHSA Handbook. See your principal.

(Please Post)

Figure 41. Reprinted with permission from the Illinois High School Association.

1. All eligibility rules as stated in the conference manual will apply to all regularly scheduled contests.
2. A contestant may make only one change in the level of competition during one season between varsity and frosh-soph teams.
3. No contestant in the spring sports may change teams more than once during the season.
4. A contestant may not be a member of two teams at the same time.
5. No contestant shall be given permission to play or practice with outside teams if he is at the same time a member of a high school team.

6. No contestant shall play on any two teams during the same day.
7. No contestant shall play in a junior varsity or freshman game following participation in a varsity or frosh-soph game.
8. No contestant shall play in a freshman B game following participation in a freshman A game until the next freshman A game has been played in that sport.

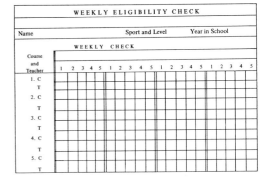

Figure 42.

TABLE LI

DIRECTIONS

I. *Athlete:*
  1. Fill in name, sport, and class and months of season.
  2. Fill in name of subject taking and name of teacher.
  3. Take to teacher *each Monday* for eligibility check.

II. *Teacher:*
  1. Initial by week if boy has passing accumulative grade.
  2. Do not initial (leave blank) if boy is failing on accumulative grade.

Some schools use the full semester to determine eligibility, others use a six-week period. Some states have advocated using a one-week period in determining the eligibility of an athlete.

5802040

ELIGIBILITY CARD FOR ATHLETES

RECORD OF

Return This Card to the Office Each Wednesday Night Before Leaving Building

Week Ending					

*By "Passing work" is meant the contestant shall be doing work of such a grade that credit would be entered on the records were credits given at the time of the issuance of the certificate.

Figure 43.

PALATINE TOWNSHIP HIGH SCHOOL DISTRICT 112

GRADE DISTRIBUTION SHEET

Grading Period _____ Nine Weeks

Teacher _____

SUBJECT	A	B	C	D	E	F	INC.	PASS	FAIL	TOTAL
TOTAL										

Figure 44.

GRANVILLE HIGH SCHOOL DISTRICT 119

STUDENT ELIGIBILITY LIST

WEEK ENDING _____

Name	Failing Subjects	Near failing Subjects	Ineligible to _____	Comments

Assistant Superintendent

Figure 45.

GRAND RAPIDS HIGH SCHOOL DISTRICT 112

ATHLETIC ELIGIBILITY

DATE _____ ATHLETE'S NAME _____

SPORT _____

COACH _____

SUBJECT	TEACHER'S SIGNATURE	PASS	FAIL	INC.	COMMENTS

Figure 46.

There is probably more of an opportunity for schools within a conference to exercise uniformity in their eligibility rules and regulations than on a state level. This is due in part at least to the close proximity of the schools to one another. One of the reasons a conference is formed in the first place is to provide equal competition on a comparable level. Thus, a conference will be composed of schools with comparable enrollments, financing, facilities, and usually, comparable philosophies, objectives, and outcomes.

However, there are instances where this is not true especially in a situation where a conference is formed with schools surrounding a large city. There, communities with divergent viewpoints regarding philosophy, objectives, unequal financial backing, and different social and economic stratification may make up the conference. As a result of this situation, there can be wide differ-

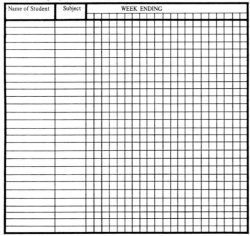

WEEKLY ATHLETIC ELIGIBILITY CARD

RETURN TO MAIN OFFICE BY NOON FRIDAY OF EACH WEEK

The following boys have maintained to date a passing average for the current semester in the following subjects:

NOTE: If pupil is maintaining a passing average the instructor should sign initials; if below passing, a horizontal line should be drawn through space for the particular week; if near failing mark X.

Figure 47.

There are many who believe, and justifiably so, that the only eligibility rule for an athlete is that he is a *bona fide* student in the school. Interscholastic athletics are a part of the total educational program and no student should be deprived of this opportunity. He should be allowed to learn from these experiences. The administration is obligated to protect these opportunities for the student. Winning has been the reason for establishing eligibility rules. Many unethical people within the school and community will violate sound educational practices in order to win. Eligibility rules have been developed to prevent this from happening. It is only fair to expect uniform regulations among schools to assure equal competition.

Local or School Plans

It is understandable that there will be local school systems that will be more interested in certain aspects of the eligibility problem than others. It is their prerogative to set up rules of their own choice as long as these rules comply with and are not more lenient than those which are used by the state association. On the other hand, it is conceivable that some schools may have local regulations that exceed the state eligibility requirement regulations. Some schools might require a student to do satisfactory work in fifteen hours during a semester while another might require twenty hours. The regulations pertaining to other aspects of eligibility, such as practice periods, number of semester hours carried by the student, attendance, etc. might be in excess of what is required by the state rules.

Frequently, the coach, athlete, and other interested people feel that the athlete is being discriminated against by setting up rules which will prevent his participation in athletics, an extracurricular ac-

ences of opinion regarding eligibility rules and their purposes.

There are many people that feel that if a student has grades high enough to stay in school, he then should be permitted to participate in all the activities within the school, including athletics. This sounds reasonable. However, it does have its ramifications because this could mean that a student could participate in athletics and not pass a single subject. Many schools allow the student to remain in school regardless of his or her grades. They even allow the student to graduate with a special diploma. Again, the basic principle behind this thinking is that athletics is a part of the educational curriculum, and therefore, the student will gain from this educational experience. Assuming that this is true, then they ask the question: Why is athletics any different from any other subject within the school system? Why is it different from math, English, or history when it comes to determining eligibility?

tivity, while, using the same criteria, his friend is allowed to participate in other extracurricular activities, including band, orchestra, dramatics, debate, etc.

Suggested Local Academic Eligibility Rules

1. An athlete must take at least four hours of academic credit to be eligibile.
2. Eligibility of players will be determined on a week by week basis according to the following rules.
   A. A student must pass three academic subjects or be placed on academic probation.
   B. If a student fails to do passing work in the week while on academic probation he will be suspended from athletics for a minimum period of one week or until he or she brings the work up to minimal acceptable standards.
3. If a student is expelled from a class by a teacher the first violation calls for a conference with the principal, and the second warrants a two-week suspension.
4. If an athlete is on detention he will perform extra duties in practice as determined by the coach.
5. If an athlete has an unexcused absence from class which requires disciplinary action, the first and second violations should result in suspension from the next scheduled contest; the third violation should result in suspension for the sport season.
6. An athlete who is in academic good standing and receives an incomplete will be suspended from athletic contests until his work is complete. He or she must attend all practices and be with the team but not suit up at all contests. The principal may make exceptions in cases of extended illness.
7. An athlete must be in school the full day on the day of a contest in order to participate. With prior notification given to the coach, exceptions can be made at his discretion.
8. Students must be in attendance in classes 80 percent of the days of the sport season. (No eligibility—the principal may make exceptions in cases of extended illness).
9. Athletic letters remain the property of the school until the student graduates from high school. The letter may be taken back at any time before graduation for misconduct by the student.

A Workable Eligibility Plan

A system which not only affects the athlete but all students in any extracurricular activities is one way to eliminate partiality. The plan offered here places all activities on the same basis. It can, of course, be adjusted to fit local situations and is not the complete answer to a very difficult problem. There are many other workable plans which are equally as good.

Under this system it is possible for the student who has the leading role in the school play to be declared ineligible for this play after long and tedious rehearsals. This could also be true of person in the band, choral groups, or any other activity.

The following extracurricular activities could be affected by a plan of this kind: athletics, school clubs, cheerleading, student council, newspaper, band, chorus, dramatics, G.A.A., honor study hall, etc.

Using this suggested plan, a student is ineligible if he is failing in two or more academic subjects. Physical education, band, chorus, driver training, and remedial reading are not considered academic courses. A student is eligible if he receives three D's and one F. However, anytime a student receives two F's in an academic area, he is automatically declared ineligible. This ineligibility lasts for one week; that is the week following. The student may not practice for that week and must raise his grades by the end of that week or he will be declared ineligible for the rest of that season. This should happen only when he is reported two weeks in succession. In the case of band, chorus, etc. he would be ineligible for the entire semester.

The student would be declared ineligible only if his accumulation grade average at that time is an F. The student's grade each week would be summarized with the anticipation that he will transfer on Monday. Each teacher should be held accountable if a student is declared ineligible and there are no grades in the record book. This brings about consistency in regard to athletics and to a certain extent, would eliminate personal prejudice.

The eligibility sheet or weekly report form is divided into three parts, namely: (1) failing list, (2) warning list and (3) poor study hall students. Each of these three divisions has three columns to be filled in, the name of the student, subject, and apparent reason for failing. However, it is imperative that those students should be placed on the warning list prior to being placed on the failing list. No student should be failed without first being warned. This plan not only warns the student but gives the coach, band director, etc. time to replace the student with someone else and also to administer some guidance in the student's behalf.

Those individuals whose names appear on the warning list would be border-line students, and unless an improvement is shown, should be placed on the failing list.

The third division on the report sheet is for those students not studying in study hall.

Each teacher would be responsible for notifying the student that his name is on one of three lists. This would be done by giving each student a number at the beginning of the year and then as his name appeared on one of the lists in the teacher's record book, his number would be read in class. In this way any questions that the student might have can be taken care of immediately after class.

The eligibility sheet would be placed in the mail boxes of staff members Wednesday of each week and returned to the principal's office prior to leaving school on Friday.

The office staff should be delegated the responsibility of compiling the records and sending the results to the athletic director or coach. He, in turn, would inform those who are ineligible. All other students would be notified by their respective teachers.

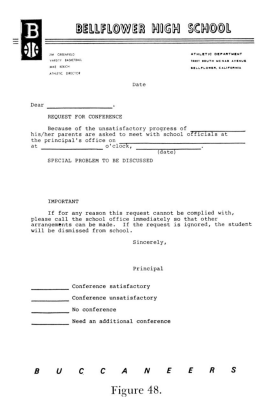

Figure 48.

This system of eligibility is more effective if the school has the full cooperation of the parents. Two letters should be sent to the parents, one of which informs the parents that the student has had his name placed on the warning list. The teacher should write a letter to the parent informing the parent why the student's name is on the list and what can be done to have his name removed. If the student's name is then placed on the failing list, the following week another letter should be sent to the parent. Unless the parent comes to the school for a discussion of the problem, the student is removed from school until such a conference can be arranged.

The enforcement of the school work load ruling is a problem of each individual school administration. It is their responsi-

New London High School

NEW LONDON, CONNECTICUT 06320

INTERSCHOLASTIC ATHLETICS

SALVATORE A. AMANTI   WILLIAM L. FOYE   GEORGE H. GREGORY
Director of Athletics   *Principal*   *Faculty Manager*

Date _____

Dear _____ :

    Your son/daughter, _____ , is having difficulties in certain areas in the course, _____ . We would appreciate your assistance in helping him/her remedy these difficulties as soon as possible.

AREAS OF UNSATISFACTORY PERFORMANCE:

_____ ATTENDANCE _____
_____ CONDUCT _____
_____ STUDY HABITS _____
_____ SKILL AREA _____

Instructor's Comments:

    If no improvement is noticed, we will arrange a conference to discuss this matter with you. You also are welcome to discuss the above comments at this time. Simply telephone the school office, Tel. No. _____ , for an appointment.

        Sincerely,

        _____
        Teacher

        _____
        Principal

jj

Figure 49.

BAY SHORE PUBLIC SCHOOLS

516-665-1700   RAYMOND R. HOWARD, *Superintendent of Schools*

DEPARTMENT OF PHYSICAL EDUCATION
102 EAST MAIN STREET, BAY SHORE, NEW YORK 11706

WILLIAM W. MAHON   Date
Director of Health, Physical Education and Recreation

    To the Parents of _____

    Mr. and Mrs. _____

    With much regret, we must inform you that your son, _____ , has decided to drop from our sports program. This program meets from _____ to _____ every school day during the season. Your son has indicated to his coach that his reasons for dropping from the _____ squad were due to one or more of the following:

_____ Academic
_____ Medical
_____ Economic
_____ Lack of interest
_____ Extra-curricular activities
_____ Others (explained on reverse side)

    We feel that your son would benefit from this program. If you would like more information about this matter, please call his coach, Mr. _____ , at the high school at your earliest convenience. Thank you very much.

        Sincerely,

        _____
        Director
        Department of Athletics

gg

Figure 50.

LAWSON TOWNSHIP HIGH SCHOOL DISTRICT 112

WEEKLY REPORT

For Week Ending _____ Teacher _____

Pupils who, if grades were to be given now, would be failing. This list determines interscholastic eligibility.

STUDENT	SUBJECT	APPARENT REASON

Pupils who would be passing but whose work has been unsatisfactory during the week. This is a warning list.

Pupils who seem to have no studying to do when they are in the study hall.

These reports are to be turned in at the office on Friday night before you leave the building.

Figure 51.

bility to be certain that all their competing athletes are academically eligible. This, of course, is handled differently in the various schools. It is of major concern, and no one plan will fit every situation. Another plan is one in which the athlete must be passing in three solids (major subjects). A weekly report is required on all athletes. If the athlete is not passing in three solids in a given week, he is ineligible for the following week. If at the end of the semester, he is still failing, he is ineligible for the entire following semester. At the beginning of the season, the coaches submit a list of the candidates for their teams to the office and a weekly eligibility list is prepared from the passing or failing reports submitted by the academic teachers.

In addition to the regular academic requirements set forth by schools, other standards are required over and beyond the academic requirements. For example, before any student may participate in athletics at many schools, his parents must sign a permission card which relieves the school of any liability as a result of an injury. However, many schools underwrite accident insurance for every student. Several states include this feature in their programs. Other requirements may be listed.

The compiling and gathering of weekly grades to determine a student's eligibility to participate in athletics is an administrative problem and is handled differently in different school systems. Many schools allow the student to carry a card with him to each instructor who signs the card and gives the grade. There is always the possibility that the student might forge the instructor's signature, especially if the school system is a large one where this might not be detected easily. This system of carrying the cards to the instructor each week is acceptable, however. This is one method of checking the weekly grade to determine eligibility.

The following method could be used to help eliminate any tampering of grades or records by students. Eligibility sheets with the names of all the players are given to the teachers every Wednesday morning and are dated the Saturday of the following week. The teacher indicates, by placing a check mark in the correct space, if the student has been in class and an E if the student is failing, or a U if he is in danger of failing. The previous semester's grades would be checked to ascertain eligibility of students participating in sophomore sports. Athletic record cards would be made out for every athlete. The details for carrying out the record keeping are very important and usually this is the direct responsibility of the principal's office.

Most schools require that to be eligible a student must have passed a satisfactory physical examination, be insured against accidents, pass three solid courses during the period of participation as well as the previous semester, and meet other state requirements dealing with residence, school attendance, out of school competition in sports, outside awards, and age limitations. Most schools allow the coach to recommend students for awards based on participation, training, sportsmanship, cooperation, and attitude. Many schools do not drop students from the freshmen and sophomore squads on the basis of lack of athletic ability unless the coach, athletic director, and principal all feel it is in the best interests of the individual. Usually students participating in one sport are not permitted to switch to another sport that season without being released by the first coach. No student should be allowed to practice and compete in two sports the same season.

Schools should take a long hard look at their eligibility requirements. Is the athlete being discriminated against? Is he required to meet more rigid academic and disciplinary regulations than other students participating in other extracurricular activities? Is keeping him off the team being used as a means of keeping him in line? Are teachers and administrators using athletics as a disciplinary measure? On the other hand, is the student staying in school just to participate in athletics? Is this wrong? These are some of the questions which must be answered.

BEHAVIORAL OBJECTIVES

After a person has read this chapter, he should be able to:

1. Define eligibility as it pertains to high school athletics.
2. Explain the value of athletics in the education curriculum.
3. Compile and explain the benefits derived from athletic eligibility requirements.
4. Identify the two types of eligibility. Select and explain some of the rules under each type.
5. Identify the four organizations determining eligibility requirements and compare the purposes of each.
6. State some of the purposes and benefits of keeping permanent eligibility records by the schools.
7. Propose a plan of eligibility which will include all of the extracurricular activities within a school system.
8. Enumerate the various ways whereby eligibility information can be disseminated to players and explain the merits of each.
9. Explain why eligibility lists are important in high school athletics.
10. Develop an eligibility plan within a given school system whereby all athletes may obtain all the information necessary regarding athletic eligibility regulations.
11. Give opinions both pro and con as to why or why not athletes must meet eligibility requirements while their friends do not need to meet the same requirements to participate in other extracurricular activities.
12. Explain why some conferences have different athletic eligibility regulations even though the schools within these conferences may occasionally compete against one another. List some examples of rules that might be different. Analyze the reasons for these differences.
13. Interpret the differences between the purposes of the national, state, and local eligibility regulations. Explain why it is necessary to have these regulations.
14. Explain the two reasons why eligibility requirements are established.
15. Analyze several of the benefits derived from eligibility requirements.
16. Identify some of the reasons the state association relieves outside pressure on school authorities to lower standards.
17. Explain the importance of keeping permanent eligibility records.
18. Explain why eligibility lists are exchanged between schools and analyze the importance of these lists.
19. Compile a list of extracurricular activities within a school system that might be included in an all inclusive plan of eligibility.
20. Prepare a statement of philosophy of your own regarding eligibility.
21. Differentiate between national, state, conference, and local eligibility regulations.
22. Enumerate several rules which apply to most states regarding eligibility.
23. Visualize several problems that might arise in keeping the permanent eligibility records of the athletes.
24. Summarize the advantages of having the principal responsible for all eligibility.

ACTIVITIES

1. Form two groups of students enrolled in the class and debate the issue: Should eligibility of athletes be different from those students participating in other extracurricular activities?
2. Form two groups of students enrolled in the class and debate the issue: Is it right for a student to attend school just so that he can play athletics even though he is passing his subjects?
3. Send for several state eligibility regulations and compare them as to the following: age, limit on competition, semesters in school and others.
4. Visit a school and talk to the athletic director about his philosophy regarding athletic eligibility regulations. Discuss these viewpoints in class.
5. Talk with a professional and a college athlete and enumerate some of the values he received from participating in athletics.
6. Form a committee of class members and talk with the principal of a high school. Find out the procedure that exists in his school regarding athletic eligibility.

SUGGESTED READINGS

1. AAHPER: Athletics in education—A platform statement. *Journal of Health, Physical Education, and Recreation,* September, 1962.
2. ———: Attention athletes! You are not eligible. *The Illinois Inter-Scholastic,* May, 1973.
3. Briggs, Paul: The opportunity to be relevant, *Journal of Health, Physical Education, and Recreation,* May, 1970.
4. Bucher, Charles, and Dupee, Ralph: *Athletics in Schools and Colleges,* New York, The Center for Applied Research in Education, 1965.
5. Forsythe, Charles and Keller, Irvin: *The Administration of High School Athletics, Englewood Cliffs,* P-H, 1972.
6. Forsythe, Charles E.: *Administration of Physical Education.* New York, P-H, 1959.
7. ———: *The Athletic Directors Handbook.* Englewood Cliffs, P-H, 1956.
8. George, Jack F., and Lehmann, Harry: *School Athletic Administration.* New York, Har-Row, 1966.
9. Grieve, Andrew: Why eligibility regulations. *Athletic Journal,* October, 1968.
10. Griffin, John Harold: *Athletic Directors Handbook,* Interstate, Danville, 1960.
11. Hixson, Chalmer: *The Administration of Interscholastic Athletics.* New York, Lowell Pratt, 1967.
12. Johnson, Page: The courts and eligibility rules: Is a new attitude emerging? *Journal of Health, Physical Education and Recreation.* February, 1973.
13. Resick, Matthew, Seidel, Beverly, and Mason, James: *Modern Administrative Practices in Physical Education and Athletics.* Reading, A-W, 1970.
14. Voltmer, Edward, and Esslinger, Arthur: *The Organization and Administration of Physical Education.* New York, Appleton, 1967.

CHAPTER 11

The Budget

ANY SCHOOL'S FINANCIAL problems are centered around its budget. It takes a great deal of money to run a school. The athletic expenses are just a very small part of the total amount that is needed but it should be considered a very important part. The school budget is an organized plan for receiving and expending funds for a specific period of time. The school time usually runs from July 1 of each year to the following June 30. This constitutes one academic year. The budget is a general statement of the expenses that will be anticipated for that particular year or for a specified period of time. The athletic budget, of course, will be based entirely on the number of sports that will be conducted. An adequate budget will tie together the athletic and educational plan and the financial plan for the school. The budget should present a message to the administration. This message should give a brief summary of the conditions, policies, and plans for the interscholastic athletic program in the school which underlie the financial proposals. The message should be based on detailed information and data which have been used by those persons making the budget. This data should support the request for money and should be readily available to the school administration, board members, community officials, and, if necessary, the general public.

DEFINITION OF BUDGETING

There are many definitions of the term budget. It depends to some extent on what it applies to. Bartizal[1] says, "... budget is a forecast in detail of the results of an officially recognized program of operation based on the highest reasonable expectation of operation efficiency."

Koonty and O'Donnell[2] define it as, "... essentially the formulation of plans for a given period in the future in specific numerical terms. As such budgets are statements of anticipated results."

Roe[3] would define the educational budget as, "... the translation of educational needs into a financial plan which is interpreted to the public in such a way that when formally adapted it expresses the kind of educational program the community is willing to support, financially and morally, for a one-year period."

Forsythe[4] defines it as, "... an estimate of probable income and expenditures."

The Purpose or Function of the Budget

The primary purpose of any budget, regardless of the area in which it is functioning, is to proportion the expenditures in

[1]Bartizal, J.R., *Budget Principles and Procedures* (Englewood Cliffs, New Jersey: by permission of Prentice-Hall, Inc., 1942), p. 1.

[2]Koonty, Harold and O'Donnell, Cyril, *Principles of Management* (New York, McGraw Hill, 1955), p. 435.

[3]Roe, William, *School Business Management* (New York, McGraw Hill, 1961), p. 81.

[4]Forsythe, Charles and Keller, Irvin, *Administration of High School Athletics*, 5th ed., (Englewood Cliffs, New Jersey, by permission of Prentice-Hall, 1972), p. 237.

265

relation to the estimated income. It should show a planned program for the immediate and long-term needs of the department. It shows the financial needs of the program to the administration and allows them to plan the use of the monies. It should provide an estimate of income and expenditures, and it should be planned ahead of time. It should, if it is to be effective, be reviewed yearly to evaluate the results of the previous year.

In regard to athletic budgeting, it is a means by which the expenditures which are planned for the athletic program are proportioned in relation to the amount of money that is available for this purpose. This amount will vary from school to school and will depend entirely upon the financial structure of each community or district in which the school is located. Very few schools are able to completely finance the athletic program from gate receipts so that a good share of the money must come from general revenue. In most schools the budget is broken down into individual sports. How this is done and the amount of money that is appropriated for each sport is entirely dependent upon the administration of each school. There is no magic formula that will determine how much each sport should receive.

The athletic director will usually take the initiative in setting up the budget. He will give direction, encouragement, and guidance to those people in his department that are involved in the budget-making procedure. Usually the coach of each particular sport will be required to estimate his expenses for that sport. The director will assemble these budgets from the coaches of the various sports and determine where the cuts must be if any are required.

The budget in itself should be thought of as a financial plan and a means by which the philosophy of the department of ath-

letics is stated in dollars and cents. The specific purposes of the budget are listed by DeYoung[5] as follows:

1. The budget is a servant of education.
2. It gives an overview.
3. It aids in analysis.
4. It develops cooperation within the school.
5. It stimulates confidence among the taxpayers.
6. It estimates the receipts.
7. It determines the tax levy.
8. It authorizes expenditures.
9. It aids in administering the school economically.
10. It improves accounting procedures.
11. It aids in extracurricular activities.
12. It projects the school into the future.

Forsythe[6] explains, "Its preparation is of value to those in charge of high school athletic programs because it necessitates that they anticipate, as far as possible, all probable factors involved."

Importance of the Budget

The importance of the budget to the athletic department as well as other departments within the school system is unquestionable. A budget makes possible the maximum use of available funds.

An athletic program necessitates the expenditure of large sums of money. It is a rare occasion when the gate receipts from athletic events is large enough to finance the athletic program. It is, therefore, of extreme importance that the budget and budgetary procedures be understood if maximum use of the funds available are to be obtained. The preparation and administration of the athletic budget must conform to an acceptable process which is used by the entire school system. This simplifies the bookkeeping procedures and places all

---

[5]DeYoung, C.A., *Budgeting in Public Schools* (London, Doubleday Doran and Co., 1936) , p. 9.

[6]Forsythe, Charles and Keller, Irvin, *Administration of High School Athletics*, p. 237.

budgetary procedure on the same basis.

Howard and Masonbrink[7] stress the following points in budget making as being important to the department:

1. Budget making stimulates planning for the present as well as for the future. It requires that decisions be made with respect to where money shall be spent, and when it shall be spent on any item or project.
2. The budget requires a review of operation costs for the program. Such a review shows where the money has been spent, the items which are receiving the larger share of the funds, and those which may need more money.
3. The budget permits determination of the worth of outcomes in terms of goals being sought and the cost involved in reaching them.
4. The budget controls program development according to an institutional rather than a departmental pattern.
5. The budget makes it possible to secure more of the items and services which a department needs because it provides the means to acquire them in its plan for spending money.

It is important for every athletic administrator to have a knowledge of budget making. It is to their advantage to have a background in business administration but this is rarely the case. The athletic administrator must know enough about budget procedures to make out the budget for his department, something about the budgetary procedures used by the school district and the correct management of departmental funds or monies.

Setting up the budget has long been a headache for the athletic director and perhaps more so in recent years because of the rising prices and fluctuating cost of equipment, supplies, and personnel. Any depart-

ment within the school system must operate under certain budgetary procedures and restrictions. The budget will serve as a guide in keeping records of all financial transactions in the department and at the same time protect the personnel from suspicion of misuse of funds. It will serve as a guide in establishing equalization of funds within departments and between departments. While there is no set rule which will apply to all situations because of differences in the economics and philosophies of school systems, certain fundamental principles can be applied by all athletic directors who prepare budgets in all situations. Fessenden[8] has listed these principles as follows:

PRINCIPLES OF BUDGET MAKING

1. Estimated expenditures should never exceed 90 percent of anticipated income.
2. Allocations should be made on the basis of demonstrated need, and never on a hard-and-fast basis of a certain percentage to each respective sport.
3. Averages computed over a period of three years should carry significant weight in budget preparation. Actual figures, not guess work should be used as a basis for estimation.
4. All personnel concerned with the administration of the budget should be consulted before it is submitted for final approval.
5. All budgets should receive the approval of an authoritative body, athletic boards, school boards, or some type of an overlooking body.

Howard and Masonbrink[9] makes the following important observation regarding the budget:

The budget for a department should reflect the plans, goals, and policies of the department. The chairman in pre-

[7]Howard, Glenn, and Masonbrink, Edward, *Administration of Physical Education* (New York, Harper and Row, 1963), p. 111.

[8]Fessenden, Douglas, "Planning the Athletic Budget," *Scholastic Coach* (December, 1952), p. 20.

[9]Howard, Glenn, and Masonbrink, Edward, *Administration of Physical Education*, p. 128.

paring the budget, will be mindful of the amount of money which he will have and will plan for its most effective utilization. He also will look ahead in order to initiate processes by which additional funds can be secured to meet goals which the department and the institution agree are worth achieving.

Need for the Budget

Every school business and athletic department need a budget. When public funds are being used, it is absolutely imperative that requests for money are made and records are kept of how it is spent. It can be used as a guide for purchasing equipment as well as for a record of money spent. The public has a right to expect this type of procedure in handling tax funds. The director of athletics must adhere to the following rules:

1. He should attempt to use the same type of bookkeeping that is being used by the school system.
2. He must keep a record of every purchase he makes.
3. He must keep his spending within the budget.
4. He must be accurate in his bookkeeping so his books will balance and there will be no shortage of funds at the end of the year.
5. He must be eternally vigilant so that he does not commit any kind of an act which will create any suspicion of misuse of money in any way.

Requirements of the Budget

A great amount of forethought must precede budget making because the budget must represent an entire department as well as an entire school and community. There are certain requirements which the budget must fulfill if it is to do the job it is expected to do. Scott[10] has listed these as

[10]Scott, Harry, *Competitive Sports in Schools and Colleges* (New York, Harper and Brothers, 1951), p. 307.

follows:

1. It should reflect the philosophy, purposes and aspirations of the athletic department.
2. It should reflect the changing directions of institutional or departmental policies.
3. It should take into account the economic conditions of the times.
4. It should provide sufficient funds to meet the needs of the proposed program which it covers.
5. It should be confined to a period of time for which dependable estimates can be made.
6. It should reflect the current financial conditions of the institution and of the department.
7. It should be detailed, showing the exact purposes for which the funds are to be used.
8. It should be sufficiently flexible to provide for emergency requirements.
9. It should reflect the combined thinking of representatives of all phases of the program which it covers.
10. It should be subject to hearings before final adoption.

Estimates of income and expenditures should be based on analyses of previous budgets covering a stable period of from three to five years.

Advantages and Disadvantages of the Budget

A desirable characteristic of an athletic budget is that the estimated expenditures and incomes should be determined as near the needs as possible. If the coach knows what has been spent in the past, he can use this information as a guide for preparing future budgets. The budget should be flexible enough so that unusual situations as well as emergencies can be taken care of. It should be possible to transfer funds from one account to another and to allow for less important items to be removed so that more important items may replace them. Some of the disadvantages as revealed by Hixson are that the program may be designed and developed to fit the budget instead of the budget fitting the program. The budget may also be padded out of all proportion to the actual needs. One of the most flagrant disadvantages of the budget is that money is spent to purchase unneeded items because of the fear that if the money is not spent the budget will be cut the next year.[11]

Types of Budgets

Fundamentally there are two types of budgets. These types are given different names, the short- or long-range budget, and the yearly or continuous budget. Both can be used simultaneously or separately and both serve a purpose and in most cases are necessary.

The short-term budget usually involves the planned expenditure of money over one year or a short period of time. The long-term budget involves a number of years of long-range planning. The schools and athletic departments within the school usually are concerned mainly with the short-term or yearly type of budget. However, some long-range budgeting is necessary.

Budget Restrictions

While it is important that every athletic department regardless of size should operate within the confines of a budget in order to accomplish its purpose, it must be understood that budgets have serious limitations. George and Lehmann[12] listed these limitations very adequately as follows:

1. The budget is not a watchdog of the treasury.

2. The budget cannot be substituted for good administration.
3. The budget will be as good as the executive who makes it.
4. The budget improves as administration improves.
5. The budget should not be discarded because of failure to use it advantageously.
6. Responsibility should not be placed in the budget.
7. The budget should not be followed blindly.
8. Judgment should be used. Remember the budget is based on estimate.
9. The budget should not be allowed to run the school and kill initiative.

Benefits of Budgeting

Any athletic department will function better if it operates on some kind of budgetary plan. The budget should be thought of as a financial plan for a specified period of time. It states in dollars and cents the amount of money that can be spent. It determines the amount and quality of materials and number and type of personnel. It also determines the emphasis which is placed on athletics as well as which sports are to be stressed and which are not.

Roe[13] lists the following as benefits of budgeting:

1. Establishes a plan of action for the coming year.
2. Requires an appraisal of past activities in relation to planned activities.
3. Necessitates the establishment of work plans.
4. Provides security for the administration by assuring the financing and approval of a year's course of action.
5. Necessitates foreseeing expenditures and estimating revenues.
6. Requires orderly planning and coordination throughout the organization.
7. Establishes a system of management controls.
8. Provides an orderly process of expan-

[11]Hixson, Chalmer, *The Administration of Interscholastic Athletics* (New York, Lowell Pratt and Co., 1967) , p. 83.

[12]George, Jack F., and Lehmann, Harry A., *School Athletic Administration* (New York, Harper and Row, 1966), p. 115.

[13]Roe, William, *School Business Management*, p. 83.

sion in both personnel and facilities.

9. May serve as a public information device.

Use of the Budget

Obviously there is no reason for going through the work of making a budget if it is not going to be used. However, it is a protection for those persons using public funds so that they are more or less protected against any accusations of the misuse of these public funds.

The budget may be used in various ways. It indicates to the director the following:

1. The amount of money that can be paid for salaries of coaches, including the coaches of various sports.

2. The amount of extra pay that a coach may be paid who is also teaching an academic subject.

3. The amount of money that can be allowed for equipment so that enough is left for salaries of coaches.

4. The amount of money that can be spent for new equipment.

5. The amount of money that should be allowed for equipment repair.

6. The amount of money that should be allotted for equipment replacement according to an organized plan.

7. The amount of money spent for athletics compared to the amount spent in other schools of equal size and with like emphasis on athletics.

Budgetary Procedures

The budget is an extremely important item in the functioning of the school system. Money or lack of money will govern the way any organization, whether it is a school system or business, is managed and the way it succeeds. Schools must have financial support to have a good program.

There must be a fundamental identity between school policy and school finance. The methods of bookkeeping and budgetary procedures must be the same for each department. Scott[14] emphasizes this fact in the following comment:

A bookkeeping system should be established to conform to the items or lines provided, in the central financial office, no particular problem arises for the department, since uniform procedures are established by the school or college, which are the same for athletics as for other areas of the institution. This, of course, is the recommended procedure, and is a prerequisite to complete institutional control of interscholastic or intercollegiate athletics.

The expenditure of budget funds should be made with the greatest of care and in accordance with approved business practices. It is essential that all funds of the department be centrally controlled and that one person, usually the head of the department, be designated to authorize expenditure of such funds. In this connection, it is also well to have another person authorized to act in the place of the chairman of the department in emergencies in approving expenditures such as issuing checks in payment of bills or meeting the payroll of personnel. This may be the individual next above the chairman. In the case of athletics, this second person may be the chairman of the faculty committee on athletics, or the bursar of the institution. Before any financial commitment is made involving the funds of the department, it should be determined from the bookkeeper if funds are available in the account to which the expenditure is to be charged. Having been satisfied as to the availability of the funds, the next step is to determine the specifications of the items to be purchased. These specifications are then turned over to the vendor, who will provide samples and give price quotations.

---

[14]Scott, Harry, *Competitive Sports in Schools and Colleges,* p. 308.

Criteria Used in Making the Budget

If a budget is to be made to fulfill the needs of a particular area, such as inter-scholastic athletics, it is necessary that certain criteria be established that can be used as a basis for budget preparation. While it is true that every situation if different because of various and sometimes obvious reasons it is also true that well-established and sound criteria can be used in preparing the budget in most situations. Bucher[15] has listed the following criteria as representative of the kind that can be used in most situations:

1. The budget will clearly present the financial needs of the entire program in relation to the objectives sought.
2. Key persons in the organization have been consulted.
3. The budget will provide a realistic estimate of income to balance the expenditures that are anticipated.
4. The possibilities of emergencies is recognized through flexibility in the financial plan.
5. The budget will be prepared well in advance of the fiscal year so as to leave ample time for analysis, thought, criticism, and review.
6. Budget requests are realistic, not padded.
7. The budget meets the essential requirements of students, faculty, and administrators.

Scott[16] states that:

The local institution will designate the administrative personnel to whom the departmental budget is to be presented. If a faculty committee on athletics is in control of the program of competitive sports, the head of the department should work closely with this group in preparing the budget. Before it is passed on to the administrative authorities of the institu-

tion, it should be approved by the faculty committee on athletics. In the operation of the program of athletics it frequently becomes necessary to collect funds for others. For example, taxes are collected on ticket sales for the federal and sometimes the local government; tickets are sold on the home campus of a rival institution when the game is to be played on the rival's grounds and payments are made to visiting teams according to their contemplated share of the net gate receipts. In drawing up the budget these transactions ordinarily should not become a part of the document when they represent neither income nor expenditures; the department is simply serving as the agent of another party. Once the budget is adopted, the department is obligated to make every effort to conform both in letter and in spirit to its provisions.

Preparation of the Budget

In preparing the athletic budget, it is important that it is prepared in a consistent form and content with other departments within the school system. It should be broken down into separate units or sports and as a result there should be considerable input from the coaches of the various sports. The philosophy of the school and community will have a direct bearing on the amount of money spent on athletics and also on the different sports. By breaking the budget down into the different sports it clearly indicates where the money is being spent and in what areas the stress is being placed.

A complete and accurate inventory is of the utmost importance in solving the budget problem. The athletic director must know the amount and condition of all the equipment. This is important so that no athlete uses any poor equipment and so that any poor equipment can be replaced. Equipment should be replaced by buying some new each year. Never wait until all

---

[15]Bucher, Charles, *Administration of Health and Physical Education Programs* (St. Louis, The C.V. Mosby Co, 1971), p 473.

[16]Scott, Harry, *Competitive Sports in Schools and Colleges*, p 307.

of the equipment has to be replaced. This will necessitate having to buy heavy in one area and light in another in order to balance the budget.

The first step in preparing the budget is to determine the needs of the program. The needs will determine to a large extent the amount of money that is required. After these needs have been determined, the budget should be prepared to reflect these needs. There are various sources of information which are used in the preparation of the budget. It should reflect the combined thinking of several people and depends to a large extent on the size of the school and of course the economic and financial status of the school district. The organizational setup of the school will also determine whose responsibility it will be to make out the budget. In some schools the principal may determine what the needs are for the athletic program and he alone may make the decision as to the amount of money available for athletics. The budget may be determined by the superintendent of schools along with other departmental budgets. The most popular and democratic method would be for the director of athletics to assume this responsibility.

TABLE LII
CONCORD HIGH SCHOOL
Athletic Department
ATHLETIC BUDGET AND FINANCIAL STATEMENT

RECEIPTS	Actual 1973 - 74 Receipts	1973 - 74 Budget	Estimated 1973 - 74 Receipts
Activities Association	$ 3,000.00	$ 3,050.00	$ 2,500.00
Balance expected, past year	951.85	600.00	....
Baseball	131.50	50.00	50.00
Basketball	2,396.00	2,462.52	1,750.00
Football	4,469.75	6,756.27	4,850.00
Track	225.30	....	50.00
From Board of Education	5,272.02	5,484.45	8,629.00

Actual Receipts 1973 - 74 .... $16,446.70
1973 - 74 Budget Allocations .... $ 18,403.24
Estimated 1973 - 74 Receipts $17,999.00

EXPENDITURES

General Expenditures:			
Baseball	$ 969.02	$ 750.00	$ 845.00
Basketball	3,401.11	3,127.93	3,021.00
Football	6,770.83	8,099.31	7,528.00
Golf	86.50	175.00	180.00
Skiing	96.03	80.00	70.00
Swimming	141.19	125.00	150.00
Tennis	164.75	200.00	180.00
Track and Cross Country	649.14	580.00	575.00
Volleyball	44.08	150.00	150.00
Wrestling	623.20	606.00	695.00
Miscellaneous Expenditures:			
Athletic Numerals	326.37	$ 250.00	$ 250.00

EXPENDITURES — (cont.)

Emergency	....	200.00	150.00
Faculty Outing	208.67	250.00	250.00
Freight Charges	29.58	50.00	50.00
Insurance and Dues	572.18	550.00	550.00
Laundry and Dry Cleaning	1,239.00	1,000.00	1,000.00
Medical Aid and Service	91.00	100.00	100.00
Medical Supplies	188.69	500.00	400.00
Meetings and Conferences	272.77	200.00	200.00
Motion Pictures	69.40	75.00	100.00
Office Supplies and Equipment	33.02	50.00	50.00
Repairing and Reconditioning of Equipment	1,000.32	900.00	1,000.00
Supplies, Cheerleaders	44.00	225.00	....
Trophies	44.00	100.00	150.00
Towel Replacement	....	....	300.00
Miscellaneous	11.00	60.00	60.00

Actual 1973 - 74 Expenditures $17,050.72

1973 - 74 Budget Allocations .... $ 18,403.24

Estimated 1973 - 74 Expenditures $17,999.00

Estimated 1973 - 74 Receipts $17,999.00

Estimated 1973 - 74 Expenditures .... $ 17,999.00

Total 1973 - 74 Athletic Budget $17,999.00

TABLE LIII
FULTON HIGH SCHOOL DISTRICT 122
SAMPLE ATHLETIC BUDGET

Football	$ 5,173.00
Shoe Rental Reimbursement	673.00
	4,500.00
Cross Country	400.00
Basketball	1,545.00
Wrestling	1,360.00
Swimming	650.00
Gymnastics	700.00
Baseball	1,900.00
Track	1,800.00
Golf	350.00
Tennis	550.00
Tape & First Aid	1,400.00
Pictures, Trophies, Engraving, etc.	100.00
Special Braces for Injuries	100.00
Miscellaneous (Freight, Newspapers, Coaching Directory, Cleaning, etc.)	300.00
TOTAL	$15,655.00

EXPENDITURES — (cont.)

SPECIAL APPROPRIATIONS

Porta Phone Model C-2 with 500-Foot Extension Unit (Football)	250.00
Mat Carts (Wrestling)	225.00
Twenty Protective Baseball Helmets ($8.00 each)	160.00
Total	$ 635.00

RECOMMENDATIONS

1. Four glass backboards, replacing the metal boards, in new & old girls gym.
2. Paint a large Spartan Head on East Wall of Spartan Gym.

Regardless of who takes this responsibility he must have the cooperation of many people. The athletic director should seek the help of the coaches of the different sports in order to determine the needs of that particular sport. Who knows more about the needs of a particular sport than the person in charge of that sport? The coach does not necessarily need to have had experience in budgetary procedure as a special form may be provided for this purpose. This plan has two advantages. In the first place it secures the necessary information upon which the preparation of a good budget is dependent. In the second place, and just as important, it gives the coach a feeling of being a part of the organization and contributes to a good *esprit-de-corps*

NORTH JACKSON HIGH SCHOOL DISTRICT 130
JACKSON, OREGON

ESTIMATED EXPENSES 19 ____

ATHLETIC BOARD ALLOCATION _____

SCHEDULE (AWAY)	Travel Unit	Lodging	Meals	Trans.	Officials*	Guarantee	Other** Specify	Est. Cost Per Event	Encumb. Balance	Free Balance
SCHEDULE (HOME)										
TOTALS										

Clinics	
Pub. Rel.	
Recruitment	

SCHEDULE LIMIT _____
Home _____
Away _____

Figure 52.

within the department.

The director of athletics and the coach of each sport should review the inventory sheet of each sport and on this information determine the needs of the sport for the coming season. On the basis of these needs the budget for that sport should be determined. This meeting should be held as soon after the season is completed as possible.

The budget should then be analyzed in every detail for every sport. Only by securing detailed information can a budget be accurately prepared. Every proposed expenditure should be listed even though some of them amount to a few cents.

In preparing the budget it must be kept in mind that the most difficult task is to estimate the necessary expenditures for the year for which the budget is being prepared. There are certain factors which must be considered.

1. To look ahead is to insure the future; but to avoid the use of past experiences is folly. It is important to plan ahead as many as three years to insure a continuing plan on which to operate.

2. Prices fluctuate from season to season. The changes in the cost of equipment should be taken advantage of and purchases should be made when the prices are down. The athletic director should be aware of this situation and take advantage of it.

3. The number of participants in the sports program should be considered. If there is a decrease or increase in the number of sports that are being offered then this must be taken into consideration when the budget is being prepared.

4. Consideration should be given as to whether any new type of equipment designed to provide better preparation for the athletic teams are desirable.

5. Consideration should be given to the elimination of items that were customarily placed in the budget but are no longer needed. The fact that an item has always been in a budget does not necessarily mean that it should remain there.

Hixson[17] makes the following comment about preparing the budget:

In preparation of the budget the estimated expenditures should be determined as near the needs as possible. Budget work sheets should be distributed to those responsible for the various units in the department. Logically, the head coach of each sport in consultation with his assistants best qualifies to assess the real needs for his sport. The work sheets completed for each category of expenditure in the budget, detail specifications as to colors, materials, sizes, catalog numbers and unit cost. To determine the budget the athletic director and coaches need the following information:

1. The number of students expected on each squad.
2. The number of contests on the schedules of the various sports.
3. Current and accurate inventories of equipment and supplies.
4. The current prices and cost of materials and services.
5. The extent of travel, meals, and lodging to fulfill schedule responsibilities.
6. The number and cost of officials for all contests, varsity, reserve, junior varsity, freshmen.
7. The cost of game administration.
8. Medical costs, including insurance premiums.
9. The costs of reconditioning of equipment and estimated laundry and dry cleaning service.
10. Estimated cost of teaching aids including motion pictures of practices and games.
11. In service education and expenses to coaching clinics, workshops, and institutes for members of the staff.
12. The guarantees to be paid to visiting

[17]Hixson Chalmer, *The Administration of Interscholastic Athletics*, p. 81.

opponents.

13. The guarantees to be received from games played away from home.

14. Admission prices for students, adults, and season tickets.

15. Estimated game attendance.

16. The estimated income from additional sources for the fiscal year.

Guides for Preparing Athletic Budgets

The persons responsible for preparing the budget must not only be familiar with the philosophy of the school and the athletic department but must also have a complete knowledge and sufficient information to enable them to help in its preparation. There are certain guides, however, that lend themselves well and can be used in preparing the budget. Certain information must be known in order to prepare the budget and certain guidelines must be followed. Several of these are listed.

1. Records should be carefully kept on all expenditures involving the athletic program. The amount of money spent for each sport will provide a basis for determining the budget for the next year.

2. New equipment for the next year can be determined from the inventory forms used by the department. These forms should indicate all equipment needs.

3. The athletic director or school business manager should keep an accurate record of all monies collected at the gate.

4. The estimated budgetary needs should be accurate. It is common procedure to *pad the budget* so that the needed money will be available if the budget is reduced as it customarily is in many instances. This is not an acceptable practice but unfortunately it is a common one.

5. Provision should be made for emergency expenses. The amount will vary according to unforeseen circumstances that arise which were not planned for in the overall budget. It is possible through the proper authority to shift funds from one item to another should this occur. However, the best procedure is to expect these emergencies and make provisions to meet them by budgeting for them.

6. The coaches and athletic director should be familiar with athletic equipment and its cost. The coach should indicate on his equipment request the make and cost of each piece of equipment and where it can be purchased. This should be done on all items.

7. The athletic director should assume the responsibility of gathering the budgetary information from the coaches and assembling it in final form for presentation to the proper authorities for their approval or disapproval.

8. All coaches should present their budgets to the athletic director. It is advisable in a large school where there are a number of coaches employed to have a general staff meeting at which time the budget should be discussed.

9. Athletic equipment should be purchased soon after the money is available.

Scott[18] suggests the following guides should be considered in constructing the budget:

> It should reflect the philosophy, purposes, and aspirations of the department and of the institution.
>
> It should reflect the changing directions of institutional or departmental policies.
>
> It should take into account the economic conditions of the times.
>
> It should provide sufficient funds to meet the needs of the proposed program which it covers.
>
> It should be confined to a period of time for which dependable estimates can be made.
>
> It should reflect the current financial

[18]Scott, Harry, *Competitive Sports in Schools and Colleges*, p. 307.

conditions of the institution and of the department.

It should be detailed, showing the exact purposes for which the funds are to be used.

It should be sufficiently flexible to provide for emergency requirements.

It should reflect the combined thinking of representatives of all phases of the program which it covers.

It should be subject to hearings before final adoption.

Estimates of income and expenditures should be based on analyses of previous budgets covering a stable period of from three to five years.

The Budget in Relation to Purchasing Procedures

The most important aspect in the purchase of equipment is that it must be needed and it must fit the program. Extraneous purchasing is inexcusable. It must always be remembered that all purchasing of equipment should be done in a business-like manner. The funds used to purchase equipment whether from gate receipts, student fees, or tax monies belong to the school to be used wisely and frugally. Purchases should be made only by authorized personnel and then only by following the regular procedure as outlined by the administration. The purchasing could also be done by bidding.

The person entrusted with the task of purchasing the athletic equipment should take the time to investigate prices and attempt in every way to purchase wisely yet not sacrifice quality. He should make every effort to keep accurate books and be able to justify every purchase he makes in light of the program he is administering.

Time to Purchase

Purchases should be made during the season of the year when prices are the lowest. There are times during the off season when supplies of certain athletic equipment are more plentiful than at other times. Usually prices are lower at this time and it is advantageous to purchase equipment. Athletic departments should check on these times and adopt a time schedule to guide them in purchases of their equipment.

Kinds of Athletic Purchases

Most coaches have a preference as to the type of athletic equipment they want their players to use. Purchasing different kinds of equipment should be held to a minimum since better prices can usually be obtained on standardized equipment and the same kind of equipment. It is much easier to purchase, to requisition, to deliver, and to account for only one type of equipment. Also, it is good economy to buy good quality equipment and not rely on a larger amount for a lesser price.

Securing Bids

Most school systems require bids on all purchases over a certain amount. Most of the time this results in better prices and better buys. However, this practice does not allow for emergency purchases unless provision is made for it.

The bids should be sent to several firms in order to get good coverage. The information given to the bidders should include exact specifications so that the bidders will be bidding on the exact article and not substitutes. This is good practice even though it may not be required by law. The companies may be selected or it may be thrown open for competitive bidding. If the latter is true, then the letting of the contract should be widely advertised. Usually this is done through the news media.

The larger school systems, in order to make it more convenient for the supplier,

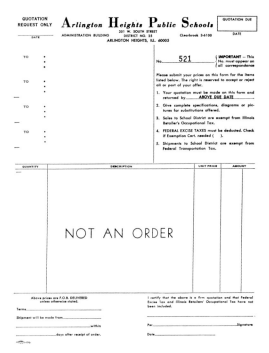

QUOTATION REQUEST ONLY

Arlington Heights Public Schools
ADMINISTRATION BUILDING
301 W. SOUTH STREET
DISTRICT NO. 25
ARLINGTON HEIGHTS, ILL. 60005
Clearbrook 3-6100

QUOTATION DUE
DATE

No. 521

IMPORTANT — This No. must appear on all correspondence

Please submit your prices on this form for the items listed below. The right is reserved to accept or reject all or part of your offer.

1. Your quotation must be made on this form and returned by ___**ABOVE DUE DATE**___
2. Give complete specifications, diagrams or pictures for substitutions offered.
3. Sales to School District are exempt from Illinois Retailer's Occupational Tax.
4. FEDERAL EXCISE TAXES must be deducted. Check if Exemption Cert. needed ( ).
5. Shipments to School District are exempt from Federal Transportation Tax.

QUANTITY	DESCRIPTION	UNIT PRICE	AMOUNT
	NOT AN ORDER		

Above prices are F.O.B. DELIVERED unless otherwise stated.
Terms___
Shipment will be made from___
___within
___days after receipt of order.

I certify that the above is a firm quotation and that Federal Excise Tax and Illinois Retailers' Occupational Tax have not been included.

Per___Signature
Date___

Figure 53. Reprinted with permission of Arlington Heights Public School District no. 25, Arlington Heights, Illinois.

will furnish him with a bidder's blank which will give him all the information relative to the nature of the items on which he is bidding, specifications, and other details.

Bidding has become prevalent over the past few years and has come about because of unfair business transactions and political issues.

Ashton[19] makes the following comment:

To insure equities and to protect public monies, many institutions require that bids be let on purchases over a specified amount. This practice is time-consuming, but the saving is often worth the time. The administrator simply schedules request earlier so that bids may be taken. The type, quality, and quantity

of materials needed are specified in the bid letting. Therefore a low bid with inferior merchandise could be rejected.

Amount to Purchase

Usually large purchases can be obtained at a lower price. Not all athletic departments are able to purchase in large quantities because of obvious reasons, among them being lack of funds at the time of purchase, storage space available, and supply. The large schools where a larger amount of athletic equipment is needed are able to take advantage of large purchases. Over ordering of equipment that is not used, however, is poor economy and care should be taken that this does not happen.

Delivery and Checking of Supplies

Unless the school system is a large one, the equipment is usually delivered directly to the athletic department. This can result in a great deal of difficulty in determining whether the exact amount and the right kind of equipment has been delivered. In order to avoid any problems in this respect a system of checking the equipment as it arrives should be established to determine if the quantity, quality, and condition of the purchase is as it should be.

Purchase Order

A purchase order is the next step after bids have been received. A purchase order is usually made out in response to the requisition providing the necessary authority has been given.

Ashton[20] explains it in this fashion:

Upon completion of requisitions and bids, if necessary, purchase orders are written. These orders carry the requisition number and usually are prepared in duplicate or triplicate. Standard

[19]Ashton, Dudley, *Administration of Physical Education for Women* (New York, The Ronald Press, 1968) , p. 221.

[20]Ashton, Dudley, *Administration of Physical Education for Women*, p. 221.

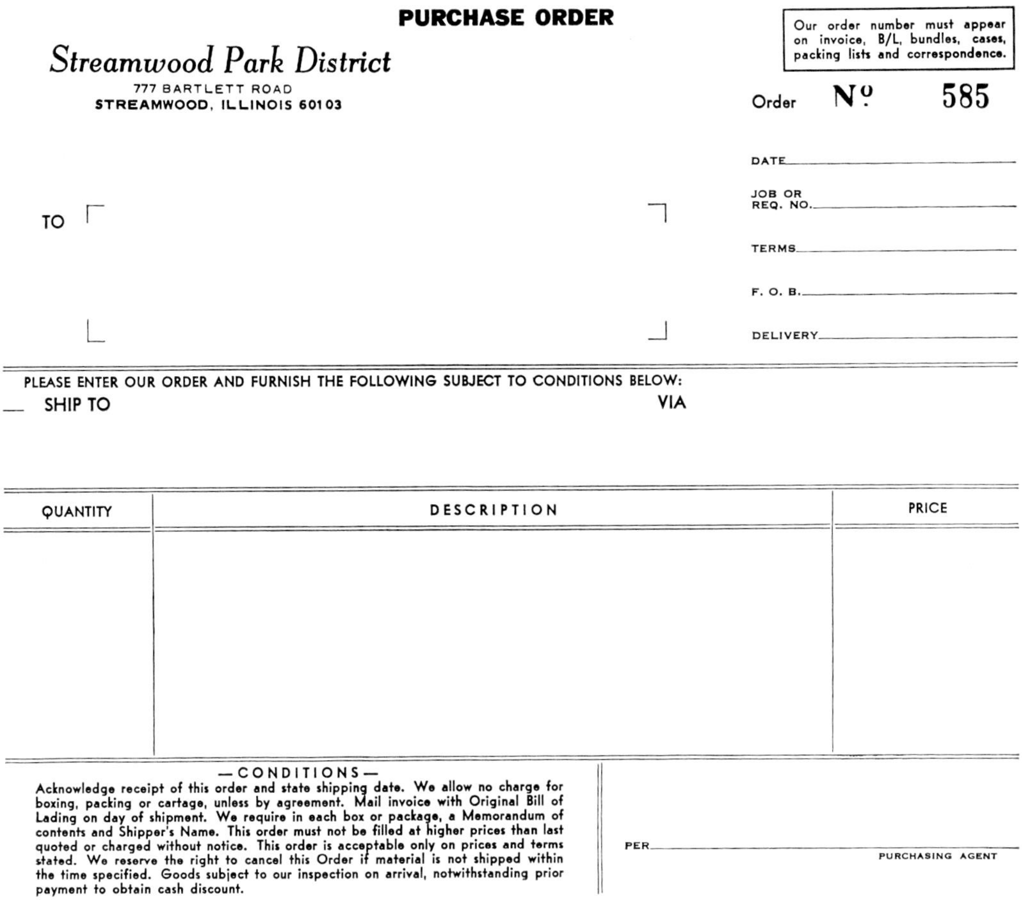

PURCHASE ORDER

Streamwood Park District
777 BARTLETT ROAD
STREAMWOOD, ILLINOIS 60103

Our order number must appear on invoice, B/L, bundles, cases, packing lists and correspondence.

Order **N?** **585**

DATE_____

TO ⌐   ⌐

JOB OR
REQ. NO._____

TERMS_____

F. O. B._____

⌐   ⌐

DELIVERY_____

PLEASE ENTER OUR ORDER AND FURNISH THE FOLLOWING SUBJECT TO CONDITIONS BELOW:

__ SHIP TO   VIA

QUANTITY	DESCRIPTION	PRICE

—CONDITIONS—

Acknowledge receipt of this order and state shipping date. We allow no charge for boxing, packing or cartage, unless by agreement. Mail invoice with Original Bill of Lading on day of shipment. We require in each box or package, a Memorandum of contents and Shipper's Name. This order must not be filled at higher prices than last quoted or charged without notice. This order is acceptable only on prices and terms stated. We reserve the right to cancel this Order if material is not shipped within the time specified. Goods subject to our inspection on arrival, notwithstanding prior payment to obtain cash discount.

PER_____

PURCHASING AGENT

Figure 54. Reproduced with permission from the Streamwood Park District, Streamwood, Illinois.

forms are used and voucher sheets for use by the supplier accompany the purchase order. At this point the commitment is firm and can only be voided by the inability of the supplier to furnish the materials under order.

Requisitions

Requisitions are requests from the department for items that are needed in order for the department to function.

Ashton[21] explains requisitions in the following manner:

Requisitions are written to cover the

[21]*Ibid.*, p. 220.

department's needs. Each requisition should carry the department budget number and should carry a purchase order number. Every requisition should be in writing and should carry at least one carbon for departmental records. An oral order has questionable legality and can lead to difficulties in executing the budget.

The method of requisitioning of these supplies will differ within each school system and many times is known only to those people whose responsibility it is to request these supplies. Requisitioning is important because unless this is done and a properly signed requisition blank has been received,

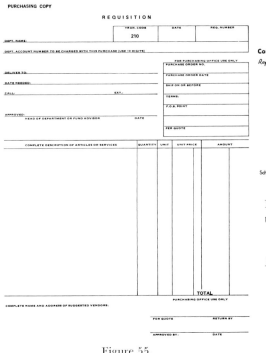

PURCHASING COPY

REQUISITION

TRAN. CODE	DATE	REQ. NUMBER
210		

DEPT. NAME:

DEPT. ACCOUNT NUMBER TO BE CHARGED WITH THIS PURCHASE (USE 10 DIGITS)

FOR PURCHASING OFFICE USE ONLY
PURCHASE ORDER NO.
PURCHASE ORDER DATE
SHIP ON OR BEFORE
TERMS:
F.O.B. POINT
PER QUOTE

DELIVER TO:
DATE NEEDED:
CALL: EXT.:
APPROVED: HEAD OF DEPARTMENT OR FUND ADVISOR DATE

COMPLETE DESCRIPTION OF ARTICLES OR SERVICES	QUANTITY	UNIT	UNIT PRICE	AMOUNT
			TOTAL	

PURCHASING OFFICE USE ONLY
COMPLETE NAME AND ADDRESS OF SUGGESTED VENDORS:
FOR QUOTE RETURN BY
APPROVED BY: DATE

Figure 55.

proper accounting of supplies and equipment cannot take place.

Invoices

The invoice is a record or a written statement which accompanies the order and is usually enclosed with the package. This should be checked carefully against the items which have been shipped. Ash-

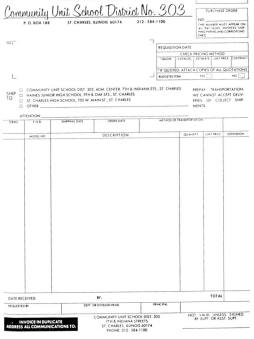

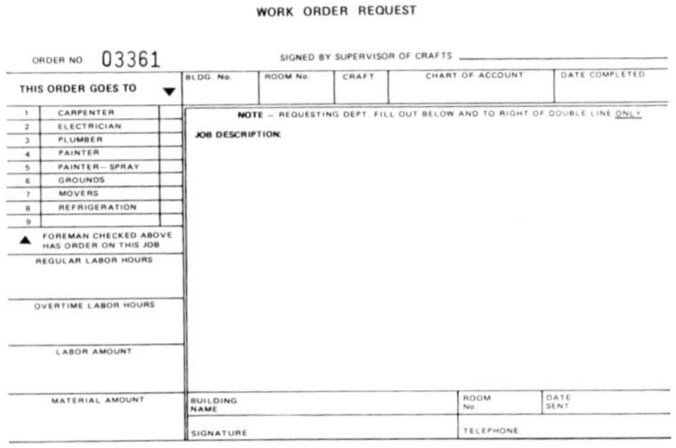

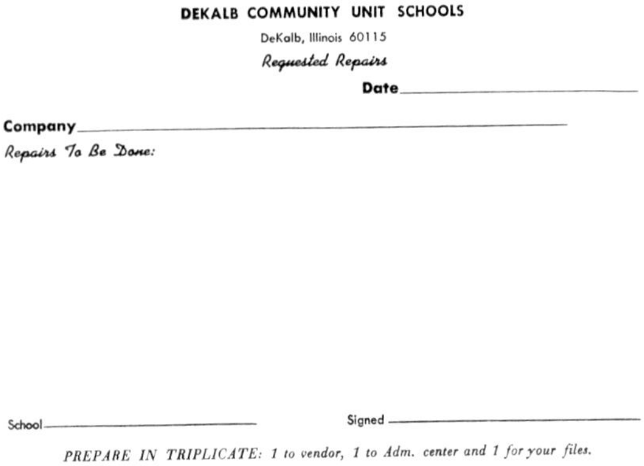

WORK ORDER REQUEST

ORDER NO 03361 SIGNED BY SUPERVISOR OF CRAFTS

THIS ORDER GOES TO ▼ | BLDG. No. | ROOM No. | CRAFT | CHART OF ACCOUNT | DATE COMPLETED

1 CARPENTER
2 ELECTRICIAN
3 PLUMBER
4 PAINTER
5 PAINTER – SPRAY
6 GROUNDS
7 MOVERS
8 REFRIGERATION
9
▲ FOREMAN CHECKED ABOVE HAS ORDER ON THIS JOB

NOTE – REQUESTING DEPT. FILL OUT BELOW AND TO RIGHT OF DOUBLE LINE ONLY
JOB DESCRIPTION:

REGULAR LABOR HOURS
OVERTIME LABOR HOURS
LABOR AMOUNT
MATERIAL AMOUNT

BUILDING NAME | ROOM No. | DATE SENT
SIGNATURE | TELEPHONE

Figure 56-A.

DEKALB COMMUNITY UNIT SCHOOLS
DeKalb, Illinois 60115
Requested Repairs
Date

Company
Repairs To Be Done:

School Signed

PREPARE IN TRIPLICATE: 1 to vendor, 1 to Adm. center and 1 for your files.

Figure 56-B. Reprinted with permission from the DeKalb School District, DeKalb, Illinois.

PURCHASE ORDER – REQUISITION
Community Unit School District No. 303
P. O. BOX 188 ST. CHARLES, ILLINOIS 60174 312 - 584-1100

CODE
PURCHASE ORDER
NO.
THIS NUMBER MUST APPEAR ON ALL PACKAGES, INVOICES, SHIPPING PAPERS AND CORRESPONDENCE

TO

REQUISITION DATE:
CHECK PRICING METHOD
*QUOTE | CATALOG | ESTIMATE | LAST PRICE | CONTRACT
*IF QUOTED, ATTACH COPIES OF ALL QUOTATIONS
BUDGETED ITEM YES NO

SHIP TO
☐ COMMUNITY UNIT SCHOOL DIST. 303, ADM. CENTER, 7TH & INDIANA STS., ST. CHARLES
☐ HAINES JUNIOR HIGH SCHOOL, 9TH & OAK STS., ST. CHARLES
☐ ST. CHARLES HIGH SCHOOL, 705 W. MAIN ST., ST. CHARLES
☐ OTHER

PREPAY TRANSPORTATION. WE CANNOT ACCEPT DELIVERIES OF COLLECT SHIPMENTS.

ATTENTION

TERMS	F.O.B.	SHIPPING DATE	ORDER DATE	METHOD OF TRANSPORTATION

MODEL NO.	DESCRIPTION	QUANTITY	UNIT PRICE	EXTENSION
			TOTAL	

DATE RECEIVED: BY:
REQUESTED BY | DEPT. OR DIVISION HEAD | PRINCIPAL

• INVOICE IN DUPLICATE
ADDRESS ALL COMMUNICATIONS TO:
COMMUNITY UNIT SCHOOL DIST. 303
7TH & INDIANA STREETS
ST. CHARLES, ILLINOIS 60174
PHONE: 312 - 584-1100

NOT VALID UNLESS SIGNED BY SUPT. OR ASST. SUPT.

Figure 57. Reprinted with permission from the Community Unit School District No. 303, St. Charles, Illinois.

ton[22] makes the following statement:

> An invoice or statement of shipment accompanies every order. These should be checked against the written order to be

[22]*Ibid*, p. 222.

LYONS TOWNSHIP HIGH SCHOOL
CHECK REQUISITION

Date ....

PAYABLE TO: ....

ADDRESS: ....

....

FROM: ....

(Name of Organization or Account)

SPONSOR ORDERING: ....

FOR:	PRICE

Club Sponsor-or Chairman: ....

Club Treasurer: ....

Check No. .... Approval: ....

Figure 58. Reprinted with permission from Lyons Township High School, LaGrange, Illinois.

sure the shipment carries the same materials. If not, the package should be rejected. If the shipment is correct and in order, the invoices are signed. There is no redress after the invoice is signed.

Use of Funds

When using public funds, extreme care should be exercised. The director of athletics is in a position of great responsibility financially because of the large amount of money which is entrusted to his care. This money can take various forms, such as gate receipts, guarantees, and appropriations from the general education fund. He should keep a detailed set of books and an

INVOICE	PHONE 756-9910

TERWILLIGER'S INC.
UNIVERSITY CITY
DEKALB, ILLINOIS 60115

INVOICE NO.
DATE OF INVOICE
YOUR ORDER NO.
OUR ORDER NO.

SOLD TO: SHIPPED TO:

DATE SHIPPED	SHIPPED VIA	F.O.B.	SALESMAN	TERMS

QUANTITY SHIPPED	QUANTITY ORDERED	DESCRIPTION	PRICE	UNIT	AMOUNT

Figure 59. Reprinted with permission from Terwilliger's Inc., DeKalb, Illinois.

accurate account of all monies spent. He should be able to give to the proper authorities a detailed record of every purchase at a moment's notice. One way a director of athletics can get himself in a great deal of trouble is through slipshod methods of handling public funds. Scott[23] stresses this point in the following comment:

> The expenditure of budgeted funds should be made with the greatest of care and in accordance with approved business practices. It is essential that all funds of the department be centrally controlled and that one person, usually the head of the department, be designated to authorize expenditure of such funds. In this connection, it is also well to have another person authorized to act in the place of the chairman of the department in emergencies in approving expenditures, such as issuing checks in payment of bills or meeting the payroll of personnel. This may be the individual next above the chairman. In the case of athletics, this second person may be the chairman of the faculty committee on athletics, or the bursar of the institution. Before any financial commitment is made involving the funds of the department it should be determined from the bookkeeper if funds are available to the account to which the expenditure is to be charged. Having been satisfied as to the availability of the funds, the next step is to determine the specifications of the items to be purchased. These qualifications are then turned over to the vendor, who will provide samples and give price quotations.

Presentation of the Budget

Presenting the budget is a very important aspect of the budgetary procedure and as such should be given careful consideration. The expenditure of any public funds should be justified and this is the responsibility of the people who request these expenditures. The budget should be based on authentic and detailed information. A complete analyzation of the budget should be provided in writing to the person or persons designated to approve it. This presentation may need to be made to several persons or groups of persons before final approval is given. This helps explain the necessity for detailed information and justification. Usually the budget request moves from the coach to the athletic director, to the principal, to the superintendent, and eventually to the board of education.

Hixson[24] makes the following comment on assembling the information for making the budget:

> The athletic director assembles all requests and worksheets compiling them into a complete departmental budget. In this process he prevents duplication and at the same time coordinates and integrates the budget. For example, if the wrestling and basketball teams are going to compete on the same day at the same school, he can consolidate the transportation, meals, and lodging, thereby realizing substantial savings. If the estimates are unreasonable in terms of the expected financial support or seem unnecessary in view of the present inventory, the director in consultation with the coaches can revise the budget before presenting it to the approving authorities. The director prepares a summary statement of the budget as well as the detailed budgets submitted by each sport.

Probably the most important presentation is made by the athletic director to the principal. Usually the administration works together very closely, and if the principal approves the budget request, an attempt will usually be made to substantiate this request. The budgets for all sports should be presented to the principal by the athletic director for his approval. To

[23]Scott, Harry, *Competitive Sports in Schools and Colleges*, p. 309.

[24]Hixson, Chalmer, *The Administration of Interscholastic Athletics*, p. 82.

TABLE LIV
**CONCORD HIGH SCHOOL
ATHLETIC DEPARTMENT
ATHLETIC BUDGET AND FINANCIAL STATEMENT**

RECEIPTS: ITEMIZED BY SPORT

	Actual Receipts 19_____	Budget 19_____	Estimated Receipts 19_____
BASEBALL			
Gate Receipts	$ 79.00	$ 50.00	$ 50.00
Advertising	52.50	....	....
	$ 131.50	$ 50.00	$ 50.00
BASKETBALL			
Gate Receipts	$1,331.50	$1,662.52	$1,150.00
Guarantees	500.00	500.00	100.00
Share in Regional Tournament	564.73	300.00	300.00
	$2,396.28	$2,462.52	$1,750.00
FOOTBALL			
Gate Receipts	$3.619.75	$5,906.27	$4,000.00
Guarantees	700.00	700.00	900.00
Advertising	150.00	150.00	150.00
	$4,469.75	$6,756.27	$4,850.00
WRESTLING			
Gate Receipts	$ 188.80	....	$ 200.00
Advertising	36.50	....	20.00
	$ 225.30	....	$ 220.00

EXPENDITURES: ITEMIZED BY SPORT

	Actual Expenditures 19_____	Budget 19_____	Estimated Expenditures 19_____
BASEBALL			
New Equipment	$ 200.24	$ 256.00	$ 350.00
Meals	341.30	169.00	175.00
Officials	42.90	25.00	50.00
Repairs	138.00	100.00	50.00
Transportation	220.99	150.00	200.00
Advertising	25.54	....	....
Emergencies	....	50.00	....
	$ 969.02	$ 750.00	$ 845.00
BASKETBALL			
New Equipment	$ 893.23	$ 888.93	$ 800.00
Films	....	25.00	24.00
Game Expense	175.00	125.00	125.00
Guarantees	350.00	250.00	250.00
Meals on Trips	597.00	470.00	450.00
Officials	429.90	432.00	400.00

TABLE LIV—(cont.)

Tickets and Advertising	150.00	100.00	100.00
Transportation	706.05	737.00	672.00
Emergencies	....	....	100.00
	$3,401.11	$3,127.93	$3,021.00

	Actual Expenditures 19_____	Budget 19_____	Estimated Expenditures 19_____
FOOTBALL			
New Equipment	$3,657.17	$3,676.31	$3,600.00
Equipment Repairs	484.97	1,000.00	1,000.00
Field Expense	4.63	100.00	100.00
Motion Pictures, Books, etc.	71.98	200.00	300.00
Game Expense	26.00	50.00	50.00
Guarantees	900.00	900.00	400.00
Meals and Rooms on Trips	356.00	510.00	440.00
Officials	311.40	297.00	300.00
Programs	180.00	200.00	200.00
Scouting and Use of Car	139.90	150.00	150.00
Tickets and Advertising	153.83	250.00	250.00
Transportation	414.75	566.00	498.00
Clinic	....	....	40.00
Emergencies	70.20	200.00	200.00
	$6,770.83	$8,099.31	$7,528.00
GOLF			
New Equipment	$ 36.00	$ 100.00	$ 120.00
Meals and Transportation	50.50	75.00	60.00
	$ 86.50	$ 175.00	$ 180.00
SKIING			
Meals and Transportation	$ 56.03	$ 50.00	$ 50.00
Trophies	40.00	25.00	25.00
	$ 96.03	$ 75.00	$ 75.00
SWIMMING			
Meals and Transportation	$ 41.19	$ 50.00	$ 50.00
New Equipment	100.00	75.00	100.00
	$ 141.19	$ 125.00	$ 150.00
TENNIS			
New Equipment	$ 104.00	$ 100.00	$ 100.00
Meals and Transportation	60.75	100.00	80.00
	$ 164.75	$ 200.00	$ 180.00
TRACK			
New Equipment	$ 409.75	$ 225.00	$ 275.00
Meals	87.50	115.00	125.00
Officials	55.00	65.00	75.00
Tickets and Advertising	50.00	50.00	50.00
Transportation	46.89	100.00	50.00
	$ 649.14	$ 580.00	$ 575.00

TABLE LIV—(cont.)

VOLLEYBALL

New Equipment	$ 21.00	$ 50.00	$ 50.00
Meals and Transportation	23.08	100.00	100.00
	$ 44.08	$ 150.00	$ 150.00

WRESTLING

New Equipment	$ 179.75	$ 320.00	$ 360.00
Meals	162.50	56.00	75.00
Officials	155.00	80.00	100.00
Repairs	8.00	25.00	....
Transportation	109.35	100.00	125.00
Advertising	8.60	25.00	25.00
	$ 623.20	$ 606.00	$ 685.00

BOARD OF EDUCATION–COMMUNITY HIGH SCHOOL DISTRICT #92   Check One: AT_____

BUDGET REQUESTS   W_____

     Y_____

Check One		DEPARTMENT _____	Supplier: _____
E563.1 Capital Equipment	[]	Instructional	Address: _____
E502.39 Instructional Supplies	[]	Area _____	

Room No. _____   Cat. No.: ¯¯¯¯¯¯¯

INSTRUCTIONS   Dept. Chairman's Signature _____

Page___of___Pages

(1) Please number pages consecutively (2) List only one supplier per page (3) Prepare in triplicate, department chairman retains one copy, forwards two copies to principal who retains one copy and sends original to District Business Office (4) All deletions from the original must be initialed by the individual making the deletion.

Catalog Page No.	Catalog Number	Quantity	Nomenclature and/or Specifications	Unit Cost	Total Cost

Figure 60.

avoid misunderstandings a full explanation of various items in the budget can be given at this time. The budget should include all information relative to cost, quality, order number, make, and other specifications of each item.

The budget request is now sent to the superintendent of schools, who combines it with the other departmental budgets for presentation to the board of education for their approval.

Tonigan[25] makes these five suggestions for presenting a budget. If the budget is

[25]Tonigan, Richard, "How to Prepare a Budget for Tight Times—and Get It Approved," *School Management* (February 1971), p. 30.

well planned and properly presented the chances of getting it approved are greatly increased.

1. Be sure the department is in good order.
2. Convince the administrators that everything humanly possible has been done and the only thing left that is needed is money.
3. Demonstrate the flexibility and innovative ability of the staff.
4. Conduct a good follow-up. After submitting the budget keep checking with the administration. Be ready to answer any and all questions about the budget.
5. Communicate effectively. Submit a budget that is clearly and concisely stated so that no one can fail to understand it.

Approval of the Budget

The budget for athletics in high school usually is first approved by the principal, then by the superintendent and finally by the board of education.

The director of athletics should be ready at all times to defend every item in the budget. It is necessary, therefore, that he understands exactly every procedure and the need for every item included in the budget. Very seldom is a proposed budget accepted without question. Athletic directors and coaches must employ effective techniques for presenting the budget for approval. Problems in areas must be anticipated and preparation for defending them should be done.

Bracken[26] suggests that the budget message in order to obtain approval should include:

1. The money spent for each item or sport.
2. Reasons for increases or decreases in the money spent.
3. Any new sports or programs to be added.

[26]Bracken, Charles, "Presenting the Small City School Budget," *American School Board Journal,* March, 1966, p. 19.

4. Any other conditions that will influence the cost.

Administration of the Budget

There is no real reason for making a budget unless it is used. The budget is nothing more or less than a plan to follow in spending appropriated funds. This does not mean that alterations or changes cannot be made if this is deemed necessary. There may be unforeseen circumstances that arise that will necessitate the use of certain monies in different areas or on different items that had previously been decided on for another item. For example, expenditures for equipment may be larger than anticipated in some areas while expenses in another area may not be as great.

Care should be taken, however, that this practice is not carried to an extreme. By and large all monies should be spent on items that were requested.

Every athletic department should have a financial accounting system which would enable the athletic director and coaches to know at any moment how much money remains in each appropriation item. Each coach should know how much money he has left in his budget by merely asking the athletic director. Most school systems will require a monthly statement showing the status of the finances of the school system.

The size of the budget request will be determined to some extent by the money allocated the previous year, unless unforeseen circumstances arise such as increase in enrollment and the money available.

Revisions of the budget are usually made after the requests from all departments are reviewed. This means that if the amount requested for athletics is reduced, then the athletic director will need to study the requests for each sport and make the necessary adjustments in order to bring them in line with the total budget cut.

The athletic director should have the

responsibility of administering the budget.

One of the problems in the budgeting of athletic funds lies in the fact that there are some sports like football and basketball that are revenue producing sports. Others such as track, tennis, golf, etc. earn very little through gate receipts. This creates the feeling that the sports that produce the most money should be allowed to spend it. On the other hand if the value of athletics lies in the fact that it is a part of the educational curriculum then each sport should be treated equally regardless of the amount of revenue it produces. There should not be any difference in the amount of money spent for equipment on a need basis.

Evaluating the Budget

After the budget is accepted and put into action, it is necessary to see if it is functioning. Often this is not an easy procedure because it is difficult to foresee all

REQUEST FOR REPAIRS, ADDITIONS, ALTERATIONS

BOARD OF EDUCATION
COMMUNITY HIGH SCHOOL DISTRICT 88
Du PAGE COUNTY, ILLINOIS

Willowbrook ________
York ________
(Check one)

Requested by: ________________ Date of Request: ________

Please make this request in a neat, clear and detailed form.

Description of existing condition and recommendation:

Location of the problem situation:

Any special date wanted:

Comments:

Request approved by ____________ Date: ________
Principal

Acknowledged by: ____________ Date: ________
(Sup't. Bldgs. & Grounds)

Work completed: Date ________ Approved by: ____________
Foreman / Sup't. Bldgs. & Grounds

Copy for Superintendent Buildings and Grounds

Figure 61. Reprinted with permission from Community High School District 88, Du Page, Illinois.

TABLE LV
FULTON HIGH SCHOOL DISTRICT 122
PAYMENT FORM

____________ High School Athletic Association

To the Treasurer: Date ____________

Please issue checks to:	Amount	Charge to Number
____________	$________	________
____________	$________	________
____________	$________	________
____________	$________	________

Expenses	*Sport*
1. Labor	Football
2. Scouting	Cross Country
3. Printing	Basketball
4. Medical	Swimming
5. Federal Tax	Wrestling
6. Officials	Baseball
7. Meals	Track
8. Transportation	Golf
9. Repairs	Tennis
10. Equipment	Miscellaneous
11. Miscellaneous	

____
(Athletic Director)

the conditions that may arise during the year which could make a tremendous difference in the expenditure of funds that had not previously been planned for. Emergencies arise that could drain the budget and make it appear that it was not a good budget. The discrepancies between estimated and actual expenditures could be quite large in some instances and yet justifiable. It is because of this situation that budget planners sometimes allow plenty of leeway between estimated expenditures and estimated income to provide for a balanced budget at the end of the fiscal year. They are then accused of padding the budget. This practice defeats the purpose of the budget yet it is sometimes justified. It should be kept in mind, however, that the purpose of the budget is to provide for accuracy and efficiency in the procurement of supplies and equipment.

BEHAVIORAL OBJECTIVES

After a person has read this chapter, he should be able to:

1. Discuss the relationship of budgeting to the democratic process.
2. Explain the function of the school business official in the budgeting process in interscholastic athletics.
3. Determine where an athletic director would go to get help on budgeting.
4. List the principles of budget making and discuss their function on the basis that a principle is a guiding rule for action.
5. Define budget and interpret its meaning in terms of the athletic budget.
6. List the two types of budgets and explain how each are used in preparing an interscholastic athletic budget.
7. Differentiate between the purpose and the outcomes of the athletic budget.
8. List and explain several limitations of the budget and apply them to the in-

terscholastic athletic program.
9. Explain how an athletic director could operate an athletic program on a smaller budget than last year if he was required to do so.
10. Discuss the functions of the budget.
11. List and analyze the requirements of a good budget and apply them to a specific situation.
12. Present arguments for and against a budget.
13. Explain the purpose of the athletic budget.
14. Differentiate between the benefits and requirements of the budget and list several of each.
15. List and explain several criteria that are used as a basis for budget making.
16. Explain what is meant by padding the budget and explain the consequences of such a practice.
17. Criticize the practice of padding the budget.
18. Compare the relative functions of the athletic director and the principal in budget making. Which of these should play the leading role?
19. List any further principles, if any, under the three steps of budget making.
20. List the advantages there might be in using standardized and uniform budget forms.
21. Outline a plan which the athletic director might follow in securing the cooperation of the coaches in budget making.
22. List the steps the athletic director should take to ascertain whether his budget is well proportioned as to all sports.
23. List and explain several purposes of the budget and apply them to the interscholastic athletic program.
24. List several guides for preparing athletic budgets and discuss the informa-

tion that should be furnished to use these guides.

25. List and analyze several factors which have a direct bearing on the preparation of the budget.

26. Explain the procedure or steps used in most high schools in the presentation of the athletic budget.

27. Differentiate between the following: preparing the budget, presenting the budget, and administering the budget.

28. Differentiate between requisitions and purchase orders, and explain when each is used.

29. Explain the advantages and disadvantages of bidding.

30. Draw up a proposed athletic budget for a new senior high school of 1000 students with seven sports.

31. Outline the various categories which would be included in the development of an interscholastic budget including the following sports: football, basketball, swimming, baseball, track, tennis, and golf.

32. Explain the responsibility of the individual coach in budget preparation.

33. Differentiate between the responsibilities of the coach, the athletic director, and the principal in preparing the budget.

34. Determine what percentage of the school budget for your school district is allocated for athletics.

35. Identify some of the current practices regarding ticket sales for athletic contests.

36. Explain the responsibility of the individual staff members in budget preparation.

37. Describe the principal's role in the preparation and administration of the athletic budget.

38. Describe the athletic director's and coach's role in the preparation of the athletic budget.

39. Explain the purpose of the budget.

40. Differentiate between policy and budget and explain how each complements the other in preparing the athletic budget.

41. Define the budget. Recall and explain the types of budgets used in the department of athletics in high school.

42. Describe in detail the major steps in the preparation of the budget for athletics and apply each step to the purchasing process.

43. Describe the use of the budget and explain its function in the department of athletics.

ACTIVITIES

1. Select several budgets and compare their contents. Make a list of the strengths and weaknesses of each.

2. Find out what the laws of your state are regarding school budgets.

3. Interview several athletic high school directors and try to categorize their philosophy of budgeting.

4. Obtain and examine the budgets of several athletic departments in schools of equal size and note the differences among them in form, organization, detail, understandability, etc. Select one as the poorest and report in class.

5. Draw a diagram or flow chart showing in detail the participation of each athletic coach in the budgetary process.

6. Consult with a high school athletic director regarding the preparation of his budget.

7. Consult with a high school coach and find out from him his responsibilities in budget making.

8. Make a pie chart showing the percentage of money spent on each sport in a typical school.

9. Form two groups of students and de-

bate the issue of having gate receipts as the only revenue for the support of athletics.

10. Arrange for a high school athletic director to talk to the class on the preparation of the budget.

11. Prepare and explain a purchasing method for the athletic department.

12. Prepare a five-year budget spread for introducing a new sport into the program.

13. Develop a form for reporting gate receipts for athletic contests.

14. Visit a high school in your neighborhood and ascertain how the athletic department is financed.

15. Draw up a proposed budget for a new senior high school of 2000 students including six major sports.

16. Outline the various categories that would be included in the development of an interscholastic budget including the following sports: football, basketball, and track.

17. Study the athletic budgets of several schools. After determining their strengths and weaknesses report the findings to the class for discussion.

18. Obtain several budget record forms and discuss them in class.

19. Plan a workable athletic budget for a school of 1000 students. Make a presentation to the class using them as a board of education. Justify all expenditures.

20. Obtain the budgets from several schools. Determine their strengths and weaknesses and report the findings to the class for recommendations.

SUGGESTED READINGS

1. Ashton, Dudley: *Administration of Physical Education for Women.* New York, Ronald, 1968.

2. Bartizal, J.R.: *Budget Principles and Pro-*

cedures. Englewood Cliffs, P-H, 1942.

3. Boyd, William: Sample purchasing proves practical method. *American School Board Journal,* March, 1965.

4. Bracken, Charles: On presenting the small city school budget in the small city school district *American School Board Journal,* March, 1966.

5. Bucher, Charles: *Administration of Health and Physical Education Programs.* St. Louis, Mosby, 1971.

6. Burrup, Percy: *Modern High School Administration.* New York, Har-Row, 1962.

7. Cass, James: First things first. *Saturday Review,* October 16, 1971.

8. DeYoung, C.H.: *Budgeting in Public Schools.* London, Doubleday, 1936.

9. Evans, Robert and Menaphac, Joseph: Relevant and accountable athletic department spending. *Scholastic Coach,* Jan. 1971.

10. Fessenden, Douglas: Planning the athletic budget. *Scholastic Coach,* December, 1952.

11. Forsythe, Charles and Keller, Irvin: *Administration of High School Athletics.* Englewood Cliffs, P-H, 1972.

12. Furno, Orlando: How effective is your budget. *School Management,* January, 1971.

13. George, Jack F., and Lehmann, Harry A.: *School Athletic Administration.* New York, Har-Row, 1966.

14. Hixson, Chalmer: *The Administration of Interscholastic Athletics.* New York, Lowell Pratt, 1967.

15. Hughes, William, French, Esther, and Lehsten, Nelson: *The Administration of Physical Education for Schools and Colleges.* New York, Ronald, 1962.

16. Knezevich, Stephen: *Administration of Public Education.* New York; Har-Row, 1962.

17. Koontz, Harold and O'Donnell, Cyril: *Principles of Management.* New York, McGraw, 1955.

18. Masonbrink, Edward, and Howard, Glenn: *Administration of Physical Education.* New York, Har-Row, 1963.

19. Roe, William: *School Business Manage-*

ment. New York, McGraw, 1961.

20. Scott, Harry: *Competitive Sports in Schools and Colleges,* New York, Har-Row, 1951.

21. Successful financial plans for school athletic departments. River Grove, *Wilson Sporting Goods Company,* 1961.

22. Tonigan, Richard: How to prepare a budget for tight times and get it approved. *School Management,* February, 1971.

23. Wilsey, C.E.: Budget for equipment replacement, *American School Board Journal,* May, 1967.

24. Wray, J.A.: Costs of secondary school athletic programs. *School Management,* November, 1972.

CHAPTER 12

Purchase and Care of Athletic Equipment

THE PURCHASE AND CARE of equipment is a big problem for every high school athletic director and coach. Because of the tremendous growth and interest in interscholastic athletics the purchase and care of equipment has become a subject of extreme importance. The use of the taxpayers' money should *receive* the undivided attention of every athletic director and coach. At the very beginning of athletic competition in the schools the player traditionally supplied his own equipment. As the interest in athletics grew and became more popular and more a part of the school curriculum, the schools began supplying the equipment for the athletic teams. This practice varied in different localities, and still does, depending not only on the philosophy of the school district but on the financial condition as well.

Many athletic directors and coaches know very little about buying and maintaining equipment. Each year millions of dollars are wasted by poor purchasing practices and improper maintenance procedures. During the past few years, however, purchasing practices have been standardized. This has resulted in a more knowledgeable athletic director. Purchasing requires knowledge as to where and what to buy, quality of goods, placing orders, and checking of incoming equipment and shipments. Maintenance involves making inventories and issuing all types of equipment as well as keeping all equipment in

the highest possible repair. Very few schools have persons who are knowledgeable about equipment maintenance. Therefore, this responsibility is inherited by the athletic director and coach.

It is important to establish some sound guidelines for purchasing, maintaining, and storing equipment in order to get the most out of each and every precious piece of equipment a school or team may possess. There is nothing more aggravating than to see a good piece of equipment go "down-the-drain" just because someone did not know how to care for it properly or to see a substandard piece of equipment have to be replaced prematurely just because someone got a "bargain."

Kaczmarek[1] has this to say about purchasing equipment:

> The wise purchasing and maintenance of athletic equipment is the responsibility which school authorities cannot avoid. The administrative responsibilities for selecting and purchasing athletic equipment must be clearly defined and delegated. Athletics in a school system involves the health and safety of all the participants; therefore, the selection and purchase of such equipment must meet high standards of workmanship, quality, and safety, to protect each participant. It is most essential, therefore, that a harmonious relationship exist in all the facets of purchasing and securing athletic equipment, namely, between

[1]Kaczmarek, John, "Equipment Care Cardinal Obligations," *American School Board Journal* (August, 1966) p. 29.

the coach and the athletic director; athletic director and the school administrator or the person delegated to act in his behalf.

Cost of Equipment

Costs have skyrocketed not only in athletic equipment but in other areas of the athletic program. This has caused a great deal of concern with school administrators, school boards, and the persons who are footing the bills. It has caused drastic curtailment of the athletic program in many schools throughout the United States. While there is not much that can be done about the high cost of equipment, there could be more consideration given to the purchasing practices and general overall care of equipment so that it will last longer.

Some sports such as football, track, and baseball require a great deal of expensive equipment, while others require very little. This will be one determining factor as to whether a school engages in the sport or whether they do not.

It is not the purpose here to discuss in detail the cost of equipment for every sport that might be offered in the high school athletic program. All prices on athletic equipment of any kind are subject to change and will be affected by the economic conditions of the country just as prices of other consumer products are affected. Other changes and differences in prices of equipment will be determined by the quantity purchased, the company from whom the merchandise is purchased, and the conditions under which it is purchased.

There is also the factor of how much and how little equipment is needed for the sport which is to be played. However, there are basic items of equipment that every player should have. The following lists of equipment for various sports are offered as rough guidelines in estimating the equipment costs for each sport. Prices will vary with the state of the economy, the rate of inflation, and the quality of the item.

TABLE LVI
GYMNASTIC EQUIPMENT

No. 407	Parallel Bar with Floating Counterbalance	$775
No. 405	Uneven Parallel Bar Conversion Kit	$248
No. 212	Apparatus Transporter	$100
No. 208	Low Parallel Bar	$175
No. 460	Side Horse	$660
No. 253	Combination Buck and Short Horse	$460
No. 209	Cabled Ring Frame	$530
No. 690	Collegiate Rings	$160
No. 615	Horizontal Bar	$415
No. 203	Chalk Stand 2/$80 ea.	$160
No. 249	Reuther Board	$125
No. 201B	Port-a-Score 2/$105 ea.	$210
No. 770	Trampoline	$840
No. 394	Permanent Suspension 4/148 ea.	$600
No. 398	Traveling Spotting Belt Suspension	$200
No. 1306	Twisting Belt	$ 80
No. 1304	Spotting Belt 4/$25 ea.	$100
No. 840	Tumbling Mat	$970
No. 839	Crash Mats 2/$50 ea.	$100
No. 841	Fitted Mat for Side Horse	$240
No. 842	Fitted Mat for Side Horse	$230

LVI—(cont'd.)

No. 843	Fitted Mat for Buck	$230
No. 838	Mat for High Bar	$200
No. 23	Floor Plate 16/40 ea.	$640

| | | |
| Total | $8348 |

CROSS COUNTRY EQUIPMENT
(12-Man Team)

ITEM	QUANTITY	UNIT PRICE	TOTAL PRICE
Athletic Supporter	24	$ 1.11	$ 26.80
Socks	24	.86	20.70
Sweat Suits	12	3.29	39.50
Sleeveless Jerseys	12	2.13	25.60
Practice Jerseys	12	2.88	34.60
Pants	12	1.29	15.50
Shoes	12	12.95	155.40
Stop Watches	3	14.50	43.50
Clipboards	3	1.50	4.50
Whistles	3	.98	2.94
Twine	1	1.98	1.98
Starting Gun	1	31.95	31.95
Gun Blanks	50	3.75	3.75
		Total	$439.52

WRESTLING EQUIPMENT

Wrestling shoes	$9.00/each
Sweat socks	$1.25/each — 6 pr./wrestler
Shoes (for running)	$9.00/each
Athletic supporters	$2.25/each
Gym shorts	$1.50/each
Work-out gear	$10.00/each
Head gear	$10.00/each
Kneepads	$3.50/each
Wrestling uniform (meets)	$16.00/each
Warm-ups (meets)	$20.00/each
Gear bags	$3.50/each

SAMPLE EQUIPMENT BUDGETS
Girls Athletic Budget

Sports	*Salaries*	*Officials*	*Transportation*	*Supplies & Equip.*
Softball	$280	$120	$160	$986.76
Golf	260		120	120.00
Gymnastics	260	60	120	120.00
Track	320	60	180	300.00
Field Hockey	320	60	160	475.00
Tennis	260		120	120.00
Volleyball	260	120	180	120.00
Basketball	320	160	180	200.00

Swimming	260	60	120	120.00
Badminton	260	120	180	120.00
	$280	$760	$1520	$2676.76

Misc. Expenses		*Total Budget Expenses*	
Cleaning	$360	Salaries	$2800
Physicals	160	Officials	760
Printing &		Transportation	1520
Postage	160	Supplies &	
Clinic &		Equip.	2676
State Meets	340	Misc. Expenses	1400
Reconditioning			$9156
Expenses	160		
Custodial			
Expenses	220		
	$1400		

SOFTBALL BUDGET

Quantity	Brand Name	Description	Unit Cost	Total
24	Lady Champ.	Sweat Shirt	12.00	288.00
24	Lady Champ.	Sweat Pant	9.80	235.20
24	Lady Champ.	Pinnies	1.74	41.76
12	Rawlings	Bats - 15G	3.10	37.20
12	Rawlings	Game Balls MC120	34.25 (doz.)	34.25
12	Rawlings	Practice Balls 812	1.90	22.80
Set	Rawlings	Bases - F	11.00 (set)	11.00
1	Rawlings	Home Plate - 3w	19.25	19.25
1	Rawlings	Pitcher's Plate 2PP	10.55	10.55
1	Rawlings	Catcher's Mask SB	6.65	6.65
1	Rawlings	Chest Protector 3GP	13.95	13.95
1	Rawlings	Catcher's Glove DB35	20.45	20.45
1	Rawlings	First Baseman's Glove XFB50	19.25	19.25
20	Rawlings	Fielder's Gloves DW15	9.65	193.00
1 pr.	Rawlings	Shin Guards 5CW-1	16.95	16.95
1	Rawlings	Equipment Bag DB8	6.00	6.00
1	Rawlings	Scorebook 80SB	1.95	1.95
1	Rawlings	Bat Bag 12SVB	8.55	8.55

FIELD HOCKEY

Quantity	Cat. #	Description	Unit Cost	Total Cost
30	CH 92p	Style "Diane" pants royal blue w/white trim. Stripe 1" Split legs	4.50	135.00
30	CH 92s	Sleeveless shirt royal blue w/white trim neck & sleeve ½". White #s back 6". WOODSTOCK 6" front	8.25	247.50
30	Sox	Royal Blue	1.05	31.50
1	CR1246	Field Hockey Goalie Glove		9.25

1	CR744	Reed Horn		2.75
12	CR910	Leather Hockey Balls	4.00	48.00
24	CR929	Rubber Hockey Balls	2.50	60.00
6	M 0041	Indian Head Hockey Sticks	9.00	54.00
		Salaries		320.00
		Transportation		160.00
		Officials		60.00
		Misc. Expenses		157.50
				1285.50

TABLE LVII
SAMPLE EXTRACURRICULAR BUDGET

	Supplies	Travel	Capital Outlay	Contracted Services	Rental	Totals
FORENSICS	$ —0—	$ —0—	$ —0—	$ 750.00	$ —0—	$ 750.00
ATHLETICS						
Baseball	210.00			600.00		810.00
Basketball	472.00			1400.00		1872.00
Cheerleaders	—0—					—0—
Cross Country	49.00			150.00		199.00
Drill Corps	—0—					—0—
Football	980.00			1800.00	2500.00	5280.00
Golf	25.00					25.00
Gymnastics	129.00			300.00		429.00
Intramurals	280.00			500.00		780.00
First Aid	1149.00					1149.00
Swimming	84.00			350.00		434.00
Tennis	126.00			350.00		476.00
Track	350.00			200.00		550.00
Wrestling	441.00			600.00		1041.00
Trophies & Awards	600.00					600.00
General	280.00			1850.00		2130.00
	5175.00			8100.00	2500.00	15775.00
Total Athletics	200.00					200.00
MUSIC						
STUDENT						
PUBLICATIONS						
Barblet	1000.00			3500.00		4500.00
Kalibre	550.00			6500.00		7050.00
Total Stu Pub	1550.00			10,000.00		11550.00
TOTALS	6925.00			18850.00		28275.00

Purchasing Equipment
Responsibilities

The administrator can save many dollars by wise purchasing and the judicious handling of equipment. Purchasing procedures and methods vary from state to state according to the size of the school or type of item purchased, but the principles underlying wise purchasing remain the same.

Kaczmarek[2] suggests that:

> The tragedy of mistakes made in purchasing equipment is multiplied many times because of the lack of understanding, communication, and resourcefulness between administrators.
>
> Administrators would be wise to establish sharp lines and patterns of communications between all involved. Regular procedures must be followed. A school athletic council should be composed of athletic directors, all head coaches, the purchasing agent of the school, the principal and/or superintendent or the delegated authority, and the director of physical education.
>
> As schools have increased in size, and as they have continued to move in the direction of supplying more materials without charge to the student body, the administration of this service has become an increasingly more important part of the principal's job. Budgeting for, purchasing, storing, and filling requisitions for supplies requires managerial ability on the part of the principal. Needless to say, the more systematized and simplified the system used, the more time the administrator will have for some of the more important problems of school administration.

One of the major difficulties in the purchase of athletic equipment is the fact that no one person is qualified to make all purchasing decisions. It cannot be expected that the purchasing agent in a large school system will know all about every-

[2]Kaczmarek, John, "Equipment Care Cardinal Obligations." p. 29.

thing that should be purchased by the school district. He must lean heavily upon the shoulders of those people within the different departments where the equipment is to be used to give him the necessary information that will enable him to purchase wisely. This means, of course, that someone or several people within each department is knowledgeable enough about the equipment to work out the necessary details and supply needed information. The athletic director in collaboration with the coaches would be the logical persons to assume this responsibility in the athletic department. Therefore, there must be a close relationship between the coach, who uses the equipment, the athletic director who is held responsible for obtaining the best equipment at the best price and the school administrator who is responsible for the disbursement of the money.

Kaczmarek[3] stresses the fact that:

> The administrative responsibilities for selecting athletic equipment must be clearly defined and delegated. Administrators should make sure that everything relating to budgeting, selection, care, maintenance, and inventory are clearly understood by those persons who are responsible for them. He proposes the following.
>   1. Select the best designed item and best material
>   2. Make sure the equipment affords the best protection possible
>   3. Select the best quality
>   4. Make sure the equipment is of proven utility and can be easily maintained
>   5. Make sure the price is right

Schools differ in size. This, of course, will have a direct bearing and influence on the purchasing procedures. The schools have in recent years furnished more and more of the athletic equipment used by the athletic teams. This necessitates more

[3]*Ibid.*

managerial ability on the part of the administration.

It can be seen that the larger the school the more difficult purchasing of equipment becomes. However, regardless of the size of the school, a pattern must be established which will minimize mistakes and simplify purchasing procedures. Burrup[4] has made the following comment regarding the patterns used in purchasing of equipment in the different sized schools:

> In general there are three patterns used in the purchasing of supplies and equipment: (1) the larger systems usually employ a purchasing agent in the central office to do all purchasing, (2) somewhat smaller systems use the school board clerk or secretary to perform this job as a part of his over-all assignment; and (3) the small school districts usually delegate the district superintendent of schools to carry out this assignment. The use of a purchasing agent allows for savings to be made because of large orders and competitive bidding. The purchasing agent usually knows the market and the places where more favorable costs can be obtained. The same advantages apply to the second method, but to a lesser degree. The third method favors more staff participation in the selection of materials and usually provides more benefits for local businesses. The costs may be higher, but the problem of storage and delivery is minimized by the use of this method of purchasing. An added advantage to having the superintendent or principal purchase his own supplies is that price is secondary to the selection of high quality or name products. Under other methods, the impersonal ordering is often done entirely in terms of competitive costs. This does not guarantee economy in the long run and often results in the teacher or administrator receiving materials or equipment which do not meet his specifications.

Even though procedures and patterns are established, there are still many problems which exist relative to the purchase of athletic equipment. These problems are not always the same in each school system. In fact, many of them are unique to a particular school system because of factors which exist only in that particular school system. For example, the bookkeeping procedures alone would tend to create a problem in a large system unless each departmental chairman was aware of the exact procedure used.

French and Lehsten[5] present their opinion regarding the problems in purchasing equipment in the following suggestion:

> The purchase of expensive physical education and athletic equipment is a business matter which should be conducted in a business-like manner. The funds used to purchase equipment, whether gate receipts, student fees, or tax monies, nevertheless belong to the institution and are to be used to provide the best possible service to students in the most economical way. Several individuals are involved in each school and college if the purchase and care of equipment is properly administered. The director, with the assistance of his staff of physical education teachers and coaches, will select the materials to be purchased. In larger institutions there will be a purchasing agent to buy the equipment; a custodian to store, issue, repair and otherwise care for it; and janitor-and-maid service in locker rooms to safeguard equipment and the personal belongings of students. In small schools, where one man and one woman constitute the staff, they must assume many responsibilities ordinarily performed by the purchasing agent, the custodian, the janitor and the maid, or else make other arrangements to get these jobs done. Unfortunately many overburdened directors find it difficult, if not impossible, to do all these things, and consequently the

---

[4]Burrup, Percy, *Modern High School Administration* (New York, Harper and Brothers, 1961) , p. 281.

[5]French, Esther, and Lehsten, Nelson, *Administration of Physical Education in Schools and Colleges*—3rd ed. (New York, The Ronald Press Company, 1973) , p. 471-2.

care of equipment is largely neglected. One of their major tasks, therefore, is to convince boards of education and college trustees of the importance of providing adequate personnel to solve the equipment problem.

The Coach's Responsibility for Purchasing Equipment

The coach knows the kind of equipment he wants as well as the equipment which appeals to the players. He is close to the situation so he should assume the responsibility of equipment selection but he must work very closely with the athletic director. The coach in many respects is legally responsible for allowing the player to use faulty equipment so he should take special interest in obtaining the best equipment he can.

The Athletic Director's Responsibility for Purchasing Equipment

The athletic director, of course, makes the final approval on the purchase of all athletic equipment. His decision is tempered and determined to a large extent by the money available. He should act as a consultant to all the coaches and possibly meet with them in their discussions with athletic equipment salesmen whenever possible. The director should be fair in his treatment of all coaches and the amount of money allocated to each sport. He should not favor one over the other.

The School Administrator's Responsibility for Purchasing Equipment

Athletics is part of the educational program and should be thought of as such. The administrator should, therefore, take an active interest in the purchasing of athletic equipment. He should in many respects be a liaison between the coach and the athletic director in all matters where there is a controversy about price, kind of equipment and appropriations for each sport. As the school administrator, it is his responsibility to see to it that adequate equipment is provided for the athletic program. He must provide for a workable system of budgeting, selecting, purchasing, storing, and adequate accounting for athletic equipment.

The Athletic Council's Responsibility for Purchasing Equipment

Many school systems have established athletic councils where some of the responsibility of providing athletic equipment can be placed. This council can be composed of coaches, principal, athletic director, and students. This arrangement takes a great deal of pressure from any one person and distributes the responsibilities more evenly. The council can meet several times a year to discuss equipment problems, draft, and decide on the budget, and establish equipment procedures for the school system. It can help set up uniform procedures in all problems concerning athletic equipment.

The Role of the Athletic Director and Coach in Purchasing Equipment

The director and coach will need to depend upon the equipment salesman to a certain extent to furnish them with much of the needed information on the type of equipment which will fulfill their needs. However, even though they do rely on this information, it is necessary that they have some knowledge as to the types of equipment which are needed for specific activities and materials which are used in the manufacture of this equipment. Players, coaches, and directors have their own likes and dislikes and their desires are governed accordingly. This in itself will determine to some extent at least, the kind and type of equipment which will be purchased. However, the most important aspect of equipment purchasing is knowing what the piece of equipment is going to be used for. For example, the lineman in football will require equipment somewhat different than the ends or backs. This will also be true in the use of shoes by the field man and track man, the goalie, forwards, and fullbacks, in soccer as well as in the different positions in other sports. The director and coach should, therefore, have a thorough knowledge of the types of equipment needed for playing the various positions in each sport. They also should have an understanding of the materials that are used in the manufacture of athletic equipment. There are many substitutes that are now being used in the manufacture of athletic equipment, many of which have not been thoroughly tested. The purchase of these substitutes should be avoided if at all possible. It is not good economy and certainly not fair to the player.

The coach and director will also need to be alert to sizes needed in all types and kinds of equipment and purchase accordingly. The coach will need to obtain the different sizes of each player for each piece of equipment worn by that player. This pertains especially to game equipment.

Purchasing Regulations

The best time to purchase equipment is after the completion of a particular season. The coach and director are aware of the needs at this time. If purchases cannot be made at this time because of budgetary procedures the next best thing would be to prepare a list of needs directly after the season is over and file it so it will be available when it is possible to order the equipment.

There are various regulations which govern the purchase of athletic equipment by the school. These regulations affect all forms of school supplies and equipment. They can be very rigid in some schools and yet very free in others.

The amount of equipment purchased will, to some extent, determine the price. The practice of purchasing equipment in large quantities is used successfully in many school systems, New York City is a good example.

> The State's Division of Standards and Purchase does all the purchasing for the various state institutions, as well as any school district that wishes to use their services. It was found in a study by Whited that although not all the school districts used the system, it did save a great deal of money and the state contract purchasing technique worked so well that the prices were well below the prices asked by sporting distributors in the state.[6]

Roe[7] makes the following statement regarding state regulations for purchasing school equipment:

> Purchasing is regulated by state law, court decisions, and local school board policy. All states have deemed it necessary to pass legislation controlling certain aspects of purchasing. The most common are (1) laws which make it mandatory that purchases above a certain amount (usually from $1,000 to $1,500) be submitted for open bids and (2) laws which prohibit board members and executives of the school from selling goods to the district in which they are employed from receiving personal rebates on goods purchased for the district.

---

[6]Whited, Clark, "These Purchasing Pointers Help Cut Sports Costs," *American School and University* (August, 1968), p. 31.

[7]Roe, William, *School Business Management* (New York, McGraw Hill Book Company, 1961), p. 127.

Williams and Brownell[8] make this interesting statement regarding the difficulties encountered in regulating purchasing practices, to the satisfaction of everyone.

It is difficult to suggest a satisfactory method of determining the budget for each athletic activity, owing to the range in amount of equipment needed, the varying cost of this equipment, the popularity of the sport, and its educational value. These items never are comparable. Football is more expensive than track, and basketball costs more than tennis, but expense is not the sole criterion. Intramural athletics usually provide greater educational value than interschool competition, but the latter affords outcomes that the former never can provide.

Under the system of admission fees, the sport which contributes the largest number of dollars to the athletic fund receives the lion's share of the budget. This is unfortunate because it assumes that money pouring into the athletic coffer is synonymous with the educational value of the activity. It would be just as logical to assume that the person paying the largest tax for the support of education should receive the greatest benefit from the schools.

Guidelines for School Policies on Purchasing of Equipment

The purchasing guidelines will vary in every school district. This is understandable because of the various circumstances that surround the situation and the political aspects that must be dealt with. If the school is situated in a small community, it is understandable that much of the school equipment including athletic supplies probably will be purchased locally. Many individuals feel that this is as it should be because the money for purchasing the equipment was obtained in a large

[8]Williams, Jesse and Brownell, Clifford, *The Administration of Health Education and Physical Education* (Philadelphia, W.B. Saunders Co., 1951), p. 68.

measure from local tax funds. In the large school system much of the purchasing is on a bid basis and local purchasing does not play such a great role.

SYCAMORE HIGH SCHOOL
ATHLETIC SUPPLIES – Requisition Form – Departmental

Name of School _____ Date _____
Principal's Signature _____ Date Order Filled _____
Order Filled by _____

ITEM DESCRIPTION	CATALOG & NO.	PAGE IN CATALOG	SPECIFICATION Size, wt, ht, etc.	REQUESTED	ORDERED	REJECTED

Figure 62.

REAVIS HIGH SCHOOL
DEPARTMENT REQUISITION FORM

Department _____ Date _____

Quantity	Items Desired	Estimate Cost*	Actual Quotation	Supplies	Equipment	Repairs	Name of Suggested Dealer

Note: Please describe items desired as definitely as possible.
*One or the other must be stated.

Signed _____ Department Chairman
Approved _____ Superintendent

Figure 63.

Regardless of the situation, however, there are certain guidelines that should be adhered to in order for the school to get the most for their money. Roe[9] states these guidelines:

1. Purchasing should be a centralized function of the school.
2. Those who use materials should have a decision in the selection of materials.
3. Supplies and equipment must be so handled that there are checks and balances at each step of supply administration from their selection to the time they are used up or become obsolete.
4. Purchasing should be so organized that the user will have the right quantity and quality of equipment at the appropriate time.
5. There should be sufficient flexibility in the purchasing program to allow for experimental programs, unusual expansions, or changes in curricula and emergencies.
6. Means should be provided to assure the proper use, care, storage, and control of equipment and supplies.
7. New and untried materials should be purchased in quantity only after a period of experimental use.
8. Scientific selection and testing of materials should be undertaken to the limits appropriate to the size and capacity of the school district.
9. The educational welfare of the child should be a foremost consideration when making any purchase.
10. The public should expect the greatest possible return for every dollar spent.
11. All records of the purchasing office should be open to public scrutiny. Absolutely no activities should take place which would throw a cloud of suspicion on the integrity of the school.
12. Making and controlling the budget for equipment and supplies and the purchasing function are highly related and should be centralized. Expenditures on supplies and equipment, like all expenditures, should be subject to budgetary control.

---

[9]Roe, William, *School Business Management*, p. 131.

Sample Schedule for Purchasing Equipment

There is an opportune time for doing most everything. This holds true in the purchasing of athletic equipment. The smart administrator will set up a purchasing time schedule which will provide him with the opportunity to take advantage of off-season prices. He can take advantage of this opportunity by adhering to the following schedule.

1. As soon as possible, after January 1 of each year, each individual head coach should meet with the athletic director to:
   A. Review the sports up-to-date athletic inventory.
   B. Recommend the type of additional or replacement equipment and supplies needed.
2. Coaches and athletic director should make every effort to visit showrooms or have equipment samples brought to them for their thorough inspection before purchase.
3. Upon the completion of all meetings the athletic director should compile a detailed preliminary budget to include:
   A. Current compensation paid for coaching.
   B. Anticipated custodial overtime.
   C. Contractural services—officials, dry cleaning, laundry, reconditioning, ticket takers, ticket sellers, police, student parkers, scorekeeper, announcer, timer, statistician, crowd control men.
   D. Requested supplies and equipment.
   E. Requested travel allowances—scouting, clinics, conference meetings.
   F. Transportation costs.
   G. Capital outlay items.

This budget should then be presented to the superintendent, the principal, and the business manager, on or before the date specified by the superintendent.

4. The athletic director should then prepare a bid list and submit it, with a list of acceptable bidders, to the business manager.

5. Upon receipt of the sealed bids, the athletic director should prepare a list showing the low and second low bidder. If the low bid is rejected a satisfactory explanation will be given by the athletic director.

6. Upon final approval of the budget, the athletic director should meet with those suppliers involved, review bids, and submit purchase order requests.

7. Equipment and supplies should be delivered between July 1 and August 1. The athletic director will keep records of orders and delivery of all items. He also should approve purchase orders for payment by the business office.

8. Coaches are to make *NO* school purchases without previous approval of the athletic director. Items purchased, and not approved for purchase, should become the responsibility of the person involved.

Rules for the Purchase of Athletic Equipment

The buyer can save a great deal of money if he follows certain rules such as the ones compiled by the Rawlings Sporting Goods Company[10] in their *Athletic Equipment Digest.*

1. *Order early.* By ordering early you assure yourself of delivery of the proper equipment, carefully made, ahead of your deadline. You then have time to make necessary adjustments in sizes and to order any additional items.

2. *Standardize requirements.* Measurements of players change from season to season, often even within a season.

By 'buying for the team' rather than for individual players you will be able, with few exceptions, to fit your squad properly.

3. *Measure properly.* When players are to be fitted to individual measurements be sure to take these measurements properly. Read DIRECTIONS!

4. *Buy quality equipment.* Needless to say, quality is as important in the purchase of athletic equipment as it is in any other commodity. In buying protective equipment it is of paramount importance.

5. *Buy from reputable sources.* Buy from a dealer who will give you the service you need. It is also important that he carry nationally known brands made by manufacturers who back up their products—manufacturers who have a reputation for making quality products.

6. *Keep accurate records.* Detailed records should be kept on all equipment and a practical checkout system should be developed. An up-to-date inventory is an absolute necessity.

7. *Buy the best protective equipment available.* If it is necessary to cut corners in buying equipment, adjustments should be made in items other than protective gear. Never sacrifice quality in helmets and protective pads.

8. *Know your equipment.* Keep abreast of the changes in design, materials, protective features, etc. Arrange for your athletic equipment dealer to show you samples of new equipment.

9. *Know the rules.* The rules of baseball, basketball, football and other sports are very specific regarding equipment requirements. Know these requirements and keep up with changes in the rules.

10. *Check incoming shipments.* Check all deliveries and arrange for the immediate return of defective or inferior items. See that all equipment is properly checked in, identified and stored.

Hixson[11] emphasizes the importance of

[10]Rawlings Sporting Goods Company, *Athletic Equipment Digest,* Fourth Edition (1966), p. 3.

[11]Hixson, Chalmer, *The Administration of Interscholastic Athletics* (New York, J. Lowell Pratt and Co., 1967), p. 101.

purchasing good equipment by stressing the fact that:

Equipment which fulfills official specifications should always be selected. For example a shot which is too light is no bargain regardless of its initial cost. The administrator of athletic sports strives for the greatest value of each dollar invested in equipment and supplies. Verified and established needs determine purchases. Excess and unused equipment on a shelf in the school storage room ties up money, which if available could provide additional opportunities for participation. A bargain which deteriorates or is destroyed or lost while stored is no bargain at all; it is a total loss. The highest quality of equipment should always be purchased. This is especially true of protective equipment on which the safety and welfare of the athlete depends. If choices must be made to economize then the reductions in quality should come in nonprotective equipment or that which is unessential for excellence in performance.

Administrative Guides
in Purchasing Practices

The Athletic Goods Manufacturing Association[12] offers the following list of recommendations as a guide in establishing good equipment administrative practices:

1. Adequate equipment should be provided for every participant in athletics. The equipment should be of proven high quality and afford maximum safety to the participant.
2. Selection of athletic equipment should be a major responsibility of the coach. The head coach of each sport should either purchase new equipment or be consulted before purchases are made.
3. Care and maintenance of equipment should be the responsibility of the head coach of each sport. In schools with full time equipment managers, a major portion of the responsibilities

[12]Athletic Goods Manufacturing Association, 805 Merchandise Mart, Chicago, Illinois.

will be delegated to the equipment manager.
4. All sports participants should be instructed in the use and care of equipment.
5. The school administration has an obligation to see that plenty of equipment is provided for a complete athletic program. No sport should be slighted simply because it does not produce revenue.
6. Equipment purchasing, budgeting, and maintenance policies should be established cooperatively by the coaching staff, athletic director, business manager, and school administrator. An athletic council can be established to achieve this purpose.
7. Quality of equipment should never be sacrificed for price.
8. Uniform procedures should be established in all problems concerning athletic equipment.
9. Adequate space should be provided for a partitioned stock room where bins and cabinets can be utilized for storing and handling cleaned and soiled equipment. Some schools use the stock room for storage of out-of-season equipment.
10. The scope of athletic and physical education programs should be the basic blueprint for the schools athletic budget. The budget should reflect the school's entire program. The budget should be prepared by coaches, athletic directors, school business managers, and school administrators. It should include all anticipated expenditures and receipts—and should be itemized by sport.
11. New equipment needs should be determined and budgeted one year in advance.

Higdon points to the fact that equipment follows two categories. It is either slanted toward safety for the participant or toward improved performances. The administrator should be aware of the kinds of athletic equipment that is being purchased because of these two reasons. The first reason is a very humane and reasonable one, that of protecting the student athlete. The second reason is also a very obvious one, it being for the legal protection of the school should it be proven that an athlete was injured and it could be shown that the injury was due to lack of or defective equipment.[13]

Centralization of Purchasing

If the purchasing of athletic equipment for all school supplies is centralized so that one individual can do all the purchasing, there are many advantages. Such a person must, however, understand equipment of all kinds and devise a system whereby the athletic department can obtain the kind and type of equipment it wants. In the large school system often the purchasing agent will want to make substitutions on equipment and as a result inferior equipment may be obtained. It will help to standardize equipment, and if this can be done better prices can be obtained. This standardization of equipment also allows for competitive bidding and enables the purchasing agent to buy in quantity at a much lower price.

Williams[14] suggests some of the advantages of purchasing all supplies through one office or purchasing agent:

> Efficiency in the purchase of supplies and equipment involves a careful study of community and school needs, existing prices, the quality of workmanship, and satisfactory materials. Formerly the director controlled the purchasing for his department, and this plan still persists in numerous cities in spite of the fact that such antiquated practices have been abolished in other administrative matters. Indeed, years after teachers ceased to act

as venders of pencils and paper, one often finds the physical educator peddling sneakers, towels, and soap. Teachers of physical education should be taken out of the merchandising business.

The purchase of all school materials through one central office, presided over by a person known as the business manager or purchasing agent, is both economical and effective. It is his duty to keep on hand adequate records relating to standardized materials, requisition blanks, and a card index of supply houses. Purchasing is greatly facilitated if adequate records are kept. He checks the receipt of materials with respect to quantity and quality, distributes them to their proper destination, and insures prompt payment on contracts made. The business manager or purchasing agent is guided in the selection of goods by the departmental director who recommends the amount and quality of equipment needed but the actual buying of all school supplies is best confined to a single office.

Every athletic director and coach is interested in purchasing the kind of equipment that will give optimum protection to the athlete. Higdon[15] states that the American Medical Association's Committee on the Medical Aspects of Sports recommends four basic principles for optimum protection:

1. The best available athletic equipment should be purchased. The selection of equipment should not be dictated by reasons of economy.

2. Equipment should be carefully fitted to the individual.

3. Equipment should be maintained conscientiously and checked periodically as to continued proper fit and absence of acquired defects.

4. Equipment should be worn at all appropriate times, whether in practice or in games.

---

[13]Higdon, Hal, "How to Reduce Athletic Injuries," *School Management* December, 1968, p. 52.

[14]Williams, Jesse and Brownell, Clifford, *The Administration of Health Education and Physical Education,* p. 69.

[15]Higdon, Hall, "How to Reduce Athletic Injuries," p. 54.

Procedures Used to Purchase Athletic Equipment

There is a great deal of information relative to how to buy athletic equipment. Everyone has his own opinion on what, where, and when to buy. The first prerequisite is to know and study the existing market conditions at the time of purchase. Prices do not remain stable and, therefore, there seems to be a right time and a wrong time to buy. Be that as it may, there must be certain uniform and standardized procedures that can be followed. This facilitates accurate and uniform accounting procedures which are necessary in any reputable business venture.

The importance of setting up procedures for purchasing equipment and supplies for athletics is emphasized by Stier.

He suggests that a purchasing agent must be appointed (preferably the head of physical education or the athletic director) who has the knowledge of equipment and can identify quality and at the same time knows what is needed. He maintains that the buyer should adhere to the old proverb which says ". . . to obtain the highest quality for optimum results does not necessarily mean buying the most expensive equipment." The quality of the equipment is dependent upon the use it is going to receive. The buyer should use care in selecting a firm to purchase from.[16]

Steps in Purchasing Equipment

There are certain standardized rules that must be followed in purchasing any school supplies where public funds are expended. These rules must be strictly adhered to in order to justify the purchase and use of any athletic equipment. These steps are as follows:

[16]Stier, William, "Policies Concerning Procurement of Equipment and Supplies," *Coach and Athlete* (August, 1968), p. 22.

1. DETERMINING THE NEED: The coach checks his equipment inventory and decides on what he needs.
2. CONSULTATION WITH SUPERIOR: The coach consults with the director of athletics and in some cases with the principal depending on the size of the school.
3. REQUISITION: The director of athletics approves, with or without reservations or changes, and sends a requisition to the purchasing agent who could be the principal, superintendent, or in a large city school system a special purchasing agent.
4. STAFF ACTION: The purchasing agent consults with the superintendent if the school is large and with the board of education if the school is small. The size of the school will be the determining factor in this case. If the staff action is favorable, the requisition is approved.
5. BIDS: The purchasing agent sends the order to several firms in order to secure the best possible price.
6. PURCHASE ORDER: After all bids are returned, the purchasing agent selects the firm from which the purchase is to be made. He then fills out the purchase order in quadruplicate. One copy is sent to the firm that will furnish the equipment, one copy is sent to the board of education, one copy to the athletic director, and one copy is placed on file in the business office.
7. FOLLOW UP: The purchasing agent conducts a follow-up if the equipment is not received in a specified time.
8. RECEIPT OF EQUIPMENT: The purchasing agent receives the equipment and checks it to make certain it meets the specifications and is what was ordered.
9. PAYMENT OF BILL: The purchasing agent presents the bill to the board of

education for approval for payment. It is then given to the correct person who in turn pays the bill.

10. DISPERSEMENT OF EQUIPMENT: The purchasing agent sends the equipment to the athletic director who turns it

Local Controls on Purchasing

The monies for running the local schools come to a large extent from local taxes. The people are naturally interested in how their money is being spent. Definite policies should be set up and clearly de-

TABLE LVIII
ARGO HIGH SCHOOL DISTRICT 122

INTERNAL BUDGET REPORT

_____ to _____

	Department	
	SUPPLIES	*EQUIPMENT*
BUDGET		
SPENT TO DATE		
BALANCE*		

*Does not include current purchase orders or bills received after last date shown above

DUNBAR HIGH SCHOOL DISTRICT 121

ATHLETIC DEPARTMENT EQUIPMENT RECORD

PURCHASE ORDER #	DATE ORDERED	DATE RECEIVED	SIGNED FOR BY	WHERE STORED	TURNED OVER TO COACH & DATE

Figure 64.

over to the coach of the sport for which it was ordered. Many of the schools, large or small, will have the equipment sent directly from the athletic supply company to the athletic director in the specific school.

fined so that this information can be properly disseminated to the general public.

There seems to be no specific pattern that is followed in all school systems. However this is due in part to the general make-up of the school district itself, such as size, financial condition, and the general overall philosophy. There are some general overall policies that can be followed. Forsythe and Keller suggest that only quality equipment should be purchased. It is also important that the equipment should be purchased at a regular time each year so that advantage may be taken of seasonal price changes. Another policy that should be strictly adhered to is to purchase only from reputable companies. It is also a wise procedure to use the standard school purchase order, and only authorized people should fill out and sign these purchase orders. One of the most important aspects of purchasing equipment is need and purchase of the right kind. In order to do this, it is necessary that inventories of equipment be taken regularly to ascertain the kind and amount of equipment that is needed.[17]

Roe[18] makes the following statement regarding legal controls from a local basis:

> Boards of education must perform the purchasing function in the manner prescribed by law. There is no alternative. Permissive legislation does, however, give the boards wide discretion in the way they may operate within the law. Local school boards must then establish policies and procedures which provide for the most intelligent application of these laws and rulings according to local needs and circumstances.
>
> Clearly stated, carefully considered policies show the public that there is nothing to hide in one of the most sensitive areas of operation in the public school. Policy statements should present the best judgment and thinking of the board on problems which might become critical issues and result in emotional conflicts. They should seek to eliminate petty politics, "favor doing," and patronage. They should be clear-cut guides which translate laws into action.

School board policy in regard to purchasing should include the following:

1. An interpretation or summary of state statutes affecting purchasing
2. An interpretation or summary of state court cases having implications for local purchasing
3. A summary of administrative rulings on purchasing by state boards of education or state departments of education
4. A statement on authority and responsibility in purchasing for the district
5. A designation of the purchasing agent for the school district
6. An outline of steps for approval and disapproval of purchases, des-

ignated different situations according to amount and type of purchase
7. A clarification of local purchasing practices
8. A statement clarifying how those who use materials and equipment shall work with the purchasing agent in selecting supplies and equipment.

Specifications for Equipment

If the director and coach expect to get the kind of equipment they want, they must not only order correctly, but must specify exactly the equipment they want. Gabrielson[19] has listed the following suggestions or steps for the preparation of the specifications:

1. Determining what is actually needed or wanted according to existing inventory.
2. Become acquainted with the different trade brands usually available of each particular item to be purchased.
3. Select reliable, well-known manufacturers and their merchandise; however, thoroughly investigate new products. Sample them or obtain recommendations from other users.
4. A full description of each item or a reference number should be given.
5. Detailed specifications are most essential in permanent equipment.

Selection of Equipment

There should be some general overall guidelines that must be considered and used in the selection of equipment. The *first* consideration is how much money is available to spend. This is the most important consideration because it will determine to a large extent the quality of the equipment that can be purchased. The money must be available to pay for the equipment as it is the responsibility of the

[17]Forsythe, Charles, and Keller, Irvin, *Administration of High School Athletics* 5th ed., (Englewood Cliffs, New Jersey, by permission of Prentice-Hall, 1972) , p. 205.

[18]Roe, William, *School Business Management,* p. 130.

[19]Gabrielson, Alexander, and Miles, Caswell, *Sports and Recreational Facilities for Schools and Community* (Englewood Cliffs, New Jersey, by permission of Prentice-Hall, 1958) , p. 335.

director of athletics to live within the budget that has been established. He should buy on credit only if he is sure that the money to pay for the equipment will be forthcoming in the immediate future. Even this type of procedure can get him into trouble if unforeseen circumstances prevent monies from becoming available within the payment time limit established by the company from whom the equipment was purchased.

The *second* guideline is the purpose for which the item is to be used. This will result in certain requirements which the equipment must meet in order to perform the function for which it was intended. This means that the equipment must meet specifications. This in itself will limit the buyer to purchasing only certain types of equipment of a specific quality but, more important, equipment designed for specific needs or use.

The *third* guideline is the consideration to purchase equipment of a standard type or open stock so that it can be added to as it is worn out or used up. This practice will save a great deal of money because it will allow keeping and using equipment that is in good condition because an exact replacement can be obtained which will be an identical match to the original equipment.

The selection of athletic equipment is of extreme importance and should be given a number one priority in time, effort, and money.

Lande[20] points out this fact very aptly in the following statement:

There are many reasons why the selection, purchase, and care of athletic equipment constitute an important phase of the athletic sports program, whether it is promoted by school, community, club, or professional agencies. In brief, these are the factors of (1) cost,

(2) durability, (3) safety, (4) styling, and (5) team morale. In the matter of cost, it is now well recognized that economies should not be practiced at the expense of quality. Seeming bargains are not true ones if durability is sacrificed for cheapness, particularly with articles whose wearing powers should outlast a single season. And it stands to reason that any equipment needed for protective purposes needs to be the very best or the objective of safety is being overlooked. And, as for styling, every team has the right to appear in the latest approved sporting apparel, traditional to the respective sport, and the distinctive colors of the school or other sponsoring agency. Whenever the players know they look their best—that they are being protected by modern safeguards against injury— that they look 'smart' when they run onto the field—then the important asset of team morale is being definitely improved. Theirs is the psychology that leads to pride in appearance and in performance as well.

Criteria Used in Athletic Equipment Selection

The selection of athletic equipment should receive the same consideration as any other merchandise that is expected to give long service, and be both practical and economical. There should be sound criteria established and basic considerations made as a basis for selecting any athletic equipment. The Athletic Goods Manufacturing Association[21] has offered the following basic considerations:

1. *Design and Material:* The design should be in keeping with the times and of a practical nature so that it will not need to be changed too often. The material should be serviceable and fit the occasion in that it should wear well and not be too much on the experimental side.

2. *Utility and Cost of Maintenance:* All athletic equipment should fit the

---

[20]Lande, Leon "The Selection of Athletic Equipment," *Coach and Athlete* (January, 1966), p. 38.

[21]Athletic Goods Manufacturers Association, 805 Merchandise Mart, Chicago, Ill., p. 14.

needs of the particular sport or activity it was designed for. It should also be easy to maintain.

3. *Safety Factor in Protective Equipment:* The first consideration in purchasing or selecting any equipment is whether it is safe. There is absolutely no justification regardless of cost to purchase equipment that will subject the wearer to injury of any kind. Every precaution should be taken to avoid the selection of faulty equipment and under no circumstances should this be done.

4. *Quality and Workmanship:* These two items complement each other. Usually the cheaper the material the poorer the workmanship. Athletic equipment is like everything else and therefore as a general rule, you get what you pay for. It is poor economy to sacrifice either quality or workmanship.

5. *Source of Supply:* Oftentimes schools make a practice of purchasing locally if at all possible. This practice is a good one if quality merchandise can be obtained. Sacrificing quality and price should not be done at the expense of the taxpayer. All purchases should be made only on the basis of obtaining the best equipment.

6. *Price:* Price alone should never be the determining factor in purchasing equipment.

The Do's and Don'ts of Equipment Selection

There are many factors involved in the selection of athletic equipment. The following do's and don'ts should provide a helpful checklist for evaluating buying habits and techniques and are suggested by the Athletic Goods Manufacturing Association.[22]

DO'S

1. Standardize equipment requirements. More and more coaches are finding that standard sizing of equipment for an entire squad is more efficient than individual fitting because team members grow

so rapidly in a short period of time that preseason fitting to each player usually results in ordering undersize equipment. Standard sizes, recommended by the manufacturers, will meet 95% of your requirements.

2. Budget for some replacements each year even though you start with a new set of uniforms or equipment at the start of the season. Even the most expensive garments will be worn out by a few of your players during one season.

3. Buy the best protective equipment; even if it means fewer units.

4. Buy only from recognized sources of supply.

5. Order proper sizes carefully. The ordering of proper sizes is as important as the quantity of each size. Use the data available from your own records and recommendations from the manufacturers.

6. Scrutinize your inventory carefully. Order what you need for replacements and for additional squad members.

7. Try to avoid too many special orders. Special orders are usually expensive and cannot be exchanged.

8. Keep accurate records of your present equipment. Note sizes, catalogue numbers, brand names, year purchased, price, etc. Use these records to help you order new equipment

9. Place your new equipment orders EARLY!

DON'TS

1. Don't be careless about equipment selection. Careful equipment selection is as important as team conditioning. Your successful season actually starts with good equipment, of high quality, purchased well in advance of your first practice.

2. Don't attach numerals to jerseys in too large a size, since it is likely the elasticity in the garment will be eliminated. In most high schools and college sports, the official rules specify maximum and min-

---

[22]*Ibid.,* p. 15.

imum numeral sizes.

3. Don't buy on price alone; there is no substitute for quality.
4. Don't forget to order athletic equipment early.
5. Don't buy a new type of material or equipment without first checking its quality, ability to take game wear, and how well it will clean. Buy and test a sample first to make sure.
6. Don't buy poor materials. You risk your reputation and possible injury to the user by equipping your teams with inferior merchandise.
7. Don't try to get one more season out of wornout protective equipment.
8. Don't take a boy's word for the correct size. Most boys seldom know their sizes. See that all equipment fits your team members. Have them try on equipment for proper fit.
9. Don't buy on impulse. Most coaches plan their game schedules one or two years in advance. Plan in advance on equipment, too! ORDER EARLY!

The Purchasing Agent

The purchasing agent can be any one of a number of people. Strictly speaking, however, he is the person who makes the final arrangements for the actual purchase of the equipment. The administration can save many dollars by wise purchasing practices and almost as many by proper handling and caring for this equipment. Naturally purchasing procedures are going to vary from school to school because of the rules governing the handling of funds, bidding procedures, etc.

Regardless of the size of the school, the purchasing agent, whether he is the athletic director or coach in the small school, the principal, or superintendent, he must perform certain functions. Roe[23] makes the

[23]Roe, William, *School Business Management,* p. 126.

following comment regarding these functions. The organizational structure of the school will be a determining factor in the functions.

The person doing the purchasing for a school performs a service function and has two major responsibilities: (1) to furnish supplies and equipment of the right quality and quantity when needed, and (2) to purchase supplies and equipment at the lowest possible cost. Often these obligations may seem at odds with each other and the necessity of effecting a compromise which will satisfy both is a heavy responsibility.

The purchasing function is considered one of the most touchy jobs in public service. When it is performed fairly, judiciously, and with good management techniques, few people outside the purchasing department concern themselves with it. Let any questionable practices come to light, however, and the public spotlight focuses with ruthless intensity upon the total organization. Mismanagement in purchasing can throw an entire organization into turmoil and disrepute. Thus the purchasing agent is placed high on the staff level. He must be a person of impeccable reputation, a man who operates on principle, who will not allow anyone—either the fawning backslapping salesman with an offer of gifts or entertainment or the important citizen with an interest to serve—to sway him from the honest and unbiased performance of duty. In addition he must be a person with the technical know-how and the ability to handle the intricate process of purchasing.

The board of education, by policy and regulation, should appoint a purchasing agent. In the small school the superintendent may act as the purchasing agent; in the medium-sized school the administrative assistant or business manager is the logical person to choose; and in the large city school a full-time purchasing agent who reports directly through the assistant superintendent for business is warranted.

There are various patterns in schools throughout the nation, but two trends have been apparent in the last twenty years. First, the purchasing function may be centralized under a single person or department; and second, the purchasing agent may be established as an important member of the administrative staff.

There are differences of opinion in regard to the person who should be responsible for purchasing equipment. For example French and Lehsten[24] make the following suggestion:

> Opinion is divided regarding who should purchase equipment. In many of the larger institution, equipment is purchased by a person especially trained in the knowledge of materials and values, known as the purchasing agent. Large organizations, including business, find the employment of a purchasing agent to be a money-saving plan. If one is provided, he should consult with the director or coach who knows specifications and materials as well as particular needs.
>
> In smaller institutions, and in many of the larger ones also, the director, teacher, or coach does the buying. He may purchase direct or through the principal, business manager, or purchasing agent. If any directors believe they know physical education and athletic equipment better than the purchasing agent possibly can know, they would use him as legal agent rather than as buyer. However, if the purchasing is done through such a specialist, the director should cooperate with him by helping to determine needs, select materials, and check incoming shipments.

Purchasing the Equipment

The director or coach should not make the mistake of trying to cut down expenses by buying less expensive or cheap equipment. Buy on the policy that the best is none too good. Most high school directors and coaches need to rely upon the word of the salesman as to the quality of the equip-

ment. This necessitates purchasing the equipment from good and reliable sporting goods houses. Beware of bargains, seconds, and close-outs. Many of the less reputable houses offer discounts on athletic equipment as an inducement. The buyer should be wary of this type of practice.

The high school director or coach should cooperate with the local merchant whenever possible, providing the merchant offers the same quality goods at the same price.

If the coach is interested in saving on equipment he may do so by buying early or during slack months. Fall equipment should be bought in the spring if it is possible to do so. Buying in quantity will sometimes reduce the price.

There are bargains in athletic equipment as well as in other lines of merchandise. The coach who knows athletic equipment can recognize and take advantage of these bargains. But unless the coach knows equipment thoroughly, he must rely upon the integrity of the companies with whom he deals. Buying from respectable firms will prove more satisfactory and more economical in the long run.

Most coaches feel that it is wise to buy the best equipment. It has been proven on numerous occasions that quality merchandise fits much better, looks better, wears longer, and can be repaired more easily than the cheaper equipment. The practice of purchasing poor quality equipment for reserve and freshmen teams has not proven to be economical. It is far better to pass down the varsity-squad, quality material in good repair than to provide a cheaper grade of equipment that must last for the season but gives little promise of being suitable for reconditioning.

The coach should not overlook the advantages of early buying. Fall equipment should be ordered in the spring and the

[24]French, Esther, and Lehsten, Nelson, *Administration of Physical Education in Schools and Colleges*, p. 472.

spring equipment in the fall. Early buying also aids the manufacturer. He is better able to estimate the expected volume of business and prepare for it. In addition the reputable manufacturer has the opportunity to replace material that is defective or not up to standard.

The sporting goods concerns, by knowing what to order and buy in quantity, can give a better price.

Gabrielson[25] makes this comment on the quality vs. the quantity in buying equipment.

> The importance of top quality merchandise cannot be over emphasized. The very nature of athletic activities suggests roughness and toughness. In no other field of activity is there greater need for sturdy, safe and durable equipment. The old adage, 'Penny wise and pound foolish' has direct implications for the purchaser of athletic equipment.

It is far better to buy one piece of quality equipment that will give top-notch service over a long period of time than to purchase an inferior piece of equipment that will give poor service and wear out in a short time.

Ordering of Athletic Equipment

The ordering and purchasing of athletic equipment should be thoroughly systemitized. The easiest way to save time and avoid problems is to use purchase order forms, copies of which give a record of exactly what was ordered, its description, and date of order. This is only one part of the ordering procedure. The athletic director of a large school or the head coach of all sports in a small school should follow the same general buying procedure. The Athletic Goods Manufacturing Association[26] suggest the following:

[25]Gabrielson, Alexander, *Sports and Recreational Facilities for School and Community*, p. 334.

[26]Athletic Goods Manufacturing Association, p. 15.

1. *Some person must determine what is to be purchased.* Usually this will be the coach of the individual sport concerned. He will make recommendations based upon a report of an inventory of equipment on hand.
2. *The determining of what is to be purchased must be passed on to the one who is to place the order.* An additional step may be necessary if approval at some higher level is necessary. Or it may be eliminated if the coach places the order personally, if he has that authority. The latter procedure is recommended unless the item is definitely known by number and brand.
3. *The order is then placed with the dealer, and the coach should receive a duplicate copy of his purchase order.* If a copy is not given to the coach, he should receive some type of notice to keep in his files. This insures the coach that the equipment has actually been ordered.
4. *The invoice is received either prior to, with, or after the shipment of goods.* The invoice should be examined, approved, and sent to the paying official. The actual disposition of the invoice will vary according to a school's individual financial system.
5. *The goods, when received, should be examined and approved as to the quantity and the quality ordered.* This is sometimes accomplished through the receiving report. After an examination of equipment, the items should be placed in the current inventory.

This procedure will, of course, vary from school to school. But it is important that the coach adopts a systematic purchasing procedure. The purchase order should always have proper approval of the chief school administrator. This is your best purchasing safeguard.

Use of Equipment

An affluent society has brought about an indifferent attitude among young people in the use of public property. The use of athletic equipment is no exception, as many of the schools furnish virtually all of the equipment needed by the player to enable him to compete. Every attempt should be made to impress upon the users of the equipment that the equipment does not belong to them but that it does belong to the school which, in essence, is the tax-payers of the community. The player should be told and made to understand that the school has not given him the equipment that he is using but has loaned him the equipment so that he is able to participate in any sport regardless of what his financial situation happens to be. Every player should clearly understand that when equipment is issued to him, he is responsible for that equipment, and that he must return it in good condition, taking into consideration reasonable wear and tear which will result from hard usage.

Hixson[27] has this interesting comment about the use of athletic equipment:

The money to purchase athletic equip-

ABRON HIGH SCHOOL ATHLETIC DEPARTMENT

REPORT OF THEFT

Name of student making report_____

Address_____ Telephone_____

Class_____ Period_____ P. E. Instructor or Coach_____

P. E. or Athletic Locker No._____ Do you have lock?_____ Make_____

Articles lost_____

Please give a detailed account of all circumstances regarding the loss or theft, and answer the following questions:

1. Have you been sharing a locker in P. E. or Athletics?_____

2. Was your lock on your locker and locked?_____

3. Have you ever given your combination to anyone?_____

4. Do you lock your locker when you shower?_____

5. How many times have you lost articles during P. E. or practice?_____

Other details:

Check:

☐+ P. E. Teacher or Coach

☐ Athletic Director

File this with Mr. Smith

Figure 65.

TABLE LIX
BISHOP TOWNSHIP HIGH SCHOOL
BISHOP, ILLINOIS

Date _____

REPORT OF LOSS

DESCRIPTION OF ARTICLE LOST:

Date first missed _____ Time or class period _____

Was article marked with your name? _____

Was it taken from your gym locker? #_____, or clothes locker? _____

Who knows your combinations? _____

Have you checked all possible places where article was used? _____

OTHER INFORMATION:

_____
Student's signature

Date: _____

ment and supplies is usually 'mined' out of the pockets of the student body, the parents, and the general public. In this respect equipment really belongs to

no individual but to all those students who have ever been enrolled or who are presently enrolled or will ever be enrolled in the future. It is, therefore, community property which athletes are privileged to use. Students must learn early that participation on a school athletic

---

[27]Hixson, Chalmer, *The Administration of Interscholastic Athletics*, p. 98.

squad is a privilege; and the school owes the athletes nothing for having participated. In reality, the athletes are indebted for having had the privilege of participation. Therefore they have no right to help themselves to sweat socks, tee shirts, shoes or other athletic equipment.

The Equipment Manager

It is unusual to have a full-time equipment manager in the high school. However, it is important to have someone, if it is at all possible, in charge of the equipment room. If it is not possible to have some responsible individual in charge of the equipment room on a full-time basis, perhaps arrangements can be made to have a custodian in charge on a part-time basis. If the plan cannot be worked out then responsible students can be appointed to work in the equipment room either for free or on a paid basis. In any event it is the responsibility of the athletic director and coach to be responsible for equipment care.

Kaczmarek[28] suggests that:

Assignment of personnel to handle equipment, storage space, and inventories must be administered properly if length of service of an item is to be realized. It is essential that guidelines be established. A policy in maintenance and administrative responsibility should be clear to all in the program. All directors or coaches must be made responsible for the basic care of equipment. Information must be given to those responsible as to the proper handling of leather goods, athletic shoes, inflated materials, all rubber equipment, fabrics used in athletic uniforms, hard plastic protective equipment, and laundering factors. The do's and don'ts properly interpreted from the time equipment is unpacked until it is discarded as 'worn out' are essential.

The importance of the equipment man

cannot be underestimated. The biggest problem is to convince the administration that it would be profitable to hire one and justify it by pointing out the amount of money that could be saved. This can be done if the proper technique is used. There are various ways in which an equipment manager can be used depending upon the size of the school. If the school is small, he could serve as a part-time custodian or bus driver. He could also be used as a maintenance man or groundman during the fall and spring.

There are those who believe that hiring an equipment manager would be worthwhile. Others feel that only the large schools need a manager who can serve in this position. Oosting comments that in a study of a large school system with a combined elementary high school enrollment of 6,000 students it was found that after two years of work by the equipment manager there was a savings.[29]

Oosting[30] stresses the importance of the equipment manager in the following comment:

Would hiring an athletic equipment manager be worthwhile? Is there a minimum size a school district must be to realize any economic advantages from having a manager? What should this employee's duties be?

If a school system is large enough to have full-time work for a manager and if a skilled person is available, then the district would profit from hiring one.

Enrollment in our combined elementary and secondary school districts exceed 6,000, and we have found after two years' service by an athletic equipment manager that the arrangement is not only worth continuing, but that we can prove savings.

A director of athletic equipment

---

[28]Kaczmarek, John, "Equipment Care Cardinal Obligations," p. 29.

[29]Oosting, Bernard, "Does Sports Equipment Require a Manager?" *The Nations Schools* (May, 1964), p. 92.
[30]*Ibid.*

should be expected to perform these duties for a district:

DUTIES OF THE EQUIPMENT MANAGER

1. The equipment manager is directly responsible to the athletic director.
2. Be responsible for his own selected student managers and help supervise team managers.
3. Take sole possession and administer the complete operation of the laundry room.
4. Assist coaches in their team equipment rooms with supplies and equipment.
5. Follow the specific assignments provided by the athletic director as to the extent of duties, responsibilities, and authority.
6. Maintain and repair equipment if the equipment has not reached a state where repair no longer is worthwhile.
7. Issue equipment.
8. Maintain a record of inventory. Keep track of to whom the equipment is issued and note when it is returned.
9. Assume custodial responsibility for an assigned area.
10. Have plenty of initiative for tackling new problems.

Machinery and tools for repairing equipment must be provided, of course. One such item is a heavy-duty sewing machine —it will be needed for patching and rebuilding wrestling mats, for example. A large stock room with adequate work area could be home base for the athletic manager.

The Equipment Room

The equipment room is a very important part of equipment care and use. It is very unusual for any school to have adequate facilities to take care of the equipment in the way it should be taken care of.

According to Hixson:[31]

In the ideal situation there should be two separate equipment rooms. One in which off-season equipment is kept and

the other in which in-season equipment, that is presently being used, on a daily or seasonal basis, is stored. The equipment room should be near the locker room. It should be clean, dry, and well ventilated. It should be so arranged that the equipment can be issued easily and with dispatch. The general stockroom for out-of-season storage must be provided with the greatest degree of security. Fewer persons should have access to this room than to any other equipment facility. A minimum number of keys should be available with which to open the stockroom; the principal and the custodian should have keys in the event of emergencies; and one additional key might well serve the needs of the athletic department for access to the general storeroom. Devices for the regulation of temperatures, humidity and light should be provided. Racks, bins, shelves, and hangers of all types should be available on which to store equipment for long periods of time. Only clean and repaired equipment should be stored in this facility. A general storage room located immediately adjacent to locker room areas while convenient, is unnecessary, since the facility is used infrequently. Maximum security, controlled conditions, and storage devices facilitate the long range preservation of equipment and supplies.

Drying Room

Very few schools can afford the luxury of a drying room. A drying room is as the name implies a room which is used for drying equipment. The drying room should be well ventilated and equipped with a large number of racks upon which equipment may be hung to dry. It should be possible to heat this room to a high temperature to increase the drying rate. Hixson[32] makes the following comment regarding the drying room:

Heat and ventilation must be con-

---

[31]Hixson, Chalmer, *The Administration of Interscholastic Athletics*, p. 104.

[32]*Ibid*, p. 105.

trolled in order to force-dry equipment. There is less security in the facility than either of the other two. Greater access must be granted to a larger number of individuals. Hangers holding all of the equipment issued to an individual athlete are especially valuable. Such hangers can be arranged on racks to increase the ventilation and shorten the drying time required in a typical dressing locker. A drying room provides greater control of equipment than individual dressing lockers housed in a locker room. Daily inspections are possible and the managers and equipment handlers can be trained to recognize damaged and abused equipment, which can readily be replaced with equipment in good repair. Certain materials should be excluded from the drying room when forced drying is required. Leather goods, for example, should not be force dried. An issue room should be located in the locker room. Less security is maintained than for the storage room. Nevertheless, access is still limited; and, not every one should be admitted to the issue room. Equipment for the seasonal sports in progress is stored here. The materials have been brought from the storage room to the issue room to be readily available for daily use. It should be equipped with bins, racks, hangers, and those tools and supplies necessary for daily repair and care.

Providing Player Equipment

Because of the tremendous expense involved in the purchase of athletic equipment, it is understandable that policies should be established for the use of the equipment. Most schools now furnish most all of the equipment used by athletic teams. There are others, however, that furnish certain equipment that can be re-used by other team members and require personal items, such as shoes, etc. to be furnished by individual players. It is necessary that the policies be understood by players, parents, athletic directors, and coaches before any issuing of equipment takes place.

Problems can develop because of a players' inability to purchase the necessary equipment. In some cases it could prevent the player from participating unless other arrangements can be made.

It is recommended that if it is at all possible, all equipment be furnished by the school. This necessitates careful planning and a thorough knowledge of purchasing procedures.

Schools should be very careful to provide adequate sports equipment for all players who participate in interscholastic athletics. It should meet the highest standards of safety and it should be constantly improved. The equipment should not be sold or given away. It must be known to the user that it is loaned to them to be kept at the school, properly used and cared for, and must be returned immediately upon the close of the sport season for which it was issued or at any time the student may be dropped from the sport. Under no circumstances should school-issued equipment be worn except for interscholastic athletics.

Students should be held responsible for the care and return of all equipment issued to them and should pay for it in case it is lost. No school credit should be given until all equipment issued is returned or paid for. The protection of equipment is largely a matter of proper instruction and education. This is a function of the coach and the athletic director. However, sometimes in spite of these instructions, students willfully damage equipment. The coach should use every means at his disposal to prevent it.

The best means used by the athletic director and the coach to prevent loss of equipment through theft or misplacement is to keep accurate inventories.

System of Checking Equipment

It is a problem in every high school to keep track of athletic equipment since it has the habit of walking off by itself and can seldom be found again. Wide awake and efficient managers will eliminate this sort of thing to a great extent. However, there should be a system worked out whereby both the coach and the manager can keep a constant eye on all equipment.

ARGO HIGH SCHOOL DISTRICT No. 161
BASKETBALL EQUIPMENT CHECK OUT SHEET

Team _____ Year_____ Coach_____

| NAME | PRACTICE EQUIPMENT | | | | GAME EQUIPMENT | | | | | | OTHER |
	SHIRT	TRUNKS	SHOES	MLS.	SHIRT white	TRUNKS white	WARM UP jacket	WARM UP pants	SHIRT dark	TRUNKS dark	

Figure 66.

Most of the high schools furnish practice and game equipment. The game equipment should be given to the players before

FOOTBALL EQUIPMENT FORM

Locker_____
Lock No._____
Combination_____

Name_____ Insurance_____ Physical Exam_____
Birth Date_____ County_____ Year in School – Frosh ☐ Soph.☐ Jr.☐ Sr.☐
Family Doctor_____ Phone No. _____
Home Phone No._____ Coach_____

Articles	No.	Color	Date Issued	Date Returned

Received by_____ Date_____

Figure 67.

each game and should be turned in after each game. Each player has his own uniform which he uses for every game. The practice equipment, however, presents a

TABLE LX
CASEY HIGH SCHOOL DISTRICT NO. 3

BASKETBALL

Issued by _____ High School

Name of athlete _____ Age _____

Address _____ Tel. No. _____

Home Room _____ Locker No. _____ Grade _____

List of Equipment

Shoes _____Size_____No._____   Jacket _____Size_____No._____
Knee Pads _____Size_____No._____   Trunks _____Size_____No._____
Sweat Socks _____Size_____No._____   Jersey _____Size_____No._____
Supporter _____Size_____No._____   Sweat Pads _____Size_____No._____

All the equipment checked above has been issued to me. I promise to take care of it and return it at the end of the season or at the request of the coach or superintendent or pay the penalty determined by the school officials.

_____   _____
Date   Player's Signature

Figure 68.

HIGH SCHOOL ATHLETIC EQUIPMENT RECORD											
Name ___ Age ___ Height ___ Weight ___ Physical Checked ___											
FOOTBALL			**BASKETBALL**			**BASEBALL**			**TRACK**		
Practice Equip.	Out	In	Practice Equip.	Out	In	Practice Equip.	Out	In	Practice Equip.	Out	In
Pants			Pants			Shirt			Pants		
Blocking Pads			T Shirt			Pants			T Shirt		
Shoulder Pads			Jersey			T Shirt			Shoes		
Helmet			Sweat Shirt			Socks—Sweat			Sweat Shirt		
Sweat Shirt(J's'y)			Sweat Pants			Socks—Long			Sweat Pants		
T Shirt			Socks—Sweat			Supporter			Socks		
Supporter			Socks—Track			Cap			Supporter		
Socks			Supporter			Shoes			Sweat Shirt		
Knee Pads			Knee Pads						Sweat Pants		
Shoes											
Lock			Lock			Lock			Towel Fee		
Game Equipment			**Game Equipment**			**Game Equipment**			**SWIMMING**		
T Shirt			Pants			Shirt			Sweat Shirt		
Jersey			Shirt			Pants			Sweat Pants		
Pants			Sweat Jacket			T Shirt			Robe		
Storm Coat			Sweat Pants			Socks—Long			Swim Suit		
Socks—Long			Shoes								
			Equipment Bag								
									Lock		
Towel Fee			Towel Fee			Towel Fee			Towel Fee		

greater problem but should be handled in a similar manner.

All players who answer the first call should be given cards to fill out. Each card has a number and as each piece of equipment is issued, it is checked on the card which bears the name of the individual who is getting the equipment. This card should be kept on file in the equipment room and the office. Every sport should have a special colored card. The cards can be kept separate according to sports and filed alphabetically or they can be kept in one file. They are easily identifiable as to sports because of their color.

If it is impossible for each player to have his own locker to store his practice equipment, other means of storage must be provided. If only one large dressing room is available, the following plan may be used.

Long rows of hooks can be placed in the equipment room with numbers above each hook corresponding to the numbers on the cards in the files. The player remembers the number assigned to him and his practice equipment is hung on his hook. He asks the manager for his equipment each day by number. Under no conditions should any one except coaches and manager be allowed in the equipment room. This same set-up may be used in the drying room.

There are, of course, other systems, of which a few are described here.

USE OF THE LOCKER SYSTEM FOR EQUIPMENT STORAGE: Probably the most widely used method of storing player equipment during the playing season is lockers. If the lockers are large enough to accommodate all the personal equipment, this system is entirely satisfactory. This system places the responsibility directly on the player himself. He or she is assigned a locker, given the equipment and assumes the responsibility of keeping the locker door locked, turning in dirty equipment to the equipment manager, and receiving clean equipment at stated intervals as designated by the coach. The coach or athletic director has the lock combination so that if it is necessary for him to get into the locker he can do so.

USE OF THE BASKET SYSTEM FOR EQUIPMENT STORAGE: This method saves space and can be used in the same manner as the locker system. This really is the only advantage.

CHECK OUT SYSTEM FOR EQUIPMENT: The value of a good method of checking out equipment cannot be underestimated. The secret to this of course is to have a good card system of keeping track of all equipment that is issued and returned by each player. This can be done more efficiently if the coach will designate specific times when this must be done. The players must conform to this rule and unless it is an emergency, should not be allowed to receive or return any equipment except at the designated time to do so. No partiality should be shown to any one player no matter who he is; otherwise the entire system will break down. Each player should be held accountable at the time he fails to turn in or reports equipment loss. The coach should be so informed and take the necessary action which has been previously decided upon when this situation arises.

GREENVILLE COMMUNITY HIGH SCHOOL

ATHLETIC EQUIPMENT CHECK LIST

Name_____

Address_____

Class_____

Sport_____ Year_____ Assigned Locker No. _____

Equipment Issued	Out–date	In–date	Comments
Initial of Issuer			

Figure 69.

COMMUNITY HIGH SCHOOL

Athletic Department

INDIVIDUAL PROPERTY CARD

Sport_____ Inventoried by_____

Description	Size	Specifications	Year Purchased	Condition	Where Stored	Box No.

Figure 70.

GLENBARD ATHLETIC EQUIPMENT RECORD

NAME_____

	19—		19—		19—		19—		COMMENTS
	OUT	IN	OUT	IN	OUT	IN	OUT	IN	
FOOTBALL									
Helmet									
Shoulder Pad									
Practice Jersey									
Game Jersey – Lt.									
Game Jersey – Dk.									
Forearms Pad									
Rib Pads									
Hip Pads									
Practice Pants									
Game Pants – Lt.									
Game Pants – Dk.									
Thigh Guards									
Knee Pads									
Shoes									
Warm-up Jacket									
Med. Equip. & Misc.									
CROSS COUNTRY									
Sweatsuit									
Game Shirt									
Game Pants									
Shoes									
Warm-up Jacket									
Warm-up Pants									
Med. Equip. & Misc.									
WRESTLING									
Sweatshirt									
Sweat Pants									
Game Jersey									
Game Pants									
Warm-up Jacket									
Rubber Jacket									
Shoes									
Knee Pads									
Head Gear									
Jumping Rope									
Med. Equip. & Misc.									
GYMNASTICS									
TT Bars									
Tights									
Hand Guard									
Shoes									
Game Jersey									
Warm-up Jacket									
Med. Equip. & Misc.									

Figure 71.

NUMBERING OF EQUIPMENT: There are various ways of numbering equipment. The composition of the equipment itself will dictate to some extent the method that should be used. Some suggestions are as follows:

1. Stencils should be used for clothing such as shirts, pants, warm-ups and shoes.
2. Stamping should be used for all leather goods.
3. Painting should be used for balls.

A good method of inventory and equipment checking will require a uniform method of numbering equipment. The numbering system can be one of many in

TABLE LXI
ACORES HIGH SCHOOL DISTRICT NO. 24

Equipment Request Form

Date _____

SPORT _____

NAME _____

Equipment Issued	Quantity
_____	_____
_____	_____
_____	_____
_____	_____
_____	_____
_____	_____
_____	_____
_____	_____

COMMENTS:

Signed _____

Equipment Manager _____

TABLE LXII
PALO HIGH SCHOOL
PALO, NEBRASKA

LOST ATHLETIC EQUIPMENT REPORT FORM

Owner of _____

Date Lost _____   Time _____

Article Lost _____

Description of Article:

Details of how and where it was lost:

Circumstances under which it was lost:

signed _____

use today. Whichever one is used, it should designate the year the equipment is purchased along with the number for the equipment. For example the articles can be numbered consecutively, such as 1, 2, 3, 4, 5. The year the piece of equipment was purchased would be 175. This method of numbering will enable the coach to judge how durable the equipment is. There are other numbering systems just as effective. The inventory should be available to the coach to examine and use for future reference in composing future requi-sitions for equipment.

PENALTIES FOR EQUIPMENT LOSS BY PLAYERS: A great deal of athletic equipment is lost during the course of a season of play. Every effort to curtail and lessen this equipment loss should be exercised by every coach and athletic director. An affluent society has brought about a feeling of apathy toward an attempt to require the student to either replace or pay for equipment that is lost. There are several methods that can be used, however, which will help to curtail this loss of equipment which seems to be so prevalent in our schools to-day. Some of the methods used are with-holding the player's grades, withholding the athletic award, prohibiting the player from further competition, and withholding the diploma if he is a senior.

Much of the equipment is lost through carelessness on the part of the user. He leaves it lying around the locker room while he takes a shower or he may leave it on the practice field. Oftentimes during a track meet sweat clothing is left at the starting blocks. When the runner returns after the race to pick it up, it has disap-peared. The coach should arrange to have one of the managers pick up all sweat clothing at the beginning of the race and have it available for the athlete after he has completed the race. However, the ath-lete himself should realize that the ath-letic equipment is given to him to use and that he is responsible for it. If stiff penalties are imposed on those who loose this equip-ment, they will be more careful. Another problem which presents itself is the prac-tice of keeping equipment. This practice can be abolished if penalities are imposed for all lost equipment.

MARKING OF EQUIPMENT: The loss of equipment can be serious because if it be-comes habitual it can cost the department a great deal of money and untold difficulty. In order to avoid this, all items should be marked so that they can be easily identi-fied. The marking of equipment can cut down loss and save a great deal of money. There are several methods of marking equipment. An ideal method is offered by George and Lehmann.[33]

A Plan for Marking Pants

The following is a simple but effective plan for marking pants so they can be

readily identified by sizes:
1. Use a fabric pen or indelible pencil.
2. Place a permanent number in the inner waistband to the right of the fly.
3. Use a different series of hundreds for each size, e.g.

size 28	#1-99
size 30	#100-199
size 32	#200-299
size 34	#300-399
size 36	#400-499

4. This plan may be modified to fit a particular age group.

A Plan for Marking Balls

The following system provides a means for easy identification and also for determining the length of useful life for balls of the inflated type:
1. Leather balls should be marked with an electric branding iron.
2. The marks should be in the same relative position on all balls.
3. Recommended marks are the school's initial-year-number: Example would be "BHS-6$_4$-1," "BHS-6$_4$-2."

Care and Maintenance of Athletic Equipment

Large sums of money are expended every year on equipment for baseball, foot-ball, basketball, softball, and other team sports by schools, colleges, and organiza-tions of all types and sizes throughout the country. Most of this equipment, which is produced by manufacturers of quality ath-letic equipment, is designed to withstand hard play on the court or in the field. It is also designed for continued use *provided* it receives proper care, cleaning, and main-tenance. Here are ten basic principles for good equipment maintenance as suggested by the Athletic Goods Manufacturing Association.[34]

1. There must be a definite policy re-garding the care of athletic equip-ment.
2. Players must be instructed in the care

[33]George, Jack, and Lehmann, Harry, *School Athletic Administration* (New York, Harper and Row, 1966), p. 183.

[34]Athletic Goods Manufacturing Association, p. 15.

of athletic equipment.

3. The head coach should be directly responsible for the care of athletic equipment.

4. An accurate record must be kept of all equipment, including condition, size, and age.

5. All athletic equipment must be marked for size and identification number —also date when issued into service.

6. There must be a definite system regarding the issuance, use, and return of athletic equipment.

7. If an equipment manager is utilized, there must be a clear understanding of his duties and responsibilities between the coach and manager.

8. Athletic equipment must be correctly cleaned and laundered if possible after every game. Practice equipment should be cleaned about every two or three days. Equipment should be air dried after use.

9. Equipment should be stored, repaired, and maintained in accordance with manufacturer's recommendations.

10. Proper methods of out-of-season storage should be utilized.

It is universally accepted by coaches and athletic directors throughout the country that the care of athletic equipment presents a very great problem. This is true because of the philosophy of various administrators regarding adequate help and the delegation of responsibility in this particular area. This philosophy can be due in part to the lack of funds and different situations. There are certain rules which apply to the care of athletic equipment which must be followed regardless of the situation.

Athletic equipment is expensive. The students of today have been living in an affluent society. They are careless with equipment yet on the other hand they should be provided with the best equipment if at all possible. This would avoid possible injury and better performance might be forthcoming. However, this does not entitle the athlete to misuse equipment that does not belong to him. Proper use of equipment will lengthen its service and thereby save money. Both coaches and players should be provided with the necessary information on the proper use and care of athletic equipment. There are basic principles which should be taken into consideration for proper equipment care. These principles are listed by The Athletic Goods Manufacturing Company:[35]

1. Definite policies regarding the care and maintenance of all equipment falling under the administrative responsibility of the director of the program or programs should be developed.

2. Program participants should be carefully instructed in the use and care of any equipment employed in activities provided.

3. Staff personnel responsible for various phases of the programs should assume direct responsibility for the care of equipment used in their fields of specialty.

4. Accurate records should be maintained on all equipment including condition, size, age, and number.

5. All equipment used in health education, physical education, and recreation should be marked for identification purposes according to a system devised for each particular situation.

6. An efficient system should be developed for the issuance, use, and return of any equipment employed on a daily, seasonal, or annual basis.

7. Student leaders should be utilized to carry out numerous duties and responsibilities for controlling the various kinds of equipment.

8. Every maintenance precaution should be taken to keep equipment in operating order with particular emphasis being placed upon drying, cleaning, and repairing.

9. Equipment should be used, stored, repaired, and maintained in accordance

---

[35]Athletic Goods Manufacturing Association, p. 37.

with manufacturers' recommendations.

10. Plans should be made for the storage of all equipment when not in use so that all items are protected from deterioration, theft, and unauthorized use.

The equipment purchased today is safe, comfortable, and well fitted. It will stand up under extremely hard usage. It is made to stand a great deal of wear and use provided it receives the proper care; this includes proper cleaning, maintenance, and care when not in use. More equipment is ruined while not being used than ever was while being used. Athletic equipment is like clothing; it will wear out faster if it is dirty and if it does not fit correctly.

Preseason Care of Equipment

Uniforms should be given proper care the minute they are delivered and placed in the equipment room. They should be left in the containers until ready for use after they have been checked for size, color, and type of material. Usually wool garments are shipped moth protected but it might be wise to double check this fact. The uniforms should be stored in a clean, dry area away from the humidity that might come from the shower room.

During the Game Care

The treatment given the uniform during the game is important, especially the warm-up pants and jackets. Players have the habit of throwing these on the floor or expecting the manager to take care of them after they remove them to either start the game or enter the game. Very often players will leave them on the bench upon returning to the dressing room. This will happen more often away from home where there is more of a chance of their being lost. The players should be informed by the senior manager that this is their responsibility.

Each player should remove the jacket and pants when he is ready to do so, carefully fold each garment, and place it on the bench. If he is removed from the game, the manager should have his jacket and warm-up pants ready for him as he approaches the bench. The players should be cautioned that they are to receive this equipment graciously and not grab it and start throwing it about. This not only embarrasses the coach, but also the manager.

After the Game Care

All uniforms should be hung in a clean, dry room on separate hangers. Each athlete should have his own hanger and all of his equipment should be kept together. There should be plenty of air in the room, and it should be warm to induce the drying of the uniforms. Wood or rust-proof hangers are necessary. This can be taken care of very satisfactorily at home but the care of uniforms while the team is away from home presents another problem. Frequently there is very little or no time at all to dry out the uniforms after the game and before the team starts it trip back home. If the team is on an extended trip, the manager should make arrangements to have the uniforms dried as soon as possible. If the individual players are handling their own uniforms, they often can hang them up in their hotel rooms after the game.

Postseason Care

The close of the season presents the biggest problem regarding the care of equipment. The uniforms should first of all receive a thorough drying. They should hang for several days in the drying area so that they will be perfectly dry when they are sent to the cleaners. The cleaner should be instructed to do any repair work such as loose lettering, snags, etc. All necessary repairs should be made before the uniform is cleaned. All uniforms should be moth-proofed by the cleaner and packed in moth-proof boxes. They should be stored in a clean, dry place. The coach, along with the manager, will need to decide at this time what replacements are necessary.

The Do's and Don'ts of Equipment Maintenance

Properly interpreted "the care of athletic equipment" includes care taken of equipment from the time it is first unpacked in the storeroom until it is destroyed. Such a broad interpretation involves care by all personnel including coach, managers, players, cleaners, launderers, repair personnel, and anyone having anything to do with the equipment. Here is a list of do's and don'ts which can serve as a guide in the efficient use and care of all types of athletic equipment as suggested by the Athletic Goods Manufacturing Association.[36]

DO'S

1. Have one man in charge of equipment.
2. Mark all equipment with date and identification marks.
3. Give athletic clothing the same care you would give your own clothing.
4. Dry out equipment as soon as possible after using.
5. After equipment has dried, brush off mud and foreign matter.
6. Pack all wet equipment in separate containers, prior to washing or cleaning.
7. Clean or launder equipment in accordance with manufacturer's recommendations.
8. Pack wet jerseys separate from pants.
9. Clean all equipment at the end of each playing season. Keep an equipment inventory for color, size, and number and have the

record kept in the equipment room. Each trunk or carton of equipment should be numbered or identified as to contents.
10. Clean muddy gear immediately.
11. Store equipment during the off-season in a clean, dry, cool room.
12. Make certain the storage room is well ventilated.
13. Inventory your equipment at the end of your sport season. Determine your new equipment needs for next season. And ORDER EARLY!

DON'TS

1. Don't permit dirt and untidiness in the locker room.
2. Don't allow the equipment storage room to become overcrowded, dirty, and junky. Keep it clean.
3. Don't store equipment in a dark, damp place.
4. Don't fold garments when wet. Dry out flat and place wrapping paper between each jersey or over the numerals if a light color.
5. Don't mix colors washing garments.
6. Don't use excessively cold rinse water after washing garments in a lukewarm wash. This will cause an increase in shrinkage.
7. Don't use excessively hot water in cleaning; it will also shrink garments.
8. Do not hang garments on nails to dry. Use nonrust hangers. Knit jerseys should be dried flat.
9. Do not let gear lie in a muddy pile for several weeks or even several days. Clean it at once, or send it to a reliable reconditioner.
10. Don't try to get an extra season out of worn out equipment. Replace it. And order new equipment EARLY!

Cleaning Equipment

Cleaning is an economical way to preserve equipment because clean equipment will last much longer. This applies to all types of equipment but especially to equipment such as woolen and cotton garments

---

[36]Athletic Goods Manufacturing Association, p. 15.

that have a tendency to deteriorate when soiled. Arrangements should be made with a commercial laundry if the school does not have its own.

Storage of Equipment

The problem of equipment storage is serious to a number of smaller high schools as well as some of the larger ones. Very few have adequate storage room and are forced to store equipment in rooms poorly lighted and ventilated. Equipment deteriorates in poorly ventilated, overheated, and damp rooms. Equipment should be taken care of immediately after each sport season is finished. Any long delay can result in lost equipment and problems. After all the equipment is returned, it should be checked to determine what should be stored, what should be sent to the cleaners and what should be discarded or sent out to be repaired. Proper storage will prolong the life of equipment and thereby save an untold amount of money. It is well worth the money that needs to be spent to provide proper storage space.

French and Lehsten[37] make the following comment about equipment storage, "Storage of equipment is as important as its care while in use, and for that reason adequate storage is a 'must' if equipment is to be properly maintained. The life of athletic equipment depends in large measure upon the care it receives."

Even though ideal storage space cannot be provided in many schools, it is possible to take advantage of seldom used areas and with a little ingenuity and foresight these areas can be converted into usable storage rooms.

George and Lehmann[38] give these stand-

[37]French, Esther, and Lehsten Nelson, *Administration of Physical Education in Schools and Colleges*, p. 488.

[38]George, Jack F., and Lehmann, Harry A., *School Athletic Administration*, p. 181.

ards as being necessary for rooms in which athletic equipment may be stored.

1. Roomy, light and cool.
2. Well-ventilated and dry.
3. Free from damp or sweaty pipes or walls.
4. Protected against moths, roaches, and rodents.
5. Provide space for all department equipment.
6. Provide space for handling, marking, and making minor repairs.
7. Contain facilities and materials for marking and repairing equipment.

If it is possible to have a large room for the storage of equipment, careful planning should be done to take full advantage of it. If at all possible, there should be a window placed in this room. This will give proper ventilation which is a must in proper storage of athletic equipment. Shelving should be installed to store wearing apparel. Bins should be provided for shoes, basketballs, footballs, baseball bats, etc. Large racks should be placed in the center of the room. The proper placement of these items will minimize the problem of proper storage. All equipment should be stored systematically so that all items of the same kind are together and therefore easily accessible when needed for use or for inventory.

All equipment should be protected against mildew, rodents, and moths.

JERSEYS AND PANTS: The jerseys should be hung on coat hangers and then hung on racks far enough apart so that they are not touching. Woolen jerseys should be sprayed with a moth preventative. Another plan is to send them to the dry cleaners and after they are cleaned, have them packed in boxes and sprayed by the cleaners. They are then ready for storage.

SHOES: The shoes should be stored in bin compartments if space is available.

SOCKS AND SUPPORTERS: These articles should be washed and packed in boxes to prolong their life, should be laundered often when in use, using lukewarm water and a good soap.

BALLS: All balls should be stored in individual bin compartments. The molded ball is not deflated.

COTTON MATERIALS: All materials should be washed and placed on shelves or in cardboard boxes.

WOOLENS: All woolen materials should be cleaned and stored in boxes or bins. They should be moth proofed.

LEATHER GOODS: Leather goods should be completely dry before storage. In order for all leather goods to hold their shape, such as shoes and helmets, forms should be placed inside them. All leather goods should be stored in a dry airy room to avoid mildew and rot. It is a good plan to oil all leather before storage. This will help avoid cracking, drying out and general deterioration. Leather goods should always be dried out *slowly* to avoid excessive shrinkage. The two common enemies of leather are high temperatures and moisture.

WOOD: All wood equipment should be protected by varnish or paint and weather proofed. If this is not done, moisture will penetrate the surface and the wood will lose its strength and finally disintegrate.

RUBBER AND PLASTIC EQUIPMENT: A great amount of athletic equipment is now made out of rubber or plastic. This type of equipment must also be stored in a clean dry place. Sunlight can cause this type of equipment to disintegrate. Grease and oil are both enemies of rubber and plastic goods.

LAUNDRY: Laundering equipment, such as socks, towels, supporters, T shirts, etc. does not present a major problem if funds are available. There are many laundries that will pick up this equipment, wash and dry it, and return it the next day. They can do this at a cost that cannot be equaled by the school having its own laundry.

According to Hixson:[39]

A laundry facility should be readily available to the department of athletics. It can be commercial grade equipment or washers and dryers purchased through the home economics department at greatly reduced prices. The athletic laundry can be operated by student managers or by student employees. The useful life of jerseys and tee shirts, is increased by regular laundry and clean equipment not only lasts longer, but improves the sanitary conditions for protecting the welfare of athletes.

Equipment Repair

Keeping athletic equipment in good repair is a major problem for every athletic director and coach. The question arises as to what extent the repair work should be done locally and how much should be sent to professional cleaning and repair companies. The determining factors in this respect will be the size of the school, the amount of money at hand, and the skilled personnel available. At the present time very few high schools have personnel on their staff that can repair athletic equipment. The usual procedure is to make simple repairs and to send the remainder to professional repair and cleaning companies. Often a custodian will be assigned the task of equipment repair and sometimes he will do this along with his other duties as custodian. This often happens in smaller schools.

It has been proven that in the large high school where a great deal of equipment is used, it is most economical to hire a full-time equipment and repair man. This man will more than make up his salary in the amount of money he will save the school in repairing and cleaning ath-

---

[39]Hixson, Chalmer, *The Administration of Interscholastic Athletics*, p. 105.

letic equipment. A hiring of a full-time equipment manager who is skilled in repairing equipment is a wise move if it can be done.

Voltmer and Esslinger[40] have made this observation regarding equipment repair:

> Good judgment and common sense must be used in repairing equipment. Up to a certain point it is good economy to recondition athletic materials, but beyond that it is a waste of money. Some directors make the mistake of repairing old equipment that will not give them enough service to pay for the repairs made. It is more advisable to sell old equipment to cleaning and reconditioning firms and apply the money to new equipment.

Kaczmarek[41] suggests that:

> Maintenance of any athletic equipment is a cardinal obligation of the administration. Large sums of public funds can be squandered on maintenance because of inefficiency, lack of good judgement, poor discipline by the coach, and the failure to teach participants the proper care of an item. Equipment is designed and manufactured to withstand hard play on any play area, provided it receives the proper care, cleaning, and storage.

The athletic director and especially the coach have a moral as well as a legal obligation to see to it that all athletic equipment is in good repair. The coach should never permit the use of equipment by the athlete when he knows it is defective. Some have learned this through bitter experience in the courts, which usually hold the coach guilty of negligence if injuries are caused in such cases.

---

[40]Voltmer, Edward and Esslinger, Arthur, *Organization and Administration of Physical Education,* (New York, Appleton Crofts, Inc. 1967), p. 448.

[41]Kaczmarek, John, "Equipment Care Cardinal Obligations," p. 29.

Inventory

Inventories of all equipment should receive the undivided attention of every athletic director and coach. It is not only a good business procedure, but it is a necessity if the funds used to purchase the equipment are to be employed efficiently. By listing each piece of athletic equipment, it is possible to know at all times exactly how much equipment is available, what it is, and the condition it is in. A systemized manner of taking inventory should be installed and a uniform timetable for taking inventory should be established. It can be done on a monthly, yearly, or a three-year period depending on the kind of equipment that is being inventoried. A good inventory system will help eliminate loss of equipment. A numbering system should also help keep track of all equipment.

The numbering of equipment will place a great deal of the responsibility on the players themselves. Lost equipment can be easily identified and equipment that has been mixed up by player exchange can be straightened out very easily.

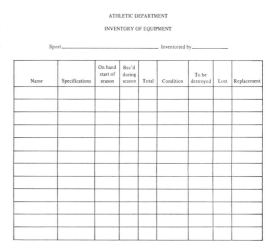

LANARK COMMUNITY HIGH SCHOOL DISTRICT 112

ATHLETIC DEPARTMENT

INVENTORY OF EQUIPMENT

Sport_____   Inventoried by_____

Name	Specifications	On hand start of season	Rec'd during season	Total	Condition	To be destroyed	Lost	Replacement

Figure 72.

LENA TOWNSHIP HIGH SCHOOL DISTRICT 219
INVENTORY OF EQUIPMENT

School_____   Inventory taken by_____

Room No. or Sport_____   Verified by_____

Division Head_____   Inventories taken following sport season

Name & Description of Equipment BME Allowance and BME #	Date of Purchase	Number Verified and Condition 19__	19__	19__	19__
____ BME# ____ or Supplies ____		Good___ Fair___ Poor___ Total___	Good___ Fair___ Poor___ Total___	Good___ Fair___ Poor___ Total___	Good___ Fair___ Poor___ Total___
____ BME# ____ or Supplies ____		Good___ Fair___ Poor___ Total___	Good___ Fair___ Poor___ Total___	Good___ Fair___ Poor___ Total___	Good___ Fair___ Poor___ Total___
____ BME# ____ or Supplies ____		Good___ Fair___ Poor___ Total___	Good___ Fair___ Poor___ Total___	Good___ Fair___ Poor___ Total___	Good___ Fair___ Poor___ Total___
____ BME# ____ or Supplies___		Good___ Fair___ Poor___ Total___	Good___ Fair___ Poor___ Total___	Good___ Fair___ Poor___ Total___	Good___ Fair___ Poor___ Total___
____ BME# ____ or Supplies ____		Good___ Fair___ Poor___ Total___	Good___ Fair___ Poor___ Total___	Good___ Fair___ Poor___ Total___	Good___ Fair___ Poor___ Total___
____ BME## ____ or Supplies ____		Good___ Fair___ Poor___ Total___	Good___ Fair___ Poor___ Total___	Good___ Fair___ Poor___ Total___	Good___ Fair___ Poor___ Total___
____ BME# ____ or Supplies ____		Good___ Fair___ Poor___ Total___	Good___ Fair___ Poor___ Total___	Good___ Fair___ Poor___ Total___	Good___ Fair___ Poor___ Total___

Figure 73.

The numbering and marking of equipment also makes it easier for the manager to care for it. Usually a competent manager will take a hurried inventory of equipment each day so that if a loss is discovered it can be tracked down quickly. The manager should be responsible for a complete inventory after the season has been completed. This inventory should be submitted to the coach and should contain an itemized list of all equipment pertaining to the particular sport along with the estimated value and condition. The yearly inventories from each sport should be filed so that they are easily accessible from one year to the next. This type of inventory is valuable because it can be used each year as an example of what equipment is needed. A good inventory will answer the following:

1. The equipment that should be repaired or discarded

2. The equipment that can be used the next year and the condition it is in

3. The equipment that must be replaced

4. The equipment that will need to be purchased before the next season starts

5. How efficient the manager was

6. How much equipment was stolen or lost

The best way to keep track of equipment is to list each piece on forms which are provided for this task. There are many types of forms that may be used; the important consideration is that these forms be uniform and used throughout the school system.

The inventory should consist of two different listings. The first sheet (and a separate form should be used for this) should consist of such items as basketballs, uniforms, scorebooks, etc. that are used in games. The second sheet should consist of expendable items such as towels, first-aid supplies, practice jerseys, etc.

Collin[42] stresses the importance of a simplified method of inventorying athletic equipment. The plan offered enables the department to record efficiently all the essential information with a minimum of effort. He suggests that several five by eight note cards be taped to the inside of a three-ring type notebook in photo album style. The following headings are then typed across the top of each card: (1) name of the item, (2) quantity on hand, (3) present condition, and (4) the date of inventory. A title for each card is printed in the lower left-hand corner, so that all card titles are visible when the notebook cover is opened. The titles are arranged in alphabetical order to simplify the location of a

[42]Collins, Don, A Workable Athletic Equipment Budget," *The Athletic Journal* (April, 1971), p. 64.

certain item. For example, the items could be pads, gymnastics, footballs, etc.

LOCKPORT TOWNSHIP HIGH SCHOOL
ATHLETIC DEPARTMENT
EQUIPMENT INVENTORY

SPORT__________ YEAR__________

EQUIPMENT	GAME				PRACTICE				NEEDED		REMARKS
CONDITION	NEW	USED	NEED REPAIR	NO GOOD	GOOD	FAIR	NEED REPAIR	NO GOOD	GAME	PRACTICE	

Date of Inventory__________19___ COACH__________

ATHLETIC DIRECTOR__________

Figure 74.

BEHAVIORAL OBJECTIVES

After a person has read this chapter, he should be able to:

1. Select a sport and list the essential equipment required to conduct it along with how to care and repair this equipment.
2. Prepare a plan for staff responsibility for equipment for a specific sport on a daily, seasonal, and annual basis.
3. Explain the need for adequate protection for all types of athletic equipment.
4. Indicate some of the advantages and disadvantages in the use of a custodian as an equipment manager.
5. Explain the importance of the establishment of sound criteria and practices in the purchase of athletic equipment.
6. Identify some of the problems which might arise by having players furnish some of the athletic equipment needed to participate in a specific sport.
7. Explain the role of the coach, the ath-

TABLE LXIII
PIPER CITY HIGH SCHOOL DISTRICT NO. 3
INVENTORY OF ATHLETIC EQUIPMENT

__________ HIGH SCHOOL __________
(DATE)

__________ YEAR __________
(COACH)

Equipment for Sport	Previous Count	Number Purchased During Year	Total Number	Present Inventory (Good)	Present Inventory (Fair)	Present Inventory (Poor)	Est. No. New Needed

NORTH JACKSON HIGH SCHOOL DISTRICT 130

INVENTORY—BUDGET

Item No.	Budget Code No.	Description	Unit Price	Inventory		To Be Ordered	Total Price	Other
				On Hand	Recomm.			

Figure 75.

letic director, the principal, the super-intendent, purchasing agent, and the board of education in the purchase of athletic equipment.

8. List and explain several vital rules or practices which should be adhered to in the purchase of athletic equipment.

9. List and explain the three, overall guidelines which should be considered and used in the selection of athletic equipment. Apply these guidelines to specific situations.

10. Distinguish between the selection and purchase of athletic equipment. Discuss the ramifications of each.

11. Select one sport and prepare a complete breakdown of equipment needs for that sport, both on a team and individual basis. Include types of equipment needed as well as the cost of each item.

12. List several important criteria which can be used to advantage in the selection of athletic equipment.

13. List several important necessities pertaining to the equipment room and its importance in the overall athletic program.

14. Explain the purpose of the drying room and discuss its role in the high school athletic program.

15. Identify and explain several administrative guides which can be used in purchasing athletic equipment.

16. List and explain the steps in purchasing athletic equipment.

17. Explain the importance of specifications in the selection of equipment.

18. List and explain the criteria that can be used in the selection of athletic equipment.

19. Explain the purpose and use of an inventory.

20. Recall and analyze several basic principles of good equipment maintenance.

21. List several criteria or standards for a storage equipment room.

22. Select several do's and don'ts which can be applied to buying habits for athletic equipment.

23. Identify some of the duties of the equipment manager and explain his importance in the athletic program.

24. Explain the importance of the proper storage of athletic equipment.

25. Identify several important points in the location of the athletic equipment room.

26. Discuss the advantages and disadvantages of buying athletic equipment through a purchasing agent.

27. List the advantages of early buying. Quality buying. Quantity buying.

28. Enumerate suggestions for special care in in-season and out-of-season athletic equipment.

29. List the considerations that should be undertaken by the buyer in determining where to buy.

30. Explain the importance of providing protective equipment that meets all specifications and official regulations.

31. Explain the relationship of the issue and collection of equipment, inventory of equipment, and purchase of equipment.

32. Enumerate some of the common unsanitary practices in the use and care of equipment. Suggest reminders for such practices.

33. Set up a plan for coaches' responsibility for equipment on a daily, seasonal, and an annual basis.

34. Explain the advantages and the limitations in the use of a custodian for equipment issue and collection.

35. List the essential equipment for a football player.

36. Describe an acceptable plan for issuing ordering and storing athletic equipment.

37. Explain the importance of providing protective equipment that meets all specifications and official regulations.

38. List the responsibilities of the equipment manager in the small, medium, and large high schools.

39. Differentiate between the issue of equipment, inventory of equipment, and the purchase of equipment.

40. Differentiate between the use of the equipment room, the laundry room, and the drying room.

41. Enumerate some of the bad practices in the use and care of athletic equipment.

42. Distinguish between supplies, equipment, commodities, materials, and gear.

43. Select the best time for ordering athletic equipment and justify your reason.

44. Enumerate suggestions for the special care of equipment in-season and out-of-season.

45. Develop a marking system for athletic equipment.

46. Explain the importance of correct storage of equipment and analyze some of the methods.

47. Select and describe several important and recent developments in athletic equipment.

48. Enumerate the duties of the equipment manager, the trainer, and the team physician.

49. Describe an acceptable plan for storing, requisitioning, and delivering athletic supplies in a large school system.

50. Indicate what is meant by the statement: Equipment should conform to specifications and what are the implications.

51. Explain the advantages and disadvantages of buying athletic equipment through a purchasing agent.

52. List the arguments for and against central purchasing of athletic equipment.

ACTIVITIES

1. Select one of the new synthetic materials used in athletic equipment and trace its use under as many conditions as possible and the type of care it requires as opposed to the old type of material.

2. Visit both a large and small high school. Examine the system of checking equipment in both schools.

3. Suppose you were appointed director of athletics in a large suburban high school. Set up a workable system of purchasing athletic equipment.

4. Visit a large high school and talk with the person in charge of equipment.

5. Design an equipment storage room and a drying room.

6. Obtain copies of purchase orders, requisitions, and vouchers from several high schools. Examine them as to similarity and use.

7. Interview several athletic directors in large and small schools and obtain from them information relative to purchasing procedures.

8. Seek the opinions of several high school coaches and athletic directors relative

to putting athletic equipment purchases out for bid.

9. Arrange for an athletic equipment salesman to talk to the class.

10. Obtain several athletic equipment sales catalogues from different companies. Compare the price and quality of the same merchandise.

11. Develop an equipment form for dispensing athletic equipment.

12. Visit an athletic equipment wholesale store and factory.

13. Form a panel of students and arrange a debate on whose responsibility it is to do research on athletic equipment, the coach or equipment manufacturer.

14. Debate the best methods of transporting athletic equipment on out-of-town trips.

15. Debate the issue: Equipment should be purchased from several concerns because this creates competitive bidding.

16. Debate the issue: All equipment should be purchased by the athletic director or by the school purchasing agent.

17. Debate the issue: All athletic equipment should be purchased through the athletic director rather than through central purchasing at the school district level.

18. Formulate a plan for the distribution of athletic equipment.

SUGGESTED READINGS

1. Athletic Goods Manufacturing Association, 805 Merchandise Mart, Chicago, Illinois.

2. Bucher, Charles: *The Administration of School and College Health and Physical Education Programs.* St. Louis, Mosby, 1967.

3. Burrup, Percy: *Modern High School Administration.* New York, Har-Row, 1961.

4. Collins, Dan: A workable athletic equipment budget. *The Athletic Journal,* April, 1971.

5. Czarnicki, John: Eliminate equipment shortages. *Scholastic Coach,* January, 1971.

6. Forsythe, Charles and Keller, Irvin: *Administration of High School Athletics.* Englewood Cliffs, P-H, 1972.

7. Gabrielson, Alexander: *Sports and Recreation Facilities for School and Community.* Englewood Cliffs, P-H, 1958.

8. George, Jack F., and Lehmann, Harry A.: *School Athletic Administration.* New York, Har-Row, 1966.

9. Higdon, Hal: How to reduce athletic injuries. *School Management,* December, 1968.

10. Hixson, Chalmer: *The Administration of Inter-Scholastic Athletics.* New York, Lowell Pratt, 1967.

11. Hughes, William, French, Esther, and Lehsten, Nelson: *Administration of Physical Education for Schools and Colleges.* New York, Ronald, 1962.

12. Kaczmarek, John: Equipment care cardinal obligation. *American School Board Journal,* August, 1966.

13. Lacy, E.H.: The issuing of equipment. *Athletic Journal,* November, 1956.

14. Lande, Lion: The selection of athletic equipment. *Coach and Athlete,* January, 1966.

15. Oosting, Bernard: Does sports equipment require a manager? *The Nations Schools,* May, 1964.

16. Ralston, John and White, Mike: *Coaching Today's Athlete,* Palo Alto, Natl Pr, 1971.

17. Rawlings Sporting Goods Company, *Athletic Equipment Digest,* 1966.

18. Resick, Matthew, Siedel, Beverly, and Mason, James: *Modern Administrative Practices in Physical Education and Athletics.* Massachusetts, A-W, 1970.

19. Roe, William: *School Business Management.* New York, McGraw, 1961.

20. Stier, William: Policies concerning procurement of equipment and supplies. *Coach and Athlete,* August, 1968.

21. Voltmer, Edward and Esslinger, Arthur: *Organization and Administration of Physical Education.* New York, Appleton, 1967.

22. Whited, Clark V.: These purchasing pointers help cut sports supply costs. *American School and University,* August 8, 1968.

23. Williams, Jesse and Brownell, Clifford: *The Administration of Health, Education and Physical Education.* Philadelphia, Saunders, 1951.

24. Wilson Sporting Goods Co.: *How to Select and Order Athletic Equipment,* River Grove, Illinois.

CHAPTER 13

Crowd Control

ADMINISTRATORS OF HIGH school athletics have become increasingly aware and alarmed during the past few years over the behavior of spectators during and after athletic contests between schools. Many schools have discontinued all night football games and have limited spectators to students only to all athletic contests. Vandalism, muggings, fighting, rioting, beatings, and even murders are frequent occurrences during and after these athletic contests. Games are constantly being disrupted, players are harassed and viciously attacked for no apparent reason. This has continued without abatement to the point that many schools have considered complete abandonment of their athletic program.

The conduct of spectators at interscholastic athletic contests has developed to the point that it is almost out of control. O'Neil verifies the concern of many sports-minded enthusiasts regarding the behavior of spectators at athletic events. He describes the lack of spectator control as one of the disturbing trends in today's athletic program. He feels, however, that many of the problems are caused from sources outside of the school's control. Nevertheless, the school must assume the responsibility and leadership in helping to remedy this situation. The blame can be placed partially on the fact that although the competing players are benefiting from a true learning experience and displaying sportsmanship, their fellow students are, as spectators, not gaining this experience at all. If this situation is to be corrected, then school administrators, athletic directors, and staff members all must combine their efforts to remedy it by assuming the responsibility to promote sportsmanship in both school and community.[1]

The following comment was made by Luby[2] which illustrates the danger to spectators and at the same time emphasizes the seriousness of crowd control as well as the threat to interscholastic athletic programs:

> An explosion of social dynamite in the mid-1950s in Detroit resulted in the elimination of most night games in the public schools' athletic program. A more recent explosion resulted in even more stringent athletic program policies and procedures.
>
> In March, 1965, national wire services carried a picture of an unusual basketball game, a district finals in the Michigan State Championship Basketball tournament involving two Detroit area schools. The picture showed two teams playing a tournament game on a Saturday morning without any spectators in the stands.
>
> The decision to ban spectators had been forced by violence which occurred several nights earlier when nine spectators were stabbed while leaving this same

[1]O'Neil, Lee, "Spectator Control—Whose Responsibility?" *The Coaching Clinic* October, 1969), p. 29.

[2]Luby, Robert, "Detroit Resolves Problems," *School Board Journal* (August 1966), p. 30.

gymnasium at the conclusion of an earlier tournament game. The violence had tragic consequences for more than the nine innocent victims who were assaulted. The entire community was aroused, and an air of bitterness and excitement was created which indicted an entire student body and threatened the racial peace of a large city.

Individuals act differently while a member of a crowd than they would act if alone. The social scientists explain that the frequency of antisocial behavior during and after athletic contests is the result of the feeling that the individual gains by being a member of a large, sometimes strange group of people. Any individual inhibitions that a person might have, if he is acting on his own, will be completely different if the individual is associated with a crowd. Any feelings of hostility the individual might have are easily triggered by the fact that his identity is easy to hide in a crowd.

A crowd of people enables the individual to commit certain acts which he can blame on the entire group. He, therefore, can use the crowd as a disguise to commit acts which, if done alone, would get him into trouble. Crowds at athletic contests are usually boisterous and unruly because of the very fact that they are watching a physical contest between opponents who are trying to win the contest. It is natural, therefore, that the spectators might become physical in one way or another. Very few constructive suggestions have been offered to administrators of athletic contests for use in successful crowd control.

There are several indirect methods of handling crowds. (1) Prevent a focal point by attempting to change the object of attention from one subject or object to another. (2) Make it difficult for the crowd to focus on one particular object by keeping them from milling. (3) Try and use various methods in attempting to reach these goals. (4) Use every conceivable method to alleviate crowd anxiety.

Frank,[3] Superintendent of Schools in Toledo, Ohio, voiced his concern about protecting their athletic program from being discontinued as a result of the increasing misconduct of a few spectators. He felt that athletics was an opportunity for the community to come together, to develop an interest in their schools and work together toward a common cause. The program initiated attempted to educate the fans to the philosophy of the school system. A program was developed in three areas in an attempt to prevent unruly behavior by spectators at athletic events. These areas included education, involvement and enforcement. The program relied on the cooperation of students, parents, police, and the courts. Before each major sports season, the Commissioner of Athletics brought together all of the principals, athletic directors, head coaches, game officials, police, and fire and city officials to discuss preventive steps to be taken at each contest.

Causes of Problems

The past few years have brought forth many changes in the attitude of people toward law and order and other peoples' rights. Many young people now make deliberate attempts to ignore, abuse, and ridicule what they call the system. This attitude makes it necessary for school administrators to establish and maintain proper behavior of both spectators and players at all athletic contests. They must first of all determine the primary causes of these disturbances and stamp them out before they have had a chance to multiply into a full-fledged conflagration.

[3]Frank, Dick, "Spectator Sports, Opportunity or Nightmare," *National Association of Secondary School Principals* (May, 1971) , p. 185.

The Sixth National Conference of City and County Directors[4] has listed the following causes of crowd control problems:

1. Lack of anticipation of, and preventive planning for, possible trouble.
2. Lack of proper facilities.
3. Poor communication resulting in lack of information.
4. Lack of involvement of one or more of the following: school administration, faculty, student body, parents, community, press, and law enforcement agencies.
5. Lack of respect for authority and property.
6. Attendance at games of youth under the influence of narcotics.
7. Increased attitude of permissiveness.
8. School dropouts, recent graduates, and outsiders.

Precontest Arrangements

Precontest arrangements are of extreme importance in crowd control planning. Prior to the beginning of any athletic season an administrative meeting could be held which could include athletic and administrative personnel. This could include the following persons: assistant administrators, athletic directors, administrators of special services, student activities director, custodial people, head coach, school health service, concessions director, police counselor of the school, local police, cheerleader sponsor, band director, safety committee chairman, and student representatives. The larger the school system, the more people there are to become involved. Proper precontest management will not only assure the administrative success of the contest but will make it an enjoyable experience for players and spectators alike. Regardless of cautious plans, crowd control still presents a problem.

A survey by Kozak[5] was sent to seventy selected athletic directors across the nation asking about practices for spectator control. Based on a 75 percent return, results were as follows: disturbances at athletic events occurred occasionally in 41 percent of the systems; seldom in 50 percent, and frequently in none. The survey also revealed that 50 percent of the school systems evaluated attitudes of coaches, players, and spectators following the game performance, 61 percent evaluated the quality of officiating by coaches and 15 percent evaluated the officiating by the athletic commission, 65 percent established programs of human relations within and between schools, 82 percent reviewed facilities for athletic events for maximum safety and security, and 59 percent established a local athletic advisory committee to review and recommend policies for athletic events.

Hartford, Connecticut's Supervisor of Health and Physical Education, Robert M. Pate,[6] believes that crowd control at athletic contests is one of the most pressing responsibilities of the director of health, physical education, and recreation.

> Ideally, we function to provide a vigorous physical activity program that is geared to the needs of all pupils. We aim to reach all children with a good health education program. We try our best to make our programs such that pupils will understand the value of physical activity and enjoy it enough to continue participation for years to come.
>
> Too often, however, our total programs are judged by the 'success' of the athletic teams at the high school level. School boards or city councils look at gate receipts from athletic contests when setting school budget figures. We could

[4]Sixth National Conference of City and County Directors (Washington, D.C. December 8-10, 1968), *Approaches to Problems of Public School Administration in Health, Physical Education, and Recreation* (AAPER Washington, D.C., 1968), p. 17.

[5]Kozak, George, "Crowd Control at Athletic Events," *Journal of Health, Physical Education, and Recreation* (April, 1969), p. 29.

[6]Pate, Robert, "Crowd Control at Athletic Events," *Journal of Health, Physical Education and Recreation*, April, 1969, p. 30.

TABLE LXIV
CHECK LIST OF ARRANGEMENTS AND PREPARATIONS
FOR SPECTATOR CONDUCT AND CONTROL IN A LARGE CITY

Game: Football _____ vs _____

Field _____ Time _____ Date _____

ESTIMATE OF TENSION (Check one) HEAVY _____ MEDIUM _____ LIGHT _____

Check each item below indicating attention given; remarks, if any.

STUDENT INFORMATION AND EDUCATION

_____ Sports Assembly _____
_____ Transporation Information _____
_____ Field Seating Arrangement _____
_____ Field Dispersal Plan _____

FACULTY PERSONNEL

_____ Faculty Representative in Charge _____
_____ Explanation of duties; Station Assignment: (Field, Building, Bleachers)
_____ Pre-Game _____
_____ During Game _____
_____ After Game _____

STADIUM AND FIELD MANAGEMENT

_____ Faculty Representative in Charge _____
_____ Seating Arrangements _____
_____ First Aid Station _____
_____ Comfort Stations _____
_____ Locker Rooms _____
_____ Ticket Sellers _____
_____ Ticket Takers _____
_____ Gatemen _____
_____ Pass Gate _____
_____ Barricades and Signs _____

POLICE DEPARTMENT SERVICE

Request for a Detail via Director's Office
_____ Local Field Control Plan Discussed with Police _____
_____ Dispersal Plans Discussed with Police _____
_____ Name of Police Officer in Charge at Game _____

TRANSPORTATION ARRANGEMENTS

_____ Local Request from School Authorities _____
_____ Local Request from City _____
_____ Date _____

Signature of Person Completing Check List

_____

High School

succeed in some of our ideal duties, but if we fail in properly administering athletic contests, we can be so severely criticized that we become ineffective in our overall function. These are the hard facts of life.

Responsibility of Crowd Control

The high school principal is usually the person to whom the responsibility of crowd control is given. He may delegate responsibility and usually does, but ultimately he is the one who must assume the final responsibility. This is part of his job. Therefore, he must delegate these responsibilities in such a way that he will be able to pinpoint the failure of any one person not doing his job. It is natural, therefore, for the principal to lean heavily upon the athletic director and expect him to assume a very large share of this responsibility. It is evident, then, that crowd control at athletic contests rests in the hands of the athletic director. Therefore, it is his responsibility to call the meetings of all those people who may be involved in one way or another with crowd control. He should delegate the responsibility of each person and be sure that they understand these responsibilities and exactly what is expected of them.

It is the director of athletic's responsibility to develop a set of procedures and guidelines to be used for crowd control at all athletic contests. The Division of Health, Physical Education, and Safety of the Chicago Public Schools has developed a checklist of arrangements and preparations for spectator control which can be used with modifications in any school system.

O'Dell[7] makes the following comment in regard to supervision of athletic contests

in the Minneapolis, Minnesota Schools:

> The example that the coaches, cheerleaders, and team set has a determinative effect on adult behavior. Plain clothes and uniform policemen generally are assigned to control adult conduct. Lavatories are policed. Campaigns are conducted to have parents attend night games with their children.
>
> It is highly desirable to have entrances and exits for spectators at opposite ends of the fields. The same procedure should be followed for team entry and exit. The city police are notified of teams that are playing. The police in turn will patrol the area, including bus stops, from the home school to and from the playing site. School buses hauling students are highly desirable. These, of course, are chaperoned.
>
> While the procedures as stated are of benefit in correcting deviations from established procedures, the basic strength of any successful program of spectator control resolves itself into careful preparation through the in-school instructional program.

Jorndt[8] feels that both the home and the visiting school share equal responsibility for the organization and follow-up of all operations concerning spectator conduct and control. A continuous program of educating the student should be carried out throughout the year. School assemblies should be used to give students the necessary information about transportation and seating arrangements and to talk to them about personal conduct at the game. Coaches should talk about the sportsmanship of the team members and spectators at every opportunity. Faculty members should help out in every way possible. Faculty and police should be in constant contact throughout the contest. All should work together.

[7]O'Dell, Griffith, "Administrative Vigilance Pays," *American School Board Journal* (August, 1966), p. 32.

[8]Jorndt, Louis, "A Plan of Operation for Spectator Conduct and Control at Football and Basketball Games," *School Activities* (September, 1968), p. 17.

Personnel Selection and Responsibilities

The selection of personnel and the delegation of their responsibilities in crowd control is of the utmost importance. Just what persons should be selected? Should these persons be from within the school system or from without?

Kozak's survey[9] of seventy selected athletic directors across the nation reports that 51 percent of the reporting school systems had faculty supervision at the athletic contests; 25 percent of the schools paid their faculty for the supervision; 5 percent reported no school personnel used at athletic contests.

This study indicates that there are still many schools that use faculty to help supervise athletic contests. There are, however, several disadvantages in using faculty. Perhaps the main one is that they are not trained in crowd control tactics and students sometimes resent them in situations outside the classroom. The students feel that they are not under the direct control of school officials at athletic contests and as a result may even attempt to provoke a teacher with whom they have had trouble in a classroom situation. Usually faculty will have better control in the small school and less in the larger suburban type school.

Types of Personnel

School

There are many persons who are directly or indirectly responsible for crowd control in the school system. Some of these people include the following.

Coaches

The coach plays a very important role in crowd control. He sets the tempo of spectator behavior by his actions from the bench. He can show his displeasure by his antics and actions and can incite the spectators into frenzied action. The following excerpt from a newspaper and written by a high school principal,[10] is a splendid illustration of the importance of the coach in crowd control.

> At times during close and hard fought ball games, actions of a coach or players can engender bitterness and retaliation on the part of the crowd. For these embarrassing situations, the coach should have to answer to his administration, board of education and community . . . . The coach is responsible for the attitude of his team, his players' reactions to the referees, and the immediate postgame control of those under his jurisdiction. It is the actual staging of the game which gives the coach his shining hour. All preparation that goes into the game plan, no matter how carefully detailed, can be useless if the team is not disciplined.
>
> To be competitive in today's world one must be self controlled in crisis. Nothing teaches alertness and discipline as well as the actual competition of the game. Young athletes learn how to compete. They come to know that every game in life has rules and expectations that must be followed. They learn to give all they have to win and to take defeat with the same grace with which they have earned victory. Discipline of the team goes hand in hand with the coach's own example of self-control. No matter how well organized a coach may be during the week, if he is not well organized at critical moments during the game his demonstration before a crowd can become a foolish travesty. All this, in competition, comes under the scrutiny of an audience which sometimes can be critical and even hostile. In the time of crisis, the coach is definitely coaching more than his team. He has the responsibility not only to his athletes, but also to the student body, to his administration, and

---

[9]Kozak, George, "Crowd Control," *Journal of Health, Physical Education, and Recreation* (April, 1966) , p. 29.

[10]Walters, George, "Letters to the Editor," *The DeKalb Daily Chronicle* (February 25, 1969) , p. 8.

to the community in which he lives.

The spirit of competition is one of the great things in our American society. While physical facilities at a given institution may be the greatest, it is the man who is honored with the name of coach who ties the whole thing together. A well-controlled coach in a cow pasture is better for society than the dubiously dedicated coach with the greatest team in the country.

The coach in many cases holds the key to the action by the spectator. His actions before, during, and after the contest will have a direct affect on the spectators watching the contest. He should be aware of this and govern his actions accordingly. The general tone he sets and the feeling he instills in the student body will to a large extent determine the conduct of the students during and after the game.

Parris[11] has this to say about the influence of the coach on crowd control:

> Coaches influence not only the conduct of players under their direction but also that of the student spectator, school faculty, parents of squad members, and interested citizens who attend athletic contests. Since the coach is so influential in setting the tone of conduct, he must visibly show that he values self restraint, fair play and sportsmanship conduct.

The latest interpretations of the National High School Federation Basketball Rules say a coach may walk in front of his bench. However, this does not give him license to agitate unsportsmanlike conduct by yelling, throwing towels or otherwise acting in a manner unbefitting a well-disciplined leader. When there is a question of interpretation of a rule, the coach's conduct should not inordinately excite the spectators. Public dissension on a ruling is one of the major causes of crowd discontent. For this reason, a coach should be careful how he approaches the official for the discussion and how he acts during the discussion. The coach must be sensitive to explosive situations.

Kozak[12] makes the following observation regarding the coach's influence:

> The coaches and players should be exceptionally aware of the influence they have on school behavior, not only at games attended, but also in their daily behavior around school. Coaches and athletes giving talks at neighborhood elementary and junior high schools will minimize difficulties in the neighborhood where the contest is held. Many of our problems are caused by junior high pupils who reside in the area of the athletic field.

Players

The players themselves can exert a tremendous influence on the general behavior of the spectator at athletics contests. It is important, therefore, that the players should be taught the real purpose of athletics. They should be schooled to accept the official's decisions and show the proper respect to them. They should be taught to play hard, play to win and yet, at the same time, show good sportsmanship, fair play, and accept defeat when it comes like a gentleman. This kind of attitude on the part of the players has a decided effect on the spectators, coaches, opposing players and officials.

Parris[13] stresses the importance of player conduct in the following statement:

> The player's conduct can influence actions of spectators, therefore, it places a serious responsibility on the athlete. The player who concentrates on the game and takes little notice of the audi-

[11]Parris, Wendell, "Conduct of Coaches, Players, Officials Helps to Guide Fans," *American School Board Journal* (August, 1966), p. 33.

[12]Kozak, George, "Practices and Methods of Crowd Control at School Athletic Events," *Approaches to Problems of Public School Administration of Health, Physical Education and Recreation* (Washington, D.C., AAHPER, December 8-10, 1968), p. 8.

[13]Parris, Wendell, "*Conduct of Coaches, Players, Officials Help to Guide Fans.*"

ence is less likely to behave poorly on the court or playing field and thus arouse the spectators.

Spectators will tend not to 'boo' and 'hiss' if they see players conducting themselves with proper decorum and good manners. When spectators see a player respecting the ruling of an official, shaking hands with a player on the team of an intense rival, helping an injured opponent or congratulating a team for its performance, they quickly get the idea that good spectator conduct is the only acceptable conduct.

Players should avoid 'show boating,' using unsportsman like gestures or harassing an opponent. Players on the bench should not heckle opponents or officials. They should cooperate with officials at all times. Basketball players should raise one hand without gestures when a personal foul is called on them. Players should avoid 'rabbit ears' or any invitation for spectator disapproval by showing feigned surprise or irritation.

The players must assume their responsibility in crowd control. They can do their part by abiding by the rules, showing their respect for their opponents, and attempting in every way possible to display good citizenship. The players can also help by refraining from fighting for any reason whatsoever. This has become a major concern the past few years. This situation must be corrected and Mr. Clifford Fagan,[14] Executive Secretary of the National Federation of State High School Associations, has recommended the following remedies:

1. The head of the school and the director of athletics must impress upon the coach that fighting by players will not be tolerated. Coaches must support the premise that an athletic contest is an educational experience and fighting is not a part of it.
2. Coaches must accept that one of their principal obligations is to control the

members of their squads.
3. Coaches must make certain players representing their schools do not intimidate nor attempt to intimidate opponents or officials.
4. Athletic directors must make certain they engage and then aggressively support only those officials who administer the game according to the letter and spirit of the rules.
5. Those who are responsible for hiring athletic coaches must engage only coaches who have the proper athletic philosophy for inter-scholastic competition and they must know what the philosophy of the coach is before they hire him.

Faculty Supervisors

Many schools use faculty members for crowd control. However, not all teachers are well suited for this type of duty. They must be strong disciplinarians and respected by the students; otherwise, the students will take advantage of them. The faculty members must also be well known by the students and be able to communicate with them. Some schools are now using women faculty members with considerable success as they, in turn, will communicate well with the girls. O'Dell[15] states that:

Minneapolis Public Schools believe that spectator control at athletic contests require continual vigilance. The system has for years used teachers as supervisors of students along with paid uniform police. The supervisor should adhere to the following suggestions.
The supervisors:
1. Should arrive early, be on duty for the entire game and remain until the playing site area has been cleared.
2. Should move about wherever the students congregate.
3. No smoking is permitted in the arena proper.
4. Drinking alcoholic beverages will not be tolerated in any area.
5. Throwing debris is an annoyance

[14]Fagan, Clifford, "Players Brawls Must Be Eliminated," *Physical Educator* (May, 1972), p. 59.

[15]O'Dell, Griffith, "Administrative Vigilance Pays."

which the supervisor should see and stop.

6. Fighting of any kind is not to be permitted.
7. Supervisor identification should be made known to the policeman on duty in order to have police help in handling difficult situations.
8. Supervisors should be alert for abusive or profane language by any spectator.
9. A report should be made to the school athletic director giving the names of any students who need to be checked upon return to the school.
10. Each supervisor is to wear an identifing arm band.
11. Only official signs must be permitted.

The Council of City and County Directors[16] has suggested the use of supervisory school personnel as a partial solution to the problem of crowd control. The following criteria are suggested:

1. Select carefully teacher supervisors who are attentive and alert to signs of possible trouble.
2. Identify faculty members by arm bands or other means.
3. Provide for communication by means of walkie-talkie systems.
4. Assign some faculty members to sit behind the visiting fans; this reduces verbal harassment of visitors.
5. Employ paid ticket takers and paid chaperons to mingle strategically among the crowd and to remain on duty throughout the game, including halftime.
6. Issue passes to junior high physical education teachers to provide more adult supervision.

Use of Out-of-Season Coaches

Coaches of out-of-season sports can be used effectively for crowd control during

[16]Proceedings of Sixth National Conference of City and County Directors, "Approaches to Problems of Public School Administration in Health, Physical Education and Recreation," *American Association of Health, Physical Education and Recreation* (December 10, 1968), p. 20.

athletic contests. Most of the coaches will be known by the students. The coaches are also well versed in handling students and are well acquainted with athletic fans. They usually know about the athletic facilities and are able to answer many questions about facilities, personnel, and the different rules and regulations which have to do with the contest that the ordinary faculty member cannot answer.

Custodial Staff

The custodial staff is an important link between faculty and students. They usually identify very well with both. The custodians' role in crowd control is confined mainly to facilities and equipment. He should confine his efforts to these areas and not attempt to supervise students or fans. This is not his job. However, he can help to make the contest run smoothly by being available to replace broken equipment, sweep floors, etc.

Student Organizations

Students are assuming more responsibility, and rightly so, in all phases of education. By giving them this responsibility it indicates that the school authorities have confidence in them. They should not, however, be expected to take the place of faculty supervisors or the police at athletic contests. There are many tasks connected with crowd control that they can perform if given a plan of action. There are several student organizations that lend themselves to this type of service.

LETTERMAN'S CLUB: The members of this organization may act as ushers. The members should wear their letter sweaters so that the spectators can easily identify them. They should be stationed in strategic areas and remain there throughout the contest. Their very presence will tend to have a steadying influence on the crowd. Razor suggests the use of letterclub members as "hosts" to teams from other schools as a means of promoting good public relations. The athletes would be representing different sports. Their responsibilities could include directing visiting teams to lockers, playing areas, washrooms, etc. The hosts would stay with the team and be in the approximate area of the visiting team during the contest.[17]

The Minneapolis, Minnesota school system has for a number of years used students to supervise at athletic contests. The schools have done an excellent job through homerooms and student councils. They believe in the education of the young people through the athletic program and therefore feel that the students themselves can be used as leaders to keep down rowdiness at all athletic events.

PEP CLUB: Usually the members of the pep club sit in one area or cheering section of the bleachers. Their actions and conduct will have a decided affect on the crowd. They can set the tone of crowd behavior. This, along with urging the team to a greater performance, is their main function.

BOOSTER CLUB: This organization is usually composed of sportsminded people in the community who are interested in the athletic program. The booster club people will be able to help control the crowd if they have the respect of the students and the paying public. Most of the people in a booster club will be concerned with the type of activity that goes along with an athletic event. They should be made aware of the rules and regulations that are to be enforced. The social conduct of the crowd is what the boosters are concerned about. The athletic event may serve as a laboratory for learning the ideals concerned with

personal respect and group consciousness. The boosters should try and show generous treatment to opponents, fine expressions of sportsmanship, generosity, and other social qualities.[18]

The booster club should:

1. Try and safeguard the health of each person present.
2. Display a good attitude toward opponent's play.
3. Be leaders in praise of officiating.
4. Be friendly to hostile people so they cool down.
5. Be a guide to behavior at the athletic event.

CHEERLEADERS: The purpose of the cheerleaders at an athletic event is to create enthusiasm from the audience and inspire them to cheer the team on to victory or encourage them in the face of defeat. Cheerleaders can, however, do a great deal to help crowd control. They must be given instruction and help in this particular function and realize their importance in this area. The atmosphere the cheerleaders create will be carried by the crowd (be it good or bad) almost as much as that of the coach. Because of their direct contact with the crowd, their importance in crowd control cannot be minimized.

Bolden[19] stresses the importance of cheerleaders in crowd control in the following statement "Well-trained cheerleaders, choosing the right cheer at the right time, can have a tremendous influence on proper spectator conduct. Their primary function should be to stimulate and control crowd response. The atmosphere the cheerleaders create will carry over to the spectators, be

---

[17]Razor, Jack, "Hosts for athletic contests," *The Clearing House* (January, 1971), p. 305.

[18]Hixson, Chalmer, *The Administration of Interscholastic Athletics* (New York, J. Lowell Pratt and Co., 1967), p. 138.

[19]Bolden, Frank, "The Role of Cheerleaders," *Journal of Health, Physical Education, and Recreation* (April, 1969), p. 29.

it good or bad."

Parris[20] stresses the fact that, "the cheerleaders are an important part of any athletic contest. They can be either a great help or a hindrance depending upon their training. They should realize that their primary purpose is to stimulate and control crowd response. They are not there to entertain the fans."

The cheerleaders help control the contest by:

1. Introducing themselves to the visiting cheerleaders.
2. Helping the visiting cheerleaders find the facilities that are available.
3. Keeping the audience busy cheering.
4. Showing pep and enthusiasm.
5. Stop any booing or other unwanted activity.
6. Facing the crowd when doing cheers.
7. Talk so the crowd can understand.
8. If the crowd starts any unwanted activity, the cheerleaders should start a cheer so the booing will subside.

The cheerleaders should fully understand their role. They should never take their position lightly and one of the criteria used in selecting them should be emotional stability in the face of adversity. Parris[21] stressed the importance of the position of cheerleaders in the following statement:

> There should be no 'horseplay' on the court or playing field at halftime. All cheers should be under the leadership of the cheerleaders. Pep bands and noise-makers such as bells, horns and clackers should be discouraged at indoor contests. Well-trained cheerleaders, choosing the right cheer at the right time, can have a tremendous influence on proper spectator conduct. Their primary function should be to stimulate and control crowd response. It is not their function to put on a show or per-

---

[20]Parris, Wendell, "Conduct of Coaches, Players, Officials Helps to Guide Fans."

[21]*Ibid.*

form for the audience. They are cheerleaders and their job is to lead the crowd in cheers, not to entertain with dance routines. The cheerleaders' gestures should be pleasing to watch and easy to follow. Firm, definite movements instead of little wiggles and shakes are appropriate. Care should be taken in making certain that words used in a cheer are not suggestive or have a connection which would inflame an audience.

Principals should insist that pupils remain silent when the other team is cheering or being penalized. Pupils should be cautioned against throwing objects on the floor or playing field. This is not only unsportsmanlike but extremely dangerous.

STUDENT COUNCIL: The student council is usually composed of the student leaders within the student body. The council can and should accept part of the responsibility in establishing methods of crowd control at athletic contests. The student council should take the responsibility of organizing the student body and should rely heavily on the individual student members. The council should establish stated objectives which represent the thinking of the students in regard to accepted conduct and behavior at an athletic contest.

Community

There are many people in the community who are more than willing to help out in the supervision of crowds at an athletic contest. The use of people in the community for this purpose can help to prevent many incidents from occurring because spectators know them and are, therefore, reluctant to start trouble. When community organizations are used for crowd control purposes, care should be taken to inform those people involved of their specific duties and to keep them under the direction and supervision of the school's administration. Only those people should be used who will act in a professional manner and be aware of their responsibility. Several organizations that can be used in this capacity are booster clubs, mothers and fathers clubs, etc.

The Council of City and County Directors[22] suggest some approaches to solving the crowd control problem by informing the community and doing the following:

1. Request coaches and athletic directors to talk to service groups and other community groups.
2. Stress the need for exemplary conduct of coaches at all times.
3. Invite community leaders (nonschool people) to attend athletic events.
4. Post on all available notice boards around town, in factories and other public places, posters showing the Sportsmanship Code of Ethics and Guidelines in brief.
5. Release constructive information and positive statements to news media and request publication of brief guidelines on sports pages.
6. Provide news media with pertinent information as to ways in which the community may directly and indirectly render assistance in the crowd control problem.
7. Avoid overstressing the winning of games.
8. Discontinue double headers and triple headers.
9. After-game incidents away from the proximity of the stadium or gymnasium are out of the control of school officials, but cause bad public reaction.

Police

The use of the local police department to help in crowd control at athletic events is more common in large cities than in small communities. This is understandable. If police are used, the officers in charge of special services in relation to athletic con-

tests should be notified well in advance of the day of the game regarding provision for police supervision in and outside of the field, stadium, or gymnasium. This may be accomplished by an informative letter, previous arrangements from past years, and the preseason meeting. This information should include the size and nature of the crowd anticipated and whether trouble is expected and from what source. Many games have more tension surrounding them than others. It is also necessary for the police to know the transportation routes and the general plan for crowd dispersal after the game.

The faculty representative in charge of the contest should identify himself to the police officer in charge sometime before the game starts. They should, at that time, discuss their plans for crowd control and if any changes from the previously agreed upon plan is made, it should be done at this time.

The police can perform many duties in crowd control, such as controlling the flow of automobile traffic and supervising at the ticket gate. The use of the police in dispersing disturbing groups is essential. The police should be dressed in their uniforms and the salary they receive will depend upon the agreement made between the school officials and the chief of police. The sight of uniformed police officers at any contest will give spectators, participants, and school officials a sense of protection, safety, and control.

Luby[23] suggests the following rules to follow to obtain liaison between schools and the police at athletic contests. It is essential that:

1. A meeting be scheduled at the start of each school year between top-level school and police officials to routinely

---

[22]Proceedings of Sixth National Conference of City and County Directors, "Approaches to Problems of Public School Administration in HPER" (December 10, 1968), p. 19.

---

[23]Luby, Robert, "Detroit Resolves Problems," p. 31.

review the details of athletic event supervision. Police and faculty assignments would be made as a result of this review with specific supervisory responsibilities spelled out for each professional. High school principals or their delegates were charged with official responsibilities for the conduct of the game.

2. Football and basketball games be scheduled so that not more than one game shall be scheduled within one police precinct on any one day. This would relieve pressures on police precincts and permit better coverage of games.

3. Loitering near athletic events should be eliminated by police, since the no-gate-sale policy would permit only people with tickets to be in the vicinity of athletic facilities.

The Council of City and County Directors[24] suggest the following ways of involving law enforcement personnel:

1. Police and other security personnel should be strategically located so as to afford the best possible control.

2. Law enforcement professionals should handle *all* enforcement and disciplining of spectators.

3. Strength in force may be shown by appearance of several policemen, motorcycles, police cruise cars, etc. at and near the site of the game.

4. Women police may be stationed in women's rest roms.

5. Civil defense organizations could patrol parking areas.

6. A faculty member from the visiting school may be used as a liaison with police and local faculty in identifying visiting students.

7. Attendants, police, county sheriffs, deputies should be in uniform. Uniformed authority figures command greater respect.

Private Agencies

Another selection of personnel and the most well-known professional organization

[24]Proceedings of Sixth National Conference of City and County Directors, p. 20.

that can be used at all types of athletic events is the Andy Frain Crowd Engineering Inc. with its well-dressed and mannerly ushers who courteously handle over 30,000,-000 persons annually at sports, political, and industrial events. Andy Frain has offices in seventeen cities throughout the United States. Professional organizations, and there are several, are best used at athletic contests as ticket takers or ushers for reserved seating. They can be used when tournaments are being held or championship games are played. Their use is more common in large cities. These types of organizations believe that crowd behavior is less predictable than crowd flow. They have well-devised methods for outwitting gate crashers. To do this, they place a man at the door who admits only those who show tickets, another man fifteen feet back to collect tickets and a troubleshooter roving between them.

Communication

Excellent communication is absolutely necessary to assure and maintain crowd control. Anytime a crowd is expected at an athletic event, all supervisors and officials should be present with proper identification. This is very important because of the aspect of authority which these people hold and in turn communicate to the crowd. There should be no question as to the status of this authority and the spectators should be well aware of this. Proper identification also provides a better opportunity for the officials to help those people who are in need or to answer any questions.

The size of the school will have a direct bearing on the type of communication system that should be used. Most of the smaller schools have little need for identification of the supervisors because they are already known to most of the spectators.

Means of Identification of Supervisors

There are various ways by which supervisors may be identified, among them being the use of buttons or cards with the word OFFICIAL printed on them. The buttons may be pinned to the coat lapel. Cards with the word OFFICIAL printed on them may either be pinned or placed in the upper pocket of the coat. Blazers or jackets may be worn for identification purposes and some schools use athletes who wear their letter sweaters.

Use of Communication Systems

If crowd control is to be accomplished, communication is very important. A system of communication should, therefore, be established which can cope with all the eventualities which accompany the handling of crowds. Most important is the use of telephones because they are both accessible and economical. Other means of communication are walkie-talkies which are used quite extensively by many police departments. Short-wave radios are also used, but the cost is prohibitive in many instances. Hand and light signals may also be used for directing traffic.

Physical Factors Affecting Crowd Control

Every person attending an athletic contest, including players and coaches, have a right to expect protection from physical violence. However, in the past few years there have been many occasions when this was not true. Oftentimes, the facilities themselves help produce situations which are conducive to violence in one form or another. Therefore, the physical plant and facility factors are extremely important in crowd control. Some of these factors are as follows.

Signs

Most people arrive at an athletic contest just a short time before it begins. In so doing, they create a problem if they are not completely familiar with the surroundings. Many will be attempting to find out where they are going to sit. It is, therefore, important that signs are properly placed so that the people are kept moving along smoothly and long waits in line are eliminated. This tends to aggravate many people and makes them restless, short-tempered, and irritable.

Exits

The exits should be numerous and well marked. It should be made possible for the home and visitors' fans to leave by different exits. The fans should be separated as much as possible.

Concessions

The concession stand has created many crowd control problems at athletic contests. On the other hand, it has been instrumental in giving the spectators something to do at halftime, a period where there is nothing to do and trouble could start. Tempers could erupt. If there are too few concession stands and people need to wait in line, they will be late in returning to the game. In order to prevent hard feelings, the exact price of all items sold at the stand should be posted. Care should be taken that all items are palatable. The cold drinks should be cold and the hot drinks, hot. It is better to have more than enough food than too little. Shortages create hard feelings and could result in some disorder.

Concession Personnel

Pleasant, personable, and alert persons should be employed in the concession stands.

Rest Rooms

An adequate number of rest rooms should be available and they should be clean and airy. These rest rooms should be clearly marked and conveniently located. Proper supervision of these rest rooms should be provided as trouble often starts here, especially if rooters from both teams use the same rest rooms. Oftentimes high school students use the rest rooms for smoking and drinking areas and trouble can easily develop.

Smoking Area

Even though smoking is being discouraged as a definite health hazard, many still smoke. Therefore, a smoking area should be provided so that people who do not smoke will not become irritated, and perhaps cause trouble. No smoking signs should be placed in conspicuous places to inform the public that there is to be no smoking in certain areas. Signs should also be placed in these same areas informing the spectators where smoking will be permitted. It is important that all signs be placed where they can be seen.

Parking

A great deal of agitation can be generated by inadequate parking spaces for fans and lack of supervision of parking areas. The larger the crowd attending the contest, the bigger the problem of crowd control. The parking of cars, including the entering and exiting of them, is not the only major problem. Vandalism can occur. Therefore, all parking lots should be well supervised. All parking attendants should be well identified and instructed in the proper rules and regulations regarding the proper techniques to be used.

The attendants should be properly equipped to do the job. The school officials should enlist the help of the state and local police whenever possible as they are experienced and well qualified to direct the flow of traffic effectively and quickly, thereby avoiding agitating drivers who could start trouble. Everything possible should be done so that spectators will be able to quickly depart from the school after the contest.

Emergencies

Wherever there are large numbers of people gathered together, there will be incidents that call for emergency treatment. How these emergencies are handled becomes very important because in the case of injury or illness it could result in very serious consequences. Some of the factors which must be considered from an emergency standpoint in crowd control are as follows: (1) have a doctor on duty at all times; (2) have an ambulance on call at all times and in the case of football, an ambulance should be stationed near the field; (3) have a centrally located first-aid station with qualified help in attendance; (4) have an emergency lighting system available in case of power failure; and (5) have an electric portable scoreboard available.

Tickets

Long lines of people waiting to purchase tickets can result in many disgruntled and unruly fans. This should be avoided if at all possible. This can be done in a variety of ways; the first, of course, is to have enough ticket sellers so that there will be no long period of waiting to purchase tickets. Other ways might be to sell season tickets ahead of time to the general public. The students can be encouraged to purchase student activity cards as a way to avoid waiting to purchase tickets at the gate.

Crowd Movement

A great deal of thought must be given to the control of the crowd as it moves about before the contest begins, during the time it is in progress, and after it is over. The traffic pattern of spectator movement should be one in which direct spectator movement in one direction takes place so that the movement of one group of spectators is not moving against another group coming from the opposite direction. Every effort should be made to keep all spectators off the playing area. If check rooms are provided, they should not be in the main line of traffic. Access to telephone, toilet facilities, and refreshments should not interfere with spectator movement to and from the game. These are the areas where there will be congestion and, wherever it is possible to do so, these facilities should be spread out.

Crowd Control Mediums

There are many mediums that influence the attitude and consequently the behavior of spectators at an athletic contest. Many can be used successfully in helping to control the spectators' behavior if some pre-planning is attempted. These mediums can be divided into those that influence the spectators' attitude before the game begins, during the game, and after the game.

Newspapers

The effect that the newspaper as a medium has over crowd control can be overwhelming. Every effort should be made by school administrators and coaches to build a good relationship with the newspaper. This can be done in various ways, but the best one is to treat the sportswriters in a courteous, friendly manner and make known to them that in their sports write-up they should include information on the importance of sportsmanship, honesty, and fairplay as being part of athletics. Do not tell them how to write a story but do tell them what to include.

School Publications

Usually the school publication is not quite as outspoken as the city or community newspaper. Yet, it is read by the student and to some extent does influence the students' thinking and attitude which in turn would have some effect on crowd control. The school publication, however, usually confines its remarks to team accomplishments and makes no attempt to editorialize.

Radio and Television

Certainly radio and television can influence the attitude of the average fan. Consequently, in the interest of crowd control at the contests every effort should be made to create a wholesome atmosphere between the radio and television announcers and the school administration and coaches.

Treatment of Visiting Teams

One of the main purposes of athletics is to promote good will, friendly competition, and rivalry. Therefore, the friendly treatment of the visiting team helps a great deal in promoting a healthy relationship between opposing team members. Good treatment afforded the guest team members will, in turn, determine to a certain extent the actions of the team on the field of play. If the two teams display good sportsmanship, it will avert to some extent any anti-social behavior of the spectators and visiting team fans.

Public Address System

The purpose of the public address system is to give a running account of the progress of the game and to convey informa-tion relative to the two teams to the specta-tors. The announcer should refrain from making any derogatory remarks about any of the opposing players or team. To do so might have an adverse affect on the specta-tors who might resent it to the extent that it could cause hard feelings. The announcer should in no way incite the emotions of the crowd.

Team Dress

It would seem that the way a team dresses should not make much difference as far as crowd control is concerned, but in many cases it does. Dress seems to reflect the personality and sometimes the attitude of the person or persons wearing the cloth-ing and uniforms. If a team is dressed neat-ly and in team blazers, it creates a very favorable impression on the spectators. This is especially true when playing away from home. Gaudy clothing and uniforms seem to have an adverse effect on the spec-tators and build up a feeling of resentment by the spectators. This should be avoided if at all possible.

Crowd Control Tactics Before the Game

The pep rally is one of many mediums that can be used to influence students' be-havior before an athletic contest. This per-tains particularly to football and basket-ball. The pep rally should be more than just a series of yells to excite the students. It should also include some of the follow-ing: talks by faculty, alumni, coaches and students; band playing; singing of school songs; introduction of coaches and players; short skits; novelty yells; stunts; clinics on rules; competitive cheering; discussion on sportsmanship and specialty acts. Although perhaps the main purpose of the pep rally is to inspire the team, the general atmos-phere that is created is usually carried over

into the contest by players and students alike. It presents a wonderful opportunity to teach good sportsmanship and proper spectator behavior.

The City and County Directors have indicated in the proceedings of the Sixth National Conference[25] several approaches to crowd control by intensifying communi-cations before the game using the follow-ing methods:

1. Arrange for an exchange of speakers at school assembly programs; the prin-cipals, coaches or team captains could visit the opposing school.
2. Discuss with appropriate personnel of the competing school the procedures for the game, including method and location of team entry and departure.
3. Provide superintendent or principal, athletic director, and coach with a copy of written policy statement, guidelines, and regulations.
4. Meet all game officials and request them to stress good sportsmanship on the field.
5. Meet with coaches and instruct them not to question officials during a con-test; stress the importance of good sportsmanship and the fact that their conduct sets the tone for spectator reaction to game incidents.
6. Instruct students what to expect and what is expected of them.
7. Schedule preventive planning confer-ences with local police to be assured of their full cooperation and effective-ness in spectator control.
8. Encourage as many students as pos-sible to be in the uniforms of the athletic club, pep club, booster clubs, band, majorettes, cheerleaders.
9. Bus participants to and from the site of the game.
10. Have participants dressed to play be-fore leaving for a game or contest.
11. Adhere to established seating capacity of stadium and gymnasiums.
12. Request home team fans to remain in their own stands until visiting team fans have left.

[25]Proceedings of the Sixth National Conference of City and County Directors, p. 19.

13. Try to arrange for a statewide athletic association regulation prohibiting all noise makers including musical instruments except for the school band or orchestra under professional supervision.

14. Request the assistance of visiting clubs.

15. Educate cheerleaders, student leaders, band captains, pep squads, and faculty supervisors by means of a one day conference program.

16. Keep spectators buffered from the playing area as much as practical.

17. Request that elementary school children be accompanied by an adult.

18. Teach good sportsmanship throughout the school and the community.

19. Begin education in good sportsmanship in the earliest grades and continue it throughout the school life.

20. Make frequent approving references to constructive and commendable behavior.

21. Arrange for program appearances by faculty members and students jointly to discuss the true values of athletic competition including good sportsmanship.

22. Make use of all news media through frequent and effective television, radio, and press presentations and interviews, commentaries, and frequent announcement of good sportsmanship slogans.

23. Distribute a printed Code of Ethics for Good Sportsmanship.

24. Include the good sportsmanship slogan in all printed programs at sports events.

25. Urge the use of athletic events as an example in elementary school citizenship classes, stressing positive values of good conduct at games, during the raising of the flag and singing of the national anthem; courtesy toward visitors.

26. Involve teachers in school athletic associations, provide them with passes to all sports events and stress the positive values of their setting an example of good sportsmanship.

Crowd Control Tactics During the Game

There are many factors regarding crowd control during the game or contest that must warrant serious consideration because it is at this time that trouble begins and the spectator mood is developed. Some factors of importance are as follows.

Officials

The officials of the contest play an extremely important role in crowd control in interscholastic athletic programs. Poor officiating can arouse a crowd to a frenzy of dissatisfaction and do much to bring on rioting and all kinds of trouble. The officials more than anything else affect the mood of the spectators. It is important to hire good ones. The most important attribute of an official is to have the ability to control the game, even though he may make a wrong call, without antagonizing the athletes or spectators.

Crowd Control Tactics at Halftime

Halftime entertainment can help a great deal in crowd control. Good entertainment takes the spectator's mind off of the game at a time when he might be in a highly emotional state and very resentful of the preceeding halftime play of his team. The halftime entertainment should be of the type that will be entertaining and include spectators participation in activities such as cheering and singing.

Crowd Control Tactics After the Game

This is the time when a great deal of the trouble starts. It is important that all supervisors, including students, faculty, and police are alert and remain at their posts after the contest. It is an absolute must if the contest is at night to have the parking area and the area between the field or building where the contest is held and the parking area well lighted and supervised. Parris[26] emphasizes this fact in the following statement.

> Too much stress cannot be placed on the orderly departure of spectators and cheerleaders from an athletic contest. Most trouble at a contest generally takes place late in the last quarter when spectators begin to leave. These 'early leavers' stand around the edges of the field or players court, which makes play difficult and causes tempers to flare. Well-planned teacher supervision will help control this situation.

Kozak[27] makes the following observation regarding crowd control after the game:

> Every effort should be made to dissipate traffic from the area of the contest as quickly as possible. Schedules of all contests, day or night, should be delivered to the police chief or safety director before the season begins; also, throughout the season they should receive current reminders of the games scheduled for the week with anticipated attendance given for each game.

Spectator control is becoming an increasing problem especially in urban areas. Many times athletic contests seem to act as a magnet in attracting undesirable individuals who are not really interested in the game but want to cause trouble. The most serious problems occur after the game. Fewer problems occur during the daylight; consequently, many schools are abandoning night football games and are also playing basketball games in the afternoon. Constant vigilance not only pays but is essential for the protection of the fan and player and also to preserve and protect interscholastic athletics from total extinction.

[26]Parris, Wendell, "Conduct of Coaches, Players, Officials Helps to Guide Fans," *American School Board Journal* (August, 1966), p. 33.

[27]Kozak, George, "Practices and Methods of Crowd Control at School Athletic Events," p. 28.

BEHAVIORAL OBJECTIVES

After a person has read this chapter, he should be able to:

1. Explain what is meant by the term crowd control and discuss briefly why administrators are concerned.
2. Recall several major indirect methods of handling crowds and explain each in relation to athletic contests.
3. Identify and explain several causes of crowd control problems at athletic contests.
4. Differentiate between pregame, during the game, and after the game arrangements for crowd control at athletic contests.
5. Select several people who are directly responsible for crowd control at athletic contests and indicate why.
6. Explain the influence the coach might have in spectator control and summarize what he can do to keep the crowd under control.
7. Explain the role the faculty plays in crowd control at athletic contests.
8. Recall several suggestions the faculty supervisor should adhere to in his duties as supervisor at athletic contests.
9. Explain several ways in which students can help in crowd control at athletic contests.
10. Explain how out-of-season coaches may be used in crowd control.
11. Explain the use of cheerleaders in crowd control and give examples.
12. Summarize the reasons for the use of the booster club in crowd control.
13. Recall several ways in which the cheerleaders help control spectators behavior and justify each.
14. Summarize the role of the cheerleader in crowd control.
15. Explain the role of the student council in student spectator behavior.

16. Recall several approaches which might be used in crowd control by the community.
17. Explain the use of the police department in crowd control at athletic contests.
18. Recall several rules which may be followed to obtain liaison between the school and the police in attempting to obtain better spectator behavior at athletic contests.
19. Recall several ways of involving law enforcement personnel in crowd control at athletic contests.
20. Recall several ways in which supervisors at athletic contests may be identified and explain each.
21. Select several physical factors affecting crowd control and explain each.
22. Identify several crowd control mediums, explain their importance and at what period of the contest they can be used.
23. Identify several approaches to crowd control by intensifying communications before the game.
24. Summarize the importance of good officiating in crowd control.
25. Identify several factors regarding crowd control during the game and explain each.

5. Write to several large and small high schools for their organizational and administrative set-up for crowd control at athletic contests and compare them.
6. Arrange to have an athletic director and head football and basketball coach talk to the class about their role in spectator behavior at athletic contests.
7. Form two groups of students and debate the issue: All night athletic contests should be abolished.
8. Debate the issue: All junior high school students should be accompanied by a parent or guardian when attending high school athletic contests.
9. Arrange to have a member of a high school student council talk to the class on student behavior at athletic contests.
10. Seek the opinion of several high school athletic directors on night versus day athletic contests.
11. Talk with several high school faculty members who act as supervisors at athletic contests and obtain their opinions on student behavior.
12. Arrange to have a high school cheerleader talk to the class about his role in crowd control.
13. Write to several athletic directors and inquire how they take care of emergencies at athletic contests.

ACTIVITIES

1. Attend a night contest and report to the class on the crowd control efforts.
2. Arrange for a local policeman to talk to the class on crowd control tactics.
3. Visit with an athletic director in a large high school and learn from him how he administers the program of crowd control.
4. Visit with a principal in a large, medium, and small-sized high school and get his opinion on the use of faculty and student supervision at athletic contests.

SUGGESTED READINGS

1. Ambrose, W.L.: Guidelines for good spectator sportsmanship. *School and Community,* October, 1965.
2. Barham, Walter: Crowd control at athletic events. *Approaches to Problems of Public School Administration in Health, Physical Education and Recreation.* Washington, D.C., Sixth National Conference of City and County Directors, AAHPER, December, 1968.
3. Bolden Frank:The role of cheerleaders. *Journal of Health, Physical Education, and Recreation,* April, 1969.

4. Bucher, Charles: *Administration of School Health and Physical Education Programs.* St. Louis, Mosby, 1967.

5. Fagan, Clifford: Players brawls must be eliminated. *Physical Educator,* May, 1972.

6. Hughes, William, French, Esther, and Lehsten, Nelson: *Administration of Physical Education for Schools and Colleges,* New York, Ronald, 1962.

7. Jorndt, Louis: A plan of operation for spectator conduct and control at football and basketball games. *School Activities,* September, 1968.

8. Jorndt, Louis: A reference paper on big-city approach to crowd control for interscholastic competition. *Approaches to Problems of Public School Administration in Health, Physical Education, and Recreation.* Washington, D.C., 1968.

9. Jorndt, Louis: Crowd control at athletic events. *Journal of Health, Physical Education, and Recreation,* April, 1969.

10. Jorndt, Louis: Crowd control in a big city sports program. *School Activities,* September, 1968.

11. Killian, George: Involvement: The key to success. *Coach and Athlete,* June, 1969.

12. Kozak, George: Crowd control. *Journal of Health, Physical Education, and Recreation,* April, 1969.

13. Kozak, George: Practices and methods of crowd control at school athletic events. *Approaches to Problems of Public School Administration in Health, Physical Education, and Recreation.* Washington, D.C., AAHPER, December 10, 1968.

14. Lang, Kurt and Engel, Gladys: *Collective Dynamics.* New York, Crowell, 1961.

15. Leach, Glenn: *Spectator Control at Inter-scholastic Basketball Games.* Sportshelf, New Rochelle, N.Y., 1959.

16. Lehmann, Harry: Right in your own back yard. *The Physical Educator,* 1958.

17. Luby, Robert: Detroit resolves problems of Crowd Control. *American School Board Journal,* August, 1966.

18. Murphy, Hilton: Crowd control. *Journal of Health, Physical Education, and Recreation,* April, 1969.

19. O'Dell, Griffith: Administrative vigilance pays. *American School Board Journal,* August, 1966.

20. O'Neil, Lee: Spectator control: Whose responsibility? *The Coaching Clinic,* October, 1969.

21. Parris, Wendell: Conduct of coaches, players, officials helps to guide fans. *American School Board Journal,* August, 1966.

22. Pate, Robert: Crowd control. *Journal of Health, Physical Education, and Recreation,* April, 1969.

23. Pate, Robert: Crowd control: A pressing responsibility for city directors. *Approaches to Problems of Public School Administration in Health, Physical Education, and Recreation.* Washington, D.C., Sixth National Conference of City and County Directors, AAHPER, December, 1968.

24. Perry, James: Community football clinics. *Scholastic Coach,* May, 1953.

25. Sixth National Conference of City and County Directors. *Approaches to Problems of Public School Administration in Health, Physical Education, and Recreation.* Washington, D.C., 1969.

26. Walters, George: Letters to the editor. *De-Kalb Daily Chronicle,* February 25, 1969.

CHAPTER 14

Public Relations

PUBLIC RELATIONS SHOULD not be confused with publicity, although the two are closely related. Public relations, according to Cutlip:[1]

> . . . has become a common-place term in the language and thought of twentieth century America. Its function is the planned effort to influence opinion through acceptable performance and two-way communication.
>
> Public relations is often mistaken for and used as a handy synonym for some of its functional parts, such as publicity, propaganda, press-agentry, and advertising. This is a misconception—these become tools of public relations, not its equivalent.

Defining Public Relations

There is some difficulty encountered in defining public relations because of the various ramifications it has and areas it encompasses, which in turn, can be included as a functional part of the public relations program. It should be remembered, however, that these areas may be parts of the whole in relation to public relations, but the sum of the parts does not equal the whole.

Robert Heilbroner,[2] writing in 1957, commented on how difficult it is to define public relations, "In a word, public rela-tions covers a lot of acreage—blurring out into advertising, slopping over into selling, dipping down into publicity, and touching —or at least aspiring to the making of public opinion itself."

The following definitions are typical. Professor Byron Christian[3] says that, "Public relations is the conscientious effort to motivate or influence people primarily through communication, to think well of an organization, to respect it, to support it, and to stick with it through trial and trouble."

Webster[4] defines public relations thus, "The promotion of rapport and goodwill between a person, firm, or institution and other persons, special publics or a community at large through the distribution of interpretative material, the development of neighborly interchange, and the assessment of public reaction."

The American Association of School Administrators[5] defines it as, ". . . seeking to bring about a harmony of understanding between any group and the public it serves and upon whose goodwill it depends." This definition is an excellent one for public relations, as it relates well to interscholastic athletics.

---

[1]Cutlip, Scott, and Center, Allen, *Effective Public Relations* 2nd ed. (Englewood Cliffs, New Jersey, by permission of Prentice-Hall, 1958) , p. 3.

[2]Heilbroner, Robert, "Public Relations—The Invisible Sell" *Harpers Magazine* (June, 1957) , p. 24.

[3]Cutlip, Scott and Center, Allen, *Effective Public Relations,* p. 4.

[4]*Websters New International Dictionary* 3rd ed. (Merriam Co. 1961) .

[5]Public Relations for America's Schools, Twenty-eighth yearbook, (Washington, D.C.), *American Association of School Administrators* (1950) , p. 12.

Benjamin Fine[6] defines public relations as being ". . . more than a set of rules, it is a broad concept. It is the entire body of relationships that go to make up our impressions of an individual, an organization or an idea."

Public Relations Applied to Athletics

The importance of public relations in athletics cannot be over emphasized. However, there is a difference in the publicizing of athletics because of its tremendous popularity and the way in which it lends itself to publicity. Since interscholastic athletics involves the school and the school is supported by public funds, it is natural that many people are interested in it.

Duke[7] makes the following comment about public relations as it applies to athletics:

Public relations has been defined as '90 percent doing something worth while and 10 percent telling about it.' It has also been said, 'A public relations program is only as good as the product it represents.' Either aptly fits the public relations program for athletics conducted by the nation's colleges and universities.

The objectives of an overall athletic public relations program are,

1. Constant review and evaluation of intercollegiate athletics as an expression of and an important contribution to the American way of life.

2. Development of a proper perspective of athletic competition by everyone participating in the athletic program.

3. Emphasis on the advantages of competitive athletics to the individual, his institution, and his community.

4. Encouragement of support from the press and other media of communication in carrying out an intercollegiate athletic program.

5. Development of positive public support for the continuance and further development of intercollegiate athletics and an appreciation of its purposes and objectives.

Resick, Seidel, and Mason[8] make the following interesting interpretations of public relations as it applies to the schools and the way in which the public forms its opinions regarding the school.

The public relations field evolved from the publicity, and in the minds of many it still remains synonymous with it. Since public relations is a relatively new field of endeavor, there are more definitions of what it is not than concise definitions of what it is. A definition of school public relations must include the management function which sees the problems of the school in terms of public interest and initiates communication between the school and the public in order to inform the public about the school's program and thus gain its approval.

A school system cannot avoid public relations. Relations with the public may be either good, bad, or somewhere in between. The public has opinions about the school, its personnel, and its programs, including physical education and athletics. These opinions are formed from impressions gained by contact with students, school programs, and school personnel. Sometimes these impressions are formed by reading newspaper releases and by other less objective means. Unfortunately, the picture may not be in focus with that which actually exists.

Public relations must begin with the bold premise that the public has a right to know everything about the school and not just what the administration and the board of education wishes to know.

Public relations has become a way of life in America. Competition for the almighty dollar in education as well as in

---

[6]Fine, Benjamin, *Educational Publicity* (New York, Harper and Row, 1943), p. 255.

[7]Duke, Wayne, "Public Relations and Athletics," *Journal of Health, Physical Education and Recreation* (October, 1959), p. 17.

[8]Resick, Matthew, Seidel, Beverly, and Mason, James, *Modern Administrative Practices in Physical Education and Athletics* (Reading, Mass., Addison-Wesley Publishing Company, 1970), p. 225.

business has presented a totally different picture because education is big business. Education is competing for that dollar and it is successful only through good public relations.

Dudley Ashton[9] makes this summarizing statement regarding sound public relations:

> Sound public relations are a function of daily living patterns in the classroom, in the barber shop, in the grocery store, at church, at bridge parties, at the backyard barbecue, on the playground and athletic field, in the pool and in the gymnasium. One cannot afford to forget the results of one's words, attitudes, and actions upon persons or other groups.

The Need for Public Relations in Athletics

If public funds are being spent in any endeavor, then the public has a right to know how they are being spent. The public should also know the purpose and reason for the program of athletics. If the facts which are presented to the public are realistic and meaningful, they will be generally accepted. The American Association of School Administrators[10] presents some very interesting ones in the following statement:

1. School public relations must be honest in intent and execution.
2. School public relations must be intrinsic.
3. School public relations must be continuous.
4. School public relations must be positive in approach.
5. School public relations must be comprehensive.
6. School public relations should be sensitive to its publics.

7. The ideas communicated must be simple.

According to Hesse and Damore public relations in many schools is handled reluctantly and ineffectively. To do an effective job in publicizing sports, they suggest that it must be thought through carefully and a program for public relations should be set up in all schools. A well worked-out program involving the newspapers, radio, and the community is necessary if the desired results are to be obtained.[11]

The Purpose of Public Relations

Everything that is labeled public relations is done to influence public opinion in a particular area. Public relations in athletics is carried out with the express purpose of benefiting the program and creating a good impression on the general public so that it looks upon it favorably. This is very important.

Cutlip[12] emphasizes this point by stating that:

> There can be no escape in today's world from the grinding wheels of public attitudes. This is the era of 'The public be pleased' more than ever 'the genius of the people' must be consulted. The practice of public relations is predicated on the belief that only an informed public can be a wise public. One of the basic precepts is 'People are essentially rational by nature; they respond to facts and want the truth; and they will ultimately find it and act upon it.

Public relations involves impressions made to parents, fellow teachers, administrators, school board members, and the general public. The purpose of public relations, then, is to sell the program to these people in such a way that they will see the

[9]Ashton, Dudley, *Administration of Physical Education for Women* (New York, The Ronald Press, 1968) , p. 99.

[10]American Association of School Administrators, *Public Relations for American Schools, Twenty-eighth Yearbook* (Washington, D.C., 1952) , p. 16.

[11]Hesse, Robert, and Damore, Patrick "A Program of Public Relations for Sports," *Coach and Athlete* (October, 1969) , p. 38.

[12]Cutlip, Scott, and Center, Allen, *Effective Public Relations*, p. 71.

need for such a program and be willing to support it. The public must be made aware of the values derived from a good athletic program. An understanding of the values of such a program will clear up any misunderstandings and remove negative attitudes. The real purpose of public relations in athletics is to sell the program to the public.

Ashton[13] comments on this point of view by stating that, "Solving the problem of establishing the fine values that may accrue from varsity athletics without antagonizing local pressure groups often places relations in the category of a fine art."

Resick, Seidel, and Mason[14] make the following observation regarding the role of the publicity in school athletics:

> The chief problem in school publicity, especially in the areas of physical eduacation and athletics, is to secure, organize, and present information to the mass communications media. A cursory examination of any daily newspaper shows the enormous amount of space that is devoted to school sports news. The schools could not begin to buy this space in a competitive market.
>
> Publicity can be as unfavorable as it is favorable. It can be subject to misinterpretation and misunderstanding. If it is overdone, it can bring out an unfavorable reaction from the group it is trying to influence.
>
> Publicity cannot stand alone. It must be part of a total program of public relations.

Frey,[15] in discussing how to build an effective school-community relations, indicated that:

. . . a good program can do much to build

[13]Ashton, Dudley, *Administration of Physical Education for Women*, p. 99.

[14]Resick, Matthew, Seidel, Beverly, and Mason, James, *Modern Administrative Practices in Physical Education and Athletics*, p. 227.

[15]Frey, George, "How Can We Build an Effective School-Community Relations," *Today's Education* (January, 1971) , p. 14.

constructive school-community ties. The one big problem could be the reluctance of school people to involve themselves with the community. However, if they do, they will find that the program will yield many rewards and can quickly become a reality and a benefit to the total school community. There are several basic ingredients among them being honest with parents and students, keep all promises and a good community relations advisor.

Responsibility for Public Relations

A tremendous responsibility for public relations rests upon the shoulders of the athletic director and the athletic coaches in the high school. The school is often judged by the way in which the athletic program is administered because this is often the only time many people observe any part of the school program in action.

It has been said that the athletic program of the high school is a window through which the general public views the entire school program and as a result, it forms its attitudes from these experiences. It is important that these experiences be the kind that provide the general tax-paying public with the kind of experiences that will send him away satisfied that the school is being administered properly and that his tax dollar is being spent wisely.

It has been difficult over the years to justify interscholastic athletics as a part of the educational program and as such to be financed from the general school fund. The program is constantly being scrutinized by skeptics and those who are outrightly opposed to the program. These people welcome the opportunity to level any criticism they can against the athletic program. This is one reason public relations relating to the athletic program is of such great importance and should command the individual attention of all those people who are directly or even indirectly associated with it. In order that the general public has a clearer understanding as to the value of athletics as an integral part of the educational program, Hixson[16] has suggested the following course of action which will help achieve this goal:

1. Correct misunderstandings of the athletic program.
2. Establish community confidence in the judgment and purposes of the athletic faculty and administration.
3. Rally community support for interscholastic sports for boys and girls.
4. Develop general community awareness of the importance of athletics in education.
5. Establish the concept of cooperation between parents and coaches in athletics.
6. Evaluate the program of the athletic department for the community.

Importance of Public Relations

Good public relations is the backbone of any program that is supported by public funds. Its importance cannot be over emphasized. The high school athletic program is no exception and can benefit greatly through a good public relations program. Its importance is dramatized by Cutlip[17] in the following statement:

The power of public opinion to control human affairs has been recognized through the centuries. Though the term 'public opinion' was not coined until the eighteenth century, the force of people's opinion was demonstrated and recognized in ancient times. Public relations, perhaps, began when neolithic man traded flint for the hindquarters of a sheep. With recognition of the power of people's opinions, there came in response practices we now call public relations.

While it is true that public relations in all areas has the same basic purpose, that of selling the general public as to the value of a specific product, program, or person, it is true that school-athletic-community relations are different from the usual school-activity-community public relationship situations. This is true, in part, to the belief that success in athletics is measured by John Q. Public in terms of the number of games won or lost and in some measure on the ability of the program to support itself financially. This is an unfortunate circumstance, and it is because of this feeling that it is important to have a strong public relations program in athletics to counteract this belief. Every attempt should be made to have people believe that win or lose, the athletic program is valuable as a part of the total educational program. The director of athletics or the coach should use every medium at their command to keep people informed about the program which takes place under their guidance. So important is the place of high school athletics in our present-day society, that a good sound program presents a tremendous public relations potential for the school and community. It is, therefore, essential, because of this widespread interest, that the public not only be informed of its existence but is shown the vast benefits that can result from such a program. Everyone connected with the program should be constantly alert to come to the defense of the program and to protect it from any situation that might bring discredit to it.

The importance of publicity in public relations cannot be underestimated because without favorable publicity no program can be successful. The value of publicity is very well stated by Harris[18] in the following comment:

---

[16]Hixson, Chalmer, *The Administration of Interscholastic Athletics* (New York, Lowell Pratt and Co., 1967), p. 131.

[17]Cutlip, Scott, and Center, Allen, *Effective Public Relations*, p. 16.

[18]Harris, William, "Stimulate Curiosity," *Journal of Health, Physical Education, and Recreation* (February, 1968), p. 44.

The value of well-organized publicity is recognized and appreciated by many different enterprises, and should be especially so regarded by the schools which depend upon favorable public opinion for their support. Much of the information about the schools comes to a community through its children, who occasionally fail to report the facts accurately. To ensure as accurate a presentation of facts as possible, it becomes doubly necessary to have a well-balanced publicity program.

Publicity is information with news value. It may involve action, speech, or written material which secures public notice. Publicity has the broad, general meaning of attracting public attention. It is an effective way of influencing public opinion as the purposes and objectives are not so evident that the public is likely to develop a defensive frame of mind. Publicity is only a part of public relations, of course. Public relations is a reflection of the quality of teaching, relationships with others, ideals, and principles for the entire program.

Public relations has always been a factor in athletics. Constantz and Scott[19] were aware of the importance of public relations in athletics as far back as 1951 and made the following observation at that time:

Publicity may not make the world go around, as is commonly claimed, but it certainly greases the ballbearings of the athletic program. A well-planned publicity program can be justified on several vital counts. It (1) interprets your program to the community and builds good will, (2) performs a real service for the local press, (3) increases gate receipts, thus providing the wherewithal to support the nonpaying sports.

History of Public Relations

Public relations has affected men's lives since the beginning of time, as Cutlip[20] has

so aptly put it, "The effort to deal with the force of opinion and to communicate with others goes back to antiquity. Only the tools, degree of specialization, and intensity of effort required today are relatively new."

The attempts at different periods of time in history to use public relations to sway public opinion can be easily traced through its early beginnings to the present time.

History has shown public relations as a prime agent in the struggle for power among people. Public relations was used to establish public opinion for or against certain people or peoples. The Boston Tea Party is an excellent example of the value of using created events to dramatize a point of view or a situation. The Boston Tea Party was a direct attempt by Adams to influence the colonists to revolt against the British, which they did. He accomplished this purpose, and then through the efforts of Benjamin Franklin who was a master at public relations, spread the news of the ensuing battles at Lexington and Concord. History is filled with such incidents, many of which have resulted in momentous decisions which have shaped the destiny of the world.

Guidelines for a Public Relations Program in Interscholastic Athletics

What responsibility does public relations have in the area of interscholastic athletics? It must help to establish a program of promotions to get backing and financing from the school administration, student body, businessmen in the community, and the "everyday Joe" in the community, who basically is the guy who helps keep the interest alive in the program by attending and supporting the athletic events.

The one person who must thoroughly understand that there are certain guidelines which are basic to any good public

[19]Constanz, Quinn and Scott, James, "Sports Publicity Program," *Scholastic Coach* (November, 1951) , p. 40.

[20]Cutlip, Scott, and Center, Alan, *Effective Public Relations*. p. 16.

relations program in athletics is the athletic director. He must use these guidelines and add to them as the opportunity and need presents itself. These guidelines are many and only a few can be listed here. The athletic director must assume the leadership and have the full cooperation of the staff if the public relations program is to succeed.

1. Profit by past mistakes. Analyze previous strategies and select those which were successful and discard those that were not. Construct or design a public relations plan on this basis.

2. Work on the theory that everyone counts, everyone is important, and everyone is an important part of the team, every coach, equipment man, custodian, player, and teacher. Make them feel their importance and make everyone a contributing team member.

3. Develop the *we* spirit and forget the *I* complex that is so prevalent in our present-day society. Most losers are *I* men. Winners are *we* men. *We* is the word in public relations, and not *I*.

4. Show concern for the program. Take the initiative, be a builder and a leader. Be a cooperator. Be creative. Move forward. Do not remain static.

5. Keep the staff informed so they know what is going on in the department. Relate the thinking of the administration to the coaches and the students. Make them feel that they are an important part of the program and that their presence is essential to the program.

6. Be progressive. Cast aside outdated and outmoted ideas and rules that will hinder the program. Do not handcuff the program by subjecting it to rules and regulations that will deprive the boys and girls of the opportunity to participate in a varsity sport.

7. Be aggressive! Find out the answers to the why's. Rebuild the interest in the athletic program by casting aside the old ways of doing things. Be modern! If something has not been working discard it for a better idea.

8. Establish a departmental organization that will provide for continuous attention to all phases of the public relations program such as the department newsletter, coaches manual, staff meetings, etc. Do not slight one area or phase of the program at the expense of the other. All are important to someone.

9. Remember that if interscholastic athletics are to survive, they must compete for attention in the nation's news media. Professional sports are gradually taking over the limelight and like an octopus, are slowly squeezing the life blood out of the high school athletic program.

10. Develop and cultivate a good understanding between the coaches and the sport writers. Both need to be "educated" and kept in balance.

11. Keep in constant contact and in the good graces of the editor of the local newspaper. It will pay off!

Basic Sources of a Good Public Relations Program

Coaching Staff

To have a successful public relations program, the athletic director must have the complete cooperation and dedication of his coaching staff. They have the everyday contact with parents and students. They must be willing to speak at service clubs, put on clinics, etc. The athletic director must provide his coaching staff the tools with which he can get the job done in the best interests of the athletes under his guidance and direction. No program will be successful if all of these people who are involved in the program are not on the same team.

Another important basic ingredient of every good community public relations program is the necessity for coaches and the athletic director to know their community by understanding its background, its strengths and weaknesses, its ambitions, its operations, its local pride, and prejudices. In short, one must understand its personality. Only then will the personnel of the high school athletic program fit harmoniously into the local scheme of things athletically.

Any successful community public relations program, whether it be via radio, newspaper, or any other means of communication, requires a detailed knowledge of the day-to-day community patterns of life within the community as well as a considerable understanding of how it got that way and why it stays that way. Field[21] emphasizes the fact that, "The basic ingredient essential to all public relations is the ability to get along with others. No one operates through life alone, the need for friendship is too vital to existence. Getting along with people is foremost in life."

The Administration

It is important, therefore, that the department of athletics must work cooperatively with the administration if the desired results are to be obtained. Large sums of money are spent for the athletic program and this money must be appropriated and approved through administrative action. Therefore, the good will of the administration must be obtained and encouraged. This can only be done through a good public relations effort and a program that

will enlighten the administration as to benefits derived from the athletic program. The administration should be given firsthand information regarding every aspect of the program of athletics and be made to feel that they are an intricate and important part of athletics in the school program.

The Parents

No program of interscholastic athletics can be successful without the complete cooperation of the parents. Parents who do not believe in or are reluctant to support the program will sound the "death knell of athletics" in the school program. It is, therefore, of extreme importance that every effort be made to enlist the support of the parents in every way possible. Parents not only provide the participants, but help finance the program. Some of the ways in which a program of public relations with the parents can be instigated will be discussed later in this chapter. Field[22] stresses "The importance of the coaches' relationship to players and parents off the field. He noted the tremendous amount of influence a coach has on a boy and off the field a coach can assist a young man in many ways by cooperating with the parents."

The Faculty

The attitude of the coach and athletic director toward the total school program is of prime importance in public relations within the school structure itself. The athletic department must have the backing of the entire faculty if it is to survive and be successful in meeting the aims and objectives which justify its existence. This means that the personnel of the department must be a working part of the entire faculty.

---

[21]Field, Charles, "Faculty and Coach Relationship," *Coach and Athlete* (October, 1971), p. 26.

[22]*Ibid.*

OFFICE OF:
DIRECTOR OF PHYSICAL
EDUCATION
DIRECTOR OF ATHLETICS
BOOTH STREET
TELEPHONE FA 2-6954
EXT. 69

Reno High School
DEPARTMENT OF ATHLETICS
RENO, NEVADA

Dear Parent:

Your son/daughter has shown an interest in becoming a member of the _____ team at _____ High School. We are pleased to be able to offer a wide variety of competitive opportunities through athletics to the high school youth of our community. Our fine coaching staff will give your son/daughter the opportunity to learn the fundamentals and techniques of his/her chosen sport plus the self-discipline necessary to become an excellent athlete.

To maintain the high standard of our athletic programs at _____ High School, every participant must comply with certain rules. First, an athlete in our program must strive to maintain a high standard of personal behavior at all times so as not to discredit himself/herself, his/her teammates, or his/her school. An athlete, being in the public eye, is subject to constant scrutiny. He/she must be conscious of the "image" he/she is projecting. Second, an athlete must maintain the scholastic average as prescribed in the eligibility requirements of the Illinois High School Association. We must strictly enforce these requirements. The athlete must organize his/her time to be able to maintain the highest possible scholastic standing while fulfilling his/her commitment to the team. Third, each athlete is asked to follow these training rules:

1. No smoking
2. Do not drink alcoholic beverages
3. Do not use illegal drugs
4. Keep proper hours as specified by coaches
5. Proper diet
6. No gambling
7. Maintain the proper boy/girl relationship

We expect our athletes to comply with these rules all twelve months of the year. If you have questions about these rules, contact the athletic director or any coach.

Violating any of these rules is a serious offense and may result in dismissal from the team.

To show that both parent(s) or guardian and participant(s) are aware of the rules for athletic participation at _____ High School, the parent(s) or guardian and the athlete are asked to sign this letter and return it to the head coach before the first practice session.

This letter is sent to inform you and your son/daughter of the rules by which all members of our teams must abide.

_____ Parent or Guardian

_____ Athlete _____Date

Figure 76.

They must attend staff meetings or send a representative if they are not able to attend, serve on committees, and fulfil their obligations as a teacher as well as a coach. It is true that after-school coaching assignments make this very difficult, but it must be done if the coaching staff expects to maintain faculty status and preserve good public relations with the other teachers within the school. The members of the athletic staff must be familiar with the total school program and take their place within it.

The Coach

Even though behavioral patterns have changed the past few years, basically the conduct of the coach is an important factor in influencing the attitude of the players and students. These patterns of behavior, dress, actions, and moral standards still set the pattern for student and player behavior and do much to establish the moral tone of the entire school community. Their actions dictate, to a very large extent, the attitude of the community toward athletics as well.

The coach would do well to set himself up as an example and practice what he preaches if he expects exemplary behavior from his players and respect from the business community.

Tener[23] comments on the importance of the coach in public relations by making the following statement:

There are vast opportunities for public relations possibilities, but the crux of public relations is the coach himself, his department and the way he perceives his position and its responsibilities. Does he focus upon his athletes as to what is beneficial to them? Does he resort to good educational policies and practices? Does he appreciate what the sport can do for its participants? If he can say yes to these questions, he has a firm spring board from which to start. Attitudes of the coach are reflected upon his players.

Many coaches have not recognized the need for a carefully developed public relations program. In brief, the coach should consistently appraise himself, study the community, understand his players, identify areas of negativism and develop an organization for carrying through a positive program of public relations.

The coaching personnel must be active members of the school staff. They should participate in all school activities. They should offer help when needed. They can organize recreation activities and can be an active force and influence over students in teaching them to respect school rules and regulations. Many coaches have and still do give the impression that they are not members of the academic staff and place themselves apart from the regular

[23]Tener, Morton, "Public Relations in Athletics," *Coach and Athlete* (November, 1968), p. 24.

teaching staff. This is wrong. This type of coach does not belong in the teaching field.

Visiting Teams

Another important ingredient of public relations is the treatment of visiting teams and their followers. During the past few years a trend away from the feeling that the opponents are guests and should be treated as such has developed. Oftentimes the players are harassed by local spectators and the visiting team fans are subjected to indignities of all descriptions. This type of treatment should not happen. Instead the visiting players and fans should be treated with respect. Special seats in reserved sections should be provided for them. The players should be met by a player host who takes care of their needs before, during, and after the game. Field[24] touches on the importance of this type of public relations in the following observation, "He calls it sportsmanship and indicates how important it is to other coaches. It helps to maintain a firm relationship. This carries over to be a gentlemen to officials as well."

Guiding Policies Basic to Public Relations in Athletics

The director of athletics must establish guidelines or policies which will be the determining factors in all the decision making which will be done within the department in regard to publicity. These guiding policies which will be used in making the decisions will result in problems being solved uniformly and judiciously. Nothing will do more to produce discord within the department and misunderstanding throughout the community than slipshod decisions made on the spur of the moment and based on the whims of only those people involved. Hixson[25] suggests the following policies to guide the director as he administers the program of public relations:

1. Honesty in public relations instills confidence and trust.
2. Emphasize the true values of athletics rather than sensational or controversial issues.
3. Fairness in public relations prevents the favored from expecting special privileges and the unfavored from resorting to acts of retribution.
4. Centralization of responsibility eliminates unnecessary contradiction and duplication and prevents omissions from athletic department publicity.
5. Positive public relations are more effective than negative ones.
6. Continuous public relations impress the community with the sincerity of athletics.
7. Two-way flow of information in public relations develops mutual respect.
8. Timely news releases and public relations activities find a more receptive public.
9. Public relations designed to meet particular characteristics of each group included in the community will be more effective.

Guiding Principles of Public Relations

A principle is a guiding rule for action. It is necessary to establish these guiding principles or rules before any action can take place. The purpose of this procedure is of course to obtain uniformity in all endeavors, regardless of the area in which decisions are being made.

The American Association of School Administrators[26] gives the following principles which apply to all school systems regardless of the different areas which it encompasses:

---

[24]Field, Charles, "Faculty and Coach Relationship," p. 26.

[25]Hixson, Chalmer, *The Administration of Interscholastic Athletics*, p. 132.

[26]*American Association of School Administrators*, p. 16

1. To inform the public as to the work of the school.
2. To establish confidence in schools.
3. To rally support for proper maintenance of the educational program.
4. To develop awareness of the importance of education in a democracy.
5. To improve the partnership concept by uniting parents and teachers in meeting the educational needs of the children.
6. To integrate the home, school, and community in improving the educational opportunities for all children.
7. To evaluate the offering of the school in meeting the needs of the children of the community.
8. To correct misunderstandings as to the aims and activities of the school.

Harmon,[27] in discussing the principles of public relations, indicates, "That of great importance was telling the truth, treating all equally, being respectful of all colleagues, and keeping yourself as neat as possible. Other important aspects of public relations was the persons concern for the students, and maintaining good contact with the parents."

Areas of Concern in Public Relations

A good athletic public relations program will explore, take advantage of, and implement all avenues in order to obtain the desired results. In order to accomplish this, it is necessary to use every means available. The athletic director and his coaching staff must marshall all their resources to "tell the school's athletic story," and tell it effectively. There are various ways in which this may be done. However, first and foremost, the program must have direction so that it will produce these desired results. This direction must come from the athletic director with the help of the coaches.

There are various areas into which public relations may be divided to be effective. All of them are important, some more than others. These areas can be listed as follows: alumni, parents, faculty, students, community, publications, radio, and television.

Alumni

An important and often neglected phase of the athletic public relations program in the high school has to do with the alumnus. It is unfortunate that so many graduates are forgotten once they have graduated. This is especially true of the athletes and it is understandable because although tradition has its merits, it cannot take the place of immediate present goals and objectives. The coaches, students, and players are interested in winning the present games and place their efforts and achievements on these games and forget about the past.

Many students and athletes remain in the community or immediate vicinity after graduation. Their loyalty to their alma mater and their convictions toward the athletic program will remain with them. They should be given the opportunity to express these feelings by various means. There are numerous ways in which public relations can be used to help keep the alumni active supporters of the athletic program.

Parents

Usually, the best boosters of the athletic program are the parents. This applies not only to the parents of the players, but others as well. Parents who believe in the program will support it. Their attitude toward it will come as a direct result of how their children react to the program and the information they bring home to the parents about it. Their enthusiasm and loyalty to the athletic program will do much to formulate their parent's belief as to the value of it.

[27]Harmon, J. J., "Public Relations — A Necessity," *School and Community* (December, 1971) p. 17.

It is necessary, therefore, that the parents receive the right image of the athletic program through the eyes, feelings, and beliefs of the students. There is a golden opportunity for the athletic staff to work closely with the parents in many ways for the betterment of the athletic program. Their cooperation and help should be solicited in every way possible. Their moral, as well as financial support, is valuable and will be fully given if they can see the beneficial results to their children.

Troppman[28] stresses one way in which coaches and parents may work closely together:

> Most coaches contact the parents by letter before the season starts to explain the overall picture for the coming year. Included in this letter can be the following points: (1) Training rules for the coming season. (2) Schedule of the preseason practice. (3) Schedule of games. (4) General outlook for the season—prospects, etc. (5) Diet for team members such as the daily menu, prepractice, and pregame menu. (6) Study habits and eligibility requirements of the school and league. (7) Dating and use of automobiles during the season. (8) College requirements and what members of last year's squad are doing now. (9) Advantages a boy gets when he plays football or participates in athletics for the school. In closing the letter, the coach should set a time for the parents to visit a practice session or a time when they can meet him and talk over any problems which will tend to interfere with the coming season.
>
> A day may be set for the parents to visit a practice session, see just what system is being employed, and get a firsthand look at the team and the coaching staff in action. A good day, especially during the football season, is the second Saturday of preseason practice. The coach can introduce all the members of his squad, explain his system through

demonstrations given by team members, and have an intrasquad scrimmage. Then the athletic director can explain the insurance coverage, equipment a boy needs, physical examinations, and all other details that should be taken care of before a boy participates in a sport. This is also a good time for the coach to go over items covered in the letter, such as training rules, diet, etc.

> This meeting presents an excellent opportunity to show the parents the type of equipment that is worn by the boys. A team member can show the pads, and extra pads can be passed among the parents so they can look at the equipment and see how their tax money is being spent. After the demonstration, a coffee and doughnut social hour can be arranged by the letterman's club.

Tener[29] makes this comment about parents and public relations:

> A unique but an informative technique in establishing good rapport is to extend an invitation to parents to attend a practice session so that they may witness first hand what their youngsters experience daily. It is an ideal opportunity to demonstrate the fact that team instruction has educational values and coaching is teaching in every sense of the word.
>
> Communication releases should be submitted periodically to the local papers from the athletic department to sensitize the community of the team's progress, problems and activities. The team's progress and all members of the team should be given prominence instead of concentrating on just a few members.
>
> Bulletins sent home describing comprehensively the objectives, benefits, and projected program could promote profound parental support and understanding. This technique provides an effective method to reduce 'sport dropouts.'
>
> Bridging the gap could also be substantial through parent booster clubs. Booster parents can offer new ideas to increase the sport's image in the community, stimulate interest and often

---

[28]Troppman, Bob, "The Place of the Parent in High School Athletics," *The Athletic Journal* (February, 1958), p. 36.

[29]Tener, Morton, "Public Relations in Athletics."

change potential critics into advocates of the school's athletic program.

There should be a close relationship between the coach and the parents of the players if at all possible. The players are under the direction and guidance of the coach under very emotional and trying circumstances. His decisions will be a guiding influence on many youngster's attitude toward life. The coach is a second parent to many of his players. It is difficult to meet the parents of all the players if the school system is large, but the coach or his assistants should make every effort to communicate with them. There are a number of ways that this may be done, several of which will be discussed.

Troppman[30] makes the following comment on the importance the parent might have in the high school athletic program:

> Sometimes high school coaches and administrators feel that parent groups, other than the PTA and community booster clubs, do more harm than good. This tendency stems from many high-pressure college organizations which are inclined to run the sports program, and try to make the teams a separate part of the institution. Then the sports program becomes an affair of the whole community and not just a small part of the overall educational picture. In some schools an unhealthy situation has been the result of interference by these groups.
>
> At the high school level the athletic teams are an integral part of the whole educational set-up and many benefits can be derived through having strong parent and alumni interest.

It is always difficult in the coaches' and parents' busy time schedule for them to arrange for a meeting. A social hour should be planned, and if possible, a parents' group or club can be formed to support the athletic teams. There is, however, always some danger in this type of venture. It

[30]Troppman, Bob, "The Place of the Parent in High School Athletics."

should be understood that the support should mean over and above what is provided by the school budget. In some schools, this group is called the booster club or dad's club.

BILLINGS SENIOR HIGH SCHOOL

BOB THORSON
TICKET MANAGER
PHONE 248-6202

RAY COLLINS—Principal
PHONE 245-6127
JIM DUTCHER—Director of Physical Education
AND ATHLETICS
PHONE 252-6608

January 8, _____

Dear Parents:

    The Billings High School Athletic Department is sponsoring its first Basketball Dinner before the game on Friday, February 7th. All fathers and mothers who have sons on the varsity team are invited to attend. The dinner will be buffet style and served in the small gym immediately preceeding the game.

    We have a special section reserved in the bleachers for all parents. After the dinner we hope that you will stay and enjoy the game.

    During halftime we plan to introduce all mothers and fathers. When your name is called, please stand and remain standing until all parents have been introduced.

    You will receive tickets for the dinner within the next week or so from your son. The ticket also entitles you to free admission to the game.

    Please enter the school between 5:30 and 6:00 p.m. through the north doors.

    We are looking forward to seeing all of you on Friday, February 7th.

                        Sincerely,

                        Athletic Director

jj

Figure 77.

The sole purpose of the group is to work with the administration and the coaching staff in any way necessary to aid the athletic program. Some possible projects include the following:

1. Annual sports banquet.
2. Films of some of the games to be used as instructional aids for the team as well as enjoyment by the parents and the student.
3. Awards at the end of the semester.
4. Purchasing of shoes, insurance, and other items for needy players.
5. Weekly or semimonthly chalk talks and get-togethers for the parents and the coaching staff.
6. Food for trips, (sandwiches, milk, and apples) games when the players will be getting home late, or snacks for the play-

ers to eat in the locker room at home games.

7. The parents would be able to enjoy comradeship with the parents of other team members as well as share an interest with a teenage son or daughter.

These activities can be financed in many ways, such as selling food at home games, selling season tickets at home games, a theater party, showing of sport films, and other means the parents may suggest. A good way is for the organization to give a dollar's value for a dollar received. It should not be a charitable organization. An example would be through the sale of season tickets. They could be sold to the parents at a reduced rate. Thus, the school derives a profit and the parents see the games at reduced prices, and both parties benefit.

Parents definitely have a place in the high school athletic picture, and the high school will be a much better place if they share these experiences with their sons and daughters.

If one were to pick out one area that would be judged to be most important in influencing any high school athletic program or more specifically a team, it would be the parents of the players. They are the first and usually the direct source of outside influence on the player. Good public relations with the parent result in positive relations between the coach and the players.

Faculty

The faculty certainly should not be slighted in the public relations program for athletics. There are times when the faculty members who have the athletes in class can cooperate and help the program.

Duke[31] presents the following ideas for

communicating with the faculty:

1. Rotate faculty members into game day situations, including pregame mail, pregame preparations, locker room at halftime and after the game. Pioneered by the University of Texas, this practice is now followed by a number of colleges and high schools.

2. Conduct a brief clinic each spring for faculty and students to provide better understanding of the game and coaching problems.

3. At halftime of televised games show a film devoted to outstanding faculty members and educational achievements. This practice is followed by member institutions of the Atlantic Coast and Big Ten Conferences.

4. Schedule gym nights once a week for faculty men to encourage knowledge and participation in various sports.

5. Stress the relationship of scholarship to athletics by adopting conference or institutional honors for the athlete who excels in the class room as well as on the playing field. Faculty members can play an important part in the selection of recipients for such honors. Most of the major conferences now are selecting all-academic, all-conference teams.

School papers should carry accounts of the coming athletic event; a lengthy article about the contest written by a student reporter after an interview with the coach would be interesting. Student assemblies may be held to arouse student interest. It is the student who will be receiving the benefit of an athletic event and this should be pointed out to them.

Baley[32] comments on the part the school plays in publicity:

Bulletin boards, posters, student newspapers, and faculty bulletins should all be utilized to publicize the gymnastics program within the school itself. Interesting articles (newspaper or magazine) and pictures of gymnastics can be

[31]Duke, Wayne, "Public Relations and Athletics," *Journal of Health, Physical Education and Athletics* (October, 1959), p. 52.

[32]Baley, James, "Public Relations," *The Journal of Health, Physical Education and Recreation,* (November, 1961), p. 27.

posted on strategically placed bulletin boards. Stories and pictures of the home group should be prominently displayed. Bulletin boards should be attractive and neat– materials should be changed frequently.

Art departments may design or produce posters for you, or this may be done commercially. Posters should be eye-catching and stimulating. This requires some thought and planning. Do not clutter up a bulletin board or poster. Illustrations should be large enough to be seen from a distance.

The faculty news bulletin can be used to inform your colleagues of coming events or of progress made. More of the story can be told through letters and the student newspaper. Announcements of coming activities can be prepared to be read to classes by all teachers.

Students

Efforts should be made by members of the athletic faculty to develop among the students a sense of the value of the athletic program. It is necessary that the students know why the program is important. Students who understand that athletics is more than just fun for the participants, more than a big show for the spectators, more than just a contest to show supremacy in a particular sport will back the athletic program and be loyal supporters of it. These students will have gained the insight and developed positive attitudes toward the athletic program and, as a result, they will be staunch boosters when they become parents, adults, and taxpayers.

It should always be remembered that public relations start at school with the contacts the coaches, athletic director, and everyone connected with the athletic program make with the students. These people really have no choice as to whether they wish to engage in public relations. It is in the final analysis, the kind of public relations in which they engage in daily and the affect it makes upon the students, that

is important. The students will be affected one way or the other because they come face to face with the results of the program every day. It will be accepted or rejected depending upon the nature of the impact which the athletic program makes upon them. It is, therefore, important that the public relations program be the kind that will show that not only is the athletic program essential to the total education program, but that it deserves the support of the students. How this is accomplished depends upon many people. Its importance cannot be questioned.

Tener[33] makes the following comment regarding the students and public relations:

> Interpreting the sports program to the rank and file of the student body is an essential consideration. Like the teacher in the classroom, the nucleus of a good public relations program is the coach himself. The most constant means of communication to the home is that furnished by pupils. Consequently, most opinions held by parents have been molded from the reactions of their children. This is often where coaches are remiss. Usually too much concentration is directed to the 'stars' of the team and limited consideration is given to the marginal players, junior varsity players and especially the student who has a keen desire to participate but is not proficient to make any of the teams representing the school.

Community

The athletic program holds a very prominent and important place in American society. It has been justified only on the basis that it is an integral part of the educational program. It must be kept that way and this can be done only by convincing the general public that it is accomplishing this purpose. The people

[33]Tener, Morton, "Public Relations in Athletics."

within the community are generally aware of *what* the athletic contest is, *where* it will be held, and *how* the decisions are made. Therefore, the public relations program must provide the general public with information as to *why* the athletic program should be continued. This can only be done by communication through a good public relations program. The people must be given a regular presentation and interpretation of the achievements, problems, purposes, proposed goals, and objectives of the athletic program. The athletic department must continually bring to the attention of the people of the community, as they are the ones who determine the course of education, the contributions made by a program of interschool athletics. A good program of public relations will bring about favorable public reaction to the athletic program so the public will support it. This is the responsibility of the athletic director and coaches. There are various ways in which to do this and a number of them will be listed. It should be kept in mind that citizens who can participate will be interested.

Tener[34] makes the following comment about the community and public relations:

Neglected in most cases, public relations are predicated upon wins and losses. Though the amount of wins a team may achieve is still a very important factor in a community's attitude, individuals in this current era are more cognizant of the educational values in sports. Consequently, a team's record does not have to be the only criterion for success. An athletic public relations committee should be established in order to explore, take advantage, and implement all public relations possibilities.

A standard avenue used to expose the community to the school's athletic activities is newspaper coverage. It is usually adequate, but not always limited to a game's action. It is fair to all con-

cerned that the public be given the opportunity to take a look behind the scene. Parent-teacher study groups are not unfamiliar in current school systems. Why can't this be applied to athletics? Evening sessions could be offered for parents to learn the mechanics and rules of the sport and to incite interest. A genuine understanding of the program and its problems can also be brought to the surface.

Voltmer and Esslinger[35] make the following observation:

In recent years many coaches have endeavored to develop effective public relations by weekly letters to alumni, supporters, faculty, parents, and other interested individuals. Other coaches have weekly meetings with local groups. Some coaches write letters to parents. All these methods are of value in transmitting correct information to interested groups, and if they are well done, supporters are gained. Much of the antagonism toward coaches and teams is the result of misinformation.

A civic organization will often help promote an athletic event. Many of these men are in business, and they can spread the word concerning the coming athletic event. It might be possible to get several of the businessmen to purchase a considerable quantity of tickets to give away to loyal customers. The cost of the tickets could be deducted from their income tax. In many communities booster clubs or parent organizations play an active part in the promotion of athletics in the high school. These organizations, sometimes consisting of the players' fathers, could assume the responsibility of ticket sales and help in the promotion of the contest.

Posters are often put in windows of leading business places or other prominent

---

[34]*Ibid.*

[35]Voltmer, Edward, Esslinger, Arthur, *The Organization and Administraton of Physical Education* (New York, Appleton-Century Crofts, 1967), p. 473.

establishments. The best publicity for future athletic events is through people who have watched previous athletic events at the high school.

Publications

Publications can be used in public relations in the athletic program. This will be dependent on the financial situation of the athletic department and the personnel needed to pursue such a program. The most important publication media is the brochure or handbook. This contains a complete summarization of the department's philosophy, aims, and objectives. The amount of material included in the brochure will depend upon the desires of those individuals planning, preparing, and bearing the responsibility for its publication. Its length will range from a few pages to an elaborate publication including pages of written material, pictures, and advertisements.

The main problem confronting publications is the cost. There are various ways that publications can be used and a few of these will be discussed.

The principle publicity media employed in public relations are newspapers, magazines, radio, and television. In high school athletics, the local newspaper and radio would certainly qualify as being the most important. Newspapers are the basic media in public relations because they are read by many local people, enjoy the confidence of the readers in most cases, exert a tremendous influence on public opinion, provide good coverage of the areas in which they circulate or appear frequently.

A knowledge of the news functions of newspapers, radio, and television is desirable in the preparation of news releases and relations with the press. Not all coaches, and for that matter, athletic directors, are fortunate enough to have this knowledge

or experience. For most coaches, the first serious recognition of the public relations problem comes with the first visit from the local sports editor or sportscaster. It is a bit late at that point to try to acquire a working knowledge of public relations. All the people connected with the athletic program are directly involved in press and radio relations, from the receptionists who greets the sports writer, the office worker who answers the phone, the coaches and the athletic director. The principle responsibility for press relations rests with these persons who determine the policies which creates news, those who execute the policies, and those who meet the press. The athletic director and the coaches are the ones generally involved.

In regard to publicity, it should be remembered that the publication of news stories and pictures are most effective in encouraging those who take part in the activity. The members of a team feel that the attention given their activity by the newspaper lifts that activity a bit above the ordinary and that it gives the activity added prestige and importance.

If the athletic program is a good one, it is never difficult to get publicity, especially through the newspaper. The newspaper should be kept informed and aware of what is being planned. They should be given schedules, programs, and announcements well in advance.

Gathany[36] comments on the newspaper and publicity as follows:

> Newspapers cannot begin to cover all high school football, basketball, or baseball games in an area without some assistance. They must rely upon correspondents in the individual localities to supply information. That correspondent may be the coach, a student, a reporter for the town daily or weekly newspaper,

---

[36]Gathany, Ted, "Pressing for a Good Press," *The Athletic Journal* (November, 1959), p. 60.

or even an interested team follower. However, the responsibility for getting the information to the correct sources rests on the shoulders of this individual.

If this correspondent follows four basic and simple rules, press coverage of an athletic program can be as effective and broad as allowable, and coaches will reap the benefits in player and town morale. The four basic principles are: (1) know whom to contact and when, (2) know what the newspapers want, (3) be honest and objective, (4) be reliable.

Radio and Television

Spot comments over local broadcasting stations along with taped interviews with celebrated coaches are methods used in informing many people about the athletic event. During the week prior to the contest, the host coach should conduct a five- to ten-minute interview describing the history of the event, commenting on the top performers and previewing some of the happenings that are to take place the evening or day of the contest.

Baley[37] states the following regarding radio publicity:

> Radio is another useful communication media, but presentations must contain qualities of vitality. Here one can appeal to loyalty to school, community, or friends. Stimulate curiosity by painting word pictures. Interviews with student participants or the coach can be interesting.
>
> Tape recordings of interviews with children enrolled in our tumbling classes at Mississippi Southern College were made. The proceeds from these classes completely financed our comprehensive gymnastic program, including the purchase of most equipment, all uniforms, expenses of travel, entry fees, etc. This was possible in large part through good publicity.

Many of the athletic contests can be broadcast by the local radio stations even though the school may be small. Arrangements should be made in advance with the station so that there is no misunderstanding either from a financial standpoint or concerning privileges. This should be done in writing.

The opportunities to utilize television as a medium will be limited, but wherever possible, short announcements should be made on the contest, and possibly a short taped or live interview should be arranged. For large and important contests this is one medium that should be used a great deal.

Certain events lend themselves well to television coverage. Gymnastics is a good example. Baley[38] makes the following comment:

> Gymnastics lends itself well to television. Good planning results in contin-

Hannibal Senior High School

H. V. MASON, Principal

TELEPHONE 2733   4500 McMASTERS AVENUE

Hannibal, Missouri

Mr. _____

Radio Station _____

_____

_____

Dear Mr. _____:

    As the Athletic Director of _____ High School, I would like to confirm Radio Station _____ as the broadcaster of our athletic events, and grant you the rights and privileges to broadcast.

    Payment of fees for these rights and privileges of broadcasting, Radio Station _____ agrees to pay $_____ for the athletic events.

    Radio Station _____ and _____ High School mutually respect this letter as an agreement between the two.

            Sincerely,

            Athletic Director

Acknowledged:

_____
  (Radio Station)

By_____

on_____

Figure 78.

---

[37]Baley, James, "Public Relations."

[38]*Ibid.*, p. 27.

TABLE LXV

APPLICATION FOR RADIO BROADCASTING AND TELEVISING SPENCER CONSOLI-
DATED HIGH SCHOOL FOOTBALL OR BASKETBALL GAMES: _____ 19____

Address all applications and other correspondence to the athletic director of the high school involved.

Name of Station _____ City _____ State _____

Game or games requested _____ Date _____

Date _____

Date _____

Date _____

Date _____

Will broadcast or telecast be sponsored or unsponsored? _____

Sponsor and its product or service will be _____

Mail press box tickets to _____

(Limit 2)

FOR STATIONS REQUESTING COMMERCIAL PRIVILEGES

We agree to make payment to Spencer Consolidated High School in the amount of _____
_____ at least one week in advance of the date of each broadcast or telecaast. We
have read the School District broadcasting and telecasting policy and agree to abide by its provisions.

Signed: _____

Position: _____

Address: _____

Date _____

Approved _____

TABLE LXVI
JEFFERSON HIGH SCHOOL DISTRICT 122

RADIO AND/OR TELEVISION BROADCASTING OF HIGH SCHOOL ATHLETIC EVENTS
Permission for commercial radio and/or television stations to broadcast high school athletic events may be granted by the Athletic Director under the following conditions:

1. Exclusive broadcasting or telecasting privileges shall not be granted to any one station. If there is insufficient space to accommodate all applicants, local stations will be given preference. However, at least one visiting station shall be granted broadcast space. The high school athletic director shall notify teams in their leagues of this policy.

2. A broadcast privilege fee shall be charged for both sponsored and unsponsored play-by-play broadcasts, and the fee shall be the same for all stations.

3. Stations carrying play-by-play broadcast or telecast of football games will be charged privilege broadcasting fees as follows: _____ for local and out-of-town stations. The play-by-play broadcast or telecast of basketball games will be charged privilege broadcasting fees as follows: _____ for local and out-of-town stations. (State association approval must be given for telecasts).

   (A commercially-sponsored broadcast or telecast is considered as one for which any part of the time consumed is paid for by one or more sponsors; or by one where before, during or after the broadcast or telecast, the name or names of sponsors, their products, businesses, or professions are mentioned.)

4. Delayed or tape broadcasts must also request the broadcast privilege, and stations using such broadcasts shall be charged the regular broadcast fee.

5. The school district reserves the right to reject any or all applications for broadcast or telecast privileges whether noncommercially or commercially sponsored. The superintendent

may approve or reject the product or service which desires to sponsor a broadcast or telecast. No beer, wine, or tobacco sponsorship shall be permitted. No tavern or other establishment serving alcoholic beverages will be accepted for sponsorship. Combination businesses, such as drug stores, hotels, or restaurants which may dispense or distribute alcoholic beverages may be acceptable as sponsors, but no part of advertising messages shall refer to the dispensing or distribution of alcoholic beverages, beer, wine, or tobacco, or to a bar, cocktail lounge, or other facility dispensing alcoholic beverages.

6. Local arrangements for broadcast or telecast of athletic events shall be made with the athletic director of the school involved at least one week before the broadcast or telecast, and an agreement form shall be executed between the program director of the radio or television station and the athletic director.

7. Each station given permission to broadcast football games shall be limited to two seats in the broadcast area of the press box. No other complimentary tickets will be available to station representatives.

8. All installation costs incurred by radio or television stations in connection with broadcasts or telecasts are to be met by the station or stations concerned.

9. If two or more stations are included in a multistation commercial broadcast or telecast of school games, the privilege-fee for broadcasting or telecasting as indicated in (3) above shall be paid by each station involved, one week before the broadcast or telecast.

10. Broadcasting privileges shall be requested at least one week in advance of the game.

ARDMORE CITY SCHOOLS
ATHLETIC DEPARTMENT
TELEPHONE 405 / 223-2471 • P.O. BOX 1709 • ARDMORE, OKLAHOMA 73401

HOME OF THE
ARDMORE TIGERS

Date

Dear Mr. _____:

This letter is about the policies of the press and photographers which our school officials have set up for this coming year. They basically are the same as in the past. However, in the case that you have acquired some new assistants, we again would like to review them for you. The policies have been set up with the best interest of all the people concerned in mind, and we feel that they will assist you in doing your job not only better, but with less inconvenience to yourself and others.

Press Policies

1. All newspapers within a 50-mile radius will receive two tickets

2. Tickets are not transferable

3. Seats will be reserved in the press box

4. Coaches will not be interviewed one-half hour before or after the game

Photographer Policies

1. Pictures will be taken from the end lines except those taken from the vicinity of the press box

2. Pictures will be the property of the host school or the photographer

3. No pictures will be allowed to be taken that would interfere with the performance of any contestant

Sincerely,

Athletic Director

Figure 79.

uous movement, with no stage waits. Use colorful costumes and select the most interesting stunts to provide a better program. TV presentations should possess the qualities of freshness, daring, and spontaneity. Because gymnastics provides many opportunities to display both skill and daring, it is especially effective on television.

Several days before the group is scheduled to make a television appearance, you should visit the TV station to measure the working area and the ceiling height. When this has been determined, the group should rehearse the show under as nearly identical circumstances as possible.

An example of television programming, with a different message promulgated on each show, might be as follows. On the first show, present balance beam and free exercise activities, demonstrating the inherent opportunities for artistic self-expression. At another performance, presenting rebound tumbling and mat tumbling, point out the opportunities for the development of physical courage. On a third show present side horse and parallel bar work, indicating the possibilities for the development of perseverance as well as strength. With complete knowledge of the field and a little imagination, the possibilities are limitless. However, be careful not to exaggerate or to misrepresent. As educators, we should use publicity media to broaden our effectiveness in achieving educational goals, not to add glory or fanfare to our own program.

To achieve more with less effort, you might also produce a movie of your group and its activities.

Treatment of News Media

The treatment of the news media should merit the undivided attention of every member of the athletic staff. It is through this means that the most good can be done in the area of public relations. Extreme care should be taken so that the news media is given every opportunity to exercise all their talents in giving the public the information that will be beneficial to the athletic program. Keep the news media well-informed, work closely with them. Never be too busy to see them. Give them the cooperation they deserve. Assist them in every way possible.

The press and radio are dedicated to the task of disseminating the news as they see it. They cannot be biased, although local sports writers are usually anxious to do what they can to help the coach in producing winning teams. It is much easier to write about a winner than a loser, and most sports writers enjoy doing it. Most sports writers will help as long as the ethics of his paper are not violated. They can help build up the fighting spirit of a team or inspire confidence in a worried team. This is ethical help and many times badly needed by the coach at crucial times during the season.

The athletic department should provide good working conditions for the press and radio including adequate space for the writers and radio men. They should be provided with a good point of vantage with an unobstructed view of the activity. The radio men should have space enough to hold all of his equipment.

With a mutual understanding of needs and procedures, the athletic department and news media can work together for the mutual benefit of both parties and gain better athletic news coverage to the local community.

The coach plays an important part in public relations and its effect upon the press. The coach must attempt at all times to be completely honest and never, at any time, give false impressions or attempt to deceive a sports writer for personal gain.

Canfield[39] has listed the following do's and don'ts in dealing with the press:

> Do's
> Be friendly, polite, and even-tempered.
> Be helpful
> Be accurate
> Be truthful
> Be frank
> Be thorough
> Be fair
> Be patient
> Don'ts
> Don't lie

ATHLETIC DEPARTMENT

ELYRIA **HIGH SCHOOL**

ELYRIA, OHIO 44035
TELEPHONE 322-6387

Date

Dear Sports Editor:

This letter is in regard to the annual basketball tournament held at Elyria High School, December 26-31, 19___. This tournament has consistently drawn some of the best teams in the state. This year's tournament, from all indications, promises to be no exception.

We have been proud of the tradition this tournament has developed and proud of the enthusiasm it has generated throughout the twenty-five years it has been held.

The tournament has been successful for many reasons. It has first and foremost been conducted from an educational standpoint with the winning having second priority. This has been the theme and philosophy of the tournament since its inception twenty-five years ago. We wish to keep it that way.

Most important, however, this tournament has always been received enthusiastically by the news media. It is with this in mind that we solicit your help, encouragement and backing. Without this help it cannot hope to be successful.

We hope your help will be forthcoming and all of us working together can make this year's tournament the best ever.

Sincerely,

Athletic Director

kk

Figure 80.

[39]Canfield, Betrand, *Public Relations* (Homewood, Illinois, Richard Irwin, Inc., 1964), p. 466.

Don't bluster
Don't lose your temper
Don't Exaggerate
Don't write opinion, just facts
Don't blame a reporter for his paper's
   policies
Don't be self-important
Don't expect miracles
Don't give up

Types of Material Given to the News Media

The kinds and types of news that is given to the news media will vary according to the philosophy of the school regarding the place of athletics in the school, the size of the school, the personnel, and the interest the local news media takes in the program.

The athletic director should make it as convenient as possible for the news media to obtain the information they want. The following guides will help encourage coverage.

The coach should prepare a statement for the press concerning the coming athletic event. The local paper will almost always print such statements, and if the coach will prepare several lead stories about various performers and aspects of the particular event, a great deal of fan interest can be aroused. Another attention-getter is to publish weekly summaries of the top performances given by various members of the conference in an athletic event. If the performances are very good, they can be compared to the performance of other individuals in the area. Near the date of the contest, a picture of the queen along with the top performers from her school could be placed in the paper. This is particularly effective in individual-event meets such as track, swimming, golf, etc.

Letters should be sent to all sport writers in the vicinity informing them of the policies that are to be followed in regard to press admittances, passes, seating accommodations, and facilities available to them.

Photographers should be given sideline passes and told about the area from which they may take pictures. All such personnel should be told where to present their passes for admittance, the location of the pass gate, and the procedure to be followed in admitting them to the event.

The school newspaper and the daily bulletin should be used to promote the events among the students, telling them of the teams involved, time of the contests, and the price of admission. Posters should be distributed to the various schools and the various communities.

Baley[40] explains how to tell the story of the athletic program:

> Newspaper articles and pictures are important publicity media. The first step in using news services is to visit the newspaper offices, particularly the sports writers. Learn their deadlines; then stick to them. Find out how they want stories prepared. Size of paper, double spacing, wide margins are all standard, but they may have other special requirements. Ask about preparing the information in note or story form. In typing the release be careful of spelling, punctuation, and neatness as well as the accuracy of the facts. Finish paragraphs on the page rather than continuing to the next page. Make the story complete but not long-winded; reporters and editors can condense and shorten an article but they cannot fill in the facts. Editorializing in your news stories is not permissible.

Public Relations Activities

Annual Awards Party

The annual awards party is probably the most popular and one of the best opportunities for public relations afforded the high school athletic department. It provides an opportunity for a great many

---

[40]Baley, James, "Public Relations."

TABLE LXVII
DAVIS HIGH SCHOOL DISTRICT NO. 99

PRESS PUBLICITY GUIDE

1. Identify team members
    - a. Age
    - b. Year in school
    - c. Weight
    - d. Height
    - e. Position
    - f. Experience
    - g. Family relationship to previous members
2. Identification of coaches
    - a. Number of years coaching
    - b. Alma mater
    - c. Coaching record
    - d. Honors received
    - e. Other positions held
3. History of school sports program
    - a. Early years
    - b. Best year
    - c. Outstanding coaches
    - d. Athletic record
    - e. Rivalries
    - f. Traditions
4. Student manager system used
    - a. Present managers
    - b. Past managers
    - c. Duties
5. Schedule
    - a. Conference members — Final conference standings last season — strong contenders this season — new gyms and fields — new coaches (see identification of coaches) — conference affiliations — distance to travel.
    - b. Nonconference members — strong contenders — new gyms and fields — new coaches (see identification of coaches) — conference affiliations — distance to travel.
6. Cheerleaders
    - a. Name — years of experience — family relationship
    - b. New candidates
    - c. Past cheerleaders
    - d. Dress
    - e. Method of selection
    - f. Duties
    - g. Training
7. Administration
    - a. Tickets
    - b. Gatekeepers
    - c. Programs
    - d. Publicity
    - e. Parking
    - f. Ushers
    - g. Concessions
    - h. Timers
    - i. Scorers
    - j. Care of guests
    - k. Accounting
    - l. _____
8. Pregame releases for press
    - a. Opponent
    - b. Time
    - c. Place
    - d. History
    - e. Significance — conference standing — victory string — Homecoming, etc. — first game last
    - f. All-time won and loss records
    - g. Band
    - h. Pep squad
    - i. Special features
    - j. Probable line-up
    - k. Officials
    - l. Coaches
9. Postgame write-up
    - a. Score — effect on conference standing — size of crowd — injuries — unusual occurrences
    - b. First score and by whom — style of offense and defense and effectiveness — strength or weaknesses
    - c. Box score
10. Photographs
    - a. Squad pictures
    - f. Individual

b. Cheerleader costumes
c. Biggest boy
d. Coaching staff
e. Brothers
g. Smallest boy
h. Comparison: smallest/biggest
i. Returning lettermen
j. Scrubs
11. Other basis for feature write-ups
   a. Lettermen — what became of them — college record — success in community or political affairs — military record — members from same family — records held
   b. Former captains (see above)
   c. History of conference
   d. Tournament history
   e. Homecomings
   f. Traditions
   g. Records — likely to be broken — unlikely — holders of the records
   h. State association affiliations

TABLE LXVIII

KANSAS HIGH SCHOOL DISTRICT NO. 115

SAMPLE PREGAME PUBLICITY RELEASE

_____ vs. _____

Opponent Nickname

Game Date _____ Day _____ Time _____ _____

Tentative
Lineup   WE   THEY   OFFICIALS

_____   _____   _____
_____   _____   _____
_____   _____   _____
_____   _____   Coach WE
_____   _____   _____
_____   _____   Coach THEY
_____   _____   _____
_____   _____
_____   _____

No. times played in past _____ We won _____ They won _____

Their lettermen   _____   _____   _____
                  _____   _____   _____
Our lettermen   _____   _____   _____
                  _____   _____   _____

Outstanding players and what is outstanding about them
We _____
_____
They _____
_____

Conference Record to Date   WE _____   THEY _____
All Game Record to Date   WE _____   THEY _____
Interesting Historical Data _____
_____

Miscellaneous _____
_____

TABLE LXIX
BATAVIA HIGH SCHOOL DISTRICT NO. 22

Preseason Publicity Information Sheet

Lettermen _____   _____   _____
_____   _____   _____
_____   _____   _____
_____   _____   _____

Last season won _____ lost _____ Conference won _____ lost _____
Conference affiliation _____
Non-   _____   _____   _____
lettermen
prospects   _____   _____   _____
_____   _____   _____

New buildings, _____
equipment,
etc.   _____
Coach _____ College attended _____
    All time win _____ loss _____ Last season win _____ Loss _____
    Other _____
Assistant Coach _____ College attended _____
    All time win _____ loss _____ Last season win _____ loss _____
    Other _____
New   _____
opponents
tourneys   _____
Season   _____
prospects
_____

N. B. The schedule of games at home and away are attached to this sheet.

TABLE LXX
PERSONAL DATA SHEET

Name _____   _____
HOME ADDRESS _____
HOME PHONE _____ BIRTH DATE _____
MARITAL STATUS _____ NUMBER OF CHILDREN _____
YOUR HOME TOWN _____
DEGREES HELD & SCHOOL _____
_____
_____

ATHLETIC PLAYING EXPERIENCE   (High School, College, Professional)

_____
_____
_____
_____

COACHING EXPERIENCE   (Sport & School)

_____
_____
_____

HONORS WON AS PLAYER OR COACH

_____ _____
_____ _____
_____ _____

WHAT SPORTS ARE YOU COACHING AT GLENBARD EAST? LEVEL?

_____ _____
_____ _____
_____ _____

TABLE LXXI

STARTING LINEUPS FOR _____ GAME

_____ vs. _____

No.	Receiving Team	Pos.	No.	Kicking Team
_____	_____	LE	_____	_____
_____	_____	LT	_____	_____
_____	_____	LG	_____	_____
_____	_____	C	_____	_____
_____	_____	RG	_____	_____
_____	_____	RT	_____	_____
_____	_____	RE	_____	_____
_____	_____	QB	_____	_____
_____	_____	HB	_____	_____
_____	_____	HB	_____	_____
_____	_____	FB	_____	_____
Captain	_____			

people to gather together at a prearranged function for the sole purpose of honoring the athletes and coaches. It brings parents, coaches, and players together in a manner which can be rewarding, educational, and beneficial to everyone.

There are certain procedures which should be followed in planning an all awards party. The very first thing that must be done is to arrange for someone who is willing to take over the responsibility. Often this can be a service club in the community or within the school itself. Sometimes an interested parent will assume this responsibility. Whoever does accept this responsibility should be assured that he will be given the full cooperation of the director of athletics, coaches, and the principal because it is a herculean task to make all the arrangements necessary to make the party a success. A faculty member may be enticed into acting as master of ceremonies. This type of party affords a golden opportunity to promote excellent public relations.

Decorations

Any championship event should include decorations. The use of banners or pennants of the competing teams can be placed around the competition area in full view of the audience. A large banner with the name of the tournament can be placed at a central place, such as over the entrance to the gym. The decorations should be as colorful as possible. Any championship game or tournament is an exciting affair and colorful decorations add to that excitement. This is a definite part of a good public relations program.

ANNOUNCER'S PLAYER IDENTIFICATION CHART

School_____

L E No.	L T No.	L G No.	C No.	R G No.	R T No.	R E No.

Q B No.

L H No.	F B No.	R H No.

COACH_____

ASST. COACH_____

CAPTAIN_____

Figure 81.

Dressing Accommodations for Officials

Separate locker and shower areas for officials should be provided. It is good public relations to provide a coaches-officials hospitality room (coffee, rolls, etc.) where officials can relax before and after the competition and during prolonged intermissions.

Publication of Top Scholars in Athletics

The recognition given to top scholars who participate in athletics affords a good opportunity to dispel the image of the dumb athlete that some people have. Over the years, people in general, have developed an attitude that students involved in athletics are scholastically inferior to the average student. Actually, many top disciplined athletes also perform well in an academic role because the discipline they practice in athletics carries over to their performance in the classroom. The public can be made aware of the academic benefits of athletics. This can be accomplished through publicizing the many top scholars who are participants in athletics.

Clinic for Players' Parents

Whenever students are involved in athletics at any grade or age level, the parents either directly or indirectly also become involved in the athletic program. If a clinic for the parents is organized for each sport, it will give the coach an opportunity to explain to the parents what he is trying to accomplish in his program. This will help to bridge the gap that often develops between the parents and the coach because of a lack of communication.

Basketball Preview Night

A good program designed to enlist the support of the parents and promote good public relations is a preview night which is held prior to the season. The parents and general public are invited to see all the players of each team introduced in uniform and to observe a scrimmage. A social hour of coffee and donuts can follow the program.

Athletic Checklist for Teachers

One way of promoting good public relations between the athletic department and academic teachers and at the same time further the cause for the athlete who is enrolled in an academic course, is the athlete's checklist. The checklist includes the player's name, his coach's name, and items of difficulty that the student may encounter in class. The teacher is asked to check the particular area where the student has problems. The coach then attempts to arrange a conference between the student, parents, and the teacher in an attempt to solve the problem.

Clinics for Students of Elementary Schools

Young people today have things to attract their interest and to consume their time. Coaches must be prepared to sell their programs to these people before they enroll in high school. This is true in all sports but is particularly true in the so-called minor sports. High school coaches can put on clinics to build good public relations and at the same time create an interest in these sports for students in the elementary schools. There are several kinds of clinics that a high school coach can promote at this level. One effective way to reach a great number of youngsters is through an all-school, athletic assembly program. Another kind of clinic is the visit to the high school athletic practice sessions. A third type of clinic which is very effective is to invite the elementary students and coaches to the high school on a Saturday for a formal coaching clinic. Still another clinic that is effective is an off-season program, allowing students to come to the high school several times a week and participate in an instructional program taught by the high school coaches and athletes.

Hosts for Dressing Rooms

A wonderful opportunity for good public relations with the visiting school presents itself when they visit the campus for an athletic contest.

Upon arrival at the gymnasium or field house, the team is met at the door by an appointed host. This person should be dressed neatly and appropriately, so that he will be recognized by the visiting team. He should introduce himself and escort the team to their dressing room. The host should be friendly and courteous and offer his services to the visiting coach. It is very important that the student host make a good impression at the outset if he is to be of value. This could be the first visit to the school by the other team; first impressions often leave a lasting mark.

The host's duty does not end there. As the host, he should make himself available to the visiting coach for whatever purpose the coach should deem necessary.

Once the visiting team is dressed and ready to leave the room the host locks the room. He then makes himself readily available at halftime and during any emergency in which the visiting team finds itself.

At the end of the game, the host checks the dressing quarters for equipment that has been left behind and escorts the team to the door, providing any services that might be of some help along the way.

It is of the utmost importance that the host be discrete and inconspicuous at all times. He must use good judgment in all his actions, being careful never to offend and yet always be ready to serve and assist whenever he can.

Monthly Newsletter and Sports Calendar

Both the newsletter and the sports calendar can be of help in promoting the high school athletic program. These publications inform fans on the progress of each team and when they will be in action. The newsletter should give full coverage to all sports.

The sports calendar should be distributed to all interested parties, particularly alumni and booster club members. Dates of all athletic contests and other school activities should be posted in public places and at the main entrance to the school.

Players Making Trips

Providing an opportunity for students to visit other school campuses is one aspect of athletics that can be a very important educational experience if properly administered. An athletic team can reflect the image of its school and community. When players visit another school, they should act as guests and try to promote good interschool relations. If the members of a visiting team are dressed presentably, this will project a far better image of the school and community than if they appear sloppy and unruly. Visiting teams and their coaches should think of themselves as goodwill ambassadors representing their school and community and dress and conduct themselves accordingly. The public relations effects will be far reaching and very worthwhile.

Players Dressing for Home Games

A successful team has pride in its appearance as well as its performance. Warmup jackets and pants must always be clean and worn correctly. Uniform tops must be neatly tucked inside the bottoms. Every member of the team must have the same type of shoes and socks.

Every member of the team, from the captain down to the third string, should have pride in his appearance. Proper dress and appearance is public relations at its best.

Scoreboard

The scoreboard will add tremendously to the enjoyment of the game by the spectators and is essential if any game is to progress smoothly. Its main function is to inform the participants and spectators. Every scoreboard should clearly display the score, inning or quarter, and time remaining if time is used. Other information may be added if it is not confusing and does not distract from the appearance.

The scoreboard or boards should be placed where they can be viewed by every player and spectator. They should be far enough from the playing area so as not to cause a safety problem. The scoreboard should be checked before each contest to be sure that it is operating correctly. Any burned out bulbs should be replaced. Finally, the operation of the scoreboard during a contest should be performed by an experienced person who knows the exact procedure for operation. Hand timers and official scorebooks should be kept nearby in case of scoreboard breakdown.

Fathers Sitting on the Bench

Inviting fathers to sit on the bench can provide a wonderful opportunity to create and generate parental support and give recognition to the parents of the athletes and student managers and any of the other students that are directly concerned with the sport. Parent support is very important when trying to have a successful athletic program.

One possible bad point when having "Fathers on the Bench" is that it could produce some type of pressure, on the players that might not be there if the father was in the stands. This pressure could cause good effects as well as bad effects.

Use of the Local Radio Station

The radio station is a good media for public relations. Community interest can be developed and encouraged through this media. It offers a very good opportunity for advertisement, interviews with important personnel in the community, parents of some of the athletes, and even some of the athletes themselves. It should be used in every way possible as it affords an opportunity to reach the people in the community and surrounding area.

Athletic Handbook on Philosophy

The Athletic Handbook on Philosophy can do much for the public relations of an athletic department. The parents, athletes, community members, school staff, and the coaching staff can see and read the purposes, aims, goals, and objectives of a particular school's philosophy on athletics. This book may be used by counselors, school boards, press agents, and for teacher recruitment to express the school's attitude about athletics. Everyone has his own idea about what the philosophy should be, so there is a need for one central idea that is stated in writing.

Superintendent's Letter to Parents of Participants

A letter to the parents who have a child participating in sports can be in the form of an insurance policy. Parents will appreciate the fact that someone cares enough to send a letter thanking them for letting their child participate. A simple letter of concern and thanks can go a long way and may cause the parents to show more interest. The parents may be asked to help in such matters as training and fitness of their child. A letter may help to explain what the school stands for in the way of athletics and also the academics of its athletics. The letter should contain a request for the parents to contact the school in any matters they wish to talk about.

Schedules—Team Synopsis Sent to All News Media

The practice has grown in recent years for high school athletic departments to prepare a team synopsis which is made available to all local sportswriters and sportscasters in the area. This synopsis contains pertinent information about the team and includes the names of all squad members, with data concerning age, height, weight, experience, year in school, position, and the potential of the athlete. The previous season's record and the outlook for the present team are indicated in this synopsis. It also includes a complete biography and record of the head coach and his assistants. This method of providing information to all news media is a valuable technique for public relations.

Picture Displays of Games and Players

Picture displays can be used in several ways. One of the most common is the hallway display of outstanding athletes (Wall of Fame). This kind of display should be located in a prominent place in the school, and should feature individual champions and championship teams in all sports. Another kind of picture display can be used in the work-out area or locker room. The display case in the school can be used each week to promote interest in upcoming sports events. These pictures could be portraits, action shots, comedy shots, or anything that will draw attention. It is a wonderful public relations gesture and a motivating force for better performance by the athletes.

Faculty Representation at the Games

In the interest of good public relations, a good administrator will make sure that members of the school's faculty attend the games. It would seem that teachers would show enough interest in the school and its students to want to get involved. However, many times this is not the case in today's society. Most faculty members will not take on extra duty without being paid. Free passes can be given to faculty members and a kind word of thanks from an athletic staff member will also do much toward uniting the athletic program with the rest of the school's programs and provide the right kind of public relations.

Coaches' Corner

It is customary in many communities to sponsor a coaches' corner each week on radio to stimulate interest in the athletic programs. These programs are sometimes presented before and after games. This affords the coach an opportunity to educate the average fan in game strategy, sportsmanship, etc.

Handbook for Each Sport

The handbook is an excellent way to promote good public relations. Before the season begins for each sport, the head coach can compile the majority of the information that is to be included in the handbook. The content of the handbook should be determined by the members or the athletic department and could be very elaborate or very simple. The booklet, depending on the size of the school, can be mimeographed or offset printed, with pictures, etc.

When finished, the handbook can be distributed to the administration, faculty, townspeople, and athletes. Once the material is compiled, it is easily kept up to date from year to year.

Blown-up Pictures of Athletes

Most athletes like to be well thought of. An athlete can be honored for excellent performance by having his or her picture enlarged and placed in a location where a great number of people can see it. The athlete probably desires this type of recognition more than most other people. (This fact probably stems from the idea of pride and honor which is closely associated with athletic achievement.)

The use of this method of paying tribute to an outstanding performance can be a very successful means of obtaining good public relations. It can be considered an ever-existing type of publicity because it would be impossible to place every athlete in a picture gallery of this type.

Secondly, a good location for the display should be selected. It should be an area which allows the greatest number of students and adults to see the pictures. This location probably would be near the main gymnasium or fieldhouse.

Thirdly, a predetermined method of arrangement should be planned to place athletes in location by sport.

The development of a picture gallery honoring outstanding performances can most assuredly be of great value in obtaining good public relations. It pleases the parents, athletes, and students alike to see an outstanding athlete's picture placed where the entire public audience may reflect upon the student's athletic achievement.

Dad's Night

Dad's night can be another valuable way to promote good public relations between the community and the school's athletic program. Dad's night can be an occasion in which all the dads of the members of the team would be honored. The dads, along with the rest of the members of the family, can be admitted to the athletic event free of charge. During halftime, the dads can be introduced to the fans and given a momento of the event. An after-the-game activity can also be held to honor the dads. This is a valuable means of introducing the sport to the athletes' parents. They may find they enjoy it and return on later occasions.

Parents' Night Scrimmage

Parents' night scrimmages can be one of the most important nights of the year for a coach. Emerson once wrote, "He who has a thousand friends, has not a friend to spare, but he who has one enemy will meet him everywhere." For the coach, who has to satisfy or justify the way he handles young men, these words are most meaningful.

This particular night can be used to inform the parents about the objectives and rules of the program and the actual work and sacrifices that they and their child must make. The system of play that will be used during the year can also be discussed.

The use of an informal coffee and donut session will afford the coach and his staff an opportunity to meet the parents individually and to open lines of communication for the coming year. Name cards can be given to each parent to provide a personal touch. It will also help the staff introduce themselves to the parents and the parents to each other.

High School Coaches' Speakers Bureau

An excellent way to promote the high school athletic program is to have the various coaches speak to different organizations throughout the community. It is possible that many persons in the community do not know too much about the high school athletic program because they are not involved with it in any way. An explanation of the program can be given to these people. An opportunity should be provided those who have questions regarding the program.

A Weekly Interview with Coaches

The athletic program of the local high school can be given valuable publicity by providing an opportunity for the coaches to be interviewed and to have them express their views to the public. This can be done in several ways. A local radio station can have a weekly interview with a coach of a team at various times during the season. For example, the football and soccer coaches could be interviewed on alternate weeks from September to November. In some areas where cable television is available, it is possible to conduct interviews with coaches weekly on sport shows. Another excellent idea is to have the coach write a weekly column in the community newspaper. In this way, townspeople would be able to follow the progress of the various athletic teams and to know more about the program.

After the Game

After the game, public relations may set up a talk session for those parents who might want to talk about why coaches and players did certain things.

After the game get-togethers should be held twice a year and usually during the start and end of the season. During these meetings coaches and parents get to know each other better.

Organization of this meeting is very important and the wise coach and athletic director will try and schedule these meetings after playing teams of lower calibre. It is much easier for the coaches to go to the meeting as winners than as losers. Refreshments should also be served.

Contest Programs

A very good public relations opportunity presents itself in the form of contest programs. Programs list names and positions of players in the contest.

It can be very frustrating and discouraging to people if they have taken time to attend an athletic event and cannot distinguish one player from another.

The program can be responsible for developing a good rapport with the business men of the community by giving them a chance to advertise their product to the people of the community. At the same time, money can be made from selling this advertising space.

Parents can be given information on the rules and strategy of a particular sport through the use of the program. Some of the less popular and more difficult to understand sports such as wrestling, gymnastics, and football can be made easier to understand using this approach. This particular gesture is well appreciated and in turn results in good public relations.

Discussion of Schedule with News Media

An important public relations gesture would be to invite the sportswriter of the local newspaper and the sports announcer of the radio station to attend a preseason luncheon where they could meet the coaches, talk over the schedule, prospects for the season, and needs of the news media.

Furnishing of Pictures to Newspapers

It should not be left to the newspaper photographer to furnish all the pictures for the local newspaper. Pictures can be taken before the season begins and prints should be made available to the news media. A photographer should be at each game, and pictures he has taken should be available to the press.

Custodial Services and Maintenance

Athletic administrators place custodians and grounds personnel high on their list of important staff members. Without them,

playing areas would not be available and safe. Let them know you appreciate their help through acknowledgement or complimentary tickets and personal thanks. Neat and clean facilities usually correspond with safe facilities.

Availability of Coaches

Coaches should be available to visit with the parents and students at specified times during the week. There should be concern for not only academic problems but also personal problems. By becoming involved with his players, the coach can accomplish a great deal as far as helping his players cope with life. Parents will have more respect for the coach because they know he is concerned about their child. The coach's concern will serve as an excellent public relations gesture and will help the athletic program when it needs community support. If people feel that someone is really concerned about them, they are more willing to make sacrifices for that person.

Window Display

Athletic departments attract considerable interest from many segments of the community. Persons from every walk of life attend the athletic contests and identify with the school. An attractive window display could further enhance the relationship between the students, the school, and the community. The display can provide information and promote interest in all areas of athletics. This display should tell everyone who, what, when, where, and why. It should be attractive and eye-catching. The window display could be utilized effectively in the downtown stores as well as school window. This type of display can do a great deal for the public relations of the athletic department.

The window display could be looked

upon unfavorably if it is used incorrectly. By only using the display for fund-raising projects or for ticket sales, the community could become disgusted or disinterested. On the other hand, the community could identify with the program if the window display is used effectively. By attractively advertising the coming events or highlighting past events, the community would become more aware of the programs. The displays could draw more and wider support if they showed all types of athletic contests rather than only the "big sport" in the community. If these ideas are kept in mind, the window display could be very beneficial to the athletic department.

Booster Club

The need for people to become involved with the school athletic program has encouraged the formation of such organizations as the booster club. The members of these groups provide services and resources to build and develop facilities as well as provide equipment and supplies necessary to expand the athletic programs in many communities. These activities help to involve many dedicated citizens in the school program. They tend to hold a collective goal and a collective identity around which to build loyalties and around which they rally to a cause. These organizations may seek to serve their own purposes, however, rather than those of the school; they should not become so narrow and specialized that they neglect other areas of the total school program. The values of entertainment, victories, and community prestige should never dictate policy. The educational welfare of the student body, athlete and spectator alike, must be of primary concern in the formation of policies and procedures for administering the interscholastic athletic program.

Public Address System

The public address system is an excellent aid to the enjoyment of the game by the spectators. The system should be heard by all people in attendance. The speakers must be properly placed and the system continually maintained for trouble-free performance. The public address system is an excellent aid especially when it is manned by an experienced announcer. The announcer should be a mature person with good judgment and emotional stability. He must refrain from criticizing the performances of players, officials, or coaches in the contest for his responsibility is to provide the information necessary for the enjoyment of the game. The announcer should not use the techniques of the radio broadcaster in describing every detail of the play. He should provide only the information the spectator cannot secure from the scoreboard or personal observation.

The public address system is also extremely useful in case of emergency, but many individuals in local communities have attempted to exploit the local athletic situations by having their name publicly announced. A special policy and procedure needs to be established to control this problem. Spectators expecting calls during the contest should leave their seat numbers or special instructions with the box office. The ushers could then contact them directly without special announcements over the loud speaker. Of course emergencies will always arise where no provisions have been made. In such instances a system for the approving of special announcements should be provided.

Calling Cards Printed for Coaches

A calling card can be a great asset to a coach. These cards provide an easy and business-like way for the coach to inform people where he may be reached.

Calling cards can be printed in the school's own print shop if this facility is available. The amount of money spent for these cards will vary according to the needs of the individual.

The cards should include the school insignia, the coach or coaches' names, their addresses, and telephone numbers. The team schedule or any other important information may be printed on the card. All cards should be small enough to fit easily into a wallet.

Distribute calling cards to salesmen, opposing schools and coaches, the press, college coaches, and parents.

Posters

Attractive posters can be valuable aids to anyone who is trying to publicize an athletic event. Posters, if utilized correctly, can induce greater participation among the student body and a better understanding among the public.

A good poster is one that is eye-catching yet pleasing to look at. The poster should tell what the event is and where and when it will take place. Admission charge, phone numbers, and any other information may be added to the poster if necessary. A special slogan on the poster is also a good idea.

When making a poster, the most important things to remember are (1) keep the poster simple, (2) make sure every letter and word is legible, and (3) display the poster in a place where it will be seen by the greatest number of people.

Availability of Tickets for Community

All tickets for athletic contests not reserved for students, faculty, and press should be made available to the remainder of the community. These tickets can be sold at the door on the day of the game or at other locations throughout the community on days prior to the game.

Local merchants are usually happy to promote athletics by posting game schedules in their store windows. Some will also be interested in handling advance ticket sales.

The best thing is to be fair in distributing tickets. Season tickets are an excellent idea, especially when you consider the problems involved with postseason tournaments. Generally, season ticket holders have first choice on tournament tickets. This will guarantee a ticket to the fan who has followed the team all season.

The efficient handling of ticket distribution is appreciated, and it is a step in the right direction toward developing good public relations.

A Letter as a Method of Developing Good Public Relations from the Coach to the Parents

A letter from the coach to the parents of his players is an excellent idea, but very few coaches utilize this method of developing good public relations. Periodic letters to the parents can give them first hand information about the progress of the school team.

Coaches can use these letters to discuss a variety of topics. His philosophy, objectives for the season, or any other matter that he deems important can be discussed.

The coach should encourage the parents to respond to any questions or problems that may arise. Most parents will be happy to assist the coach in anyway they can. The coach should take the time to thank parents either by phone or through a letter. A letter to a parent shows that the coach is interested in the player's family and not just the player. Coaches can obtain much valuable information from the parents that may help him in working effectively with their child.

Concessions

The principles behind concessions at an athletic event are to provide an alternate means of income, while providing programs, refreshments, and other paraphernalia that expands the interest, enthusiasm, and color of the audience.

The athletic director must take advantage of the concession aspect of sports to involve not only different school departments but also to enlist support of the community. As an example each department may manage a concession for a particular or series of events to raise funds for that club or for a community organization.

Filing of Contest Data

The athletic administrator should assign the responsibility of filing athletic contest data to either the athletic sports information director, athletic director, coach, or student manager. The efficient handling of athletic contest results by local radio stations, newspapers, school newspapers, etc. could improve community, school, and student relations. Also the school, athletic department, and team's *esprit-de-corps* would be strengthened.

Ushers

It is always a good idea to provide qualified ushers for athletic events which draw a large number of people. Ushers should see that spectators enter and leave the building or stadium in an orderly fashion. They should also make sure that the spectators abide by any special rules concerning crowd behavior.

The usher spends most of his time before the game seating spectators if their tickets provide for a reserved seat. During the game ushers should keep the aisles clear.

Ushers should wear some type of uniform or other identification so that the spectators will know who he is. Ushers should be neatly groomed and dressed, looking as professional as possible. Using students as ushers is a good idea, provided they know their duties and how to react in emergencies. Ushers should always be courteous. A warm welcome to the spectator is most appreciated. Spectators should feel free to ask any usher for assistance if needed. The ushers are there to serve the spectators, and a thoughtful usher can do much to improve public relations.

Interpretation of the Athletic Program to the Students

Often students do not have the opportunity to learn the rules, understand the game, and know the players. An assembly program where the coaches of the sports in season discuss the rules and game strategy as well as introduce the players by position will provide the students with a much better knowledge of the game.

Involvement in Community Affairs

Every athletic director, coach, and for that matter, every teacher should become a member of the community. One way in which this can be done, and at the same time create good public relations, is to become involved in community projects such as March of Dimes, service clubs, blood bank drives, and programs for the retarded. By helping in these affairs and demonstrating that they are interested in helping others, the coaches are in a better position to ask for help for their own athletic program.

Parents' Night

An excellent public relation gesture is to set aside a time for recognizing and honoring parents of the athletes. They have sacrificed much and endured many hardships for their athletic offspring. The athletes themselves should feel happy and proud to recognize their parents' contribution to their athletic endeavors. It is a simple way to say thanks, and this program is always well received. The responsibility for this program can be undertaken by the student council. A letter to the parents requesting their presence at a certain date and time is essential. The usual time could be before a swimming or wrestling meet, and at the halftime of football or basketball games. The parents should be informed of the date and time of the event and be requested to attend a small get-together in the school cafeteria following the meet.

When parents arrive, they should be presented with a corsage (for mom) and boutonniere (for dad). For sports where numbered uniforms are worn by the athletes, the parents can be given their child's number to wear. A special seating arrangement can be made to place the parents together in an advantageous position.

As the ceremony begins, the parents' names are announced, "Mr. and Mrs. LeRoy Cisar, parents of Dawn and Dan." At this time the athlete(s) escort their parents to a position along the home sideline and stand with them. After the contest, over refreshments, the coaches can give a short talk and mingle with the parents.

Use of Service Clubs
for Transporting Athletes

There are athletes who, following athletic practice after school, have difficulty obtaining a ride home. This is not such a big problem in urban communities, but it can be in rural situations where there are many farm children involved in athletics. Some athletes have to be home at a certain time in order to do their portion of the farm chores. If they are not there, these chores are neglected and eventually the parents will force the child to give up athletics because of its interference with the work on the farm.

This problem can be solved by contacting one of a number of local organizations, such as Lions, Elks, etc. A ride service can be arranged to pick up the athletes at school after practice and drive them to their out-lying homes. A schedule of driving stints can be coordinated by the chairman of the group and the head coach. Any athlete who needs a ride should be ready at a certain time. A driver will then pick up a carload of students going in the same general direction and chauffeur them home.

This action benefits the school two ways: it involves those in the community who are interested by letting them be a part of the program and it keeps the athletes on the better side of their parents in relation to arriving home in time for chores.

Special Sport Season Tickets for Parents

These tickets are made available for parents of athletes turning out for the sport regardless of the level of competition. The criteria to be used for the issuance of these tickets must be established so that the practice is not abused.

Inspirational Awards Winner

This award is given to the player who has in the opinion of the coaches, done the most to inspire team members to do a better job. Usually the award should be given at the annual awards dinner. It can be given for each sport and be presented at the separate sport dinner.

Annual Spring Sports Festival

The total school can become involved in an annual sports festival. This is a tremendous public relations medium as it provides an opportunity for the students to learn something about the sport itself and to become acquainted with the individual athletes in these sports. Participation in the various sports is encouraged with coaches and athletes supervising the activities. Explanation and talks are given by coaches and players describing the sport, techniques, and rules.

Outstanding Athlete Recognition

A selection committee is established for the purpose of recognizing the outstanding achievements of the school athletes. Names are placed on a large plaque. The selection committee can include coaches, teachers, administrators, and students. A plaque can be used for each sport and the outstanding athlete for each sport can have his name inscribed on the plaque or the outstanding athlete for all sports can be recognized.

Fathers' Club

One of the most important aspects of public relations is personal contact. Through the proper use of clubs like the fathers' club, this personal contact can be accomplished. Through the fathers' club, information can be disseminated and a better understanding between school personnel and citizens of the community can be achieved.

Parents in the fathers' club can assist school personnel in different activities needed to make the event run smoothly. One of these jobs could be to help in the sale of tickets. There is always a need for people to assist in this area. Also, it makes citizens of the community a part of the program. Another job for the fathers' club could be for certain people to park cars before the event. This may help recruit additional fathers for membership in the club. A third job for the fathers' club might be to set up a coffee hour one night a week to view films of the previous week's activities. This could be one night a month or twice a month. The important thing is that citizens from the community should be given ample opportunities to view the program. This also may give them a chance to speak up and be heard if they have any ideas that may help the program.

Gold Passes for All Senior Citizens

Public relations means that the opinion of the community must be taken into consideration. Public opinion is very powerful and the success or failure of an athletic program depend a great deal on its influence. Athletics particularly, needs to bring about an understanding among parents, teachers, school administrators, and other citizens in the community. With one of the main purposes of public relations being to build confidence in the schools, what better way is there than to establish a good relationship with the senior citizens?

Basic psychological needs for the aged do not differ radically from those of any other age group. But many senior citizens are living on reduced or fixed incomes which limit or deny the leisure activity they may participate in. By establishing a gold pass for senior citizens, it not only alleviates a problem for them but also enhances the possibility of getting support and help from a senior citizen club.

In setting up a gold pass system for senior citizens for athletic events, a service could also be obtained from them. In performing such a service they will be given the feeling of becoming a part of the program. They could perform such services as selling programs, refreshments, or taking tickets at the door.

At various athletic events throughout the year, if it is not feasible for every athletic events, a section can be reserved for seating senior citizens wishing to attend. Recognition should be given to their presence at the athletic event.

Principal's Letter to Parents

Having the principal write a letter to the parents of those athletes who are participating in minor sports merits consideration as a public relations gesture. There are several points that can be covered in the letter which will further good public relations. The idea of just sending a letter has significant merit because in most cases it will be viewed by many parents as a goodwill gesture on the part of the school administration. Not only will the student develop a feeling of recognition and belonging but the parents will also develop a feeling that the school is interested in their child and what he does.

Statistics Available for Press

Statistics supply a source of information to the public and thus become one more phase of good public relations. Statistics is another form of developing an awareness of the importance of athletics in the total educational program.

Statistics made available to the press should be of significant interest and informative. The readers should be able to understand or interpret those statistics. In order to make this possible, short articles explaining each statistic should accompany the report if it is to be valuable as a public relations medium.

Any statistics that are released should be kept current. Regular statistic sheets that are kept by the coaches or managers should be transferred to regular forms that can be readily translated by not only the press but also the reader. Articles that accompany those statistics should point out any accomplishments that deserve recognition on the part of the athletes. Regular or standard statistic's sheets make reading and translation much easier.

Press and Radio

The press and raido should be given special attention not only on game day but throughout the school year. A school should be careful not to concern itself with the media only when it wants coverage of an athletic contest.

After a good base has been set for communications, the school should put forth a little extra effort on game day to please the media. Make sure pass tickets are sent, and that all help working the contest gate area are aware of the passes that have been given out. Provide a table near the scorer's bench or a spot in the press box for the media to conduct their work. Score cards, stat sheets, schedules, rosters, and interesting articles about the schools participating will be appreciated by the press and radio crews. A room for relaxation for halftime or postgame interviews should be provided. A little effort towards helping the media can bring many rewards to a school and its athletic program.

Transportation

Transportation should be arranged well in advance of an athletic contest. The day before the contest a note or call to the people responsible for the transportation should be made to reconfirm the arrangements and lessen the chance for error. An administrator must make arrangements with a reliable transporting company to insure smooth operations. The coach should instruct his athletes about their behavior while on the trip. Arrangements should be made by the visiting teams to allow their bus driver to enter the game with a pass. Both parties should discuss bus routes, time tables, and parking before departure.

Dressing Accommodations for Contestants

It is desirable to have a separate home team dressing room in those high schools that conduct a broad interschool athletic program. Multiple use of rooms provides for better supervision, and installation of large lockers furnishes adequate space for bulky equipment. For visiting teams one or more rooms of sufficient size to take care of peak loads are recommended. This arrangement allows for privacy desired by the visiting teams.

The accommodations should include all of the benefits that the home team receives. It is good public relations to provide halftime refreshments, such as oranges, and to provide ample towel service. A student from the lettermen's club could be assigned to help accommodate the visiting team. He could run errands and supply the visiting team with the necessary items that they need.

The dressing room should be neat and orderly. It should be well lighted, properly heated and ventilated, well supplied with lockers, and all of the necessary shower and lavatory facilities. Proper accommodations are definitely a positive factor in good school relations.

Athlete of the Week Award

The selection of the athlete of the week can be made by the coaches, the sports staff of the local newspaper, a combination of both and in some cases a group of knowledgeable fans. A feature story on the selection for each week should appear in the newspaper and an athlete of the week award certificate signed by the selection committee is given to the athlete.

Awards Dessert

At the conclusion of each sport season an awards dessert can be held at which time awards are given to the recipient. This is in the evening, and parents and athletes are guests of the athletic department at a social hour that follows the giving of awards. The dessert can be served by the home economics department, the P.T.A. the mother's club, or service club. A parent of one of the award winners may be given special recognition and asked to address the gathering of parents and award winners.

Bulletins to Parents

Most parents appreciate any attention that is given to their child. A knowledge of what he is doing after school hours is appreciated. Bulletins sent home explaining the objectives and purposes of the athletic program will result in parental support, understanding, and enthusiasm from them. It will do much to cement relations between parents, players, and coaches. It is a public relations technique that should not be overlooked.

Linebacker Club

This group is similar in many respects to the boosters club. The club is made up of local football fans. It can meet at noon for lunch, and films of the previous games can be shown. A short talk on the upcoming game can be given by one of the coaches or a knowledgeable fan.

Athletic Family of the Year Award

Any family having three or more athletes who have participated in sports during the year can be given recognition at the annual banquet by giving them a plaque. This can be done on an individual sports basis or by combining all the sports.

Sideliners Club

This club is also similar to the booster club except that it meets every Monday morning for breakfast. Anyone interested can belong to the club and a nominal fee is charged. The sole purpose of the club is to promote the local athletic program and the meeting consists of sports talk. Different projects which will benefit the athletic program are undertaken by this group.

Letters of Appreciation

These letters of appreciation are sent to anyone that has helped the athletic program. This could include medical people, musicians, ticket takers, ushers, or just anyone within the school community who has helped in some special way.

Grade School Students Invited To High School Games

Permitting grade school students to attend high school athletic contests free of charge is an excellent way to develop interest and loyalty from students who will be attending high school in the future. The grade school youngsters will have a golden opportunity to become involved early with the high school athletic program. Hopefully, the grade school youngsters will witness some fine athletes in action and can learn by studying the performance of these athletes. It will serve as an incentive to them.

It might be a good idea to have a special seating area set aside for the grade school students. In many cases these students will contribute to the spirit generated by the rest of the crowd.

Press Book

The press book which contains information relative to players, coaches, etc. is given to all news media and parents. This helps build spirit and public support.

Newsletter

Each school in the system including the elementary and junior high school could send a newsletter to every parent each month with information about the athletic program. This is a wonderful media for selling the athletic program to the parents and at the same time placing news of other phases of the school curriculum before the parents as a total educational program of which athletics is an important part.

Spartan Supporter First Class Award

This award is given at the annual awards banquet to one individual who has been, in the opinion of a committee, the number one supporter of the high school athletic teams. This award would usually go to someone outside the school but could go to a principal, teacher, custodian, or anyone who has been a staunch supporter of athletics.

Taped Recordings for Local Radio Station

Weekly tapes of talks with each head coach during the season is another good vehicle of public relations. Coaches should be well prepared, however, because this could result in a poor image of their program if the coach does not present himself well in this mode of communication.

Loan Out an Athletic Kit

An excellent public relations gimmick is to put together a special kit which would include horseshoes, volleyball net and ball, badminton equipment, softballs and bats, football, and a basketball. These kits can be loaned to service clubs, churches, groups for outings, and booster club picnics.

Parents

There may be parents who are qualified to hold the sideline chains at the football games. This would be good public relations and the parents would feel privileged to do this.

Coaches' Directory

A coaches' directory would give the addresses of all the coaches and the sport they coach. Such a directory could be made available to all parents whose child is participating on an athletic team. It could be, however, given to any person who might deserve the book.

Weekly Sports Release

It is poor public relations on the part of any coach or athletic director to withhold information about certain aspects of the athletic program until it leaks out and results in inaccurate news coverage. To avoid this, a weekly news release should be given bringing all the information about the program, the coaches, players, games, etc. up to date. This is good public relations and will result in people believing in the department.

Free Passes for Local Doctors

Many high schools have working agreements with the doctors within the community to furnish their services at all the football and basketball games. This relationship can result in good rapport with the doctors who make all the assignments themselves and inform the high school athletic director which doctor will donate his services for each particular game. In return all the doctors who participate, are given a pass for themselves and their wives which continues indefinitely.

Films on Local High School Athletic Programs

Rich dividends in good public relations can be realized by filming the various aspects of the school athletic program and show them at various community gatherings such as the P.T.A., service clubs, chamber of commerce, church and civic groups. The educational aspects of the program should be stressed and the film should be slanted in this direction. The educational advantages of the athletic program should be given high priority instead of placing the stress on winning.

Certificates Given to All Athletes

These certificates can be given to all the athletes who make all-star, all-conference, or all-state teams. These certificates can be signed by the athletic director or the superintendent of schools or both.

Organization of a Pledge Club

Members of this club pledge a certain amount of money for a specific purpose. In return the members may be given an opportunity to purchase a season ticket in appreciation for their original pledge of money. They also may be given a year or several years' free admission depending on the amount of money pledged.

Pictures of Teams, Coaches Sent to All Newspapers

This can involve some expense but it is worth it. Most newspapers do not have the personnel to make periodic trips to the school to interview coaches, players, and to take pictures. Most of them are most happy to receive pictures with a story along with it and will print it. A faculty member or a student can take these pictures with a minimum of expense.

Contact with Former Players or Alumni

Many former athletes are members of the community. They should not be forgotten as they will be staunch supporters of the athlete program. Some have gained prominence and leadership in the business community. These former players are more than willing to assume leadership roles in the promotion of the athletic program. They, along with outstanding teams of the past, can be honored during regular season contests. Public relations of this type are invaluable.

Opening the Gym One Night Per Week

In communities where recreational facilities are limited, a wonderful opportunity for public relations is available by opening the school gym to the community. Coaches can organize and provide leadership for basketball, volleyball, badminton, archery, and many other activities for interested people within the community. This will provide an opportunity for the coaches to become acquainted with parents and other members of the community. It can create good will and good public relations.

Working with Local Groups in the Promotion of Their Athletic Activities

There are many opportunities for high school coaches to use their talents and work with local groups. They can help with little league and pony league baseball teams, boy scouts, camping trips, kite contests, punt and pass contests, and other athletic and recreational activities that they are familiar with and proficient in which are being promoted by the same community-minded citizens that are boosting the high school athletic program. This is public relations at its best.

Brochure Made Available to Incoming Freshmen and Parents

An informative type of brochure especially published for freshman and parents is good publicity. The information con-

tained in the brochure should pertain only to items which directly affect the player or parent, such as time and days of practice, length of practice sessions, grades, eligibility, and information which will have a direct bearing on the player or parent. This type of information is greatly appreciated and is a good public relations media.

Passes

A very impressive public relations gimmick is to issue passes to the many people in the community who have helped in any way to promote the athletic program in the high school. It is a way of saying thank you for their help. Some of these people may never use the pass but still appreciate the gesture of receiving the pass. Care should be taken, however, that this practice does not get out of hand.

Annual Coaches' Party

If there is more than one high school within the city or if the high school is a large one, an annual coaches party can be a very important means of public relations. A golf dinner or a picnic with a social hour could be included. Good public relations should begin with the staff. It will help to relieve any hostility or jealousy between coaches within an individual school staff or between schools within the community or district.

Work Cooperatively with Other Youth Groups

Representatives of other groups that work with young athletes such as the C.Y.O., Y.M.C.A., churches, etc. should be given free passes to athletic gatherings and invited to banquets where they should be introduced and given recognition for their contributions to the youth athletic program. The coaches should volunteer their services to the athletic endeavors of these groups.

Pot Luck Dinners

These types of banquets can be held often as the expense incurred is nominal. The parents bring the food. Milk, coffee, ice cream, and soft drinks can be furnished by the booster club.

Honor an Outstanding Sports Citizen

Honoring an outstanding sports figure either from the school or community is an excellent way to promote special games or meets and improve public relations. Interest may be increased if people know that a popular sports figure will be attending the game. Having special days in their honor lets the athletes know that their athletic achievements have been appreciated.

Presenting the guest with some sort of trophy or plaque is also a good idea. This provides the guest with a special gift to remember the occasion.

Be sure when selecting someone to receive an honor, that this person is well deserving of that honor. Naming a field or building after an outstanding athlete is an important honor, so any decisions regarding such an honor should be studied carefully. Above all, avoid any situation that might cheapen the honor being bestowed.

Sports Writers Invited to Banquets

As in any other event involving athletic teams, invitations to all athletic banquets should be extended to the local sports writers. This is the first step toward securing good public relations with the press.

In order to assist the press covering the banquet, arrangements should be made to provide proper accommodations for the writers. This includes providing each writer with a summary of the program and answering any questions they may have.

Seating the press at a special table is a good idea. It is also good practice to introduce all of the sports writers in attendance to the rest of the audience.

Some newspapers present special awards to outstanding athletes. The banquet is the ideal time to present such awards. The sports editor or some other important figure from the newspaper will usually make the presentation.

Finally, at the conclusion of the banquet, arrangements should be made for the writers to conduct any interviews.

Invite the Community Ministers to Give a Pregame Prayer

This is a fine gesture and will meet with the approval of almost everyone. The dates and time can be given to the ministerial association in the community and they can arrange among themselves when each minister would give the prayer. Some of the ministers will often mention this in their Sunday service.

Camera Day

During the football season, a day may be set aside when all interested persons may take pictures of the football players. The parents are allowed on the practice field for certain periods during which time pictures may be taken. A full-scale scrimmage is conducted after this, and the parents are allowed to roam the sidelines and take action pictures. A question-and-answer period is held after the scrimmage and is conducted by the coaches.

Articles and Feature Stories Written by Coaches

Too often coaches feel that all they must do is coach. The reality of the situation is that the coach is as much a PR man as he is a coach. His personality can do as much to draw fans and bring attention to his squad as a winning team. The ability to communicate with the public is one of the greatest assets a coach can have. By using his ability to communicate, a coach can create an atmosphere of caring about the public. Writing articles for local newspapers can only serve to heighten spectator interest. Stories about players, opposing teams, and game strategy are all items that will allow fans to aquaint themselves with the coach. People like to read about themselves and people they know. They also like to feel as though they are a part of something. By sharing his thoughts and ideas, the coach can create an atmosphere of involvement for all. The entire community will feel as though the team is theirs and this feeling can help when it comes time for a referendum.

Intermission Programs

If properly planned, intermission programs can add life and enthusiasm to the game. Basketball games afford the best opportunity for well-planned programs. There are no weather conditions to worry about.

Although performances by the school band are the usual mode of entertainment, other possibilities could be used with great success. School activities could be used such as gymnastics, wrestling, girls' activities in gymnastics, volleyball, basketball, and others. These activities would not only entertain the fans but also give lesser known activities some exposure. All athletes like to perform before an audience and these types of programs would give the athletes a chance to perform.

Involving elementary and junior high school students in halftime or between game demonstrations can help cement relations between the schools. It will also bring their parents, who will eventually be a

part of the high school athletic picture. This could lead to a good relationship between parents and the athletic department. Public support could help when it is time for a referendum to be voted on.

Athletic Films Available for Use by Clubs

Showing athletic films could involve a weekly meeting of local citizens in a booster's club. Films could be shown of the previous week's games. This will build interest since people see many things on films that they may have missed when viewing the game previously.

BEHAVIORAL OBJECTIVES

After a person has read this chapter, he should be able to:

1. Define public relations as it applies to athletics.
2. Differentiate between propaganda and public relations. Cite an example of each in athletics.
3. Summarize the public relations aspects of the use of school gymnasiums by community groups. Identify some of the problems.
4. Explain the role of the parent in the athletic program.
5. Develop and explain a plan for parent's night in football.
6. Develop and explain a plan of leadership for a high school athletic program.
7. Explain and develop a technique or plan for the orientation of parents for a particular sport.
8. Distinguish between the public relations program in athletics and the academic areas.
9. Explain what a good public relations program in athletics should do in addition to informing the public about athletics.

10. Cite an example of how public relations has benefited the athletic program in your school.

11. Distinguish between public relations and publicity in athletics.

12. Explain the purposes of public relations and apply this to athletics.

13. Explain the importance of public relations in athletics and predict its future in the high school program.

14. Explain the effects on the public relations program in athletics of a football death of a member of the local high school team. Propose some ways which could be used to counteract the adverse publicity this might bring about.

15. Identify some historical facts about public relations and explain what effect they can have on the situation.

16. Recall one incident in history when public relations was used to advantage.

17. List several guidelines which are basic to any good program in athletics and apply these guidelines to specific situations.

18. Select three basic ingredients of a good public relations program and apply them to the athletic program in a large and small community high school.

19. Recall several guiding policies which are basic to public relations and relate them to specific examples.

20. Select several do's and don'ts in dealing with press and radio and appraise each as to their significance.

21. Select three areas into which public relations may be divided and give examples.

22. Cite an objective of a public relations program. Apply this objective to an athletic program, a business, and a product.

23. Explain how the faculty in a school may help with public relations for athletics.

24. Appraise the public relation program in athletics in your school.

25. Explain what is meant by public relations media. Cite several examples.

26. Differentiate between propaganda, public relations, and gossip.

27. Recognize the advantages that can be obtained by cooperation by the faculty and explain and illustrate each.

28. Identify several good and poor public relations in athletics which you can recall from your own experiences.

29. Describe the changes in policy that have taken place in athletic public relations programs in high schools the past few years. Explain the reasons for these changes.

30. Explain the role of the athletic director and coach in the schools public relations program in contrast to that of the principal, superintendent, and classroom teacher.

31. Assess the attitude of the athletic director toward the press.

32. Suggest several practical approaches that the high school might take in order to improve school-community relations in athletics.

33. Differentiate between internal and external public relations in athletics and give several concrete examples of each.

34. Explain the ways in which coaches and athletic directors can work closely and cooperatively with the news media.

35. Define public relations as it pertains to school athletics.

36. Suggest several ways in which a high school could initiate to improve public relations between athletics and other departments in that school.

37. Explain the purpose of a good public relations program in athletics other than to promote interest in gate receipts.

38. Distinguish between a public relations

program for interscholastics, business, or industry.

39. List some of the problems faced by athletic directors in developing good human relations within a staff.

40. List several factors that the athletic directors should be aware of in developing good human relations within the department.

41. Formulate a theory of good human relations. Describe the public relations problems which might be encountered in the use of athletic facilities by recreational groups.

42. Identify three mass media that could be used in forwarding the athletic program in high school.

43. Explain the phrase, "a picture is worth a thousand words," and give examples.

ACTIVITIES

1. Prepare a handbook or brochure for coaches in a large high school and a small high school.

2. Survey the opinions of two or three high school athletic directors relative to the value of the public relations program in their school.

3. Visit a school that has had winning teams. Find out about how their athletic public relations program differs from others in similar schools.

4. There are a number of real sources of influence on high school athletics. Some are state and national, while others are local. Make a list of organizations that in some way had, or may continue to have, an influence on the athletic program.

5. Interview the public relations director of an industrial firm. Find out from him some ideas that could be used in promoting the high school athletic program.

6. Develop a paragraph stating the rela-

tionship between public relations and publicity.

7. Obtain a copy of a public relations manual from an industrial concern. Apply some of the principles used by them to the athletic public relations program.

8. Seek the opinion of several school administrators relative to the value of athletics as a public relations gimmick for the entire school program.

9. Prepare a two-hundred-word statement relative to the value of the athletic program as a public relations media.

10. Arrange for an athletic director to talk to the class and explain some of the things that are done in his school in public relations.

11. Formulate a policy for the use of athletic facilities by outside groups. Write some regulations to control the situation.

12. Interview a principal or superintendent about the processes he employs to be sensitive to community expectations about the athletic program.

13. Formulate a few simple questions pertaining to the athletic program in the high school of your community and use these questions to interview a number of citizens. Note the similarity and diversity of their opinions.

14. Interview a number of teachers, a number of pupils, and a number of parents in a particular school system and ask them what they consider important aspects of the athletic program. Note the similarities and differences in the responses.

15. Set up an effective public relations program for a school athletic program.

16. Set up a public relations brochure for athletics.

17. Prepare a workable plan for promoting sportsmanship among players, coaches,

and spectators.

18. Develop some principles to recommend to the school board concerning the use of athletic facilities by outside groups.

19. Prepare a plan for parents' night.

SUGGESTED READINGS

1. American Association of School Administrators: *Public Relations for American Schools,* Twenty-eighth yearbook. Washington, D.C., 1952.

2. Ashton, Dudley: *Administration of Physical Education for Women.* New York, Ronald, 1968.

3. Avedision, Charles: Interpreting the total athletic program via home visits. *The Athletic Journal,* January, 1958.

4. Baley, James: Public relations. *Journal of Health, Physical Education, and Recreation,* November, 1961.

5. Bubos, Vic: Promote attendance by a ladies night clinic. *Coach and Athlete,* March, 1961.

6. Canfield, Bertrand: *Public Relations.* Homewood, Richard D. Irwin, 1964.

7. Constantz, Quinn, and Scott, James: Sports publicity program. *Scholastic Coach,* November, 1951.

8. Cutlip, Scott, and Center, Allen: *Effective Public Relations.* Englewood Cliffs, P-H, 1958.

9. Damore, Patrick, and Hesse, Robert: A program of public relations for sports. *Coach and Athlete,* October, 1969.

10. Davis, Michael: Put some public relations in your swimming. *The Athletic Journal,* October, 1967.

11. Duke, Wayne: Public relations and athletics. *Journal of Health, Physical Education, and Recreation,* October, 1959.

12. Field, Charles: Faculty and coach relationship. *Coach and Athlete,* Ocotber, 1971.

13. Fine, Benjamin: *Educational Publicity.* New York, Har-Row, 1943.

14. Frey, George: How can we build effective school-community relations. *Today's Education,* January, 1971.

15. Gathanay, Ted: Pressing for a good press. *The Athletic Journal,* November, 1959.

16. Harmon, J.J.: Public relations, a necessity. *School and Community,* December, 1971.

17. Harris, William: Stimulate curiosity. *Journal of Health, Physical Education, and Recreation,* February, 1968.

18. Hesse, Robert, and Damore, Patrick: A program of public relations for sports. *Coach and Athlete,* October, 1969.

19. Hixson, Chalmer: *The Administration of Interscholastic Athletics.* New York, Lowell Pratt, 1967.

20. Heilbroner, Robert: Public relations—The invisible sell. *Harpers Magazine,* June, 1957.

21. Kozloff, Edward: The public relations gap . . . can we close it? *The Physical Educator,* October, 1969.

22. O'Quinn, Mickey: Booster club boosts team through films. *The Athletic Journal,* June, 1964.

23. Resick, Mathew, Seidel, Beverly, and Mason, James: *Modern Administrative Practices in Physical Education and Athletics.* Reading, A-W, 1970.

24. Shroyer, George: Inform, don't let them guess. *Journal of Health, Physical Education, and Recreation,* February, 1968.

25. Singer, Robert: Communicate or perish. *Journal of Health, Physical Education, and Recreation,* February, 1968.

26. Tamerelli, Al: The coach is a public relations man. *Coaching Clinic,* December, 1971.

27. Tener, Morton: Public relations in athletics. *Coach and Athlete,* November, 1968.

28. Troppman, Bob: The place of the parent in high school athletics. *The Athletic Journal,* February, 1958.

29. Voltmer, Edward and Esslinger, Arthur: *The Organization and Administration of Physical Education.* New York, Appleton, 1967.

30. *Webster's New International Dictionary,* Third Edition, Merriman, 1961.

CHAPTER 15

The Student Manager

T HE USE OF STUDENT managers for inter-school athletic programs has been prevalent for many years. From the beginning, they have played an important part in the program of competitive sports. Hixson[1] verifies this position by the following statement:

> Traditionally student athletic managers have been used to improve and expand the athletic program in our secondary schools. This practice provides a variety of educational experiences for these students; and, it in turn enables them to make a valuable contribution to their schools. Many details of practices and games can be effectively administered by qualified student managers.

The efficiency of an athletic program often depends on the role played by the student athletic manager. The student manager is to the coach as the nurse is to the doctor. In studying the duties of the student manager it can be readily seen why the manager is of extreme importance to the coach and why his presence is indispensable.

George and Lehmann[2] make the following statement relative to the importance of the role of the manager:

> Student managers are necessary for all interscholastic squads. They may be

elected or appointed and a plan should be formulated concerning their selection and advancement. In order to insure continuity in the managerial ranks, it is a good plan to have representatives from all classes serve in each sport. The managers' specific responsibilities should be clearly defined. Their tasks may involve the care and issue of equipment, scoring, charting, public relations, and such pregame and postgame chores as may be assigned.

Most every coach in every sport will appreciate the efforts of a good manager. If the coach is smart, he will make every effort to install a reliable and workable managerial system and use every means possible to make it work. The initial effort that it takes to organize and initiate such a system will pay rich dividends and make the coach's job much easier.

Most authorities will attest to the value of a good managerial program. As proof of this Forsythe[3] offers this following comment:

> Student managers should be not only necessary but valuable aids in administering a local school athletic program. They may be made the connecting link between faculty control—athletics and the student body and athletes themselves. In this capacity a student manager may be invaluable to his coach. He has the students' point of view and may

---

[1]Hixson, Chalmer, *The Administration of Interscholastic Athletics* (New York, J. Lowell Pratt and Company, 1967), p. 64.

[2]George, Jack, and Lehmann, Harry, *School Athletic Administration* (New York, Harper and Row, 1966), p. 286.

[3]Forsythe, Charles, *Administration of High School Athletics*, 3rd ed., (Englewood Cliffs, New Jersey, by permission of Prentice-Hall, 1959), p. 155.

be of real aid in making the program run smoothly.

It is difficult to assess the value of a good student manager. He can be a very important asset to any athletic team and his contributions can be almost unlimited. The coach must realize this and as a result put forth a tremendous effort to have a good manager or managers. Most coaches will adhere to this belief and attempt to secure good managers because they know that without them the team will not function nearly as well. The value of a capable and dedicated manager is unlimited.

This is brought out very forcefully by Daughtrey[4] in the following statement, "Student managers are necessary for efficient administration of the interschool program. Not only are they indispensable to the coach in the daily operation of his program, but they also serve as public relations agents while associating with the students and faculty."

Halperin thinks in terms of what the manager can contribute to the team. He feels that the coach needs a good group of managers to enable him to devote all of his time toward building a winning team. The managers can play an extremely important role in the success or failure of a season.[5]

Recruitment of Managers

If the program of manager recruitment is to be successful, then some time and effort should be spent on it. If outstanding students are to be sought, a means of attracting these students should be devised. It is important, first of all, to attempt to get the freshman and sophomore student interested in joining the managerial organization. By doing this, it assures the coach that even though some of the candidates will become discouraged, disenchanted, or dissatisfied, there will be those who will want to continue in the program and remain until they are seniors and become a head manager. There will always be a few students who will receive enough self satisfaction from being a manager that they will want to remain in the program. Many students find it difficult to receive any other type of recognition and the prestige gained from a high-class managerial organization allows them to obtain this recognition. It is a very satisfying experience for them.

Kowalk[6] points out the prestige factor very clearly in the following statement:

> The manager's position on the team must be regarded as a highly respected function of the coach, the squad, and the school. This respect can only be developed when coaches become aware of the real importance of the manager, and when they employ a young man who will bring enthusiasm, concentrated effort, and pride to the job which he has undertaken. As one fine manager said, 'You must have a keen desire to be a manager.'

One of the secrets to success in coaching is good organization. Good organization not only saves time and energy but creates confidence in the players because they feel that the coach knows what he is doing, and he usually does if he is well organized. Good organization gets more done because the players as well as the coaching staff know exactly what is expected of them. There is no time wasted; there is no time for bickering and fault finding. When everything is running smoothly and on time, things get done and the objectives which were outlined before are accomplished. It creates a feeling of ac-

[4]Daughtrey, Greyson and Woods, John, *Physical Education Programs* (Philadelphia, W.B. Saunders, 1971), p. 430.

[5]Halperin, Gary, "A Syllabus for Basketball Managers," *Coaching Clinic* (April, 1972), p. 16.

[6]Kowalk, Clayton, "Basketball Managers—A Key to Organization Success" *The Athletic Journal* (Sept., 1964), p. 28.

TABLE LXXII
APPLICATION FOR STUDENT ATHLETIC MANAGER

Please fill out the following statements.

I.   Name _____ Homeroom number _____ Age _____

                                                        Homeroom advisor _____

II. Grades for last semester.

                    Subject   *Grades*

III. Grades per semester for physical education.

      Fr. _____   Soph. _____   Jr. _____

      Fr. _____   Soph. _____

IV. Responsibilities held now or have held in school activities or in community activities.

V.   Persons who are my closest friends.

VI. Teachers who know me best.

VII. Physical education teacher. _____

VIII. Favorite sports. _____

Write a statement as to why you would like to become a leader, what your qualifications are to become an athletic manager and what you think this program will do for you.

Signed _____

Date _____

complishment which otherwise would not exist. This type of organization should carry over into the managerial ranks. Good organization on this level will create good morale at every practice session and at every game. The efficient handling of equipment and other managerial duties can keep this morale at a high pitch. The coach should insist on and the manager should do everything to keep it that way. All managers should be well informed of his duties and then organize his time so that he can perform them quickly, efficiently, and effectively with a minimum of friction.

The manager must have the full co-operation of the coaching staff. He cannot do an efficient job without the help and complete understanding of the coaches. They must exercise tact as well as skill in helping the manager do his job. All coaches should respect the manager and help him develop a plan by which he will be able to carry out his duties. It is the coach's responsibility to inform all players of the managerial duties and to impress upon them that these duties are all that he is expected to do. It should be made very evident to the players that the manager is not a valet to them and that he is not expected to wait on them. He is only expected to perform the duties assigned to him. This can be accomplished in several ways. For example, Forsythe[7] suggests the following:

> Athletic directors must remember that student managers are youngsters and that their duties must be well laid out for them. Successful plans have been followed in some schools of having daily work assignment sheets prepared for managers. These special assignments may be in addition to their routine daily duties. It takes a little time for the athletic director to fill out one of these assignment sheets but it should result in definite accomplishments.

The coach can do a great deal to educate the players as to expected treatment of the managers by outlining the duties of the managers and informing them that the manager will be his right-hand man and that they will be directly responsible to him for many of their actions.

The coach should train the managers as he trains his team. By doing this, he removes many of the problems he would otherwise have to face. These problems involve equipment, trips, etc. An experienced manager will be of great assistance in issuing equipment at the start of the season and checking it in at the end of the season. The managers should be made to feel that their work is important to the success of the team. The coach should give the manager enough responsibility to make him feel that he is doing a special job and not just something anyone else could do. He should have specific duties to perform that he alone should do. No one else should be allowed to perform these duties, and the manager should be given to understand that this is his responsibility and his alone.

The coach should learn to lean heavily upon the manager for the many game details that should be his to perform. He should take him into his confidence in many things other than those that are personal, both regarding himself and his players. He should be friendly but never familiar.

Care should be taken, however, not to place the manager in a vulnerable position. After all, he still wants to keep his friends and does not want to have them feel that he has turned his back on them. He should not be expected to take the place of a faculty member or assistant coach and assume their responsibilities and duties.

Forsythe[8] explains this situation very aptly in the following statement:

> The responsibilities of the student manager should be delegated ones entirely and should not extend beyond the school. The care of equipment and the attending to specific details in connection with visiting teams, game officials, home-game arrangements, and practice sessions —these and many more should be jobs performed most efficiently by student managers.

Managerial Organization

Any organization, to operate effectively and efficiently, must be organized in such a way that there will be an opportunity for promotion from within the ranks. This is true in a managerial system in interscholastic athletics. All personnel performing managerial duties must be aware of what is expected of them. He also must have a complete knowledge of the basis for promotion and awards should he perform these duties satisfactorily. If this situation is not in evidence and no provision is made for this type of situation, then there will be hard feelings, bickering, and a complete

---

[7]Forsythe, Charles, *The Athletic Director's Handbook* (Englewood Cliffs, New Jersey, by permission of Prentice-Hall, 1956) p. 327.

[8]Forsythe, Charles, *The Administration of High School Athletics* 3rd ed., (Englewood Cliffs, New Jersey: by permission of Prentice-Hall, Inc., 1959) , p. 155.

collapse of the organization.

This situation is explained very well by Forsythe[9] in the following statement, "An efficient organization for carrying on the athletic program is as important as a well-coached and well-balanced team. The student manager always should remember that his contribution is a vital part in the whole athletic scheme of things even though it may not be very conspicuous."

The foresighted coach will look far enough ahead to avoid the situation which will leave him without an experienced manager no matter what happens. He can do this by careful planning, by setting up a permanent organization, one which will be self perpetuating and will function from year to year. A system propogates itself and uses an award and promotional system that allows students to be continually promoted in rank until they eventually become the head manager. This type of system breeds loyalty and insures the coach that there will always be an experienced manager to step in and take over. It also provides for a managerial staff that knows what is expected of them and how they can become head manager.

A staff of three to four training in service for the head manager position are called manager candidates. This system works ideally in the large school.

Manager Requirements

It takes a certain type of student to be a good manager. He is constantly being placed in a position of compromise between the coach and the player. He can be a tremendous help by serving as liaison man between the coach and the players. This means that he must have the trust of both. This is a very difficult position to be in. He must hold on to his status with the players because many of them are his

friends. If he has their respect, he can be a tremendous help to the coach. Oftentimes it is very difficult for him to inform the coach of things that are being done by the players that he knows will jeopardize the team's chances of winning. If he tells the coach, many of the players will stamp him as an informer and he will lose their friendship. He is in a position to know about the little as well as the big things that happen to members of a team that he is in close contact with for a long period of time. These things include players accusing others of inferior play, hogging the ball, shooting too much or failing to feed off. Often this type of situation can be well hidden by the players from the public and the coach. The manager knows because he is in a position to know. Should he confide in the coach? If he does, the problem can often be solved. He takes the chance of losing his friendship with the players involved, but he also knows he will be helping the team in the long run.

Kowalk[10] makes the following interesting observation as a good explanation of the situation, "The prerequisites for the position of manager include (1) a desire to work, (2) a keen interest in the sport in which he is manager, (3) good personal habits, (4) a good sense of humor, (5) confidence with humility, and (6) ability to organize time."

For example, some years ago a young inexperienced coach was having a fine season until for no apparent reason the team went sour. The team's scoring fell off and Jerry, the team's leading scorer, could not maintain the scoring ability he had previously established. Finally, his student manager came to him and explained the problem. It seemed that Jerry's teammates resented his failure to pass off to them when

---

[9]*Ibid.*

[10]Kowalk, Clayton, "Basketball Managers—A Key to Organization Success."

they were open for a shot even though the coach had told him to shoot often because he was the best shot. The coach immediately called a team meeting and explained that Jerry had been instructed to shoot and it was to the team's benefit for him to do so. He convinced the team members that it was not selfishness on Jerry's part. The improvement was instantaneous and the team went on to a fine season's record. The student manager could be given the credit for doing what he felt was right.

Qualifications of Student Managers

1. Interest in the particular sport.
2. Enthusiasm for work.
3. Ability to assume responsibility.
4. Punctuality.
5. Personality.
6. Ability to get along with others.
7. Honesty.
8. Good grades.
9. Willingness to sacrifice along with members of the team.
10. Willingness to abide by training rules.

Types of Student Managers

The student managers can be classified under three categories, namely, (1) head managers, (2) assistant managers, and (3) manager candidates.

HEAD MANAGERS: The head manager naturally assumes the major responsibility and, therefore, it is best that he is a senior. He should follow the promotion procedure and become a senior manager only by the accepted method of promotion. Any other type of appointment will destroy the initiative that should be inherent in the organizational pattern of managerial selection. An image that the position of manager is a coveted and respected position in the athletic program should always be striven for. It should symbolize a position of trust and dignity among the players, student body,

and faculty. The manager should be made to feel that his position is necessary and without him the team would suffer. He needs to feel this trust and that all his efforts should be directed toward the best interest of the team. He needs to understand that he must place himself above the petty jealousies that cause dissension and hard feelings, and that he may lose some friends. However, in the long run he will gain the respect of the right kind of friends and mostly of himself because he is doing his job, the way he understands and knows it should be done.

This philosophy and understanding can only be gained through his experience of promotion through the ranks as a manager candidate and an assistant manager.

The head manager should be the type of person that can accept responsibility and not be afraid to say no to his friends. He must make it plain too that he will treat everyone alike while he is performing his managerial duties. He must maintain discipline and be fair in his supervision of those managers working under his direction. He should not take advantage of his position of authority and trust and use it for private gain. He must not assume a dominating, domineering attitude and be unreasonable in his demands from his subordinates. He should do his job and make it as pleasant as possible for others to do theirs.

His character should be above reproach, and his conduct on and off the field should reflect the responsibility and trust which is placed in him. He should be an example to his subordinates as well as to the players. He will, in this way, command the respect of everyone and help his team, his coach, and his school immeasurably.

ASSISTANT MANAGERS: This position requires a certain type of an individual, and this is one of the reasons why a system of promotion for managers is desirable. It is a very difficult position to fill because the recognition received for it is very minimal. The assistant manager must be the type of person who is satisfied to remain in the background knowing that his turn will come. He will need to be the type of person who is willing to take orders from his friend without resentment. The assistant managers should preferably be juniors.

MANAGER CANDIDATES: The manager candidates are "low men on the totem pole." It is the "bottom of the ladder" in terms of position, authority, and recognition. It is the starting place which may lead to the position of head manager. The individual holding this position should realize this and act accordingly. He must be content to do the menial tasks and bide his time because eventually, through the promotional procedure, he will become head manager. An ideal situation would be if the school has a freshman team, and the manager candidate can assume more responsibility by managing this team.

Selection of Student Managers

Forsythe[11] states that:

The student manager should remember that he has been selected for his job because of his honesty, faithfulness, and dependability. In many cases he will have access to records and to equipment valued in hundreds of thousands of dollars. He should treat such material as his own and attempt to safeguard it accordingly. He should remember that the coach is a busy man. Whenever he assigns a task to him, it should be possible for him to consider it as good as done.

Further evidence that the selection of managers is a very important part of the success of the program as emphasized by

Hixson.[12] He states that:

These student athletic managers will have ready access to important records, equipment, and substantial sums of money; they should be carefully selected. Not only must they be able to meet such responsibilities but they must be able to work cooperatively with coaches, be able to work also with athletes and other student managers. The system of selection will provide continuity from year to year and season to season so that in no instance will there be a complete turn over of student managers for a particular sport. Students from the various classes move through a sequence of increasing responsibility from freshmen to senior manager. This procedure allows the experienced student manager to provide the program of preparation by which the inexperienced students can be qualified and assigned their duties.

Forsythe[13] makes the following observation:

Some student managers are elected to their positions; others are appointed by the principal, athletic director, or coach. Sometimes they are boys who, because of being over age or having too many semesters of enrollment, are ineligible for further athletic competition. Evidently, though, the most successful type of student manager is not the ex-athlete who has become ineligible. Too many times he is too likely to concern himself with practice and play instead of performing his duties.

The managerial system described in this chapter requires that enough preplanning be done so that the right kind of students are selected for this important position. The students selected as managers should be the kind that can assume responsibility, take orders, and be aware of the complexity and importance of their duties. The manager must have organizational ability of

[11]Forsythe, Charles, *Administration of High School Athletics,* 3rd ed., (Englewood Cliffs, New Jersey: by permission of Prentice-Hall, Inc., 1959), p. 155.

[12]Hixson, Chalmer, *The Administration of Interscholastic Athletics.*

[13]Forsythe, Charles, *Administration of High School Athletics.*

TABLE LXXIII
PALO HIGH SCHOOL
PALO, NEBRASKA

Athletic Manager Candidate Selection Form

_____ has applied for a position as manager of
(Candidate's Name)

the _____ team. If you know the candidate well enough to supply
(sport)

the information asked for below would you please do so? Please return the form with the

needed information to _____.
(Athletic Director)

<table>
<tr><td></td><td>yes</td><td>no</td><td>not sure</td></tr>
<tr><td>Is he emotionally stable? _____</td><td></td><td></td><td></td></tr>
<tr><td>Is he trustworthy? _____</td><td></td><td></td><td></td></tr>
<tr><td>Is he a good worker? _____</td><td></td><td></td><td></td></tr>
<tr><td>Can he accept responsibility? _____</td><td></td><td></td><td></td></tr>
<tr><td>Does he get along with other students? _____</td><td></td><td></td><td></td></tr>
<tr><td>In your opinion will he be a good manager? _____</td><td></td><td></td><td></td></tr>
<tr><td>Is he a leader? _____</td><td></td><td></td><td></td></tr>
<tr><td>Is he a follower? _____</td><td></td><td></td><td></td></tr>
<tr><td>Is he honest? _____</td><td></td><td></td><td></td></tr>
<tr><td>Does he cooperate? _____</td><td></td><td></td><td></td></tr>
<tr><td>Is he mature? _____</td><td></td><td></td><td></td></tr>
<tr><td>Is he easily influenced? _____</td><td></td><td></td><td></td></tr>
<tr><td>Is he courteous? _____</td><td></td><td></td><td></td></tr>
</table>

Signed _____

Faculty Member

---

his own in order that he can correlate the duties of those individuals under his direct supervision.

It is important that a great deal of time and effort be put into the selection procedure to insure outstanding managerial candidates. After carefully screening the candidates, they should be asked to sign up for the position of manager. Each one should be given a personal interview by the coaches and athletic director. Such things as grades and personal background should be part of the selection criteria. During this interview each candidate should be informed about the time he will need to spend doing the job and the duties he will need to perform. He should be asked about why he wants to become a manager. He should also be warned about the responsibilities and that he will be called upon to assume a position of authority which might jeopardize his friendship with his fellow-students. He must thoroughly understand what the position entails and give his consent freely without any pressure being brought to bear which might influence his decision.

The selection of a manager should require careful thought and planning on the part of the athletic staff. Time spent in planning the selection procedure will alleviate many problems later on. A good manager is worth the time and effort spent in selecting him.

Kowalk[14] emphasizes the importance of obtaining the right kind of students to assume the managerial duties of the athletic teams on the interscholastic level. He sug-

---

[14]Kowalk, Clayton, "Basketball Managers—A Key to Organization Success."

gests the following method of selection of a varsity manager:

> The varsity manager should serve three years in the program. He should serve as the reserve squad manager as a sophomore, be promoted to student trainer as a junior, and then become the varsity manager during his senior year. Thus, the program and the manager benefit from three years of experience. After serving this length of time it will be found that many of the so-called incidental functions and some of the major activities of the program have been developed by a sharp, conscientious student manager, who has relieved the coach of many headaches and time-consuming activities.

There are various ways in which the student manager may be selected. These may be listed and summarized as follows:

1. The manager may be elected to the position by the athletes.
2. The manager may be elected by popular vote of the coaches.
3. The manager may be elected by popular vote of the student body.
4. The manager may be appointed by the athletic director.
5. The manager may be selected by the senior manager.
6. A competitive plan on an all-year basis may be used.
7. A system whereby the manager is appointed by the coach, athletes, athletic association, or any other organization delegated that authority.
8. A selective plan based on individual merit may be used.

It is surprising the large number of managers that are selected by the coach, but some students come to the coach and ask to be a manager. Also, the coach can pick out a person he knows and ask him to be manager. This is permissible, of course, but certainly does not place much prestige on the assignment. The manager can be as good as he wants to be. He can lead or he can follow, and if he is the latter he is not much good to anyone. He could be a detriment if he is this type of person. He can, on the other hand, be a second coach, and a real help, rather than a fault finder and a real hindrance. The plan in which the student is selected, first of all on his merits, and then works his way up through the ranks is most satisfactory because it makes the person feel that he was selected on his merits rather than on his knowing someone.

Cousy and Power[15] suggest that:

> The selection of the manager should be made by the coach with consultation with his staff, graduating managers, equipment manager. They found great success with freshmen squad members who played freshman basketball but did not make the next level team. Because of the experience as a player they were very efficient because they knew the organizational setup and wanted to be a part of the group.

If the coach is new on the job, he can use various ways to obtain information from his fellow teachers who in some cases are in a position to know many of the candidates. The principal may also help in contacting good candidates. Information may be obtained from previous or present managers. After due consideration of the candidates, two managers could be selected on the sophomore level. They should be informed that they are on a trial basis and can be dropped if they do not measure up after a year's time.

Two ranking managers should be on the varsity squad and they should preferably be juniors and seniors. The head manager should always be a senior. The coaches should at all times impress upon all personnel that the senior manager is in charge. A

---

[15]Cousy, Bob and Power, Frank, *Basketball Concepts and Techniques* (Boston, Massachusetts, Allyn and Bacon, 1970), p. 14.

monthly report should be made by the senior manager on all managers under his direct supervision. They should be evaluated on the following: (1) willingness to work, (2) promptness, (3) his ideas on how to improve himself as a manager, (4) punctuality in reports, (5) cooperation, (6) ability to follow directions, and (7) ability to get along with people.

It should be explained to all managers that it is their prerogative to talk to the coach at any time should they feel that they are being treated unfairly. However, they should meet with the coach in the presence of the head manager to state their complaint. The coach should listen to both of them and then make his decision. The head coach should be the final authority on all decisions of this nature.

Duties of Student Managers

The duties of the manager are many and varied. If the coach spends enough time instructing his managers properly, he will save himself many headaches during the course of the season. The coach should have the manager's duties written and outlined for him the day before each contest. A check list is advisable. It is the coach's responsibility to think of every possible situation that could arise before, during, and after the game. If these things are not foreseen, the coach will find himself, in the excitement of the game, performing duties that could have been done by managers. The coach should not take the manager's duties lightly. Managers need and want something to do. These duties make the manager feel needed and a part of the team. A coach will lose good managers if he does not instruct them in their duties.

Vannier and Fait[16] stress the fact that

the selection and duties of managers should be important considerations for the athletic coach. The student should first of all be interested in the job. He should be reliable and cooperative. These qualities can sometimes be discovered in classrooms. The authors list eight general duties of managers regardless of the sport.

1. Taking charge of equipment
2. Cleaning and storing equipment
3. Providing towels and water
4. Assisting players during games
5. Posting notices from the coach
6. Keeping statistics, scrapbooks, etc.
7. Assisting officials and visiting teams
8. Officiating at practice sessions

During the basketball season the head coach should make out a daily list of duties or materials he needs for the manager to take care of. The manager should report to the office each day to pick up this list. It should be his duty at all times to keep supplies on hand and to inform the coach if he has not been able to secure them. The coach should provide the manager with shot charts and weight charts.

If the coach desires the manager to perform the many duties expected of him, then he should inform him daily just what these duties are. A list should be prepared by the coach and the manager should pick up this list from the coach's office early enough in the day so that he will have time to study it.

Specific duties, such as charting shots during practice sessions, keeping time, keeping score, etc. should be done by the senior manager. The senior manager should set himself up as an example by being the first person on the practice floor. He should be ready at any time to step in and do the enumerable jobs so necessary in every practice session. He might even be called upon to referee the scrimmage or take care of any other eventuality which might arise.

[16]Vannier, Mary Helen and Fait, Holles, *Teaching Physical Education in Secondary Schools* (Philadelphia, W.B. Saunders Co., 1969) , p. 422.

The senior manager should be in close contact with the coach each day and report to him sometime before practice begins, preferably, the first thing before school starts. This will give the coach an opportunity to arrange for a change in plans if this is necessary. For example, the coach might be delayed for practice which might necessitate a change in plans which the manager could handle.

The senior manager should be responsible for gathering information regarding the opposition. He can cut clippings from newspapers and paste them on the bulletin board or file them for future reference. The coach can use them as he needs them in planning his strategy against future opponents. This is vital information and can save the coach long hours; the time saved can be spent in other vital areas. The clippings placed on the bulletin board can mentally prepare the players and start them thinking about the opposition.

Coaches more than anyone know the value of a good manager. A good manager enables the coach to spend this time on the important duty of coaching the team rather than managing it.

The coach and manager must work hand in hand to get the job done. Through this joint cooperation the necessary objectives can be accomplished to produce a winning team.

The coach will determine to a very large extent the value of the manager in promoting a winning season. He must coach his manager as he does his players, giving him advice and helping him to adjust to the many duties required of him throughout the season. These duties will be many and varied and will not be the same for every locality. The manager will need the ability to adjust quickly and cheerfully to every situation. He must meet every problem head on with a smile and

hard work. If he does this, he can be as instrumental to the success of the team as the most valuable player.

One of the important duties of the senior manager is to be certain opponents are greeted as they arrive at the host school. He can do this himself or assign one of his subordinates the task. The manager assigned should guide the team to the dressing room and provide them with the courtesies expected from the host school.

The tasks of the manager will not always be the same for the various sports. To emphasize this fact, the following duties are listed which apply to the game of basketball. With some modification they can be fitted to other sports.

Suggested Duties of Basketball Managers

I. Basketball Care
  A. Inflate all balls.
  B. Mark each ball.
  C. Clean all balls every week.
  D. Check all balls in and out each practice.
  E. Keep reserve balls ready for use.

II. Care of Game Uniforms and Practice Clothes
  A. Issue all game suits.
  B. Check all articles in after each game.
  C. Assume responsibility for the cleaning of uniforms.
  D. Keep a record of all equipment that is sent to the cleaners and returned.
  E. Keep a record of all game and practice equipment that has been issued to each player.
  F. Hang game uniforms up neatly after each game.
  G. Collect game uniforms the next day after the game.

H. Be responsible for sending uniforms to be repaired.

III. Practice
A. Have all practice shirts ready for use.
B. Have rebound ring ready for use.
C. Check attendance.
D. Keep free throw and shot chart records.
E. Keep all students out of the gym.
F. Lock all gym doors to players at 3:30 P.M.
G. Keep ample supply of shoelaces, soap, extra shoes, etc.
H. Consult the coach before discarding any equipment.
I. Keep first-aid kit filled.
J. Make sure a manager is on duty.
K. Check out all special equipment.
L. Check with the coach before practice.
M. Check bulletin board; remove unnecessary material.
N. Keep bulletin board up to date.
O. Check all first-aid problems.
P. Pull down baskets into position.
Q. Check weight of team members before and after practice.
R. Guard and watch all equipment.
S. Record daily attendance of team members.
T. Have stretcher on hand.

IV. Additional Duties
A. Keep a record of all physical examinations of all players.
B. Arrange for the proper treatment of all officials and teams.
C. Make all locker assignments and help keep all records.
D. Keep statistical records of each game.
E. Keep the bulletin board up to date.
F. Keep a record of the amount of time each player plays.

V. Preseason and Postseason Duties
A. Preseason
1. Head manager should make an appointment with the coach for discussion of problems.
2. Have equipment ready for use.
3. Contact and assign duties to assistant managers.
4. Check the lockers.
B. Postseason
1. Arrange for the cleaning of all uniforms and equipment and their storage.
2. Report to the coach any equipment which was not collected.
3. Wash and store the balls.

VI. Managerial Duties Pertaining to Games
A. Home games
1. Take care of the visiting team and officials.
2. Have the game uniforms ready for use.
3. Have gum or oranges for halftime use.
4. Have the scorebook ready and appoint an efficient scorekeeper.
5. Check the timers for clocks and horn.
6. Give the ball to head official fifteen minutes before the game.
7. Check the nets on the baskets.
8. Get the ball racks ready for use.
9. Check chalk or black boards in both coaches dressing rooms.
10. Put first-aid kits in proper places.
11. Collect the game uniforms.
12. Present the checks to the officials.
B. Trips
1. Arrange for the timers and

scorers.

2. Have gum and oranges for halftime use.

3. Make a check list of the duties for each game away from home.

4. Have the equipment and uniforms packed.

VII. Equipment Duties
    A. Assist the coach in inventory.
    B. Issue out and check in equipment.
    C. Keep equipment clean.
    D. Make sure all equipment is returned.

VIII. Final Report at End of Season
    A. Suggest in writing any improvements to the coach.
    B. Turn in all keys.
    C. Check bulletin board.
    D. Suggest needed changes.

IX. Locker Room Duties
    A. Make a list of phone numbers, addresses, and class schedules of all players so that they can be reached in a hurry.
    B. Cut out all new items regarding the team and place in scrapbook or on bulletin board.
    C. Suggest improvement in locker room administration to the coach.
    D. Check all lockers before leaving after practice.
    E. Pick up loose clothing.
    F. Keep a close check on all towels and other equipment.
    G. Lock all doors after practice.
    H. Supervise the cleaning of the locker room.

CHECK LISTS: The importance of the check list cannot be minimized. No matter how conscientious the manager may be, he will forget some duty that he is expected to perform. This usually happens at a critical time and not only embarrasses certain individuals but oftentimes results in a delay of the game. The following basketball check list will serve as an example. This list may be changed to fit other sports.

Suggested Basketball Manager's Check List

BASKETBALL

I. Before and After Practice Session
    A. Check the medicine kit.
    B. Do minor taping.
    C. Check out the equipment.
    D. Take the attendance.
    E. Have all the practice equipment in the gym (balls, clock, jerseys, etc.) .
    F. Have one manager with each team in gym.
    G. Hand out the towels.
    H. Collect all the equipment.
    I. Clean the locker rooms, and hang up all the equipment.
    J. Hand in a list of missing equipment.

II. Before All Games
    A. Clean all the balls.
    B. Have all the medical equipment ready for use.
    C. Make sure there is chalk, clipboards, and paper and pencil ready for use.
    D. Issue all the equipment.

III. Before Home Games
    A. Arrive at the gym one hour before game time.
    B. Hand out the uniforms.
    C. See that the officials have towels and soap.
    D. See that the clock and scoreboard are ready for use.
    E. Pass out firm grip.
    F. Have the chalk and blackboard ready for use.

G. Have the medicine kit in the gym.

H. Bring towels and drinking cups to the gym.

I. Check the locker room to make sure everything is locked.

IV. During Home Games

A. Sit on the bench and be ready to help at all times.

B. Give water and towels to players when they are needed.

C. Collect balls when they are not in use.

D. Collect and put away all warm-up uniforms.

E. Be ready to administer emergency first aid.

V. After Home Games

A. Take all the balls and jerseys and put them away.

B. Refill the medicine kit.

C. Collect, count, and bundle all towels.

D. Help remove tape.

E. Check all the lockers to see that they are locked.

F. Put away the clock and horn.

G. Make sure the equipment rooms are locked.

VI. Before Leaving for Away Games

A. Arrive at the gym forty-five minutes before the bus leaves.

B. Check all the equipment.

C. Pack the medicine kit.

D. Check to see that the equipment room is left clean.

E. Pack the towels.

VII. Arrival to Away Games

A. Get all the equipment off the bus.

B. Hand out the equipment.

C. Collect all valuables.

D. Follow the same routine as at the home games.

VIII. Departure from Away Games

A. Collect all the equipment.

B. Collect the towels.

C. See that no equipment is left behind.

D. Return all the valuables.

E. Load the bus.

IX. Arrival Home from Away Games

A. Check to see that nothing is left on the bus.

B. Collect and hang up the uniforms.

C. Put the first-aid kit away.

D. Count the towels and put them away.

E. Lock up everything and check to see if everything is done.

X. During Halftime

A. Have oranges cut and ready to hand out to the players.

B. Have towels and water ready.

C. Help with the equipment.

D. Assist the coach.

Suggested Manager's Daily Duties

1. Report to the training room or equipment room immediately after school.

2. Check with your coach to see what equipment is needed for that day's practice unless you already know.

3. Get out any equipment that the coach wants out.

4. Put out clean towels and bags.

5. Put bags of dirty towels back in laundry room.

6. Pick up any equipment left out in the locker room and put it in the lost and found.

7. Squeegee floor.

8. Pick up any towels or soap left on the floor and report this to your coaches.

9. Any locks left unlocked are to be turned in to your coaches.

10. Keep all doors locked when areas are not in use.

11. Check schedule of duties.

12. Keep a supply of soap in the shower room.

13. Make sure all equipment is put back where it belongs.
14. Clean foot powder bath as needed.
15. Sweep office floors.
16. Sweep training room floor.
17. Sweep equipment room floor.
18. Sweep laundry room floor.
19. Check bulletin boards daily.
20. Have first-aid kit conveniently located on the practice floor.
21. Report to the coach for any special duties.

CARE OF EQUIPMENT: The care of equipment is one of the main duties of the manager as he has complete charge of all equipment after it has been issued to the players.

Usually there are three ways in which equipment may be issued to the players all of which are satisfactory to some degree. However, each situation along with the wishes of the coach will dictate the way in which the equipment is handled.

One method used to issue the equipment is allow the players to keep it for the entire season. The chances of losing the equipment are much greater using this method but the burden of responsibility is on the player.

Another method of issuing equipment is to give it to the player before each game and have it returned after the game. This system places the responsibility upon the manager because he will need to check each uniform out and in for each game.

The third method is to have all the uniforms placed on hangers in one room. The players themselves, under the supervision of the manager, pick up their uniforms before the game and return them to the equipment room after the game. This system makes it very inconvenient and awkward after the away-from-home games. It does allow the manager to check all the equipment to see if each piece is returned.

Regardless of the system used, the danger of losing equipment is always present. Often, equipment has a way of disappearing through no fault of the player or the manager. Good equipment costs a great deal of money so it should be protected against loss. Good equipment care will lengthen its use. Most of the present-day equipment is like clothing; give it good care and it will wear longer. More equipment is ruined through poor care than by hard use.

EQUIPMENT CARE BEFORE THE SEASON: Equipment care begins at the time of delivery from the manufacturer. As soon as it arrives, it should be taken from the containers and checked for size, color, and type of material. All equipment should then be stored in a dry, well-lighted, clean equipment room.

EQUIPMENT CARE DURING THE GAME: Equipment gets the hardest use during the game. The manager should work out a system with the players for taking care of warm-up pants and jerseys so that they will not be thrown on the floor. After each player removes the warm-up clothing, it should be stacked neatly near the bench. This practice will also help to prevent the clothing from being lost. If a player is sent into a game that is in progress he should remove his warm-up clothing, hand them to the manager who in turn folds them and places them on the bench. If a player is removed from the game, the manager should have his warm-up clothing ready for him to put on as he approaches the bench. The players should be instructed to receive their equipment graciously and not start throwing it about.

EQUIPMENT CARE AFTER THE GAME: This is the time when most of the equipment is lost and special attention should be given to this period of time so that this loss can be prevented. This is also a time when everyone is in a hurry to get away and clothing is left in piles until the next practice session. A good manager will prevent this from happening but it does take a special effort on his part. All equipment should be put on hangers in the drying room if one is available. If the game is away from home, then the manager should instruct and inspect to see that players hang their uniforms up in their motel room. If the team is on an extended trip, the uniforms should be cleaned.

EQUIPMENT CARE AFTER THE SEASON: Good equipment care after the season is completed is of utmost importance. This is the time when equipment needs the best care. If it is neglected at this time and not taken care of until the next season rolls around, it will deteriorate to the point that it will be useless. All equipment should first be thoroughly dried out for several days and then sent to the cleaners. The cleaner should be instructed not only to clean the equipment but also to repair it. The equipment should be carefully checked after the season to determine what replacements are needed.

Managerial Award System

There are various systems of awards for managers. The requirements for these awards will vary in each school as the regular athletic awards do.

George and Lehmann[17] suggest the following requirements:

> The senior manager should be awarded the school monogram with 'M' superimposed. Only one such monogram shall be awarded. Junior managers upon successful completion of their duties shall be awarded the J.U. letter with the 'm' superimposed. The number of such letters awarded will not exceed the number of junior managers specified for that sport. The assistant manager, upon completion of their duties shall be awarded the lightweight (or felt) letter with an 'm' superimposed. No more than four such letters shall be awarded.
>
> The coach and athletic director must agree that any manager's work has been satisfactory.

The importance of these awards should not be overlooked. Their value to the recipients cannot be measured and certainly not compared to others who receive the playing award. This award may be the closest athletic award the manager will ever receive. It represents his contribution to any success the team may have had. Hixson[18] emphasizes the importance of this award by commenting that, "At no time should these students be omitted from the awards banquets or the recognition assembly. Their contribution to the athletic teams as well as their own growth and development warrants recognition."

Motivation is always a big factor in producing a winning team. The smart coach will attempt to provide this motivation. If he has the right kind of managers, they can exert a tremendous influence on the players and their desire to win. Knowing this, the coach should make winning attractive. He can do this by the following method.

He can foster a plan of motivation by making it possible for the varsity manager to be allowed to make additional points if the school is on a point system. For example, if the school is on a point system, the manager would be allowed extra points if the team were league champion.

Motivation can also be promoted by allowing the assistant managers to receive additional points for winning teams. This type of motivation serves as an incentive to both players and managers alike and is an important aspect of the athletic program.

[17]George, Jack, and Lehmann, Harry, *School Athletic Administration*, p. 248.

[18]Hixson, Chalmer, *The Administration of Interscholastic Athletics*, p. 65.

Halperin[19] feels that there should be a basis of promotion and awards for managers and offers the following suggestions:

1. Promotion should be based on the efficient manner in which the season's work is accomplished and the attitude which accompanies the work.
2. The head manager should be a senior, the assistant manager a junior, managerial candidates should be freshmen or sophomores.
3. One of the two assistant managers should be promoted to varsity manager.
4. The varsity manager should be eligible for a varsity award and a membership in the varsity club. Assistant managers should be eligible to receive a minor award.
5. The manager should prepare and get all equipment ready before the season and store all equipment after the season.

Rewards of Student Managers

Resick, Seidel and Mason[20] state that:

In most high schools it is a policy to present awards to student managers for efficient service. These awards should differentiate the type of service rendered. Some schools make awards to senior managers only; others recognize juniors and sophomores as well. When awards are granted to senior, junior, and sophomore managers, they should be indicative of the student's position in the managerial hierarchy. Managers should be subject to the same eligibility and scholastic rules as members of the team they manage.

Not all those individuals who indicate a desire to be a manager are looking for an immediate and visible award. They are looking for the type of experience that can be gained only from the association with coaches and players that takes place during a season of competition. This type of experience can exert a tremendous influence on the manager and can result in his being able to better adjust himself to similar problems which he faces during the season and later on in life. There will be a carry over in his ability to face life situations where the emotional aspect of athletics will coincide with those of everyday living. He will learn to work with people and for a common cause. He will learn to abide by the rules and to run a "tight ship." He will learn to sacrifice personal gain for combined gain. He will learn to sacrifice personal prestige for group prestige. He will learn to live for and by group approval. He will learn to live better in a democratic society.

Forsythe[21] has this comment regarding rewards:

Schoolmen should keep the fact in mind that we learn by doing and that more students will be brought into the program by use of the student manager system. In virtually all instances they are more than glad to be of service. Usually they need not be paid but they should be given recognition by being awarded a school letter or some other suitable emblem.

George and Lehmann[22] make the following comments regarding rewards for managers:

The degree of interest in serving as student assistants in the athletic program is usually closely related to school morale, and to the status given to persons serving in these capacities. Coaches and administrators should do everything possible to make assignments as student managers, trainers, and other student assistants attractive. A system of awards and rewards can help to create and maintain interest. Some possible incen-

[19]Halperin, Gary, "A Syllabus for Basketball Managers."

[20]Resick, Mathew, Seidel, Beverly, and Mason James, *Modern Administrative Practices in Physical Education and Athletics* (Reading, Massachusetts, Addison-Wesley Co., 1970), p. 133.

[21]Forsythe, Charles, *Administration of High School Athletics.*

[22]George, Jack, and Lehmann, Harry, *School Athletic Administration,* p. 288.

tives for managers and other assistants can be listed as follows:

1. Qualifications for awards
2. Status in the eyes of their peers
3. Group membership and a sense of belonging
4. Team and school pride and spirit
5. Feeling of achievement and a sense of service.
6. Team trips and banquets
7. Notation on permanent school records.
8. Recommendation for college entrance or job applications.
9. Excellent work experience.
10. Such recognition as names on programs and squad rosters.
11. Special uniforms or other means of identification, such as arm bands, blazers, sweaters, or jackets.

The manager will also learn to live close to the players, sharing their emotional experiences of winning and losing. He will learn many lessons of life that he will need to face up to later on. He will need to be firm in his convictions of what is right and wrong, and what should and should not be done. His duties as manager will present many challenges which will make him a better person.

Other rewards may be classified as follows:

1. The development of leadership qualities
2. Learning the acceptance of responsibility
3. The development of initiative and executive ability
4. Foresight in planning for efficient administration and organization
5. The satisfaction of rendering unselfish service
6. Giving and receiving cooperation in dealing with men

Halperin stresses the fact that a good selling point when trying to recruit managers is to inform them that they will be assuming a responsibility for the organization and supervision of detailed work that will parallel most vocations. The manager will have the opportunity of having personal contacts with players, coaches, alumni, etc. They can also feel that they are a big part of the team.[23]

Dress of the Manager

An appropriate uniform for the manager will do a great deal to enhance his prestige. He should be as well dressed as the players at all times. He should never be allowed to dress in cast-off clothing such as an old sweat shirt and pants. Uniforms in school colors should be provided and the shirts or jackets should be inscribed with the lettering "Varsity Manager," "Freshman Manager," etc. This will add dignity and class to the position of manager. All other materials that the manager will need in the performance of his duties should be furnished by the school.

BEHAVIORAL OBJECTIVES

After a person has read this chapter, he should be able to:

1. Define the term manager as used in this text.
2. Explain the ideal organizational managerial setup.
3. Explain the relationship between the student athletic manager and the coach.
4. Describe and explain the most desirable method of recruiting student athletic managers.
5. Complete a list of requirements needed for the student athletic manager and apply these requirements to specific situations.
6. Identify several qualifications of student managers and analyze their importance.
7. List the three types of student man-

---

[23]Halperin, Gary, "A Syllabus for Basketball Managers."

agers and explain and analyze in detail their duties.

8. Identify and explain the various ways in which the student manager may be selected.

9. Develop a managerial plan based on merit.

10. Distinguish between the duties of the head manager and assistant manager.

11. Identify and analyze the duties of student managers.

12. Develop a manager's checklist for football and basketball.

13. Compile a list of the personal attributes of the student athletic manager.

14. Develop an awards system for the student manager.

15. Identify and analyze the rewards which may accrue from being an athletic student manager.

16. Explain and analyze the proper dress for the athletic student manager.

17. Distinguish between the duties of the basketball manager before, during, and after the game.

18. Develop a list of duties for the basketball manager during the game.

19. Identify several ways which schools use in caring for athletes' injuries.

20. Outline the duties of the student athletic trainer in high school.

21. Propose a plan for the training of the student athletic trainer.

22. Select three attributes which are most important for the student athletic manager to possess and explain why.

23. Explain why it is important for the coach to have a good manager.

24. Identify and analyze several requirements that the athletic student manager should possess.

25. Prepare a list of qualifications which the athletic student manager should possess.

26. Prepare a selection plan for student athletic managers in a large high school.

27. Identify several ways in which student athletic managers are selected.

28. Develop an athletic student managers' checklist in football for the day of the game.

29. Identify several methods by which students may be encouraged to become managers of athletic teams.

30. Compile a list of the responsibilities of the student manager.

31. Compile a list of the advantages and disadvantages of having a student athletic manager.

32. Differentiate between an award system and reward system for student athletic managers.

ACTIVITIES

1. Visit several high school football and basketball games and observe the athletic managers regarding duties, dress, and general behavior.

2. Attend a high school practice session and observe the rapport between the manager, coach and players.

3. Interview a high school coach and obtain his opinion as to the value of the student athletic manager, his duties and his position relative to the coach and players.

4. Seek the opinions of several coaches as to the specific duties of the student athletic manager.

5. Write to several athletic directors of large high schools and ask for their student athletic managerial plans which they use.

6. Contact several school athletic directors and find out how they select their student athletic managers.

7. Visit a school and talk with a student athletic manager regarding his philosophy, duties, responsibilities, and rap-

port with the coach, players, and school officials.

8. Write to several athletic directors and ask them how they recruit their student athletic managers.

9. Write a ten-item checklist of specific phases of managership that could be used at the high school level.

10. Develop a student manager system that will continue for a period of years and be reasonably successful.

11. Develop a plan for the selection, retention, and rewarding of student athletic managers.

SUGGESTED READINGS

1. Cousy, Bob, and Power, Frank: *Basketball Concepts and Techniques.* Boston, Allyn, 1970.

2. Curtis, P.D.: Hard lot of the team manager. *Times London Education Supplement,* August 22, 1969.

3. Daughtrey, Greyson, and Woods, John: *Physical Education Programs.* Philadelphia, Saunders, 1971.

4. Damren, Jerry: The High School Manager. *Athletic Journal,* February, 1953.

5. Forsythe, Charles: *Administration of High School Athletics.* Englewood Cliffs, P-H, 1959.

6. Forsythe, Charles: *The Athletic Director's Handbook.* Englewood Cliffs, P-H, 1956.

7. George, Jack F., and Lehmann, Harry A.: *School Athletic Administration.* New York, Har-Row, 1966.

8. Halperin, Gary: A syllabus for basketball managers. *Coaching Clinic,* April, 1972.

9. Healey, William: The student manager for basketball. *School Activities,* November, 1967.

10. Hixson, Chalmer: *The Administration of Interscholastic Athletics.* New York, Lowell Pratt, 1967.

11. Kowalk, Clayton: Basketball managers—a key to organization success. *The Athletic Journal,* September, 1964

12. Resick, Mathew, Seidel, Beverly, and Mason, James: *Modern Administrative Practices in Physical Education and Athletics,* Reading, A-W, 1970.

13. Vannier, Mary Helen, and Fait, Hollis: *Teaching Physical Education in Secondary Schools,* Philadelphia, Saunders, 1969.

CHAPTER **16**

The Athletic Trainer

THERE IS A TREMENDOUS need today for the services of an athletic trainer in the high school athletic program. However, most budgets do not provide for a full-time trainer or even a part-time trainer except in the larger high schools. All schools engaged in athletics attempt to do something regarding the care of athletic injuries. Most of these attempts fall into one of the following categories: (1) full-time trainer, (2) part-time trainer, (3) coaches taking over training duties, (4) local physician on call, (5) student trainers, and (6) school nurse.

Definition of the Athletic Trainer

Athletic trainers, as recommended by the National Athletic Trainers Association's educational program, are instructors who are medical technicians working directly under the supervision of a team physician and in cooperation with the coaching staff and administration of their schools. In this role of dual responsibility, one to athletics and one to medicine, the athletic trainer serves as a close liaison between the coach and the team physician. The athletic trainer serves as a medical counsel to the coach.

What Is Athletic Training

Athletic training is an auxiliary function of medicine. It is involved with the prevention and care of injuries associated with competitive athletics. This is done in the following ways:

1. Preparation and utilization of a program of conditioning for athletes in cooperation with the coaching staff.
2. Administration of first aid to injured athletes.
3. Application of devices, such as strapping, bandaging, or bracing designed to prevent or protect against injury.
4. Administration of therapeutic techniques under the direction of the team physician.
5. Development and supervision of rehabilitation programs for injured athletes under the direction of the team physician.
6. Proper selection, care, and fitting of athletic equipment in cooperation with the coaching and equipment staffs.
7. Supervision of all athletic training menus and diets for athletes.
8. Supervision of the safety factors involved with all athletic playing areas by insuring that all undue hazards are eliminated.

Importance of Athletic Training

Sports, by their very nature, invite injury. The all-out effort required of the participants, the speed of movement, throwing and striking of missiles, and the rapid change of direction which is necessary are among the hazards inherent in sports activities. These are the hazards that

424

are responsible for the various injuries suffered by athletes.

There is no comprehensive estimate of the number of athletes injured annually in athletic competition. Insurance companies report that tens of thousands of athletes suffer fractures, sprains, strains, abrasions, and contusions annually. Statistics also indicate that the annual number of injuries resulting from athletic competition, especially football, have been increasing steadily. This is a major concern among parents and coaches. They realize that something must be done to not only prevent these injuries but to provide a means by which the athletes can be taken care of after the injury has occurred.

The blame for this increasing number of athletic injuries does not, however, rest with the nature of the activities alone. The increase is also due in part to the increased participation of youth in the sports programs of today. An example of this involvement is the estimate that more than 810,000 young men in over 14,000 high schools alone participate in football each year. To this add the thousands of other athletes who participate in the many other sports that are a part of the athletic programs in the schools throughout the nation.

If the risk of injury in sports competition is to be justified, then the administrators of every sports program are morally obligated to do everything within their power to (1) prevent injury whenever possible, (2) minimize the severity of the injury, and (3) treat each injury promptly and properly, with total rehabilitation of the athlete as their goal. In order to fulfill this obligation, each school would need to develop an athletic training program which would include the appropriate personnel to carry out such a program. This is the goal of the National Athletic Trainers Association and could become a reality in the near future.

The Need for an Athletic Trainer

Considerable progress has been made in the field of athletic training at the professional and collegiate levels. However, much remains to be done at the secondary school level. Too few high schools have a professionally trained person on their instructional staff to fill the position of an athletic trainer. The importance of an athletic trainer in the high school athletic training program is compounded by several factors.

First, the coaching staffs at the high school level are often small in number. This limits the amount of time that the staff members have in order to cover the day-to-day services of an adequate athletic training program.

Secondly, many high schools in smaller communities have problems due to a lack of physicians who are experienced in sports medicine.

Thirdly, the high school athlete is less mature and is not as well developed physically as he will be when he is in college. Therefore, high school athletes need closer observation for physical disabilities.

Duties and Responsibilities of the Trainer

Because of the nature of the trainer's duties and responsibilities, and because of the legal liability which could result from the carrying out of these duties, it is very important that they be very carefully spelled out. Because every situation is different, it is very difficult to state these duties in anything except in very broad and general terms. However, there are some that can be listed as being those which could be classified as general and would apply to most situations. These are as follows:

1. Working cooperatively with the coaches in setting up and carrying out a program of conditioning for athletes.
2. Administering first aid to injured athletes on the field, in the gym, or in the training room.
3. Applying protective or injury-preventive devices, such as strapping, bandaging, or bracing.
4. Working cooperatively with and under the direction of the physician in respect to:
   a. Reconditioning procedures
   b. Operation of therapeutic devices and equipment
   c. Fitting of braces, guards, and other devices
   d. Referrals to the physician, health services, or hospital
5. Working cooperatively with the coaches and the physician in selecting protective equipment and gear and in checking it for safety.
6. Supervising the training room, which includes the requisitioning and storage of supplies and equipment, keeping adequate records, maintaining a standing and running inventory, and maintaining a budget.
7. Supervising and instructing assistant trainers and other staff members under his jurisdiction.
8. Counseling and advising athletes and coaches on matters pertaining to conditioning and training, such as diet, rest, and reconditioning.
9. Conducting himself at all times as a responsible professional person.

The athletic trainer of today will find himself working with the team physician or school doctor and it is from them that he will receive his technical advice. It is very important, therefore, that the trainer follow closely the directions of the physician, and that he should not under any conditions take it upon himself to use any authority such as that vested in the physician.

Rumph[1] makes the following comment regarding the trainer:

> The head athletic trainer must adhere to the high standards of conduct set by the National Athletic Trainers Association and be willing to carry them out at all levels. He must be dedicated to serving people and committed to improving standards of performance. He should set high standards for training procedures, correlated with the school's educational policy. He must be impartial in his efforts and interests, working to enrich all branches of athletics. He must not show partiality in dealing with athletes, treating the team hero and the last member of the squad in the same way. The trainer is in a good position to help the coaches instill the ideas of fair play and sportsmanship among athletes.
>
> Through cooperation and communication, the trainer must work to achieve mutual respect and a harmonious working relationship with all coaches, personnel, and team physician.

Training of the Athletic Trainer

Athletic trainers of the past were a totally different type of person than their counterpart of today. They first made their appearance and became a part of the athletic program at the college level. They had always, to some extent at least, been a part of professional athletics. College athletics flourished after World War I and with it came the trainer. He had no formal training and what he knew came from experience. As the college program grew in stature and became recognized as a part of

---

[1] Rumph, Robert, "The Training Room Staff," *Journal of Health, Physical Education and Recreation* (October, 1974), p. 31.

college life, the demand for better trained coaches became prevalent especially for a coach who could formulate a program for the prevention of injury to athletes.

The colleges struggled through a period of the coach-type trainer until the time when individuals became interested in working in the college athletic program strictly as an athletic trainer. This type of arrangement continued until recently at which time a number of colleges and universities began offering formal curriculum in athletic training. While it is true that these colleges are not large in number, they are steadily increasing in number spurred on by the demand from colleges, universities, and high schools for qualified athletic trainers.

The National Athletic Trainers Association

The National Athletic Trainers Association was established in about 1947 and has its offices in Gardner, Kansas. Its purpose was to unify and establish an educational program, and the procedures and testing which would be required for certification of athletic trainers. The official publication of the association is the *Trainer*.

The approved program is as follows.[2]

APPROVED PROGRAM OF EDUCATION FOR THE ATHLETIC TRAINER

In the NATA approved program of education the athletic trainer should be encouraged to act as liaison with the departments of physical education and student health. The program highly recommends a major study in physical education and health and/or another secondary education field with the necessary

courses required by states for a teaching license. Also entered in the degree program are prerequisites for entry to schools of physical therapy as suggested by the American Physical Therapy Association.

The basic minimal requirements as recommended by the NATA are as follows:

I. A major study including teaching license in physical education, health, and/or a secondary education field variable, by states.

   A. Total of 24 semester hours in biological and social sciences.

      1. Biology—zoology (anatomy and physiology)—8 hours

      2. Social sciences (at least 6 hours in psychology) — 10 hours

      3. Electives strongly advised —minimum of 6 hours Additional biological and social sciences; physical education such as group activities, dancing, etc.; hygiene; speech; physics; chemistry

II. Specific, required courses (if not included in I, these must be added)

   A. Anatomy—one or more courses which will include human anatomy

   B. Physiology—circulation, respiration, digestion, excretion, nerve, brain and sense organs (Note: One course will not meet the two requirements listed above)

   C. Physiology of exercise

   D. Applied anatomy and kinesiology—the muscles; emphasis on their functions in and development for specific activities

   E. Psychology — one advanced course beyond the basic general course (could be sports psychology)

   F. First aid — minimum of advanced Red Cross first aid certification

---

[2]National Athletic Trainers Association Professional Education committee, changes in the NA&A Eduational Program for Trainers, *Journal of Health, Physical Education and Recreation* (October, 1973), p. 10.

G. Nutrition and foods
   1. Basic principles of nutrition.
   2. Basic diet and special diet
H. Remedial exercise, therapeutic exercise, adapted exercise, or corrective exercise — exercises for a typical and/or both temporary and permanent handicap
I. Personal, community, and school health
J. Techniques of athletic training—basic general course (acceptable course for all coaches)
K. Advanced techniques of athletic training
   1. Special course or courses for athletic training candidates with full academic background
   2. Laboratory practices (six semester hours credit or two years equivalent work of 600 clock hours)

III. Recommended courses
A. Laboratory physical science—six semester hours in physics and/or chemistry (should be required of students continuing on with a study in physical therapy)
B. Pharmacology — specific side effects of drugs
C. Histology—tissues and methods of studying them
D. Pathology — laboratory study of tissues in pathological condition
E. Organization and administration of health and physical education programs
F. Psychology of coaching
G. Coaching techniques
   1. Highly recommended: football, basketball, and track coaching technique courses
   2. Also recommended: courses in baseball, soccer, wrestling, and preferred sports by geographic areas

IV. To become an NATA Certified Athletic Trainer the student must complete the above course of study, present proof of one year of active membership in the NATA immediately prior to application for certification, and then pass practical and written examinations given at designated sites on specified dates under the supervision of the NATA Board of Certification.

The Student Trainer

Many schools cannot hire a full-time trainer because they are unavailable or because they cannot afford one. In order to overcome this difficulty it may be possible for many schools to hire a teacher-trainer or to appoint a student who is sincerely interested in training. The best plan is to hire a full-time trainer and to allow him to be in charge of training those students or coaches who are interested in learning more about athletic training. The interested students are known as student trainers. What are the duties of a student trainer? (1) Primarily to assist the head trainer and team physician in routine procedures, and (2) to be responsible for the general cleanliness and physical condition of the training room.

In order to become a better trainer, the following tips may prove helpful.
1. Be the first man on the job and the last one to leave.
2. Keep the training room clean and neat but do not spend time cleaning when there are players needing attention.
3. Let the coach make and enforce the rules. They are his responsibility, not yours.
4. Put all supplies away before going home at night.
5. Find things to do in slack moments.
6. Prepare a "want list" of needed supplies.
7. Always keep the first-aid kit properly packed.

8. Always remember that the trainers hands are his most important tools. Keep them clean.
9. Although a special uniform is not needed, the trainer should dress neatly.
10. Do not experiment with new methods until you have learned the merits and disadvantages of the old ones.
11. Even though the trainer may not have as good a training room as his neighbor he should do the best with what he has.
12. Do not have pets or favorites.
13. During the game or practice, pay close attention to those you know have some sort of injury, and check every player at halftime or as occasion permits.
14. Use your eyes and ears to improve the efficiency of your hands.

Rumph[3] makes the following comments regarding the student trainer:

> The student trainer's chief function is to relieve the trainer and coach of many small chores necessary for daily practice and athletic events. He sometimes acts as a liaison between the team physician, coach, and trainer and athlete. With basic knowledge of strapping, rehabilitative exercise, and therapy, he helps with preseason conditioning, rehabilitation, and immediate treatment of injuries. He reports injuries to the coach and trainer so that first aid can be administered. He keeps an updated record on all player injuries and treatment.

Training of the Student Trainer

Student trainers are not capable of handling the varied duties of the fully qualified trainer; therefore, their duties must be confined to first aid. However, many schools have adopted a student trainer system. In order for a student to become a trainer, he should complete a detailed correspondence course devised and regulated by Kramer Brothers of Gardner,

Kansas. When a student has satisfactorily completed this basic course, he should have acquired the fundamental knowledge to assist in daily minor training room duties. However, he should not be allowed to treat any injuries other than those connected with first aid.

Awards and Rewards for Student Trainers

The student trainer should be given the same recognition as his fellow athletes. He plays an important part in their success as an athlete. This the athlete should know. He should realize that the student trainer's importance to the team should be reflected in the same way as that of the star player. The athlete should, therefore, consider the student trainer as a valuable member of the team, and as such he should receive the same type of rewards and awards.

The Training Room

The ideal training room should be light and dry. It should be well ventilated. It should be kept at 78 degrees F. The floor should be a light color and kept dry at all times.

The Layout of the Training Room

The arrangement of equipment in the training room is very important. If the equipment is not arranged and placed properly, it can cause a great deal of confusion during periods of heavy use. The proper arrangement of equipment can also save the trainer or coach many headaches when the training room is being cleaned. All the equipment should be arranged so that all patients can be taken care of quickly and efficiently. All arrangements must be practical and take into consideration the patient's welfare at all times. They should not contribute to the possibility of further

---

[3]Rumph, Robert, "The Training Room Staff."

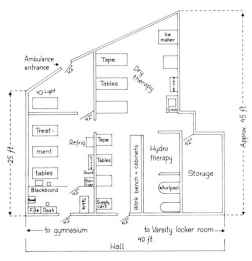

Figure 82.

injury. The arrangement should be such that it will save the time and effort of the trainer.

Organizing the Use of the Training Room

In order to better organize the use of the training room, a permit should be issued. This will aid in keeping the records and the proper use of the training room. These permits would also eliminate the boy who is looking for a place to kill time. Requiring a training room permit would also enable the trainer to plan more wisely for the future practice sessions. Training rooms should have a definite detailed set of rules, and these rules should be placed where everyone can see them.

Trainer's Check List

A. DAILY

1. Report to training room immediately after school each day.
2. Help coaches care for any injuries needing first-aid attention.
3. Make sure training room Johnnies are not late for practice.

PROVISO NORTH HIGH SCHOOL DISTRICT 112

TRAINING ROOM PERMIT FORM

NAME_____ DATE_____

COACH_____ ACTIVITY_____

TIME IN_____ TIME OUT_____

HELD FOR FOLLOWING TREATMENT

REPORT BACK_____ TRAINER_____

PROVISO NORTH TOWNSHIP HIGH SCHOOL

ATHLETIC DEPARTMENT

Date_____

This is to certify that_____ is a member

of the_____ squad in_____ (Sport). He is to receive

medical attention by the school doctor.

Nature of injury:

_____

_____

_____

Signature of Coach _____

This form must be returned to the coach upon return to school accompanied by a report from the doctor to the coach.

Figure 83.

CHARLESTON HIGH SCHOOL DISTRICT NO. 114

PLAYER INJURY REPORT SHEET

Date_____

NAME	INJURY	DATE INJURED	EXPECTED RETURN	TREATMENT	LIMITATIONS
1.					
2.					
3.					
4.					
5.					
6.					
7.					
8.					
9.					
10.					
11.					
12.					
13.					
14.					

Figure 84.

4. Make sure locker room doors are kept locked and none other than players and coaches come into the locker rooms.
5. Keep first-aid supply container full.

TABLE LXXIV
HARRIS HIGH SCHOOL DISTRICT 99

Training Room Rules

1. No one will be sent to the training room for treatment during the school day except as follows:
   (a) At a time when a trainer is on duty as shown below:

Hour	Day	Trainer
1		
2		
3		
4	When	Eiserman
5	Possible	
6		
7	Everyday	Birong
8	Everyday	Volling

   (Note) Both Joe Birong & Cliff Volling have satisfactorily completed a student training course.
   (b) At a time other than stated above when extreme emergency arises.
   (c) Unless the person recommending treatment be present with the student.
2. No student will give himself first-aid treatment in the training room:
   (Note) If treatment is needed, attention will be given such treatment only by a trainer, a coach, or an instructor.
3. The training room will be locked at all times when no one is on duty to care for injuries.
4. To all coaches:
   If at any time there is a shortage of training room supplies or items that you would like to order please let me know.

   COACH _____

6. One trainer must be with the teams during practice sessions with their kits. All trainers should be available for games.
7. Keep whirlpool and foot powder bath clean.
8. Keep training room spotless.
9. Keep daily inventory on ace bandages and ankle wraps and get them washed and dried.
10. Keep supply of soap in the shower rooms.
11. Check foot sprays in shower rooms.
12. Report to your coach before leaving.
13. Lock all doors and turn off lights.
14. Keep ice cube trays filled at all times.
15. Keep all equipment in its proper place.
16. Check your first-aid kits daily.

B. WEEKLY AND GAMES
   1. Report all first-aid supply shortages or needs to the coach.
   2. Be present at all games.
   3. Have all necessary first-aid equipment at the bench during the game.
   4. Do not leave training room until all players are dressed and leave the locker room.

C. DURING GYM CLASSES
   1. Report to the coach for any special duties.
   2. Keep all locks in lock room on their respective hooks.
   3. Help squeegee floors.
   4. Help with towels and towel bags.

D. GENERAL
   1. Keep yourself neat and clean at all times and wear the equipment

issued to you. Always have clean equipment for games.

2. Tell one of the coaches if you cannot be at practice or a game.

Training Supplies and Costs

The training supplies and equipment for the training room will depend upon many factors, the most important one being the amount of money available to spend. Another factor is the space that is available for use as a training facility. Still another important factor is the qualifications of the person or persons in charge of this area. The entire high school training program has presented a problem because of these three factors along with the general philosophy which exists in most communities regarding the treatment of injuries by anyone except a qualified physician. Therefore, in staffing the training

area and preparing the budget, these things must be taken into consideration.

The following training budget as well as the sample equipment supplies are only suggestions and must be adapted to a particular situation as it applies to that situation. Also the cost of the various items are not authentic and will also vary with the economy of the times.

BEHAVIORAL OBJECTIVES

After a person has read this chapter, he should be able to:

1. Define athletic training.
2. Recall the early history of the National Athletic Trainers Association.
3. Explain the function of athletic training as it relates to medicine.
4. Identify several ways in which athletic training relates to medicine.
5. Explain the responsibilities of the ad-

TABLE LXXV

Budget for Athletic Supplies and Equipment for High School

SUPPLIES ORDERED ANNUALLY	
Bandages	$ 200.86
Dressings	509.60
Instruments	158.20
Liquids — consumable	10.44
Liquids — nonconsumable	147.03
Tablets — consumable	72.50
Tablets — nonconsumable	4.50
Ointments & Powders	104.11
Protective Materials	383.04
Tape and Related Products	379.58
Tape	2174.20
Miscellaneous Items	119.08
	$4263.14
PERMANENT EQUIPMENT (not ordered annually)	
Rehabilitation Equipment	$ 715.25
Hydrotherapy Equipment	2540.00
Dry Room Therapy Equipment	1450.00
Training Room Equipment	2039.00
Trainer's Office	601.00
	$7345.25
GRAND TOTAL	$11,608.39

TABLE LXXVI

BANDAGES

Item Description	Quantity	Unit	Unit Price	Total
Elastic Bandage — Johnson & Johnson (Rubber) 5 yds. x 4"	6	doz.	$7.98	$ 47.88
Elastic Bandage — Johnson & Johnson (Rubber, Dynaflex) 5 yds. x 6"	6	doz.	$11.31	67.86
Conco Elastic rubber — pressure Bandage #883 8: x ⅛"	6	doz.	$3.65	21.90
Conco Elastic foam rubber pressure Bandage 4" x ⅛"	6	doz.	$2.95	17.70
NU Wrap Bandage rolls #7212, 28 x 24 gauze 2" width 90 rolls/box	2	doz.	$10.75	21.50
Kling Nonsteril Bulk foam-self-adherring Bandage, #6902, 2 x 5 yds. 1 doz/pkg., 8 doz/cs	2	doz.	$12.01	24.02
				$200.86

DRESSINGS

Item Description	Quantity	Unit	Unit Price	Total
Band-Aids — A plastic telfa adhesive band-aid with an unmedicated sterile pad in individual wrapper. 100/box.				
1" x 3"	50	box	$1.35	$ 67.50
¾" x 3"	15	box	$1.10	16.50
Telfa Pads (100/box.)				
2" x 3"	50	box	$2.19	109.50
3" x 4"	40	box	$3.41	136.40
Special Purpose Band-Aids Blastoplast Elastic Dressing knuckle coverlets, size 1½ x 3", Duke #385, 50/box	12	box	$1.95	23.40
Wing coverlets for elbow and hand injury, overall size 3" x 3", Duke #385, 50/box	12	box	$3.05	36.60
Nonsterile gauze sponges, Bulk packed, Bike #2346, 3" x 3", 12 ply packed, 4000/cs.	2	box	$37.17	74.34
Sterile Gauze pads #6132 individually enveloped 3" x 3" 12 ply, 100 box, 12 boxes/cs.	2	box	$22.68	45.46
				$509.60

INSTRUMENTS

Item Description	Quantity	Unit	Unit Price	Total
Needle Holder, Mayo Heger Box Lock 8", Stainless Steel	1	ea.	$5.00	$ 5.00

TABLE LXXVI — (cont.)

Item Description	Quantity	Unit	Unit Price	Total
Operating Scissors, Straight Points, sharp/sharp, 5½" stainless steel	6	ea.	$1.75	10.50
Operating Scissors, curved points, sharp/sharp, 5½" stainless steel	6	ea.	$1.85	11.10
Tissue Forcepts, 2 x 3 teeth, 5½" stainless steel	6	ea.	$1.60	9.60
Thumb Dressing Forceps 5½" stainless steel	6	ea.	$1.35	8.10
Bard Parker #3 Scalpel, Blade Handle	6	ea.	$2.10	12.60
Bard Parker #11, Scalpel, Blade	4	doz.	$2.00	8.00
Bandage Scissors — Chrome Plated 7¼" Su 2006	12	ea.	$2.15	25.80
Tape Cutters Gilcrest	12	ea.	$2.00	24.00
Fingernail Drill, chrome plated with 3 drill points	2	ea.	$4.75	9.50
Revlon Toenail clippers #2330	6	ea.	$4.50	27.00
Helmet Cutters	2	ea.	$3.50	7.00
				$158.20

LIQUIDS — CONSUMABLE

Item Description	Quantity	Unit	Unit Price	Total
Kaopectate®, 8 oz.	12	ea.	$.87	$ 10.44
				$ 10.44

LIQUIDS — NONCONSUMABLE

Item Description	Quantity	Unit	Unit Price	Total
Alcohol, 70% Isopropyl (Gallon)	6	ea.	$2.10	$ 12.60
Baby Lotion, (1 Gallon container)	6	ea.	$3.45	20.70
Physohex®, Winthrop, (Gallon container)	3	ea.	$10.00	30.00
Zephiran, Chloride® (Gallon)	12	ea.	$6.00	72.00
Collodion (flexible) (Merck) 4 oz. bottles	3	ea.	$1.31	3.93
Dacriose Eye solution 30 cc.	6	ea.	$.55	3.30
Merthiolate®/pints	2	ea.	$2.25	4.50
				$147.03

TABLETS — CONSUMABLE

Item Description	Quantity	Unit	Unit Price	Total
Aspirin, 5 gr., Norwich, 1000/bottle	1	bot.	$1.10	1.10
Gelusil® Tablets 1000/box	1	box	$16.90	16.90
Dextrose Tablets, 25 grain dextrose 500/box	3	box	$3.25	9.75
Salt Tablets, 5000/box	5	box	$8.50	42.50
Potassium	3	box	$.75	2.25
				$ 72.50

TABLE LXXVI — (cont.)

Item Description	Quantity	Unit	Unit Price	Total
TABLETS — NONCONSUMABLE				
Nonrust Tablets	1	box	$4.50	4.50
				$ 4.50

| **OINTMENTS & POWDERS** | | | | |
Item Description	Quantity	Unit	Unit Price	Total
Vitamin A and D ointment (Pharmodern) (1 lb. jar)	6	jar	$2.35	$ 14.10
Neo-Polycin®, 15 gram tubes	24	tube	$1.60	38.40
Desenex® ointment, 0.2 cr. Av.	1	case	$27.16	27.16
Zinc Oxide (Pharmodern) (1 lb. jar)	3	jar	$1.15	3.45
Foot & Body Powder, TA15, (25 lb. fiber drum)	2	ea.	$10.50	21.00
				$104.11

| **PROTECTIVE MATERIAL** | | | | |
Item Description	Quantity	Unit	Unit Price	Total
Orthoplast Isoprene Splinting Material, Perforated Sheets, 12" x 20", (4 sheets/cs.)	4	case	$37.45	149.84
Foam Rubber Sheets				
21 x 36 x ½"	4	ea.	$3.15	12.60
21 x 36 x 1"	4	ea.	$5.00	30.00
Adhesive Felt (Zinc Oxide Adhesive Mass)				
6½" x 1 yd. x 1/16" — white	2	ea.	$1.70	3.40
6½" x 1 yd. x ⅛" — white	2	ea.	$1.90	3.80
Moleskin, 7" x 1 yd. C 44	2	ea.	$ .70	1.40
Safe-T guard Mouth Piece, Form Fit to individual mouth, Model 5510, without strap — Madison Dental Co.	200	ea.	$ .80	160.00
Ankle wrap webbing, Bike #47 2" x 72 yds.	4	ea.	$5.50	22.00
				$383.04

| **TAPE & RELATED PRODUCTS** | | | | |
Item Description	Quantity	Unit	Unit Price	Total
Adherent: Precision Lab skin tough Aerosol can, 24 oz. 12 cans/cs	3	case	$13.80	$ 41.40
Cramer Product QDA, aerosol can 6 oz.	12	ea.	$1.05	12.60
Under Wrap, Bike 8 wrap 40/case	4	case	$35.64	142.56
Under Wrap, Bike pro-wrap 50/case	6	case	$28.52	171.12

TABLE LXXVI — (cont.)

Item Description	Quantity	Unit	Unit Price	Total
Tape Remover, TA-31, Gallon	2	case	$5.95	11.90
				$379.58

TAPE

Item Description	Quantity	Unit	Unit Price	Total
Johnson & Johnson, zonas, porous athletic tape, 1½" x 15 yd. cuts, 32/case	80	case	$14.68	1174.40
Johnson & Johnson, Coach, porous athletic tape, 1½" x 15 yd. cuts 32/case	20	case	$13.24	264.80
Johnson & Johnson, Jonas 1" x 10 yd. cuts, 12/tube	24	tube	$2.80	67.20
Bike Conform, 2" x 7½ yds. 24 cuts/pack	24	pack	$15.18	364.32
Johnson & Johnson, Elasticon, 3" cuts 4/tube, 12" x 5 yds.	96	tube	$3.00	288.00
Demicil Surgical tape, 1½" cuts 3/tube, 4½" x 5 yds.	2	case	$7.74	15.48
				$2174.20

MISCELLANEOUS

Item Description	Quantity	Unit	Unit Price	Total
Ammonia Capsules 100/box	10	ea.	$4.95	$ 49.50
Analgesic Balm Mild TA-3 — Train Aid 5 lb. can	3	ea.	$9.00	27.00
Hot TA-3 — Train Aid 5 lb. can	3	ea.	$10.00	30.00
Arm Sling — Adult Size	4	ea.	$2.50	10.00
Polyethyl Spray Bottles 802 #-22-8 without imprint 8 oz.	12	ea.	$ .50	6.00
Non-sterile cotton #5026 Dixwell — 16 oz. rolls	3	ea.	$ .80	2.40
Combination or Composite Padding Roll, Absorbant, Size 8" x 20 yds.	12	ea.	$4.24	50.88
Crutches — straight grained, hardwood, adjustable, 48" x 60" (arm cushion and tip included)	12	ea.	$5.25	63.00
Hair Clippers — continuous multi-out blade — SH S9-400	3	ea.	$11.50	34.50
Woolen Blanket — 100% processed wool 62" x 82"	3	ea.	$7.50	22.50

TABLE LXXVI — (cont.)

Item Description	Quantity	Unit	Unit Price	Total
Sling Psychorometer soc-853 with slide rule construction for quick reading — telescopes into handle	1	ea.	$15.75	15.75
Tongue Depressors (500/box)	6	ea.	$2.10	12.60
Cotton Tipped applicators, 10,000/cs	2	case	$14.50	29.00
White Petrolatum (5lb. can) ta-17	6	ea.	$6.75	40.50
B & D Thermometer	6	ea.	$ .75	4.50
B - D 08 Plastic-leak proof spring loaded, theremometer-case — with bakelite cap and pocket clip	6	ea.	$1.35	8.10
All metal garbage drums — metal handles	3	ea.		15.00

Item Description	Quantity	Unit	Unit Price	Total
5 Gallon cooler, bottom push button spout, Vacucel insulation, plastic exterior, 2 metal side handles, orange exterior with white lid, Poloron Products, Inc., New Rochelle, N.Y.	12	ea.	$6.00	$ 72.00
Ankle Wrap Roller — Metal SHS	2	ea.	$4.50	9.00
Splints				
Alumaform 4" x 16"	6	ea.	$3.00	18.00
Vobst Air Splints — complete set	3	ea.	$39.95	119.85
Penlite — push button with pocket clip with batteries	6	ea.	$1.50	9.00
Sundry Var Set 5 piece labeled set with stainless steel covers labeled gauze, cotton, applicators, bandages, and tongue depressors, Var Size 4" x 7"	2	set	$12.50	25.00
Stretcher (folding)	2	ea.	$22.50	45.00
				$719.08

ministrator in helping to avoid athletic injuries.

6. Indicate several reasons why too few high schools have a professionally trained athletic trainer on their staff.

7. Explain what Congress is doing regarding the employment of athletic trainers in the high school. Cite several implications, effects, and consequences.

8. Recall several duties of the athletic trainer and explain each.

9. Summarize the early history of athletic training and identify it with present-day training.

10. Compare the role of the present-day athletic trainer with that of the past.

11. Explain the course requirements as set up by the NATA. Analyze them in relation to the needs of the athletic trainer.

12. Explain the duties of the student trainer.

TABLE LXXVII

ITEM	DESCRIPTION	QUAN-TITY	UNIT	UNIT PRICE	TOTAL PRICE
REHABILITATION EQUIPMENT					
J. A. Preston Corporation PC 2051 Quadracepts Boot Iron Weight	With bar and screw on collars, 5 lbs.	1	ea.	$ 7.00	$ 7.00
PC 2055 Quadracepts Boot Aluminum	With bar and screw on collars (bar and collars weight 1½ lbs.)	1	ea.	$ 8.25	$ 8.25
J. A. Preston Corporation PC 2041 Hospital Department Weight Set	Consists of 194 lbs. of disc weights in the following quantities: 12 each — 1¼ lbs. / 10 each — 2½ lbs. Iron / 10 each — 5 lbs. / 10 each — 10 lbs. / 6 each — ¼ lb. Aluminum / 4 each — ⅝ lb.	1	ea.	$100.00	$100.00
J. A. Preston Corporation PC 6008 Treatment Table	78" long, 30" wide, 34" high. Legs 3" made of hardwood, aprons made of hardwood. Padded with polyfoam and upholstered in green nylon plastic.	6	ea.	$100.00	$600.00
HYDROTHERAPY EQUIPMENT					
Whirlpool Ille Model HT100DLX Therapeutic Tub	The complete unit consists of a heavy gauge all stainless steel tub (seamless — completely and continuously electrically welded — leakproof) with covered corners, stainless steel trim shield supporting base, handle operated DLX type 2" drain valve and a 2" full-flow overflow with a separate tank outlet, and 3½" dial thermometer mounted inside tub. Inside tub dimensions: 7' long, 2' wide, 20" deep. Rm. Width 2½", Overall height 28".	2	ea.	$1010.00	$1010.00

Optional Item

Item	Description	Qty	Unit	Price	Total
Model TP100 and RL100	Electric Turbine Ejector and Aerator and Raising and Lowering Device for attaching to end of tube. Fittings polished chrome.	2	ea.	$385.00	$ 385.00
					$1395.00
Whirlpool Ille Stationary Model THM105-54 (S)	Stainless Steel Tank (fully welded-leakproof) powerful Electric Turbine Ejector and Aerator with 1/3 HP high speed motor, raising and lowering device, 3½" dial thermometer and floor drain valve; for operation on 115 volts, 60 cycles AC.	1	ea.	$705.00	$ 705.00
Adjustable Suspension Seats for Whirpool Stainless Steel for 22, 24, or 25" inside tank width	HMA14T Adjustable Suspension Seat HMA14 20" inside tank	1	ea.	$ 52.00	$ 52.00
		1	ea.	$ 46.00	$ 46.00
					$ 98.00
Arm Rest for Whirlpool, Stainless Steel	HMA11	2	ea.	$ 21.00	$ 42.00
Whirlpool Formica Bath Table School Health Supply	Will fit all whirlpools with dimensions up to 22' wide. Outside dimensions: 48" x 30". Seats are 12" x 12", stands 34' high. Zinc-plated steel legs with sure grip rubber tips. Model SHSW-2	1	ea.	$300.00	$300.00

TRAINING ROOM EQUIPMENT
(Miscellaneous)

Item	Description	Qty	Unit	Price	Total
Scotsman Super Flaker Ice Maker	Produces up to 1050 pounds of Super Flakes per day. Stores up to 300 pounds. Occupies less than 8½ square feet. Aircooled condensing unit. Gray Hammer finish, with bin. SF-3WS	1	ea.	$1484.00	$1484.00

TABLE LXXVII — (cont.)

ITEM	DESCRIPTION	QUAN-TITY	UNIT	UNIT PRICE	TOTAL PRICE
Freezer - Refrigerator Philco 14.3 cu. ft. No frost, Model RD14K7	102 lb. Frost freezer with 3 fast-freeze ice cube trays, portable ice cube keeper, freezer storage door and separate freezer adjustable cold control. No frost refrigerator section has: deep shelf storage door, porcelain-enamel meat keeper, 2 porcelain enamel crispers, automatic interior light and separate adjustable cold control. 14.3 cu. ft. total capacity. Dimensions: 60½" high, 30" wide, 28⅞" deep. Color: avocado	1	ea.	$300.00	$300.00
Taping Table	Constructed of seasoned hardwood natural finish in green upholstering with heavy legs made of 3" stock; top of 5 ply veneer, well-padded with urethane foam upholstering and covered with green waterproof and acid resistant vinyl, leatherette mitred cross braces.	3	ea.	$ 85.00	$255.00
DRY THERAPY ROOM Medco Dublett Dual Ultrasound	Synchronized Ultrasound. Selected and synchronized with electrical muscle stimulation (Medcalator) and Medical (DC) Galvanism (Iontophoresis) *Accessories:* 2 — "PF" Ultrasound/Stimulator Applicators 2 — 4" x 4" pads w/Lead Cords 2 — 18" Velco Stretch Straps 2 — 25" Velco Stretch Straps 2 — 40" Rubber Straps				

1 — 16 oz. Dispensor — Medico Lotion
1 — AC Line Cord
1 — Lift-Out Strap
Specifications:
FCC Approved — U310
  Solid State Design
Ultrasound — 20 Watts
Effective Radiating
Effective Intensity
  Area 10 sq. cm.
Max. 2 Watts per sw. cm.
Frequency 1 — Megahertz
Variable Pulse ($\frac{1}{2}$% to 20% Duty Cycle)
Variable Surge ($\frac{1}{2}$% to 20% Duty Cycle)
The New Solid State, Velvet Smooth
Medcolator Current for Application
  with Metal Electrodes
Medco Green
115-125/v-60 HZ
Meets new hospital safety requirements
  with .5 ma line filter
Dimensions/Weights:
Console
25$\frac{1}{4}$" width, 30" high, 18" deep
43 lbs. weight .... 1 ea. $1450.00 $1450.00

TRAINER'S OFFICE
General Office Desk
Rehabilitation Products 1710L
Single pedestal with 3 box drawers on
right and center drawers 45" wide,
30" deep, 29" high. Steel construction
with desk top of linoleum, mist green. .... 1 ea. $140.00 $140.00

TABLE LXXVII — (cont.)

ITEM	DESCRIPTION	TITY QUAN.	UNIT	PRICE UNIT	PRICE TOTAL
Swivel Office Chair Rehabilitation Products 17130	Foam rubber seat and back. Tenite arm rests. Two inch ball-bearing casters on base, mist green. Fabric — naugahyde.	1	ea.	$ 70.00	$ 70.00
Side Chair Rehabilitation Products 17140	Steel panel back, saddle seat upholstered over left cusion, naugahyde, mist green.	1	ea.	$ 20.00	$ 20.00
File Cabinet, Letter Size. Rehabilitation Products 17164	Steel, when heavy loaded, drawers roll like a ball, close without rebound, perfectly aligned, rigidly steel constructed framework, four drawers, mist green, with lock.	2	ea.	$125.00	$250.00
Dazor Surgical Examination Lamp Rehabilitation Products 15036	UL approved, arm extension is 34". A 60 watt bulb. Finish gray baked enamel over bonderizing.	1	ea.	$ 33.00	$ 33.00
J. A. Preston Corporation PC 6143 Utility Cart	Solid stainless steel construction. Size of top and shelves is 15½" x 24." Height, 31¾". 3½" casters. Carrying capacity 200 lbs.	1	ea.	$ 88.00	$ 88.00

TABLE LXXVIII
MANUFACTURERS OF ATHLETIC TRAINERS SUPPLIES

Cramer Products Incorporated
Gardner, Kansaas 66030

Kendall Company
Bike Athletic Products Division
309 W. Jackson Blvd.
Chicago, Illinois 60606

Logan Incorporated
848 Fair Oaks
Pasadena, California 91103

Mueller Chemical Company Incorporated
Praire du Sac, Wisconsin 53578

School Health Supply Company
300 Lombard Road
Addison, Illinois 60101

MANUFACTURERS OF ADHESIVE TAPE
Johnson and Johnson
New Brunswick, New Jersey 08911

Kendall Company
Bike Athletic Products Division
309 W. Jackson Blvd.
Chicago, Illinois 60606

MEDICAL SUPPLIES
American Hospital Supply
2020 Ridge Avenue
Evanston, Illinois 60201

Johnson and Johnson
New Brunswick, New Jersey 08911

Kendall Company
Bike Athletic Products Division
309 W. Jackson Blvd.
Chicago, Illinois 60606

School Health Supply Company
3000 Lombard Road
Addison, Illinois 60101

SPLINTS AND STRETCHERS
(arm, leg, elbow, wrist, and fingers)
Ferno - Washington, Incorporated
Drawer 79
Greenfield, Ohio 45123

THERAPEUTIC MEDICAL EQUIPMENT
Burdick Corporation
Milton, Wisconsin

Medco Products Company
3607 E. Admiral Place
Tulsa, 12, Oklahoma

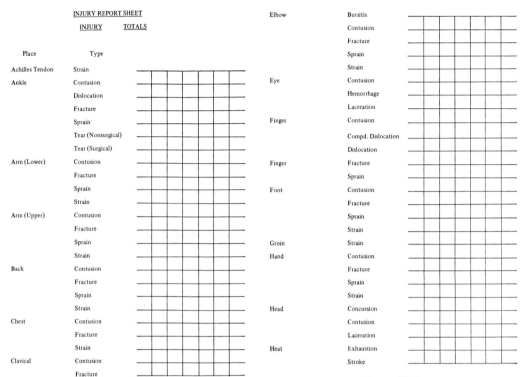

Figure 85-A.

Figure 85-B.

13. Explain the methods by which the student trainer can receive his training.
14. Recall several ways in which the trainer may do a better job.
15. Explain the importance of equipment placement in the training room.
16. Explain the use of the training room permit and discuss its value.
17. Identify several ways in which the schools attempt to care for their athletic injuries.
18. Explain what is meant by athletic training.
19. Explain the relationship between the athletic trainer and the physician.
20. Compile a list of reasons why any school should employ a full-time athletic trainer.

ACTIVITIES

1. Write to an insurance company for their policy on athletes and discuss this in class.
2. Ask a local insurance agent to talk to the class and explain the company policy on athletic protection.
3. Seek the opinion of several athletic directors regarding the values of having an athletic trainer on the staff.
4. Write to several colleges and obtain their course curriculum for the major in athletic training. Compare these.
5. Debate the question as to whether the athletic trainer should teach health or other subjects.
6. Prepare a list of reasons why each school should have an athletic trainer.

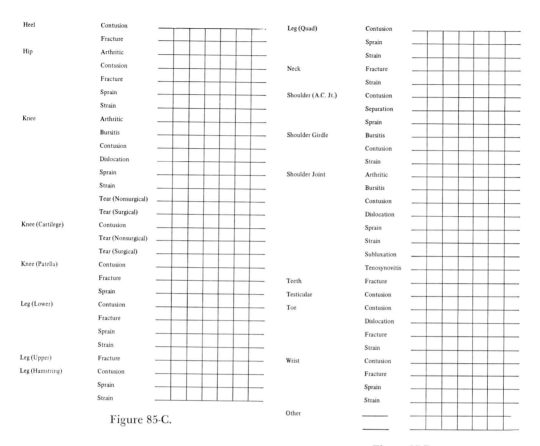

Figure 85-C.

Figure 85-D.

7. Arrange to have a high school or college trainer talk to the class.
8. Visit a large high school and observe their training personnel.
9. Visit a high school training room and list the equipment. Compare this to the essential equipment that is needed.
10. Prepare an equipment list for a training room in a large and small high school.

SUGGESTED READINGS

1. Atty, Alex: Some problems of the high school trainer. *The Mentor,* Feb.-March, 1952.
2. Bevan, Roland: *The Athletic Trainer's Handbook.* Englewood Cliffs, P-H, 1958.
3. Brashear, Robert G.: Basic areas of pre-vention of athletic injuries. *Journal of the NATA,* Fall, 1960.
4. Brown, B.J.: *Complete Guide to the Prevention and Treatment of Athletic Injuries,* West Nyack, Parker Pub, 1972.
5. Dickinson, A.D.: A philosophy of training. *Journal of the NATA,* Sept., 1956.
6. Dolan, Joseph P.: *Treatment and Prevention of Athletic Injuries.* 2nd ed. Danville, The Interstate, 1967.
7. Feurig, James S.: Legal liabilities of team physicians. *Journal of the NATA,* Nov., 1963.
8. Godfrey, Paul E.: Athletic injuries, a coach's responsibility. *Scholastic Coach,* March, 28, 1958.
9. Hrata, Jr., Isao, J.: *The Doctor and the*

Athlete. Philadelphia, Lippincott, 1968.

10. Harsha, William N.: Legal ramifications of athletic injuries. *Journal of the NATA,* Fall, 1961.

11. Matthews, David O., and Thomson, Richard A.: *Athletic Injuries: A Trainer's Manual and Textbook*. Dubuque, W.C. Brown, 1963.

12. Morehouse, Laurence E. and Rasch, Philip J.: *Sports Medicine for Trainers*. 2nd ed. Philadelphia, Saunders, 1963.

13. Mutchner, John: Developing a training room. *Scholastic Coach,* Jan., 1966.

14. National Federation: Moving an injured player. *Scholastic Coach,* May, 1960.

15. O'Donoghue, Don: *Treatment of Injuries to Athletes*. Philadelphia, Saunders, 1972.

16. Prelax, Edward J.: The trainer's 'warbag.'

Scholastic Coach, Jan., 1958.

17. Railey, Jimmy H.: The coach-trainer relationship: College coaches report. *Journal of the NATA,* August, 1963.

18. Ryan, Allan J.: Survey shows up lack of physical exams. *Journal of the NATA,* June, 1965.

19. Ryan, Allan J.: Survey shows up lack of physical exams, part II. *Journal of the NATA,* Sept., 1965.

20. Stromgren, George: Evaluation of the athletic injury care program. *The Mentor,* Summer, 1960.

21. Strong, Elliott S.: Relation of trainer to team physician. *Journal of the NATA,* May, 1963.

22. Troppmann, Bob: Relationship between the team physician and the coach. *Athletic Journal,* Jan., 1964.

CHAPTER 17

Tournaments

O NE OF THE MOST important administrative duties of the athletic director or coach could be to conduct a tournament. It could be an invitational tournament in soccer, basketball, tennis, or some other sport that lends itself to tournament play. Without previous experience or a thorough knowedge of the many duties involved, this could be a momentous task. It is important, therefore, that the director and coach thoroughly understand the many duties connected with conducting the tournament. There are many problems that need to be worked out, many of which can be partially solved ahead of time by perseverance and long-range planning. The success of any tournament can be traced to good and efficient management, so it is imperative that every detail is taken care of. Often the school administration is judged by the way the tournament is managed. It is a direct reflection on the coach, and he is criticized if the tournament administration is lax and ineffective.

It is important to the coach, athletic director, and school to make every effort to see to it that the tournament is conducted in such a way that it will cause the least amount of dissatisfaction for both spectator and participant. This requires wise and thoughtful planning of every detail as well as knowledge of administrative techniques on the part of the director or coach.

The tournament, if administered correctly, can be an educational experience for both the spectator and participant. It, therefore, should be conducted in such a way that will be in keeping with the educational values and goals considered important for the entire school. The tournament, if properly conducted, can contribute to the education of all people involved in the administration of it. It provides an opportunity for students and faculty to participate in and experience an activity where many of the objectives of education are being emphasized.

All the duties need not fall upon the shoulders of one or two individuals. Other departments in the school should be asked to cooperate in one way or another. For example, the art department can make posters, cover designs for programs, etc. The speech department can help in announcing the different events. The English department can prepare any script, dialogue, or narration which might be used. The home economics department may work on costumes for extra acts used in connection with the tournaments or may be in charge of meals which are served to the participants. The industrial arts department can construct any platforms or benches that may be needed. The journalism class can help handle the publicity in the school paper. The printing department can assist in the printing of programs and circulars. The music department can furnish band and record music. Boyden and Burton emphasize preplanning in the following observations:

> Probably the most important factor in the conducting of any tournament is the advance planning that is accomplished by the sponsoring organization weeks and months prior to the tournament. It makes little difference whether it be a badminton, volleyball, handball, basketball, or some other kind of tournament, the same basic and thorough planning is necessary to insure success on the day of the event. Too often a tournament committee waits until a few weeks before the event and then hurries to prepare and mail what turns out to be incomplete information about the tourney; orders trophies and/or medals that eventually come late and have to be sent to the winners; fails to check equipment and does not allow enough time following the close of entries to send out pairing information. These are but a few of the problems that can cause trouble when advance planning is lacking.

> Even if a tournament is to be a small affair conducted on an intramural basis by a school, college, YMCA, or church, there should be careful planning, organizing, and directing. Following the event an evaluation should be made by the sponsoring committee and tourney participants. Too often, those responsible for tournaments accept their responsibility too lightly, with the result that the contest becomes just another program.[1]

Committees

No one person could ever conduct a tournament of any magnitude without help. All planning committees should meet regularly. The number of these committees will depend to a large extent upon the number of teams in the tournament along with many other things. The planning committee should plan the tournament. This committee is important with one of its main duties placing the right people including faculty administrators and students on the various committees. These committees will vary in size, purpose, and duties.

The Planning Committee

People placed on tournament committees should be those who have indicated a keen interest in the program and are willing to work diligently. The director should appoint an assistant and a planning committee as this will save him the burdensome task of making all the decisions. To avoid confusion it is suggested that the planning committee chairman give each of the other committee chairmen selected a copy of the tentative tournament program with a detailed list of instructions to be followed. The successful tournament depends upon each committee's fulfilling its obligations on time. A series of time deadlines for each committee should be worked out in order to keep things moving at a prescribed rate of speed. Care should be taken that duties of one committee will not overlap the duties of another. Sometimes certain duties must be followed in sequence and one task must be finished before another can be started. The planning committee will need to coordinate the work of all the committees and perhaps work out a check list so that when each committee is ready to begin its work, it will not be delayed because of the negligence of other committees in the performance of their duties. It will take perfect coordination of all the committees to get the job done.

Care should be taken that all members of each committee are willing to be placed on a particular committee. In contacting the person to serve on the committee, it should be made certain that everyone understands his duties and is willing to accept them.

The systematic organization of the committees and the selection of efficient person-

[1]Boyden, Douglas, and Burton, Roger, *Staging Successful Tournaments* (New York, New York, Associated Press, 1957) , p. 42.

TABLE LXXIX
TOURNAMENT COMMITTEE PLAN

Tournament Committee
(chairman, secretary, supervisor or director)

Tournament Executive Committee
(tournament chairman, secretary, director and finance chairman)

maintenance committee	announcer	program committee	first aid committee	concession committee	ushering committee	publicity committee	awards committee
			Finance Committee	Miscellaneous Committee			

nel to man these committees are important elements in the administration of the tournament. The success of the tournament will depend to a large extent on how well the committees function. They will furnish the key to the proper administration of the tournament. It must represent the best there is in thought and planning and should provide for those elements which will facilitate its operation. Administration is the means by which the tournament is created and its success is in direct proportion to the right kind of administration, care, and thought in reaching the objectives.

The purposes of the tournament should be reflected and should, therefore, be the guidelines by which every committee functions. There should be no values except those which are stated from the beginning and these must be understood by every member of every committee.

The committees should be formulated in a democratic fashion and the members should be made aware of the purposes of the tournament and how it is to be administered.

Committee Appointments

The appointment of committee chairmen and committee members is very important, for the success of the tournament is directly proportional to the ability and concern of the committees, especially the chairmen. The chairman of each committee should be contacted and his permission obtained before he is appointed. He should understand that this appointment involves a great deal of work, but also some recognition. If the school is large, a number of committee chairmen may be members of the physical education department. However, some of the committees will require other faculty members to be chairmen, as the duties of the committee will involve different departments. For instance, the chairman of the music committee would be a member of the music faculty. He would pick his own committee in order to work closely with each member. He would naturally pick students and faculty from his department.

Qualifications of the Committee Chairman

The most important member of the committee is the chairman and he should be appointed by the director rather than elected by the group. This appointment should be based first of all on his knowledge of the task at hand. Some other attributes might be whether he will or can present those facts to the group for their consideration. He should also be the type of person who will ask the committee members for their suggestions and make them feel that they are a well-knit group working for a common goal. He should have the ability to steer the discussion along channels of mutual agreement so that a decision which is agreeable to all may be reached. He should have the ability to coordinate and pull together the different ideas that have been presented in such a way that no one will be offended, yet the outcome will be a group decision.

A good chairman will take an active part in committee undertakings. He will get the meetings started on time, will push the committee through its work, coordinate the thinking of the group, and reach definite conclusions. He must be a person of integrity, initiative, and "know-how"; one who has the ability to lead and contribute. He must be able to keep the committee members on the task at hand and not let them wander in their discussions. A strong chairman will speak often and is not afraid to say what he feels he should say.

Assignment of Specific Duties

The assignment of specific duties to each committee is the responsibility of the director. This should be done after the first meeting of all the chairmen, during the first week of the time that is to be devoted to the organization of the tournament. After the duties have been assigned, the chairman should select his committee. He should meet with the director of the tournament and carefully go over the specific duties of his committee. The chairman should then meet with his committee and the director and again go over the duties. Suggestions may be made and questions answered at this meeting. Any questions or problems of the committee may then be carried from the chairman to the director personally and worked out between them. The chairman should be in close contact with every member of his committee and should be able to meet with them at short notice. Each chairman should have in his possession a list of the duties assigned to his committee. This list may be added to or subtracted from, as the situation dictates. He may make assignments as he sees fit, depending upon the ability of the committee members. The chairman should work through the director whenever possible; however, if the problem involves another committee, he may bypass the director to save time. Any major problem, however, should be handled through the director.

The success of the tournament administratively depends to a great extent upon

TABLE LXXX
TOURNAMENT COMMITTEE ASSIGNMENTS

February _____, _____

To: All Personnel Concerned
From: Mr. John Jones, Director of Physical Education
Subject: Committee Appointments for Basketball Tournament
December 26, _____.

Director	John Jones	Physical Ed. Dept.
Tournament Supervisor	Fred Smith	Physical Ed. Dept.
Announcer	Dean Brown	Speech Dept.
Student Personnel	Eric White	Physical Ed. Dept.
Publicity	Jack Johnson	English Dept.
		Art Dept.
		Home Ec. Dept.
		Ind. Arts Dept.
Maintenance	Bill Howard	Custodian
Equipment and Supplies	Howard Dill	Physical Ed. Dept.
Music	Floyd Fellows	Music Dept.
First Aid	Sue Black	Nurse
Programs	Frank Brown	Ind. Arts Dept.
Parking and Police	Mike Whitson	Chief of Police
Concessions	Roger Miller	Varsity Club
Facilities	Duane Alexander	Physical Ed. Dept.
Hospitality	Bill Rodney	Physical Ed. Dept.
Planning	Dwight Reading	Physical Ed. Dept.
Tickets	Joe Freend	Business Dept.
Ushering	Fred Jones	Social Science Dept.

The first meeting of the committee chairmen will be held Monday, February 26, _____ at 3:30 P.M. in the faculty lounge.

the work of the committees. The smoothness of the tournament proceedings is in direct proportion to the efficiency of the committees.

Policies

It is important in the administration of any tournament, if it is to function smoothly and efficiently, that the planning committee establish guiding policies or rules as a basis upon which all committees should operate. All committee members should be made aware, through published material which is given to them, of the rules and regulations upon which the entire school operates. Any decisions made by the planning committee or any of the other committees must be made with these in mind. Policies will differ in local situations and may, in many cases, deviate from the generally accepted ones thought to be applicable to most situations. The policies must be modified to meet local conditions but must coincide with those under which other departments and the entire school system are governed.

Decisions relative to the operation of the tournament should be carried out through the regular chain-of-command for all school functions. Where certain policies or normal procedures do not fit the situation, an all-out effort should be made to modify them so that they will fit into the general pattern of school procedures. If this is not possible, then a temporary policy should be offered to the school governing body for acceptance before any action is taken. It should be kept in mind that the general public will be viewing the tournament and every effort should be made to promote good public relations and create a good impression. Any policies or rules which might appear on the surface to be objectionable should be abandoned for the moment in favor of some which will be more suitable to the situation. Arrangements must be made for meetings to be held at regular intervals whereby the aims, purposes, objectives, and policies may be worked out to the satisfaction of everyone concerned.

It is important, therefore, that a great deal of thought be placed on the selection of the committee members and especially the chairman. If the committee is to function effectively, it must have the following attributes:

1. A strong chairman who is acceptable to the majority of the committee members. It is not necessary for him to be able to win a popularity contest, but he should have a likeable personality and not have an antagonistic attitude or "rub people the wrong way."

2. A free hand to make decisions without too much interference from supervisors. Every committee tends to feel that the decision they have agreed upon after careful study and deliberation will be accepted in good faith as the proper solution to the problem. Intelligent people do not like to feel that they are serving a useless function, that all their efforts, their time, and their energy have been expended in vain. Therefore, they should have authority to carry out their assignment.

3. An opportunity to obtain all the information that is needed for the proper functioning of the committee. It is most important that all information needed to make decisions should be made available to the committee. Provisions should be made for a feedback on the results of committee decisions. A knowledge of how these decisions are being received by others is necessary in order to facilitate further the work of other committees.

4. An opportunity to reward the efforts

of those individuals on the committee who have done a good job. There is always a place for a good word or a pat on the back; however, group awards will do more for overall morale than singling out certain individuals.

5. A chance to evaluate the results of the work of the committee. It is the duty of the director to work closely with each committee and make periodic checks to see if the job is being done.

DUTIES OF COMMITTEES

Committees are necessary in tournament planning. Each committee should have specific tasks to perform and should be under the direct supervision of the director, who works closely with them at all times. The number of committees will be determined by the director and will depend upon the type of tournament, the number of people involved, the desires of the director, and the use of other departments. The duties of each committee will be determined by the director and will be dependent to some extent on the abilities of the personnel as well as the desires of the director. The duties may be of a general nature, with the chairman taking a great deal of responsibility, or they may be very detailed and circumscribed, in which case the committee will know exactly what is to be done, but will have little initiative in the planning, and will be deprived of making any original contribution to the tournament. On the other hand, if the duties are detailed, it will afford less chance of errors which might result from slipshod thinking, planning, and execution of duties.

The chairman assumes the major share of the work and responsibility of the committee. Because of the very nature of the duties which will be performed by the committees and because of the overlapping of these duties, it is necessary for the committees to work very closely together for maximum efficiency. Complete harmony must prevail at all times within each committee and between all the committees. Their functions should be clearly defined so that each may know its sphere of responsibility and will not entrench on the duties of some other committee.

It should be clearly understood by the members that the committee was formed to perform a definite function and not for effect, an unfortunate occurrence which sometimes takes place.

The success of the committee depends upon the chairman. He should have skill at impartial presiding. Rare is the man who has talent for setting forth his own ideas and at the same time encouraging others to do the same. Nevertheless, he should try to preside impartially. A chairman should be the servant of the committee, not the master, or even the wise man of it.

The director should spell out the limits of the power, duty, and responsibility of the committee before it is organized. There should be an understanding of these duties among the other committees. This will eliminate much of the confusion among committees' relationships.

The first and foremost item in setting out a committee's duties and responsibilities is to determine whether it shall simply pass information upward or serve the broader function of passing on recommendations for action. The committee should not be run just as an advisory body to decision-making individuals.

Limiting the committee in power and in scope limits it in its decision-making. The committee therefore cannot adequately offer advice unless it has responsibility.

The general duties fall into three distinct categories, namely:

1. To furnish group judgment where a problem overlaps into another element of the tournament.
2. To study and analyze the problems, then recommend action to the director who must eventually make the decision.
3. To carry out the specific duties as outlined by the director and supervisor.

It should be remembered by the reader that all the duties of the committees that are discussed here need not be used in every situation. They are discussed here with the idea that many of them can be used, and it is up to the individuals presenting the tournament to select those which are apropos. There are some that overlap and those duties are to be given to the committee which is able to do them more effectively in a particular situation.

Maintenance Committee

The maintenance committee should realize that its duties and responsibilities bear an important relationship to the success of the tournament. The director should instruct the committee members as to the following:

1. An understanding of the school's policies regarding the adaptation of school facilities to the educational program.
2. Explanation of all duties and responsibilities. Each member should be given a carefully prepared outline of the duties to be performed, besides other information pertinent to the assignments.
3. A firsthand demonstration of all the duties required with an opportunity to practice these duties.
4. A full explanation of the time the members will be required to be on duty.
5. An acquaintance with all supplies, ma-

terials, cleaning and operating tools, equipment, storage, and other facilities, with an opportunity to ask questions.
6. An orientation period long enough to thoroughly acquaint each member with the duties he is expected to perform.

LINES OF COMMUNICATION: Definite lines of communication should be established between the maintenance committee and other committees, as well as all school personnel, since this committee, in performing its duties, will of necessity come in contact with all phases of the school program and all types of school personnel. The lines of communication, already established within the school system from the board of education and the superintendent and the principal through the director of athletics should be adhered to as closely as possible.

DUTIES AND RESPONSIBILITIES: The maintenance committee's responsibilities and duties are innumerable and never ending. These duties may differ depending upon school policy. Many of these duties are custodial in nature. The committee merely sees to it that they are done.

1. Cleaning of the school building in general and the gymnasium in particular.
2. Care of walks, halls, and areas related to the tournament.
3. Reporting of all needed repairs.
4. Security of the school building, including doors, windows, stair treads, and panic bolts against fire and the weather.
5. Elimination of all hazards likely to cause injury.
6. Maintenance of proper temperature and ventilation within the gymnasium.
7. Checking of all lights, and prevention of any damage or destruction whenever possible.
8. Helping with the conduct of pupils.
9. Maintaining a courteous manner at all times.

10. Delivery of supplies.
11. Performance of routine building inspection.
12. Inspecting all equipment for needed repairs.
13. Placement of all needed equipment.

SAFETY: State and local building codes provide for adequate safety standards in all school buildings. Older buildings, however, do not usually meet the standards required in the newer buildings. A critical analysis should be made of all possible hazards in and around the building. This might include inspecting heating and ventilation systems, checking fire escapes, seeing that doors have panic bolts and are unchained, checking the condition of stair treads, anticipating hazardous weather conditions, removing obstructions when necessary, repairing all equipment used in the tournament and inspecting all electrical equipment involving possible fire hazards.

Safety is the business of everyone connected with the tournament, and everyone must assume responsibility for it. Nothing will put a damper on a function of this type more quickly than an accident of any kind. Therefore, everything possible should be done to avoid any mishap.

MAINTENANCE BY CLEAN-UP COMMITTEE: There should be a clean-up committee comprised of students that work through the tournament chairman. The chairman of this committee must have his duties outlined and assigned well in advance of the tournament. He will appoint subcommittees to take down chairs, sweep the gym floor, clean the locker rooms, clean the lobby, remove all posters and decorations, and return all equipment to its proper place.

The duty of special clean-up will be the responsibility of the chairman. These duties will be more specific than the regular janitorial duties and will include such

things as removing signs, posters, banners, decorations, or any special markings used in the tournament. Removing any additional chairs or bleachers following the tournament as well as a general cleaning of the area at the conclusion of the tournament games will also be included. Whoever is delegated the authority for being in charge of the special clean-up group must first of all remember that, however the clean-up is to be handled, the people he selects must be capable, responsible individuals willing to work. This is no job for lackadaisical or irresponsible personnel, since in most cases the facilities used for the tournament will also be needed for the following day's school activities and will have to be put in order immediately after the tournament.

Usually sufficient personnel can be selected from students who are willing to accept the added responsibility and work. This would probably be the most economical way to handle the situation.

All the equipment needed for the special clean-up should be secured ahead of time, such as brooms, mops, disposal containers, chair carts, etc. and should be at the immediate disposal of the group as soon as the area is cleared following the tournament.

It will also be the duty of the individual in charge to brief the clean-up group on each person's job, or he may separate the workers into four or five groups with one person in charge of each of the areas to be cleaned.

MAINTENANCE BY CUSTODIANS: The custodian should play an integral part in the overall planning of the tournament. He can be of assistance by giving advice in the planning and preparation of the facilities used during the tournament and helping in many other areas.

It will be his duty to arrive well in advance of the starting time of the tournament in order to open the building and check on proper heating and ventilation. He should remain on duty and be of assistance to committees that have maintenance duties. After the tournament he should see that the building is in order, the lights are out, and the building is securely locked.

In most schools it is the policy of the school or organization to pay the custodian for his services. This should be taken care of by the tournament chairman after the conclusion of the tournament.

IMPORTANCE OF CUSTODIAN: The custodian is one of the most important members of the school personnel. All committee members will find it necessary to seek his services and help at one time or another.

FIRE PROTECTION: Fire protection is important, especially when a large number of people are involved. The custodian should check all fire regulations and see that all exit doors leading to the street or to the fire escapes are equipped with panic bolts. He should see if all fire exits are indicated by illuminated signs. The electric fire alarm should be checked to be sure that it is in good working order. The custodian should cooperate with the fire marshall in every respect.

CLEANING OF REST ROOMS: The custodian must be sure to check on all rest rooms before the tournament to see if they are unlocked and clean. The corridors of the school and the lobby of the gymnasium should be made presentable.

GYMNASIUM TEMPERATURE: The problem of temperature in the gymnasium is important, and the custodian should be aware of this and regulate the temperature according to the need.

GYMNASIUM LIGHTING: The lighting of the gymnasium usually will be the responsibility of the custodian, although this duty may be delegated to a responsible student.

CLEANING OF FLOORS: The floors, windows, and all equipment should be cleaned before the tournament.

Programs

It is almost a necessity to furnish the spectator a program for the tournament. The determining factor in furnishing this program is that it is virtually impossible to distinguish one player from another without the aid of a program giving the number of each player. Many of the spectators will be watching teams play that they are not familiar with. A program can help them identify the players. Another factor is, of course, the distance which exists between the player and spectator and also the number of players going in and out of the game almost constantly.

The announcer, no matter how efficient he is, cannot hope to keep the spectator informed at all times as to who the players are that are playing; consequently, a program is a necessity. The program need not be elaborate although many schools produce such a program for homecoming.

A small amount of advertising may be used but it should be kept in mind that the purpose of the program is not to place the names of certain businesses before the public but rather to help the spectators enjoy and understand the game better. Advertising, therefore, should be held to a minimum and used only to help defray the cost of the program.

In order not to create any ill will among the advertisers, every effort should be made not to pressure anyone into subscribing to an ad.

The determining factors in deciding upon the type of program to be issued should be the importance of the game and the size of the student body and the community. The best policy is to make the program

TABLE LXXXI
FIRST PAGE OF PROGRAM

WELCOME

All of us at _____ are sincerely pleased to have you as our guests again for this basketball tournament. We are sure there will be many exciting moments for all of us during these games, and we are making every possible effort to provide the best in facilities and service for all of you.

The High School Association joins us in asking each of you to help make this tournament a memorable success by remembering at all times that these are games played in the vigorous American tradition of wholesome youthful competition.

We think it is important that every person involved in the tournament, be he player, student or adult spectator, coach, or school official, should strive to exhibit on all occasions the sportsmanship which we want all youth to learn from such an experience.

Thank you for your enthusiastic support and cooperation!

TOURNAMENT OFFICIALS NEEDED

Tournament Manager .... _____

Tournament Director .... _____

Ticket Manager .... _____

Custodial Service .... _____

Score .... _____

Timer .... _____

Announcer .... _____

Statisticians .... _____

Band Director .... _____

TABLE LXXXII
GENERAL INFORMATION SHEET

  I. School Location

 II. Gym opening

Inform the competing schools and public as to what time the gym will be open. When two games are played on the same night the gym shall open at 6:15 P.M. and when only one game is played it shall be open at 7:15 P.M.

III. Smoking

Inform the schools and public of the smoking rule. No smoking in the building. Adults only may secure passes and smoke outside.

IV. Photographer

Only professional newspaper photographers should be allowed to take pictures from the floor. Students and spectator photographers will not be allowed on the floor.

 V. Spectator Conduct

Any rules of the State High School Athletic Association or rules of the host school should be brought to the attention of all school officials and spectators, such as: Some state associations do not permit the use of mechanical noisemakers, whistles, signs, banners, and placards at its basketball tournaments.

VI. School Administrators

School administrators should remind their faculty members not to call tournament officials or come to the door seeking free admission. If one such request is honored, all must be and this is obviously unfair and impossible.

VII. School Lettermen

Will be on duty to assist spectators and officials.

TABLE LXXXII — (cont.)

VIII.   Names and numbers of local sporting goods stores, names of their representatives and telephone numbers.
  IX.   List of cleaning establishments
   X.   Information on the following:
        A.   How participants were selected
        B.   How pairings were made
        C.   Date and sites
        D.   Starting times of each game
        E.   Opening ceremonies
        F.   Medical and liability
        G.   Transportation
        H.   Officials
        I.   Eligibility
        J.   Tickets
        K.   Housing
        L.   Coaches meetings
        M.   Practice sessions for teams
        N.   Uniforms
        O.   Squad size
        P.   Ball to be used
        Q.   Films
        R.   Radio provisions
        S.   All tournament teams

---

simple, informative and at as low a cost as is possible without making it look cheap.

Program Committee

The program committee should meet after the type of program and time of the program have been decided upon.

TYPE OF PRINTED PROGRAM: The program committee should first discuss which kind of printed program is suitable. The choice will probably be one of these types:

1. A professional program done by a local printer. The following plan should then be followed.

   a. Put the program up for bids.
   b. Secure advertising to help pay for the program.
   c. Gather and arrange all material to be included in the program.
   d. Make sure all material reaches the printer on time.
   e. Arrange to have the programs de-livered to the school or to have them picked up.

2. A program done by the school print shop. The following plan should then be followed.

   a. All the above steps should be carried out.
   b. Close cooperation with the department head should be obtained, as students will be doing the work and need more time to make up the program.

3. An inexpensive program done on the duplicating machine. Secure permission from the principal to use the machine and materials.

ADVERTISING AND COSTS: If a professional program is desired, it will be necessary to solicit advertising and determine the charges for space. A list of potential advertisers should be made. Sources are advertisers in past programs (or if no previ-

TABLE LXXXIII
ADVERTISING CONTRACT

_____ High School   Date _____

The _____ agrees to take _____

(individual organization)

page or pages of advertisements in the _____ tournament program

(date)

in the amount of $_____.

_____	_____
Tournament Representative	Individual or Organization

_____
(date)

---

ous programs have been attempted those sponsoring ads in football and basketball programs are good possibilities) and local service groups.

ORGANIZATION AND DELIVERY OF MATERIAL: The organization and delivery of material will mean close cooperation with the head of the program committee. He should help compile a list of events and names of participants. This can then be prepared, checked thoroughly, and sent out on time.

NUMBER NEEDED: There are three determining factors influencing the number of programs needed. These are the number used at previous tournaments, the seating capacity of the gym together with the number of games that will be held, and the advance ticket sale.

ATTRACTIVE COVER AND THEME: The theme of the program will help determine the program cover. Cooperation and aid will usually be given by the school art department or by the printer, if it is a professional program.

PAYING BILLS: It will be necessary for one member of the committee to collect all bills and submit them to the committee which in turn will approve them and send them to the proper authority for payment. Prompt attention to financial matters will be of the utmost importance. A financial

secretary for the entire tournament would be a great aid to all who must obtain materials.

OBTAINING HELP IN PROGRAM ARRANGEMENT: The committee should work under the supervision of an adult. This could be done by students. If there is no sponsoring organization, it might be possible to get the lettermen's club to help with folding and arranging programs.

DISTRIBUTION AND COLLECTION: The committee should distribute the programs. There should be a central supply to draw upon and ample help at each entrance. If the programs are sold, an adult should be in charge of change and central supply to aid the students distributing the programs.

DESIGNING: The front page of the program should be discussed with the head of the art department. One or more classes could be given the assignment of designing a cover which would be fitting to the event. Recognition should be given inside the program cover to the student and the art department.

INTERIOR: The interior of the program gives the order of events, the names of the participants, and the various times of each performance; it must be arranged, typed, mimeographed or stenciled, and rolled off. The cooperation of the business department should be obtained. The instructor

PROGRAM INFORMATION DATA SHEET

We want to give recognition to your team on your program. Please help us by sending us the following information. USE THE ENCLOSED STAMPED ENVELOPE.

Player's Name	Number Dk Lt	Position	Weight	Height	Class

Superintendent_____Principal_____

Coaches_____ _____

Team Nickname_____ Colors_____

Student Managers_____ _____

Cheerleaders _____ _____ _____

_____ _____ _____

Other Data _____

Figure 86.

CLASSIC BASKETBALL TOURNAMENT

PROGRAM SALES REPORT

_____ Invitational Tournament   Date _____

Name	Change Received	Returned	Sold	Amount
1._____				
2._____				
3._____				
4._____				
5._____				
6._____				
7._____				
8._____				
9._____				
10._____				

Totals _____

Programs Received   _____

Complimentary Copies   _____

Number Sold   _____

Number Returned   _____

Athletic Director

Figure 87.

may assign each phase of the work and this work, in return, gives the students experience which is beneficial to them and to the school.

COST: The cost of printing the program can be held to a minimum by the use of interschool departments and the use of school supplies. There may or may not be a charge for the program to the spectators, but a small donation may be accepted in case no charge is made.

THANKS TO HELPERS: A special thank you in appreciation of all aid in arranging the program should be given immediately, either through a page in the rear of the program or a direct letter to each helper. This will assure close cooperation in the future when planning other programs.

First-Aid Committee

The chairman of this committee should be concerned with the safety and welfare of both participants and spectators. There should, therefore, be provisions made to take immediate care of anyone who is in need of first aid.

Usually the school has definite procedures to follow in case of any accident or illness on the part of a pupil or school personnel. These procedures should be followed as closely as possible and with as few changes as possible to fit the situation.

The committee should be charged with the responsibility of mimeographing these procedures and giving them to those in-

TABLE LXXXIV
SAMPLE SHEET OF GENERAL INFORMATION TO BE INCLUDED IN PROGRAM

1. Smoking rule, whether permitted or not
2. Location of lavatories.
3. Location of first-aid room
4. Drinking fountains.
5. Purchase of refreshments and area for eating.
6. Location of lost and found department.
7. Rule of the Illinois High School Association pertaining to noisemakers, signs, banners, or placards at its basketball tournament.
8. Respect for the tournament officials and treat them kindly.
9. Conduct during free throws (being quiet).
10. Loitering or loafing of persons who give evidence of not being interested in game will be asked to leave building.
11. Rhythmical stamping or swaying in bleachers is not permitted on advice of safety experts.
12. Lettermen attired in letter sweaters are on duty to help crowd whenever possible.
13. Crowd should remain seated until end of each game.
14. Confetti is not to be used in the gym.
15. Drive safely going home.

dividuals. Accident report forms should be made available to the first-aid chairman. Instructions should be given as to how these forms are to be made out.

EMERGENCY TREATMENT ROOM: During the regular school day, this room may also serve the purpose of being an office, lounge, concession room, lecture room, or any other room that meets certain minimal standards. The size and equipment for this area will vary some according to the size of the school, the available space, and the budget. There are certain minimum standards for such a facility which would be desirable for every tournament.

The following facilities should not only provide for any emergencies, but should also be conducive to parental appeal and approval. The first-aid room should be immediately adjacent to the playing area and should contain an adjoining bathroom equipped with a sink, hot and cold water, soap, toilet, mirror, and towels. The general consideration of the layout should provide good ventilation, adequate heat-ing, and sufficient lighting. Air conditioning is advisable but not mandatory. The items of necessity should include a cot, pillows, sheets, blankets, training table, desk, chairs, phone, waste cans, stretcher, refrigerator or ice container, and medicine cabinet or table. Smaller equipment of equal importance includes splints, crutches, walking cane, ice bags, hot water bottle, paper cups and dispenser, flashlights, tourniquet, and thermometer.

NURSE AND PHYSICIAN: The first matter to be considered should be that of providing a nurse for the tournament. In larger schools where a school nurse is available, it would be advisable to engage her services. In smaller schools where a full-time nurse is not on duty, the services of the local doctor's nurse should be obtained if possible. A physician should be present on the night of the tournament. However, a nurse must be on duty if a doctor is not available. It should be remembered that first aid is the first temporary treatment given to an injured person in an emergency. It should be given only by an experienced and trained person. Second aid should be given by a doctor. The actual purpose of first aid is to offer temporary and immediate care to the victim of an accident or sudden illness until the services of a physician can be obtained.

If a doctor is not readily available, provisions should be made to have a phone installed in the first-aid room with the phone number of a local doctor easily accessible. Arrangements should be made with the doctor so that he is alerted.

FIRST-AID HELPERS: A faculty sponsor should be in charge of the first-aid helpers, if possible, but the actual work is carried on by the student helpers. There should be a director of first aid in charge of the station. The qualifications necessary to hold this position are successful completion of an American Red Cross First Aid Course, and at least one year of experience. The director of first aid is appointed by the faculty sponsor. During the tournament there should be two attendants present. The junior attendant should have also successfully completed the requirements of an American Red Cross First Aid Course or one year of experience. After the junior attendant has successfully completed one year, he automatically becomes a senior attendant. If no students with the above qualifications can be found in the school, a call for students with previous first-aid experience in the boy scouts or some other organization along this line should be made.

The student first-aid helpers' responsibilities are these: a record of all services should be kept, the main purpose of which is to protect the school, should any charges be made against the first-aid helpers; only those services listed in the *American Red Cross Manual* should be rendered, no internal treatments should be given; should

the immediate services of a physician be needed, either the student is taken to a neighborhood physician, or a physician is called to the school. In the first-aid station there should be posted a list of physicians and the time each is available.

In concluding it might be said that student first-aid helpers through this experience get a chance to develop leadership, a cooperative spirit, and an appreciation of the value of first aid.

EMERGENCY EQUIPMENT AND TRANSPORTATION: Emergency equipment which may be needed at a tournament should include an oxygen tank. This could no doubt be obtained from the local fire department. Although it will probably not be used, it is a good idea to have one available and ready for use. An ambulance should also be on hand at any tournament involving a large number of participants. All participants involved in the tournament should be informed ahead of time as to where they should go to receive first-aid treatment in case of minor injuries such as floor burns, blisters, minor cuts and abrasions, headaches, etc.

FIRST-AID SUPPLIES: In addition to the first-aid room, a kit should be available near the area of the tournament. The kit should be neat in appearance and well organized in content. It should also be available to both spectators and participants, but at the discretion of a qualified school official. The first-aid kit should include the following:

Sterile dressings: 4″ × 4″ and 3″ × 3″ gauze
        pads
        adaptable-type roll bandages (1-, 2-, 3-inch)
        cotton and cotton balls
        band-aids in various sizes

Nonsterile items: bandages and wraps
        elastic-reinforced   5-yard

bandages (2-, 3-, 4-inch widths)
ankle wrap
arm sling and safety pins

Adhesive tape: regular
elastic

Pads: felt
foam rubber

Solutions: alcohol (70%)
tape remover
eye wash
tincture of benzoin, spray container
aromatic spirits of ammonia
mild antiseptic

Equipment: tongue depressors and applicators
scissors, surgical and bandage
eye dropper or eye cup
razor and blades
tweezers
nail clippers
oral screw
needles

Concession Committee

Concessions at the tournament can be profitable if handled in an efficient manner. The arrangements will vary from school to school and will often depend on the size of the school. In large schools, where there may be a sizable attendance at a certain event, the cash may become too difficult for school organizations to handle, and this service is often transferred to a commercial group that is better able to cope with the large volume of business. Under this system, the school may derive a percentage of the sales. In other situations, organizations from within the school, the athletic association, the student coun-

cil, the senior class, or some other such group, may handle this money-raising activity.

EXTENT OF CONCESSION ENTERPRISE: The extent of the enterprise will be determined by the attendance. In some cases there will be a great variety of items available for purchase; in others, the variety may be quite limited. The advisability of offering a considerable choice will usually be determined by previous experience.

SUPERVISION OF CONCESSIONS: As with any phase of a school activity, these concessions should be supervised. If the authority to sponsor such an activity is delegated to a particular school group, an advisor of this group should be responsible.

SELLERS: An adequate number of sellers should be selected to work at the concessions stand. Too many sellers will only be in the way and will slow down the operation. On the other hand, not enough sellers will cause much confusion and smaller profits.

CONCESSION RECORDS: Students who function as sellers should complete standard forms indicating the cost of items purchased, the items sold, items returned, and the total sales. This will prove to be a valuable record in determining future purchases.

SOURCES FOR PURCHASING ITEMS: Most items needed for the operation of a concession stand may be obtained through any wholesale company. If more than one source of supply is available, it would be wise to compare prices and service before buying.

PRICE OF ITEMS: Almost all items to be sold have a standard retail price. The cost of the items purchased should determine the retail price. It is best to keep prices low and make a fair profit than to have prices high and limit the number of sales.

TABLE LXXXV
CONCESSIONS REPORT FORM

Date _____   Event _____

Sales	Units	Unit Price	Total		
Soda	____	____.___	____.___		
Hot Dogs	____	____.___	____.___		
Candy	____	____.___	____.___		
Popcorn	____	____.___	____.___		
_____	____	____.___	____.___		
_____	____	____.___	____.___		
Total Sales	____		____.___	____.___	
Cost of Sales			____.___		
Soda	____	____.___	____.___		
Hot Dogs	____	____.___	____.___		
Candy	____	____.___	____.___		
Popcorn	____	____.___	____.___		
_____	____	____.___	____.___		
_____	____	____.___	____.___		
Cost of Items	____		____.___	____.___	
Profit on Sales				____.___	
Expenses					
_____	____	____.___	____.___		
_____	____	____.___	____.___		
_____	____	____.___	____.___		
Total Expenses	____		____.___	____.___	
Net Profit			____ ____	____.___	

CHANGE AND CHANGE BOXES: To try to operate a concession stand with a limited amount of change is a serious error. If most of the items will be selling for a dime it is well to keep a good supply of nickels on hand for change. If the stand is rather large, and there are several sellers, an extra change box or two may help to speed sales.

CONCESSION SIGNS: Signs indicating the items that are available and the prices of each should be placed where customers can see clearly. Signs will aid in helping customers to make their selection and help to speed sales.

CONTAINERS: An ample supply of trash containers should be placed within close proximity to the stand. This will help to facilitate clean-up.

Ushering Committee

The ushering can be handled in various ways. It is best, however, to have an adult in charge if students are to be used. Faculty members can be used, but students do a very commendable job. The ushers assist the public in finding seats and help to enforce laws and rules which have been set up by the administration.

ORGANIZATION: The chairman of the committee should be responsible for the organization of the ushering crew. It is most important to select reliable personnel to serve as ushers because these individuals will have direct contact with the general public. These ushers should be given special instructions in how to greet and serve the public. There should be enough ushers to insure smooth operation and each usher should know his duties well for his area of work. These people should be selected on the basis of their personality and courteous manner.

RESPONSIBILITY: The ushers should be responsible for enforcing the rules and regulations of the building as well as directing people to their seats. They should control the entrance of late comers so that the audience is not distracted from the program. They also should control the traffic of small children going in and out of the gymnasium.

They should be ready and willing to help out in an emergency, should they be called upon to do so. They should always bear in mind that they are the direct contact between the public and the administration of the school.

HEAD USHER: A student may be appointed as a head usher. He should be stationed just inside the door of the main entrance and direct the spectators to the proper sections of the building. He should know where these sections are as well as know the exact duties of all the other ushers. All ushers should come directly to him for any needed information, and he, in turn should seek needed advice from the chairman of the committee. The latter should be stationed in the immediate vicinity and be readily available. The head usher is responsible for all seating arrangements and all decisions regarding seating.

USHERS: The ushers should be students. Because of their duties, they are most directly and most continuously in contact with the spectators. The head usher should assign one or two of the ushers to each aisle of the building. One should be stationed at the front of the aisle and one at the rear. This will allow for little movement on the part of the front usher as the spectators come to him. The ushers should

enforce the rules and regulations in regard to safety, smoking, etc. During the performance they must see to it that the spectators are not disturbed by movements of people.

DRESS: The ushers should be distinguishable from other helpers. They may be dressed in white shirts or letter sweaters for the boys. All should wear arm bands. The girls may be dressed in white with arm bands for identification.

Publicity Committee

The publicity committee should do everything possible to make sure that the overall publicity given the tournament will be favorable and enhance the program. This is its primary function. Although the committee should assume this responsibility, every one connected with the program must share in making the tournament a success.

GUIDELINES FOR PUBLICIZING A TOURNAMENT: There are several policies which may be used as guidelines by the committee in establishing a working arrangement for publicizing a tournament.

1. The committee needs to work in close harmony with the regular school publicity program.
2. The committee should be well informed as to the policies and procedures of the school as well as those set up for the tournament. These policies must be agreeable to all committee members.
3. The committee should agree on the type of facts that are to be stressed in publicizing the tournament.
4. The committee should single out the media of publicity which will help the most in the particular situation.
5. The publicity committee should assume the full responsibility for using all public relations media, including

newspaper stories, radio and television interviews, films, slides and pictorial materials, public addresses, student newspapers, etc. It should be the policy of the committee to treat all public relations media the same in regard to the release of news at the same time.

6. The chairman of the committee should be either the person who handles all of the school's publicity or someone appointed by the chairman who will act in this capacity. His job would be to make the news regarding the tournament available to the press, radio, and every other news media. He should be available to talk personally to the representatives of the press and be fully responsible for the channeling of all news to the correct destination. He should proofread all material so that there will not be any mistakes.

7. The committee should meet with the school principal and explain to him the policies under which the committee will function.

8. All news media personnel should be invited to cover the event.

9. Whenever possible, photographs should be furnished to the newspaper. Permission should be given for pictures to be taken.

10. The money needed for the tournament should be appropriated from the general fund. All money received from gate receipts should be placed in the general fund.

THE ROLE OF THE NEWSPAPER AND RADIO: There will be many problems that will come up during the course of planning for the tournament which will result in policies being made for each particular situation.

There are many facets of public relations, all of which will be important in publicizing the tournament. The news-

paper and the radio will take precedence. Therefore, one of the prime tasks of the committee will be to prepare and schedule press releases to the newspapers.

Most families within a community subscribe to the local newspaper, and since all pay taxes, the mention of a school function will usually catch the reader's eye. Information of this type can be conveyed to the public in various portions of the newspaper so as to attract attention to a wide variety of readers. For example, the various aspects in which this information may appear are the news column, sports page, school news, community news, or advertisement section in the form of a purchased ad.

Compose and release articles, with pictures if possible, so that maximum effects may be achieved. In most communities the local newspaper will welcome news from the public schools. Usually, simply typing the article and giving it to the newspaper is enough to have the article printed. But a few simple rules must be followed in organizing the story to save the editor time and hold the interest of the public. The article should be as brief as possible and the information must be complete and accurate. Also, details should be arranged in order of importance so that if the story is condensed before publication, the essential items will appear.

When writing the article, the publicity committee should remember that it is of paramount importance to use clear and correct English. Names should be used whenever possible and should be correctly spelled.

It is the responsibility of the committee to present the story to the newspaper as they would like to have it written. The chairman should ask the editor how he wants the story written. If pictures are to be furnished, they should be good ones and show the tournament to its best advantage.

The newspaper photographer may be good at taking a picture, but he may take the wrong picture at the wrong time. What the newspaper thinks is interesting to the public may not be important in the opinion of the athletic department.

All editors must face deadlines. This means that a story brought in close to the deadline has less chance of being published in the next issue, and there is a good chance that it will be cut, with a great deal of the interesting and important details eliminated.

Each school system should have at least one person responsible for dealing with the press, and this person should be chairman of the publicity committee. He should, therefore, become acquainted with newspaper, radio, and television personnel, and with public officials in the community. All information about the tournaments should be channeled through the committee, with the chairman responsible for all personal contacts with news agencies. This does not mean that the chairman will be responsible for answering all the questions himself, but he will work closely with those people engaged in publicity to find the answers. This will cut down the number of people the press will need to contact to get the story. The committee will need to check with school officials concerning policies which govern the release of school news. The chairman, if he is connected with the school news service, can be of assistance in this respect.

TICKET COMMITTEE: The problem of tickets should not be a difficult one. In larger schools, the student print shop should handle the printing. The local printer is usually quite reasonable in price and can serve the needs of the smaller high school. One or two men from the business department should handle the ordering and distribution of tickets. They should also take care of the state tax forms if they are necessary.

All spectators should be required to pass the ticket stand. The price of the tickets should be reasonable so that all people who desire to attend may do so. Very few complimentary tickets should be given. When the tickets go on sale, the ticket seller should have a box with petty cash for change. The tickets for people helping in the tournament should be sent out ahead of time. The tickets for the contestants should be in the coach's folder that is given to him as the team arrives at the playing site.

Student tickets should be sent to the visiting schools in advance and only adult tickets should be sold at the window on the day of the event.

TICKET SELLERS AND TAKERS: The two positions of ticket seller and taker require reliable personnel. Whoever is employed for these jobs should be paid for their help. The personnel should be told, both orally and in written form of their duties, responsibilities, and areas of work.

When there is need for more than one group of sellers and takers, a supervisor should be named and each person in that group should be responsible to him.

The chairman of all the ticket committees should make sure that all stations are supplied with adequate tables, chairs, change, tickets, and report forms. The supervisor of each group along with the chairman will be in charge of both setting up and cleaning up of all ticket stations.

The supervisor of each group should watch for such things as scalping of tickets, persons having the wrong tickets for that session, and the misuse of complimentary tickets and passes.

PASSES AND COMPLIMENTARY TICKETS: There are many types of passes that exist. It will be up to the host school to set up

TABLE LXXXVI
CEDAR FALLS TOWNSHIP HIGH SCHOOL
CEDAR FALLS, ILLINOIS

Ticket Sales Form

Date of Activity _____

Total Number of Adult Tickets Sold	_____	
Total Number of Student Tickets Sold	_____	
_____ Adult Tickets Sold # $1.00		_____
_____ Student Tickets Sold # .50		_____
AMOUNT OF MONEY ENCLOSED	_____	_____

Signature of ticket seller _____

Note: Please return this blank with money and unsold tickets to ticket
        office on or before _____P.M., _____

TICKET SALE FORM

_____
       Date

_____
                 Activity
_____

Tickets issued to	Tickets issued	Tickets returned	Money returned	Tickets sold

Summary	Number of tickets	Selling Price	Total Value
Tickets issued	_____	_____	_____
Tickets returned	_____	_____	_____
Tickets sold	_____	_____	_____

O.K. _____   _____
                                        Signature

Figure 88

which ones will be allowed and which ones will not.

Once a pass has been lost, the person who lost it should be charged for admittance. Passes should have the name of the person (s) it is issued to on it and should not be transferrable.

The head coach should take care of the distribution of team passes which should include the players, managers, cheerleaders, and assistant coaches.

Financial Committee

The financial committee is, of course, a very important committee because the tournament cannot be conducted without money.

FINANCIAL REPORT: All expenses incurred in conducting the tournament should be itemized and a financial report should be formulated as soon after the tournament ends as possible.

SUGGESTED FINANCIAL BREAKDOWN OF SIXTEEN-TEAM BASKETBALL TOURNAMENT

All schools should receive a flat rate of _____ per mile based upon the shortest possible route both to and from games. However, this includes only one round trip per day. The remainder of the money should be distributed on the following percentage basis.

I. First Round, December 26
   A. First Session
      1. 15 percent of each school
        of total net proceeds   60%

TABLE LXXXVII
CEDAR FALLS TOWNSHIP HIGH SCHOOL

TICKET SELLER'S REPORT

Tax			
	Date _____	Event _____	
	Adult Tickets	Color _____	
	Ending No.	_____	
	Beginning No.	_____	
_____.____	Sold	_____ at _____.____ = _____.____	
	Child Tickets	Color _____	
	Ending No.	_____	
	Beginning No.	_____	
_____.____	Sold	_____ at _____.____ = _____.____	
	_____ Tickets	Color _____	
	Ending No.	_____	
	Beginning No.	_____	
_____.____	Sold	_____ at _____.____ = _____.____	
	Value of tickets sold		
_____.____		_____.____	
	Amount of money returned	_____.____	
	Over or Under	_____.____	

Signature of ticket seller

2. 40 percent for the host
   school   **40%**
          TOTAL   **100%**

B. Second Session
   1. 15 percent for each school
      of total net proceeds for
      the session (15% × 6)   **90%**
   2. 10 percent for the host
      school   **10%**
           TOTAL   **100%**

C. Third Session
   1. 15 percent for each school
      of total net proceeds for
      the session (15% × 6)   **90%**
   2. 10 percent for the host
      school   **10%**
           TOTAL   **100%**

II. Quarter Final, December 27
   A. Fourth Session
      1. 20 percent for the two
         winners of total net pro-

ceeds for the session
(20% × 2)   **40%**
2. 15 percent for the two
   losers of total net pro-
   ceeds for the session
   (15% × 2)   **30%**
3. 30 percent to the host
   school   **30%**
        TOTAL   **100%**

B. Fifth Session
   1. 20 percent for the two
      winners of total net pro-
      ceeds for the session
      (20% × 2)   **40%**
   2. 15 percent for the two
      losers of total net pro-
      ceeds for the session
      (15% × 2)   **30%**
   3. 30 percent to the host
      school   **30%**
           TOTAL   **100%**

TABLE LXXXVIII
CEDAR FALLS TOWNSHIP HIGH SCHOOL

TICKET SELLERS REPORT FORM

Date _____

COLOR   NAME OF ACTIVITY

Last Ticket No. _____   _____ Football

First Ticket No. _____   _____ Basketball

Tickets Sold _____   _____ Baseball

Price _____   _____ Track

Amount _____   _____ Tennis
                          Total
                          Sales ....   _____ Golf
                                                          _____ Wrestling
Sig. Ticket Seller _____
                                                          _____ Play

_____ Other Income _____   _____ Dance

_____ From _____ For _____   _____ Demonstration

_____   _____ _____

_____

_____

_____

_____

                          Total Income _____
                          Plus Change _____
                          Deposit   _____
                          Deposit
                          Receipt No. _____

III. Semifinals and Finals, December 28   FINANCIAL AGREEMENT
     A. Sixth and Seventh Session   MILEAGE: Each participating team
        1. 20 percent for each school   will receive _____ per
           of total net proceeds for   mile for each trip to
           the session (20% × 4)   80%   and from the tourna-
        2. 20 percent for the host   ment.
           school   20%   LODGING: _____ will be allotted
                          TOTAL   100%   per man per night

(maximum of 12 persons) for each school that travels 100 miles or more. Also, an additional room for two coaches or a coach and his wife will be provided at _____ per night. We must have at least two weeks notice in order to make reservations.

MEALS:

Teams staying over night will be provided with three meals per day starting after their first game. All meals will be provided in the _____ _____ cafeteria. All other teams may receive one meal immediately after each game they participate in. These meals are also in the same facility.

TEAM SHARES: Each team will receive tournament shares dependent upon the number of games they play. One half of the total profit (Expenses subtracted from income) will be divided into shares and distributed according to the tournament results.

STATEMENTS: The tournament director is responsible for preparing a statement of finances and must distribute this to the local coach, athletic director, principal, school superintendent and to the competing school officials.

CLASSIC BASKETBALL TOURNAMENT TAX REPORT FORM

TYPE OF TICKET	NUMBER SOLD	PRICE	CITY TAX RATE	NET AMOUNT	TOTAL CITY TAX	AMOUNT
TOTALS						

Attendance at Tournament:
  Paid Admissions

  1. Reserved _____
  2. General _____
  3. Half-time _____

Student Paid Admissions:

  1. Activity tickets _____
  2. Complimentary admissions _____

Total Attendance _____

Gross Receipts:
  Cash at Tournament _____

  Gate Receipts _____
  Programs _____
  Student tickets _____

  Total Receipts _____

(Signed)_____
           Athletic Director

Figure 89.

CLASSIC BASKETBALL TOURNAMENT FINANCIAL REPORT FORM

TOURNAMENT, held at _____, Illinois, on _____, 19___

RECEIPTS

GATE RECEIPTS

_____ Tickets @ _____ : $ _____
_____ Tickets @ _____ : $ _____
    TOTAL GATE RECEIPTS $ _____
ANY OTHER RECEIPTS . . . . $ _____
GRAND TOTAL RECEIPTS . . . . $ _____

EXPENDITURES

LOCAL SCHOOL EXPENSE
Officials' Fees: *Name*   *Fee*
_____ $ _____
_____ _____
Advertising . . . . _____
Tickets . . . . _____
Other Expenses (Itemize)
_____ $ _____
_____ _____
TOTAL EXPENSES OF TOURNAMENT. . . . . $ _____

BALANCE
TO HOST SCHOOL 60% . . . . $ _____
TO COMPETING SCHOOLS 40% . . . . $ _____
TOTAL FUNDS DISTRIBUTED . . . . $ _____

_____   _____
(Signed by Manager)   (Signed by Principal)

Figure 90.

TABLE LXXXIX
SAMPLE BASKETBALL TOURNAMENT

FINANCIAL REPORT

19_____

TOTAL RECEIPTS:		$10,080.25
EXPENSES:		
Officials	$1,190.00	
Tickets	163.01	
Tourney Luncheons	50.00	
Boylan Cafeteria (meals)	573.60	
Hospitality Room	70.00	
Statistics	50.00	
Tournament Manager	150.00	
Ticket Manager	150.00	
Ball and Scorebook	29.90	
Promotions	36.00	
Postage and Telephone	62.50	
Trophies	123.50	
Police	330.00	
Coaches Smoker	40.30	
TOTAL	$3,019.71	$ 3,019.71
TEAM EXPENSES:		
HOUSING	$ 614.00	
MEALS (Breakfast and Nite)	$ 903.00	
MILEAGE	$ 632.40	
TOTAL	$2,149.40	$ 2,149.40
TOTAL EXPENSES:		$ 5,169.11
TOURNAMENT PROFIT:		$ 4,911.14
SPONSORING SCHOOLS SHARES (50% of NET)		
Auburn	$ 613.89	
Boylan	$ 613.89	
Guilford	$ 613.89	
Harlem	$ 613.89	
	$2,455.57	$ 2,455.57
PARTICIPATING SCHOOLS SHARES: (38 shares $64.62)		$ 2,455.57
		$ 4,011.14

ESTIMATE OF SIXTEEN-TEAM BASKETBALL TOURNAMENT EXPENSE: Every tournament director must have a general concept of the cost involved when sponsoring a tournament. Locality, parking, lockers, and shower facilities are a prime consideration. Is the facility centrally located? What income can be realized? Will there be advanced ticket sales? What will the cost of tickets be? What is the anticipated ticket sale receipts? The tournament director must determine what percent of the gate the host team should receive. Twenty to thirty percent would be a logical sliding scale. The remainder could then be distributed among the other teams.

TABLE XC
CLASSIC BASKETBALL TOURNAMENT

FINANCIAL REPORT FOR SINGLE GAME

School _____   Date _____

Advance change $_____.____

Receipts

Gate $_____.____

Guarantees   _____.____

Concessions   _____.____

Other (itemize)   _____.____

_____   _____.____

_____   _____.____

Total Receipts   _____.____   _____.____

Disbursements

Officials   _____.____

Food   _____.____

Travel   _____.____

Guarantee   _____.____

Police   _____.____

Other (itemize)

_____   _____.____

Total Disbursements   _____.____   _____.____

Deposit _____   _____.____   Gain
     date   or loss   _____.____

O. K. _____   _____

ESTIMATED EXPENDITURES
FOR THE TOURNAMENT

1. Two officials ($35 per game for 16 games) — $560.–
2. One policeman ($50 per day for 3 days) — $150.–
3. Two ticket sellers (3 days at $15 per day) — $ 45.–
4. Three janitors ($25 per day per janitor for 3 days) — $225.–
5. Public address announcer — $ 30.–
6. Ten sets of tickets (1,500 tickets per set at $15 per set) — $150.–
7. Two basketballs ($26.35 each) — $ 52.70
8. Two scorebooks — $ 5.–
9. Three nets — $ 5.–
10. First-aid equipment — $ 50.–
11. Four trophies (assorted and engraving included) — $155.–
12. Towel service (450 towels at 10 cents each) — $ 45.–
13. Art department (decorations) — $100.–
14. Electricity ($50 per day for 3 days) — $150.–
15. Tournament manager — $150.–

Grand total $1,872.70

TOTAL RECEIPTS: $2 per ticket × 4,000 tickets = $8,000.00

Receipts $8,000.00
Expenses $1,872.70

Balance $6,127.30

NOTE: The host school also can increase their funds through concession sales, souvenirs, programs, etc.

TABLE XCI
SAMPLE TOURNAMENT FINANCIAL REPORT

at _____   date _____

Receipts

Ticket sales _____ at _____		$_____
_____ at _____		$_____
	Total sales	$_____
	Less state & city taxes	$_____
	Net Sales	$_____

Program receipts
    Sales ....
    Advertising ....
    Other income (specify) ....
    Total receipts ....

Disbursements

I. Promotion Expense
    1. Advertising $_____
    2. Supplies   _____
    3. Postage   _____
    4. Telephone and telegram   _____
    5.   _____

II. Ticket and Administration Expense
    1. Printing tickets $_____
    2. Ticket sellers and takers   _____
    3.   _____
    4.   _____

III. Official Expense
    1. Officials fees $_____
    2.   _____

Committee for Awards

The selection of the different types, quantity, and quality of awards is the responsibility of the committee for awards. Generally, the committee will follow a previously arranged plan for giving awards, purchasing them from available funds, and storing them until plans have been determined for presenting them.

PRESENTATION OF AWARDS: After the conclusion of the championship game, arrangements should be made for a brief awards presentation ceremony. Award pre-sentations should be made by one of three individuals: (1) state association representative, (2) host principal, (3) tournament manager. A state association member should be first choice for presenting of awards.

ALL-TOURNAMENT TEAM SELECTION: A committee for selecting the "All-Tournament" team and the "Most Valuable Player" to be announced following the championship game should be designated by the tournament manager.

TABLE XCII
CLASSIC BASKETBALL TOURNAMENT

19_____ FINANCIAL REPORT

SCHOOL	HOUSING	BREAKFAST	NITE MEALS	MILEAGE	SHARES	SHARE AMOUNT	TOTAL
ANTIOCH			$ 35.00	$ 117.00	3.5	$ 226.17	$ 378.17
AUBURN					2.0	129.24	129.24
BOYLAN					4.0	258.48	258.48
CHICAGO CARVER	$153.00	$ 31.50	$105.00	$ 56.40	4.0	258.48	604.38
DIXON			$ 35.00	$ 50.40	2.0	129.24	214.64
FULTON	$102.00	$ 21.00	$ 70.00	$ 54.00	2.0	129.24	376.24
FENTON	$ 51.00	$ 10.00	$ 35.00	$ 68.40	1.5	96.93	216.83
GUILFORD					3.5	226.17	226.17
HARLEM					2.0	129.24	129.24
JEFFERSON		$ 10.50		$ 12.00	1.5	96.93	119.43
JOLIET CATHOLIC	$153.50	$ 31.50	$140.00	$ 57.60	2.0	129.24	511.34
PRINCETON	$ 53.00	$ 10.50	$ 35.00	$ 44.40	1.5	96.93	239.83
WINNEBAGO			$ 35.00	$ 12.00	2.0	129.24	176.24
WOODSTOCK		$ 21.00	$ 70.00	$ 70.20	2.5	161.55	322.75
WOODSTOCK MARIAN		$ 10.50	$ 35.00	$ 46.80	1.5	96.93	189.23
ZION - BENTON	$102.00	$ 21.00	$140.00	$ 43.20	2.5	161.55	467.75
TOTALS:	$614.00	$168.00	$735.00	$ 632.40	38	$2,455.56	$4,604.96

TABLE XCIII
DEPOSIT ENVELOPE

Amount _____ Date _____

Source _____

Credit to _____ account.

Anyone depositing money

Deposited by _____

TABLE XCIV
CLASSIC BASKETBALL TOURNAMENT
EQUIPMENT ORDER

No.	Quan.	Size	Description	Price	T.P.
x107	2	—	Basketball - Official	$ 21.95	$ 43.90
s987	1	—	Last Built Official N. C. A. A.	1.50	1.50
s938	2	Flight Check	Nets	3.35	6.70
					$ 52.10
AWARDS					
1579a	1	15"	Walnut wood base Collegiate top, cadet size figure No. 628	21.50	21.50
1579b	1	16"	”	22.50	22.50
1579c	1	17½"	”	23.00	23.00
1479d	1	19½"	”	23.00	23.00
					$ 90.00
ENGRAVE					
1579a			Fourth Place	.99	.99
1579b			Third Place	.90	.90
1579c			Second Place	.99	.99
1579d			First Place	.90	.90
					$ 3.78
			TOTAL PRICE OF ORDER		$145.88

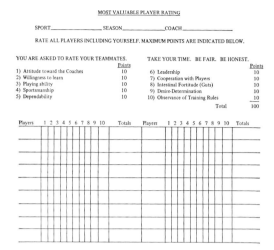

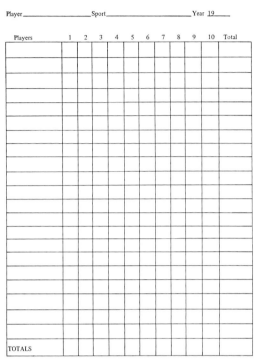

Figure 91.

Figure 92.

The Announcer

QUALIFICATIONS AND PERFORMANCE: Since the position of an announcer is very important to the presentation, it is essential that the individual performing this task have a good clear voice, have command of the English language, and be well acquainted with basketball. He should be able to establish close contact with the spectators and make the game interesting to them. Spectators attending a tournament should go away feeling that they have enjoyed the game and understood what was occurring. A member of the speech department, such as the debate coach or another qualified faculty member could do this job adequately or a talented speech student if he understands basketball.

The announcer should consult with the director and have all the needed information relative to what he is going to say. This should be written down so that there will be no repetition, no hesitation; all the pertinent facts should be given. These facts should be organized and planned ahead of time in such a way that they follow a definite pattern and are in perfect sequence with the entire program. Writing down the information will clarify his thinking and lead to an effective announcement of what is to transpire. He does not have the opportunity to arrange the program, so he must do the best he can to create a unified presentation, fitting everything together harmoniously with smooth transitions.

The announcer should speak in a full voice. He should speak clearly, keep his mind on what he is saying, and speak directly to his audience. The old saying that, "You stammer in speech because you falter in thought" is an adage worth remembering. A firm and pleasing voice will command the attention of the audience. Know what to say and say it. Do not clutter up the talk with ah's, uh's, but's, and well's.

TABLE XCV
SPORTSMANSHIP RATING FORM

Date _____ 197____

_____ vs. _____
(Team Rated)
Visitors rate home teams; home groups rate visitors.
LOCATION OF THE CONTEST _____

Rating Scale: 100-90   (Good Sportsmanship)
                   89-90   (Fair Sportsmanship)
                   79-70   (Poor Sportsmanship)
                Rate each division separately

   I.   ....GENERAL BEHAVIOR OF SPECTATORS.
  II.   ...........SPORTSMANSHIP DISPLAYED BY MEMBERS OF THE TEAM.
 III.   ...........PROFESSIONAL SPIRIT DISPLAYED BY COACH.
Scored by: ...Spectator   ...Coach   ...Player   ...Official

SOME SUGGESTED RATING CRITERIA

Spectators:
    Did they conduct themselves in a commendable manner?
    Did they control their tempers and avoid starting quarrels and fights?
    Did they accept the rulings of the officials in a sportsmanlike manner?
Team Sportsmanship:
    Did they play a clean game and avoid display of temper and use of profane language?
    Did they show friendliness toward opponents and readily accept rulings of the officials?
Coach:
    Was he calm and sportsmanlike, with professional poise under pressure?
    Did he make the most of limited facilities or other handicaps?

A few well-chosen words are better than a great many. Remember that a story is a good one only if it drives home a point. The announcer should always speak slowly and distinctly. He should not run his words together. Every word is important in his remarks and should be clearly conveyed to each member of the audience. He should talk to an audience as if he were talking to one person.

The qualities that go into the making of a good announcer are a pleasing personality, charm, naturalness, sincerity, conviction, enthusiasm, spontaneity, accuracy, culture, and salesmanship. Add to these a fine voice with an excellent vocabulary, and you will have an ideal announcer.

The quality of any program will depend, in part, upon the qualifications of the announcer and how well he can achieve rapport with spectators as he coordinates the various factors that are in the program.

THE ANNOUNCER'S SKILLS: Announcing can be learned. It is a highly specialized speech activity, but the student having the proper qualifications and a desire to improve can learn announcing just as readily as he can any other speech activity. Announcing is nothing more than an attempt to communicate information, to make something known. There is complete communication only when the announcer succeeds in four fundamental responsibilities. First, he must gain the attention of the listener; second, he must get the listener interested in his message and hold that interest despite distractions; third, he must evoke the listener's comprehension; and fourth, he must interest the listener in the forthcoming activity.

The announcer's skills are: (1) communication of ideas, (2) communication of emotion, (3) projection of personality, (4) pronunciation, and (5) voice control.

MICROPHONE TECHNIQUE: The announcer who speaks into the microphone in such a manner that his speech faults are minimized and its excellences magnified is said to have "mike technique." To acquire this technique the announcer should acquaint himself with the different types of microphones currently in use and know the speech input characteristics and peculiarities of each. He should know the rated response to the pitch range, the directional features, and the sensitivity of each microphone commonly used.

In addition to acquiring technical knowledge about microphones, the announcer should work for personal knowledge. He should know the response of each microphone to his own voice and be aware of the heightening of some voice peculiarities by certain ones. He should know at what distance to stand before the microphone for the best voice reception. He should know how to make use of the live and dead sides of the microphone for effects and for most complete interpretation.

Miscellaneous Items

There are many details that the director of the tournament and his principal as well as the assistant director will need to decide. Some problems can be ironed out with the help of the various committees. The following material is offered as suggestions for conducting a basketball tournament. Some of the material will be applicable to all situations and some will need to be revised to fit certain definite situations.

OBTAINING OFFICIAL APPROVAL FOR CONTESTS: Most states now have regulations governing the playing of athletic contests. This is particularly true where there are a number of schools involved. It is necessary to obtain permission from the state office to conduct the contests. The athletic association eligibility rules should be followed. No nonmembers should be allowed to participate, and all entry lists should be accompanied by an eligibility list.

LOCATION OF HOST SCHOOL: All information, including directions to the host school, access to and lay-out of the gym should be diagramed and mailed to each participating team.

TOURNAMENT RULES: Tournament conducting will follow those rules established by the state association and the host school. Players in the tournament must present evidence of having a physical examination as well as a parental consent form before participating. Verification of players' eligibility will be determined according to regulations established by the state association.

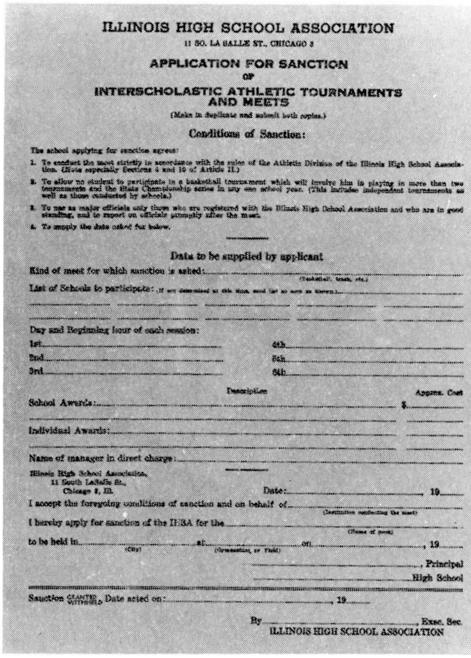
ILLINOIS HIGH SCHOOL ASSOCIATION
11 SO. LA SALLE ST., CHICAGO 3

APPLICATION FOR SANCTION
OF
INTERSCHOLASTIC ATHLETIC TOURNAMENTS
AND MEETS

(Make in duplicate and submit both copies.)

Conditions of Sanction:

The school applying for sanction agrees:

1. To conduct the meet strictly in accordance with the rules of the Athletic Division of the Illinois High School Association. (Note especially Sections 4 and 10 of Article II.)
2. To allow no student to participate in a basketball tournament which will involve him in playing in more than two tournaments and the State Championship series in any one school year. (This includes independent tournaments as well as those conducted by schools.)
3. To use as major officials only those who are registered with the Illinois High School Association and who are in good standing, and to report on officials promptly after the meet.
4. To supply the data asked for below.

Data to be supplied by applicant

Kind of meet for which sanction is asked: ____________ (Basketball, track, etc.)

List of Schools to participate: ____________

Day and Beginning hour of each session:
1st ____________ 4th ____________
2nd ____________ 5th ____________
3rd ____________ 6th ____________

Description — Approx. Cost

School Awards: ____________ $ ______

Individual Awards: ____________

Name of manager in direct charge: ____________

Illinois High School Association,
11 South LaSalle St.,
Chicago 3, Ill.

Date: ____________, 19____

I accept the foregoing conditions of sanction and on behalf of ____________

I hereby apply for sanction of the IHSA for the ____________ (Name of meet)

to be held in ______ (City) at ______ (Gymnasium, or Field) on ______, 19____

____________, Principal
____________ High School

Sanction GRANTED / WITHHELD, Date acted on: ____________, 19____

By ____________, Exec. Sec.
ILLINOIS HIGH SCHOOL ASSOCIATION

Figure 93. Reprinted with permission from the Illinois High School Association.

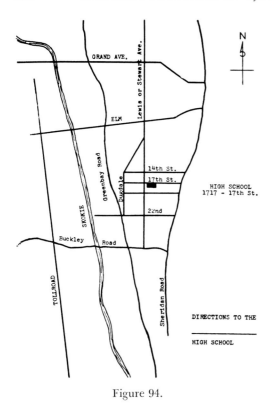

Figure 94.

WALTER M. WILLIAMS HIGH SCHOOL

ATHLETIC DEPARTMENT

BURLINGTON, N. C. 27215

Date

To the High School Principal and Coaches:

The _____ High School and the city of _____ extend to you a cordial invitation to participate in the _____ Basketball Tournament. We are looking forward to welcoming you and your boys to what we hope will be an enjoyable and prosperous experience.

In order to answer any questions that might arise, I am outlining some information for your convenience which I am enclosing.

The administration at _____ High School is anxious that this year's tournament be conducted in the same traditional manner that has been true in the past, keeping the educational values of a tournament of this kind uppermost in mind. With this objective as a goal, every effort will be made to protect the welfare of the participant and to provide an opportunity for him to benefit from this experience. Therefore, we urge you to cooperate to the fullest in making this tournament an educational experience for everyone concerned.

Sincerely,

Athletic Director

Figure 95.

TOURNAMENT LENGTH: The host school, in compliance with the state association, should determine the length of tournament, designated dates for play, and number of teams playing on a given night or successive nights (Monday through Friday).

TEAM SELECTION FOR AN INVITATIONAL TOURNAMENT: Whenever setting up an invitational tournament, the problem of selection of teams arises. Do you want teams with outstanding win records, or teams with equal ability that would insure close games and create interest? If you want to look at it financially, local teams would surely have to be considered.

Whatever you decide, you must remember that invitations have to be sent well in advance so the coaches can get prior permission from their administration to enter the tournament.

OVERNIGHT ACCOMMODATIONS: Another thing to consider when planning a tournament is the type of accommodations available for those schools that need to stay overnight. The area motels and hotels will have to be contacted as to the type of accommodations they may have available during the tournament. The tournament manager may want to assign this job to a reliable person to relieve himself of the added work.

TEAM BEHAVIOR: The actions of the coaches and team are a reflection of the school they represent. Consequently, not only on the playing field but also in public the actions of the team should be the type that would present a good image to the public.

COACHES' DECORUM: During the course

of the game the coach should refrain from dramatics which may incite the crowd's reaction to the game. Because most fans lack the knowledge of the game that the coach possesses, they will follow the actions of their teams' coach during the game.

LOCKER ROOMS: Before the date of the game, teams should be given information as to which locker room they are going to dress in. Upon arriving at the school the team should be led to the locker room by a member of the host school. The host should also educate the visiting team on the use of any extra equipment located in the room. During the visitor's stay, the locker room should be watched by a member of the host school, allowing only those connected with that school in the locker room area.

LOCKS AND TOWELS: If the host school is to furnish towels and locks to the visiting schools, the visitors should be notified. The visiting school should receive this information prior to the game date so that they can prepare themselves for the trip.

TOURNAMENT LOCATION: The tournament will be conducted in the host school's gymnasium. If this is not the situation, the participating schools shall be notified of the location. Every effort should be made to make participating schools comfortable. The tournament site should also be desirable to spectators and their needs.

SEATING: Every effort should be given to see that spectators are comfortable. The management is primarily responsible for their safety. All fire regulations should be met and seats should be marked for easy accessibility. Careful planning should be considered for segregation of participating schools.

PLAYING AREA: All possible hazards should be removed and floors should not be allowed to become unsanitary or unsafe. Check for repainting and refinishing. Finishes for gym floors are on the market.

ELIGIBILITY: One hour is allowed before the first game to name ten players who will be in the tournament. A list of the players should be given to the management in time to prepare the scoreboard panel cards. The coach should turn a form into the gate attendant, which contains names of the remaining team members, if they arrive late.

UNIFORMS: The light colored jerseys will be the home team and will be listed on the upper line of a single bracket. The lower line will wear dark jerseys. In order to have time for schools to comply, this rule will be determined in advance. Numbers on the jerseys need not correspond but all uniforms must meet association requirements and other required rules.

GYM ENTRANCE, PRACTICE AND WARM-UP PROCEDURES FOR PARTICIPATING TOURNAMENT TEAMS: The following provisions regarding the use of the tournament facilities by tournament teams will coordinate practice and actual game times to insure a better tournament.

Participating teams should have the opportunity to schedule an optional practice session on Saturday prior to the opening of the tournament. Teams who want to use the floor for a practice should sign up for their one-hour allotted time and plan to use the gym during this designated time only.

The gym should open at six o'clock (6:00 P.M.) for any team arriving for the early game. The first game will begin at 7:00 P.M. with a warm-up period beginning at 6:40 P.M. The second game will begin fifteen minutes after the end of the first game, allowing the participating teams a fifteen minute warm-up period.

PLAYERS' BENCHES: There should be no more than ten chairs on the sidelines. Five of these should be provided for the players, two for managers, two for coaches, and one for the host letterman who should be available to help the team. In order to keep the sidelines clear, this arrangement should be strictly enforced. All others will remain in the stands. Any unusual circumstance requiring arrangements other than these shall be discussed with the tournament manager.

SQUAD SIZE: There should be a maximum of ten players in uniform. These players may be substituted for up until the game begins. No substitutes should be permitted for any reason after the start of a contest.

OFFICIALS: It is of utmost importance that officials selected for tournament play should be satisfactory to all concerned. Contracts should be signed well in advance of the tournament date to ensure the hiring of desired officials. This should be taken care of by the state association for state sponsored tournaments and by the athletic director or tournament manager for local tournaments.

OFFICIAL'S LOCKER ROOM: There should be a room solely for the use of basketball officials. This special room will provide officials with a dressing room and a rest area. Therefore, it should be near the gym. Every effort should be made to have this room away from the locker rooms as well as the spectators.

THE SCOREBOARD: For a tournament to run smoothly, the scoreboard must be in proper running condition. The names and numbers of the players should be on the scoreboard or printed on cards next to the scoreboard. Place the title of the tournament near the scoreboard.

FILMS: Since many school officials desire films of the games, be sure arrangements are made for this. Teams wishing to have games filmed must agree to handle all costs. This information should be made known in order to avoid any misunderstanding.

SCOREKEEPER: The official scorer should wear an official shirt for easy identification. The official scorer should be a faculty member associated with the host school. The scorekeeper should be seated at the scorer's table at center court. It is very important that the scorers be thoroughly acquainted with their duties. The home team's time and book are official, and the two teams' scorers should cooperate with each other to avoid discrepancies. During tournaments, scorers should be assigned by the tournament director.

TIMERS: Timers should wear a striped shirt for easy identification and sit at the scorer's table. The timer should be trained for his job and should be responsible, efficient, and not get easily excited. He must have a thorough knowledge of the timing

WALTER M. WILLIAMS HIGH SCHOOL
ATHLETIC DEPARTMENT
BURLINGTON, N. C. 27215

Date

Officials of Rogers High School
Invitational Holiday Basketball Tournament

The administration of Walter Williams High School welcome you to the Invitational Holiday Basketball Tournament to be held December 26, 27, and 28, 19___. This year's tournament has many outstanding teams and promises to be the best yet in a long list of previous tournaments.

The teams are some of the strongest in the state and are evenly matched. Your assignments are enclosed. However, there are several things that you will want to know about. They are as follows:

1. You will be paid before each game by check.

2. You will dress in the coach's room directly west of the gymnasium playing floor.

3. You will enter the gymnasium by way of the west door by using the enclosed pass.

4. You will park in the special parking lot right next to your entry door.

5. You will stay at the Howell Motel near the high school.

Sincerely,

Tournament Manager

Figure 96.

procedures necessary in a basketball game.

STATISTICIANS: If statisticians are desired by the state association, accommodations should be made for them. A table should be set up near the scorer's table, and the person who takes the shot chart, individual scoring, and fouls should be stationed at the officials' table. Copies of their charts should be made available to each coach and the press at halftime.

It is important to record the following data:

1. the number of shots attempted by each player
2. the number of shots made by each player
3. the number of shots attempted by each team
4. the number of shots made by each team
5. the field goal percentage of each team

All of this is recorded by the statisticians on a shot chart.

A shot chart can be made by mimeographing a page with two basketball "keyholes," one on each side for the two teams. As each player attempts a shot, his number is recorded approximately from where he shot. If he scores, his number is circled. The statistics can be compiled at halftime and at the end of the game.

The scorebook will provide a cross reference for this data. It will also give attempted foul shots, foul shots made, and the number of fouls. These statistics can be compiled in order to obtain player and team averages throughout the season.

RADIO: It is important that schools be contacted in regard to whether or not a broadcasting team is going to cover their game.

BASKETBALL TO BE USED: Home basketball coaches should send information pertaining to the type, brand name, and color of the basketball used in competition. This practice is in keeping with code of ethics of coaching basketball. The home team displays its hospitality by providing practice balls for warm-up drills. It is a rule that a game ball be used a maximum of two games and one extra ball be available if needed.

RESPONSIBILITIES, REQUIREMENTS, AND VALUES OF CHEERLEADERS: School cheerleaders are responsible for and required to conduct themselves in a proper manner and to set a good example. The cheerleaders main value is in their leadership of their respective fans and supporters.

TOURNAMENT PAIRINGS: When the state association conducts an eight-team tournament, the teams are paired in an upper and lower bracket in respect to how they are rated by the coaches.

There are many ways of pairing teams for invitational tournaments. The most democratic method is placing school names in a hat and drawing for pairings, but this often produces an inferior tournament. More desirable methods included the pairings of rival teams, weak vs. strong teams, or on the basis of the strength of teams. When the latter method is utilized, the number one team should be matched with the number three team in the upper bracket. The number two team and the number four team would be paired in the lower bracket. This procedure is followed until all teams are represented.

The rating method for this procedure is to have each school entered in the tournament rate the other teams. A number should be awarded to the teams on the basis of the strengths of teams. The strongest team would receive the number one, the second team would receive the number two, and so on until all teams are included.

ENTERTAINMENT: Entertainment at halftime is important. Although many people like to leave the stands at halftime, there are those who prefer to remain. Some enjoy the halftime entertainment and it is

Figure 99.

Figure 97.

a welcome interlude to the excitement of the game. The halftime entertainment can include a gymnastic exhibition by the gym-

Figure 98.

nastic team, majorette girls or a jazz band. The entertainment should not delay the start of the second half.

DECORATIONS: Decorating provides a festive atmosphere and adds color to the tournament. The decorations can include banners of the competing teams and streamers of all kinds.

WORKERS' INSTRUCTION SHEET: The following is a list of the duties for some of the individuals, groups, companies, and organizations that should help in the tournament.

I. Ushers

  A. Report twenty minutes prior to the opening of the gates. The doors should open at the following times.

    1. For morning sessions 8:15 A.M.

    2. For afternoon sessions 12:30 P.M.

    3. For evening sessions 6:00 P.M.

  B. Report to the manager's office and get instructions as to the procedure used in seating the spectators.

C. Assign each usher a section that he is to be responsible for.

D. Seat people before the games begin only, and at time out, quarters and halftime periods.

E. Do not let the fans sit in the aisles.

F. Issue arm bands.

II. Program Sellers

A. Report fifteen minutes prior to the opening of the gates. The doors should open during the tournament as follows.
1. For morning sessions 8:15 A.M.
2. For afternoon
   sessions   12:30 P.M.
3. For evening sessions 6.00 P.M.

B. Inform each seller of the area in which he is to work.

C. Upon arrival, report to the office and pick up programs, change, and aprons.

D. The cost of the program is _____ each.

E. After each session, report back to the office and return all equipment, unsold programs, and money.

III. Ticket Sellers

A. Report fifteen minutes prior to the opening of the gates. The doors should open during the tournament as follows.
1. For morning sessions 8:15 A.M.
2. For afternoon
   sessions   12:30 P.M.
3. For evening sessions 6.00 P.M.

B. Pick up the cash and tickets at the manager's office.

C. Obtain a seating plan of the gymnasium.

D. Ticket sales should end at half-

time of the final game of the session.

E. Check in with the manager immediately after the sale of tickets has ended.

IV. Ticket Takers

A. Report fifteen minutes prior to the opening of the gates. The doors should open during the tournament as follows.
1. For morning sessions 8:15 A.M.
2. For afternoon
   sessions   12:30 P.M.
3. For evening sessions 6.00 P.M.

B. Issue arm bands.

C. Inform each taker of the area in which he is to work.

D. Take the tickets until the second half of the final game of each session.

V. Art Department

A. Make banners, pennants, and other decorations for the gym.

B. Take down as many decorations as possible and save them for the following year.

C. Make posters advertising the tournament.

VI. Janitors

A. Bleachers must be cleaned the day before the tournament and also swept out after each day's game.

B. The floor must be swept between halves of each game and also swept after the completion of each session.

C. Clean washrooms and dressing rooms daily.

D. Give the janitors a schedule of when the games will be played so they can schedule accordingly.

VII. Campus Police

A. Two policemen should direct traffic to and from the lots, before and after each session.

B. The traffic police should be given a schedule and be requested to report to duty one hour before the start of each session.

C. Two policemen should be on duty in the gym at all times.

VIII. Purchasing of Tickets

A. Bids should be let for the purchase of tickets.

B. Information concerning tickets
1. Seven sets of tickets with 1,400 tickets to a set should be purchased.
2. The tickets should be 4 inches long and $1\frac{1}{2}$ inches wide.
3. Each set of tickets should be a different color with blank letters.
4. After the purchase of the tickets has been decided, a blueprint of the gymnasium showing all the sections, rows, and seats should be sent to the company from whom the purchase is made.

IX. Public Address Announcer

A. Introduce the starting line-up three minutes before game time.

B. Immediately after this, the National Anthem should be played.

C. Give a summary of the scoring and statistics at the halftime of each game, and then give the final total immediately after the game.

X. Equipment Order

If equipment is needed for conducting the tournament, the cost of this equipment should be charged to tournament expense.

GENERAL INFORMATION SHEET

I. School Location

II. Gym Opening

Inform the competing schools and public as to what time the gym will be open. When two games are played on the same night the gym shall open at 6:15 P.M. and when only one game is played it should be opened at 7:15 P.M.

III. Smoking

Inform the schools and public of the smoking rule. No smoking in the building. Only adults may secure passes and smoke outside.

IV. Photographer

Only professional newspaper photographers should be allowed to take pictures from the floor. Students and spectator photographers should not be allowed on the floor.

V. Spectator Conduct

Any rules of the State High School Athletic Association or rules of the host school should be brought to the attention of all school officials and spectators. Some state associations do not permit the use of mechanical noisemakers, whistles, signs, banners, and placards at its basketball tournaments.

VI. School Administrators

School administrators should remind their faculty members not to call tournament officials or come to the door seeking free admission. If one such request is honored, all must be and this is obviously unfair and impossible.

VII. School Lettermen

School lettermen will be on duty to assist spectators and officials.

VIII. Names and numbers of local sporting goods stores, names of their representatives and telephone numbers

IX. List of cleaning establishments

X. Information on the following:

A. How participants were selected

B. How pairings were made

C. Date and sites

D. Starting time of each game

E. Opening ceremonies

F. Medical and liability

G. Transportation

H. Officials

I. Eligibility

J. Tickets

K. Housing

L. Coaches' meetings

M. Practice sessions for teams

N. Uniforms

O. Squad size

P. Ball to be used

Q. Films

R. Radio provisions

S. All-tournament teams

TOURNAMENT CHECKLIST

I. Pretournament Planning

A. Obtain official approval or sanction for conducting the tournament from the State High School Association. The sanction should include the following information.

   1. The names of the schools participating in the tournament.

   2. All the information regarding the awards to be given to the participants.

B. Schedule a meeting with the superintendent of schools and the tournament manager to delegate definite duties to the different organizations within the school.

   1. Place the pep club or some other school organization in charge of the concessions.

   2. Arrange to have the letterman's club members take tickets and usher at the tournament.

   3. Send a letter to the head custodian inquiring about janitorial help for the tournament.

   4. Arrange to have faculty members sell tickets.

   5. Arrange to have varsity football players sell programs.

   6. Arrange to have the junior varsity football players act as squad hosts.

   7. Arrange for parking attendants.

   8. Arrange for faculty members to serve as timer and scorekeeper.

   9. Arrange for the art department to decorate the gym and to make posters.

C. Send letters to all of the schools that are to be represented in the tournament including the following information in the letters.

   1. Financial guarantees.

   2. Date of the tournament.

   3. Place of the tournament.

   4. Type of tournament.

   5. Time of games.

   6. Squad limit.

   7. List of officials available.

   8. Color of uniforms to wear according to brackets.

   9. Ticket information and the policy to be followed regarding the issuing of tickets.

D. Send letters to the coaches of the participating teams.

   1. Ask for information on squad pictures and squad roster.

   2. List the dressing room assignment for each team.

   3. List the pairings.

   4. List the game times for each team.

   5. List the officials.

E. Plan first-aid arrangements and facilities including the following:

   1. Arrange to have a doctor at all games.

   2. Send complimentary tickets to all necessary officials.

   3. Give the teams needed informa-

tion regarding the use of the training room.

F. Send a letter to the police department.
　1. List special duties to be performed by police.
　2. List the time and the date the games are to be played.
　3. Work with the school faculty on all tournament arrangements.

G. Check the fire regulations for the gymnasium and other areas to be used.
　1. Arrange for all exits to be cleared and well lighted.
　2. Make fire extinguishers available and accessible.

H. Arrange for the tournament programs to be printed.
　1. Make plans for the securing of pictures, rosters, etc.
　2. Arrange for individuals to sell advertisements to defray the cost of the printing.
　3. Secure the bids for the printing of the programs.
　4. Make sure the programs will be ready at least two weeks before the tournament is held.
　5. Decide on the purchase price for the programs.

I. Make arrangements for the selection of tournament personnel and send instructions to each of the following.
　1. Ushers
　2. Parking attendants
　3. Ticket takers
　4. Ticket sellers
　5. Decorating committees
　6. Faculty supervisor of programs
　7. Public address announcer
　8. Police
　9. Janitors

J. Determine the number of personnel needed for each of the following duties.
　1. Ushers—14
　2. Ticket takers—4
　3. Ticket sellers—2
　4. Police—3
　5. Janitors—3
　6. Public Address Announcer—1
　7. Faculty supervisor of programs—1 to 5
　8. Parking attendants—4

K. Make the ticket arrangements
　1. Secure bids for the printing of the tickets.
　2. Arrange for the tickets to be made available at least a month before the tournament takes place.
　3. Arrange for ticket distribution.

L. Make arrangements for the broadcasting of games.
　1. Check on recording services to tape the games.
　2. Make arrangements with any of the schools who want to tape their game to replay for delayed broadcast on local radio stations.
　3. Reserve four seats for the announcer and the engineer.

M. Arrange for extending courtesies to visiting schools.
　1. Send schools complimentary tickets.
　2. Make provisions for seating cheerleaders.
　3. Arrange for adequate locker space for visitors.
　4. Arrange for drying room facilities.
　5. Provide for enough towels for each team.
　6. Provide access to the drying room.
　7. Provide adequate seats for the players who elect to stay for other games.
　8. Be sure that dressing rooms and

washrooms are cleaned up.

9. Provide a guide to meet visitors on arrival and be at their service until they leave.

10. Provide a safe place for visitors' valuables.

11. Arrange to have the dressing room locked and have a key with the guide.

12. Arrange to have all the needs of the visitors taken care of during halftime.

13. Provide blackboard and chalk for the dressing room.

N. Check on all the equipment that was ordered.

1. Basketballs—2
2. Scorebook—1
3. Nets—3
4. Trophies—3

O. Arrange for proper newspaper coverage.

1. Make provisions for sportswriters.
2. Arrange to have reports phoned in to the local newspaper.

II. Post-tournament Planning

A. Arrange to have the financial report sent to members of the tournament committee.

B. Send letters of appreciation to all the following personnel:

1. School officials of each competing school, including superintendent and coach
2. Police
3. Doctors
4. High school staff members
5. Letterman's club

C. Arrange for a meeting with the superintendent, tournament manager, coach, and the heads of the various tournament committees to discuss the tournament and to determine what procedures should be changed and what can be done to improve the administration of the tournament.

D. Keep tournament records for future reference.

CHECK LIST FOR ATHLETIC DIRECTOR

_____ 1. School notified: Asked for eligibility lists, rosters, enrollment, coaches, administrators, etc. for programs

_____ 2. Schools sent info: Pregame time schedule, tickets, lockers, cheerleader regulations, etc.

_____ 3. Call meeting of tourney coaches. Rated list of twenty officials sent to state office

_____ 4. Letter sent of officials regarding parking, pass gate, schedule, etc.

_____ 5. Nurse contacted, if needed

_____ 6. Scorer, announcer, and timer hired. Set pay

_____ 7. Band and risers arranged for—pads in front

_____ 8. Arrange for additional bleachers if needed

_____ 9. Rims repainted. Put up new nets

_____10. Sell adds for program (Approximately $600.00)

_____11. Read printer's proofs (twice)

_____12. Welcome letter to cheerleaders for meeting

_____13. Publicity (Brackets, favorites, seedings, etc.)

_____14. Make up list for custodial staff

_____15. Write announcements

_____16. Coordinate custodians' work schedule with basketball, gymnastics and track. *See that baseball is kept out.* Have coach call meeting

_____17. Assign statisticians with supervisor

_____18. Assign workers thru lettermen— Officials (2) Ropes (10) Runners (3)

Popcorn (10) Statistics (4)

              + Supervisor

Program (6) Catcher (?)

Hosts (4)

Officials (2)

Sweepers (2)

_____19. Notice to coaches regarding use of gyms and locker rooms during tourney

_____20. Arrange for hospitality room (and tickets)

_____21. Assign teams to locker rooms

_____22. Check scoreboard and "Home" sign

_____23. Starter pistol and air horns and scorebook

_____24. Emergency scoreboard control

_____25. Display trophy

_____26. Arrange for presentations of trophy

_____27. Game ball

_____28. Letter to officials

_____29. Reserve parking for officials

_____30. Ladders, custodian, and knife for presentation of nets (last night)

_____31. Wet-mop floor every day

_____32. Clean backboards. Dry-mop bleachers

_____33. Get ropes if needed

_____34. Pep club signs (8) for gym

_____35. Check room

_____36. Concessions

_____37. Clean coaches locker rooms

_____38. Clean all four locker rooms

_____39. Blackboards and benches

_____40. Press table and radio table

_____41. Meet with workers

_____42. Final ten for scoreboard

_____43. List of workers, radio, etc. to pass gate

_____44. Starting line-ups to announcers

_____45. Regulate free play, intramural etc. during tourney

_____46. Thank those buying ads

_____47. Have keys for hosts (4) and offi-

cials (2) (Gym area)

_____48. Arrange for calling scores to news service

_____49. Check speaker systems

TOURNAMENT REPORT

High School	Date	YOUR ESTIMATE			Needs improve-ment in Item Number	Comment
		Superior	Average	Poor		

SPECIAL NOTE: Give location and date of interpretation meetings or clinics you attended during the past month.

1.   2.   3.

REMARKS:

Figure 100

BEHAVIORAL OBJECTIVES

After a person has read this chapter, he should be able to:

1. Distinguish between an invitational and a state conducted basketball tournament.

2. Identify and explain three types of basketball tournaments.

3. Identify the method of selecting teams for the invitational tournament, and explain its importance for a successful tournament.

4. Distinguish between the methods of conducting the pairing of teams in the invitational tournament and the state conducted tournament.

5. Identify several methods of pairings in the invitational tournament, and explain how each is accomplished.
6. Distinguish between what is meant by seeding and bracketing of teams.
7. Explain how the teams may be placed in brackets and list several reasons why it is done in this manner.
8. Explain the purpose and procedure used in declaring the eligibility of the players who are to play in the tournament.
9. Outline an acceptable policy on admissions for spectators, coaches, and players, and justify your thinking.
10. Prepare an acceptable method of distributing passes for the tournament.
11. Analyze the reasoning behind the desirability of having a separate dressing room for officials.
12. Propose a set of procedures which will determine the number of players allowed for the tournament and a uniform; the bench arrangements for players, coaches, and players.
13. Develop a set of rules for the press and press room which would be fair to both local and out-of-town press officials.
14. Identify and explain the duties and dress of the announcer, scorekeeper, timers, and statisticians.
15. Propose a method for the selection of an all-tournament team.
16. Compile a list of workers needed for a sixteen-team basketball tournament.
17. Suggest several programs which could be used for halftime entertainment.
18. Analyze the financial breakdown of a sixteen-team basketball tournament.
19. Prepare a list of the duties of the workers needed for the tournament.
20. Estimate the expense of a sixteen-team basketball tournament, and justify your answers.
21. Explain the bench arrangement for players so that there is no partiality shown to either teams.
22. Propose an ideal locker room arrangement for each team, and explain the procedures necessary for its use.
23. Develop a procedure whereby provisions are made for all teams to practice before the tournament play is begun.
24. Explain the statement: Coaches are the key to much of their fans' behavior.
25. Analyze the statement: Many times the school administration is judged upon the way in which the tournament is conducted.
26. Explain the value of postseason planning.

ACTIVITIES

1. Write to your state director of interscholastic athletics and obtain the rules and regulations regarding the conducting of the state tournament. Discuss this in class.
2. Ask the local basketball coach to talk to the class about the regulations for financial arrangement for competing teams in an invitational tournament.
3. Talk with the local high school principal regarding his role in tournament participation both from a state and invitational level.
4. Prepare a financial statement for a sixteen-team basketball tournament.
5. Survey several high school basketball coaches, and obtain their opinion on the selection and seeding of teams for the invitational and state tournament. Discuss this in class.
6. Write a letter inviting teams to a tournament to be conducted at your school.
7. Work out a detailed expense account for a sixteen-team tournament.
8. Work out a complete halftime arrangement for entertainment for a sixteen-team tournament.

9. Prepare a financial statement to be sent to each competing school after the tournament is over.
10. Prepare a complete summary of the duties of the statistician.
11. Prepare a worksheet to be given to each tournament worker.
12. Prepare a complete financial statement for the completed tournament.
13. Make a poster advertising the upcoming tournament.

SUGGESTED READINGS

1. Boyden, Douglas and Burton, Roger: *Staging Successful Tournaments.* New York, NY Assoc Pr, 1957.
2. Bucher, Charles: *Administration of Health and Physical Education Programs.* St. Louis, Mosby, 1971.
3. Christenson, Irv: Basketball tournament management. *Scholastic Coach,* October, 1954.
4. Daughtrey, Greyson and Woods, John: *Physical Education Programs.* Philadelphia, Saunders, 1971.
5. Daughtrey, Greyson: *Method in Physical Education and Health for Secondary Schools.* Philadelphia, Saunders, 1967.
6. Forsythe, Charles and Keller, Irvin: *Administration of High School Athletics.* Englewood Cliffs, P-H, 1972.
7. Gilbert, Clark: Hosting a high school basketball tournament. *School Activities,* December, 1963.
8. King, Carroll: Tournament preparation. *Athletic Journal,* December, 1952.
9. Mihm, William: How to run a wrestling tournament. *Coach and Athlete,* January, 1969.
10. Muller, Pat: *Intramural Sports.* New York, Ronald, 1960.
11. Schakel, Douglas: Tournament preparation and organization. *Coaching Clinic,* October, 1969.

CHAPTER 18

Team Travel

ONE OF THE PROBLEMS confronting the coach and athletic director is planning for and organizing the out-of-town trips. However, if proper plans are made far enough in advance, many of these problems can be solved before they take place. This will, however, necessitate some wise and thoughtful planning on the part of both the coach and athletic director. Their efforts and forethought can pay rich dividends in trouble-free trips for the athletic teams. It can be time and effort well spent.

Parents' Permission

It must always be uppermost in the minds of coaches and athletic directors that boys and girls of high school age who are participants on interscholastic athletic teams are often minors. It should, therefore, be of major concern to the coach and athletic director that permission for making the trip should be obtained from the parents or guardians. It must be remembered that obtaining this permission does not obsolve the coach, athletic director, or school from the usual responsibility connected with negligence. Obtaining permission may be done by two methods. The first method requests the parents or guardian to simply sign a prepared statement to the effect that permission is granted by them for the student to make the trip using the kind of transportation specified by the school for the entire season. The permission slip is returned by the parent or guardian and placed on file for future use if the need arises. The second method is to issue permission slips for each individual trip. The second method is much more complicated because it entails the very same routine as the first method, yet it is done each time a trip is made. The one advantage that it does have, however, is that it eliminates any chance of a change in the date of a contest. When using the first method there could be a chance that the permission blanks would not be obtained if a date change was made. Also, some of the players who started the season may not be members of the squad later on, or, for that matter, even before the first trip, and therefore, it would not be necessary to have the permit blanks signed at all.

Preparing the Itinerary

The coach and athletic director should be mindful of the concern of parents when their children are away from home. They should make every effort to keep parents informed of the whereabouts of their children because very often children forget to tell their parents where they are going or worse yet, they do not tell them they are going. A detailed itinerary can be prepared with a minimum of effort and this should be the coach's responsibility. The itinerary should be sent to the parents of each player who is making the trip. It will be greatly appreciated by them and do a great deal to cement relations between the parent,

TABLE XCVI
LACANA HIGH SCHOOL
LACANA, OREGON

PARENTS' TRIP CONSENT FORM

Activity _____ Date _____
Destination _____ Purpose _____
Time of Departure _____ Date of Departure _____
Approx. Time of Return _____ Place of Return _____
Means of Transportation _____ Cost to Student _____
Coach of Sport _____
    I hereby grant permission for _____
                                                      Student
to make the trip explained above. In doing so, I agree that the school will not be held responsible for any accidents which might occur.
                            Signed _____
                                       Parent or Guardian
                          Address _____
                      Telephone _____
                              Date _____

school, and coach. It assures the parent that their child's welfare is being taken care of in an efficient and thoughtful manner. The itinerary should also be placed in the hands of all key people. This will enable them to know where the coach and team members can be reached at all times in case an emergency arises. It will save time and in many cases a great deal of trouble.

Forsythe[1] makes the following comment:

> Some schools do not think it is desirable or necessary to require permission of parents of students for each out-of-town trip that the school athletic team takes. They feel that the original permission for the student to participate covers scheduled trips as well as actual play. This opinion is reasonable. Other schools have forms that they require the student to take home, have signed by one of the parents, and return to the coach, faculty manager, or principal before he may go on the trip with the team. These forms usually state the loca-

tion, date, and time of the contest. They also indicate the type of transportation to be used, hour of departure, probable hour of return, and a source where information may be obtained in case the return trip is delayed. In signing such a form the parent usually indicates that the school is released from any liability in case of accident. Just how much this apparent release of liability amounts to is questionable. The chief justification for a procedure of this kind is that it keeps parents informed of the school's efforts to cooperate with them in the care and safety of their son or daughter.

Player Dress and Behavior

Although times have changed a great deal the past few years in the dress and behavior of young people, there still should be standards set in this respect when they are representing a school and community. Our present-day society, with its civil rights movement, has allowed a greater amount of freedom in dress and all around behavior than ever before. However, there are those people who still believe that the impressions the team members make on

[1]Forsythe, Charles, and Keller, Irvin, *Administration of High School Athletics* 5th ed., (Englewood Cliffs, New Jersey, by permission of Prentice-Hall Inc. 1972), p. 191.

TABLE XCVII
HIGH SCHOOL BASKETBALL ITINERARY

Trip to _____, Feb. 1, 19_____

Friday, February 1, 19_____

8:00 A. M.	Arrive at high school gym
8:10 A. M.	Check out equipment
8:30 A. M.	Board bus
8:30 A. M.	Leave high school
12:00 A.M.	Stop at Hudsonville for lunch. Marine Cafe.
1:00 P. M.	Leave Hudsonville
2:30 P. M.	Arrive at motel in Marionville. (Roadside Motel)
2:30 P. M.	Sign up for rooms — Rest
4:00 P. M.	Eat pre-game meal — East Side Cafe
5:00 P. M.	Take brisk one mile walk
6:00 P. M.	Back to motel — get ready to go to gym
6:30 P. M.	Board bus for gym
6:45 P. M.	Arrive at gym
7:00 P. M.	Dress for game
8:00 P. M.	Game
10:00 P. M.	Return to motel and eat following the game (East Side Cafe)
11:00 P. M.	Bed

Saturday, February 2, 19_____

9:00 A. M.	Get up — dress
9:30 A. M.	Eat breakfast (East Side Cafe)
10:30 A. M.	Board Bus, leave for home
12:00 A. M.	Stop Morgantown. Eat. (West Side Cafe)
1:00 P. M.	Board bus
3:30 P. M.	Arrive high school gym

Conduct on Trips:

All boys are expected to conduct themselves as gentlemen at all times on our athletic trips. Foul language and unmanly actions will not be tolerated.

All teams are expected to go and return on the school-chartered bus. All vehicles are covered by insurance and are well supervised.

All class work that is missed by members of athletic teams because of trips for games *must* be made up. It is recommended that each student make plans with his instructors to make up his work or hand in his assignment *prior* to the periods missed if possible.

Strive always to go first class in appearance, conduct, and performance.

other people are a direct reflection on the school, its students, its faculty, and the community which they represent. The coach should set up rules which will regulate the conduct of the players on all trips and he should see to it that these rules are enforced. While it is difficult to require specific clothing to be worn, the rule can be made that it be clean. Many schools furnish travel jackets or sport coats in the school colors. This often solves the dress problem and enables the players, who sometimes cannot afford appropriate clothing, to be dressed the same as his team members. This always makes a very favorable impression to have all team members dressed alike.

The players' as well as the coaches' behavior in all eating establishments should reflect good taste. All horseplay should be held to a minimum; otherwise it can get out of hand. All athletes should be expected to conduct themselves in a respectful and dignified manner both on and off the field and in such a way that it will be a credit to their school and their community. They should be leaders, who will be respected and admired by the student body as well as the faculty. Coaches should set a definite pattern of behavior on all trips. Such common sense rules as no hanging out of windows, no yelling at pedestrians, no card playing, no swearing etc. should be in order and rigidly enforced. Each team member should be informed of the consequences if the rules are broken. After arriving at their destination, the players should stay together as much as possible. They should not be allowed to wander about on their own and mingle with the crowd. The coaching staff should remain with the group and supervise them at all times.

Coaches have a great responsibility to young athletes in teaching them the social obligations that they must perform to become accepted members of society. They must be taught to accept these responsibilities, and this is just one of the many opportunities coaches have because of their unique position to develop mature students.

The coaches and players should assume the responsibility to leave all locker rooms and lockers which have been used for dressing purposes in as good, if not better, condition than they were found.

Rooms

Usually high school athletic teams do not stay over night. Occasionally, however, this might happen, such as during a tournament. Should such a situation arise, it is advisable if not imperative to make arrangements in advance by letter. These accommodations should be arranged for as far in advance as possible. By doing so, a better chance of rooms is possible as well as, perhaps, a better price. The accommodations should assure a quiet atmosphere so that the athletes will be able to get a good night's rest. A smaller motel in a quiet neighborhood is much better than one with large crowds of people and a great deal of hustle and bustle. This type of atmosphere is wearing and tends to unnerve the young athlete because it is something to which he is not accustomed. Players never sleep as well away from home and this might be the first time some of them have spent a night away; therefore, everything should be done to make things as relaxing and homelike as possible. It might make the difference between winning and

Figure 101.

losing the game the next night. It will make for a more pleasant experience for the athlete, one which he will remember.

If it is at all possible, no more than two players should be housed in one room. This helps prevent the possibility of horseplay which almost always takes place when there are several players housed in one room. Each player should have a separate bed.

Outside noise should also be a factor in selecting a motel. A motel situated near a busy truck route, near a stop sign, or on an incline where trucks must shift gears should be avoided. Nothing can be as distracting or disturbing as heavy traffic noises especially if the players are not used to this type of noise. It can result in a sleepless night which must be avoided. Prearranged plans can help avoid this possibility.

Meals

Most high school athletic teams are restricted as to the amount of money that can be spent on items such as meals, either before or after a game or while on an extended trip. Many schools do not furnish any meals unless the team is staying overnight. However, if meals are furnished, every effort should be made to give the players good meals after games and an additional light meal before games. The meals are very important. The old adage that, "an army travels on its stomach" will hold true with athletic teams. However, overeating should be avoided as this can do more harm than undereating. Meals should be arranged for in advance if at all possible. This will avoid confusion and long delays in being served. If a pregame meal is planned, then previous arrangements are necessary. This can be done by phone or letter. If an after-the-game meal is planned, the meal can be ordered before the game starts. It is best to eat in a restaurant that has a private dining room al-

though this is not mandatory. The purpose of this kind of arrangement is to keep the team members away from opposing fans as much as possible especially if there is a keen rivalry between the two schools. There is no reason to ask for trouble. It is much better to go out of the way to avoid it.

Figure 102.

If at all possible it is best to try and order meals that correspond to the kind the players have at home. A change in eating habits and food can upset the player. Overeating should be avoided and watched closely by the coach. Most of the players will eat two meals a day at home during the week and all his meals at home during the weekend.

The pregame meal should be eaten from three to four hours before game time and it should be a light meal. There are many differences of opinions as to what constitutes a good pregame meal. The main thing is not to overeat. The after game meal is not as important, but the

Date __________________ 19____

SPECIAL TRIPS

Request for Bus Service

Bus service requested for: ______________________ (Group)

Bus service requested for: __________ (Number) students on __________ (Date)

To go to: ______________________ (Exact Destination)

Bus to leave from: ________________ at: __________ (Time)

And return to: ________________ at: __________ (Time)

Trip sponsored by: ______________________ (Signature of faculty member)

To be Paid by ______________________

Approved by: ______________________ (Signature of administrator)

Driver: ________________ Bus No.: __________

TIME REPORT

Group Transported:	Arrived at bus ________	Mileage Report Speedometer Readings
	Arrived destination ________	
Destination:	Left destination ________	Beginning ________
	Left bus ________	Ending ________
Group Transported:	Arrived at bus ________	Beginning ________
	Arrived destination ________	
Destination:	Left destination ________	Ending ________
	Left bus ________	

Emergency Expenses	Item	Amount	Paid by

Figure 103.

coach should never give money to the players with the expectation that they should get something to eat. Usually they will fill up on fried foods or not eat anything at all and keep the money. On the other hand, some of the players do not want a heavy meal after playing a hard game and are satisfied with one or two hamburgers and a milk shake. Their wishes should be considered. Others may prefer something else. It is, of course, impossible to ask each player what he wishes for an after-the-game meal. Therefore, if it is necessary to order the after game meal ahead of time, a random poll of the squad will indicate likes and dislikes and the coach can make a decision accordingly. The important thing for the coach to remember is that likes and dislikes differ as far as food is concerned. The player's diet should be kept as routine as possible, and he should not be forced to eat food he is not used to and does not like just because the coach might think that it is the proper food for him to eat at a particular time. It is just good philosophy to keep the same routine as they have at home in so far as possible. This holds true for the days activities as well as the eating habits of the players. The belief here is, of course, that any new adjustment is disturbing to the nervous system and can bring undesirable results which in turn can influence the play of the athlete at a given time and place. This is the one thing the coach should try and avoid.

Mode of Transportation

The accepted practice now is for all athletic teams to travel by school bus. These buses are available in most cases because of consolidation. A few may go by car, especially on short trips.

Responsible persons must be the drivers and they must also have the proper amount of insurance coverage in case of a serious accident.

Care should be taken to make the ride, no matter how short it may be, as comfortable as possible. Players cannot perform up to their capacity if they are forced to sit in a cramped or crowded position for any length of time.

If a bus is used to make the trip, then the coach should ride with the team unless the circumstances are such that he is unable to do so. If he cannot ride in the bus, then some other responsible person should take his place and serve in this capacity. All forms of horseplay should be avoided en route to the game. The players should be in a serious state of mind at this time. If the trip is made by car, the coach and manager should assign the players to the cars. This practice helps to break up cliques

TABLE XCVIII
JACKSON CONSOLIDATED SCHOOLS
District 190
TRAVEL REQUEST AND VOUCHER

Request for travel to _____

For the purpose of _____

_____

Number of pupils to make the trip _____

Departure Date _____ Departure Time _____

Estimated time of return to _____

Type and number of vehicles requested:

School Bus _____ School Automobile _____ Pupil Carrier _____

Date of

Name of person making request _____ Request _____

Names of additional certificated staff included in this trip _____

_____

Estimated Costs: Travel _____; Lodging _____; Meals _____;

Other (Specify): _____ Total _____

Approved _____ Date _____

(Building Principal)

Approved _____ Date _____

(Assistant Superintendent)

Approved _____ Date _____

(Superintendent)

— — — — — — — — — — — — — — — — — — —

Request for travel reimbursement: Date _____

Travel: No. of miles _____ @ ._____ = _____

Lodging _____

Meals _____

Other _____

Total _____

Attach receipts Signed _____

MAKE REQUEST IN 4 COPIES. SUBMIT ALL 4 COPIES TO THE BUILDING PRINCI-PAL. After superintendent's approval: Copy 1 and 2 to person making request. Copy 3 to the building principal. Copy 4 to the director of transportation. After trip has been made, complete copy 1 and transmit to business office.

---

getting together and creates a more friendly and healthy attitude among the players. Forsythe[2] stresses the importance of arranging for the transportation of athletic teams in the following observation:

This is one of the most important items in connection with games away from home. Decide on the use of common carrier, school bus, or private car

transportation. The first two listed are most preferable, in that order. Make certain that contracts are signed if necessary; that leaving and returning times are understood; that the place of departure is designated; that the number in the party is determined; and that the cost of transportation is established.

The mode of transportation used by the athletic teams as well as other extra-mural activities is often determined by the financial conditions of the school. How-

[2]Forsythe, Charles, and Keller, Irvin, *Administration of High School Athletics.*

SPECIAL TRANSPORTATION REQUEST - ST. CHARLES COMMUNITY UNIT SCHOOL

☐ Educational Excursion   ☐ Athletic Trip   ☐ Other ....

DESTINATION ....   DATE OF TRIP ....   APPROVED ....

ADDRESS ....   TOWN ....

TIME — LEAVE ....   RETURN ....

IMPORTANT: LEAVE AND RETURN TIME SHALL BE AT POINT OF ORIGIN AND POINT OF RETURN, TO MEET OTHER TRIP SCHEDULES.

GRADE (OR TEAM) ....   TEACHER OR SPONSOR ....

NUMBER OF PASSENGERS — ADULT ....   STUDENTS ....

PRINCIPAL ....   SCHOOL ....

PURPOSE OF TRIP ....

EXTRA EQUIPMENT TO BE TRANSPORTED ....

BUS DRIVER'S REPORT

INDICATE BELOW

DATE OF TRIP ....194....   TIME ....   SPEEDOMETER READING ....   MILES

TIME: LEAVE (FROM POINT OF ORIGIN)
ARRIVE (DESTINATION)
LEAVE (DESTINATION)
ARRIVE (POINT OF ORIGIN)

TOTAL MILEAGE ....

BUS DRIVER ....   ADULT SPONSOR ....
SIGNATURE   SIGNATURE

FOR ADMINISTRATION OFFICER USE ONLY

CHARGE TO   DRIVER TO BE PAID   ADMINISTRATION OFFICE APPROVAL
Group ....   BY ....
Amount $ ....   AMOUNT $ ....   BUSINESS MANAGER

Check NO. ....   DATE ....

Figure 104. Reprinted with permission from St. Charles Community School District, St. Charles, Illinois.

take their son or daughter home with them. Have a definite time for starting the trip. Plan a definite range in time for the return trip, and notify parents accordingly. Usually team members, student managers, coaches, and school officials only should make up the party if a bus is chartered for the trip. The same applies if a school bus is used. Discipline problems are lessened to a considerable degree if no students other than team members, student managers, and possibly cheer leaders are allowed.

EXPENSE VOUCHER

Glenbard East ☐   Glenbard West ☐   Department _____

Date _____ 19 ____

Name _____

	Sun.	Mon.	Tues.	Wed.	Thur.	Fri.	Sat.	
Date								TOTAL
Breakfast								
Lunch								
Dinner								
Mileage								
Lodging								
Other								

(Please itemize other expenses.)

Attach all paid bills to this voucher.

Figure 105.

ever, most schools now use the regular school bus for transporting all athletic teams. Usually the task of arranging for athletic transportation is the duty of the athletic director. He should be very careful in making these arrangements. Forsythe[3] cites the importance of transporting athletic teams by making the following comment:

Under no circumstances should student drivers of private cars be allowed to transport athletic teams. Where such a policy is followed, school authorities may be charged with negligence in case of accident, with subsequent court action a possibility. Team members should be required to go to the entertaining school together and return the same way. The one exception to this rule is where parents personally request permission of the school official in charge of the team to

The importance of proper transportation is emphasized by Bucher[4] in the following comment:

Transporting athletes to games and contests presents many administrative problems. Such questions arise as: Who should be transported? In what kind of vehicles should athletes be transported? Is athletics part of a regular school or college program? Should private vehicles or school and college-owned vehicles be used? What are the legal implications involved in transporting athletes in school- and college-sponsored events?

It appears that the present trend is to view athletics as an integral part of the

[3]*Ibid.*

[4]Bucher, Charles, *Administration of Health and Physical Education Programs* (St. Louis, C.O. Mosby Co., 1971) , p. 254.

TRAVEL VOUCHER

For Month Ending _____ 19 ____

Name _____
      First Name   Initial   Last Name

Mail check to _____

_____

Date	DEPARTED FROM		ARRIVED AT		Auto Reimbursement		Plane, Train or Bus Fare	Lodging	Meals	OTHER EXPENSES		TOTAL
	Place	Time	Place	Time	Mileage	Amount				Item	Amount	
	Total All Columns											

MEMO REPORTING		
Amount of registration fee (\$50.00 and over)		
Amount of vehicle rental		
Payee		

I certify that the above amount is correct and just; that the detailed items charged within are taken and verified from a memorandum kept by me; that the amounts charged for subsistence were actually paid, and the expenses were occasioned by official business or unavoidable delays, requiring my stay at hotels for the time specified; that I performed the journey with all practicable dispatch, by the shortest route usually traveled, in the customary reasonable manner; and that I have not been furnished with transportation or money in lieu thereof, for any part of the journey therein charged for.

ACCOUNTING USE ONLY		
Total Expense		
Total Advance		
Balance Due	NIU	
	Traveler	

Traveler Signature _____   Date _____

Department Head or Fund Advisor _____   Date _____

Audited By _____   Date _____

Charge Expense to: _____

          Department or Fund No. and Name

Form No. 00002 (6-20; 8m)

Figure 106.

TABLE XCIX
JASON HIGH SCHOOL DISTRICT NO. 111
INDIVIDUAL OR TEAM EXPENSE ACCOUNT
Work Sheet

NAME OF TRAVELER _____

PURPOSE OF TRAVEL _____

TRAVELED TO _____

ACCOMPANIED BY _____ TOTAL NUMBER TRAVELING _____
(Include yourself, bus driver, etc.)

DATE LEFT JASON _____ TIME LEFT JASON _____A.M./P.M

DATE RETURNED JASON _____ TIME RETURNED JASON _____A.M./P.M

IF WITHDRAWAL, AMOUNT $_____ METHOD OF TRANSPORTATION

Air ____ Bus ____ Car ____ Other _____

TOTAL EXPENSES $_____

AMOUNT RETURNED _____ CHARGE TO BUDGET _____
(Name of Sport)

AMOUNT OWED TO TRAVELER _____

ITEMS BILLED: Lodging _____   Meals _____
        (Vendor and Amount)   (Vendor and Amount)

        Car Rental _____   Other _____
        (Vendor and Amount)   (Vendor and Amount)

        Air Fare _____
        (Vendor and Amount)

NOTE: Team Travel: *ALL ITEMS MUST BE RECEIPTED OR AN AFFIDAVIT SIGNED*
        Individual Travel: Lodging, Guest Meals, Registrations & *ANY PAYMENT OVER $5 MUST BE RECEIPTED.*

DISBURSEMENTS:	Receipted	Unreceipted	Total
Mileage at 10c per mile	$_____	$_____	$_____
Lodging (MUST BE RECEIPTED)	_____	_____	_____
Traveler's Meals	_____	_____	_____
Guest Meals (MUST BE RECEIPTED & NAMES) ..	_____	_____	_____
Tolls	_____	_____	_____
Parking	_____	_____	_____
Taxi	_____	_____	_____
Telephone	_____	_____	_____
Registration	_____	_____	_____
Other — List & Be Specific	_____	_____	_____
TOTALS	_____	_____	_____

Date ___/___/___

LYONS TOWNSHIP HIGH SCHOOL

REQUEST FOR TRAVEL REIMBURSEMENT

NAME _____

CAMPUS   N   S   DEPARTMENT_____
       (Circle)

Date of travel: _____

Purpose of travel: _____
                _____
                _____
                _____

Destination: _____

Expenses: (Attach receipts for room, transportation, and other items, where possible.)

                                     Amount
Room   _____

Transportation (Reimbursement shall not exceed the round trip air-coach fare from Chicago.)
(Shorter trips by car shall be reimbursed at 10¢ per mile.) _____

Other (please list)   _____
                                  _____
                                  _____
                                  _____

        Total Request for Reimbursement $_____

Signed: _____ Date _____

Department Chairman: _____ Date: _____
        Signature indicates amount
        has been budgeted

– –

FOR OFFICE USE

☐ Reimbursement approved | Vendor number _____

☐ Reimbursement disapproved | Invoice number _____

                  | Account charged _____
_____ |
  Assistant Superintendent | Amount _____

Date: _____ | Authorization _____

White — Staff Member   Pink — Purchasing Office
Yellow — Department Chairman   Gold — Personnel File

Figure 107.

educational program so that public funds may be used for transportation purposes. At the same time, however, statutes vary from state to state, and any person administering athletic programs should examine carefully the statutes in their own state.

The feeling among many administrators in regard to transportation is that athletes and representatives of the school or college concerned such as band and cheerleaders, should travel only in transportation provided by the educational institution. Where private cars belonging to coaches, students, or other persons are used, the administrator should be sure to determine whether he is in conformity with the state statutes regarding liability.

Resick, Siedel and Mason[5] make the following comment:

The arrangement of suitable transportation is one of the most important items in planning for games away from home. School buses are a useful vehicle for transporting teams; however, the laws of some states prevent the use of school buses for transportation of personnel for interscholastic contests, or they require special bonding for such purposes. When school buses are not available, buses should be chartered from a reliable public transportation company. If the money required to hire bus transportation is not available, private cars may be used, provided they are sufficiently insured and that they are driven by adult, licensed drivers. In any case team members should be required to go and return from the game as a group.

If the trip is made by bus, only the team members, managers, athletic coaches, and school officials should be permitted to travel in the official party. It is strongly recommended that when weather conditions make driving hazardous, contests should be canceled.

Grieve[6] brings out the point that:

. . . legal attitudes in the case of accidents involving school transportation differ a great deal from other school accidents. There seems to be more concern because of court action and the schools feel more responsible for such incidents. The fact that school athletics have been considered to be more a part of the total educational curriculum has changed the

[5]Resick, Matthew, Siedel Beverly and Mason, James, *Modern Administrative Practices in Physical Education and Athletics* (Reading, Mass., Addison-Wesley Publishing Co., 1970), p. 146.

[6]Grieve, Andrew, "Legal Aspects of Transportation for Athletic Events" (*Athletic Journal*, March, 1967), p. 64.

TABLE C

PLEASE FILL OUT IN TRIPLICATE

JAMES B. CONANT HIGH SCHOOL
Application for Bus Transportation

Application is hereby made for transportation for: (Please use carbon)

_____ people to leave from __ _____

(How many)   (Point of departure)

and to go to _____ on _____

(Destination)   (Date)

A.M.   A.M.

leaving at _____P.M. o'clock and to arrive back at _____P.M.

Equipment to be transported in addition to above number of persons?

_____

(Musical instruments, athletic equipment, etc.)

Name of the organization? _____

Transportation is to be paid for from _____ funds.

This application is made by _____   _____

(Date)

_____

(Signature of Sponsor of Organization)

_____

(Approved by Principal)

Date Received by

(Office Use Only)   Dir. Transportation _____

Total Miles _____   Driver Assigned _____

Total Hours _____   Bus # _____

Total Cost _____

---

attitude of school officials and eased the situation considerably.

There has always been some skepticism about the coach driving athletes to games in private cars. This may be accepted practice by some schools but it has decreased dramatically the past few years. If an accident did occur and the coach was called upon to testify, it might be proven that he did not have the necessary experience in handling large vehicles. This could place him in a very awkward position and possibly leave him vulnerable for a negligence suit.

The importance of transportation arrangements should not be minimized. Voltmer and Esslinger[7] comment on this as follows:

The athletic director must take care of a variety of details in connection with team trips. He should consult with the head coach on some of the important details, such as the menu, the time of arrival and return, the hotel, and the like. Many directors permit the team managers to handle most of these details, but the responsibility still remains with the athletic director.

---

[7]Voltmer, Edward and Esslinger, Arthur, *The Organization and Administration of Physical Education* (New York, Appleton-Century Crofts, 1967), p. 298.

REQUEST FOR TRANSPORTATION (INSTRUCTIONS ON BACK OF FORM)

PRINT NAME OF DRIVER LAST FIRST	DEPARTURE DATE & TIME	DESTINATION	PURPOSE – IF FOR OUT OF STATE USE EXPLAIN WHY PUBLIC TRANSPORTATION SHOULD NOT BE UTILIZED
OTHER TRAVELERS: NO. OF FACULTY_____ NO. OF STUDENTS_____ OTHER(S)_____	RETURN DATE & TIME	(1) SEDAN _____ (2) WAGON _____ (3) BUS _____ (4) TRUCK _____ ESTIMATED MILEAGE_____	

PICK-UP LOCATION (FOR BUS)	SIGNATURE OF STAFF MEMBER **RESPONSIBLE** FOR VEHICLE (INCLUDES) RESP. FOR VALID LICENSE OF DRIVER(S)
CHARGE TO: NUMBER; NAME (DEPT, LOCAL ACCT, BOND, OTHER)	FISCAL APPROVAL: (DEPT. HEAD OR OTHER)

| TO BE COMPLETED BY DRIVER AT TIME OF TRIP
SPEEDOMETER READING   VEHICLE MALFUNCTIONS

ENDING_____

STARTING_____

TOTAL MILES_____

VEHICLE NO._____DATE_____

USERS SIGNATURE_____
FORM NO. 147 (10M – 3/73) | TO BE COMPLETED BY TRANSPORTATION OFFICE
CAR AVAILABLE: YES_____ NO_____

COMMENTS:

VEHICLE APPROVAL – SIGN. TRANS. SUPV._____

RATE_____ AMOUNT_____ HOURS_____ |

Figure 108.

Previous Arrangements

As many arrangements as possible should be made prior to the trip. Either the coach or the senior manager should contact the coach of the opposition by letter at least two weeks previous to the contest and request all necessary information pertaining to game conditions, route to the gym, color of jerseys to be worn, officials, time of game, etc. Many schools make a

TABLE CI
PALO HIGH SCHOOL
DISTRICT 20
Palo, Nebraska

Date _____

I hereby request that my son/daughter, _____,

               (to   )

be excused from traveling (from   ) the game at _____

               (to and from)

On (Date) _____ on the bus chartered by the school. He/she will use the following means of transportation: _____

_____   _____

The reason for this request is the following: _____

_____   _____

                           (Parent's Signature)

TABLE CII
PALO HIGH SCHOOL
PALO, NEBRASKA

Trip Fund Request Form

Purpose of the trip _____

Place _____ Date of Departure _____
Sport _____ Date of Return _____
Number of players making the trip _____
Mode of travel _____ Cost $_____
Food, lodging, and other expense $_____
Staff member making the request _____
position _____
Department and fund name and no. _____

Approved by _____

Director of Athletics

practice of sending this information to the opposing school without a request. This advanced planning will save a great deal of time and will result in a more pleasant trip for everyone. The situation is usually more or less tense before a game and any irregularities, such as losing the way, etc. tends to aggravate an already nervous coach and his players. Anything that can be done to smooth out this kind of a situation will result in a more relaxed team and one that will play better. Any easing of tension at this time will be of benefit to everyone.

PALO HIGH SCHOOL

PALO, NEBRASKA

Travel Expense Form

Destination _____

Date	Items and Location	Cost
Total		

Date_____ Signed_____

Title_____

Figure 109.

BILLINGS SENIOR HIGH SCHOOL

BOB THORSON
TICKET MANAGER
PHONE 245-5202

RAY COLLINS—PRINCIPAL
PHONE 245-6127

JIM DUTCHER—DIRECTOR OF PHYSICAL EDUCATION
AND ATHLETICS
PHONE 252-6608

Date_____

Mr. _____
Principal, _____ High School
_____, _____

Subject: Football

Place: _____ Field

Suggested route to field: _____

Date: _____ Hour: _____
Officials: _____

Admission: Adults _____ Students _____
Color Suits: Home Team _____
Visiting Team: Contrasting Color
Dressing Rooms: Visiting team will enter West door of the field house where they will be met by a student manager who will conduct the team to the dressing rooms.
Complimentary Tickets: Any person having proper identification will be admitted.

Sincerely,

Athletic Director

cc

Figure 110.

It is always best to travel together as a team. If cars are used, the drivers should attempt to stay together if at all possible. Every effort should be made to make everyone feel that he is going to the game as a member of a team and not as an individual going his separate way. It should be a team effort every step of the way, before, during, and after the game. It is important that the players do not feel that they are privileged to go their separate ways after the game. They should make every effort to return with the team. This will bring about a feeling of unity and help to build strong team spirit and morale. It should be standard practice never to allow a player to go or return in any way other than the way in which he was assigned. The one exception would be for the player to go with his parents. Even then, the parents must personally contact the coach. No phone calls or notes should be accepted. If this is made a hard-and-fast rule to begin with, the players will not ask over once or twice for an exception to the rule. This rule should never, under any circumstances, be broken.

The coach should assume the responsibility of seeing to it that everyone arrives at the gymnasium or some other predetermined meeting place after the game and that each player has a way home. His responsibility should end when the players arrive at the gymnasium. This is very important and should be of major concern to the coach. He must not forget that these players are under his direct supervision and the parents have placed their trust in him. He should always keep this in mind in any decisions he makes. Voltmer and Esslinger[8] make the following comment on team travel:

[8]Volmer, Edward and Esslinger, Arthur, *The Organization and Administration of Physical Education.*

The squad should leave together, stay together after they arrive, and return home together. It is standard procedure not to permit players to return home with other individuals except their parents. It goes without saying that the coach should always accompany his squad.

All details of the trip should be arranged in advance. All the players should know who is on the traveling squad and the time and place of departure. Parents should be notified of the details of the trip. Some coaches obtain the permission of parents for their son to take the trip. The hotel, transportation, and eating arrangements should be prepared well ahead of time.

Money should not be given to the players for expenses. It is better for the coach or manager to handle the funds on trips and defray all the expenses that are incurred. He should have sufficient cash available to meet all the expected expenses of the trip. He should receive receipts for all funds expended. He is expected to account for all expenditures upon his return. Ordinarily, the hotel and transportation costs are billed to the school.

Giving Information to School Officials

Even though schedules are arranged and printed far in advance, and school officials are aware of the fact that the game is being played on a specific day, it still is necessary to inform the administration and faculty of the necessary absence from school of the team members and other personnel that will be going on the trip. Usually school officials will provide a special form, an example of which is shown, for this purpose. The names of players, managers, coaches, and anyone else making the trip are placed on this form. This form should be filled out by the coach and turned in to the school office before the team leaves. If the team is to be excused from school early on a specific day, this same form should be signed by the principal or assistant principal and given

TABLE CIII
ATHLETIC OFFICE COPY
LOMBARD HIGH SCHOOL
ATHLETIC BUS TRANSPORTATION RECORD

Date _____ Athletic Squad(s) _____ Destination _____

Mileage upon arrival at destination .... _____

Mileage upon departure from Lombard High School ...... _____

Difference _____

Mileage upon arrival at Lombard High School .... _____

Mileage upon departure from destination .... _____

Difference _____

Total Mileage _____

_____

Time of departure from Lombard High School .... _____

Time of arrival at destination .... _____

Time of departure from destination .... _____

Time of arrival at Lombard High School .... _____

Total waiting time at destination _____ hrs. _____ min.

Coach's Signature _____

Driver's Signature _____

Was locker room used at host school left in an orderly fashion?

TABLE CIV
DAVENPORT HIGH SCHOOL DISTRICT 111
OUT-OF-TOWN TRIPS OF ATHLETIC TEAMS

(Hand in to office before leaving school)

Sport _____ Leaving Time _____ By (Cars) (Bus)

Where to _____ Date _____ Signed _____

Make Trip:

1. _____	21. _____
2. _____	22. _____
3. _____	23. _____
4. _____	24. _____
5. _____	25. _____
6. _____	26. _____
7. _____	27. _____
8. _____	28. _____
9. _____	29. _____
10. _____	30. _____
11. _____	31. _____
12. _____	32. _____
13. _____	33. _____
14. _____	34. _____
15. _____	35. _____
16. _____	36. _____
17. _____	37. _____
18. _____	38. _____
19. _____	39. _____
20. _____	40. _____

to the office secretary before 9:00 A.M. the day of the trip. This will enable the secretary to get the names of the team members on the excused list for the day. This list should be sent to all teachers. The coach should then instruct each team member to meet with the teachers whose classes will be missed, turn in the assignment, and get the information regarding the next day's assignment.

If departure time is in the middle of a class period, the team member should also request permission of that teacher whose class he is attending to leave at the proper time.

The above procedure will help create a better feeling between the athletic department and the teachers.

Care of Equipment on Trips

The care of equipment on trips is very important. Many coaches prefer to have the equipment issued to each individual player and make him responsible for his own equipment. However, this plan does not always prove to be satisfactory because of the irresponsibility of some players to take care of their equipment. As a result some of them will be without their own equipment at game time. This situation results in an attempt to borrow from the opposing school. Usually the player ends up with equipment that does not fit correctly or a uniform of one of the substitutes. The outcome of this occurrence results in decreased efficiency of the player and hard feelings among team members because someone had to give up his uniform.

This system of caring for equipment on trips does have its compensations because it teaches the players the responsibility of caring for their own equipment, which in itself is a teaching process that can prove to be a valuable experience for the players.

If this method is used, individual suit-cases, in school colors, may be purchased and issued to each player before the trip and returned after the trip. This makes a good impression and solves the problem for the player who does not own a suitcase or perhaps one that is not as good as his teammates. It might help to avoid some embarrassment for some players.

Another problem that will be encountered in using this system is that many of the players will fail to dry out and air their uniforms after the game unless they are checked very closely. This, of course, can be done by the manager and it is not of major concern. Usually it will happen if the players are on an overnight trip which will not happen too frequently.

The other method of caring for the equipment on trips and one that has gained favor with many coaches, is that of carrying all equipment in one large trunk. By using this method, all the responsibility is assumed by the managers. All the equipment is placed in the trunk and is checked off the equipment list by the manager as it is placed in the trunk. Shoes, socks, and supporters are also placed in the trunk and are checked by the manager to be sure that this is done by each individual player.

One of the advantages of using this system is that all the new equipment is together and can be taken care of properly by the managers. The disadvantage is that the players become very careless and depend entirely on the manager for the care of their personal equipment.

The managers should always take several empty bags for dirty laundry. An additional bag with extra towels, socks, supporters, and an extra pair of game pants and jerseys should be taken along.

The first-aid kit should be checked by the student trainer to make sure that all necessary first-aid material is in the kit.

The kit should be the trainer's responsibility if there is a student trainer. If not, it then is the responsibility of the manager. George and Lehmann[9] make the following comment on transporting athletic equipment:

> Unless a squad is blessed with a competent staff of equipment men and managers, individual players will usually be responsible for their own personal gear. It is well to provide each athlete with a handbag or duffle bag of adequate size to hold all his individual items and to instruct the squad members on packing methods so as to avoid unnecessary crushing and warping.
>
> Each player should be provided with a check list of individual items to ascertain that he has everything he needs. Forgotten equipment creates annoying and sometimes serious problems and a pretrip check will help insure that a traveling squad is fully equipped.

Athletic Trip Insurance

Coaches should be concerned about the legal implications resulting from injuries to players which might occur on trips. These injuries might occur as a result of a traffic mishap or in some other way.

In some states the teacher is liable if negligence can be proven against him when a player is injured on a trip. Negligence can be interpreted in different ways. If private cars are used in transporting players, negligence could be interpreted to mean the circumstances under which the act is done. If the act creates a risk, even though it is done with due care and precaution, it could be interpreted as negligence. This interpretation could mean that a coach would be negligent if he allows his team to travel in a car if the driver is not completely insured.

For some time schools and teachers were considered to be outside the law of liability, but lately, not only the teachers, but also the schools have become liable under the courts and under certain circumstances. Teachers can be made to pay for their own negligent behavior when it results in injury to someone else.

Negligence is considered the failure to act as a reasonably prudent person would under the circumstances. It is also gauged by the ability to anticipate danger. So, if such foresight is reasonable, failure to seek to prevent danger is also negligence. If the coach assigns a player to ride in a car driven by an individual who is not covered by insurance, or in a car that is defective

TABLE CV
FAIRFIELD HIGH SCHOOL
Fairfield, Iowa

NOTICE OF INTENT TO TRANSPORT STUDENTS BY PERSONAL CAR

GROUP _____

DESTINATION _____

ADDRESS _____

DATE _____ TIME _____

TEACHER DRIVING _____

NUMBER OF STUDENTS TO BE TRANSPORTED _____

SIGNED: _____

APPROVED: _____

---

[9]George Jack, and Lehmann, Harry, *School Athletic Administraton* (New York, Harper and Row, 1966) p. 185.

mechanically, he could be negligent by law.

Coaches should protect themselves as much as possible, and should exhaust every other way of transporting the team before resorting to the use of private cars. They should never assume the responsibility that rightfully belongs to the school district. Coaches are prone to do this, however, and are known to be the type of person who wants to get the job done with as little waste of time as possible. Consequently, because of their desire to avoid unnecessary delay, they might create a situation that could cause them untold grief.

BEHAVIORAL OBJECTIVES

After a person has read this chapter, he should be able to:

1. Prepare a list of the various problems that accompany out-of-town trips for interscholastic athletic teams and explain how you would combat them.
2. Explain, the procedure in obtaining the parents permission to allow the student athlete to make an out-of-town trip to participate in an athletic contest.
3. Analyze the legal implication should an accident occur on an out-of-town athletic trip and negligence can be proven or cannot be proven.
4. Prepare an itinerary for an overnight trip for a football team and explain its purpose and who should receive the information.
5. Select and justify the best method of transportation for a basketball team that is playing a neighboring school. Explain why you chose this method.
6. Prepare in detailed form the complete arrangements for a basketball trip to the state tournament. This will be a three-day trip and you will be completely responsible for all details involving expenses, transportation and personnel.
7. Formulate an acceptable plan for the dress and manners which can in your opinion, and in view of present beliefs, be acceptable for both player and coaches while on trips representing the school. Analyze and explain your requirements.
18. Compile a list of the most desirable and least desirable aspects of lodging accommodations for an athletic team while on a three- or four-day trip.
19. Compile a detailed list of the important aspects of meals while playing away from home. Explain each item as it applies to your own philosophy or belief.
20. Explain the importance and philosophy of keeping things as routine as possible for the players while playing away from home.
21. Summarize and assess the importance of meals for the athletic team while on a trip which will involve eating several meals in restaurants.
22. Compile a complete list of basketball equipment that should be taken on a one-game trip for basketball.
23. Identify various ways in which athletic equipment may be handled on trips.
25. Explain why coaches should be concerned about legal implications resulting from injuries while on trips.
26. Select the best method of caring for basketball equipment while on trips.
27. Define liability, negligence, and tort. Explain, illustrate, and give an example of each.
28. Explain and illustrate how a coach can protect himself from suit involving transportation of athletes.
29. Explain how negligence must be proven.
30. Distinguish between liability and negligence and apply each to a particular situation.
31. Identify and explain several important items in planning for out-of-town athletic trips.

ACTIVITIES

1. Ask an insurance agent to talk to the class regarding insurance policies available for transportation of athletes.
2. Interview an athletic director about his insurance protection plan for the transportation of his athletic teams.
3. Talk with several coaches and solicit their feelings on how out-of-town trips should be handled regarding lodging, transportation, meals, and the dress of the athletes.
4. Invite a lawyer to talk to the class regarding legal liability for the school, athletic director, and coaches on the transportation of athletes.
5. Write a letter to the principal requesting the privilege of leaving school early to make an athletic trip to a neighboring school.
6. Arrange for a parent of a high school athlete to talk to the class and express his feelings regarding out-of-town athletic trips. Allow time for a question period.
7. Arrange for a high school principal to talk to the class regarding his problems in planning out-of-town athletic trips.
8. Plan a complete trip including the request from the principal, the parents permission, arranging for the transportation, meals, lodging, and all other details.
9. Talk with several high school athletes and obtain their opinions regarding the rules and regulations which should be established for out-of-town athletic trips.
10. Talk with several coaches and obtain their opinion as to what they think their responsibilities are regarding out-of-town trips.

SUGGESTED READINGS

1. Bucher, Charles: *Administration of Health and Physical Education Programs.* New York, Mosby, 1971.
2. Forsythe, Charles, and Keller, Irvin: *Administration of High School Athletics.* Englewood Cliffs, P-H, 1972.
3. George, Jack, and Lehmann, Harry: School Athletic Administration. New York Har-Row, 1966.
4. Grieve, Andrew: Legal aspects of transportation for athletic events. *Athletic Journal,* March, 1967.
5. Hixson, Chamber: *The Administration of Interscholastic Athletics.* New York, Lowell Pratt, 1967.
6. Hughes, Willam, French, Esther, and Lehsten, Nelson: *Administration of Physical Education for Schools and Colleges,* New York, Ronald, 1962.
7. Lankford, Sam: Problems of team travel. *Athletic Journal,* June, 1955.
8. Resick, Matthew, Siedel, Beverely, and Mason, James: *Modern Administrative Practices in Physical Education and Athletics. Reading,* A-W, 1970.
9. Uthoff, Harry: Planning your out-of-town trips. *Scholastic Coach,* March, 1959.
10. Veller, Don: Avoiding trip headaches. *Scholastic Coach,* March, 1964.
11. Voltmer, Edward and Esslinger, Arthur: *The Organization and Administration of Physical Education.* New York, Appleton, 1967.

CHAPTER 19

Athletic Awards

MEN HAVE CONTESTED for prizes from the time of the ancient Greeks and have vied for the approval of their fellow man from time immemorial. These awards have been the result of and in recognition of outstanding performances and have taken various forms. Since the beginning of history the intrinsic value of these awards has not always been in evidence and has not been a true measure of its importance. As an example, the ancient Greeks, centuries before Christ, awarded a chaplet or crown of laurel, sacred to Apollo as a symbol of victory. This was more important than any amount of wealth that could be given. Scipio Aemiduies placed crowns of roses upon the heads of the rough men of his Eleventh Legion in Carthage in 146 B.C. It was a symbol of great courage and fighting ability. His men faced death to win this coveted award. Voris[1] compares this attitude to our present award incentives. "The ancient Olympians considered the award of an olive branch as the greatest of all honors. Though simple and inexpensive, it was highly cherished by every recipient. It was the significance of the award, not its cost that counted."

Rulers, statesmen, and military leaders have long recognized that it is as important to reward the deserving as to punish the offenders. Queen Elizabeth I awarded the jeweled star and badge to Sir Francis Drake upon his return to England in 1580. Napoleon Bonaparte was well aware of the value of incentives and recognition and in 1802 founded his famous Legion of Honor to recognize outstanding civilian, as well as military achievement. This practice spread throughout the United States as its populace grew and it assumed its place with the other nations. Medals, cups, plaques, scrolls, certificates, cash, points, and trophies of various descriptions have been awarded to individuals and groups for varied and sundry achievements and accomplishments. These awards have expanded to other types of awards such as the various Hall of Fame awards given to outstanding figures in the world of sports.

Some of the reasons for presenting awards may be listed as follows:

1. To encourage students to maintain higher scholastic standings.
2. To keep students in training for the entire school year and not just for the particular sport season.
3. To place greater value on the award after it has been won.
4. To create a desire to excel.

Philosophy Regarding Awards

There are many individuals who are not in favor of athletic awards. These critics feel that awards are not educationally sound. They indicate that awards are bribes or crutches to increase participation on a false basis. They also feel that it

---

[1]Voris, Nick, "Freshman Football Incentives," *Scholastic Coach* (April, 1967), p. 44.

513

places a financial burden upon the athletic department and only a few individuals win the awards. These critics argue that students would participate in athletics even though awards were not given. They indicate that the offering of an award will have a tendency to color the philosophy of the athlete and dull his desire to compete for the thrill and love of participation. By offering awards, the athlete feels he is being bribed to participate and thereby acquires the feeling that the school owes him something, and he is doing the school a favor.

There are other individuals who applaud the award system and feel that it contributes to the overall school and academic program. These people feel, however, that strict controls on the giving of awards should be enforced and that the monetary value of the awards should be kept at a bare minimum. They feel that the participant receives his award on the value he obtains from participation and that this is a part of his education. There is a general belief among many people from schoolmen to the general laymen that if athletics is to be justified, it must be a part of the general, over-all educational program. Many coaches and athletic people are also in complete agreement with this philosophy. Forsythe[2] makes this general statement regarding the justification of giving awards:

> Participants should be the greatest recipients of benefits because of having had the chance to play. Anything they may think they have done for the school becomes insignificant in comparison with the opportunities and experiences they have had. When the athletic program is considered part of the general school curriculum, participants in it become regular class students in the sport con-

[2]Forsythe, Charles, and Keller, Irvin, *Administration of High School Athletics* 5th ed., (Englewood Cliffs, New Jersey, by permission of Prentice-Hall, Inc., 1972) , p. 217.

cerned. From that standpoint there is not much justification for rewarding them for their participation in an activity which benefits them.

Many individuals feel that the privilege of playing the sport and representing the school is reward enough; therefore, no other award should be given. The satisfaction the athlete receives from competing should be enough compensation making the award unnecessary. The enjoyment of playing the game should be sufficient, in the minds of the unbelievers.

The feeling that the athlete as well as the student participating in dramatics, band, and debate are contributing to the well being of the entire student body should be recognized and given an appropriate award indicative of the service they are rendering. This service should not go unnoticed and unappreciated and one way to show this appreciation is to give recognition in the form of a tangible award and not just a thank you. Awards are given in all walks of life as a symbol of achievement, and are a part of our culture, and as such, are justified.

Awards are symbols of achievement and should not be recognized as a prize. In Greek times, the olive wreath given to a victor was the most coveted award that could be attained by a Greek athlete. The importance of such an award was not its material value, but what is symbolized. The custom of awarding insignia or letters by school and college authorities to athletic teams in order to foster school spirit and personal pride in accomplishment and set up high ideals is almost universal. Because of the long tradition of granting awards and because of the fact that this is common practice in other activities of life, simple awards, mere symbols of achievement with little or no monetary value, seem to be justifiable. The award should be the type of award that will represent a certain achievement. There is a definite place for it in the school athletic program.

Athletic awards, therefore, can be more easily justified if they can be made part of the general award system. This giving of the athletic award should not be placed in competition with other awards in other school areas. Havel[3] has this comment:

Achievement in interscholastic athletics has traditionally been recognized through awarding some kind of recognition to successful participants. This practice when kept within reasonable bounds has merit; however, award systems have developed which go beyond the purposes originally intended. The administrator is confronted with developing an award granting procedure, both inexpensive and in keeping with recognized educational practice which rewards outstanding achievements. Ideally the major satisfactions derived from participation in interscholastic athletics come from the activity itself. Despite the efforts of educators to limit the attention devoted to school athletes, community tradition frequently contributes to an overemphasis in the practice of giving athletic awards.

The honoring of individual and team achievement can be accomplished satisfactorily by establishing wholesome approaches to interscholastic awards. Of primary consideration, any award given should be similar in nature to those provided for outstanding accomplishment in other school activities. If interschool athletics are to assume their rightful place in the educational picture, the administrator should maintain this kind of balance in recognizing successful performance.

Every school system, because of the personnel involved including school board members, administrators and coaches, will have a different philosophy regarding athletic awards. This philosophy changes with the times. Who is to say that the practice of giving awards will slacken or perhaps even disappear completely, not only in athletics but in other activities as well in the years to come.

A very interesting comment on the attitude of giving awards is made by Hixson:[4]

The basic policies and procedures to be used in the system of awards concern every administrator and athletic coach. The basic policy in the athletic department should be constant with the policy of the school concerning awards in all areas. Awards and recognition commensurate with the relative value of achievement help to keep athletics in educational perspective. Every effort should be made to prevent the awards from becoming *the* achievement. In fact, success in athletics must be measured in terms of educational goals and objectives for which athletics are sponsored. The student participates to learn, to grow, to develop, not to win a letter or trophy which is merely a symbolic memoir in recognition of his achievements.

Hughes, French, and Lehsten[5] present their views on the philosophy of giving awards in the following interesting statement:

The philosophy of the school toward athletics will have a marked influence on the award program. A basic question in the formulation of an award policy revolves around whether awards should be given as a recognition of achievement, participation as a team or squad member or whether it should be a combination of both. Few people will quarrel with the belief that participation in competitive sports is in itself a reward. On the other hand, there is no important reason why symbols and awards should not be

[3]Havel, Richard, and Seymour, Emery. *Administration of Health, Physical Education and Recreation for Schools* (New York, The Ronald Press, 1961) , p. 301.

[4]Hixson, Chalmer. *The Administration of Interscholastic Athletics* (New York, J. Lowell Pratt and Company, 1967) , p. 127.

[5]Hughes, William, French, Esther, and Lehsten, Nelson. *Administration of Physical Education—For Schools and Colleges*, 3rd ed. (New York, The Ronald Press Company, 1962) , p. 308.

given, to serve as prized mementoes of successful achievement.

Bucher[6] makes this statement of philosophy regarding awards:

There are arguments pro and con in respect to awards for intramural and extra-mural competition. Some of the arguments for awards are that they stimulate interest, serve as an incentive for participation and recognize achievement. Some of the arguments against awards are that they make for a more expensive program, a few individuals win most of the awards and that they are unnecessary since students would participate even if no awards were given, it is difficult to make awards on the basis of all factors that should be considered, and the incentive is artificial and the joy and satisfaction received are enough reward in themselves.

The conferring of awards is overdone in many cases. The practice of giving out valuable awards indiscriminately cannot be justified educationally or financially. The responsibility of the physical education department is to teach boys and girls to play for the "love of playing" without any thought of an award. The receiving of an award for achievement in athletics in the form of a ribbon, emblem, certificate, or simple medal fosters personal pride in accomplishment. Academically, we recognize students with high grades. We select valedictorians, and members of local and national honor societies. The human desire for recognition is most natural. This is as it should be because everyone realizes that praise will do more to bring out the best in a youngster than will criticism. Therefore, most people will agree that awards with certain restrictions are desirable and sometimes necessary. However, discretion is the better part of valor and there are those who are of the opinion these awards

should be curtailed in such a way that they do not have too great an influence on those people receiving them and that the monetary value of the award does not become the primary reason for winning it. Hixson[7] makes the following statement which symbolizes his thinking on the place of awards within the school system:

The awards are not something the school or community owes the athlete for his having participated. The award really symbolizes a debt which the athlete owes the school, community, parents and coaches for having provided the opportunity. While he is to be congratulated for having taken advantage of the opportunities, no one owes him anything for having done so. Local groups and individuals, well meaning in their generosity, often provide awards of excessive value. Since they are independent of the school they mistakenly believe they can provide any kind of gift or reward which they desire. Such groups need careful guidance and control since the rule defining amateur standing limits the material value of awards which can be made for athletic achievement. In addition, many state high school athletic associations stay within the spirit of the amateur rule by spelling out the nature and cost of awards regardless of sources which are approved for member schools. Athletes may not accept nor even be promised money or other valuable considerations for participating in interscholastic sports. College scholarships are acceptable; but, the amount of the scholarship must be paid by the donors directly to the college of choice and not to the athlete. The following are among the approved awards which have been used by various schools: banners, belt buckles, blankets, certificates, loving cups, miniature basketballs, baseballs, footballs, track shoes, keys, lapel pins, letters, lifetime complimentary tickets to home games, medals, numerals, plaques, ribbons, scrolls, sweaters, team pictures, tie clasps and trophies. In some states

[6]Bucher, Charles, *Administration of Health and Physical Education Programs Including Athletics,* (St. Louis, The C.V. Mosby Co., 1971), p. 215.

[7]Hixson, Chalmer, *The Administration of Interscholastic Athletics.*

nonapproved awards are also listed. In Ohio for example, the list exempts sweaters, jerseys, blazers, jackets, and any other type of wearing apparel or any award exceeding one dollar ($1.00) in value with the exception of those "athletic awards" on the approved list. Students may purchase their own letter sweaters, jackets and blazers if they so desire; but they cannot be given something materialistically useful for having participated in athletics.

There has always been a controversy on the practice of giving awards for athletics and it appears that this will always be true. The reason for this difference of opinion and attitude is not easily understood. The past few years, however, has brought about a decided change in the attitude of society in general in all areas of endeavor. No longer does the unselfish attitude exist among the young and many times the older people. People no longer want to work for the good of the cause. They either want money or recognition which in itself will lead to financial gains in one way or another. This attitude is not new to our present day society of young people. Unfortunately, it existed in the early fifties. The younger generation was beginning to place greater and greater emphasis and importance on recognition and the general feeling that nothing should be done without some sort of reward, either of a monetary nature or recognition in some form or another.

Scott[8] brought out this philosophy and attitude very ably back in 1951 when he made the following observation regarding giving awards for outstanding achievements. The same philosophy holds true today in many respects except that money is entering the picture with every passing day:

[8]Scott, Harry, *Competitive Sports in Schools and Colleges* (New York, Harper and Brothers, 1951), p. 404.

If there is any question as to the desirability of awarding outstanding achievement in any phase of educational endeavor, it concerns the proper use of incentives or devices. Sometimes, in order to stimulate individuals to engage in an educational activity, it seems expedient to set up a device or incentive designed to promote activity and through the activity, the desired learnings. Not infrequently, however, the device itself becomes more important to the learner than the lesson to be learned. If, therefore, the award for athletic prowess is the sole reason for participation, it could not be justified educationally even the activity was considerably stimulated. Athletes, particularly those in the individual and dual sports, are frequently stimulated to enter outside, open competition because of the long list of prizes that are offered. Because of these prizes, more events are entered than would ordinarily be the case. In the end, if the athlete is unusually competent, he may carry off considerable loot, which, if he is commercially minded, may be sold for cash. If not disposed of in this fashion, his trophies may be retained to tarnish and gather dust, but in any case to serve, along with his clippings, as a reminder of his former athletic prowess. Open competition, where numerous prizes are offered, should be discouraged as educationally unsound and dishonest to the extent that the athlete is exploited and bribed to enter a meet in which he would not otherwise compete. Fortunately, the award system in force in schools and colleges cannot be severely criticized as being either too elaborate or in bad educational taste. By and large an award for athletic achievement represents an earned distinction, the standards for which are jealously guarded and judiciously administered. Students wear their emblems with distinction and pride, and it is difficult to see how this phase of athletics would be materially improved if there were no awards at all.

There is a belief by many administrators and laymen that athletics are becoming a menace to education because of the many disruptions which take place because of them or as a result of them. To recognize this form of endeavor which many consider unsound educationally by awarding the participant is very difficult for these nonbelievers to justify. There are those people who would gladly abolish athletics completely and consequently the award that goes along with it. It would relieve them of many headaches and untold pressures brought about by student actions at games and the aftermath of closely contested games which has brought school officials and city police untold grief. On the other hand, there are many who fortunately realize the great educational benefits derived from a properly conducted athletic program in the schools. These people contend that athletics can be justified educational and that competition is the factor that has made America great. Who is right and who is wrong? Should the participants be awarded for athletic prowess as well as academic ability? What really is the place of awards in athletics?

Hughes and Williams,[9] suggested the following solution to the problem as far back as 1944 and perhaps it still could be the answer. He maintained at that time that:

> There is a middle ground between the policy of granting valuable awards and abolishing them entirely. Due to the long tradition of granting awards in the schools and due also to the fact that this is a common practice in other activities of life, simple awards—mere symbols of achievement with little or no monetary value—seem to be justifiable. However, as civilization progresses this practice may diminish, and finally disappear, not only in athletics but in other activities of life as well. Those in charge of athletics will miss a great opportunity to make a

valuable contribution to the education of boys and girls and at the same time set an example for society in general, if they do not show the way to 'that satisfaction which comes from doing a thing well,' a way that does not ask, 'What will you give me?' or 'How much do I get?'

There is no good reason, therefore, why awards should not be given providing they serve as mementoes of a satisfaction in achievement. Certain principles, however, are suggested as guides:

1. Athletic awards should have little or no intrinsic value; rather they should serve as symbols of achievement.
2. Major and minor award distinctions should be abolished.
3. Varsity awards should have as their base a series of awards for lesser achievement. All students should have the opportunity of attaining awards in all the sports of the curriculum.
4. Awards should come to mean more than athletic ability. Increasingly, they should stand as emblems of achievement which approach the objectives of all physical education.

Kinds of Awards

There are many kinds of awards. Usually the athlete's award consists of a school letter or emblem, a sweater, or a blanket in school colors. Often a certificate is given along with the letter indicating that the individual has won the award. This can be framed and preserved. Some schools give individual medals for members of a championship team or for winning or placing in a conference sport or meet. Meets sponsored by conference or tournament committees usually award individual or team trophies, ribbons, or prizes. There is usually a monetary limit, which is decided by the state association, placed on the award. It never has, however, been the practice of schools to give cash awards. It is the general practice for schools to limit the award given to the student to certificates, emblems, ribbons, or letters which have very little, if any, monetary value. The kinds of awards

⁹Hughes, William and Williams, Jesse. *Sports, Their Organization and Administration* (New York, A. S. Barnes and Co., 1944) , p. 331.

are governed by the cost most of the time and this is, of course, determined by the state associations in most states. Sometimes it can be determined by the local authorities. To offset this practice, policies should be determined to govern the cost of these rewards. The awards for all sports should be similar and the major/minor reward for different sports should be discouraged wherever possible. Expensive awards add to the "play for pay" incentive that the average high school athlete inherits quickly enough without this type of encouragement. Many schools will have an athletic council which will not only determine the kinds of awards to be given but also the cost. This is a good policy because it does much to promote fairness and equality in the determination of athletic awards. All policies determining awards must, of course, come under the close scrutiny of the state association. However, usually the state association is more interested in the cost of the award rather than the kind or type of award that is to be given. This council or governing body committee can be composed of students, coaches, faculty members, and even citizens of the community who are knowledgeable about school athletic amateur rules and policies and willing to contribute their services to a worthy cause.

There should be consideration given as to the number of awards one athlete may receive because if sweaters or jackets are given, one athlete might receive many and this would present a problem as far as money is concerned. George and Lehmann[10] present a sound argument for the presentation of awards:

> There is no educational logic to a plan that differentiates between different sports in the size or cost of awards. On the other hand, it would be reasonable

to develop a system of inserts (small insignia on initial award) to include with letter awards to designate each activity in this program.

George and Lehmann[11] are very emphatic in their belief that awards should be of little monetary worth and that uniform criteria should be established to determine how the award should be earned as indicated in the following statement:

> Regardless of the kinds of awards to be presented, great emphasis should be placed on their extrinsic, rather than their intrinsic worth. Their value as a symbol of achievement should be emphasized. This is a worthwhile ongoing project for the varsity club. In considering all aspects of the awards plan, the athletic council should decide whether or not to allow or encourage the presentation of special awards or insignia to members of championship teams. If authorized, such awards should not be in violation of other rules and policies that have been established.
>
> Consideration might be given to an all-sports or an all-activities award program. Such a plan would entail the establishment of a cumulative point system with credit recorded for participation and achievement in any and all recognized school activities, including the regular academic curricula. The setting up of a program of this kind would involve the establishment of various criteria and the use of weighted scores. One problem that would have to be faced is the amount of record keeping and clerical work that would be necessary. A plan of awards to students based on the complete academic and activities program may be very desirable, but considerable time and effort must go into the planning and implementation of such a project.

CAREER CERTIFICATE: Some schools will present a certificate to each graduating senior. This certificate can be presented in addition to the seasonal certificate which is earned in each particular sport. The certifi-

[10]George, Jack F., and Lehmann, Harry A., *School Athletic Administration* (New York, Harper and Row, 1966), p. 396.

[11]*Ibid.* p. 397.

Figure 111.

cate would be something the student could keep as a symbol of his achievement.

George and Lehmann[12] suggest:

These certificates may well be presented in attractive frames on high quality paper and should include the following:
1. The full name of the recipient.
2. The sports, years played, and rewards earned—e.g. varsity, junior varsity, freshman, captaincies, and any other special honors.
3. The date presented.
4. Signatures designated by the athletic council policy.

Figure 112. Reprinted with permission from Schaumbaurg High School, Shaumburg, Illinois.

[12]Ibid p. 398.

CERTIFICATES: An award certificate is given to each athlete winning a letter, numerals, or a service bar. A participation certificate is given nonaward winners.

SERVICE AWARDS: A service letter may be given a *senior* athlete who has been a full-time member of a squad for at least three years. To win this award he must not have earned a letter in that sport. The coach, in making this award, must judge the athlete to be a cooperative, contributing member of the group and that factors beyond the athlete's control prevented him from qualifying for an award in the usual manner. An athlete who was, by injury in the sport, prevented from participating fully during his senior year, may be considered for a service award. It should be strongly evident to the coach that the athlete would have qualified if no injury had occurred.

CERTIFICATES OF AWARDS: Certificates of award should be made out as follows and they should preferably be hand lettered.

1. On the first line put the recipient's name (no nickname) .
2. On the second line put the recipient's level of activity award as
   a. varsity letter
   b. a J/V letter
   c. a sophomore letter

Figure 113. Reprinted with permission from Weber Costello Company.

Figure 114. Reprinted with permission from James B. Conant High School.

d. a freshman numeral

For managers insert M.G.R. before the word letter or numeral.

3. On the third line put the sport. Do not put the level as that is taken care of on the second line.
4. On the fourth line put the year.
   a. for football and cross country the fall year only.
   b. for basketball, gymnastics, and wrestling put the two school years.
   c. for baseball, golf, tennis, and track put the spring year.

Figure 115. Reprinted with permission from Wheaton Central High School.

The individual coaches can arrange for the certificates to be properly inscribed and ready for the various signatures immediate-

ly at the end of the season's competition. The art department is usually willing to inscribe these if requested to do so sufficiently in advance. Head coaches should present all award recommendations from his sport to the athletic council. Therefore, the various coaches of a sport should make it a joint responsibility to see that the lists are on hand at the athletic council meeting.

The specific requirements for earning an award is a matter for the authorities in each school to decide. Every situation is different and the philosophy within one school system in regard to giving awards may differ completely with that of another school. However, the criteria for earning the various awards should be clearly stated so that each athlete may know just what he needs to do to earn a specific award. Consideration should be given to the athlete who has been injured.

STEPS IN THE IMPLEMENTATION OF AN AWARDS PROGRAM: George and Lehmann[13] suggest the following steps in implementing an awards program:

1. The establishment of criteria for earning an award
2. The selection of the specific award items to be presented
3. The dissemination of information to all those concerned.
4. The keeping of accurate participation records
5. The recommendations of the coach based upon participation and other established criteria
6. The approval of the director of athletics
7. The approval of the athletic council
8. The awards assembly

Award Trends and Guides

Every coach and athletic director has his ideas about awards. These are dependent upon school policies. However, trends

---

[13]George, Jack, and Lehmann, Harry A., *School Athletic Administration*, p. 399.

have developed over the past few years. Forsythe[14] states a few of them as follows:

1. State athletic associations are controlling awards more and more than in the past, at the request of member schools.
2. The National Federation of State High Schools is rendering valuable service in preventing promotions with unwarranted awards.
3. The distinction between major and minor sports with consequent direction in awards is diminishing.
4. Less costly awards are being presented in many schools.
5. Awards programs for all school activities are being combined in their presentations.
6. There is increasing realization that an athletic or activity award is given to a student as a result of his full school citizenship as well as for his athletic prowess.

Figure 116. Reprinted with permission from Conant High School.

Havel[15] makes the following suggestion as to the trends or guides which can be used in the establishment of policies for

[14]Forsythe, Charles, The Athletic Director's Handbook (Englewood Cliffs, New Jersey by permission of Prentice-Hall, Inc., 1956), p. 25.

[15]Havel, Richard, and Seymour, Emery, Administration for Health, Physical Education and Recreation for Schools, p. 302.

determining or administering of athletic awards.

Acceptable forms of acknowledgement may be developed in a variety of ways. The most common practice is to award a letter for outstanding achievement in interscholastic athletics. In some school systems, this may be accompanied by a certificate appropriately inscribed identifying the accomplishment of the individual. It has been found that by giving awards at assembly programs or at annual banquets, they are more meaningful to the recipients and allow students and other interested parties to express appreciation. The practice of presenting costly tokens of achievement should be carefully reviewed by the administrator and his staff before instituting this approach as a matter of policy. In developing any award system for interscholastic athletics, requirements of an award should be carefully defined for each activity. These will vary from one situation to another and are usually based upon percentage of total time played in team sports, points scored or places attained in individual or dual competition, and consecutive years of participation. Ordinarily, requirements are flexible and serious consideration is given to individual coaches, recommendations.

Administrating awards for interscholastic athletics should be done in accord with clearly established policy understood by both staff personnel and the student body at large.

Hughes, French and Lehsten[16] suggests the following principles which can be used as guides in the granting of awards:

A number of states limit the monetary value of an award. Other states permit the granting of a letter only or one sweater, jacket, or other award of similar monetary value.

The following principles are recommended as guides in the granting of awards:

1. Athletic awards should be symbols of

[16]Hughes, William, French, Esther and Lehsten, Nelson, Administration of Physical Education—For Schools and Colleges, p. 308.

achievement rather than gifts of high intrinsic value.

2. There should be no distinction between varsity letter awards in terms of major and minor sports distinction. Such a classification of athletic activities is outmoded and educationally unsound.

3. Every student participating in athletics should have the opportunity to attain some kind of award.

4. Varsity awards should have as their base a series of awards which identify a lesser level of achievement.

5. Awards should come to mean more than recognition of a high level of performance in sports. Increasingly, they should stand as symbols of achievement which approach the objectives of physical education.

6. The decision of who should receive an award should not rest with one individual.

7. The method used for determining awards should be clearly spelled out in writing, and should be made known to the participants and the student body through student handbook or other media within the school.

8. The awards policies should be developed by a representative group composed of coaches, school administration, and representatives of the student body.

Even though the system of awards for outstanding achievements has its problems,

it has survived for many years and if kept under reasonable control can result in many benefits. One of the main problems is allowing the system to get out of hand to the point where the "tail is wagging the dog." To avoid this the administrator must keep a level head and develop an award granting procedure which will be in keeping with the educational objectives of the school. There is nothing wrong with rewarding outstanding achievement whether it is in athletics, dramatics, or forensics, if the major satisfactions from receiving these awards is of an educational nature. By giving athletic awards it indicates and establishes athletics as a part of the educational curriculum. The wise administrator should attempt to maintain a balance of importance in all areas of extracurricular participation.

Figure 118. Reprinted with permission from Wheeling High School.

Purchase of Awards

All awards should be purchased through the regular channels and have official sanction by the proper school authorities. Most reliable sporting goods companies can supply these awards. It may be more convenient to identify with one specific company because then the letters, emblems, and

Figure 117. Reprinted with permission from Weber Costello Company.

other awards are made according to specifications. This simplifies the procedure because these specifications are kept on file where they are readily accessible if needed on short notice. Sweaters or jackets can also be ordered through sporting goods companies on bid orders. However, most schools arrange to have these items handled by local merchants. The student can order his own sweater or jacket himself and deal directly with the local merchant. He can also arrange to have the letters placed on the sweater or jacket. Forsythe suggests that usually one or two companies will supply all the awards.[17]

Financing the Awards Program

Financing an elaborate awards system can require a great deal of money. This fact needs to be kept uppermost in the minds of those individuals who are given the responsibility of making the decisions and establishing the policies as to the type of award system to be used in any particular school system. For instance, it is ridiculous to spend money for awards and go without other things within the program that are sorely needed such as equipment, adequate transportation, etc. It would be much better to use discretion on the giving of awards and spend the money on those items that are needed the most.

George and Lehmann[18] suggest that regardless of awards to be presented, great emphasis should be placed on their extrinsic rather than their intrinsic worth:

> The cost of individual awards is sometimes limited by either state association regulations or local policy. School letters, monograms, emblems, or class numerals made of felt or chenille are the most common types of awards used in the in-

[17]Forsythe, Charles, *The Athletic Director's Handbook*, p. 20.

[18]George, Jack F. and Lehmann, Harry A., *School Athletic Administration*, p. 395.

terscholastic athletic program. They are attractive and relatively inexpensive.

In many schools it is customary to accompany the letter award with a certificate, signed by the coach, athletic director, and principal, on which is noted the sport and the year presented. The exact designation of those who are to sign these certificates is a matter of local policy and may include any or all of the above and/or the director of physical education, chairman of the athletic council, superintendent of schools, and chairman of the board of education.

The presentation of such relatively expensive award items as sweaters, jackets, monogrammed blankets, and trophies is not uncommon in states where the maximum amount to be paid is not limited by the state association in control of the interschool program. However, if money is not a problem, an award system which allows each participant to gain some recognition is desirable and should be given serious consideration.

There are, however, many schools that experience serious difficulty in financing an awards program in which expensive awards are given for each sport. To offset this problem, many schools have devised and adopted a system that is not as expensive, yet gives recognition to the recipients. Even the practice of awarding a letter for each sport can be expensive. This expense can be avoided by using the following plan which in essence allows a letter winner to receive only one letter throughout his high school career in a particular sport. Each time he earns a letter after the initial one, he is given a bar which is placed on the letter and this designates that he has earned two letters in that particular sport. Under this plan it is possible for him to earn one letter and three bars which indicates that he is a four-letter winner. Each sport is identified by a small figure which is placed on the letter itself and symbolizes the sport it represents. This plan is used for each sport including freshman, sophomore, junior varsity, and varsity awards. Along with any award, the athlete is given a certificate representing his achievement. The amount of money saved over a period of years is considerable, yet the athlete receives recognition of his accomplishments.

If there is a necessity to keeping expenses down, Souza[19] has the following idea:

> Instead of giving out block letters at the freshman, sophomore and junior varsity level for each sport a boy could receive one freshman, sophomore junior varsity, and varsity letter, no matter how many sports he participated in. If an athlete would have lettered in more than one sport at the same level of competition he would receive a certificate denoting his achievement. Varsity members would receive emblems in addition to the certificates.

Every coach and athletic director must be alert to the possibility of "well-wishers" who unknowingly may be responsible for an athlete becoming ineligible by breaking a rule. These people mean well but are uninformed as to the regulations or rules under which the athlete must participate. A good example of how this can happen is given by Forsythe[20] in the following statement:

> The problem of awards from outside sources confronts schoolmen frequently, especially when a high school team has had an outstanding season as measured by number of games won or lost or championships annexed. Teams often are feted on numerous occasions. Unless the situation is watched, some well-intentioned, community-minded individ-

ual, or groups will want to present team members with awards having intrinsic values greater than school or state association regulations allow. They seem to think that the boys must be given something for what they have done. Recognition of honor brought to their school or to themselves may be all right if kept within reason. Rewards for having done that which was a benefit and pleasure for them to do are not only unnecessary but unjustifiable.

Fortunately, the state association has provided a great deal of help to the coach or athletic director who after a successful season has the difficult problem of turning down offers from appreciative fans of watches, rings, sweaters, etc. Many of these fans just do not understand why they cannot show their appreciation in this manner.

Forsythe[21] has suggested how this can be avoided:

> State athletic association regulations relative to awards are helpful limitations to which local school administrators may refer when community interests desire to give excessive gifts to team members. It behooves schoolmen to have their local athletic and other activity award policies well understood by student bodies and public alike. Publicizing them in advance will be an effective means by which the athletic program of a school may be kept in its proper place in relation to the other educational phases of the curriculum. It will help keep athletics on an even keel no matter whether a school team wins or loses all its games or finishes first or last in its city, league section or state standings.

It is of extreme importance that the awards given to athletes be within the state limitations concerning the expense of the award given. This is also true of awards in other areas of extracurricular activities. Awards need not be expensive to be meaningful. Expensive awards in any area are to

[19]Souza, George, "A Unique Award System that is Economical," *The Athletic Journal* (October, 1967) , p. 38.

[20]Forsythe, Charles, and Keller, Irvin, *Administration of High School Athletics*, 5th ed., Englewood Cliffs, New Jersey: by permission of Prentice-Hall, Inc., 1972, p. 218.

[21]*Ibid.*

be discouraged. Havel[22] states:

> . . . where outside groups wish to honor individuals or teams, they should be consoled on the award policies of the school system. Well-meaning community groups can serve as valuable sources of encouragement for the interscholastic program if fully oriented to the purposes and outcomes to be derived from inter-school competition. In cases where private groups voluntarily wish to expend large sums of money for awards, the position of the administrator becomes a delicate one. He must maintain good public relations with outside groups and, at the same time, exert every effort to keep the interscholastic program in its proper perspective relative to the total educational pattern of the community.

Requirements for Letter and Emblem Awards

Once the type of award has been determined by the administration, the method of selecting the award winners should be considered. Many schools depend entirely upon the coach for determining these award winners. There may be some merit to this plan because certainly the coach is in the best position to honestly appraise an athlete's contribution to the success of a team. The coach, however, lets himself in for a great amount of second guessing and criticism if he does not establish, in advance, what he considers award requirements. If this is done, each athlete on the squad will know exactly on what basis he is competing for an award. If this is not done, the charge of favoritism is apt to be raised over and over again by athletes who did not receive awards. The most popular plan combines the coach's judgement and the compliance with some preestablished participation requirements.

Many schools use participation as their

main criteria in the selection of award winners. Under this system, records are kept of the time the athlete has played in a contest, and the points he has accumulated. An athlete must meet the requirements to win a letter. This plan limits the number of letters given. The success of this plan depends on the coach's ability to establish fair standards upon which a letter may be won.

Most schools have set up a point system of some kind as the basis for the awarding of letters. Usually, this involves some bookkeeping but seems to be the only fair and logical way of awarding the letter. Many schools that use a system that is based primarily on game participation make some provision for an athlete who is a member of a squad for three or four years, and never qualifies for an award. This athlete, who has been loyal for all four years, has attended practice faithfully, and qualified for an award in all ways except participation, is given a service award, usually a standard major letter. While this practice takes place in many schools, some coaches feel that this is unfair to the athlete who has earned his letter through participation. However, there are others who favor this practice, believing that it gives a deserving athlete a chance to earn a letter.

Usually this proposal does not meet with any real criticism if the athlete in question is a deserving athlete and well liked in every way. It is the border-line case that will cause the coach concern. The coach, more than any one else, will know much more about the athlete and be able to justify giving the letter to the athlete.

Award requirements and methods have been devised to suit the opinions and needs of the local administrators and coaches. Award systems need to be modified according to the area in which the school is located, the size of the school, and the state

_____
[22]Havel, Richard and Seymour, Emery, *Administration for Health, Physical Education and Recreation for Schools*. p. 301.

laws governing award presentations. The awarding of letters is practiced in almost all schools, and the requirements differ in every school. This is why there are many inequities in the granting of athletic awards. However, there should be some degree of uniformity. This is understandably difficult but Hixson[23] has suggested several means by which this can be done in the following statement:

> In many schools the coaching staff selects the recipients of the various athletic awards. Granting a voice to others concerned will strengthen the process of selection. The more democratic approach helps to prevent inequities which might be caused by personal prejudices and personality clashes. Recipients should be approved by teammates, coaches, director of athletics, school athletic committee and finally the principal. A well-administered system of awards symbolizing educational achievement should encourage continued participation in interscholastic athletics.

As previously mentioned, there are many requirements for earning an award. Hixson[24] makes the following points and suggestions to sum up the criteria for the granting of awards.

1. Participation measured by appearances in a specified number of quarters, matches or minutes of play
2. Athletic skill as measured by the number of points scored for the team in dual meets or championship meets
3. Regularity of attendance at practices
4. Number of years of service to the team
5. Compliance with established rules of training
6. Extent of efforts to improve
7. Contributions to team morale
8. Sportmanship
9. School citizenship
10. Return of all school equipment

It is imperative that every prospective award winner be fully aware of the basic requirements to earn an award. These requirements could be the result of discussions or rules established by an athletic council made up of different personnel within the school system. It should be presumed that all coaches will base their judgement relative to awards on a high plane and that every attempt will be made to confirm the principle that receiving the school award is a great honor and privilege for the recipients.

Forsythe[25] has suggested a definite procedure that can be followed to assure uniformity as well as providing the necessary regulations for giving awards. These rules should be available from the director of athletics. Coaches should, prior to the season, secure a copy of these regulations.

1. At an early season practice session the coach should advise all team candidates of the award policy of the school.
2. Records of the amount of competition of each individual should be kept if that is a requisite on which awards are granted.
3. Recommended list of those to receive the school award should be prepared by the coach and submitted to the athletic director and principal.
4. The athletic director and the coach should confer with the principal in order to check on school citizenship, attitude, character and scholastic standings of those recommended.
5. Combined recommendation should be submitted to the athletic council or board of control for final approval.
6. Letter awards should be made at a school assembly as near the end of semester as possible.

There seems to be two systems of giving awards in use, namely: (1) whereby the athletic department and school administration establish the standards that every let-

[23]Hixson, Chalmer, *The Administration of Interscholastic Athletics,* p. 129.
[24]*Ibid.,* p. 128.

[25]Forsythe, Charles, *Administration of High School Athletics,* 3rd ed (Englewood Cliffs, New Jersey, by permission of Prentice-Hall, 1959) p. 234.

SAMPLE

BALLOT FOR DETERMINING BASKETBALL AWARD

Give each boy a grade from zero to one hundred for each category

NAME	IMPROVEMENT			TEAMWORK			SPORTSMANSHIP			TRAINING			TOTAL
	40%			20%			20%			20%			
	40%			20%			20%			20%			
	40%			20%			20%			20%			
	40%			20%			20%			20%			
	40%			20%			20%			20%			
	40%			20%			20%			20%			
	40%			20%			20%			20%			
	40%			20%			20%			20%			
	40%			20%			20%			20%			
	40%			20%			20%			20%			
	40%			20%			20%			20%			
	40%			20%			20%			20%			
	40%			20%			20%			20%			
	40%			20%			20%			20%			
	40%			20%			20%			20%			
	40%			20%			20%			20%			
	40%			20%			20%			20%			
	40%			20%			20%			20%			
	40%			20%			20%			20%			
	40%			20%			20%			20%			
	40%			20%			20%			20%			

Figure 119.

ter winner must meet, and (2) whereby the individual coach establishes the standards that he feels are fair and justifiable.

Usually the requirements for letter awards are well defined, although in some schools it is left pretty much up to the coach to establish rules and regulations which may be vague and subject to change from year to year. Voltmer and Esslinger[26] verify this belief in the following statement:

Recommendations for awards are initiated by the coaches, usually on the basis

[26]Voltmer, Edward and Esslinger, Arthur. *The Organization and Administration of Physical Education* (New York, Appleton Century Crofts, 1967), p. 291.

SAMPLE

BALLOT FOR DETERMINING THE FOOTBALL AWARD

NAME	ABILITY			COOPERATION			SPORTMANSHIP			HABITS		TOTAL
	30%			30%			20%			20%		
	30%			30%			20%			20%		
	30%			30%			20%			20%		
	30%			30%			20%			20%		
	30%			30%			20%			20%		
	30%			30%			20%			20%		
	30%			30%			20%			20%		
	30%			30%			20%			20%		
	30%			30%			20%			20%		
	30%			30%			20%			20%		
	30%			30%			20%			20%		
	30%			30%			20%			20%		
	30%			30%			20%			20%		
	30%			30%			20%			20%		
	30%			30%			20%			20%		
	30%			30%			20%			20%		
	30%			30%			20%			20%		
	30%			30%			20%			20%		
	30%			30%			20%			20%		
	30%			30%			20%			20%		
	30%			30%			20%			20%		
	30%			30%			20%			20%		
	30%			30%			20%			20%		
	30%			30%			20%			20%		
	30%			30%			20%			20%		

Give each boy a grade from zero to one hundred for each category

Figure 120.

of the established requirements. Generally, the coach's recommendations are acted upon by the athletic director or athletic council or both. The awards are ordinarily presented at some ceremony, such as a banquet or student assembly.

Each sport will have different requirements, but most every one has established basic or minimum requirements. Hixson[27]

[27]Hixson, Chalmer, *The Administration of Interscholastic Athletics,* p. 128.

has made the following suggestions regarding criteria for earning an award. These are considered basic:

> Participation in a particular sport is usually the basic requirement for selection of the recipient of an award. Some schools, however, use an all-sports award while still others present awards for participation in all activities in the school in which interscholastic sports are only one. Additional awards may be for captains, seniors, managers, athletc council trainers, cheerleaders, special service and honorary recognition. It is difficult, indeed, to measure the extent of achievement in educational objectives and goals. Criteria which reflect them are often used in the selection of students to receive awards.

Resick, Siedel, and Mason[28] have also stated that the granting of awards should not be haphazard, and that a definite basis must be established and followed. They have suggested the following criteria:

1. Amount of participation
2. Recommendations of the athletic coach
3. Recommendations of the athletic coach and school officials
4. Point system for participation in an individual sport.
5. Point system based on an accumulation of points for participation in more than one sport

All these requirements, of course, are based upon the student's ability to meet the academic, social, and other qualifications set up for all other students.

Scropas[29] sums this up very ably when he suggests that:

> There is more to winning a varsity sport letter than merely playing-time requirements. He feels that a participant should

---

[28]Resick, Matthew and Seidel, Beverly and Mason, James, *Modern Administrative Practices in Physical Education and Athletics* (Reading, Mass. Addison-Wesley Publishing Co., 1970), p. 133.

[29]Scropas, Ted, "New Criteria for Letter Awards," *The Athletic Journal* (April, 1949), p. 6.

be required to have an average class standing, be a disciplined follower of coaching principles, and to exact upon himself the rules of courteous player conduct. He advocates two awards, varsity and junior varsity. Point accumulations decide the candidate's claim for the award. Particular emphasis is put on the fact that a variable number 2 points can be earned with better average in grade ability, adherence to training rules, and contest conduct. The better an individual's attitude toward the sport the more limited his playing time requirements. Participation prerequisites can readily be doctored to suit any major activity difference of the season without upsetting the program. Letters are awarded from point accumulations in accordance with the following criteria: (1) Scholarship (2) Sportmanship (3) Training (4) and Participation.

Award Systems

There are many award systems used in schools throughout the United States. To say that one system is better than another would be foolhardy because one system may be ideally suited to one situation and would be a complete failure in another. It, therefore, depends on the judgement of the people in control of the particular school system to determine the type of award system to use. A number of these systems will be presented, but it must be remembered that the people within each community through their respective and duly-elected school board representatives will determine to what extent certain emphasis should be placed on the many different activities within the school. Thus, the philosophy determining the type of athletic program the school has is directly in control of the citizens of the community. This philosophy will affect the emphasis which is placed on the importance of extracurricular activities within the school program. As a result, the types of awards and the emphasis placed upon them will be differ-

Figure 121.

Figure 124. Reprinted with permission from Wheeling High School.

Figure 122.

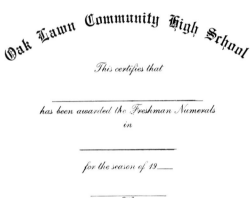

Figure 125. Reprinted with permission from Oak Lawn High School.

Figure 123. Reprinted with permission from Weber Costello Company.

ent in each individual school.

For example, in a study of twenty-five schools with enrollment of 140 to 1350, it was found that the following requirements were most common for the awarding of baseball letters.

1. Regular attendance
2. Eligibility
3. Cooperation with the team and coach
4. Responsibility for equipment
5. Obey all training rules

6. Gentlemanly conduct necessary
7. No letters given unless the coach recommended the letter
8. Dismissal from the squad results in forfeiture of the letter
9. Major letters are eight inches in size
10. Most schools issue one letter per year and then award inserts for subsequent sports.

The study also revealed striking differences in the common requirements for winning a major letter in varsity competition for basketball.

Basketball requirements:

1. Participate in 50 percent of the scheduled games.
2. Participate in 60 percent of games.
3. Participate in 40 percent of the quarters.
4. Participate in 33⅓ percent of quarters.
5. Participate in twenty quarters.
6. One school gave eight letters if the team lost out in the regional tournament, twelve letters if the team went to the state, and others based upon success of the season.
7. One school required basketball players not out for football to participate in cross country two nights a week.

The following plans for awarding of letters are typical.

Plan I

1. ATTENDANCE: The athlete must attend every practice and every game unless he is excused by the coach.
2. TRAINING: The boy must abide by the rules established by the coach.
3. ELIGIBILITY: The eligibility is to be maintained from week to week and is governed by the state association.
4. COACH'S RATING: This rating is based on loyalty, honesty, cooperation, progress, and general attitude.
5. GAME PARTICIPATION: Basketball—25

percent of all quarters played.

6. OTHER METHODS: In case of an undefeated team, all members of the varsity squad are given an award regardless of game participation. Also, any senior who has not met the game requirements is awarded a letter if he meets all other requirements.

Plan II
Varsity Basketball Award Requirements

1. To complete the season as a member of the squad, a player must have played one half of the total game quarters plus one quarter. (Quarters waivered by injuries under the discretion of the coach and athletic director.)
2. If an athlete has been on basketball squads for at least three consecutive years (injuries waivered) and has completed each season, he may be eligible for an award by playing in one fourth of the total game quarters during his senior year.
3. All letter awards are subject to the laws and by-laws of the varsity "A" club.
4. The following rules must be observed during the season:
   a. Hours are as follows: on weekdays, at home by 10:00 P.M. and in bed by 10:30 P.M.; on Saturday, at home by 11:30 P.M. and in bed by 12:00 A.M.; and on Sunday at home by 10:30 P.M. and in bed by 11:00 P.M.
   b. To attire in sport coat and slacks or suits for away games. At home games attire in clothing as good or better than worn at school.
   c. To sit in a group at both home and away games during the sophomore games.
   d. No smoking or drinking.
5. To follow rules set by the coach:
   a. To exhibit school and team spirit

and attitude (all for one, one for all attitude.)

    b. To attend practices without excuses.

    c. To attend all sophomore games.

    d. To shout, cheer, and yell at all pep rallies.

6. To be scholastically eligible. Two straight weeks on a failing list automatically drops the player from the squad.

7. To try and stay out for track and baseball unless excused by the head coach.

8. To respect all equipment and pay for some if lost or stolen.

Plan III

Requirements for earning varsity and junior varsity letter:

1. Must play in one fourth of all quarters.

2. Must meet letter club constitution requirements.

3. Must have coach's sanction.

4. Must forfeit right to letter if in trouble concerning school discipline.

Plan IV

Awards are based purely upon the appraisal of each athlete by the coach and principal, by the following standards:

1. SPORTSMANSHIP: a student, to win an athletic insignia, must maintain an attitude of true sportsmanship throughout the season.

2. SCHOLARSHIP: to receive an athletic insignia, a student must have been passing all subjects at the end of each week during that sport season.

3. ATTENDANCE AT PRACTICE AND GAMES: to receive an athletic award, a student must not have more than three unexcused absences from practice during the season.

4. PLAYING TIME: an athlete must have played at least the majority of quarters of all games.

Plan V

This plan would be based on a point system with a certain number of points given for winning, for participation, and for playing time.

1. PARTICIPATION: a limited number of points could be earned and would be based on the number of games scheduled in a particular sport. It would vary with the sport.

2. MINUTES PLAYED: the athlete would receive one point for every minute played with five hundred points being the maximum number to be earned.

3. VICTORY POINTS: the athlete would receive bonus points for playing on a winning team.

4. SCHOLASTIC POINTS: the athlete receives points for letter grades in subjects. D = O to A = 25 points.

Plan VI

1. Regular attendance at practice.

2. Cooperation with the coach and fellow teammates.

3. Loyalty to the coach, school, and community.

4. Industry—a willingness to work in practice and games.

5. Obedience to all training rules set up by the coach.

6. Participation in one half of the total quarters played.

7. A letter may be earned by participating in basketball for four years, if, in the judgement of the coaches, he is worthy of it, although he may not have played in the required quarters.

8. Good citizenship must be practiced at all times, both on and off the floor.

9. Final approval of all awards must come from the school administration.

Plan VII

Based on point system. Basketball awards are based on a twenty-game schedule.

1. Six points given for each quarter of play, making a total of 480 points.
2. Twenty-five points awarded if the athlete is eligible all season.
3. Twenty-five points for cooperation with the team and coach.
4. Twenty-five points for regular attendance at practice, making a total of 655 points possible.
5. In order to receive a letter, a total of 400 points is necessary.

The coach should reserve the right to withhold a major or minor letter from any athlete who does not conform to the accepted pattern of behavior. These behavior problems may be any one of the following: (1) poor practice habits, (2) a disciplinary case during the season, (3) missing practice sessions, (4) exhibiting poor sportsmanship, (5) breaking training rules, (6) creating problems in school, and (7) not turning in all equipment at the end of the season.

A Unique Award System Example

There are many award systems that can be used to promote, recognize, and reward excellence of performance in areas of the school curriculum in which the student demonstrates effort to pursue a laudable program of action which is above and beyond the required school program. The system described here includes various extracurricular activities and does not include only athletics but gives equal stress to all activities.

The performance of each student in each activity is evaluated by the faculty sponsor on a scale running from zero through the maximum number of points allotted for the activity. Evaluations of performance which grant to a student a number of points equal to or in excess of one-half the maximum number of points which can be earned in a particular activity are recorded and considered cumulative through the four grades of the school. A certificate of award suitable for framing is then presented to each person earning cumulative points.

As symbols of recognition of achievement, the award system embraces the use of class numerals, a school letter, a school pin, a school crest, and appropriate bars for the letter and pin. Students qualify for awards by earning point totals as follows:

Class Numerals	25
First Major Award	50
Second Major Award	100
Third Major Award	150
Fourth Major Award	200

Each subsequent major award requires an additional fifty points.

In all sports, an athlete must satisfy the following in order to be considered for points at any level:

1. complete the season (unless injury prevents this)
2. attend all practices except when properly excused
3. attend all scheduled contests unless properly excused
4. follow the established training rules for his sport

At the conclusion of the season, the coach of each sport awards points to each member of the squad. This includes managers, trainers, and statistician. Points on the awards form are filled out, signed by the coach, and handed to each individual on the squad. A duplicate copy of School Award Points Record—Cumulative Points Form is then completed, showing the list of all individuals who are to receive points.

The points earned by each individual are turned in to the athletic director.

After examination of the various methods of giving awards and of the requirements that must be met before the award can be given, it can be seen that one plan will not work for every school. The system used must meet the situation and be one that will satisfy the requirements for the one and only situation.

Whether awards of any kind should be given is purely conjecture. It depends upon the people in charge as to whether they give awards or whether they do not, the kind they give, and the method in which they are given. The monetary value to a large extent will be determined by state and federal regulations. This varies from state to state but the National Federation of State High Schools has attempted to unify the system of giving awards.

Scott[30] makes the following summarizing statement regarding awards:

> Much has been said or written in the last few years concerning the matter of awards in connection with the program of competitive sports. Since the beginning of civilization, awards have figured prominently not only in athletics but also in other types of competitive enterprises. In pointing out the evils of awards, opponents of the custom find ready reference to the unsavory practices of antiquity which rewarded the successful athlete so well that a single victory or superior performance might provide him with sufficient wealth to maintain him in luxury for the remainder of his life.

Suggested Basis for Awards in Each Sport

Baseball

Major "G" —Must engage in one half of the league games. Pitchers must pitch twenty-one in-

nings or pitch and win one complete league game.

Minor "G" —All members of the varsity squad who did not qualify for the major award. Sophomore squad members meet the same requirements as the varsity on a proportional basis.

Numerals
Major —All athletes must have played in at least two games and have met the rating chart requirements.

Basketball

Major "G" —Any athlete who has been recommended by the coach and has been in one half of the regular scheduled games.

Minor "G" —Any member of the varsity squad who has not fulfilled the major requirements. Sophomore squad members meet the same requirements as the varsity.

Numerals
Major —Must have met the rating chart requirements.

Cross County

Major "G" —Must be a member of the team that wins three meets or place first, second, or third in three meets. Must win a first place in a meet or count in the team's total points in one half of dual meets. Finish in the first fifteen of the suburban league meet or qualify in the district meet.

Minor "G" —Any athlete who has been a contestant in one half of

[30]Scott, Harry, *Competitive Sports in Schools and Colleges*, p. 403.

dual sophomore and varsity meets.

Numerals

Major —Must have met the rating chart requirements.

Football

Major "G" —Engaged in one half of the regular scheduled games or recommended by the head coach.

Minor "G" —Any member of the varsity squad who has not fulfilled the major requirements.
J. varsity and sophomore squads who have met the requirements set up on the rating chart.

Numerals

Major —Must have met the rating chart requirements.

Golf

Major "G" —Engage as regular members of the varsity team. Qualifies as a member on the championship team through excellent medal play in league or district tournaments.

Minor "G" —Sophomore squads who have engaged in interscholastic competition.

Numerals

Major —Must have met the rating chart requirements.

Gymnastics

Major "G" —Must engage in one half of the dual meets. The gymnast must score a total of fifteen or more points in dual meet competition. He may not have more than three unexcused absences.

Minor "G" —Sophomore squad members meet the same requirements as the Varsity on a proportional basis.

Numerals

Major —Must have met the rating chart requirements.

Tennis

Major "G" —Must be a member of the varsity squad and win at least one match. Qualify in the district or league meet.

Minor "G" —Sophomore squad members same as varsity except district meet.

Numerals

Major —Must have met the rating chart requirements.

Track

Major "G" —Must earn ten points in individual events, five of these must be a first place. Can be a member of a relay team in lieu of an individual first place—may substitute four team first places. In a major track event (5 teams or more) he can qualify by earning one point or fraction thereof.

Minor "G" —Frosh-soph are awarded letters on the same basis as the varsity Frosh-soph competition.

Numerals

Major —By competing in freshman or sophomore meets and meeting the rating chart requirements.

Wrestling

Major "G" —Engage in one half of the matches and win one half of the contests. Engage in one half of the league contests and win one half of them. Qualify for the state meet.

Minor "G" —Members of the varsity squad who did not qualify. Frosh-soph who qualify on the same basis as varsity with the exception of the state meet.

Numerals

Major —Must have met the rating chart requirements.

All awards must be approved by the coaches and the athletic director.

Any athlete who has been reported breaking training rules as set up in the letter sent to his parents will be investigated. He can be dropped from the squad for the balance of the season and denied his award. He can return to the sports program the following season providing his case has been reviewed by the coaching staff and one of his parents.

Suggested Girls' Varsity Award Requirements

BADMINTON: Must play in three fourths of the total game schedule and satisfactorily meet the attendance requirements for practice as established by the coach.

BASKETBALL: Must play in one fourth of the total quarters played by the team and meet the attendance requirements for practice as established by the coach.

BOWLING: Must maintain an average of 100 or more points, attend all practice sessions unless excused by the coach, and participate in all scheduled meets regardless of team level.

SOFTBALL: Must have participated in at least one half of all scheduled games and be recommended by her coach.

SWIMMING: Must accumulate points totaling $1\frac{1}{2}$ of dual meets, swim in 80 percent of the varsity meets and satisfy the attendance requirements for practice as determined by the coach.

TENNIS: Must play in at least one half of the varsity matches or place in the conference or district meet and satisfactorily meet the attendance requirements for practice as determined by the coach.

TRACK AND FIELD: Must score a total of ten points in meet competition or to place (1st thru 5th) in the district or conference meet.

VOLLEYBALL: Must participate in three fourths of all scheduled games and satisfy all requirements for attendance at practice as established by the coach.

The Meaning of the Award to the Athlete

The giving of awards and the philosophy behind the athletic program within the school coincide very closely with each other. Many coaches state their philosophy clearly to their athletes and insist that they adhere to it strictly. These coaches attempt to build a sense of belonging and bring a feeling of pride to be representing the school and the community. The coach attempts to instill in the players the philosophy behind the entire athletic program so that the athlete will be proud to receive his award and wear it knowing that others know how much he sacrificed to obtain it. This is a day and an age when the youth of this country is confused. He needs something concrete on which to base his judgments. He needs to know that there is no easy way out as far as athletics in concerned. He needs to have definite facts placed before him so that he can formulate a pattern of living which will allow him to be a part of the team. He needs something to lean on to assure him that his judgments are correct in contrast to those of his friends who are not members of teams and are not in favor of his views. He needs to feel that the award he is striving for is worth the sacrifice and worth the effort he is putting forth to win it. He needs to know that there are those people who live by these standards and the advantages far outweigh the disadvantages. He should feel that the award he receives is a symbol of the philosophy by which he has lived to win it, and that the award in itself is of no value, but that it is what it stands for that counts. He needs the assurance of those whom he respects. By putting down on paper the rules by which he must live to fulfill his obligations and win his award, the coaches are setting the standards by which all must adhere in order to be a part of the program or team to which the athlete belongs.

The Meaning of the Varsity Athletic "G"—Example

The athletic "G" at Gillespie High School is earned in a classroom that does not have four walls, a laboratory that does not have test tubes or scientific equipment. The exams take place on weekends from September to May. The tests are noisy, usually exciting, sometimes happy, often heartbreaking. The letter "G" symbolizes that the student-athlete has passed the course. What has he learned?

1. He has learned the importance of winning.
2. The importance of giving 100 percent.
3. The importance of bouncing back when defeated.
4. Recognizing excellence.
5. Taking part in a competitive activity.
6. Loyalty to self and others.
7. Respect for authority.
8. Self discipline.

Winning is important because it is the only criterion there is for measuring anything. When an all conference team of the best losers is picked, then athletics will be finished. When the game is over, it is not important whether you won. But during

TABLE CVI
VARSITY AWARD PLEDGE — EXAMPLE

All students receiving a varsity award will acknowledge that the letter is not their property, but the property of _____ Community High School. Upon graduation from school, this letter will become their property, if they abide by the following rules:

1. I will always attempt to do honor to my school and my teams by my actions both in and out of school.
2. I will abide by the training rules.
3. I will not smoke.
4. I will not drink alcoholic beverages.
5. I will not allow any other person to wear my letter.
6. I will at all times support the rules and regulations of the letterman's club.
7. I shall not steal or wear stolen equipment from my school or from other schools.

Any violations of this *Varsity Award Pledge* can result in the forfeiture of the *Varsity Award*.

Your cooperation in helping your child abide by these rules and regulations will be greatly appreciated. If at any time you would want to discuss this training code or other matter relating to your participation in athletics at _____
Community High School, please feel free to visit me at the high school or you can contact me by phone at 424-6921, Ext. 90.

Sincerely yours,

Athletic Director

---

the game, it is important that you win. Not always to look good, but to win.

And then if you have left your guts on the court or field and you can say to yourself, I left everything I had out there, and if I had to do it again tomorrow I could not do it any better, then there is no disgrace in losing.

The purpose of competition is to test yourself, not beat anybody. Perfection is not attained at that point at which nothing can be added but at that point which nothing can be taken away.

Athletics fulfills a demand for total effort. To win you must have boys who want to excel. If you are going to be a champion, you must be willing to pay a bigger price than your opponent will ever pay.

Davis[31] relates the importance of the athletic letter and what it means to each individual athlete in the following manner:

> The recipients of the athletic letter award should feel that they have been educated in the toughest kind of classroom. A classroom that does not have four walls, laboratory test tubes, or scientific equipment. The examination period comes every weekend from September until November. The tests are noisy, unusually exciting, sometimes happy, often heartbreaking. The awarding of the letter indicates his grade and that he has passed the course. It indicates that he has learned the importance of accepting defeat gracefully and bouncing back to play hard in the next game and the importance of being a team member.

George and Lehmann[32] made some valuable suggestions which will help indicate the meaning and worth of the award to not only the athlete but to others who

do not understand the meaning behind the award, what it stands for and what it takes to earn it:

> A student organization with membership limited to those who have earned varsity letter awards may, under proper guidance and supervision, be a valuable adjunct to the athletic program. A varsity club of this type would have status in the eyes of other students and could well act as a service organization whose main objective is the enrichment of the overall school activities program. In general, the proper implementation of an awards program should follow these steps:
>
> 1. The establishment of criteria for earning an award.
> 2. The selection of the specific award items to be presented.
> 3. The dissemination of information to all those concerned.
> 4. The keeping of accurate participation records.
> 5. The recommendations of the coach based upon participation and other established criteria.
> 6. The approval of the director of athletics.
> 7. The approval of the athletic council.
> 8. The awards assembly.

Presentation of Awards

One of the main problems and concerns regarding the giving of awards is the procedure used in presenting them. Many administrators believe and rightly so that the athletic program is not the only worthwhile extracurricular activity in the school. Many feel that the assembly program for the presentation of awards should be one that will include other areas such as music, dramatics, etc. An attempt should be made not to overemphasize the importance of the athletic award over all the others. The award winners in all areas should in some way be made to realize that it is a privilege to receive the award, and an honor bestowed upon them for representing the

[31]Davis, Williams, The "Meaning of the Athletic Letter Award" *Scholastic Coach* (October, 1965), p. 72.

[32]George, Jack F. and Lehmann, Harry A., *School Athletic Administration,* p. 399.

school in a creditable manner. This fact should be made clear to the recipient that the award should not be considered as payment for services rendered for the school. Many schools have an award day and give many types of awards, such as achievement in school activities, study hall supervision, student council membership, etc. The awards should be used for motivation and are not to be thought of by the athlete as a reward for something he himself has done for the school that no other person could have done just as well.

One of the main criticisms of any award system is that one area or activity is favored over another. Most likely this area will be athletics. Many administrators favor a system that will recognize the ability of the other student who may have talents in other areas, such as music, forensics, dramatics, and most of all, scholarship. The athletic award has been given special significance with a great deal of pomp and ceremony accompanying the giving of the award. Special assemblies, banquets, etc. have been given for the express purpose of presenting the recipients with the athletic award. There are those who resent this practice, feeling that other areas of endeavor in the school curriculum are important also and should receive the same attention. Watches, trophies, plaques as well as other awards are sometimes given athletes although in most cases these types of awards are disallowed by state associations.

Methods of Presentation of Awards

There are various ways in which awards may be presented; some of these ways will be discussed here. Usually there are two methods used to present these awards, at a banquet and at an assembly. The banquet is usually sponsored by a booster club, mothers' club, etc. for the express purpose of honoring the team. The coach usually presents a letter to each player at this time and makes a brief speech about each player. Usually at these affairs, an outside speaker gives the main address. The trophies are awarded for foul shooting and most valuable player etc. The general public should be invited and every effort should be made to make this event a gala affair. Forsythe[33] suggests that, "The presenting of awards should be a dignified event with a good program. It should be made one of the outstanding occasions of the school year."

Other customs are sometimes followed. In one community every even-numbered year the school sponsors what is known as a "Rose Ceremony." All varsity letter winners in basketball, wrestling etc. and their parents are invited to this ceremony. The coaching staff, cheerleaders, school administrators and board members are also invited. As the varsity coach presents each letter, the athlete and his parents are escorted forward and the mother is presented with a rose.

Special awards may be presented at this time and new members of the National Athletic Scholastic Society may be inducted. A guest speaker should be secured for this occasion and a coffee hour may be held following the program.

In the odd years an all-sports banquet may be held in the spring in place of the rose ceremony. A guest speaker may also be secured for this event. Special awards may be given at this time and new members of the National Athletic Scholastic Society may be inducted. No letter awards are presented at this banquet. All emblems, frosh-soph, junior varsity, and varsity awards during the odd-numbered years are presented at the various potluck suppers that each sport schedules. For example, fol-

[33]Forsythe, Charles, *The Athletic Director's Handbook* (Englewood Cliffs, New Jersey, by permission of Prentice-Hall, 1956) , p. 24.

lowing the sports season the coaches and players hold a potluck supper. Guests invited include cheerleaders, sports writers, and other men who have donated their time during the sports season (bus drivers, scouts, scorekeeper, ticket sellers, etc.). The frosh-soph coach should present his various letters at this supper.

Another school has an all-sports banquet which is sponsored by the pep club. At this event, each coach speaks briefly about his team and letter winners. The banquet is followed by the coronation of the king and queen of sports.

The importance of recognizing the recipient of the award is emphasized by George and Lehmann[34] in the following statement:

> Awards should be presented at an assembly of students. The practice of making awards at squad meetings and team banquets should be discouraged. The award winning athlete should be recognized and honored before as many of his fellow students as possible. Whenever possible, the parents of the athletes should be invited to these assemblies.

SAMPLE LETTER AWARDS ASSEMBLY—WINTER SPORTS
(Date)

1. Band is playing as students arrive.
2. Donald Brown makes remarks about winter sports season—thanks to various groups for support. (Don Brown is president of Varsity Club.)
3. Introduces and gives the order of speakers on the program.
   a. SWIMMING—Captain Joe Auble— (two minutes) Coach Fred introduces boys—stand—awards later
   b. SOPH. WRESTLING — Captain John Smith— (two minutes) Coach Jones introduces boys—stand—awards later

   c. VARSITY WRESTLING—Captain Don Brown— (two minutes) Coach Smith (two minutes)—introduces boys—stand—awards later
4. Brown announces second band number and second part of program.
   a. GYMNASTICS—Captain Don Smith —(two minutes)— Coach Brown introduces boys—stand—awards later.
   b. SOPH. BASKETBALL — Captain Bill Jones— (two minutes) Coach Black (two minutes) —introduces boys—stand—awards later
   c. VARSITY BASKETBALL—Captain Bill Anderson—(two minutes) Coach Green introduces boys — stand — awards later Cheerleader comments and introduce cheerleaders—awards after program
5. Loyalty—directed by student leader.

Props: Rostrum
Two gym tables Chairs for speakers
Two blankets   Chairs for award
                winners
                Microphone—
                Henry Teddle

Still another school may sponsor a banquet at the completion of a sports season which is paid for by the board of education and held in the local gymnasium. All athletes who have participated in basketball are invited to attend along with their parents. The banquet itself is prepared by the women in charge of the school cafeteria. Following the meal, all who have participated are introduced. The athletes who have earned the necessary points, come forward to receive their awards from the coach. A few words about each athlete's accomplishments are given as the player comes forward for the award. At the end of the specific sports season, each team member votes for the athlete he or she feels has been "most valuable" to the team, and also the one he feels has "improved" the most

---

[34]George, Jack F. and Lehmann, Harry A., *School Athletic Administration.*

over the season of play. The two athletes receiving the most votes are given individual trophies with the name, the inscription "most valuable" or "most improved" and the year in which he received this honor. At the end of presentation of the awards a special speaker usually talks on athletics.

Another method of presenting the awards is at a general assembly after a particular season of sports is completed. There can be three such assemblies, fall, winter, and spring. Many coaches feel that this is a much better plan than the banquet type because it makes athletics (1) a part of the whole program, (2) it creates harmony with the other winter sports, (3) players are honored before the entire student body, (4) it involves less time, (5) the program is conducted by the varsity club, (6) adults can attend free of charge, (7) the captains can take a more active part in conducting the program, and (8) school administrators feel that they have better control.

In preparing for this type of program, the captain gives a two to three minute speech. He is held to this time. To do this, the varsity club president presides over the assembly. A student timer equipped with a stop watch blows the whistle on the speaker at the end of the time limit. All players are seated in sections with the major letter winners ahead of the minor letter winners. The trophies that each team has won during the season are displayed on tables located at each side of the rostrum. The school band is invited to play inspirational music during the ceremony. The cheerleaders are honored at this assembly. The coach has the option of giving a five-minute speech about the team if the team has won a championship. After a representative for the team has spoken, the coach will introduce his assistant coach. He will then read the names for the various letter awards. As

he reads the name of each player, the player will stand. The letters are given to the athletes after the assembly is over.

This method saves a great deal of time and is in keeping with the other school-sponsored programs.

Most school authorities seem to feel that once the athletic award has been presented to the student, it loses all jurisdiction over its use and exhibition. Others, prohibit the exhibition of school letters in undesirable places, and the wearing of too many awards on one sweater or jacket. These schools want to maintain some control after the award has been presented. This control may be exercised in one or two ways, either by the athletic department itself, or by the award winners themselves through the by-laws of a varsity or lettermen's organization of some type. Many coaches feel that the authority for the control of awards is better off in the hands of the lettermen themselves. It is easier for the athlete to uncover and punish offenders than the coaches, who may have very little contact with the athletes off the playing field.

Wearing of the Varsity Award by the Athlete

The award recipient shall agree to adhere to the following policies relative to the wearing of the varsity award.

1. To abide by the varsity club code of conduct
2. To wear only the letter on a specific color of sweater
3. Only the winner of the award shall wear the letter sweater or jacket
4. To wear no type of jacket with an award on it other than the approved varsity jacket
5. To wear the bars as indicative of additional letters won on the letter
6. To wear no other type of emblems, in-

serts, or special awards except those representing the school and given by the school

Forsythe[35] suggests that a statement signed by the winner of the award be instigated to curb the practice of giving the award to other persons by the receivers. This practice can be serious if students other than those entitled to do so wear the school's athletic awards.

The lettermen club can be a powerful force in the athletic program and the school in general if handled correctly. Each club should have a constitution and by-laws if it is to function properly.

George and Lehmann[36] make the following suggestion regarding the wearing of the award:

> The wearing or displaying of an athletic award should be considered a nontransferable privilege. It may be well to include the following items in the policies:
> 1. Awards are not to be worn or displayed by anyone except the award winner himself.
> 2. Awards are not to be worn during any periods of scholastic ineligibility or academic probation or while disciplinary action for any type of misconduct is in effect.
>
> Athletes and other members of the student body should be kept well informed about awards and any new or changed policies. All coaches must also be up to date in this matter. The student handbook, the physical education handbook, the school newspaper, and the bulletin boards can all be utilized to disseminate this information. Materials regarding awards standards together with eligibility rules should be discussed by all coaches during one of the early squad meetings in each sport.

Types of Awards Given

One of the many pressing problems of presenting awards is the type of award given. Should there be specific awards for different activities or should the same award be given for all activities regardless of what it represents? Who is to say that because a student makes the athletic varsity because of his superior ability another gets a minor type of award because he has only enough ability to make the junior varsity or a second team. Both may have expended the same amount of energy, worked just as hard, spent just as much time in practice, and sacrificed just as much in every way. Why, then, should both receive different awards? Why should all not receive the same award? This is the subject of a great deal of controversy among school people. Should there be different awards for each activity? Should there be major and minor awards? Who determines this? Should the sports be rated not by the public interest in them but by their value in contributing to the complete education of the youth? Should each sport be measured by the carry-over value which it provides for later life-time activity?

Voltmer and Esslinger[37] make the following comments regarding major and minor awards:

> The majority of high schools award the same letter to all who qualify, regardless of sport. However, many differentiate the sports into major and minor categories. This is done more frequently in the larger high schools. In these schools the awards for minor sports are either a smaller monogram or the same size monogram as is awarded for the major sports but with a letter designation for the minor sport. The chief argument brought against this practice is that some sports, particularly football, demand much more

---

[35]Forsythe, Charles, *The Athletic Director's Handbook,* p. 22.

[36]George, Jack F. and Lehmann, Harry A., *School Athletic Administration,* p. 398.

[37]Voltmer, Edward and Esslinger, Arthur, *The Organization and Administration of Physical Education.* p. 290.

from the boy than fencing, tennis, golf and some of the other sports. On the other hand in discussing the advantages and disadvantages of major and minor letters, it is justifiable to grant the same letter for all sports on the theory that a boy has sufficient ability to represent his school is entitled to an award.

There are several types of letters and emblems awarded to high school athletes and many rules governing and controlling the wearing of them. A few will be discussed here as illustrations of what might be done.

MAJOR AWARD: A letter winner at the varsity level should be awarded an eight-inch letter. Only one major letter should be awarded in any given sport. If a second or third award is earned in a particular sport, a chevron should be given the winner. Since the varsity award is an eight-inch letter, it should always be worn on a sweater or leather jacket. In no case should an athlete display more than three chevrons on any one sweater or jacket. Letters should be displayed on the left side of the jacket or cardigan sweater and in the middle of the pull-over type sweater.

JUNIOR VARSITY AWARD: The junior-varsity award should be a six-inch letter. This should be the only junior-varsity letter given in this sport. The coaches should make these awards in accordance with the award requirements of their particular sports. No junior-varsity chevron should be given.

FROSH-SOPH AWARDS The frosh-soph award should be made only to a freshman or sophomore, and the award should consist of a five-inch letter. Any freshman who earns a freshman-sophomore award during his first year in more than one sport should receive only one letter. Any award for additional sports should be designated by a chevron which can be worn on the arm of a letter sweater or jacket. Any sophomore

who participated in freshman-sophomore competition for two years and did not receive a letter, should be awarded a letter on the coach's recommendation. Freshmen and sophomores should be allowed to display their awards either on a jacket or a letter sweater; either a pull-over or cardigan type of sweater. Any freshman who earns a freshman-sophomore award in his first year should only receive a repetition of the same awards in his sophomore year.

FRESHMAN AWARD: Any participant who finishes the season in good standing as a member of the freshman team should receive an emblem.

Many schools award a so-called "minor" letter that signifies one of two things, participation in a minor sport or limited participation in one of the major sports. This letter is usually smaller than the major letter. Schools may also award numerals. These are most commonly awarded to freshmen who are on school teams in schools that do not award major letters to freshmen. Emblems or patches may also be awarded for membership on a championship team. Many athletic departments have a rule that an athlete is awarded only one letter regardless of how many he may earn during his career at the school. In this case, substitute awards may be given this athlete instead of a letter. These may include a certificate, a gold pen, service stripes, or chevrons. High schools that belong to the athletic association of their state will be limited to the above awards in most cases, due to the financial limit placed on awards. Usually an athlete cannot receive an award from any source in excess of a certain monetary limit, or he may lose at least a year of eligibility.

In addition to the above mentioned awards, many schools have special awards earned only by the very few. These awards may be of two types. In one, the player's name is engraved on a permanent trophy or plaque that remains on the school premises, while the other results in an award, in addition to the letter given to the athlete, to take home with him. Educators prefer the first type, feeling that it is more of a true award and more educationally sound than the second.

An important point must be brought out at this time. Regardless of the plan in use, it is the responsibility of the athletic department to have on record, in writing, the policy of the school concerning requirements for awards. This practice will eliminate any possible unfavorable reaction by either athlete or the general public following the granting of awards.

Special Awards

There are many special awards depending on the community and the traditions that have been established and handed down from year to year. A complete list will not be attempted here but rather a representative grouping listed and briefly discussed.

THE HUSTLE AWARD: An award given for contributing the full measure of one's energy and abilities in furthering the welfare of both self and team and for making every effort to give in practice drills or games nothing less than 100 percent of himself.

OUTSTANDING PLAYER AWARD: An award given for one whose combination of skills, devotion to team welfare, and unselfish efforts have brought the greatest measure of success to the year's sport team of the high school and whose performance most nearly exemplifies the true spirit of the high school.

MOST VALUABLE PLAYER AWARD: An award given for the player's contributions to the team. Usually his teammates vote the player this award. The award signifies how the players felt regarding his value

as a team member.

REVERED PERSON ATHLETIC AWARD: The recipient of this award is usually chosen by the athletic award board of controls from among the winners of the outstanding player award from the various sports. Usually in the selection of the award winner, the board of control will screen either by vote, discussion, or both, until only two candidates are left. The winner is picked by majority vote cast for these two candidates. This award may take several forms, but an outstanding honor would be to have a large picture in sport regalia of the athlete hung in the hall of the fieldhouse.

KIWANIS AWARD: This award could be presented to the member of the team who displayed the most loyalty, diligence, leadership, desire to win, team spirit, and enthusiasm. This award can be won by the type of individual that may not score many points for his team, but when he does, he gives everything he has to do it. He always puts his team before his own personal desires and interests.

FREE THROW AWARD: This award is presented each year to the member of the varsity basketball team with the highest free-throw percentage. The winner's name is engraved on the trophy that is given.

MOST IMPROVED PLAYER AWARD: This award is given to the player who, in the opinion of the coaches, improved the most throughout the season. The winner's name is engraved on a trophy.

BEST SHOOTING PERCENTAGE LEADER: This award is given to the player who had the best shooting percentage from the field for the year.

OUTSTANDING PERFORMANCE AWARDS: There are other types or kinds of awards which are given as incentives or recognition for outstanding performance or achievement in a given sport, such as football. The purpose is to recognize individual players whose efforts are vital to the success of the team but unrecognized because few people understand their function and more important cannot see what they are doing because their attention is focused elsewhere. The following is an example of the recognition given to football players and indicates different position awards:

FOOTBALL SYSTEM OF INDIVIDUAL INCENTIVE AWARDS: Player-of-the-week awards are placed on the bulletin boards and given to the local press.

1. Game Ball (wins only)
2. Outstanding Defensive Lineman/Linebacker
3. Outstanding Defense Back/Linebacker
4. Outstanding Offensive Lineman
5. Outstanding Offensive Back
6. Big Play Award

Player of the year awards are given after the season is over.

1. Best Offensive Back
2. Best Defensive Back
3. Best Offensive Lineman
4. Best Defensive Lineman
5. Most Valuable Player
6. Most Improved Player
7. Most Consistent Player

Star awards are given for outstanding individual plays. Each time a player performs one of the plays listed below he is given a star which he places on his head gear. This practice serves as a tremendous incentive and motivator for the player to play well.

DEFENSE

1. Interception
2. Caused fumble
3. Recovered fumble
4. Blocked kick
5. Tackle on kick-off inside the twenty yard line
6. Team award for shutout
7. Quarter back thrown for a loss two or more times

8. Putting runner on his back by a tackle

OFFENSE

1. Outstanding play
2. Total net yardage of 200 yards (rush or pass)
3. Sustained scoring drive of fifty yards in ten plays or more
4. Back gains over 100 yards rushing
5. Receiver with six or more receptions
6. Punt coverage five yards or less
7. Lineman at 80 percent efficiency or better
8. Four downfield blocks

STUDENT MANAGER AWARDS: The student managers usually get the regular varsity type of letter except that the word "mgr" is written on the letter. Bars or stripes can indicate the number of years of service. Most schools will have a well-defined policy as to requirements for earning a manager's letter.

LETTERMAN'S CERTIFICATE: Most schools issue a certificate along with the letter. This certificate varies in size, but of a sufficient size so that it can be placed in a frame. This certificate is usually signed by both the coach and the principal and indicates that the recipient has fulfilled the requirements set forth by the school for earning a letter in a particular sport.

Procedures for Granting Awards

In order that the granting of awards be a part of the school policy it is necessary that a definite procedure be established which will not only be uniform and coincide with school regulations but will not be subject to change from year to year and coach to coach. Some of these procedures are listed as follows and in sequence:

1. Every participant in every sport should be informed before the season starts (preferably the first practice session) what the requirements are to win a letter in that sport.

2. The coach should devise some way in which accurate participation records are kept for each contestant. These records should be compiled at the end of the sport season to determine which players have met the requirements for winning a letter.

3. The coach should send a list of the athletes he recommends for a letter to the athletic director and/or the principal. These recommendations are based on the athletes meeting the requirements and the recommendation of the coach.

4. The principal should carefully check the list to determine if those players who have been recommended by the coach meet the scholastic as well as the citizenship, character, and attitude standards which might be part of the requirements for winning a letter in a particular school.

5. This list should then be sent to the student, faculty, or student faculty board, for their approval if the school has this type of organization.

6. The players have now met all the requirements and can be awarded the letter in any way the school sees fit to do so.

Many times the coach does not require specific requirements to be met or certain criteria to be fulfilled to earn a letter. Instead, suggestions on what can be done to earn the letter are given to the participant before the season starts with the idea that if in the coach's opinion he fulfills these requirements he will be awarded the letter.

Wrestling Award Policy (**Example**)

1. A letter award is earned, not given.
2. Under no circumstance is an award promised.
3. An award is made in recognition of your contribution to the wrestling program and of your development as a wrestler and a human being.

4. Your won-lost record may certainly be a partial indication of both your contribution and your development but it is, more certainly, not the only indication. There are many other factors which may influence the decision either to grant or withhold an award.

5. There are no specific requirements for a wrestling award. The following suggestions are made as guidelines for earning a letter award in wrestling.

A. You *must* finish the season with one of our teams. (An injury does not disqualify you but you must continue in an active role in the program even though you cannot wrestle.)

B. You may attend all practices, on time and in clean and proper uniform.

C. You may participate enthusiastically and wholeheartedly in all practices.

D. You may be ready to weigh in at all matches and tournaments regardless of whether or not you expected to wrestle.

E. You may remain willing and enthusiastic to wrestle at any weight classification and at any level of competition in order to serve the program and to further your wrestling.

F. You may attend all matches of all our teams regardless of whether or not you are wrestling.

G. You may actively support and encourage your teammates in their efforts.

H. You may strive to help younger and more inexperienced wrestlers in their attempts to learn wrestling and to "feel at home" in our program.

I. You may remain "coachable" and continually strive to improve your wrestling as directed by your coach.

J. You may assume your share of the responsibility in setting up for matches, caring for mats after matches and in performing other routine tasks necessary to the functioning of the program.

K. You may treat responsibly all equipment and facilities of the program, including personal uniform, wrestling mats, the wrestling room, etc.

L. You may strive to maintain the same dignity of being in the locker room that is required in the wrestling room, avoiding profane language, wild horseplay, carelessness with equipment, etc.

M. You may maintain a clean, neat, and well-groomed manner throughout the year. This includes the year round maintenance of an acceptable haircut.

N. You may perform conscientiously your school responsibilities, performing to the best of your ability academically and maintaining a reputation of integrity with your physical education teacher, academic teachers, and counselors.

O. You may perform with honor in victory and defeat and show respect for officials, coaches, and for all opponents, strong and weak.

Principles for Administering Athletic Awards

1. Awards should indicate achievement and should have little or no monetary value.

2. The individual should play the game for pleasure and enjoyment and not for the award that is given for excelling.

3. The opportunity for winning the awards should be available and possible for everyone.

4. The awards should be purchased by the school using school funds and not by any outside group or organization.

5. The awards should be presented to the athletes at a regular school function or awards' day program and not at any outside school organization.

6. All major and minor awards should be presented at the same time.

7. All awards should be given with the expression of citizenship, character, scholarship, and sportsmanship as being synonymous with the award.

8. Every attempt should be made to give the award as a part of the total physical education program.

9. The awards should be presented by the coach, athletic director, or the school principal and not by an outside official.

10. The major and minor sports awards should be presented at the same time.

11. The requirements for the awards should be clearly understood by the participants.

12. The requirements should be developed by a representative group of people.

13. The decision as to the award winners should be made by one person.

Award Policies

The policies governing the giving of awards in interscholastic athletics are dependent upon several factors, including the National Federation regulations, the state regulations, and the conference and local school regulations. Forsythe[38] suggests that:

Before a school establishes its award policy, it should be certain that it is in accord with the regulations adopted by the state athletic or activities association. Such information may be obtained from

---

[38]Forsythe, Charles, *The Athletic Director's Handbook,* p. 18.

the annual handbooks or yearbooks issued by these organizations. It should be remembered that the state regulations have been adopted by the duly elected representatives of all the schools of the state and have the best interests of all concerned.

George and Lehmann[39] also suggest that:

> Every school should have a clearly defined and educationally defensible awards policy, approved by the board of education. Such a policy may be the end product of studies, consultations and discussions of various committees. Any policies that are adopted must conform to limitations established by the state high school athletic association and follow suggestions and recommendations of the state group and the National Federation of State High School Athletic Association. Policies concerning awards vary from community to community and from school to school. The important thing is that the policy be well conceived and thoroughly understood and accepted by all those concerned.

The National Federation and the state associations are concerned mainly with the cost of the award and, therefore, place a monetary limit on the amount of money that can be spent for the award. Certain restrictions are sometimes placed on the types and costs of awards by the various conferences. The regulations from these three organizations, that are given by different schools, vary considerably. These variations could include the size, shape, design, and color of the letter or emblem, the number of awards given and the requirements that are placed on the winning of the award, whatever they may be.

Record of Award Presentations

It is important that records are kept of all awards that are given. These records

can be kept in the same manner as eligibility records. Usually the coach of the particular sport prepares a list of award winners. He does this by checking the game statistics record. This will inform him of the amount of actual time or quarters the athlete has played in football, basketball, soccer, etc. In the case of track the coach will be able to find out the number of points the athlete has scored or the place the player finished in a race. In baseball, it will show the number of innings the athlete has played.

Another method that is used is to have a separate card for each athlete which indicates the sport in which he earned a letter and the year in which he won it. These cards are then filed in alphabetical order so that they are readily accessible for immediate use.

GIBSON CITY HIGH SCHOOL DISTRICT 112
ATHLETIC AWARD WINNERS

SPORT_____ YEAR_____

VARSITY LETTER WINNERS	JR. VARSITY LETTER WINNERS	SOPHOMORE LETTER WINNERS	FRESHMAN NUMERAL WINNERS
Mgrs.	Mgrs.	Mgrs.	Mgrs.

Coach's Signature_____

Figure 126.

---

[39]George, Jack F. and Lehmann, Harry A., *School Athletic Administration*, p. 393.

ERIE HIGH SCHOOL DISTRICT 112

ATHLETIC AWARD LIST

Award for_____ Year_____ Coach_____

Last	First	Var.	J.V.	Soph.	Frosh.	SPECIAL
1.						
2.						
3.						
4.						
5.						
6.						
7.						
8.						
9.						
10.						
11.						
12.						
13.						
14.						
15.						
16.						
17.						
18.						
19.						
20.						
21.						
22.						

Figure 127.

ERIE HIGH SCHOOL DISTRICT 112
LETTER AWARDS' CARD RECORD

NAME_____ GRADUATION YEAR____

SPORT	FRESHMAN		SOPHOMORE		JUNIOR		SENIOR	
FOOTBALL								
CROSS COUNTRY								
SOCCER								
BASKETBALL								
WRESTLING								
GYMNASTICS								
SWIMMING								
TRACK								
BASEBALL								
GOLF								
TENNIS								

C=Certif. N=Numeral L=Letter B=Bar P=Patch Mgr.=Manager S=Sqd. Member

Figure 128.

1. Explain the custom of awarding letters by schools to members of athletic teams.
2. Differentiate between awards given for various extracurricular activities in the schools.
3. Identify the reasons for presenting awards in school athletics.
4. Prepare a philosophy of your own regarding interscholastic athletic awards.
5. Compile a list of requirements which can be used as criteria for granting interscholastic athletic awards.
6. Develop a point system for awarding of athletic awards in various sports.
7. Identify several types of athletic awards

BEHAVIORAL OBJECTIVES

After a person has read this chapter, he should be able to:

TABLE CVII

S A M P L E

LETTER AWARD RECORD

POTSDAM HIGH SCHOOL

Potsdam, Illinois

NAME _____

Sport now participating in _____

I have already received the following awards this school year:

_____Sport

_____Award (Numerals,

Soph., JV, or

Varsity)

In a previous year I received the following Varsity letters:

_____

_____

CHEERLEADERS   SAMPLE

HIGH SCHOOL AWARD RECORD

Class of _____

C = Certificate   V = Varsity Letter

N = Numeral   * = Captain's Star

S = Soph. Letter   H = Special Award

J = Jr. Varsity   CH = Chevron

Name	Year		Year		Year		Year	
	Squad	Award	Squad	Award	Squad	Award	Squad	Award

Figure 129.

which are given to participants in interscholastic athletics.

8. Explain and analyze several methods which can be used to present awards to the recipients.

9. Prepare a program which could be used for awarding athletic letters in interscholastic athletics.

10. Develop a set of rules governing the wearing of the athletic letters.

11. Develop a plan of financing an athletic awards program where limited funds are available.

12. Explain the policy regarding the purchasing of awards.

13. Develop a system of record keeping for athletic awards in the large high school.

14. Identify the various organizations which govern the giving of interscholastic athletic awards.

15. Analyze the awards policies of each of these organizations.

16. Identify several procedures which are commonly used in the granting of athletic awards.

17. Compile a list of the advantages and disadvantages of awards.

18. Identify and explain several principles used in administering interscholastic atheltic awards.

19. Prepare and develop an awards program in basketball which will give recognition to the all around player and not just the high scorer.

20. Analyze and explain the purpose of giving athletic awards.

21. Compare the giving of athletic awards with debate, dramatics, and music awards.

22. Analyze the advantages and disadvantages of giving athletic awards.

23. Distinguish between the major and minor award in interscholastic athletics.

24. Develop a plan or policy for the earning of the manager's letter.

25. Explain the value of keeping accurate records regarding letters won by participants.

26. Explain the purposes of the letterman's club in interscholastic athletics.

27. Identify several procedures for granting athletic awards.

28. Develop a procedure for the purchase of awards.

29. Develop a set of rules which can be used for wearing an athletic award.

30. Formulate a point system for an all sports award.

31. Draw up a set of training rules for participation in the athletic program in all sports.

32. Develop a set of rules which can be applied to the selection of the team captain.

33. Identify the type of award, if any, that should be given for athletic participation.

ACTIVITIES

1. Outline an award system for football, basketball, and swimming.

2. Debate the issue: The team captain should be chosen by his teammates or selected by the coach for each game.

3. Debate the issue: There should be specific criteria established for earning the award or it should be left to the discretion of the coach.

4. Set up a set of rules and procedures which could apply to the selection of the team captain.

5. Debate the issues: Awards should be abolished.

6. Debate the issue: The same awards should be given for all extramural activities.

7. Set up an awards assembly program.

8. Debate the issue: the policy for awarding sweaters to varsity athletes should be abolished.

9. Develop a system of awards for a selected senior high school.

10. Form two groups of students and debate the system of awarding letters or insignia by school authorities to members of interscholastic athletic teams.

11. Contact the athletic directors of several high schools and obtain their requirements for earning athletic awards in the various sports and compare them.

12. Write to several sporting good stores for catalogues on awards and insignia. Compare the prices, types of awards, etc.

13. Talk with a physician, farmer, lawyer, and a school teacher about their philosophy regarding awards.

14. Talk with the director of dramatics, director of the school band in respect to their philosophy regarding awards.

15. Plan and act out an assembly program for awarding athletic letters.

16. Seek the opinion of several school administrators regarding the method used in keeping records on awards.

17. Survey the opinions of two or three directors of athletics relative to awards.

18. Visit a number of schools and study their requirements for letter awards. From this information make out a point system which you can defend for awarding letters for each sport.

SUGGESTED READINGS

1. Blount, Joe: An athletic award point system. *The Athletic Journal,* February, 1955.

2. Bucher, Charles: *Administration of Health and Physical Education Programs Including Athletics.* St. Louis, Mosby, 1971.

3. Bucher, Charles, and Dupee, Ralph: *Athletics in Schools and Colleges.* New York, The Center for Applied Research in Education, 1965.

4. Dailey, John: High school letter club. *School Activities,* December, 1958.

5. Davis, William: Meaning of the high school letter. *Scholastic Coach,* October, 1965.

6. Forsythe, Charles: *Administration of High School Athletics.* Englewood Cliffs, P-H, 1959.

7. Forsythe, Charles, and Keller, Irvin: *Administration of Physical Education.* Englewood Cliffs, P-H, 1972.

8. Forsythe, Charles E.: *The Athletic Director's Handbook.* Englewood Cliffs, P-H, 1956.

9. Fox, Philip, and Lane, Ralph: What the letter club offers. *The Athletic Journal,* January, 1958.

10. George, Jack F., and Lehmann, Harry A.: *School Athletic Administration.* New York, Har-Row, 1966.

11. Griffin, John Harold: *Athletic Director's Handbook.* Danville, Interstate, 1960.

12. Havel, Richard and Emery, Seymour: *Administration of Health, Physical Education and Recreation for Schools.* New York, Ronald, 1961.

13. Healey, William: Awards in high school athletics. *School Activities,* January, 1969.

14. Hixson, Chalmer G.: *The Administration of Interscholastic Athletics.* New York, Lowell Pratt, 1967.

15. Howard, Alvin: A junior high award system that works. *School Activities,* January, 1969.

16. Huffman, Terrence: Incentive awards for baseball. *The Athletic Journal,* March, 1972.

17. Hughes, William, French, Esther, and Lehsten, Nelson: *Administration of Physical Education for Schools and Colleges.* New York, Ronald, 1962.

18. Lazarus, Marjorie: Our varsity "W" club. *School Activities,* October, 1960.

19. Meyer, Kenneth L.: Democratic system of athletic awards. *Teachers College Journal,* January, 1949.

20. Resick, Matthew, Seidel, Beverly, and Mason, James: *Modern Administrative Practices in Physical Education and Athletics.* Reading, A-W, 1970.

21. Scott, Harry: *Competitive Sports in Schools and Colleges.* New York, Har-Row, 1951.

22. Scorpas, Ted: New criteria for letter awards. *The Athletic Journal,* April, 1949.

23. Souza, George: A unique award system that is economical. *The Athletic Journal,* October, 1967.

24. Voltmer, Edward and Esslinger, Arthur: *The Organization and Administration of Physical Education.* New York, Appleton, 1967.

25. Voris, Nick: Freshman football incentives. *Scholastic Coach,* April, 1967.

CHAPTER 20

Policies for Selection and Hiring Officials

THE IMPORTANCE OF officiating in any form of athletics cannot be under-estimated. The question has often been raised, what makes a good official? Can a person learn to be a good official? Is the good official born with certain attributes that make him a good official? What are the qualities of a good official? Is a knowledge of the rules the most important ingredient or is it personality? What are the characteristics of a good official? Why can a person officiate a good game one night and an extremely poor one the next? This is proof that a knowledge of the rules is not the complete answer. Other people will insist that the best official is one who works the game, yet no one seems to sense his presence. There is no doubt that officiating is an art and everyone cannot be a good official.

A source of great concern in the inter-scholastic athletic program is and has been for some time the quality of officiating in all sports and particularly in the team sports such as football, basketball, soccer, baseball, field hockey, etc. Administrators at all levels and particularly the administrators of athletics are obligated to do all they can to upgrade the caliber of officiating which is being received by high school athletic teams everywhere.

No one can question the importance of good officiating. It is the responsibility of the administration to obtain the official whose work is conducive to good play. Much has been done by the National Federation and the state associations to insure good officiating for which coaches and players can be both proud and thankful. Capable, well-trained officials are necessary for the safe and proper conduct of the athletic contests.

Qualifications of a Good Official

There are many qualifications that a good official must have and it is difficult to determine which qualifications are the most important. The following are suggested as being important.

PERSONALITY: In the opinion of many coaches, a good official is one who, by his very presence will prevent the players from committing rule infractions. What is personality? How does an official create this impression? He can cultivate it by being friendly before the game. By his very attitude, he can give the impression that he is helping the players to abide by the rules, to play a good game, and to help the spectators enjoy the game. His reactions to certain situations will reveal his attitude. His mannerisms will have a direct influence on the players and the spectators so he must be careful to conceal his feelings at all times.

He must give the impression that he is enjoying what he is doing. However, officiating is a personal thing, and the personality of everyone is different. One person may be compatible with some people and not compatible with others. It must be said, however, that the good official is one who has good rapport with the players and one who makes the players accept his decisions and like it.

ETHICAL STANDARDS: All officials should be above reproach in all areas of moral character. There should never be any question concerning the fairness and honesty of all decisions made. There is no place in interscholastic athletics for the official who would even think of making a decision that in his own mind was not the one he firmly believed was right.

CONSISTENCY: If an official makes the calls as he sees them, he will have no trouble in being consistent. He can make errors in judgment occasionally, but if he makes all his calls instantaneous and without hesitation, he will be consistent. It is the official who tries to equalize a situation after a bad call who gets himself into trouble. He should establish a pattern upon which his calls are made and stick to it regardless of the outcome. He must realize that he cannot please everyone, but he can come close if his calls are the same under identical conditions and circumstances.

CONFIDENCE: A good official will have confidence in his ability. He should at all times believe in himself and his ability to do the job he is required to do. To establish this confidence he should prepare himself in every way to do the best job possible. This will not be easy as it takes a great deal of effort and preparation to become a good official. He must like to work with young people and not be afraid of criticism. He must not be afraid to be in the public eye and make decisions which may bring unfavorable comment from many people. He must, in his own mind, believe that every decision is the right one. In short, he must believe in himself.

CALMNESS: A good official should have control of his emotions at all times. This is not easy to do because in the excitement of a close, hard-fought game, emotions are running high, tempers are becoming short, and through it all, the official must remain calm and collected in order to make the right decisions. This takes a tremendous amount of will-power and in many cases a certain kind of person. Not all persons can do this, and so not all persons can be good officials.

JUDGMENT: The ability to exercise good judgment is essential in officiating. This attribute is very difficult to acquire, and some believe that it is an inherent one. To use good judgment is to make the type of decision that will best fit the situation. Even though the rules are written in such a way that they will cover most every playing situation in the game, there are occasions when a rule does not apply. In this kind of situation, a judgment call is needed and must be forthcoming from an alert official. While strict adherence to the rules is encouraged, the application of the same is left open to the common sense judgment of officials.

KNOWLEDGE OF THE RULES: No official should ever attempt to officiate without a thorough knowledge of the rules. To do this is to be unfair to players, coaches, spectators, and to himself. The least an official can do is to know the rules. There is no excuse not to. The rules are printed and available. Rule meetings prior to every sports season are held by all the state associations. The rules are explained at these meetings and they should be attended by all officials. A thorough knowledge of the rules and of the nature of the game are imperative so as to facilitate the implementation of skill, strategy, and physical performance. The official's job is to provide an environment which will enable the players to perform these skills within the confines of the rules and see that these variables determine the winner. He is there to see to it that the game is played by the rules.

COOPERATION: Cooperation in any endeavor is an important ingredient to success. There will be occasions when, due to unforeseen circumstances, playing dates need to be changed, games need to be cancelled because of sickness, or other causes. This will result in a change for the official. It may result in his not being able to officiate the game because of date conflicts. He should accept this unforeseen turn of events in good faith and not hold the school to the contract. He should make every effort to cooperate because he may wish the same treatment if misfortune causes him to be unable to fulfill his obligations. School administrators and officials should work closely together toward the development of a good working relationship and the solving of common problems.

APPEARANCE: The first requirement of an official in the minds of many coaches and spectators alike is to look like one. Officiating is a physically demanding profession. One needs to be in good physical condition to keep up with the play. This he owes to the players, coaches, spectators, and most of all himself. If he is not in good physical condition, he is endangering his health. Nothing is more disgusting than to see an official following the play because he cannot keep up.

Every official should wear the standard uniform and all should be dressed alike. He should present a neat, well-groomed, and tidy appearance. This in itself will tend to command the respect of both players and coaches.

DECISIVENESS: A good official makes every decision in such a way that it removes every doubt that it is not the right one. He should be decisive in all the decisions that he makes. He should stick by

his decision and give the impression that the call he made was correct.

Function of the Official

The function of any athletic official is to make sure that the game is played according to the rules set up by state and local associations. The officials should do everything within their power and ability to make sure that the outcome of the contest will be directly related to the skill and physical ability of the contestants. To assure this happening, the official must have the ability to display sound judgment and a thorough knowledge of the rules which will enable him to perform the duties expected of him. It is the main function of the official to make sure that the rules are strictly adherred to and that both teams comply and play within these established rules.

State Regulations for Officiating

All states have their own regulations regarding athletic officials. Most are similar in nature and provide for uniformity in officiating techniques. The National Federation of State High School Associations provides rule books and case books to help bring this about. Many of the states are highly organized in regard to the method by which officials are selected and allowed to officiate athletic sports.

Men who officiate in games between member schools must be registered with the state high school association. These men receive all publications and communications distributed by the association that have a bearing on officiating, and they are invited to participate in all activities that are designed to promote uniformity in officiating and to improve conditions under which athletic contests are played.

Statewide interpretation meetings are

TABLE CVIII

I L L I N O I S   H I G H   S C H O O L   A S S O C I A T I O N

BOX 2715, 2715 McGRAW DRIVE   BLOOMINGTON, ILLINOIS 61701

Dear Sir:

This statement is in response to your request for information relative to registration as an Illinois High School Association athletic official.

To be eligible for membership, the applicant must be *TWENTY YEARS OF AGE.*

Applications must be made on the enclosed forms. The APPLICATION FEE of $10.00 for one sport and $1.00 for each additional sport should accompany the application. Of this amount, $2.00 is for the registration fee and the balance for the annual membership dues. THE APPLICATION FEE WILL NOT BE REFUNDED if your application is not approved or if you fail to complete the requirements of registration within the period indicated at the top of each examination. *No reminders will be sent.*

Following the receipt of your application forms and the fee, two important steps are required for the completion of your registration. (1) The IHSA Office will write to the men whose names you give as references as to your character and possibilities of progress in officiating. If the replies should not be satisfactory, your application will be denied. (2) It will be necessary for you to receive a passing grade on a preliminary examination(s) in the rules of the sports in which you desire registration. *Note:* For football, the applicant must take *two* exams, the rules exam and the football Mechanics Exam. The tests are of the "open book" type. The rules publications in the related sports will be sent to you along with the examinations.

After the application is approved, a membership card is sent to the newly registered official. He is then supplied with contracts, monthly issue of the ILLINOIS INTERSCHOLASTIC, lists of interpretation meetings, examination centers and similar material.

An official may seek promotion to the RECOGNIZED and CERTIFIED groups. Procedures for promotions will be explained after an applicant becomes registered.

The annual membership dues are $7.00 for one sport and $1.00 for each additional sport. The dues are used to cover subscriptions to the INTERSCHOLASTIC, cost of postage, publications for officials, printed forms, and costs of interpretation meetings. Memberships begin on July 1 and end on June 30. For applications that are approved between July 1 and January 1, memberships expire on the next June 30. For those approved between January 1 and June 30, *memberships expire on June 30 of the following year.*

Names of all officials who were registered before July 1 are published in the annual Handbook, copies of which are sent to the principal of each member school and to each registered official. Only those officials who are registered with the State Association are eligible to officiate athletic contests in which member schools participate, and they may officiate only those sports in which they are registered.

Very truly yours,

Harry Fitzhugh
Executive Secretary

HF:khl
Enc.

*Reprinted with permission from Illinois High School Association.

conducted at various centers. Discussions at these meetings are based on rule and case books which are sent to all officials.

Memberships extend from a specified date to the same date the next year, and fees must be paid prior to the first date. Each

APPLICATION FOR REGISTRATION

Illinois High School Association

I hereby apply for registration as an IHSA official in the following sports:

____

I am enclosing Application Fee of $10.00 for one sport and $1.00 for each additional sport. TOTAL: $______. Data sheet is also enclosed.

(Please print following)

Name______________________________ Date__________

Street______________________________

City__________________ State & Zip Code__________

NOTE: Application fee includes membership dues to June 30 of year following registration.

Figure 130. Reprinted with permission from the Illinois High School Association.

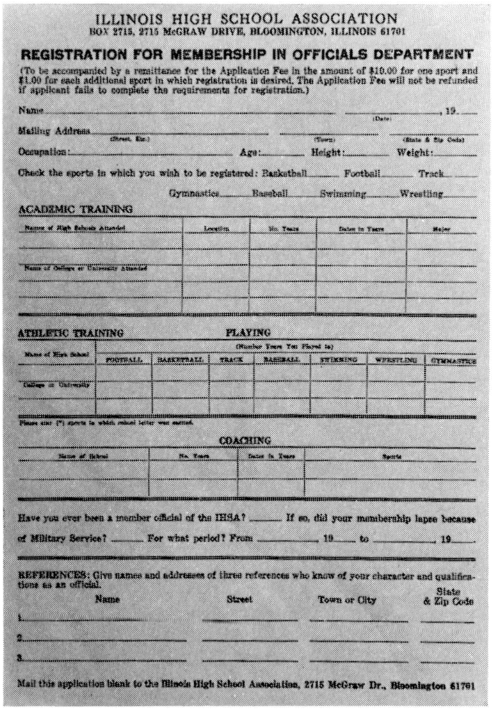

ILLINOIS HIGH SCHOOL ASSOCIATION
BOX 2715, 2715 McGRAW DRIVE, BLOOMINGTON, ILLINOIS 61701

REGISTRATION FOR MEMBERSHIP IN OFFICIALS DEPARTMENT

(To be accompanied by a remittance for the Application Fee in the amount of $10.00 for one sport and $1.00 for each additional sport in which registration is desired. The Application Fee will not be refunded if applicant fails to complete the requirements for registration.)

Name______________________________ ______________, 19____ (Date)

Mailing Address______________ (Street, Etc.) ______________ (Town) ______________ (State & Zip Code)

Occupation:______________ Age:______ Height:______ Weight:______

Check the sports in which you wish to be registered: Basketball______ Football______ Track______ Gymnastics______ Baseball______ Swimming______ Wrestling______

ACADEMIC TRAINING

Name of High Schools Attended	Location	No. Years	Dates in Years	Major
Name of College or University Attended				

ATHLETIC TRAINING — **PLAYING** (Number Years You Played in)

Name of High School	FOOTBALL	BASKETBALL	TRACK	BASEBALL	SWIMMING	WRESTLING	GYMNASTICS
College or University							

Please star (*) sports in which school letter was earned.

COACHING

Name of School	No. Years	Dates in Years	Sports

Have you ever been a member official of the IHSA? ______ If so, did your membership lapse because of Military Service? ______ For what period? From ____________, 19____ to ____________, 19____.

REFERENCES: Give names and addresses of three references who know of your character and qualifications as an official.

	Name	Street	Town or City	State & Zip Code
1.				
2.				
3.				

Mail this application blank to the Illinois High School Association, 2715 McGraw Dr., Bloomington 61701

Figure 131. Reprinted with permission from the Illinois High School Association.

state has its own particular method of the promotion of officials. One method might be as follows.

After registration in any sport, each official starts on a promotional plan that enables the better ones to rise to the *recognized* class after one year in the lower group, then to the *certified* class after two years as a *recognized* official. Reports are gathered both on the work of the official and on the general conditions surrounding the contest. Through these reports, the rating of the official and the school is determined. The four groups of officials are: (1) registered, (2) recognized, (3) certified, and (4) affiliated.

The listing of a man in the *registered* group signifies that he has registered, that he has passed preliminary rules examinations, that he is endeavoring to make use of the aids furnished by the state association and that, in the opinion of at least several responsible men, he is of the right type for a desirable athletic official.

The listing of a man in the *recognized* group in a given sport indicates that as of a specified date he has been registered for at least one year; he has passed an examination in the rules of the given sport; his composite score on examination, experience, rating received from schools, and extent to which he cooperated in meetings and the filing of reports totalled a specified number of points.

The listing of a man in the *certified* group indicates that he has served as a *recognized* official for two full years; his composite score on rules examination, rating reports, and amount of satisfactory service totalled a specified number of points; in the opinion of the executive officers of the state association he is capable of officiating satisfactorily in any contest in the sport named.

The listing of a man in the *affiliated* group indicates that he is a member in good standing in his own state association, has made application to that association for affiliation and has paid the required affiliation fee. Under these circumstances, he is entitled to officiate games between schools in the state in which he has affiliated membership. Reciprocity arrangements are made between a number of the states.

The Administrator's Responsibility in Hiring Officials

It is the administrator's responsibility to make every attempt to provide well-qualified officials for every athletic event. The administrator should operate on the theory that the best is none too good. Expense should not be taken into consideration at any time in his efforts to obtain the best officials available. This much is owed to the coaches and players who have worked long and hard to perfect the skills needed to play the game well, and to the spectators who have come to watch the players perform these skills. The administrator should engage the services of the top officials early enough so that he is able to obtain the best. The school administrator should work closely with officials' associations in obtaining good officials. School authorities should assume the responsibility of displaying openly complete confidence in the persons assigned to serve as officials.

Officials should be engaged as soon as possible. There are always many officials, but sometimes there are not enough good ones. A complete file of all correspondence with officials should be kept. Officials should be secured six months to a year in advance if at all possible. Care should be taken that all officials are registered with the state association. Officials should not be used in too many games.

Selecting of Officials

The administrator of the program of athletics, be it the athletic director, the coach, the principal, or a designated faculty member, must make every effort to obtain the best officials possible for each and every athletic contest played. The officials should be hired as early as is possible so there will be no misunderstanding on dates or fees. This will avoid cancellation of games. At the time the official is notified that he is hired, he should be given the following information: (1) the date and hour of the contest, (2) the place where the contest is to be played, (3) the teams involved, (4) the rules to be followed, and (5) the fees to be paid.

Some of the points which can be of concern in selecting officials can be listed as follows: (1) Standardize the fees. Do not try and hire an official for less than the going rate; (2) Do not hire relatives. This official might be the best, but if he is related in any way to the coach or principal, it is not a good situation and could cause trouble; (3) The official should not be hired for several games in succession. If the official is hired for several games, these assignments should be spaced, otherwise players, coaches, and spectators alike will have a different feeling toward him; (4) Every official likes to feel welcome so every effort should be made to treat him as a guest along with the opposing team members.

There are many things that must be taken into consideration before making a selection. Some of them include the following:

1. Officials must be registered for the current year with the state athletic association.

2. The officials should attend rules and interpretation meetings of the state association or local officials' associations.

3. The official must be under contract for the event.

4. The visiting school should approve the officials.

5. All conference regulations relative to

the use of athletic officials should be followed.

6. The contracts should state the amount of fees and the expense allowances for each official.

7. The officials should be reminded of the event by card or letter.

8. Student courtesy attendants should be provided to meet the officials, show them to their dressing rooms, and supply them with towels or other things they may need.

9. The coaches should support the rulings of the contest officials they have hired.

10. The officials hired should be recognized as representatives of the association they belong to.

After the officials have been selected, a contract should be made between the school and the officials. The officials should be paid before the contest. A notification should be sent to the officials preceding the contest reminding them of the site, date, and time of the event. This notification should also inform them of the parking facilities, dressing room, and motel information. When the contest is over, the officials should be rated. This rating can be used in the future when hiring the same official.

Conference Selection of Officials

The selection and use of the same officials for all conference games is becoming more and more prevalent. This practice assures more consistency and uniformity in officiating. Another practice which has become more noticeable in the past few years is that the same officials will work both the home and away conference games. This seems to be most satisfactory. Some conferences specify one person to assign all the officials for all conference games. However, this does not always prove to be satisfactory because it does not allow enough input from the coaches. Other conferences will arrange for a meeting after the football and basketball season with all the coaches where selection of officials takes place. Often this is a dinner meeting and is combined with a meeting of the principals and athletic directors who at this time can iron out other conference administrative problems.

This selection of officials by the coaches can be carried out in a variety of ways. It should not be allowed to degenerate into a bickering, fault-finding argument by the coaches, but should be kept at a high plane of discussion. One method that is generally accepted is to require every coach to submit a list of officials which is satisfactory to him. This list of officials is discussed and if there is too much opposition to any one official, his name is then taken from the list by a majority vote of the coaches. After the list of officials is determined to the satisfaction of the coaches the assigning of the officials to the conference games begin. This is done by selecting the coaches by lot as to who will have first choice, second choice, etc. The names of the officials are placed on the conference game schedule, which is in the hands of all the coaches. This process continues until all the assignments are made for all conference games. The final list is then verified, and the officials selected are contacted. Third and fourth choices for officials are selected in the same manner in case the first and second choices are unavailable. If none of the four officials selected are available, the opposing coach should submit his list of officials from which the choice must be selected.

This method of selecting officials, while seemingly rather cumbersome and time-consuming, is satisfactory because each coach has the opportunity to refuse certain officials for legitimate reasons.

TABLE CIX

ASSIGNMENT OF BIG EIGHT BASKETBALL OFFICIALS

December 15

Freeport at	*W. Aurora at*	*W. Rockford at*	*Elgin at*
E. Aurora	*E. Rockford*	*LaSalle*	*Auburn*
1._____	1._____	1._____	1._____
2._____	2._____	2._____	2._____
3._____	3._____	3._____	3._____
4._____	4._____	4._____	4._____

December 22

E. Aurora at	*LaSalle at*	*W. Rockford at*	*Auburn at*
W. Aurora	*Elgin*	*Freeport*	*E. Rockford*
1._____	1._____	1._____	1._____
2._____	2._____	2._____	2._____
3._____	3._____	3._____	3._____
4._____	4._____	4._____	4._____

January 5

E. Aurora at	*Elgin at*	*Freeport at*	*E. Rockford at*
LaSalle	*E. Aurora*	*Auburn*	*W. Rockford*
1._____	1._____	1._____	1._____
2._____	2._____	2._____	2._____
3._____	3._____	3._____	3._____
4._____	4._____	4._____	4._____

January 12

E. Rockford at	*W. Aurora at*	*Auburn at*	*Elgin at*
E. Aurora	*Freeport*	*LaSalle*	*W. Rockford*
1._____	1._____	1._____	1._____
2._____	2._____	2._____	2._____
3._____	3._____	3._____	3._____
4._____	4._____	4._____	4._____

January 19

E. Aurora at	*LaSalle at*	*Freeport at*	*W. Rockford at*
Elgin	*W. Aurora*	*E. Rockford*	*Auburn*
1._____	1._____	1._____	1._____
2._____	2._____	2._____	2._____
3._____	3._____	3._____	3._____
4._____	4._____	4._____	4._____

January 26

E. Aurora at	*Auburn at*	*E. Rockford at*	*LaSalle at*
W. Rockford	*W. Aurora*	*Elgin*	*Freeport*
1._____	1._____	1._____	1._____
2._____	2._____	2._____	2._____
3._____	3._____	3._____	3._____
4._____	4._____	4._____	4._____

February 2

W. Aurora at	*Elgin at*	*Freeport at*	*E. Rockford at*
E. Aurora	*LaSalle*	*W. Rockford*	*Auburn*
1._____	1._____	1._____	1._____
2._____	2._____	2._____	2._____
3._____	3._____	3._____	3._____
4._____	4._____	4._____	4._____

February 9

LaSalle at E. Aurora	*W. Aurora at Elgin*	*Auburn at Freeport*	*W. Rockford at E. Rockford*
1._____	1._____	1._____	1._____
2._____	2._____	2._____	2._____
3._____	3._____	3._____	3._____
4._____	4._____	4._____	4._____

February 16

E. Aurora at Auburn	*W. Rockford at W. Aurora*	*Freeport at Elgin*	*LaSalle at E. Rockford*
1._____	1._____	1._____	1._____
2._____	2._____	2._____	2._____
3._____	3._____	3._____	3._____
4._____	4._____	4._____	4._____

February 23

Elgin at E. Aurora	*W. Aurora at LaSalle*	*E. Rockford at Freeport*	*Auburn at W. Rockford*
1._____	1._____	1._____	1._____
2._____	2._____	2._____	2._____
3._____	3._____	3._____	3._____
4._____	4._____	4._____	4._____

Important:

All officials must be contacted in the order listed. If the person contacting the officials is not successful in obtaining the first official on the list, he then must contact the other officials in the order listed. If none of the four officials listed are available, he then must request the opposing coach to submit a list of officials that are acceptable. After he receives this list, he may contact anyone on the list and assign him to the game. Each coach must be satisfied with the officials before they are contacted and hired.

All conference rules regarding the selection of officials must be adhered to. Any discrepancies should be reported immediately to the President of the Conference.

Rules for Selecting Conference Officials

Some conferences establish certain rules above and beyond those set up by the state associations governing the selection of officials. Some of these rules are as follows:

1. All officials must be paid a standard fee in all games, nonconference as well as conference.
2. No officials must be used unless they are sanctioned by the state association.
3. No official may be employed by any conference school.
4. No official may be employed unless his name is on the list approved by the conference.

Assigning Officials

The assigning of officials will differ in different localities. It can be done by assignment by the conference office, assignment by officials associations, and direct employment by the host school. If the latter is true, there must be an agreement by the competing school as to the official assigned to the contest. Usually when schools assign their own officials, it is from a list approved by visiting opponents. A recent trend is to place the assignment of officials for a number of schools in a conference, a league, county, or district association in the hands of one person or one office. This system works very well providing the person is a well-qualified individual. The payment of the officials can be arranged in several ways.

Notification of Officials

Since the officials play such a major part of the successful athletic contest, it is essential that they are secured well in advance and that they have a complete knowledge of the date, place, number of games, time of the games, and the remuneration. Some schools utilize a commissioner to secure the officials, but many others assume that the athletic director is responsible for this task.

The availability of each official selected must be established, and negotiations should be completed far ahead of the first scheduled event. The official may be contacted by telephone, letter, or postcard. Some schools use a double postcard which is printed especially for this purpose. The card contains all of the information that

GADSDEN HIGH SCHOOL
607 SOUTH 12th STREET
GADSDEN, ALABAMA 35901

Office of The Principal
Phone 547-5446

Date

Mr. John C. Johnson
968 South Second Street
Anytown, Alabama

Dear Mr. Johnson:

I would like to check with you again to make sure there are no mistakes concerning the umpiring assignments. I believe these are the games you have accepted to umpire:

May 20	Wednesday	Invitational Tournament	Plate
May 21	Thursday	Invitational Tournament	Bases
May 22	Friday	Invitational Tournament	Plate

It is assumed that by your acceptance of the above assignments that you are on the approved list of the _____ High School Association and are qualified to umpire championship baseball games. As usual we are going to the set rate of $15.00 for working behind the plate and $10.00 for the bases. When a single umpire is used, the compensation is $15.00.

Cancellation is possible at a very short notice due to conflict in tournament dates, weather, or other good cause. If any changes do occur, I will make every possible effort to notify you at the earliest moment.

All games will be played at the high school baseball field. Starting time will be 4:30 p.m.

Sincerely yours,

Baseball Coach

ii

Figure 132.

ROGERS HIGH SCHOOL
NEWPORT, RHODE ISLAND

CHARLES H. TOBIN
PRINCIPAL

ATHLETIC DEPARTMENT

JOHN J. TOPPA
Athletic Director

Attention:

Officials of the 30th Annual _____
Invitational Basketball Tournament

Welcome to the 30th Annual _____ Invitational Basketball Tournament. We are sure that this will be the best managed, best played, best attended, and best officiated tournament yet conducted.

Your assignments are enclosed. However, there are a few things that will be made more enjoyable, profitable, and gratifying.

1. Your check will be given to you before the first game that you officiate.

2. 'Parking facilities will be available for officials behind the field house in the area marked B.

3. Your dressing room is on the South end of the gymnasium; an attendant will be in charge to assist you.

    4. Hotels: Hilton -- 1st and Vine
                  Rogers -- 2nd and Archer

           Motels: Fargo -- Hwy. 30
                 El Rancho -- Hwy. 40

                        Sincerely,

                        Athletic Director

Figure 133.

the official needs. The return card provides space for the official to accept the contract or to make any changes that may be necessary. Cards of this nature do not serve as contracts, but they are very helpful in making certain that all of the games have adequate officiating. Any information that the official might need could be added in a follow-up letter close to the date of the event. If the official will need overnight accommodations or a knowledge of restaurants in the area, he should be provided this information in the follow-up letter. The official should be reminded of all of the necessary details such as dates, place (with directions), times, fees, and his officiating partner.

Proper planning is essential if the event is to run smoothly. The notification of officials is one of the vital aspects that cannot be overlooked. Since the officials are so important to the success of the event, their treatment before, during, and after the activity are very important to the proper

ATHLETIC DEPARTMENT

ELYRIA HIGH SCHOOL

ELYRIA, OHIO 44035
TELEPHONE 322-6387

JUDGE'S ASSIGNMENTS

Dear Judge:

There will be a judges and coaches meeting at 1:30 for the morning session and one at 6:30 for the evening session in the cafeteria which is located just below the gymnasium.

Here are your assignments:

- -

2:30 Session   Announcer--Paul Fina

Side Horse 1. Ben Montcalm H.J.   Long Horse 1. Bob Smith
            2. John Fina   2. Geo. Fredericks
            3. Bob Kriedler   3. John Jones
            4. Bill Meade   4. Fred Gallagher
                    Penalty Zones   5. Joe Domino
Trampoline 1. Newt Loken H. J.
            2. Bob Kriedler
            3. Ben Montcalm
            4. Mike Karon
            5. John Fina - Counter and Bed area

- -

7:00 Session   Announcer--Bill Heart

Horizontal Bar 1. John Fina H. J.   Rings   1. Joe Hart
               2. Ben Montcalm   2. John Jahns
               3. Guest   3. Fred Cady
               4. Paul Fina   4. Jack Smaft

Parallel Bar 1. Paul Fina H.J.   Tumbling 1. Bob Alliza
              2. Pete Barthell   2. Fred Jones
              3. John Fina   3. John Meade
              4. Bob Kriedler   4. Fred Jones

- -

Thanks for your cooperation. I will be looking forward to seeing you (time)

                    Yours in gymnastics,

                    Director of the Meet

Figure 134.

administration of the contest.

Usually, all negotiations with the official are conducted by the athletic director or coach. However, in some of the smaller schools it can be done by the principal. In either case, the official should be notified two or three days prior to the time the game is to be played. Some schools will notify the official by sending out a master list of all games being played in a particuler sport with the dates, time, and place indicated, as well as the name of the official or officials that are assigned to the contest. Prior notification will give the official time to contact the school officials if any conflict arises.

Contracts with Officials

Written contracts usually are essential in employing an official to work an interscholastic athletic contest. In order to avoid

TABLE CX

_____19_____

Check one
☐ We would like to schedule the following with you:
☐ We would like for you to officiate the following:
☐ We are expecting you to participate in the following:
☐ We are expecting you to officiate the following:

Event: _____

Place: _____

Date: _____ Time _____A.M. Daylight Saving Time
                                       P.M. Standard Time

Terms: _____ Position _____

Remarks:

Please answer on the attached card.

Name ___ _____ Title _____

School _____

ORDER THESE ATHLETIC CORRESPONDENCE CARDS FROM
Stock No. 3   **School Aid Co., 200 Chester Ave., Danville, Ill.**
Price only $8.50 per 100 on double government postcards
Unstamped cards $3.00 per 100.

Reprinted with permission of School Aid Co., Danville, Illinois.

TABLE CXI

_____19_____

Cross   We will — will not schedule the following with you:
out   I   will — will not officiate the following:
one   We will — will not be there to participate in the following:
        I   will — will not be there to officiate the following:

        Event _____
        Place: _____
        Date: _____ Time _____A.M. Daylight Saving Time
                                           P.M. Standard Time

        Terms: _____ Position _____

Remarks:

Name _____ Title _____
School _____

TABLE CXII

MID - SUBURBAN LEAGUE
W. A. Collier - Assignment Chairman
1101 Maple Lane
Prospect Heights, Illinois 60070
537 - 1137 or 259 - 5300 ext. 72

Dear _____

        You are scheduled to be at _____

on _____
Time _____
Position _____

(DO NOT SEND A SUBSTITUTE)

misunderstanding and confusion, it is best to have in writing a contract between the official and the school. This is not only a safeguard for both parties, but good administration and in fact, good common sense. These contracts should be signed by the appropriate school officials and the official who is going to work the game or games. Many states furnish these contracts so that there will be uniformity. The contracts should contain the name of the school, dates, circumstances, and conditions under which the contest is to be played and the fee.

Most states do not want to assume the responsibility in any disputes between officials and school authorities unless forced to do so by a stalemate. In most states, the principal of the high school or a faculty representative authorized by him signs contracts.

Employment of Officials

Usually the athletic director or the principal of the host school will make the initial contact with the official. Oftentimes,

TABLE CXIII
INTERIM LEAGUE
CONTRACT FOR OFFICIALS

Deerfield — East Leyden — Glenbard East — Glenbrook — Main West — Morton West — Niles West — Prospect — Proviso West — West Leyden — Wheaton — Willowbrook.

The league of the above schools for the school year 19_____ - _____, and _____

_____, and official registered with the Illinois High School Association, do hereby enter into the following contract: The said official agrees to be present and officiate the following games or matches:

O. K.	DAY	DATE	HOUR	PLACE

If you accep*t Any of These,* write "OK" next to those dates you accept. *Draw a line* through those dates you cannot accept. In the event that you find it necessary to cancel a date, notify me at once, but *Do Not Send a Substitute.*

Signed: _____ Assignment Chairman

     O. F. Walker   Proviso West High School
     394 Park, Elmhurst — Te-4-1494

Signed: _____ Official   Home Phone _____
       _____ Address   Bus. Phone _____
       _____ City

Open Dates:

September _____   October _____   November _____

December _____   January _____   February _____

ILLINOIS HIGH SCHOOL ASSOCIATION
ATHLETIC DIVISION

CONTRACT FOR OFFICIALS

№ 146864

The_____High School and_____
                                        (Official's Name and Address)

_____, an official registered with the Illinois High School Association, hereby enter into the following agreement. The said official agrees to be present and officiate_____
                                                                        (Name of Sport)
games or meets to be played:

	Date	Day	Hour	Place	Fee	Expenses
1						
2						
3						

1. The said school will pay the said official the amount stated above for his services provided that the obligation of the school ceases if and when the official ceases to be a registered official or if the contest is cancelled because of an epidemic or similar emergency.
2. If a contract is made during a given school year for a contest to be played during the next school year and if, in the meantime, there is a change in the school principalship, the contract is valid only if and when the incoming principal has been notified of the existing contract and he has sanctioned it or has failed to inform the official of cancellation within one week after the notification.
3. If either party hereto fails to fulfill the obligation of any part of the contract, that party shall pay to the other party a sum equal to the contractual gross fee less milage allowances as damages, the remainder of the contract shall not be binding, and the breach of contract shall be reported to the Association.
4. This contract becomes invalid if not signed and returned by the Official on or before_____, 19 ____

Principal _____ Date signed _____ 19____

Official _____ Date signed_____ 19____

Home Phone Number_____ Business Phone Number_____

Figure 135. Reprinted with permission from the Illinois High School Association.

the athletic director recommends certain officials to the principal, and in turn, he assumes the responsibility of hiring the official. Naturally, the coach will have some, if not all, influence as to the selection of the officials, but he should not under any circumstances hire the officials unless it is unavoidable.

Fees for Officials

All payments to officials must be standard. No official should be hired who will attempt to work the games for a reduced rate of pay. This is not only unethical, but leads to dissatisfaction and underhanded dealings between coaches and officials. No school should attempt to hire officials for less than the standard fee which is being paid for like services in schools throughout the area. The going rate of pay should prevail whenever it is possible to do so. Most official associations will set the standard of pay in cooperation with local and state officials. It will differ to some extent in different areas and localities throughout the state.

Most conferences will stipulate the amount of money that can be paid for officials. This is an excellent practice because it discourages any attempt by the school or the official to underbid for services. The following is an example of the amount of money that can be paid under this type of regulation.

A. *Baseball*
Varsity double header (1 umpire) $25.00
(If only one game of the two scheduled is played—$16.50)
Varsity double header (2 umpires) $21.50
(If only one game of the two scheduled is played—$12.50)
Varsity single game (2 umpires) $12.50
Junior Varsity, sophomore, or freshman double header (1 umpire) $20.00
(If only one game of the two scheduled is played—$14.00)
Junior Varsity, sophomore, or freshman double header (2 umpires) $16.50
(If only one game of the two scheduled is played—$11.00)
Junior Varsity, sophomore, or freshman single game (2 umpires) $11.00
Junior Varsity, sophomore, or freshman single game (1 umpire) $14.00

B. *Basketball*
Varsity and preliminary game (2 officials) $27.50
Varsity game only $25.00
Preliminary game only $12.50
2 games below varsity level (2 officials) $15.00
1 game—junior varsity, sophomore or freshman "A" (2 officials) $10.00
1 game—freshman "B" or "C" (1 official) $10.00
2 games below varsity level (1 official) $20.00

C. *Cross Country*
League meet (any combination) $11.00

D. *Football*
Varsity and preliminary game (4 officials) $27.50
Varsity game only (4 officials) $25.00

Preliminary game only (4 officials) $12.50
1 game—junior varsity, sophomore, or freshman "A" "B" "C" (2 officials) .. $11.00
1 game—junior varsity, sophomore, or freshman "A" "B" "C" (1 official) ... $15.00
2 games below the varsity when one game has 2 officials $20.00
   and the second game has 4 officials

E. *Gymnastics*

Varsity and accompanying meet (2 officials) $16.50
Double dual meet, varsity and accompanying meet (2 officials) $22.00
Varsity only (2 officials) $11.00
Sophomore only (2 officials) $11.00
Freshman only (2 officials) .... $ 8.50
(1 official) $12.50
Varsity, sophomore, and freshman (2 officials) $25.00
League championship meet $16.50

F. *Soccer*

Any two contests in succession $20.00
Any single contest $13.00

G. *Swimming*

Varsity only (2 officials) $11.00
Any combination of two meets (2 officials) $16.50
Junior varsity, sophomore, or freshman only $12.50
Varsity, sophomore, and freshman (2 officials) $25.00
All league championship meets (2 officials) $16.50

H. *Track*

League championship varsity and sophomore meet $30.00
Freshman league meet $15.00
Varsity, sophomore quadrangular $20.00
Varsity, sophomore triangular $15.00

1. *Wrestling*

Varsity meet $16.50
Meet accompanying varsity meet $16.50
All other single meets $11.00
Combination of varsity and one other meet (1 official) $27.50
Combination of two meets other than varsity $27.50
Three level meet $22.50
(Wrestling officials' contracts for above are to
include only the 12 matches of a normal meet.)
Varsity quadrangular (24 Matches—2 officials) $33.00
Varsity quadrangular (36 round robin—2 officials) $42.00
Lower level quadrangular (24 matches—2 officials) $22.00
Lower level quadrangular (36 matches—2 officials) $28.00

Officials should be hired from lists approved by schools in each league. If sufficient names are not submitted by the schools involved, the assignment chairman should have the prerogative to hire any official he feels is qualified.

The following number of officials should be employed for each contest in various sports:

A. Varsity baseball—two
B. Other baseball—one
C. All basketball—two, except freshman "B" or "C"—one
D. Varsity and preliminary football—four, all other football—two
E. Gymnastics—two
F. Swimming—two
G. All wrestling levels—one

No parents of students who are competing should be used as officials for any league contests. The assignment chairman should assign under a rating system determined by the athletic directors, the various officials hired by each league.

Payment of Officials

The method of paying the official differs widely among schools depending upon past practices. Usually this is the task of the athletic director, although in many schools the principal will pay the official. It is not a good practice for the coach to do this, and if he is also the athletic director, the principal should pay the officials. The official should be paid before the contest so that the outcome of the game will not influence the transaction.

Because of bookkeeping procedures some schools prefer to send the payment in the form of a check as soon as possible after the game. This is acceptable and sometimes avoids confusion if a substitute official works the game and it is not known in time to make out the check to the correct person. The official should not have to seek out the director or principal in order to be paid for his services.

Hosting the Official

It must always be remembered that the official is also a guest and should be treated as such. Although many people may feel that he is paid for his services, it is not nearly enough and usually the man is officiating because he likes it. Therefore, he should be offered every courtesy and treated as a guest. Many schools will provide the official with a student host. Often this person will be an athlete. This individual will meet the official as he arrives at the door, introduce himself and escort the official to the dressing room. He will stay with him, helping him in any way possible until he leaves the dressing room to officiate. He will be available at halftime and provide the official with soft drinks and help in any way possible. He should escort the official to his car after the game.

Dressing Accommodations for Officials

Providing a suitable dressing room for the official will differ a great deal in various schools because of facilities. The official should have a separate dressing area away from both teams. It should be situated in an area where spectators will not bother the official. The athletic director should see to it that the fans, coaches, and players do not enter the officials' dressing room at any time before, at halftime, or after the game. It should be clean, neat, and tidy.

Pregame Preparation for Officials

Oftentimes there are certain circumstances and situations whereby it is necessary to discuss certain rule interpretations, floor mechanics, and other pertinent matters relating to the upcoming game with the officials. This must be done with utmost discretion and in a most courteous fashion. It should always be done with both the principal and coach, the athletic director and coach, or all three together in the officials' dressing room prior to the game and always without an audience.

Assistance before the Game for Officials

The official should be provided with the necessary items that he will need before the game. He should be given towels to be used at halftime and after the game. He should be met at the door on his arrival and escorted to his dressing room or any other place he may wish to go. If the official has any guests, they should be instructed where to sit during the game. Any game equipment, such as balls, towels, etc. should be made available to the official before game time.

Assistance During the Game for Officials

The official should not be expected to officiate the game and take care of other duties associated with the contest. This is the responsibility of the person managing the contest. However, there are certain items that the official may need during the course of the game, such as towels for cleaning the floor, an extra ball, etc., that should be readily available if needed. The student-host should be at hand to help the official in any way possible and this person should assume the responsibility of returning all equipment given to the official. Arrangements should be made for escorting the official to the dressing room at halftime.

Assistance after the Game for Officials

The official should never be left to shift for himself after the game. This could be a very trying time for him especially if the game was close and the rivalry was intense. The student-host and in some situations, the police should stay in the immediate

vicinity of the official dressing room. The official should be escorted to his car. He should be helped in any way possible and given any information regarding road directions, weather forecasts, road conditions, eating establishments, etc.

Postgame Meeting for Officials

There is an unwritten rule among many coaches that they never under any circumstances talk with the official after the game. Most officials would rather not have either the winning or losing coach in the dressing room after the contest. It can lead to nothing but trouble so why permit it? While it may be true that the coach may be a personal friend of one of the officials and meets with him socially on various occasions, it still is a wise decision to stay away from him after the game.

Athletic Code for Officials

There are many details with which the coach must concern himself in connection with athletic officials. The following is an athletic code for officials to know and understand.

1. A professional attitude and relationship which guarantees a high caliber of work.
2. A rested body and alert mind.
3. A complete knowledge of the rules.
4. A neat appearance and clean standard uniform.
5. A necessity and practice of being on time for all games.
6. A capacity for rectifying mistakes.
7. The nerve to make all calls the way he sees them and not be intimidated by coach, player, or spectator.
8. Complete control of temper.
9. Cooperation in making calls with other officials.
10. Ability to make interpretations and announcements clear to both teams.

11. The ability not to discuss teams or players in the presence of opposing coaches.

Rating of Officials

The rating of officials has been a problem for as long as there have been athletic contests that needed to be officiated. While tremendous improvements in officiating have taken place over the years and much is being done at the present time to upgrade officiating and make the art of officiating more uniform throughout the country, it still presents a problem.

Most all of the states now have official registration and make every attempt to upgrade officiating. Many states encourage and request that officials be rated for every contest and that these things are sent to the main office where the results are tabulated and brought together into a composite score for each official. The results are then sent to the schools to be used in future selection of officials.

There are other ways of obtaining information about good officials. This is important because every coach wants the best officiating that he can get. One such meth-

TABLE CXIV
OFFICIAL'S RATING FORM

Home team _____ Opponent _____ Date _____

Name of Official _____

Rater's Name _____ Position _____

Game Rating	Superior	Good	Average	Fair	Poor
	81 — 100	61 — 80	41 — 60	31 — 40	20 — 30

Evaluation _____ (Circle correct number)   *Ratings*

1. Personal: Neatness, promptness, poise, attitude	5	4	3	2	1	_____
2. Enthusiasm: Ambition, confidence	5	4	3	2	1	_____
3. Knowledge of game and Officiating techniques	5	4	3	2	1	_____
4. Consistency	5	4	3	2	1	_____
5. Control of game	5	4	3	2	1	_____
6. Agility and physical ability	5	4	3	2	1	_____
7. Decisiveness in calls and decisions	5	4	3	2	1	_____
8. Fairness	5	4	3	2	1	_____
9. Proper use of signals	5	4	3	2	1	_____
10. Spectator acceptance	5	4	3	2	1	_____

TOTAL ....

Evaluation Table

Numerical Rating	Rating	Evaluation Score
5	Superior	81 — 100
4	Good	61 — 80
3	Average	41 — 60
2	Fair	31 — 40
1	Poor	20 — 30

Probably the biggest problem encountered in the attempts to improve officiating is the fact that the remuneration received for officiating is not enough to warrant anyone making a career of it. It is true, therefore, that one needs to enjoy doing it.

od is through a school's own scouts who are scouting future opponents. These scouts are in an excellent position to judge how good an official is. Still another method and a very popular one, because it gives the young official just starting out an op-

BIG SEVEN CONFERENCE

BASKETBALL OFFICIALS RATING FORM

Please complete and return this report to Mr. Ken Trainor,
Assignment Chairman--Big Seven Conference by Winter Banquet
Meeting.

Date_____(of game)

Game |_____| at |_____|
Score   Level   Score

Official _____

Please indicate your evaluation by marking an (X) in the proper column.

	Superior	Above Average	Average	Below Average	Inferior
Appearance, bearing, physical condition	( )	( )	( )	( )	( )
Rules, knowledge and application	( )	( )	( )	( )	( )
Mechanics, position coverage, signals	( )	( )	( )	( )	( )
Manner in handling Players, bench, fans	( )	( )	( )	( )	( )
Calls on blocking and charging	( )	( )	( )	( )	( )
Calls on travelling violations	( )	( )	( )	( )	( )
Consistency of judgment	( )	( )	( )	( )	( )
Reaction to crowd pressure	( )	( )	( )	( )	( )
Hustle	( )	( )	( )	( )	( )
Promptness	( )	( )	( )	( )	( )

Please give the official a numerical rating on his overall work using the
following scale for each category: Superior - 5; Above Average - 4;
Average - 3; Below Average - 2; Inferior - 1.

Total Points_____

Comments:

Signed_____ School_____ Date_____
(of rating)

Figure 136.

NORTH SUBURBAN CONFERENCE

FOOTBALL OFFICIALS RATING SHEET

Date_____

Game_____ vs._____

Played at_____   Level of Competition

OFFICIALS   # worn   Varsity_____
                                     JV_____
1. Referee_____   Sophomore_____
2. Head Linesman_____   Frosh "A"_____
3. Field Judge_____   Frosh "B"_____
4. Umpire_____

RATING SCALE: 4-Superior   2-Acceptable
                 3-Good   1-Unacceptable (comment on reasons why)

CRITERIA	#1 R	#2 HL	#3 FJ	#4 U
1. CONSISTENCY				
a) Use of whistle____				
b) In calling fouls____				
c) Other____				
2. WORKING KNOWLEDGE OF THE RULES				
a) Knowledge of legal and illegal acts____				
b) Knowledge of proper enforcement____				
3. COMMUNICATIONS				
a) Signals and preliminary signals____				
b) Rapport with the players and coaches____				
4. HUSTLE				
a) Getting to the ball quickly____				
b) Moving to the proper position____				
c) Timing signals____				
5. MISCELLANEOUS				
a) Promptness____				
b) Proper uniform and equipment____				
c) Other--please list____				

COMMENTS--Positive or negative on either an individual officer or the team.
(Use other side of this sheet, if necessary)

Rating sheet filled in by_____   Position_____
School_____   Date_____

Mail to: Joe Smith
            Dayton High School
            Dayton, OR

Figure 137.

portunity to demonstrate what he can do,
is to use the junior varsity as a proving
ground for officials. This provides an opportunity for the head coach to observe
the official under game conditions and
affords an opportunity to pass judgment on
his ability as an official.

Regardless of the various rating systems
that are in use throughout the states, there
is no foolproof system of rating officials.
This is true because of the human element
that always enters into an evaluation technique or system. There is also the element
of judgment that every official needs to
have because oftentimes the rules that are
written by which the game should be
played do not cover every aspect of the

game. Situations will always arise that the
rules do not cover, so as a result the official
needs to make a judgment call.

However, much has been done by the
National Federation of State High School
Associations, various state associations, and
conferences to train better officials and to
make officiating more uniform. Most conferences attempt to select the same officials
for all conference games in an attempt to
secure more uniform officiating.

Improvement in Officiating

Much has been done in recent years to
unify and standardize athletic officiating.
The element of judgment will always be
a factor and as a result it is difficult to set
up any standards which cover all situations. There is still a great deal of room
for improvement. Most state associations

TABLE CXV
BIG TWELVE CONFERENCE
FOOTBALL RATING FORM

HOME TEAM	SCORE	VISITORS	SCORE	DATE

_____ _____ VS. _____ _____ _____

Varsity   F.S.   J.V.   Frosh A or B   Frosh-Soph B

OFFICIALS RATING

— — — — — — — — — — — — — — — — — — —

Name _____ Position _____

Punctuality:
1. Arrived 20 to 30 minutes early to talk over working assignments.
2. Arrived just in time for the game.
3. Arrived late with an excuse.

Dress: Wears the official uniform (1) Clean and Neat   (2) Messy   (3) Dirty

Knowledge of Rules:	(1) Excellent	(2) Good	(3) Fair	(4) Poor
Enforcement of the Rules:	(1) Excellent	(2) Good	(3) Fair	(4) Poor
Coverage of the Game:	(1) Excellent	(2) Good	(3) Fair	(4) Poor

Remarks:

— — — — — — — — — — — — — — — — — — —

Name _____ Position _____

Punctuality:
1. Arrived 20 to 30 minutes early to talk over working assignments.
2. Arrived just in time for the game.
3. Arrived late with an excuse.

Dress: Wears the official uniform (1) Clean and Neat   (2) Messy   (3) Dirty

Knowledge of Rules:	(1) Excellent	(2) Good	(3) Fair	(4) Poor
Enforcement of the Rules:	(1) Excellent	(2) Good	(3) Fair	(4) Poor
Coverage of the Game:	(1) Excellent	(2) Good	(3) Fair	(4) Poor

Remarks:

— — — — — — — — — — — — — — — — — — —

Name _____ Position _____

Punctuality:
1. Arrived 20 to 30 minutes early to talk over working assignments.
2. Arrived just in time for the game.
3. Arrived late with an excuse.

Dress: Wears the official uniform (1) Clean and Neat   (2) Messy   (3) Dirty

Knowledge of Rules:	(1) Excellent	(2) Good	(3) Fair	(4) Poor
Enforcement of the Rules:	(1) Excellent	(2) Good	(3) Fair	(4) Poor
Coverage of the Game:	(1) Excellent	(2) Good	(3) Fair	(4) Poor

Remarks:

— — — — — — — — — — — — — — — — — — —

OFFICIAL'S SHEET FOR RATING SCHOOLS

MAIL TO

ILLINOIS HIGH SCHOOL ASSOCIATION

11 S. LA SALLE ST., CHICAGO 3

N° 22603

NOTE: List schools for only ONE SPORT on a given sheet. This is for_____
(Sport)

Please list and rate all schools that played in games in which you officiated during the month specified. Report should be sent at the end of September, October and November for football and at the end of November, December, January and February for basketball.

SUGGESTED FACTORS ON WHICH TO BASE RATING: Please rate all schools on the basis of the suggested factors listed below. (Note that all ten items apply to the host school. Items 1, 6 to 10 also apply to the visiting school.)

1. Courtesy shown official by school.
2. Condition of dressing rooms for officials and visiting team.
3. Score board, measuring devices and other equipment.
4. Size, condition, marking, out-of-bounds space of floor or field.
5. Management. Time schedule. Floor or field kept cleared. Orderliness.
6. Crowd sportsmanship. Lack of booing, hissing and hoodlumism. Acceptance of decisions. Attitude toward players.
7. Sportsmanship shown by team and coach.
8. Moral tone on and off the floor or field (lack of profanity, courtesy)
9. Extent to which the administrator seemed to be in complete control of the athletic program.
10. Was there evidence of betting on the game?

In last column list numbers for ONLY THOSE ITEMS in which the school should try to improve.

School—List Below Home School First in Each Pair	Winner	YOUR ESTIMATE			Needs Improvement in Items Number	Comment
		Superior	Average	Poor		
Sample—Eaton	X	X				
Elktown			X		8, 10	Players were discourteous

Month_____Year_____   Official_____

(OVER)

TOURNAMENT REPORT

Host School	Date	YOUR ESTIMATE			Needs Improve-ment in Items Number	Comment
		Superior	Average	Poor		

SPECIAL NOTE: Give location and date of interpretation meetings or clinics you attended during the past month.

1.   2.   3.

REMARKS:

Figure 138-A & B. Reprinted with permission from the Illinois High School Association.

have set up machinery for state-wide coverage in meetings for providing opportunity to take examinations, and for keeping up-to-date on rules, changes, and officiating techniques. Such efforts have resulted in better officiating.

Clinics for Officials

Attendance by officials and prospective officials at officiating clinics can be a very rewarding experience. They are usually held in all areas of the country to satisfy the conscientious official. Not only do these clinics provide a springboard to a career in officiating, but they also bring veteran officials together for an opportunity to exchange ideas.

Any number of topics may be discussed at officiating clinics. Studying and learning rules and then passing tests may be a major part of the program for apprentice officials. Veterans may spend time reviewing recent rule changes and polishing up on old rules and officiating techniques. After attending a clinic and passing a rules test, an apprentice official may be ready to begin working on a low level. In order for him to move up to high school or college officiating, he will undoubtedly be required to pass some type of state association exam as well as have some previous officiating experience.

Veteran officials may have the opportunity to attend coaching clinics also. They may be asked to assist in rules interpretation meetings held by state and local associations. A good official will make every effort to attend officiating clinics. Even the most seasoned veteran can benefit from a well-organized clinic.

TABLE CXVI
SPECIAL REPORT
TO
IHSA ATHLETIC OFFICIAL AND IHSA OFFICE*

This form is to be used to report any matter concerning officiating that merits *immediate* attention. It shall be used to report errors in applying rules and phases of officiating in which an official should immediately attempt to improve. It may also be used to report an axceptional good job of officiating. Coaches are requested to use this channel *of filing complaints* and to refrain from protesting to officials during or following a contest. Prompt reporting to the official would help him to correct errors and improve his competency.

This form should be filled out in duplicate with the blue sheet as the original to be sent to the official and the pink sheet as a duplicate to be sent to the IHSA Office.

— —

Report for _____ who worked a _____
                          (Official)   (Sport)

contest between _____ High School, _____, Illinois,
                        (Home School)

and _____ High School, _____, Illinois
          (Visiting School)

on _____.
          (Date)

Specific item being reported:

Explanation or comment:

(Use other side if necessary)

Date _____   Signed _____, Principal

_____, High School

_____, Illinois

*Reprinted with permission from the Illinois High School Association.

Women Officials

One of the problems at the present time confronting the girls interscholastic program is the lack of qualified officials. Many of the states have already begun programs for the training of women officials. For example, the Illinois High School Association has declared that the Illinois Division of Girls and Womens Sports should be urged to work cooperatively with them in establishing and maintaining the Illinois High School Association Womens Officials' Program. This puts to work the best resources of the I.H.S.A. and the I.D.G.W.S.—O.S.A. Boards of Women Officials and adds a new

dimension to women's officiating in Illinois. The I.H.S.A. has gone on record as approving a training, rating, and registration program for women officials in basketball, volleyball, swimming, track and field, softball, field hockey, and gymnastics. This will place the women officials on practically the same basis as the men in terms of qualifications. It also means that the women will now be given the opportunity to become trained, rated, and registered officials which will qualify and challenge them to officiate in the high school girls athletic program. It will assure good officiating which will in turn result in good

TABLE CXVII
IHSA ROUTE FOR WOMEN OFFICIALS*
FACTORS WHICH DETERMINE PROMOTION

	MAXIMUM POINTS	YOUR POINTS**
I. EXAMINATION GRADE (95 or above)	30	
II. AVERAGE RATNG (1 = Superior)	40	
III. YEARS SUCCESSFUL WORK (10 or more)	10	
IV. FILING OF REPORTS	10	
V. ATTENDANCE AT MEETINGS	10	
	100	
	(Maximum)	(Your Total)

Points necessary for promotion to **RECOGNIZED** rank: 72
Points necessary for promotion to **CERTIFIED** rank: 82

**In the foregoing factors, a proportionate allowance was made for lower achievement.
*This promotional system would be used for those registered woman officials who followed the IHSA **ROUTE FOR WOMEN OFFICIALS.**
†Reprinted with permission from the Illinois High School Association.

play in the girls athletic program. This type of cooperation will eventually carry over into other states and result in a better all-around sports program for the girls. A women's classification as an I.H.S.A. woman official is determined by the current D.G.W.S.–O.S.A. rating she holds in the sport in which she is registered. She is encouraged to attend officiating training and rating sessions offered by the D.G.W.S. –O.S.A. Board of Women Officials located in Illinois to obtain a rating, renew a rating, and improve a rating. There are many factors which determine the promotion of women officials, the route for women officials, the recommended system for registration, training, and promotion of I.H.S.A. women officials.

BEHAVIORAL OBJECTIVES

After a person has read this chapter, he should be able to:

1. Discuss the importance of good officiating.

2. Enumerate and explain the qualifications of a good athletic official.
3. Explain the function of the official.
4. Distinguish between a recognized, registered, certified, and affiliated official.
5. Explain the purpose of state regulations for sports officiating.
6. Analyze the responsibility of the administrator in hiring officials.
7. Identify several criteria that govern the actions of the administrators in hiring the official.
8. Recall several points which can be of concern in selecting officials and explain each.
9. Identify the information that should be given to the official at the time he is hired.
10. Recall several things that must be taken into consideration before selecting the official.
11. Analyze the way in which conferences solve the problem of the selection of officials and explain in detail.

TABLE CXVIII
ILLINOIS HIGH SCHOOL ASSOCIATION

A BRIEF EXPLANATION OF THE RECOMMENDED SYSTEM FOR REGISTRATION, TRAINING AND PROMOTION OF IHSA WOMEN OFFICIALS:*

In those sports in which the IHSA might use DGWS rules:

> Women who register without a DGWS rating, will be accepted at the rank of REGI-STERED and will follow a training and promotional system to the rank of CERTI-FIED. (This is similar to the men officials' program.)

> Women who register with a DGWS rating below National, will be accepted at the rank of RECOGNIZED and will follow a training and promotional system to the rank of CERTIFIED.

> Women who register with a DGWS rating of National, will be accepted at the rank of CERTIFIED and will remain at the rank of CERTIFIED, provided they meet the requirements of that rank.

In those sports in which the IHSA might use National Federation girls' rules:

> All women who register, will be accepted at the rank of REGISTERED and will follow a training and promotional system to the rank of CERTIFIED.

In the future, if National Federation girls' rules are adopted in sports in which the IHSA had been using DGWS rules:

> All women who register for the first time, will be accepted at the rank of REGISTERED and will follow a training and promotional system to the rank of CERTIFIED.

> All women who register for the first time, will be accepted at the rank of REGISTERED and will follow a training and promotional system to the rank of CERTIFIED.

> IHSA Women Officials registered in that sport will maintain their same rank under National Federation rules, provided they meet the requirements of that rank. This would include passing a test on National Federation rules and attending an IHSA-sponsored girls' rules interpretation meeting on National Federation rules.

This system would involve IHSA in:

> A program of girls' rules interpretation meetings
> Development of girls' rules examinations
> Sale of girls' rules books in the IHSA Office
> A system of rating women officials by the coaches and schools

---

*Reprinted with permission from the Illinois High School Association.

12. Identify several methods of assigning officials for contests, and explain one in detail.

13. Explain one method of notifying officials of upcoming contests which they have been hired to officiate.

14. Summarize some of the advantages of having written contracts with officials.

15. Analyze the system of workable fee payment for officials.

16. Differentiate between fees paid for officiating the different sports and explain the differentiation.

17. Formulate a plan for hosting the visiting official.

18. Explain why it is necessary to have separate dressing accommodations for officials.

19. Explain the purpose of pregame preparations for officials.

20. Compile several ways in which officials can be assisted before and after the game.

21. Prepare an athletic code list and ex-

TABLE CXIX
DIVISION OF GIRLS AND WOMENS SPORTS
*ROUTE FOR WOMEN OFFICIALS**

RECOGNIZED:
1. She has registered with the IHSA Office and in the opinion of at least two responsible persons, she is of the right type for a desirable woman official.
2. She has attended an IHSA - sponsored Rules Interpretation meeting for the current year in the sport in which she is recognized.
3. She has a current DGWS - OSA Rating in the sport in which she is RECOGNIZED.

CERTIFIED:
1. She has served as a RECOGNIZED official for two full years prior to January 1 of this year.
2. She has a current DGWS - OSA Rating in the sport in which she is CERTIFIED.
3. She has attended an IHSA - sponsored Rules interpretation meeting for the current year year in the sport in which she is CERTIFIED.

OR

CERTIFIED:
1. She has registered with the IHSA Office and in the opinion of at least two responsible persons, she is of the right type for a desirable woman official.
2. She has a current DGWS - OSA National Rating in the sport in which she is CERTI-TIFIED.
3. She has attended an IHSA - sponsored Rules Interpreation meeting for the current year in the sport in which she is CERTIFIED.

---

*This route would be optional for women officials registered in sports in which DGWS rules are used.

*Reprinted with permission from the Illinois High School Association.

plain each.

22. Explain several methods of rating officials.
23. Explain several ways in which officiating can be improved.
24. Explain several ways athletic officials are selected, and elaborate on which one is best and why.
25. Explain the reason for notifying the official one week before the game which he is to officiate.
26. List some advantages of having game contracts with officials.
27. Identify some of the considerations given to the formulation of policies in the employment of athletic officials.
28. Enumerate several methods of rating officials and discuss the merits of each.
29. Explain several plans for the hiring of athletic officials.
30. List several conference rules regarding the selection of officials, and explain why it is important to have these rules.
31. List and describe the various ways in which good officials can be brought to the attention of the coach.

ACTIVITIES

1. Attend an officials' clinic and report what took place to the class.
2. Watch an official work a football or basketball game.
3. Ask a local official to talk to the class about officiating rules, regulations, and requirements.

TABLE CXX
ILLINOIS HIGH SCHOOL ASSOCIATION
ROUTE FOR WOMEN OFFICIALS*

REGISTERED:

1. She has registered with the IHSA Office and in the opinion of at least two responsible persons, she is of the right type for a desirable woman official.
2. She has passed a preliminary Part I rules examination in the sport in which she is **REGISTERED**.
3. She has attended an IHSA sponsored Rules Interpretation meeting for the current year in the sport in which she is **REGISTERED**.
4. She is endeavoring to make use of the aids furnished by the State Association.

RECOGNIZED:

1. She has served as a **REGISTERED** official for one full year prior to January 1 of this year.
2. She has written the current Part I examination for review and Part II, under supervision.
3. She has attended an IHSA - sponsored rules interpretation meeting for the current year in the sport in which she is **RECOGNIZED**.
4. Her composite score on examination, experience, ratings received from schools and extent to which she cooperated in meetings and the filing of reports totaled at least 72 points.

CERTIFIED:

1. She has served as a **RECOGNIZED** official for two full years prior to January 1 of this year.
2. She has written the current Part I examination for review and Part II, under supervision.
3. She has attended an IHSA - sponsored rules interpretation meeting for the current year in the sport in which she is **CERTIFIED**.
4. Her composite score on examination, experience, rating received from schools and extent to which she cooperated in meetings and the filing of reports totaled at least 82 points.

---

*This route would be required for women officials registered in sports in which National Federation rules are used.

This route would be optional for women officials registered in sports in which DGWS rules are used.

*Reprinted with permission from the Illinois High School Association.

4. Write to the state officials association for a rules examination and examine its contents.
5. Talk with the local principal and athletic director regarding the selecting and payment of officials.
6. Talk with an official and enumerate some of the values he received from officiating and why he does it.
7. Talk with several coaches regarding their opinions on present-day officiating.
8. Set up a complete plan for conducting an officiating clinic.
9. Attend a conference meeting in which officials are selected.
10. Form a panel and discuss the issue: Should officials be required to pass state examinations.
11. Debate the issue: Officials should work

TABLE CXXI
EVALUATION OF WOMEN OFFICIALS

Name of Official: _____

          (Miss or Mrs.)   (First)   (Last)

Date of Event: _____ Event: _____Ba, FH, Gy, Soc, Sof, Sw, Tr, Vo_____

                                         (Circle One)

Composite Rating: 1 — 2 — 3 — 4 — 5 — Site _____

      (Scale: 1 — Superior; 2 — Excellent; 3 — Average; 4 — Below Ave.; 5 — Poor)

Check below ONLY those items where improvement is needed:

1.	Knowledge of the rules	_____	5.	Influenced by crowd	_____
2.	Quick and positive decisions	_____	6.	Courtesy	_____
			7.	Appearance	_____
3.	Ability to follow routines/play	_____	8.	Judgment	_____
4.	Self control and poise	_____			

Evaluating School: _____ Signature _____

HOW TO USE CARD

Fill out one card for each official for each game both home and away.

Officials should be rated after each game as ratings should always be kept up to date.

This is a courtesy that should be extended to all officials.

the varsity game only.

12. Obtain a case study book and discuss several cases in both football and basketball.

13. Form two groups and debate the issue: Should officials be noncoaches.

SUGGESTED READINGS

1. Alderson, C.J.: Officials and coaches are on the same team. *Journal of Health, Physical Education, and Recreation,* November, 1963.

2. Billick, P.: What is an official? *Scholastic Coach,* March, 1961.

3. Bunn, John: *The Art of Officiating Sports.* Englewood Cliffs, P-H, 1968.

4. Case, R.: An indictment of officials. *Physical Educator,* October, 1971.

5. Donnelly, Richard: Relationships between athletic officials and coaches. *Athletic Journal,* May, 1957.

6. Gill, Tom: The official and the coach. *Coach and Athlete,* November, 1970.

7. Haarlow, B.: *Basketball Officiating.* New York, Ronald, 1960.

8. Kaufman, Mark: Officiating viewpoints. *Scholastic Coach,* March, 1950.

9. Lehmann, Harry: The high cost of whistle tooting. *American School Board Journal,* May, 1957.

10. Mackey, Harold: Wanted—qualified basketball officials. *Journal of Health, Physical Education, and Recreation,* November, 1958.

11. Mitchell, Elmer: *Sports Officiating.* New York, A. S. Barnes, 1949.

12. Nixon, John: Improving officiating. *Athletic Journal,* March, 1953.

13. Porter, Webb: Planning basketball officials

programs. *Whistle,* November, 1960.

14. Razor, Jack: The task of officiating. *Coach and Athlete,* January, 1971.

15. Sandlen, H.N.: Private world of a whistle tooter. *Scholastic Coach,* May, 1961.

16. Seymour, Emery: The use of ratings for basketball officials. *Athletic Journal,* November, 1955.

17. Stokstad, Lloyd: Officials performance rating form. *Athletic Journal,* November, 1957.

AUTHOR INDEX

SUBJECT INDEX

Date Due